Building Services Materials Handbook

HEATING, SANITATION AND FIRE PROTECTION

Building Services Research
and Information Association

LONDON NEW YORK
E. & F.N. Spon

First published in 1987 by
E. & F.N. Spon Ltd
11 New Fetter Lane, London EC4P 4EE
Published in the USA by
E. & F.N. Spon
29 West 35th Street, New York NY 10001

© 1987 BSRIA

Printed in Great Britain
at the University Press, Cambridge

ISBN 0 419 14310 6

British Library Cataloguing in Publication Data

Building services materials handbook.
* 1. Heating —— Great Britain —— Equipment and*
supplies   2. Air conditioning —— Great Britain
—— Equipment and supplies   3. Ventilation ——
Great Britain —— Equipment and Supplies
4. Plumbing —— Great Britain —— Equipment and
supplies
I. Building Services Research and Information
Association
697   TH7345

ISBN 0-419-14310-6

Library of Congress Cataloging-in-Publication Data

Building services materials handbook.
* Includes index.*
* 1. Building materials——Handbooks, manuals, etc.*
* 2. Buildings——Environmental engineering——*
Handbooks, manuals, etc.   I. Building Services
Research
and Information Association.
TA403.4.B85   1987   696'.028   86-33893
ISBN 0-419-14310-6

Contents

Preface   vi
Acknowledgements   vii
Structure of the handbook   viii
Scope and limitations   x
How to use the handbook   xi

Part 1 General   1
        1.1 References   3
        1.2 Advisory services   7
        1.3 Units and factors   11
        1.4 Environments   16
        1.5 Corrosion   40

Part 2 Services   47
        2.1 Space heating   49
        2.2 Water services   62
        2.3 Sanitation   76
        2.4 Fire protection   87
        Appendix: Precautions checklist   98

Part 3 Components   103
        3.1 Pipe   105
        3.2 Pipe fittings   128
        3.3 Valves   143
        3.4 Pumps   167
        3.5 Tanks   179
        3.6 Heat emitters   200
        3.7 Heat generators   211
        3.8 Controls   225
        3.9 Thermal insulation   230

Part 4 Materials   239
        4.1 Ferrous metals   241
        4.2 Non-ferrous metals   307
        4.3 Jointing and bonding   394
        4.4 Plastics   465
        4.5 Surface protection   583
        4.6 Rubbers and elastomers   632
        4.7 Sealing materials   660

Index   679

Preface

The technical enquiry service operated by the Building Services Research and Information Association (BSRIA) for the support of its members has for many years provided advice on the selection of materials for building services applications. This advice has often extended to include failure investigations, particularly in the case of heating and other piped liquid services in buildings. This service highlighted the need for some coherent guidelines for building services engineers in the selection of materials for such typical applications. This need complemented by the experience gained by BSRIA staff over many years was the stimulus to the preparation of this handbook. Its objective is to set out clearly the engineering materials available for heating and other common piped building services, to list the relevant specifications and requirements and to provide guidelines and advice on selection. In addition general information is given on the environmental exposure conditions which can be met and on common mechanisms of corrosion.

Experience has shown that while many of the actual problems arising from the use of materials are preventable the selection of appropriate materials is not a simple matter. It requires considerable knowledge to reach cost effective decisions even for typical situations. In the case of unusual projects or applications additional expert advice may be necessary. It is hoped that this handbook will be helpful in avoiding some of the pitfalls facing the building services engineer in materials selection and to indicate when specialist advice should be sought.

The bulk of the material in this handbook was compiled by T.S. Finch and P.S.G. Scurry and edited by A.G. Foster, all formerly BSRIA staff. The handbook is a tribute to the very substantial contributions made by all three main contributors. Some additional material was provided by B.M. Roberts of Brockham Design Associates Ltd, and G.P. Manly of A.G. Manly Co. Ltd undertook the task of reviewing the drafts of the sections of the handbook. BSRIA gratefully acknowledges these two important contributions.

While every effort has been made to ensure the accuracy of the data, the Association cannot accept liability for loss or damage arising from the use of information supplied.

Acknowledgements

BSRIA wish to express their gratitude for the help given by the following organisations and individuals during the preparation of this handbook:

    F.H. Biddle Ltd
    British Aluminium
    British Steel Corporation
    Brockham Design Associates Ltd
    George Fischer Sales Ltd
    Sir Alexander Gibbs & Partners
    Hepworth Industrial Plastics Ltd
    IMI Yorkshire Imperial Ltd
    Rosser and Russell Ltd
    G.P. Manly
    B.M. Roberts

BSRIA wishes to thank the publishers for permission to reproduce the following figures and tables:

Thwaites, C.J. and Berry, B.T.K.
Engineering design guide 07 – soldering, Oxford University Press: 1975
Figures 4.3/2 and 4.3/3

British Standards Institute BS219: 1977 Specification for Soft Solders
Table 4.3/4

Roberts, P.M.
Engineering design guide 10 – brazing, Oxford University Press: 1975
Figures 4.3/5, 4.3/7, 4.3/9 and Table 4.3/6

Handbook of industrial materials – first edition, Trade and Technical Press Ltd
Table 4.4/2

Carter, V.E. Metallic coatings for corrosion control, Newnes – Butterworth: 1977
Table 4.5/2

British Standards Institute BS5493: 1977 Code of Practice for Protective Coating of Iron and Steel Structures Against Corrosion
Table 4.5/3

Structure of the Handbook

The handbook is divided into four Sections:

> Section 1 – General
> Section 2 – Services
> Section 3 – Components
> Section 4 – Materials

Each of these Sections will be briefly described to show the inter-relationship.

PART 1 – GENERAL

This provides general information to support the specific content of the main body of the handbook.

First is a list of published information on a variety of related topics which provide useful references to complement the content of the handbook. The second sub-section lists organisations which may be consulted as expert advisory services in special situations where the published information is inadequate.

The units used in the handbook and those related to materials are tabulated together with other factors of general use.

Following these general information sections are two very important sub-sections providing information on the environment and corrosion – the cause and the effect relationships which are of prime importance in the selection of all materials.

PART 2 – SERVICES

All of the common piping services within heating, ventilating and public health engineering are set out separately as data sheets. Three purposes are served by the information given. Firstly, to set out norms for the operating conditions for each service as the basis for determining whether or not a particular material would be appropriate. Secondly, to remind the reader that certain features must be considered if the materials selected are to achieve the expected life; these are described as 'precautions' and are detailed separately. Thirdly, to set down the major components appropriate to each service and thereby provide a cross reference link with the next section.

PART 3 – COMPONENTS

Details of the major components are set out in data sheets. On each sheet information is given in respect of the relevant standard specifications, methods of jointing, alternative forms in which the component is available, a table of the materials called up in the listed standards and appropriate service considerations.

PART 4 – MATERIALS

The well known engineering and construction materials are described together with some newer ones that are now being introduced. The materials are collected together in sub-sections by type e.g. ferrous metals. Under each type heading a description is given of the origin and the relevant metallurgical or chemical features of the materials. Reference is made to limitations in use and the need for special measures in fabrication or protection. All the materials standards are listed at the end of each sub-section where also are to be found data sheets for each material. The data sheets primarily list out the most important physical characteristics of each material with some additional information on environmental characteristics, process and forming techniques, jointing and typical applications.

From this description it can be seen that there is a clear thread running from the Services section through Components to Materials, this being the decision process that the engineer is most likely to follow, but other forms of interrogation may be adopted as is explained later.

Scope and Limitations

The piped services, components and materials described in this handbook are selected on the basis that they are likely to be encountered by most building services engineers in the normal course of design, specification, fabrication or maintenance.

The information on materials has been collected from many sources including British Standard specifications, manufacturers' literature and reference books. Materials depend on the formulation of constituents and their processing to determine the final properties. Alternative sources of supply may offer materials which are apparently the same but which differ in some properties, especially if not produced to standard specifications. The precise value of any property which is critical to the design must be confirmed by reference to the supplier.

In Part 1 and in the preliminary text for the materials sub-sections general information has been given to support the recommendations in the Data Sheets. Where a British Standard or similar reference is quoted this would be consulted if the material and/or environment being contemplated is not familiar. Even familiarity is not a recipe for certain success. As the choice tends towards an increasing degree of unfamiliarity the more is it desirable that the engineer understands the characteristics of the material and the effect of the environment. If there are shortcomings in the information provided in the handbook other, more detailed references should be consulted or expert advice should be sought. In the end the responsibility rests with the person making the choice.

How to use the handbook

This handbook is intended to answer questions about the selection and use of materials. There are many starting points for such enquiries but, hopefully there are no dead-ends. Throughout the document the engineer is led to either a solution or a reference that will enable a deeper investigation to be undertaken or other advice sought.

Identification of a potential solution must be supported by verification that this is commercially viable and technically practical. Manufacturers, and others having an interest in the outcome, must be consulted to confirm that the proposed specification will in all respects meet the known requirements.

Two types of enquiry pattern will be discussed. Firstly, that likely to be followed by the system designer, whose interests have dictated the layout of the handbook and, secondly, the component manufacturer.

SYSTEM DESIGNER

The decision process is likely to go from system to component to material, with the environment playing a major part in the analysis. At the system level the first point to be established is whether or not the engineering requirements and other features suggest that the particular scheme is 'normal' and hence that 'standard' or conventional materials can be selected.

There are two main elements determining normality. Firstly, that the operating conditions are, and are likely to remain, within certain stated limits. This will related to both the 'engineering' features, i.e. temperature, pressure, etc., and the environment. Secondly, that basic precautions are observed so as not to create adverse conditions which good engineering practice would not tolerate. Data Sheets are provided for Services setting out both the operating conditions and precautions that define a 'normal' service. When normality is established the materials specified can be applied with a reasonable degree of certainty that a satisfactory life will be obtained.

If it is evident that the operating conditions are not normal or cannot be forecast or that normal precautions cannot be applied, a second level of analysis will be necessary. The special, i.e. non-normal, circumstances must be determined – this may be in terms of engineering requirements, environment, precautions or risk. These are discussed separately below but may be present in combination.

Engineering requirements

If it is anticipated, or intended, that operating conditions will be outside the 'normal' limits attention must be given not only to obvious engineering features, temperature, pressure, etc. but also stress, thermal or mechanical, since excess will effect the life of a material.

In a few instances it may be possible to accommodate the requirements by using a higher service specification; e.g. going from a low-temperature hot-water service specification to that for high-temperature hot water. Also, in a few cases it will be found that the specification for a particular component allows its use over a wider operating range than that designated for a 'normal' service.

Where neither of these solutions applies a detailed study of the Components and Materials sections will be necessary. When a solution appears to have been found the relevant British Standards or similar reference should be studied to ensure that there are no special constraints or limitations that have not been listed out in this handbook.

At this stage it is advisable to read the text on the chosen material set out at the beginning of each sub-section on the materials section. This should indicate any special constraints that an environment may place on a selected material and recommend particularly effective forms of protection.

If, at this stage in the investigation, no solution has appeared the designer has two courses open – either to re-design the system to eliminate the extreme requirements or seek expert advice on how best to produce a 'special' to accommodate the particular conditions.

Environment

It is difficult to be precise about the definition of a 'standard' environment. However, familiarity with the charts in the Environment section will indicate where the environment becomes hazardous for particular materials. The decision process then is an iterative one – does the material exhibit any inadequacies in the anticipated environment. If the answer is 'yes', an alternative material or a form of protection should be chosen that is described as overcoming the aggressive aspects of the environment. It will be quickly recognised that the various features of an environment will need to be accommodated in different ways.

Only to a limited degree can the environment be altered so as to be less aggressive. However, opportunities do exist, particularly at the micro-climate level. Great stress is laid in this handbook on the dangers of creating pockets of aggression and some attention to detail in design and fabrication may allow the use of a less expensive material.

Precautions

For 'normal' service from 'normal' materials the application of good engineering practice must be assumed. Whilst there is no excuse for failures arising from bad workmanship, e.g. not removing burrs from tube ends, there are occasions where it would be impossible, or extortionately expensive, to apply all precautions. One instance would be where components cannot be protected from impact, in this case the materials and construction methods must be such as to provide sufficient strength to resist damage.

Risk

For engineering designs following traditional practice in docile environments normal materials coupled to sensible precautions and assuming reasonable maintenance will give an operating period with little risk of premature failure or rapid decline in performance. Risk of premature failure or reduced performance will arise as the design or circumstances move away from the known i.e. familiar and traditional, into the unknown or less well defined or less controllable situation.

Risk will increase by substitution of materials having either less well established qualities or with less margin for error. This may arise from an attempt to optimise between the life-risk penalty and the cost advantage. This is likely to involve rational decisions and will be a calculated risk. The more difficult case to evaluate is where the circumstances, maybe the environmental conditions, are unfamiliar and hence the effect unpredictable or there are uncontrollable elements, such as the degree of vandalism, where materials must be selected conservatively, or a high risk accepted.

Clearly, for 'fine tuning' of materials selection the circumstances, in engineering and environmental terms, must be fully understood and fully predictable. All too often a higher than necessary risk is introduced into an engineering system by inadequate attention to detail, e.g. small gaps in protective coverings, non-removal of flux etc., so that a material that would have been expected to provide a satisfactory life fails prematurely. Where possible throughout the handbook an indication is given of the need to apply extra care or where diligent supervision will be worthwhile. The more hostile the environment or extreme the conditions the more will such attention to detail be rewarded.

COMPONENT MANUFACTURER

For the majority of manufacturers supplying the building services industry the problems of environment and site conditions have been recognised and catered for by engineering design and adequate installation instructions. However new firms are entering this market who cannot benefit from the long experience of traditional suppliers.

This handbook provides two main types of information for the manufacturer entering the building services market. Firstly, it provides a basic set of parameters for the most relevant services and, secondly, it sets out the wide range of environments likely to be encountered. In this latter respect, it should be noted that this handbook does not include process environments.

No attempt has been made in this document to set out the problems to be faced when designing components in respect of site conditions and practices. The site provides one of the most hostile environments that any component is likely to suffer and this has caused the downfall of more new arrivals on the building services scene than any other single factor. Unfortunately it is not a subject that lends itself to a series of recommendations. This is because most of the problems arise through either ignorance or avoidance of recommendations already in existence in terms of storage, handling, installation and testing. Manufacturers entering this market are well advised to seek authoritative advice on the hazards to be confronted and not to try to extrapolate from other experience even where this may be a related industry, e.g. petrochemicals, etc.

PART 1   GENERAL

1.1 REFERENCES

1.1.1 GENERAL

PERRY, R., CHILTON, C. Chemical engineers yearbook.
McGraw-Hill 1975.

Finishing handbook.
Sewell 1979.

Kempes - Engineers yearbook.
Morgan-Grampion 1982.

PARRISH, A. Mechanical engineers reference book.
Butterworths 1973.

KAYE, G.W.C., & LABEY, C.H. Tables for physical and chemical constants.
Longman 1978

BUTLER, G. & ISON, HCK. Corrosion and its prevention in waters.
Leonard Hill 1966.

DIAMANT, R.M.E. The prevention of corrosion.
Business Books 1971.

GRIFFITHS, J. Applied climatology.
Oxford University Press 1966.

ROSS, T.K. Metal corrosion.
Oxford University Press 1977.

SCHWEITZER, P.A. Corrosion resistance tables.
Dekker 1976.

SHRIER, L.L. Corrosion Volumes 1 and 2.
Newnes 1965.

TRESEDA, R.S. NACE Corrosion engineers reference book.
National Association of Corrosion Engineers 1980.

TREWATHA, G.W. & HORN, L.H. An introduction to climate.
McGraw-Hill 1980.

WILSON, C.L. & OATES J.A. Corrosion and the maintenance engineer.
Newnes 1968.

1.1.2 SERVICES

Chartered Institute of Building Services - Guides A, B and C.

American Society of Heating, Refrigeration and Air-conditioning Engineers - Handbooks.

Property Services Agency - Engineering specifications - Heating, hot and cold water, steam and gas installations for buildings - (M & E) No. 3.
HMSO 1974.

3

Property Services Agency - Engineering specifications - central heating and hot and cold water installations for dwellings - (M & E) No. 4.
HMSO 1970.

Property Services Agency - Engineering specifications - mechanical ventilation for buildings - (M & E) No.6.
HMSO 1971.

Property Services Agency - Engineering specifications - Air conditioning, air cooling and mechanical ventilation for buildings - (M & E) No. 100.
HMSO 1979.

FABER, O. & KELL, J.R. Heating and air conditioning of buildings.
The Architectural Press 1979.

HALL, F. - Heating, ventilating and air conditioning.
Construction Press 1980.

1.1.3 COMPONENTS

British Valve Manufacturers Association. Valves for the control of fluids.
1972.

National Water Council. Water fittings.
1980.

HOLMES, E. Industrial pipework engineering.
McGraw-Hill 1973

MARTIN, W.L. Handbook of industrial pipework.
Pitman.

PEARSON, G.H. Application of valves and fittings.
Pitman 1968.

1.1.4 MATERIALS

Copper Development Association. Copper data.
1971.

Copper Development Association. The Brasses.
1980.

Aluminium Federation. The properties of aluminium and its alloys.
1980.

Heating and Ventilating Contractors Association. TR3 - Brazing and bronze welding of copper pipework.
1976.

Heating and Ventilating Contractors Association. TR7 - Welding of carbon steel
pipework.
1980.

Handbook of industrial materials.
Trade and Technical Press.

Plastics, Volumes 1 and 2.
Morgan-Grampion 1970.

ANDREWS, D.R. Soldering, brazing, welding and adhesives.
Institution of Production Engineers. 1978.

BEADLE, J.D. Adhesives guide.
Morgan-Grampion 1969.

CARTER, V.E. Metallic coatings of corrosion control.
Newnes 1977.

ELLIOT, D. and TUPHOLME,S.M. An introduction to steel: Part 2, stainless steel.
Oxford University Press 1981.

EVANS, V. Plastics as corrosion resistant materials.
Pergamon 1966.

FOX, J.H.E. An introduction to steel selection: Part 1, carbon and low alloy steel.
Oxford University Press 1979.

HAIGH, I.P. Painting Steelwork - Report No. 93.
Construction Industry Research and Information Association 1982.

HORNBOSTEL, C. Construction materials.
John Wiley 1978.

JASTRZEBSKI, Z.D. Engineering materials.
Wiley International 1976.

MENZIES, I.A. Corrosion and protection of metals.
Institute of Metallurgists 1965.

NUTT, M.C. Metallurgy and plastics for engineers.
Associated Lithographers 1976.

POSTANS, J.H. Plastic mouldings.
Oxford University Press 1978.

POWELL, P.C. The selection and use of thermoplastics.
Oxford University Press 1977.

ROBERTS, P.M. Brazing.
Oxford University Press 1975.

ROLF, W.J. & SCOTT J.R. Fibres, films, plastics and rubbers.
Butterworth 1971.

ROLLASON, E.C.   Metallurgy for the engineer.
Edward Arnold 1963.

ROSS, R.B.   Metallic materials specification handbook.
E & F.N. Spon 1972.

SCHOLES, J.P.   The selection and use of cast irons.
Oxford University Press 1979.

SLUNDER, C.J. & BOYD, W.K.   Zinc, its corrosion resistance.
Zinc Development Association 1971.

SMITHELLS, C.J.   Metals reference book, volumes 1, 2 and 3 (4th edition)
Butterworth 1967.

THWAITES, C.J.   Capillary joining - brazing and soft solder.
Research Studies Press 1982.

THWAITES, C.J. & BARRY, B.T.K.   Soldering.
Oxford University Press 1975.

1.2 ADVISORY SERVICES

Organisation	Address	Telephone No.
Agrement Board	P.O. Box 195, Bucknalls Lane, Garston, Watford WD2 7JR.	0927 670844
Aluminium Federation	Broadway House, Calthorpe Road, Birmingham B15 1TN.	021 455 0311
Asbestos Information Centre	St. Andrews House, 22/28 High Street, Epsom, Surrey. KT19 8AH.	037 27 42055
Asphalt & Coated Macadam Association	156 Buckingham Palace Road, London SW19 9TR	01 730 0761
Association of Board Makers	3 Plough Place, Fetter Lane, London EC4A 1AL.	01 353 5222
Association of British Manufacturers of Mineral Insulating Fibres -	See EURISOL - UK	
Association of Builder's Hardware Manufacturers.	5 Greenfield Crescent, Birmingham B15 3BE	021 454 2177
Association of Building Component Manufacturers Ltd	26 Store Street, London WC1E 7BT.	01 580 9083
Association of Consulting Engineers	Alliance House, 12 Caxton Street, London SW1H 0QL.	01 222 6557
Association of Metal Sprayers	136 Hagley Road, Edgbaston, Birmingham B16 9PN.	021 454 4141
BNF Metals Technology Centre	The Grove Laboratories, Denchworth Road, Wantage, Oxfordshire OX12 9BJ.	02357 2992
Boiler & Radiator Manufacturers Association	Fleming House, Renfrew Street, Glasgow G3 6TG.	041 332 0826
Brick Development Association	Woodside House, Winkfield, Windsor SL4 2DX.	0344 88 5651
British Cast Iron Research Association (BCIRA)	Alvechurch, Birmingham B48 7QB.	0527 66414
British Ceramic Research Association.	Queen's Road, Penkhull, Stoke-on-Trent. ST4 7LQ.	0782 45431
British Gas Corporation	Watson House, Peterborough Road, Fulham, London SW6.	01 736 1212

Organisation	Address	Telephone No.
British Glass Industry Research Association	Northumberland Road, Sheffield S10 2UA.	0742 686201
British Hydromechanics Research Association (BHRA)	Cranfield, Bedford. MK43 0AJ.	0234 750422
British Lead Manufacturers Association	68 High Street, Weybridge, Surrey. KT13 8BL.	0932 56621
British Malleable Tube Fittings Association	40 City Road, London EC1Y 2AD.	01 698 8856
British Plastics Federation	5 Belgrave Square, London SW1X 8PH	01 235 9483
British Refrigeration & Air Conditioning Association	see HEATING, VENTILATING AND AIR CONDITIONING MANUFACTURERS ASSOCIATION.	
British Standards Institution	2 Park Street, London W1A 2BS.	01 629 9000
British Valve Manufacturers Association	3 Pannells Court, Chertsey Street, Guildford, Surrey GU1 4EU.	0483 37379
British Welded Steel Tube Manufacturers Association	32 Harborne Road, Edgbaston, Birmingham B15 3AQ.	021 454 6344
British Wood Preserving Association	Premier House, 150 Southampton Row, London WC1B 5AL.	01 837 8217
Building Research Establishment	1 Bucknalls Lane, Garston, Watford WD2 7JR.	0923 674040
Building Services Research and Information Association	Old Bracknell Lane West, Bracknell, Berks RG12 4AH.	0344 426511
Cement and Concrete Association Advisory Division	Wexham Springs, Slough SL3 6PL.	9266 2727
Chartered Institute of Building	Kings Ride, Ascot, Berks SL5 8BJ	0990 23355
Chartered Institution of Building Services Engineers	222 Balham High Road, London SW12 9BS.	01 675 5211
Construction Industry Research and Information Association	6 Storey's Gate, London SW1P 3AU	01 222 8891

Organisation	Address	Telephone No.
Copper Development Association	Orchard House, Mutton Lane, Potters Bar, Herts EN6 3AP.	0707 50711
Council of British Ceramic Sanitaryware Manufacturers	Federation House, Station Road, Stoke on Trent ST4 2RU.	0782 48675
Electrical Contractors' Association	34 Palace Court, London W2 4HY.	01 229 1266
Electrical Research Association	Cleeve Road, Leatherhead, Surrey.	0372 74151
Eurisol-UK	St. Pauls House, Edison Road, Bromley, Kent BR2 0EP.	01 466 6719
Fibre Building Board Organisation	1 Hanworth Road, Feltham,Middx. TW13 5AF.	01 751 6107
Glass and Glazing Federation	44/48 Borough High Street, London SE1.	01 403 7177
Heating and Ventilating Contractors Association	ESCA House, 34 Palace Court, London W2 4JG.	01 229 2488
Heat Pump Manufacturers Association	See HEVAC	
Heat Pump and Air Conditioning Bureau	30 Millbank, London SW1P 4RD	01 834 8827
Heating, Ventilating and Air Conditioning Manufacturers Association (HEVAC)	Nicholson's House, High Street, Maidenhead, Berks.	0628 34667/8
Institute of Acoustics	25 Chambers Street, Edinburgh EH1 1HU.	031 225 2143
Institute of Domestic Heating and Environmental Engineers	93 High Road, Benfleet, Essex.	03745 54266
Institute of Plumbing	64 Station Lane, Hornchurch, Essex RM12 6NB	04024 72791
Institute of Refrigeration	76 Mill Lane, Carshalton, Surrey SM5 2JR.	01 647 7033
Lead Development Association	34 Berkeley Square, London W1X 6AJ.	01 499 8422
Meteorological Office	London Road, Bracknell, Berks RG12 2SZ.	0344 420242
National Clayware Federation	7 Castle Street, Bridgwater, Somerset	
National Corrosion Service	National Physical Laboratory, Queen's Road, Teddington, Middlesex TW11 0LW.	01 977 3222

Organisation	Address	Telephone No.
National Council of Building Material Producers	33 Alfred Place, London SW1A 7EN	01 580 3344
Paint Research Association	8 Waldergrave Road, Teddington, Middlesex TW11 8LD	01 977 4427
Property Services Agency	Apollo House, Wellesley Road, Croydon CR9 2EL	01 686 5622
Rubber and Plastics Research Association	Shawbury, Shrewsbury, Shropshire SY4 4NR.	0939 250383
Steel Castings Research and Trade Association	5 East Bank Road, Sheffield S2 3PT	0742 28647
Timber Research and Development Association	Stocking Lane, Hughenden Valley, High Wycombe, Bucks HP14 4ND.	024024 3091
Vitreous Enamel Development Council	New House, High Street, Ticehurst, Wadhurst, Sussex TN5 7AL	0580 200152
Water Pollution Research Laboratory	Elder Way, Stevenage, Herts	0438 2444
Water Research Centre	Medmenham Laboratories, PO Box 16, Henley Rd, Marlow, Bucks SL7 2HD.	0491 571531
Welding Institute	Abington Hall, Abington, Cambridge, CB1 6AL.	0223 891162
Zinc Development Association	34 Berkeley Square, London W1X 6AJ.	01 499 6636

1.3 UNITS AND FACTORS

1.3.1 S.I. UNITS

The Units and their derivations are given below for those that occur within the text.

QUANTITY	UNIT	SYMBOL	DERIVATION
length	metre	m	
mass	kilogram	kg	
time	second	s	
electric current	ampere	A	
thermodynamic temperature	kelvin	K	
amount of substance	mole	mo	
plane angle	radian	rad	
acceleration	metre per second squared	m/s^2	
area	square metres	m^2	
density	kilogram per cubic metre	kg/m^3	
electric capacitance	farad	F	$1F = 1\ As/V$
electric conductance	siemens	S	$1S = 1\ A/V$
electric inductance	henry	H	$1H = 1Vs/A$
electric potential difference	volt	V	$1V = 1W/A$
electric resistance	ohm	Ω	$1\Omega = 1V/A$
electromotive force	volt	V	$1V = 1W/A$
energy	joule	J	$1J = 1N.m$
force	newton	N	$1N = 1Kgm/s^2$
frequency	hertz	Hz	$1Hz = 1s^{-1}$
heat capacity	kilojoule per kelvin	kJ/K	
heat content	joule per cubic metre	J/m^3	
heat emission	watt per cubic metre	W/m^3	
power	watt	W	$1W = 1J/s$
pressure	pascal	Pa	$1Pa = 1N/m^2$
quantity of electricity	coulomb	C	$1C = 1A/s$
quantity of heat	joule	J	$1J = 1N.m$
specific heat	joule per kilogram-kelvin	J/kg.K	
stress	pascal	Pa	$1Pa = 1N/m^2$
thermal conductivity	watt per metre-kelvin	W/m.K	

11

QUANTITY	UNIT	SYMBOL	DERIVATION
velocity	metre per second	m/s	
viscosity dynamic	pascal second	Pa.s	
viscosity kinematic	square metre per second	m^2/s	
voltage	volt	V	1V = 1W/A
volume	cubic metre	m^3	
volume rate of flow	cubic metre per second	m^3/s	
work	joule	J	1J = 1N.m

1.3.2 CONVERSION FACTORS

Multiply by	To convert	To
Linear		
25.4	inch	millimetre
0.3048	foot	metre
0.9144	yard	metre
Area		
645.2	square inch	square millimetre
0.0929	square foot	square metre
0.8361	square yard	square metre
0.4047	acre	hectare
Volume		
0.02832	cubic foot	cubic metre
28.32	cubic foot	litre
6.24	cubic foot	gallons (Imp)
0.7646	cubic yard	cubic metre
4.546	gallon (Imp)	litre
Mass		
28.35	ounces (avoirdupois)	gramme
0.4536	pounds (avoirdupois)	kilogramme
1016	ton	kilogramme
Pressure or Stress		
6895	pound force per $inch^2$ (psi)	pascal
0.06895	pound force per $inch^2$	bar
1.575	tons force per $inch^2$	kilogramm per mm^2
760	atmosphere	mm Hg @ 0^oC

Multiply by	To convert	To
Work, Heat and Energy		
1055	British Thermal Unit (Btu)	joule
1.356	foot pound (force)	joule
4.187	calorie	joule
0.2929	Btu per hour	watt
3600	watthour	joule
0.7457	horsepower	kilowatt
Thermal		
0.1442	Btu inch per hour ^{o}F	watt per metre kelvin
5.678	Btu per hour square foot ^{o}F	watt per square metre kelvin
0.6707	Btu per cubic foot	kilojoule per cubic metre kelvin
3.155	Btu per hour square foot	watt per square metre
0.1035	Btu per hour cubic foot	watt per cubic metre
Corrosion rate		
0.0254	0.001 inches per year	millimetres per year
Miscellaneous		
16.02	pound per cubic foot	kilogramme per cubic metre
0.1383	pound foot per second	kilogramme metre per second
0.001	centipoise	pascal second
1	stokes	square centimetre per second

1.3.3 MULTIPLES AND SUB-MULTIPLES OF S.I. UNITS

Multiplication Factor	Prefix	S.I. Symbol
$1\ 000\ 000\ 000\ 000 = 10^{12}$	tera	T
$1\ 000\ 000\ 000 = 10^{9}$	giga	G
$1\ 000\ 000 = 10^{6}$	mega	M
$1\ 000 = 10^{3}$	kilo	k
$100 = 10^{2}$	hecto*	h
$10 = 10^{1}$	deka*	da
$0.1 = 10^{-1}$	deci*	d
$0.01 = 10^{-2}$	centi*	c
$0.001 = 10^{-3}$	milli	m
$0.000\ 001 = 10^{-6}$	micro	μ
$0.000\ 000\ 001 = 10^{-9}$	nano	n
$0.000\ 000\ 000\ 001 = 10^{-12}$	pico	p
$0.000\ 000\ 000\ 000\ 001 = 10^{-15}$	femto	f
$0.000\ 000\ 000\ 000\ 000\ 001 = 10^{-18}$	atto	a

* non preferred

1.3.4 HARDNESS CONVERSION AND TENSILE RELATIONSHIP

Brinell No.	Newtons/mm^2	Vickers	Rockwell B
229	772	234	99
223	757	228	98
217	741	222	97
212	711	217	97
207	696	212	96
201	680	206	95
197	665	202	94
192	649	197	93
187	634	192	92
183	618	188	91
179	603	184	90
174	587	179	89
170	587	175	88
167	587	172	87
163	572	168	85
159	556	164	84
156	556	161	83
152	541	157	82
149	526	154	81
146	510	151	80
143	510	148	79
140	496	146	78
137	479	142	78
134	479	139	77
131	464	136	75
128	464	133	73
126	448	131	72
123	432	128	70
121	432	126	69
118	417	123	67
116	417	121	66
114	402	119	64
111	386	116	63

Note: 1.   The tensile strength only relates to STEEL
2.   These are only average figures and must be used accordingly.

1.3.5 STEEL PIPE SIZE RELATIONSHIP

Nominal size	Outside diameter mm	Nominal size	Outside diameter mm	Nominal size	Outside diameter mm	Nominal size	Outside diameter mm
6	10.2	80	88.9	350	355.6	850	864
8	13.5	90*	101.6*	400	406.4	900	914
10	17.2	100	114.3	450	457	1000	1016
15	21.3	125	139.7	500	508	1200	1220
20	26.9	150	168.3	550	559	1400	1420
25	33.7	175*	193.7*	600	610	1600	1620
32	42.4	200	219.1	650	660	1800	1820
40	48.3	225*	244.5*	700	711	2000	2020
50	60.3	250	273	750	762	2200	2220
65	76.1	300	323.9	800	813		

*Non preferred sizes

1.4 ENVIRONMENTS

In order to be able to isolate some of the more important factors determining the choice of materials or form of protection various 'environments' have been described below. However, in reading this Section two important limitations must be recognised in the information provided. Firstly, environments, whether natural or artificial, are complex and may change over the life time of a building services installation. The degree of protection should, therefore, err on the generous side, assuming that the conditions are likely to be worse than the evidence suggests. Secondly, no attempt has been made to cover specific environments as might be created by industrial or agricultural processes. Where these are recognised to exist specialist advise must be sought.

The following Environments are discussed:-

    Outdoor: Urban, Rural, Industrial, Marine

    Indoor: Wet Conditions, Dry Conditions

    Global Climates: Temperate, Tropical, Desert, Arctic,

    Mountainous

    Immersion:

    Buried:

    Pipes and Tanks

1.4.1 OUTDOOR ENVIRONMENTS

See Table 1.4/1

Air alone is not aggressive to the majority of materials. For atmospheric attack to be of any concern moisture and a pollutant must be present. A surface does not have to be 'wet' for attack to occur. In the case of metals they may fail almost as rapidly if the relative humidity is below 100% as they do at dewpoint. The effect seems to be related to the type of corrosion product formed. The usual explanation is that these are hygroscopic and absorb water from the atmosphere above a critical humidity. There is a critical humidity level for many metals (e.g. 70% relative humidity for carbon steel in an urban environment) above which attack is increased, particularly in the presence of aggressive pollutants. The corrosion products developed are a result of the conditions on the material surface (micro-climate) rather than the real environment. The design and shape of the material exposed will have considerable effect on the micro-climate and hence on the rate of attack.

Materials are affected differently by particular environments, coatings may react differently from unprotected metals. Sunlight will cause paints and plastics to degrade whereas it has a beneficial affect on metals by keeping them dry. Similarly, erosion by windborne sand or rain will affect quite differently protective coatings and the relatively hard metals they cover.

In Table 1.4/1 a number of factors are identified that affect corrosion in various kinds of outdoor environments, the most significant of which is geographical location, which determines whether materials are subject to industrial, rural, urban or marine derived pollutants, or a mixture.

A rural location downwind of an industrial area would have a worse problem than a similar location upwind. Equally, an industrial area located on the coast could expect extra attack from marine pollutants, as could a rural area by the sea.

1.4.2 INDOOR ENVIRONMENTS

See Table 1.4/2

The environment within buildings is complex. As well as being influenced by the external environment, each building will contain its own peculiar conditions, i.e. its own mini-climate. The materials that are attacked depend on the nature of these conditions.

A number of aggressive indoor environments are cited in Table 1.4/2 with notes of materials at risk under the stated conditions.

1.4.3 GLOBAL CLIMATES

In natural conditions it is difficult to separate the effects produced by such factors as temperature, humidity, sunlight and rainfall. Global climates can be divided into regions.

1.4.3.1 TEMPERATE REGION

The climate is intermediate between tropical and arctic. This region contains the majority of Europe, Japan, eastern USA and Canadian border, and the western sea-board of Canada and northern USA.

The characteristics range from hot summers and uniform rainfall (hottest month over 22°C) to cool summers with uniform rainfall (mean hottest month @ 22°C and 1-3 months @ 10°C). High humidities can occur.

Deterioration of materials will be more rapid in industrial and coastal locations due to local pollutants.

1.4.3.2 TROPICAL REGION

This region is characterized by high temperatures with relatively low diurnal variations (compared, with dessert regions) and by high relative humidities. A heavy rainfall may be either spread over the whole year or limited to a wet season. Generally, countries in this region lie between latitudes 23.5° north and south of the equator and include Malasia, Burma, East Indies, central and west Africa, central America, northern South America and islands such as New Guinea.

Temperature ranges from +40°C (sometimes up to +70°C) during the day and down to +20 or +25°C at night. The relative humidity can rise to +90% at night.

Exposed unprotected metal is likely to corrode in hot damp climates, especially where the atmosphere is polluted with industrial gases or marine salt. Surface moisture leads to loss of insulation resistance in electrical apparatus and bimetallic corrosion between dissimilar metals. Tropical conditions are condusive to biological growths, such as moulds, which will create new climates (e.g. surface conditions) encouraging corrosive attack.

1.4.3.3 **DESERT REGION**

Desert regions, such as those of north Africa, Arabia, Iran and central Australia, are characterized by high temperature and low relative humidity. Temperature can range from +60°C by day to -10°C at night. The maximum relative humidity is of the order of 5-10%, the maximum being observed when the temperature is lowest.

Temperature swings cause expansion and contraction of materials giving rise to warping, distortion and breakdown of seals. These variations will cause partially sealed equipment to breathe and hence introduce moisture or dust into component housings. Plastics and organic coatings may soften at high temperatures. Low humidity may cause wood and plastics materials to dry out and become brittle.

Sunlight, with its high radiant (infra red) and high ultra violet content will cause degradation of rubbers, certain plastics and paints unless they have built in inhibitors.

Dust and sand may cause abrasion of surfaces and penetrate into joints where movement due to vibration or changes of temperature may cause serious wear.

1.4.3.4 **ARCTIC REGION**

Characterised by low temperature. Although the weight of water vapour in unit volume of the air at low temperatures may be small, the relative humidity may be high. The arctic zone is divided into two classifications dependent upon the temperatures prevailing.

EXPOSED ARCTIC

A temperature of -40°C is often experienced, with occasional excursions lower. Warm temperatures of +35°C are also found. Areas such as Siberia, Alaska, north east Europe and parts of the southern hemisphere experience these conditions.

SUB-ARCTIC

The cold experienced in sub-arctic areas of southern Canada, central Europe and Asia is not so great as exposed arctic regions; temperatures of -25°C are commonly recorded.

Contraction may cause seals to leak and rigid paint finishes to crack exposing the metal substrate to attack. Plastics materials and elastomers may become brittle, whilst very low temperatures may make metals, welds, etc lose their ductility. Greases and oils will become viscous.

1.4.3.5 **MOUNTAINOUS REGION**

The climate in a particular area may be modified by the affect of altitude. High altitude may produce a reduction in temperature, such that the location would have the characteristics of another region. For example, Addis Ababa is in a region where the mean temperature for the coldest month is 18°C but because the city is located at an altitude of 2500 metres this falls to 10°C and the general climatic characteristics differ from those expected for this region. Precautions applying to a temperate region would be more appropriate in these circumstances.

1.4.4 IMMERSION

See Table 1.4/3

The corrosion characteristics of water vary with its pH, flow rate, dissolved salts, temperature and solid matter. The most vulnerable position is at the interface between the water and the atmosphere (splash line).

Further information on the corrosive affect of water types will be found in Section 1.5: Corrosion.

1.4.5 BURIED

See Table 1.4/4

Pipework buried in the soil is in a complex medium and many factors contribute to corrosive attack. The most common factors are discussed below.

1.4.5.1 SOIL COMPOSITION

The main corrosion process will be affected by the intereaction between rainfall, climate and soil constituents.

Different soil compositions or structures and varying moisture conditions from atmospheric to complete immersion, can occur in the same pipe run. As the pipe passes from one soil condition to another varying surface electro-potentials are created due to variations in oxygen, acid or salt concentrations, with the result that a current will flow from a cathodic condition to an anodic condition with corrosion appearing at the anode. Welded pipe runs are especially vulnerable because insulating gaskets are not present between pipe sections. The resistivity of the soil is an important factor in determining corrosion rate. Resistivities of up to 1,500 ohm cm are very corrosive, up to 3,200 corrosive, up to 10,000 mildly corrosive and above are non-corrosive.

The aeration of a soil is directly related to pore space and water content. Clay soils have fine particles and are closely packed with less pore capacity for moisture and gaseous diffusion than an open sandy soil with angular particles.

When a pipe trench is back-filled and compacted with soil the natural structure is lost. This can give rise to corrosion due to varying aeration along the piperun. Back-filling a buried pipe with a coarse, non-aggressive aggregate will result in an open structure which is consistant along the piperun hence reducing the likelihood of corrosion.

If the pipe is buried below the water-table then conditions similar to immersion are created, either constantly wet or alternatively wet and dry as the water rises and falls.

The effect of soluble salts depends to some extent on the local climate. In regions with moderate or high rainfall the salt solution is relatively dilute, while arid areas usually exhibit high salt concentrations.

1.4.5.2 BACTERIAL ATTACK

In water saturated clays, where air (oxygen) is excluded, microbial attack can occur. The most common form is the sulphate reducing bacterium which attacks unprotected ferrous pipes.

1.4.5.3 STRAY ELECTRIC CURRENTS

Stray D.C. electrical currents can result in the corrosion of buried pipework. This may occur in the vicinity of D.C. equipment such as welding equipment, railways, mines etc. The soil acts as the current path for flow to and return from the pipe which results in localised attack at the anode.

1.4.5.4 PROTECTION

Pipework can be protected by total isolation from the soil. This may be achieved by applying surface coatings or tapes which are compatible with the condition (see Surface Coatings). Cathodic protection using sacrificial anodes or impressed current can also prevent corrosion.

1.4.6 WATER IN PIPES AND TANKS

Water is used for a variety of domestic and industrial purpose. It is a cheap natural commodity, readily available and non-toxic with relatively good heat transfer properties. It is therefore widely used for culinary, washing and drinking purposes on a once through basis or as a heating or cooling media in a recirculatory system.

The composition of raw water will vary according to its source. Aggressive water can lead to problems with the pipe and fitting materials. The aggressive constituents in a recirculatory system may be neutralised by chemical additives. There are many formulations which specialist water treatment companies have developed and which are offered to combat specific conditions.

Many factors contribute towards materials failure, such as water source and composition, temperature and flow rate.

1.4.6.1 WATER SOURCE AND COMPOSITION

The agressive characteristics of waters, from different sources or having different constituents are described in Section 1.5: Corrosion. The most significant features are referred to in Table 1.4/5.

1.4.6.2 TEMPERATURE

Rate of corrosion normally increases with temperature. Hot zones tend to be anodic to cold zones. Corrosion occurs at heat transfer surfaces. In a closed heating circuit the rate of corrosion is related to the oxygen content which will gradually reduce. In oxygen free waters hydrogen is evolved from cast iron at 60-80°C and steel at 96°C. In open circuits the solubility of oxygen becomes zero at 100°C. With water at 70°C a zinc coating no longer cathodically protects steel; the nature of the protective film on zinc becomes altered and less adherent.

1.4.6.3 FLOW RATE

Only for copper pipes is there any specific data available. Sources agree that rate of corrosion is related to flow rate and water hardness. The Swedish Federal Building Standards brings in further variables of temperature, location and operational factors. These relationships are shown in Table 1.4/6

	Temperature - °C			
	10	50	70	90
Accessible Pipe m/s	4.0	3.0	2.5	2.0
Inaccessible Pipe m/s	2.0	1.5	1.3	1.0
Intermittant flow* m/s	16	12	10	8

* These velocities would normally be expected to give rise to erosion and are only acceptable for connections to taps, flushing cisterns etc. with intermittant flow.

Table 1.4/6: Maximum recommended with velocities in copper pipe

However, Sweden is a predominantly soft water area and higher velocities may be required for hard water areas. On this basis a general United Kingdom figure of 3m/s is suggested by the Building Research Establishment with the provisor that a lower velocity would be advisable for soft water areas. USA sources suggest a general figure of 1.3m/s whereas New Zealand prefers 2m/s. It is clearly not possible to assess all the factors totally and produce a definitive figure, even for a totally known situation but some degree of consistancy can be seen in these various recommendations.

For any pipe material erosion can occur due to severe turbulance.

Turbulance can be created by sudden changes in direction or obstructions, such as solder or weld blobs in the bore, gaskets protruding into the flow, rolled-in ends of pipe or burrs as a result of poor finishing.

1.4.6.4 SURFACE CONDITION

The internal surface conditions can affect the life of a pipe. Dirty surfaces (scales, grease, flux etc) are more likely to create local corrosion than clean surfaces. The factors involved are discussed in Section 1.5: Corrosion.

Table 1.4/1(a) Outdoor Environment – Urban/Rural

Environment	Characteristics	Materials and Protection
An urban environment is generally affected by low levels of fallout from industrial processes. Smoke emission may cause some local air contamination. Conditions may be more severe downwind from a source of pollution. Possible pollutants are sulphur dioxide, suspended particles (smoke), exhaust fumes and chemicals, such as chlorides and sulphates brought down in rain. The rural environment is generally the least polluted but it may be affected by distant industrial or marine sources according to prevailing winds or topography. The effects of salt from marine sources may extend up to 3km inland.	Dry conditions contribute little to corrosion in both urban and rural environments. Wet conditions due to rain or condensation allow corrosion to proceed by dissolved contaminants producing aggressive solutions. These solutions may flow into crevices, concentrate by evaporation, and attack the material. Even at low concentration, moisture in crevices can lead to attack through differential aeration. Wet conditions are condusive to bi-metallic attack when dissimilar metals are in contact or when dissolved metal salts may cause galvanic corrosion (e.g. drainage from a copper roof onto aluminium alloy or iron gutters). Breaks in protective coatings may promote severe local anodic attack. In rural environments the leaching out of fertilizers, etc may cause localised attack by contaminated surface water.	CARBON STEEL, LOW ALLOY STEEL, CAST IRON. Use aluminium, cadmium or zinc plating plus one coat of paint (as recommended in BS 5493), the paint thickness will depend upon the severity of the conditions and length of time before reprotection. Wrapping tapes will protect provided pretreatment is used and the covering is complete. An electroplated finish of chromium and nickel of 50 to 100 microns will protect in urban environments while in rural environments 12.5 to 50 microns is sufficient providing it is continuous. STAINLESS STEEL No treatment normally required. A coat of paint may be required to prevent bi-metallic corrosion. COPPER AND COPPER ALLOYS No treatment normally required for copper. For a bright finish use a clear lacquer. Copper alloys may need to be non-dezincifiable brass or bronze. To prevent bi-metallic corrosion with other metals the copper alloy can be electroplated with a less noble metal or an electrical insulator placed between them. ALUMINIUM AND ALUMINIUM ALLOYS Neither high purity (+ 99.5%) aluminium nor metallic coatings of aluminium and zinc on aluminium alloys require protection. Sulphuric acid anodised coatings requires a chromate seal and no painting. Chromic acid anodising requires one coat of paint. Corrosion resisting alloys, with an anodic coating of 25 to 40 microns, are satisfactory without painting providing they are washed regularly. Electroplated metallic coatings of 50 micron minimum thickness may be applied to corrodable alloys in urban environments while 25 to 50 microns are required for rural environments. Bi-metallic corrosion between dissimilar metals can be prevented by electrical insulation.

Environment	Characteristics	Materials and Protection
		LEAD

A protective oxide film forms naturally. The film is electrically insulating and the possibility of bimetallic corrosion is reduced.

PLASTICS

Very few plastics are satisfactory for long term use in direct sunlight. Even for relatively short term use ultra-violet inhibited plastics should be used. |

Table 1.4/1(b) Outdoor Environment - Industrial

Environment	Characteristics	Materials and Protection
This environment is affected by heavy fallout from industrial processes. The atmosphere may contain a mixture of gaseous pollutants (mainly sulphur dioxide), suspended particles (smoke), airborne solids (tar, ash industrial dust) and dissolved chemicals such as chlorides and sulphates washed down by the rain. These conditions may extend away from the industrial area in the direction of the prevailing wind.	Dry conditions contribute little to corrosion. Wet conditions due to rain or condensation allow corrosion to proceed by dissolved contaminants producing aggressive solutions, e.g. acids. These solutions may flow into crevices, concentrate by evaporation and attack the metal. Even at low concentration, moisture in crevices can lead to attack through differential aeration. Wet conditions are condusive to bi-metallic corrosion when dissimilar metals are in contact or when dissolved salts may cause galvanic corrosion (e.g. drainage from a copper roof onto aluminium alloy or iron guttering). Breaks in protective coatings may promote severe local anodic attack.	CARBON STEEL, LOW ALLOY STEEL AND CAST IRON. Use aluminium or zinc plating plus a full paint scheme (as recommended in BS 5493), the paint thickness will depend upon the severity of the conditions and the length of time before reprotection. Wrapping tapes will protect provided pretreatment is used and the covering is complete. STAINLESS STEELS No protection is normally required other than regular washing away of surface dirt to prevent differential aeration problems. In severe conditons or where washing is difficult use an austenitic steel with molybdenum. Bi-metallic corrosion can be prevented by applying a cadmium or zinc coating. COPPER AND COPPER ALLOYS Copper will tarnish but will require no additional protection over short periods in less severe conditions. For complete protection copper and copper based alloys should be treated with an etch primer plus a paint finish. Bimetallic corrosion between dissimilar metals can be prevented by electrical insulation. ALUMINIUM AND ALUMINIUM ALLOYS High purity aluminium requires no protection; regular washing will reduce any attack to a minimum. All corrodable aluminium alloys require protection. They may be metal sprayed with aluminium or zinc, or anodised followed by a full paint scheme including a primer. Sulphuric acid anodising gives better protection but chromic acid may be better for castings by avoiding corrosion from acid retained in pores. Bimetallic corrosion between dissimilar metals can be prevented by electrical insulation.

Environment	Characteristics	Materials and Protection
		LEAD
		A protective oxide film forms naturally. This film is electrically insulating and the probability of bimetallic corrosion is reduced.
		PLASTICS
		Very few plastics are satisfatory for long term use in direct sunlight. Even for relatively short term use ultra-violet inhibited plastics should be used.

Table 1.4/1(c) Outdoor Environment – Marine

Environment	Characteristics	Materials and Protection
This environment is associated with a high chloride content. Salt, being hygroscopic, creates conditions that are generally moist. These are ideal conditions for corrosion. The rate of corrosion falls off quickly as the distance from the sea increases. Windbourne sand causes erosion and exposes new surfaces for attack.	This environment is generally humid. An electrolyte containing chloride readily conducts electricity and is highly corrosive. The rate of corrosion for a given concentration is related to the temperature. Bi-metallic corrosion is a hazard. Deposits of sand or rock particles can lead to galvanic attack by de-aeration cells. Crevice corrosion may occur where corrosion products can concentrate by evaporation. Breaks in protective coatings may promote severe local anodic attack.	CARBON STEEL, LOW ALLOY STEEL AND CAST IRON Use aluminium, cadmium or zinc plating plus a full paint scheme (as recommended in BS 5493), the paint thickness will depend upon the severity of the conditions and the length of time before reprotection. Wrapping tapes will protect provided a pre-treatment is used and the covering is continuous. Plastics coatings (with ultra-violet inhibitors) can also give protection providing the covering is continuous. STAINLESS STEEL Austenitic stainless steel has a fairly high resistance to attack. Washing away salt, sand or rock particles will reduce the possibility of local attack. Bi-metallic corrosion can be prevented by applying a zinc or cadmium coating or by electrical insulation between contacting metals. In severe conditions or where washing is difficult use an austenitic steel with molybdenum. Crevice attack can be severe due to the lack of oxygen to regenerate the protective oxide layer. COPPER AND COPPER ALLOYS Copper will tarnish but will require no other protection over short periods. Duplex brasses may be subject to dezincification and should not be used. For complete protection copper and alloys should be treated with an etch primer plus a paint finish. Plating with cadmium, zinc or tin or the use of an electrical insulating material will prevent bimetallic corrosion. ALUMINIUM AND ALUMINIUM ALLOYS High purity aluminium requires no protection; regular washing will reduce any attack to a minimum. All corrodable aluminium alloys require protection. They may be metal sprayed, with aluminium or zinc, or anodised followed by a full paint scheme including a primer. Sulphuric acid anodising gives better protection but chromic acid may be

Materials and Protection	Characteristics	Environment

better for castings by avoiding corrosion from acid retained in the pores. Bi-metallic corrosion can be prevented by electrical insulation.

LEAD

A protective oxide film forms naturally. This film is electrically insulating and therefore the probability of bimetallic corrosion is reduced.

PLASTICS

Plastics must be protected from erosion by sand and sharp particles. Very few plastics are satisfactory for long term use in direct sunlight. Even for relatively short term use ultra-violet inhibited plastics should be used.

27

Table 1.4/2(a) Indoor Environment - Wet Conditions

Environment	Characteristics	Materials and Protection
Typical wet internal environments are swimming pools, shower rooms, laundries, kitchens, sauna baths, toilets, cold stores and glass-houses. The environment is most likely to be a combination of steam or water, with pollutants such as chlorine (in swimming pools) or industrial process liquids (such as acids).	Exposed surfaces are normally wet combined with air and any chemicals associated with the building function. The resulting liquid can be aggressive to the individual materials or may promote galvanic corrosion between different metals in contact.	CARBON STEEL, LOW ALLOY STEEL AND CAST IRON Use zinc or aluminium plating plus a paint shceme (as recommended in BS5493), the paint thickness will depend upon the severity of the conditions and time before reprotection. Zinc rich paints will provide protection if adequate preparation is carried out. Chromium plating is satisfactory but must be a non-cracking grade with copper and nickel precoats to give maximum protection. Plastic coatings will protect providing the covering is continuous. Bimetallic contact must be avoided by interposing an electrically insulating material able to withstand the environment. STAINLESS STEEL Type 302 and 304 should not require protection except in extreme conditions, in which case a coating of chlorinated rubber, epoxy, coal tar/epoxy or polyurethane paint should be applied. Type 316 is a better choice for swimming pools and industrial environments. COPPER AND COPPER ALLOYS Copper will tarnish but will require an additional protection over short periods or in less severe conditions. For a bright finish use a clear lacquer. In more aggressive conditions a complete paint system should be employed and may be based on epoxy/coal tar, polyurethane or vinyl chloride/acetate. Bimetallic corrosion between dissimilar metals can be avoided by electrical insulation. ALUMINIUM AND ALUMINIUM ALLOYS High purity aluminium will not usually require protection although anodising can be used as a decorative finish and to prevent disfigurement by surface staining. Aluminium alloys can be protected by using paint or plastic coatings. The coating must be continuous to avoid severe local anodic attack at pinholes.

Environment	Characteristics	Materials and Protection
		Crevice attack conditions should be avoided. Electroplated coatings of chromium, tin, nickel or copper may be used as protection or as decorative finishes. LEAD A protective oxide film forms naturally. This film is electrically insulating and the probability of bimetallic corrosion is reduced. Painting or bitumen coating should be applied in severe industrial conditions. PLASTICS No protection required unless exposed to direct sunlight. High temperature will reduce the physical properties of all plastics. Some household and decoration solvents will attack plastics.

29

Table 1.4/2(b) Indoor Environment – Dry Conditions

Environment	Characteristics	Materials and Protection
Typical locations are hotels, theatres, concert halls, office blocks, schools, hospitals, laboratories, stores, airport, warehouses, museums, etc. This environment will cause the least corrosion problem.	Corrosion will be insignificant under normal conditions except for bare steel. Surface attack will affect appearance but cause no significant loss of strength. The principal problem may be from condensation on cold surfaces such as windows or cold pipes where 'wet' precautions should be taken.	<u>CARBON STEEL, LOW ALLOY STEEL AND CAST IRON</u> Use zinc or aluminium plating. Decorative finishes, such as chromium plating, will protect providing complete pretreatment is applied. Zinc rich paint will protect where decorative finish is not required. Plastic coatings will give good protection providing they are continuous. <u>STAINLESS STEEL</u> No treatment normally required <u>COPPER AND COPPER ALLOYS</u> No protection required for copper or alloys. For a bright finish use a clear lacquer. Bimetallic corrosion is unlikely to be severe enough to require protection. <u>ALUMINIUM AND ALUMINUM ALLOYS</u> No protection required for high purity aluminium, and alloys with magnesium or manganese. Anodising can be used as a decorative finish or to prevent disfigurement from surface staining. Other alloys can be protected by using paint or plastic coating. Electro-plated coatings of chromium, tin, nickel or copper may be used for protection or as a decorative finish. Bi-metallic corrosion is unlikely to be severe enough to require protection. <u>LEAD</u> A protective oxide film forms naturally <u>PLASTICS</u> No protection required unless exposed to direct sunlight. High temperatures will reduce the physical properties of all plastics. Some household and decoration solvents will attack plastics.

30

Environment	Characteristics	Materials and Protection

31

Table 1.4/3(a) Immersion - Fresh Water

Environment	Characteristics	Materials and Protection
The water in rivers, reservoirs, lakes and streams will vary in composition depending on the nature of the land it flows through. Tidal regions will have a high chloride content which will vary with the tides and the seasons. Components of the water which influence its aggressiveness are the amount of dissolved solids, which determine its electrical conductivity, pH value, hardness, the carbon dioxide and oxygen content and the presence of organic matter.	The water aggressiveness will reflect its drainage area. Insoluble drainage such as rock will produce soft water; if there is decaying vegetation, peat etc. it will be acidic. Rainwater draining through chalk will produce hard water. Soft waters do not promote the formation of natural protective scales and when aggressive constituants such as carbon dioxide are present corrosion may proceed. Hard waters tend to form a calciferous layer which protects the surfaces. Water velocities above a critical value will promote erosion. Stagnant waters may promote microbial attack. Aerated water will encourage corrosion, especially in splash zones, and protection must be adequate to resist the conditions. Constructions running through water of varying composition, e.g. in layered or estuary conditions, may be affected by 'long line' corrosion due to the varying conductivity conditions.	CARBON STEEL, LOW ALLOY STEEL AND CAST IRON Use zinc or aluminium plating, plus a one coat or full paint scheme (as recommended in BS5493) depending upon water aggressiveness and length of time before reprotection. Sprayed metal coatings require sealing or painting with epoxy coal tar/epoxy or chlorinated rubber (as recommended in BS 5493); the coating must be of adequate thickness and continuous. Cast iron must be protected against graphitisation in soft acidic waters. Increased section thickness gives an extended life. STAINLESS STEEL No treatment normally required. Very aggressive waters may require type 316 alloys. Crevices in the structure should be avoided. Protection will be required in low flow conditions due to lack of oxygen to regenerate the oxide layer. COPPER AND COPPER ALLOYS Copper requires protection in soft acidic waters by surface coatings such as epoxy, coal tar/epoxy or chlorinated rubber. Fast flowing water can cause impingement; a surface coating will reduce attack or an alloy with a higher threshold velocity can be used. Duplex brasses may be susceptible to dezincification in some waters; in which case another alloy should be used. ALUMINIUM AND ALUMINIUM ALLOYS Protection is required in alkaline waters or in low flow conditions. Paints or plastics coatings should be used but must be continuous. Copper based antifouling compounds may cause galvanic corrosion. Bimetallic corrosion between dissimilar metals can be prevented by electrical insulaton.

32

Environment	Characteristics	Materials and Protection
		LEAD A protective oxide film forms naturally. This film is electrically insulating and the probability of bimetallic corrosion is reduced. In plumbosolvent and stagnant waters containing nitrates and carbon dioxide, a protective coating of paint or bitumen should be applied. **PLASTICS** No protection normally required unless exposed to direct sunlight.

33

Table 1.4/3(b) Immersion - Sea Water

Environment	Characteristics	Materials and Protection
Sea water is the natural water with the highest concentration of dissolved salts of 3500 ppm with about 2000 ppm of chloride ions. A structure can be either totally immersed, or partially due to tide changes or splash.	Structures in the tidal and splash zones tend to corrode more rapidly due to aeration than those total immersed. The presence of pollutants may influence the rate of corrosion. The oxygen content of the water contributes to the degree of attack, generally the more oxygen present the greater the corrosion rate. For stainless steel and aluminium the rate of attack is increased by a reduction of oxygen due to non replacement of the oxide. High water velocity will cause erosion which will be aggravated by water-borne solids. Every effort should be made to discourage the growth of seaweed or shellfish since these create microclimates that are likely to be aggresive.	CARBON STEEL, LOW ALLOY STEEL AND CAST IRON Use zinc or aluminium plating plus a full paint scheme using epoxy, coal-tar/epoxy, polyurethane or chlorinated rubber (as recommended in BS 5493). Antifouling paints will prevent marine growth. STAINLESS STEEL Protection is necessary for all grades; type 316 offers the greater resistance to attack. Protective coatings of epoxy, coal tar/epoxy, polyurethane or chlorinated rubber should be applied. Insulation must be used to prevent contact with cadmium, zinc, aluminium and magnesium alloys to avoid attack on the non-ferrous materials; attack on copper and copper alloys, although likely to be less severe, can also be avoided by insulation. Crevices should be avoided to prevent crevice corrosion. High water velocities with entrained oxygen are preferred conditions. COPPER AND COPPER ALLOYS Copper and copper alloys are generally attacked by polluted water, and also suffer from particulate erosion in location with high water velocity and from surface contamination. Protection from all these forms of attack can be achieved by surface coatings such as epoxy, epoxy/coal tar, polyurethane or chlorinated rubber. Duplex alloys may be prone to dezincification, use copper or bronze alloys as an alternative. ALUMINIUM AND ALUMINIUM ALLOYS Generally aluminium and alloys (except those containing copper) are not attacked. In polluted waters, protection similar to that for carbon steel should be applied. Copper based antifouling compounds may cause galvanic corrosion. Bimetallic corrosion between dissimilar metals should be prevented by electrical insulation. LEAD A protective oxide film forms naturally.

34

Environment	Characteristics	Materials and Protection
		PLASTIC

Protection will be necessary against the eroding effect of water-borne solids, particularly through narrow spaces. Some pollutants (oil, etc) may effect some plastics. An ultra-violet inhibited plastics should be used where there is likely to be direct exposure to sunlight (e.g. at low tide). |

35

Table 1.4/4 Buried

Environment	Characteristics	Materials and Protection
Soil is distinguished by its complex nature and its interaction with other environmental factors. Conditions can range from atmospheric to complete immersion depending on compactness and moisture content. The corrosion of buried objects can be influenced by factors such as stray electrical current (AC or DC) and 'long line' currents. Chemicals in the soil from fertilizers, industrial waste, brine, thawing salts, etc may accelerate the corrosion rate. Trench back-fill is an important factor as it may establish a local environment that differs from the surrounding undisturbed soil.	No two soils are exactly alike; variation in structure, composition and corrosive activity are found in different soils. Climatic factors such as rainfall, temperature, air movement and sunlight can cause marked alterations in the soil properties which relate directly to the corrosion rate of buried metals. The corrosivity of a soil is indicated by its electrical conductivity, its porosity, dissolved salts, acidity and its micro-biological activity. High risk conditions are in heavy clay and saline soils with high conductivity or pipes below the water table or in an alternating table. Low risk conditions are dry or sandy soils with low electrical conductivity. Waterlogged conditions are ideal for microbial action. Back-fill material consisting of cinder and ash attack most metals in wet conditions.	CARBON STEEL AND LOW ALLOY STEELS Isolation of the metal from the surroundings must be total. Protective with pretreatment coatings may be used, such as wrapping tapes, plastic coatings, polythene sleeves and coal tar/epoxies. Breaks in the coating will lead to concentrated local anodic attack with early failure. Zinc plating may be used but requires coating, particularly in acidic soils or where large quantities of soluble salts exist. Cut edges or welded areas must be coated with zinc rich paint. Welded piperuns should be broken into insulated sections to minimise "long line' attack. Back-fill material must have a consistant composition. Avoid damage to the protective coating by large objects falling or by builders plant. CAST IRON Waterlogged conditions can promote 'graphitisation'. This can be overcome by coating, with pretreatment, using wrapping tapes, polythene sleeves or coal tar/epoxies. STAINLESS STEEL No protection normally required. Anaerobic (i.e. waterlogged) conditions may prevent formation of oxide layer and therefore protective measures may be required, such as wrapping tapes, plastic coatings, polythene sleeves or coal tar/epoxy. Incorrect welding may promote weld decay with resultant corrosion failure in adverse conditions. In saline conditions stress corrosion may occur and total protection is required. COPPER AND COPPER ALLOYS Copper is generally satisfactory underground except in made up ground containing wet ash and cinders, acidic peat or clay. In these cases bitumen coating, wrapping tapes or plastic coatings should be used. Duplex brasses are subject to dezincification in most buried conditions and should not be used. Trench back-fill should provide drainage to prevent waterlogged conditions.

36

Environment	Characteristics	Materials and Protection
		ALUMINIUM AND ALUMINIUM ALLOYS Copper bearing alloys should be avoided. Buried aluminium and aluminium alloys should be isolated from the backfill and soil by wrapping tapes and bitumen coatings. Trench back-fill material should provide drainage to prevent waterlogged conditions. **LEAD** A protective oxide coating forms naturally and is sufficient for most conditions. In wet clays, cinders or soils with chloride and nitrate ions or which are alkalines the pipe must be protected by wrapping tape or bitumen coating. The moisture content should be reduced by using a porous trench back-fill material. Soil variations along a run of pipe can create significant potential differences, therefore the same type of back-fill should be used over the whole length. **PLASTICS** Plastics will generally withstand soil conditions without protection. Do not use large size back-fill which may fracture the pipe. Do not run plastics pipe adjacent to a hot pipe.

37

Table 1.4/5   Water in Pipes and Tanks

Environment	Characteristics	Materials and Protection
The passage of water through pipes or the storage of water in tanks may modify its composition and hence its corrosive properties. The properties of the water will be closely associated with its source. If these properties can be modified by the addition of chemicals or an ionic exchange then it may be less aggressive towards the materials in which it is in contact.	Aggressive waters have many constituents which may cause attack of the system materials, alone or in combination. The important constituents are dissolved salts (chlorides, sulphates, carbonates and bicarbonates), dissolved gases (oxygen, carbon dioxide and hydrogen sulphide), organic matter (vegetation, bacteria and marine fouling) and inorganic matter (particules and trace metals). Whether the water will deposit a protective scale or not (hard or soft water) is related to its Langelier Index. Other factors that influence material attack are temperature and water velocity. Particular forms of attack that occur in pipes and tanks (i.e. grooving, pitting and tuberculation) are discussed in the main text.	**CARBON STEEL, LOW ALLOY STEEL** Eliminate air from the system. For extra protection use an inhibitor (with biocide to prevent bacterial growth in anaerobic condition). In order to avoid erosion water velocities should not exceed 3 to 6 m/s, depending on the degree of turbulence created by and water temperature. **GALVANISED CARBON STEEL** Condition the water to remove or control undesirable constituents (waters with high carbon dioxide or are soft will attack). Do not use above 70°C. Avoid mixed metal systems where copper may be deposited. Water velocity should not exceed 6 m/s to minimise turbulence and hence avoid erosion. **CAST IRON** Water treatment to correct acidic condition will reduce graphitisation. Every effort must be made to reduce aeration of the water. **STAINLESS STEEL** Attack by chlorides can be reduced by using a stainless steel of low carbon (L grades) or one containing molybdenum. Crevices or low flow conditions creating low oxygen levels should be avoided. Air entrainment is beneficial with high flow rates above 1.5m/s to maintain the protective oxide layer. Stress corrosion can be avoided by either annealing, particularly after welding, or the use of a less sensitive alloy. **COPPER AND COPPER ALLOYS** Water treatment should be used for soft waters containing carbon dioxide. Flow velocity for potable water should be below the threshold for the particular alloy - copper 2m/s; brass 2.5m/s; cupro-nickels 4.5m/s. For seawater the threashold velocity

Environment	Characteristics	Materials and Protection
		is approximatly half that for potable water. Duplex brasses are subject to dezincification in some waters, in which case copper, bronze or a non-dezincifiable brass should be used. Cupro-solvent waters should be treated to prevent carry over of copper which could promote bimetallic corrosion of other metals in the system. Bimetallic connections should also be avoided by insulation between dissimilar metals

ALUMINIUM AND ALUMINIUM ALLOYS

Apply water treatment to maintain the pH value between 4.5 and 8.5. Avoid using aluminium or its alloys with copper in systems containing cupro-solvent water. Bimetallic corrosion between dissimilar metals should be prevented by electrical insulation.

LEAD

A protective oxide film forms naturally and is sufficient for most conditions. Plumbo-solvent waters should be treated to minimise attack. Stagnant conditions should be avoided. Lead must not be used for potable water pipe work or tank lining.

PLASTICS

Particular limitations must be recognised. The maximum velocity should not exceed 6 to 8m/s. Temperature limits must not be exceeded, particularly in pressurised applications. Adequate support must be provided, plastics pipe must not be in contact with hot pipes or surfaces. |

39

1.5 CORROSION

1.5.1 BASIC PRINCIPLES

'Corrosion' is an imprecise term used to describe the deterioration of metals under adverse environmental conditions.

At the interface between the metal and the environment a change of state occurs producing a corrosion product or debris. In some situations this process is self-defeating because the corrosion product forms an impervious coating and creates an effective barrier to the environment - the oxide coating on aluminium is an example of such a process. More usually, corrosion is a continuing process gradually converting more material into corrosion product causing weakness and eventual failure of the component.

Almost all forms of corrosion involve an electrochemical reaction in the form of a corrosion cell. Even erosion, which might be simply regarded as a mechanical process, is often accompanied by corrosion so that the overall efect is an accelerated rate of deterioration.

A corrosion cell consists of 3 parts; an anode, a cathode and an electrolyte.

The 'anode' is that part of an electrochemical system (corrosion cell) that is electrically positive with respect to other parts. In suitable conditions positive metal ions will be released and transferred to the electrolyte and then deposited on more negative surfaces. The 'cathode' provides the corresponding electrically negative area to which positive ions will be attracted.

The 'electrolyte' is invariably a liquid. It plays two related roles in the electrochemical system. It allows materials with which it is in contact to dissociate into their ionic (electrically charged) states. It also provides a conducting path between parts of the cell allowing current to flow through the transfer of ions from one place to another. Within the scope of this Handbook the only electrolyte considered is water containing dissolved impurities.

Corrosion rate can be equated to current flow in the electrolyte in that this represents the transfer of material from its intended position to somewhere else. The current flow rate, by Ohms law, depends upon the potential differences across the corrosion cell and the resistance of the system, taking account of both the electrolyte and the substrate. The relative sizes of the anode and cathode influence the local rate of attack. The smaller the anode, compared to the cathode, the more concentrated the attack.

A corrosive cell may be created by:

- local differences of composition, metallurgical conditions, surface texture, inclusions, etc which influence the anode/cathode state of the surface
- two different metals in contact with an electrolyte

local differences in the electrolyte. A common instance is where one part of the electrolyte is saturated with oxygen while another part is deficient of oxygen (de-aeration cells), such as under a deposit or tubercule, or in a crevice. Under these circumstances the oxygen rich area is cathodic to the deficient area, which results in preferential corrosion under deposits or in crevices.

All corrosion reactions require free oxygen in the electrolyte. It therefore follows that, in an enclosed liquid system, if the oxygen initially present is used up and cannot be replaced, corrosion becomes progressively slower.

1.5.2 FORMS OF CORROSION

A brief description of some forms of corrosion are given below. In many instances of corrosion more than one form may be present.

1.5.2.1 SURFACE CORROSION OR PITTING

Most atmospheric corrosion produces an even attack on the metal surface. But, in conditions where debris is deposited on the surface or tubercules are formed, localised corrosion, in the form of pits, can develop. Similarly, where natural protective layers are penetrated, local aggressive attack will occur.

By applying coatings of metals, paints, tapes or plastics that will withstand the environment and operational conditions this type of corrosion can be prevented.

1.5.2.2 BI-METALLIC CORROSION

When dissimilar metals are in contact, in the presence of water, an electrolytic cell is formed with the least noble metal corroding. Relative areas, geometry and the metals involved determine the degree of attack.

Corrosion can be prevented by choosing metals of similar electropotential (see Table 1.5/1), coating one component with a metal that reduces the potential difference between them, cathodic protection with a sacrificial anode that is less noble than the anode or by electrically insulating the components from each other.

1.5.2.3 DEZINCIFICATION

In certain environments the zinc in brass is attacked leaving a porous matrix with loss of strength. By selecting inhibited brasses, bronze or gunmetal the problem can be eliminated.

1.5.2.4 STRESS CORROSION

Tensile stress and corrosion acting together can lead to an intense, penetrating attack which may be either intergranular or transgranular. Failure can occur at stress levels far below the design strength of the component.

Materials prone to stress corrosion should not be used in a corrosive environment and should be stress relieved prior to assembly.

41

1.5.2.5   **GRAPHITISATION**

Both ductile and grey cast iron are susceptable to this form of attack in waterlogged clays, leaving behind a residue of graphite and corrosion products which is soft, porous and of low mechanical strength. The finer and more interlocked are the graphite flakes the stronger the resulting residue.

Alloy cast irons are less prone to graphitisation. Isolating the surface from the environment by surface coating or protective tapes will alleviate the problem.

1.5.2.6   **CREVICE CORROSION**

When designers allow crevices to be present where electrolyte or dirt will collect then corrosion may be instigated. The cause may be aeration cells with stagnant electrolyte creating an anode in the crevice. Materials such as aluminium and stainless steel, normally protected by an oxide film, are subject to this form of attack.

The use of alternative materials and the elimination of crevices in the design can overcome the problem.

1.5.2.7   **IMPINGEMENT**

This is associated with the velocity of liquid passing over a metal. At a critical velocity, depending on the metal and temperature, pitting of the surface will occur. If turbulance is present the corrosion product is removed exposing fresh surface for attack (erosion-corrosion). This takes place at obstructions or at sharp changes of direction.

Erosion, due to velocity, can be prevented by maintaining the velocity below a critical value, (see Section 1.4.6.3) using larger diameter pipes, eliminating all obstructions and change direction gradually. The use of a material with a higher critical velocity may overcome the problem.

1.5.2.8   **BACTERIAL CORROSION**

This generally occurs in anaerobic conditions (lack of oxygen) such as waterlogged clay, stagnant waters or under tubercles. Bacteria consume compounds, such as sulphates, and produce conditions that are corrosive to metals, particularly ferrous metals.

By creating access for air the attack by anaerobic bacteria can be reduced. The application of a protective surface coating or wrapping in tape will prevent external attack of ferrous materials.

Pipes and tanks may be protected internally by the application of a bacteriacide to the water for recirculating systems.

1.5.3   WATER SOURCE AND COMPOSITION

The composition of water plays a significant part in the corrosion process by supplying ingredients or conditions likely to promote or inhibit attack.

1.5.3.1 WATER SOURCE

RAINWATER

Composition is dependant on atmosphere pollutants. Oxygen and carbon dioxide are absorbed in significant quantities. Local sources of atmospheric pollution must be considered; industrial activities may result in highly aggressive constituants, such as sulphur dioxide, which will result in an acidic condition.

SURFACE WATER

Originates as rainwater flowing over the terrain. The catchment area will determine the nature of contaminants. Insoluable surfaces such as granite, will provide soft waters which may be acidic if decaying vegetation, e.g. peat is present. Soluble surfaces such as chalk, will impart a hardness to the water.

Lower reaches of rivers may be polluted by agriculture or urban surface runoff and industrial effulent which will require treatment before being accepted as potable water.

SEA WATER

Sea water has the highest proportion of dissolved salts, up to 20,000 mgm/1 of chlorides, and hence one of the most corrosive environments. The degree to which sea water can attack metals can vary with depth, temperature and composition changes caused by currents.

Dissolved gases are an important factor in the corrosion of metals immersed in sea water. The presence of oxygen, particularly in areas where the metal is exposed by the rise and fall of the tide and within the splash line, promotes extensive corrosion. In areas where sea water is stagnant, such as harbours, then a limited oxygen supply will reduce the rate of corrosion in this form but in circumstances where oxygen is totally deficient, corrosion may still occur due to the presence of anaerobic corrosion forming bacteria.

The flow rate of sea water can influence the rate of corrosion. High flow rates can remove corrosion products exposing the metal to further attack. Low flow rates, such as in crevices or inside immersed structures, are vulnerable areas for corrosion resistant metals that rely on oxygen to replenish the displaced protective oxide layer, such as stainless steel or aluminium alloys.

Materials can be protected by applying coatings that are compatible with the material and the environment.

ESTUARY WATER

A mixture of surface water and sea water. The proportions are likely to vary throughout the year due to floodwater. This water has a high chloride content.

WELL WATER

Formed by water perculating through sub-soil until an impervious layer is reached. This water has the most consistant composition and temperature from any source. The water is generally hard to very hard, has a high degree of bacterial and organic purity, and may be highly corrosive due to the presence of free carbon dioxide.

TREATED WATER

Treatment may be required to purify water for consumption or to remove aggressive constituents to reduce corrosion. Hard waters can be softened by lime soda, base exchange (zeolite) or ion exchange resins. Corrosion can be reduced by removing the oxygen using sodium sulphite or hydrazine. Protective surface films may be formed by using amines to inhibit corrosion. Bacterial problems may be alleviated by the use of biocides. It is important to note that water treatment is effective only if proper control is exercised.

COMPOSITION CHANGES DURING USE

Recirculation systems provide two sorts of problems. Firstly, when leakage, spray loss or aeration occurs the aggressive constituents of the water (particularly dissolved oxygen) will be replenished and allow continuing corrosion in a system that would otherwise have reached a passive state. Secondly, evaporation or steam losses (deliberate or otherwise) will cause a concentration of dissolved solids producing a more aggressive water.

1.5.3.2 WATER COMPOSITION

HYDROGEN ION CONCENTRATION (pH)

This is a measure of the alkalinity or acidity of a water. A pH of 7 is taken as neutral, below 7 as acid and above 7 as alkaline. The majority of natural waters are between 6.5 and 8 (soft water, high in carbon dioxide, may give a lower figure). Some metal oxides are soluble in both acid and alkaline solutions; there is a pH value for each material at which the corrosion rate is a minimum (e.g. aluminium 6.5, lead 8.0, tin 8.5, zinc 11.5). Most metal oxides are soluble in acid and insoluble in alkaline solution. (Nickel, copper and chromium are examples). Iron has a stable corrosion rate for pH values between 4.5 and 9 outside these values the corrosion rate is rapid.

The pH scale is logarithmic and a change of 1 is a tenfold change in strength of the solution.

DISSOLVED GASES

Oxygen - The content of water is dependent on several factors including temperature, velocity and composition. Oxygen is an effective cathode reactant and the rate of reaction increases with concentration. Differential aeration cells can be created around crevices and under deposits due to non-uniform oxygen distribution. In the total absence of oxygen (anaerobic conditions) bacterial corrosion may take place.

Carbon dioxide - Carbon dioxide influence corrosion rate by its acidic nature and its capacity to impair the formation of a carbonate protective scale. Carbon dioxide may originate from decaying organic matter. Also it can be formed in boiler steam from the decomposition of bicarbonate in make up water resulting in an aggressive condensate which attacks the steel or copper pipework.

DISSOLVED SALTS

Aggressive salts - Chlorides and sulphates are aggressive salts. They are able to break down protective films or prevent their formation, such as on stainless steel. Under anaerobic conditions bacterial corrosion of ferrous metals can take place in the presence of sulphates.

Non-aggressive salts - Carbonates, and calcium salts have inhibitive properties which restrain corrosion. These salts form surface layers which protect the metal. Hard waters may contain up to 350ppm of calcium carbonate. The Langalier Index indicates the ability of a water to form a protective scale deposit; waters registering positive values form protective layers while those with negative values do not and can actually remove a calcium protective deposit.

DISSOLVED SOLIDS

The constitution of total dissolved solids is a measure of the conductivity of the water and an indication of its purity. Conductivity is an important factor when determining a water's ability to support bimetallic corrosion or galvanic protection.

MINOR INORGANICS

Silica and metallic traces in the water are indicative of its aggressive nature or its toxicity. Silica is found in natural waters and, as silicates, forms a hard encrustations in steam equipment. Metals in solution can be deposited on metal surfaces creating bimetallic cells which may cause local corrosion (copper, as little as 0.01g/1, deposited on galvanised steel creates corrosion cells).

ORGANIC MATTER

Organic matter can be either decaying vegetable matter, e.g. peat, or living matter (algae, fungi or bacteria) which can create local changes in the water composition. Coverage of a metal surface can control the rate of corrosion. Some types of organism can attack protective layers.

BACTERIA

The two principle bacteria are the anaerobic sulphate reducing type and the iron bacteria. Sulphate reducing bacteria are found in anaerobic conditions, such as under tubercules, and produce hydrogen sulphide which aids corrosion of ferrous metals by forming acids. Iron bacteria do not change the composition of the water, nor do they contribute to corrosion. They produce fouling which leads to blockage of valves etc. and the creation of 'red water'.

1.5.4 PROTECTION

Protection from corrosion may be achieved by:-

- isolation from the aggressive environment by continuous coatings of a more corrosion resistant metal, paint, plastics or tape.
- altering the relationship between the components with respect to the environment, particularly in relation to bimetallic corrosion. This can be achieved by placing an insulating material between the metallic components, by plating with a metal that reduces the potential difference between them and thus reduces the rate of attack in a particular electrolyte or by using cathodic protection to alter the corroding component from an anode to the cathode of a system.

Various methods of protective finishings and guidance as to how to specify them are given in BS 5493 - protective coating of iron and steel structures against corrosion.

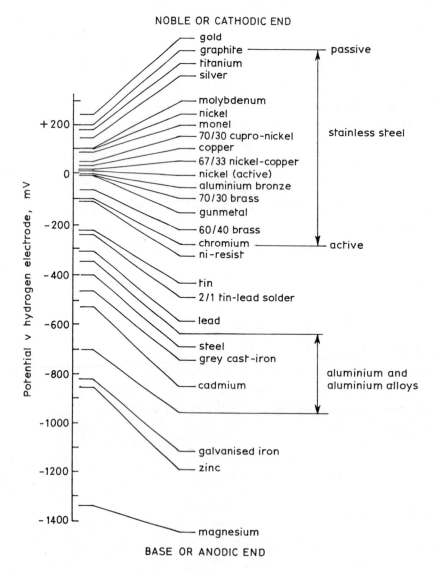

Table 1.5/1· Galvanic series of metals and alloys

46

PART 2   SERVICES

| FAMILY GROUP | SPACE HEATING | SUB-GROUP | DOMESTIC CENTRAL HEATING |

GENERAL DESCRIPTION

Domestic central heating systems range from 7.5 kW up to 45 kW. Boiler heated water is pumped through small or micro bore pipework to heat emitters. Systems may be open to atmosphere or sealed (closed). If sealed expansion of water must be accommodated by the diaphragm expansion vessel.

Either system may provide domestic hot water by means of an indirect cylinder.

SERVICE CONDITIONS

FLUID

Water generally derived from mains supply but other sources may be used. T he water is recirculated and therefore aggressive constituents are not replenished and should not represent a hazard unless there is leakage or frequent draining down.

TEMPERATURE

Open systems designed for flow temperatures between $66^{o}C$ and $82^{o}C$. Closed systems designed for flow temperatures between $66^{o}C$ and $98^{o}C$. Materials in close proximity to the heat source may need to withstand higher temperatures.

PRESSURE

Open vented systems have a maximum operating pressure determined by the static head of water plus pump head. Closed systems have a maximum recommended operating pressure of 3 bar.

STANDARD PRECAUTIONS

SEE SERVICE SECTION APPENDIX 1

A   1, 2, 3, 4, 5, 7, 8, 9, 10

B   1, 2, 3

C   1, 2, 3, 6, 8, 9

D   1, 2, 3, 4

SPECIAL CONSIDERATIONS

Various inhibitors are available for domestic systems. They are not generally regarded as essential although some installations may benefit from their use. Such additions to the water should not limit the choice of materials, but manufacturer's advice should be followed particularly with regard to innovations or non metallic materials.

MAJOR COMPONENTS

COMPONENT	DATA SHEET NO.	NOTE
PIPE		
Carbon Steel	3.1.1	BS1387 medium or heavy weight - not commonly used.
Copper	3.1.2	BS2871 Tables W, X, Y or Z.
Stainless Steel	3.1.3	BS4127
Plastics	3.1.4B	Plastics materials for domestic central heating pipework are being developed.
JOINTING METHOD		
Screwed	3.2.2	Malleable cast iron fittings to BS143 or BS1256. Brass fittings to BS864, may be either screw joints sealed on the thread or on a face washer. Sealants or washers must be compatible with the pressure and temperature.
Capillary	3.2.3	Capillary fittings are for permanent fixtures.
		BS864 or BS2051 may be either the integral solder ring or the end feed type. The solder should be to BS219 type C or G.
Compression	3.2.4	Compression fittings to BS864 or BS2051, may be used to avoid soldering or where the pipework requires breaking to facilitate maintenance or modification.
VALVES	3.3	Valves are chosen from proprietary designs to control fluid flow or to isolate sections or components. Particular attention must be paid to the selection and use of designs incorporating non metallic materials e.g. seals, floats etc.
PUMP		
Domestic glandless	3.4.2	The pump should be selected to suit the temperature and pressure of the system. 'Wetted' materials should not deteriorate under operating conditions. Pumps should be positioned so that the shaft is horizontal.
TANKS		
Feed & Expansion Cistern	3.5.1	Thermal expansion of the system contents should be accommodated; any resultant rise in temperature should not cause failure of the tank.
Cylinders	3.5.3	BS1566 Indirect copper cylinder selected to suit the system operating conditions. See also Domestic Hot Water Service Sheet 2.2.2.
Expansion Vessels	3.5.5	BS4814
HEAT EMITTERS		
Radiators	3.6.1	Cast iron, carbon steel, or aluminium capable of withstanding test pressures of 7 bar.
Convectors	3.6.2	Copper tube with non-ferrous fins or steel tube and fins galvanised after assembly.
Radiant Panels	3.6.3	Carbon steel or cast iron waterways intimately in contact with steel plates or tube continuously welded to a surface plate. Not commonly used for Domestic heating.

 **service data sheet**

COMPONENT	DATA SHEET No.	NOTE
Unit Heaters	3.6.4	Heater battery may be copper tubes and fins set into a copper, bronze, or steel header. Steel tubes, fins and header may be used with suitable corrosion protection.
HEAT GENERATORS		
Boilers		Constructed from cast iron, steel or of the low water content type using copper or steel tubes.
CONTROLS	3.8.1	Those controls having components in direct contact with the system contents must not deteriorate under normal operating conditions. Bi-metallic combinations must not generate galvanic action.

| FAMILY GROUP | SPACE HEATING | SUB-GROUP | LOW TEMPERATURE HOT WATER HEATING |

GENERAL DESCRIPTION

A system which operates at temperatures up to 95°C, ranging in size from 50kW upwards, to provide space heating. Boiler heated water is pumped through pipework to heat emitters. Heat may be used to raise the temperature of the domestic water in calorifiers or hot water cylinders. The system may be open or closed to atmosphere, if closed the expansion of the system may be accommodated.

SERVICE CONDITIONS

FLUID

Water generally derived from mains supply but other sources may be used. The water is recirculated and therefore aggressive constituents are not replenished, and should not represent a hazard unless there is leakage or frequent draining down.

TEMPERATURE

Systems may be designed for maximum service temperature 85°C. Closed systems designed for flow temperatures up to 98°C. Materials in close proximity to the heat source may need to withstand higher temperatures.

PRESSURE

Open vented systems have a maximum operating pressure determined by the static head of water plus the pump head. Closed systems have a maximum operating pressure determined by the designer in keeping with the system components and the selected expansion vessel.

STANDARD PRECAUTIONS   SEE SERVICES SECTION APPENDIX 1

A   1, 2, 3, 4, 5, 7, 8, 9, 10, 11, 12

B   1, 2, 3

C   1, 2, 3, 4, 6, 8, 9

D   1, 2, 3, 4, 5

SPECIAL CONSIDERATIONS   Corrosion inhibitors and biocides may be used to combat aggressive conditions originating from the water quality. Such additions to the water should not limit the choice of materials but the manufacturers advise should be followed particularly with regard to innovations or non-metallic materials.

MAJOR COMPONENTS

COMPONENT	DATA SHEET No.	NOTE
PIPE		
Steel	3.1.1	BS1387 medium, except for those screwed 20mm and 40mm and pipes permanently concealed which should be BS1387 heavy. BS3601 of suitable wall thickness, type, and grade.
Copper	3.1.2	BS2871 Tables W, X, Y or Z.
JOINTING METHODS		
Flanged	3.2.1	At dismantling points or component connections flanges should be used for pipework 65mm and above. Flanges to BS10 or BS4504 constructed from carbon steel and fitted with flat ring gaskets appropriate to the conditions.
Screwed	3.2.2	May be used up to 100mm where accessible. Joints in which the seal is made on the thread must have at least a taper thread on the externally threaded component. Malleable cast iron fitting to BS143 or BS1256. Brass fittings to BS864, may be screwed joints sealed on the thread or on a face washer. Sealants or washers must be compatible with the pressure and temperature.
Capillary	3.2.3	Capillary fittings are for permanent fixtures. BS864 or BS2051 may be either of the integral ring or end feed type. The solder should be to BS219 Grade C or G.
Compression	3.2.4	Compression fittings to BS864 or BS2051 may be used to avoid soldering or where the pipework requires breaking to facilitate maintenance or modification.
VALVES	3.3	Chosen from proprietary designs to control fluid flow or to isolate sections or components. Particular attention must be paid to the selection and use of designs incorporating non metallic materials e.g. seals, floats etc. Valves and cocks up to 50mm may have cast gunmetal, bronze or hot pressed brass bodies. Valves of 65mm and above may be of cast iron. Working parts should be of gunmetal or similar corrosion and wear resistant materials.
PUMPS		
Centrifugal	3.4.1	Circulating pumps of the centrifugal type with direct or indirect drive. Pumps should have isolating valves on both inlet and outlet. A facility for venting is advisable.
TANKS		
Feed/Expansion	3.5.2	Tanks may be of welded construction galvanised after manufacture to BS417 or plastics material to BS4213. Pressed steel and cast iron sectional tanks should be externally flanged and incorporate necessary stiffeners. Purpose made covers to prevent contamination of the contents must be provided.
Cylinders	3.5.3	Direct - Galvanised mild steel BS417 grade A or B. Copper to BS699 grade 1 or 2. Indirect - Galvanised mild steel BS1565 class B with detachable top. Copper to BS1566 Part 1 grade 2. Larger cylinders than above or for a greater head should be to BS853 parts 1 or 2.

COMPONENT	DATA SHEET NO.	NOTE
Cylinders (continued)	3.5.3	See also Domestic Hot Water Service sheet no. 2.2.2.
HEAT EMITTERS		
Radiators	3.6.1	Cast iron, carbon steel or aluminium capable of withstanding test pressures of 7 bar.
Convectors	3.6.2	Copper tube with non-ferrous fins mounted in casing. Also available steel tube and fins galvanised after assembly.
Radiant Panels	3.6.3	Carbon steel or cast iron waterways intimately in contact with steel plates or tube. Continuously welded to a surface plate.
Unit Heaters	3.6.4	Heating battery may be copper tubes and fins set into a copper, bronze, or steel header or steel tubes, fins and header may be used with suitable corrosion protection.
HEAT GENERATORS		
Boilers	3.7.1 3.7.2	Constructed from cast iron, steel or of the low water content type using copper or steel tubes.
CONTROLS	3.8.1	Those controls having components in direct contact with the system contents must not deteriorate under normal operating conditions. Bi-metallic combinations must not generate galvanic action.

service data sheet	SHEET NUMBER	2.1.3	1

FAMILY GROUP	SPACE HEATING	SUB-GROUP	MEDIUM TEMPERATURE HOT WATER HEATING

GENERAL DESCRIPTION

A heating system operating at temperatures between $95^{\circ}C$ and a maximum of $120^{\circ}C$ with water at pressures up to a maximum pressure of 3.4 bar. Heated water circulated by pump through pipework and controls to provide heating and, via calorifiers having temperature limiting controls, domestic hot water.

SERVICE CONDITIONS

FLUID

Water generally derived from mains supply but other sources may be used. The water is recirculated and therefore aggressive constituents are not replenished and should not represent a hazard unless there is leakage or frequent draining down.

TEMPERATURE

Range from $95^{\circ}C$ to $120^{\circ}C$. Materials in the proximity of the heat source may need to withstand higher temperatures.

PRESSURE

Systems pressurised up to a maximum of 3.4 bar by a combination of static head and pump head, and pressurisation.

STANDARD PRECAUTIONS   SEE CHECK LIST (SERVICES APPENDIX)

A   1, 3, 5, 7, 9, 10, 11, 12

B   1, 2, 3

C   1, 2, 3, 4, 6, 7, 8, 9

D   1, 2, 3, 4, 5

SPECIAL CONSIDERATIONS

Insulation is necessary for exposed pipework. Systems contained within buildings require only limited protection. External pipework above or below ground must be protected to suit the nature of the environment in which they reside. If water treatments are used to combat aggressive conditions arising from the water quality they should not limit the choice of materials, but the manufacturers advice should be followed particularly with regard to innovations or non metallic materials.

 **service data sheet**

BSRIA

| SHEET NUMBER | 2.1.3 | 2 |

MAJOR COMPONENTS

COMPONENT	DATA SHEET No.	NOTE
PIPEWORK		
Steel	3.1.1	BS1387 medium except for those screwed 20mm and 40mm and pipes permanently concealed which should be BS1387 heavy. BS3601 of suitable thickness type and grade.
JOINTING METHOD		
Flanged	3.2.1	Flanges to BS10 (imperial sizes) or BS4504 (metric sizes). Flanged joints shall be fitted with gaskets suitable for the temperature and pressure.
Screwed	3.2.2	At least the externally threaded component of the joint shall be taper threaded. Screwed fittings shall be of malleable cast iron to BS143 or BS1256.
VALVES	3.3	Chosen from proprietary designs to control fluid flow or to isolate sections or components. Particular attention must be paid to the selection and use of designs incorporating non metallic materials e.g. seals, floats etc. Valves may have non ferrous or cast iron bodies and working parts of gunmetal or similar corrosion and wear resistant material.
PUMPS		
Centrifugal	3.4.1 3.4.2 3.4.3	Circulating pumps of the centrifugal or full-way type with direct or indirect drive. Isolation valves should be installed to ease maintenance. A facility for venting the pump is advisable.
TANKS		
Feed	3.5.1 3.5.2	Tanks may be of welded construction galvanised after manufacture to BS417, or plastics material to BS4213. Pressed steel and cast iron sectional tanks should be externally flanged and incorporate necessary stiffeners. Purpose made covers to prevent contamination of the content must be provided.
Calorifier	3.5.4	Calorifiers may be of the storage type BS853 or non storage BS853 or BS3274 type 2. They may be either horizontal or vertical and adequately supported. Must be fitted with temperature limiting controls. See also Domestic Hot Water Supply Service Sheet No.2.2.2.
HEAT GENERATORS		
Boiler	3.7.1	
CONTROLS	3.8.1	Those controls having components in direct contact with the system contents must not deteriorate under normal operating conditions. Bi-metallic combinations must not generate galvanic action.

56

| FAMILY GROUP | SPACE HEATING | SUB-GROUP | HIGH TEMPERATURE HOT WATER HEATING |

GENERAL DESCRIPTION

A heating system operating at temperatures above 120°C and at pressures up to a maximum of 10.3 bar. Heated water is pumped around pipework to distribute heat to a large building or building complex. The high temperature water may be mixed with cooler water or passed through heat exchangers to lower the temperature for distribution to radiators. The system may heat domestic water in calorifiers having temperature limiting controls.

SERVICE CONDITIONS

FLUID

Usually mains water to initially charge the system and make up losses. Some systems charged with treated water, e.g. demineralised, to limit the scale and solids content of the system. Water treatment is often applied to overcome aggressive constituents and reduce the possibility of corrosion.

TEMPERATURE

Ranging up from 120°C. Materials used must withstand temperatures in excess of the maximum operating temperature particularly those in close proximity to the heat source.

PRESSURE

System pressurised up to a maximum of 10.3 bar.

STANDARD PRECAUTIONS

SEE CHECK LIST (SERVICES APPENDIX)

A   1, 3, 4, 5, 7, 9, 10, 11, 12

B   1, 2, 3

C   1, 2, 3, 4, 6, 7, 8

D   1, 2, 3, 4, 5

SPECIAL CONSIDERATIONS

Insulation is necessary for exposed pipework. Systems contained within buildings require only limited protection. External pipework above or below ground must be protected to suit the nature of the environment in which they reside. Water and chemical treatments of the system contents should not influence the choice of materials but the manufacturers advice should be followed particularly with regard to innovations or non-metallic materials.

MAJOR COMPONENTS

COMPONENT	DATA SHEET No.	NOTE
PIPEWORK		
Steel	3.1.1	BS1387 or BS3601 of suitable wall thickness, type and grade.
JOINTING METHOD		
Flanged	3.2.1	May be used for connections to valves and equipment and at dismantling points.
		Flanges to BS10 (imperial sizes) or BS4504 (metric sizes). Flanged joints shall be fitted with gaskets suitable for the temperature and pressure.
Welded	3.2.5	Welding fittings in carbon steel to BS1965 part 1 heavy seamless.
VALVES	3.3	Chosen from proprietary designs to control fluid flow or to isolate sections or components. Particular attention must be paid to the selection and use of designs incorporating non metallic materials e.g. seals etc. Valves may have non ferrous or cast iron bodies and working parts of nickel alloy, stainless steel, gunmetal or similar corrosion and wear resistant materials - manufacturers advise on pressure limitations at elevated temperatures must be followed.
PUMPS		
Centrifugal	3.4.1	Circulating pumps of the centrifugal or fullway type with direct or indirect drive. Isolation valves should be installed to ease maintenance. A facility for venting the pump is advisable.
TANKS		
Feed	3.5.1 3.5.2	Tanks may be of welded construction galvanised after manufacture - BS417, or plastics material - BS4213. Pressed steel and cast iron section tanks should be externally flanged and incorporate necessary stiffeners. Purpose made covers to prevent contamination of the content must be provided.
Calorifier	3.5.4	To supply LTHW heating circuits, calorifiers can be incorporated using HTHW for the primary heat supply. Calorifiers may be of the storage type BS853 or non storage BS853 or BS3274 type 2. They may be either horizontal or vertical and adequately supported. Must be fitted with temperature limiting controls. See also Domestic Hot Water Supply Service Sheet no. 2.2.2.
HEAT GENERATORS		
Boilers	3.7.1 3.7.2 3.7.3	Boilers shall be constructed from steel or, up to a maximum of $132^{\circ}C$ from spherodial cast iron.
INSULATION		
Thermal	3.9.1	Due to the high temperatures in the system all personnel must be protected by the application of insulation on all hot surfaces which are accessible. Insulation should comply with BS5422. The thickness is related to the declared thermal conductivity of the insulating material. BS5422 does not specify the type of material to be used but it must be compatible with the conditions.
		Material choice may be from CP3005.

FAMILY GROUP	SUB-GROUP
SPACE HEATING	STEAM HEATING AND CONDENSATE

GENERAL DESCRIPTION

Steam heating systems operating up to 10.3 bar, the actual operating pressure being dependent upon the temperature requirement of the system. Spaceheating, and the provision of domestic hot water, from steam are now usually carried out at premises where steam is used for process or similar purposes only.

Steam traps separate the condensate which is piped to the hotwell where it is collected for injection back into the boiler by the feedpump through non return valves. Make up water is added to the hotwell to compensate for evaporation and leakage losses.

SERVICE CONDITIONS

FLUID

Mains or demineralised water will be used to initially charge the system and to provide make up. The corrosion and scale potential of the supply will determine the need and nature of water treatment. The presence of mineral salts in the supply will result in the build up of solids in the boiler and, depending on the mode of system operation and size, will be the routine adopted to deal with this potential problem. The condensate will contain uncondensible gases such as chlorine, carbon dioxide and oxygen, their presence may introduce severe corrosion problems in the condense pipework.

TEMPERATURE

Temperature and pressures are inter-related. The selected design conditions must be used in the evaluation of materials and components.

PRESSURE

Three principle ranges are considered for steam services

Low pressure   -   up to 3.5 bar corresponding to 148°C

Medium pressure -   up to 10.3 bar corresponding to 186°C

High pressure   -   up to 17.5 bar corresponding to 208°C and above for superheat.
(not applicable to space heating).

STANDARD PRECAUTIONS   SEE CHECK LIST (SERVICES APPENDIX)

A   1, 3, 5, 6, 7

B   1, 2, 3

C   1, 2, 3, 4, 6, 8

D   1, 2, 3, 4, 5

SPECIAL CONSIDERATIONS

Insulation is necessary for exposed pipework.

Systems contained within buildings require only limited protection. External pipework above or below ground must be protected to suit the nature of the environment in which they reside.

Water and chemical treatments of the system contents should not limit the choice of materials but the manufacturers advice should be followed.

MAJOR COMPONENTS	STEAM HEATING

COMPONENT	DATA SHEET NO.	NOTE
PIPEWORK		
Steel	3.1.1	BS1387 heavy or BS3601 of suitable wall thickness, type and grade.
JOINTING METHOD		
Flanged	3.2.1	Used for connecting valves and equipment also at dismantling points.
		Flanges to BS10 (imperial sizes) or BS4504 (metric sizes). Joints shall be fitted with gaskets suitable for the temperature and pressure.
Welded	3.2.5	Carbon steel butt welded fittings to BS1965 care must be taken to match pipe and fitting wall thickness.
VALVES	3.3	Chosen from proprietary designs to control fluid flow or to isolate sections or components. Particular attention must be paid to the selection of designs incorporating non metallic materials e.g. seals etc. Valves may have non ferrous or cast iron bodies and working parts of nickel alloy, stainless steel, gunmetal, or similar corrosion and wear resistant materials - manufacturers advise on pressure limitations at elevated temperatures must be followed.
TANKS		
Calorifier	3.5.4	To supply LTHW heating circuits or domestic hot water calorifiers can be incorporated using steam for the primary heat supply. BS853 and BS 3274 must be fitted with temperature limiting controls.
HEAT GENERATORS		
Boilers	3.7.1 3.7.2	Boilers constructed from steel to BS855.
INSULATION	3.7.3	
Thermal	3.9.1	Personnel must be protected from contact with surfaces at high temperature. Insulation should comply with BS5422 and BS5970.

MAJOR COMPONENTS CONDENSATE

COMPONENT	DATA SHEET No	NOTE
PIPEWORK		
Steel	3.1.1	Condensate can be used as for steam but may be conducive to corrosion. BS1387 or BS3601 of suitable wall thickness type and grade.
Copper	3.1.2	Copper more corrosion resistant than steel resulting in a longer life. BS2871 part 2 selected from tables to suit pressure temperature and method of jointing.
JOINTING METHOD		
Flanged	3.2.1	Flanges to BS10 (imperial sizes) or to BS4504 (metric sizes). Similar to steam; steel or copper flanges depending on pipework. Copper flanges shall be brazed or bronze welded to the pipe. Flanged joints shall be fitted with gaskets suitable for the temperature and pressure.
Capillary	3.2.3.	Solder capillary joints must be capable of withstanding the condensate temperature without loss of joint strength i.e. standard solder (BS219 grade G) has a service limit of 100°C.
Compression	3.2.4	Compression fittings shall be suitable for the working conditions of the system.
TANKS	3.5.2.	Condensate Receiver steel plate or cast iron section depending on size. Protect against corrosion with surface coating.

GENERAL DESCRIPTION

Cold water supply systems range in size from small individual domestic installations to those for blocks of flats, hospitals, commercial and industrial premises and groups of buildings. Such systems may include the following:

i.   water supplied direct from the mains for drinking and culinary purposes and feeds to storage cisterns

ii.   cold water feeds from storage cisterns to vented primary heating circuits

iii. cold water supply for ablutionary, laundry or sanitary purposes using either a vented or unvented system

iv.   cold water feed for hot water services using either a vented or unvented system

Systems fed direct from the mains supply are termed 'unvented' and do not usually include a storage facility. Those in which the water is taken from storage cisterns open to the atmosphere are known as 'vented' systems.

Note 1: Water for Fire Protection is dealt with under Section 2.7.

Note 2: Water supplies for swimming pools, industrial and food processes and pure water for medical or scientific purposes are not included in the Handbook.

SERVICE CONDITIONS

FLUID

Water taken from natural sources may contain both desirable and undesirable constituents. The environment Section - 1.4.6 - relates some of the typical sources of water to derived characteristics. The water authority is responsible for treating the water so that it is wholesome and free from pollution or contamination. If the water is taken by the consumer direct from a natural source the quality in relation to the intended use must be assessed. If necessary treatment must be introduced to correct any undesirable characteristics.

Only in special circumstances is the storage of potable water permitted. Cisterns must be designed, installed and maintained to strict standards agreed with the water authority.

Water stored for use in secondary services is not intended for potable purposes. Such waters may need to be treated to suit the proposed use. Treatments may be required to adjust hardness, inhibit corrosion or limit biological activity.

TEMPERATURE

The supply temperature can vary throughout the year but, depending on the intended use, it may be necessary to limit the heat gain or loss by insulation and judicious routeing of pipes.

SERVICE CONDITIONS

PRESSURE

The mains pressure will vary depending on location and current demand. Water authorities do not guarantee a maximum or minimum value. Elevated locations and special duties requiring a specific pressure range may need pump boosted supplies.

Supplies provided from a cistern will operate at a pressure determined by the height of the tank above the point of use. A non-storage system will operate at a pressure determined by the setting of a pressure control valve on the supply.

STANDARD PRECAUTIONS   SEE SERVICES SECTION APPENDIX 1

A   1, 2, 3, 4, 5, 7, 8, 9, 11, 12

B   1, 2, 3

C   1, 2, 3, 6, 7, 8, 9

D   1, 2, 3, 4, 5

SPECIAL CONSIDERATIONS

System design, components, materials and sealants for potable water must conform with local water authorities' regulations. The National Water Council publication Water Fittings lists those fittings and materials which comply with the requirments of the Water Byelaws.

Storage cisterns, particularly those of plastics materials, must be supported in a manner acceptable to the manufacturers. The supports and related building structure must be of adequate strength to carry the weight of a cistern and its contents.

Aggressive water characteristics may require the use of materials to resist attack from specific conditions such as cupro or plumbo solvency, dezincification etc. Consult the local water authority to determine acceptable materials.

Plastics pipe and fittings should not be located in close proximity to hot surfaces (boilers etc.).

Pipes, fittings and valves external to buildings or exposed locations should be thermally insulated. Internal conditions may promote condensation and under such conditions impermeable materials should be applied.

MAJOR COMPONENTS

COMPONENTS	DATA SHEET	NOTE
PIPEWORK		
Carbon Steel	3.1.1	BS1387 medium or heavyweight, taper screwed and galvanised. Galvanised pipework must not be welded.
Copper	3.1.2	BS2871, Part 1, Tables X, Y or Z. Where hard drawn thin walled tube is used it should not be bent or formed.
Stainless Steel	3.1.3	BS4127
Polyethene	3.1.4A	BS3284 or BS1972
Rigid PVC	3.1.4A	BS3505
Chlorinated PVC	3.1.4B	NWC approved for use above ground for cold water.
Polybutylene	3.1.4B	NWC approved for use above ground for cold water.
Cross-linked Polyethylene	3.1.4B	NWC approved for use above ground for cold water.
JOINTING METHOD		
Flanged	3.2.1	Metal flanges shall comply with BS10 (imperial) or BS4504 (metric). For galvanised pipe flanges shall be of steel and screwed to the pipe. For copper pipes flanges shall be of brass, bronze or gunmetal and brazed or bronze welded to the pipe. Where composite flanges are used the collar shall be of steel. For plastics pipe, flanges shall be welded or screwed to the pipe. Flanges may be used at dismantling points. Jointings shall be approved by the local water authority.

Screwed	3.2.2	Screwed fittings shall comply with the following specifications:
		  Cast bronze or galvanised malleable cast iron – BS143 & 1256
		  galvanised wrought steel – BS1740
		  screwed brass or bronze – BS864, Part 2
		  or BS864, Part 3
		
		Threads shall comply with BS21. Sealants must be approved by the local water authority.

Capillary	3.2.3	Capillary fittings shall comply with BS864, Part 2. The solder shall comply with BS219. Fittings may be of integral ring or end feed types. These joints are intended to be permanent.

MAJOR COMPONENTS

COMPONENTS	DATA SHEET	NOTE
Compression	3.2.4	Compression fittings shall comply with BS864, Part 2. Compression fittings on polythylene or cross-linked polythethylene pipe shall comply with BS864, Part 3.
		These joints should be used where pipework may require dismantling or where thermal jointing methods may not be permitted or practicable.
Solvent weld		Use solvent cement recommended for the particular plastics material. Such joints are intended to be permanent.
Thermofusion weld		Use an appropriate technique for the plastics material.
Grooved	3.2.6	Permanent or temporary jointing of steel pipework. All seals and lubricants must be approved by the local water authority.
VALVES		
Gate	3.3.1	Body castings to be of cast iron, brass, bronze or gunmetal
Check	3.3.2	depending on size and water condition.
Screwdown	3.3.3	The floats of level control valves shall be plastics or copper and
Float	3.3.4	must be capable of withstanding the maximum possible temperature
Butterfly	3.3.5	likely to occur in the event of an influx of hot water from
Plug	3.3.6	expansion pipe of a hot water system.
Draw off taps		Valves shall be accessible for operation and maintenance.
Relief		Non storage systems should incorporate control valves that operate
Pressure Reducing		at the pressure design parameters.
PUMPS		
Centrifugal	3.4.1	Pumps should be of the centrifugal type with drive from a motor capable of 30 starts/hour. Pump control should be achieved by cistern float switch or pipeline pressure switches, in the latter case an air receiver should be incorporated to avoid hunting. Isolating valves should be fitted to facilitate pump removal.
TANKS		
Cisterns	3.5.1	Storage cisterns are required to supply taps and other services at a low pressure head. They should be of adequate capacity based on supply and demand relationships. Cisterns shall be covered and have suitable access to the float valve. The valve shall be suitable for the water supply pressure. Depending on size the cistern shall be of one of the following types:
		1. welded or rivetted steel, glavanised after manufacture
		2. pressed steel or cast iron sectional construction painted internally with corrosion resistant paint
		3. plastics, reinforced plastics or reinforced cement materials.

	service data sheet	SHEET NUMBER	2.2.2	1

FAMILY GROUP	WATER SERVICES	SUB- GROUP	DOMESTIC - HOT

GENERAL DESCRIPTION

The domestic hot water supply is generally provided for washing and ablutionary purposes. These systems range in capacity from small individual domestic installations to those for blocks of flats, hospitals, commercial and industrial premises and groups of buildings. Hot water may be supplied heated directly from the fuel or energy source either centrally or at the point of use. Alternatively a combined heating/hot water system provides hot water by way of a heat exchanger (indirect cylinder or calorifier) from a primary space heating circuit. Distribution to the point of use may be either by gravity, mains pressure or by pump. In large systems the hot water is recirculated by pump to limit the effect of dead-legs.

Boiler units using various fuels in combined heating/hot water system provide for water heating by way of a heat exchanger (indirect or direct cylinder or calorifier). Installations may also be designed solely for hot water supply. Heat may be derived from either a primary heating circuit (hot water or steam) or directly from the fuel source.

Information concerning the primary heat supply is included in the relevant Service Data Sheets on Space Heating. If the water is available for human consumption, the installation will be required to meet the water authorities regulations for potable water.

SERVICE CONDITIONS

FLUID

The hardness and pH value (acidity or alkilinity) of the water will influence its scale formation and/or corrosion potential and may require adjustment with the aid of water treatment. Specialists should be consulted.

TEMPERATURE

Small gravity flow systems should be designed for a flow temperature of not less than 60°C. Large systems employing circulation of the hot water by a pump suffer higher system heat losses and require an increase in flow temperature to 70°C. Scalding can occur with water at temperatures above 70°C.

To prevent legionnaires disease the temperatures must be above 60°C for storage and 50°C for distribution. Between 60-70°C scale will form in hard waters.

PRESSURE

Supplies provided from a tank will operate at a pressure determined by the height of the tank above the point of use.

Supplies from non-storage systems will operate at pressure determined by the setting of a pressure control valve on the incoming service. For pumped and recirculatory systems the pressure is determined by the height of the tank above the point of use plus the pump head.

66

STANDARD PRECAUTIONS	SEE SERVICES SECTION APPENDIX 1
A	1, 2, 3, 4, 5, 7, 8, 9, 11, 12
B	1, 2, 3
C	1, 2, 3, 4, 6, 7, 8, 9
D	1, 2, 3, 4, 5

SPECIAL CONSIDERATIONS

Movement of pipework due to expansion and contraction must be accommodated by inbuilt flexibility such as bellows and loops and must be installed in accordance with manufacturers instructions in respect of guides and anchor points.

Material selection must take account of the corrosion potential of the waters.

Galvanised steel is commonly used in domestic hot water systems. Normal corrosion protection depends on the anodic zinc (galvanising) acting as the sacrificial component to the cathodic steel but at a temperature about 60°C this polarity relationship reverses and discontinuities in the zinc will permit rapid corrosion of the steel base. Failure of galvanised pipework at elevated temperatures can be minimised in hard water areas if a layer of scale is allowed to form during the initial operations of the system. To encourage this to occur the system should be operated at a temperature below 60°C for a minimum period of six months. In areas of very soft acidic waters galvanising is not a reliable form of protection and should be avoided. Local water authorities can advise on the suitability of galvanising in their area of supply.

The combination of copper and galvanised steel in a recirculatory system can lead to attack on the galvanising depending on the water composition. Large vessels can be cathodically protected - consult specialists.

MAJOR COMPONENTS

COMPONENTS	DATA SHEET	NOTE
PIPEWORK		
Carbon Steel	3.1.1	BS1387 medium or heavyweight, taper screwed and galvanised. Galvanised pipework must not be welded.
Copper	3.1.2	BS2871, Part 1, Tables X, Y or Z. Where hard drawn thin walled tube is used it should not be bent or formed.
Stainless Steel	3.1.3	BS4127
Chlorinated PVC	3.1.4B	NWC approved up to 85°C at a pressure of 2 bar.

MAJOR COMPONENTS

COMPONENTS	DATA SHEET	NOTE
Polybutylene	3.1.4B	NWC approved up to 82°C at a pressure of 2 bar.
Cross-linked Polyethylene	2.1.4B	NWC approved up to 90°C at pressure of 2 bar
JOINTING METHOD		
Flanged	3.2.1	Metal flanges shall comply with BS10 (imperial) or BS4504 (metric). For galvanised pipe flanges shall be of steel and screwed to the pipe. For copper pipe flanges shall be of brass, bronze or gunmetal and brazed or bronze welded to the pipe. Where composite flanges are used the collar shall be of steel.
		Flange may be used at dismantling points. Jointings shall be approved by the local water authority.
Screwed	3.2.2	Screwed fittings shall comply with the following specifications: Cast bronze or galvanised malleable cast iron – BS143 & 1256 galvanised wrought steel – BS1740 screwed brass or bronze – BS864, Part 2 or BS864, Part 3
		Sealants must be approved by the local water authority.
Capillary	3.2.3	Capillary fittings shall comply with BS864, Part 2. The solder shall comply with BS219. Fittings may be of integral ring or end feed types. These joints are intended to be permanent.
Compression	3.2.4	Compression fittings shall comply with BS864, Part 2. or when used on cross-linked polyethylene pipe shall comply with BS864, Part 3. These joints should be used where pipework may require dismantling or where thermal jointing methods may not be permitted or practicable.
Solvent weld		Use solvent cement recommended for the particular plastics material. Such joints are intended to be permanent.
Grooved	3.2.6	Permanent or temporary jointing of steel pipework. All seals and lubricants must be approved by the local water authority.
VALVES		
Gate	3.3.1	Body castings to be of cast iron, brass or bronze or gunmetal
Check	3.3.2	depending on size and water condition.
Screwdown	3.3.3	The floats of level control valves shall be plastics or copper and
Float	3.3.4	must be capable of withstanding the maximum possible temperature
Butterfly	3.3.5	likely to occur in the event of an influx of hot water from
Plug	3.3.6	expansion pipe of a hot water system.
Draw off taps		Valves shall be accessible for operation and maintenance.
Pressure reducing		Control valves must operate within the systems pressure and
Thermostatic control		temperature parameters.

MAJOR COMPONENTS

COMPONENTS	DATA SHEET	NOTE
PUMPS Centrifugal	3.4.1	Electrically driven centrifugal type pumps should be suitable for the system pressure and temperature and of adequate rating to deal with the maximum demand and circulating flow requirements. Pumps to be constructed in materials compatible with the fluid conditions. Isolating valves should be fitted to facilitate pump removal.
TANKS Cylinders Calorifiers	 3.5.3 3.5.4	Calorifiers or indirect cylinders provide for heat transfer from the primary boiler circuit to the secondary HWS system and for the storage of hot water. Direct cylinders are used to store hot water in systems where there is no primary heating circuit. Both direct and indirect cylinders may contain an electrical heating element or may be heated from a central plant. To maintain heat transfer efficiency it may be necessary to clean or descale the heating element or coil either by having access to it or by chemical cleaning. When mixed metals are used the advice of the manufacturer should be obtained regarding the design and materials of construction to suit the conditions of the water supply. Calorifiers must be fitted with the statutory safety devices and fittings.
HEAT GENERATORS		Gas, oil or electrical heaters are available. The materials of construction must be selected to suit the operating conditions, temperature and nature of water supply and must be compatible with other materials used in the system. Direct gas fired heaters must be designed to cope with products of combustion.
CONTROLS	3.8.1	Heaters and heat exchangers must be fitted with all statutory controls, accessories and safety devices with any additional timing devices, alarms, etc. as may be required. System controls may include a pump control panel with failure alarm and running lights etc., pressure relief valves, pressurisation controls, water flow and temperature controls, metering instruments, tank level indicators and safety devices.

GENERAL DESCRIPTION

Water may be used as a transfer medium to dispose of surplus heat. Such requirements may be found in air conditioning, power generation sets, air compressors, process equipment etc. The principle methods of cooling are:

1 - Open type: fountains, ponds, cascades (cooling tower) etc.

2 - Closed type: fan coil 'car radiator' type

3 - Once through: river or sea water may be considered if convenient.

    - direct: water in contact with prime heat source

    - indirect: water in contact with one side of a heat exchanger with primary circuit in contact with prime heat source.

Methods 1 and 3 may create aggressive conditions; water treatment is an important factor when considering the efficient operation and life of the plant.

SERVICE CONDITIONS

FLUID

Water treatment is usually required to reduce corrosion, scale, microbiological fouling and silt problems, which may lead to conditions that affect heat transfer. A regular dosing or continuous feeding of the water system may be required. Air entrainment in the circulating water should be limited by careful design, and use of air vents.

TEMPERATURE

Temperature ranges from ambient of the recooled water to that of the heat source temperature. The actual temperature range depends on the heat load capacity of the cooling tower and the requirements of the duty.

PRESSURE

Pump pressure plus cooling tower head.

STANDARD PRECAUTIONS

SEE SERVICES SECTION APPENDIX 1

A   1, 2, 3, 4, 5, 7, 8, 9, 10, 11, 12

B   1, 3,

C   1, 2, 3, 4, 6, 7, 8, 9

D   1, 2, 3, 4, 5

SPECIAL CONSIDERATIONS

The position of a cooling tower, its orientation, wind effects and noise transmission should be considered when siting. The cooling tower may create its own mini-climate and produce corrosion problems in its immediate locality.

To maintain an efficient system chemical cleaning may be required. Water evaporation will concentrate the solids content which will have to be bled off to maintain a balance. Extra care must be taken when selecting materials for systems using river or sea waters where marine growth may be an added problem. (See 1.4 Environment).

MAJOR COMPONENTS

COMPONENTS	DATA SHEET	NOTE
PIPE		
Carbon Steel	3.1.1	BS1387, medium or heavy, or BS3601, galvanised where appropriate.
Copper	3.1.2	BS2871, Part 1, Tables X, Y or Z. Where hard drawn thin wall tube is used it should not be bent or formed.
ABS	3.1.4A	Water pressures and temperatures must be within the working limit
Polyethylene-high density	3.1.4A	of the material.
		Adequate compensation for expansion/contraction and pipe supports
Polypropylene	3.1.4A	required.
PVC-rigid	3.1.4A	
JOINTING METHOD		
Flanged	3.2.1	Metal flanges shall comply with BS10 (imperial) or BS4504 (metric). For galvanised pipe flanges shall be of steel and screwed to the pipe. For copper pipe flanges shall be of brass, bronze or gunmetal and brazed or bronze welded to the pipe. Where composite flanges are used the collar shall be of steel. For plastics pipe flanges shall be welded or screwed to the pipe. Flanges may be used at dismantling points.
Screwed	3.2.2	Screwed fittings shall comply with the following specifications: Cast bronze or galvanised malleable cast iron - BS143 & 1256 galvanised wrought steel - BS1740 screwed brass or bronze - BS864, Part 2 or BS864, Part 3
Capillary	3.2.3	Capillary fittings shall comply with BS864, Part 2. The solder shall comply with BS219. Fittings may be of integral ring or end feed types. These joints are intended to be permanent.
Compression	3.2.4	Compression fittings shall comply with BS864, Part 2. Compression fittings on polyethylene pipe shall comply with BS864, Part 3. These joints should be used where pipework may require dismantling or where thermal methods may not be permitted or practicable.
Solvent weld		Use solvent cement recommended for the particular plastics material. Such joints are intended to be permanent.
Thermofusion weld		Appropriate technique for the plastics material.
Grooved	3.2.6	Permanent or temporary jointing of steel pipework.

 **service data sheet**

| | | SHEET NUMBER | 2.2.3 | 3 |

MAJOR COMPONENTS

COMPONENTS	DATA SHEET	NOTE
VALVES		
Gate	3.3.1	Body castings to be of cast iron, brass, bronze or gunmetal
Check	3.3.2	depending on size and water condition.
Screwdown	3.3.3	The floats of level control valves shall be plastics or copper and
Float	3.3.4	must be capable of withstanding the maximum possible temperature
Butterfly	3.3.5	likely to occur.
Plug	3.3.6	
Draw off taps		Valves shall be accessible for operation and maintenance.
PUMPS	3.4	Compatible with the system requirements. Pumps should be located to ensure that the suction side is permanently primed with sufficient head to avoid cavitation. Isolating valves should be fitted to facilitate pump removal.
TANKS		
Feed	3.5.1 3.5.2	To accommodate system losses. May be incorporated in the cooling tower. Depending on size the tank shall be of the following types: 1. Welded or rivetted steel, galvanised after manufacture 2. Pressed steel or cast iron secional painted internally with corrosion resistant paint 3. Plastics, reinforced plastics or reinforced cement materials.
FANS		Fans may be used to force air through the cooling component. Usually incorporated in proprietary cooling units i.e. cooling towers, cooling radiators etc. Where wet air is being discharged, such as in cooling towers, corrosion resistant materials should be used. Fans and their motors should be compatible with the environment.
AIR CONDITIONING		
Cooling Equipment		The materials selected for condensers and cooling towers should be compatible with their respective fluids. The location of a cooling tower will influence the materials of construction, (see 1.4 Environment).
INSULATION		
Thermal	3.9.1	Pipe fittings and valves external to buildings or exposed locations should be insulated. Where required trace heating may be incorporated. Internal conditions may promote condensation and under such conditions impermeable materials should be used.

GENERAL DESCRIPTION

A recirculatory water system used to remove heat from the environment through the action of a refrigeration plant using chilled water as the transfer medium. At the plant end the refrigerant removes heat from the water in an evaporator. At the environment interface the chilled water removes heat via ducted cooler batteries, fan coil units or pipe coils. An air handling plant may use chilled water for spray washing the air.

SERVICE CONDITIONS

FLUID

Generally water, but brine or other heat transfer fluids may be used for applications other than air conditioning where lower temperatures are required.

TEMPERATURE

Chilled water, in a closed circuit, has a flow temperature of approximately 5°C.

PRESSURE

The pressure limits are determined by the static head plus the pump head of the system.

STANDARD PRECAUTIONS   SEE SERVICES SECTION APPENDIX 1

A   1, 2, 3, 4, 5, 7, 8, 9, 10, 11, 12

B   1, 2, 3,

C   1, 2, 3, 4, 6, 7, 8

D   1, 2, 4, 5

SPECIAL CONSIDERATIONS

Precautions must be taken to prevent the chilled water freezing using anti-freeze or safety cutouts. The proportion of anti-freeze will determine minimum water temperature. When used, anti-freeze solutions should include a corrosion inhibitor.

Washer circuits may require air eliminators to remove entrained air and prevent corrosion. If water treatment is required the chemicals used should not create a health hazard - expert advice should be sought.

Insulation must prevent heat gains in the chilled water. It should be continuous and where required the use of vapour barriers and mechanical protection must be considered. All materials in direct contact with the chilled water and refrigerant must be compatible with both. To maintain an efficient system chemical cleaning may be required to restore heat transfer surfaces to a clean state. Exposed metal surfaces may be subject to condensation and potential corrosion. Where lower temperatures are required, heat transfer fluids such as brine or anti-freeze are required. These fluids must be compatible with the systems materials - consult specialists.

Plastics materials will lose ductility with a reduction in temperature.

MAJOR COMPONENTS

COMPONENTS	DATA SHEET	NOTE
PIPE		
Carbon Steel	3.1.1	BS1387, medium or heavy and BS3601, galvanised where appropriate.
Copper	3.1.2	BS2871, Part 1, Tables X, Y or Z. Where hard drawn thin wall tube is used it should not be bent or formed.
Polyethylene	3.1.4A	Minimum temperature for pressure pipes; high density -18°C, low density -40°C.
Rigid PVC	3.1.4A	Minimum temperature for pressure pipe, 0°C.
Polypropylene	3.1.4A	Minimum temperature for pressure pipes, 0°C.
ABS	3.1.4A	Minimum temperature for pressure pipes, -30°C.
JOINTING METHOD		
Flanged	3.2.1	Metal flanges shall comply with BS10 (imperial) or BS4504 (metric). Flanges may be used at dismantling points. For galvanised pipe flanges shall be of steel and screwed to the pipe.
		For copper pipe flanges shall be of brass, bronze or gunmetal and brazed or bronze welded to the pipe. Where composite flanges are used the collar shall be of steel.
		For plastics pipe flanges shall be solvent or thermofusion welded, or screwed to the pipe. Flanges may be used at dismantling points.
Screwed	3.2.2	Screwed fittings shall comply with the following specifications:
		Cast bronze or galvanised malleable cast iron — BS143 & 1256
		galvanised wrought steel — BS1740
		screwed brass or bronze — BS864, Part 2 or BS864, Part 3
Capillary	3.2.3	Capillary fittings shall comply with BS864, Part 2. The solder shall comply with BS219. Fittings may be of integral ring or end feed types.
		These joints are intended to be permanent.
Compression	3.2.4	Compression fittings shall comply with BS864, Part 2. Compression fittings on polyethylene pipe shall comply with BS864, Part 3. These joints should be used where pipework may require dismantling or where thermal jointing methods may not be permitted or practicable.

MAJOR COMPONENTS

COMPONENTS	DATA SHEET	NOTE
Solvent weld		Use solvent cement recommended for the particular plastics material. Such joints are intended to be permanent.
Thermofusion weld		Use an appropriate technique for the plastics material.
Grooved	3.2.6	Permanent or temporary jointing of steel pipework. All seals and lubricants must not contaminate the water.
VALVES		
Gate	3.3.1	Chosen from propriety designs to either control flow or to
Check	3.3.2	isolate sections and/or components. All valve trim must be
Screwdown	3.3.3	compatible with the pressure and temperature limits.
Float	3.3.4	Condensation may produce conditions that cause the valve stem to
Butterfly	3.3.5	corrode and seize. Select corrosion resistant stem materials
Plug	3.3.6	or isolate the valve from the environment.
Draw off taps		
PUMPS	3.4	Compatible with the system requirements. Isolating valves should be fitted to facilitate pump removal.
TANKS		
Cisterns	3.5.1	Where required for the feed or storage of cold and chilled water
Tanks	3.5.2	Depending on size the cistern shall be one of the following types:
		1. Welded or rivetted steel, galvanised after manufacture
		2. Pressed steel or cast iron secional construction painted internally with corrosion resistant paint
		3. Plastics, reinforced plastics or reinforced cement materials.
CONTROLS	3.8.1	Control devices normally supplied with equipment. Controls for electrical, pressure, level, flow and thermal requirements must be compatible with the appropriate environment with which they are in contact.
AIR CONDITIONING		
Evaporator		Equipment materials must be compatible with the internal fluids, the chilled air and the external environment. Pressure requirements of the chilling equipment must not be exceeded.
INSULATION		
Thermal	3.9.1	The insulation must reduce heat gains to the pipework, valves, pumps and storage tanks. A continuous vapour barrier should be provided. All insulated pipework outdoors should be weatherproofed.

| FAMILY GROUP | SANITATION | SUB-GROUP | INTERNAL DRAINAGE |

GENERAL DESCRIPTION

Sanitation covers the following items:

(a) water supply.

(b) Sanitary appliances.

(c) Above ground drainage of sanitary appliances and roofs.

(d) Underground drainage.

Note: Water supply (a) is covered in data sheets 2.2.1 (cold) and 2.2.2 (hot). Sanitary appliances (b) and underground drainage (d) are outside the scope of the Materials Application Handbook, but references to their major components are given in this section.

Above ground drainage (c) includes soil pipes, soil-waste discharge pipes, ventilating pipes and waste pipes.

A soil pipe is a pipe which conveys the discharge from a water closet, urinal or slop hopper to a drain. In the 'one-pipe' and 'single-stack' systems the soil pipe also conveys to a drain the discharges from basins, wash basins, sinks and similar appliances.

A soil-waste discharge pipe is a pipe for conveying both soil and waste water.

A ventilating pipe (or soil ventilating pipe) is a pipe in a soil and/or waste pipe system which facilitates the circulation of air within the system and protects trap seals from excessive pressure fluctuations.

A waste pipe is a pipe which conveys to a drain or soil pipe the discharge from a sanitary appliance used for ablutionary, drinking or culinary purposes.

A waste ventilating pipe is a ventilating pipe in a waste pipe system.

SERVICE CONDITIONS

FLUID

Waste as discharged from a sanitary appliance used for ablutionary, drinking or culinary purposes. It is predominately water but may contain some or all of the following: detergent, soap suds, dirt, grease/fat, food scraps and similar small solids, liquid wastes from drink and meal leftovers, cigarette butts, human hair and other similar waste products.

Soil as discharged from a water closet, urinal or slop hopper. Predominatly water from flushing carrying solid and liquid human wastes, toilet tissue, etc.

TEMPERATURE

Waste may vary from normal mains water temperature of about 10°C to the temperature of domestic hot water service, say 60°C. Waste water discharged from commercial kitchens, laundries or from industrial processes may however be close to boiling point, 100°C.

Soil is usually close to the indoor ambient air temperature.

PRESSURE

Waste and soil systems are open to atmosphere and any pressure build-up is normally relieved by a system of open ventilating pipe, which are necessary to prevent pressure fluctuations from 'blowing' water seal traps.

Pressure cont'd	A stack loading of about a quarter full is normally assumed in vertical pipes. However, if a stack is blocked for any reason the waste or soil discharge held could impose a pressure equal to the static head of the contained liquid.

The terminal velocity in a vertical stack is generally 3 to 5 m/s and this is normally achieved within 2 to 3 floors in a multi-storey building.

STANDARD PRECAUTIONS SEE SERVICES SECTION APPENDIX 1

A   1, 2, 7, 8, 9

B   1, 2, 3

C   2, 3, 6, 9

D   1, 2, 3, 4

SPECIAL CONSIDERATIONS

Materials should comply with Statutory Regulations and with the requirements of the appropriate Local Authorities.

Consideration in the selection of materials and layouts should also be given to:
- fluid handled, fluid temperature, pressure including those which might be experienced under abnormal conditions (e.g. blockage).
- location, appearance, damage-resistance, ease of making joints, life expectancy and cost.

Plastics piping systems may require particular care. Pipes and fittings must be carefully stored and handled to avoid damage and open ends should be protected to avoid the risk of unsatisfactory jointing.

Pipework layouts should incoporate adequate allowances for expansion and contraction since the coefficient of thermal expansion of most thermoplastics pipes is about 5 to 12 times that of traditional metal pipes.

Some plastics materials have reduced impact strength at low temperatures. Certain plastics are also degraded by exposure to direct sunlight unless their composition includes additives such as carbon black. Natural grades of polyethylene or polypropylene are not recommended for outdoor exposure. Recommendations on the jointing methods for each material are given in Section 4.4. There are many varieties of mechanical joints available for use with plastic pipes. Some are not designed to withstand the end loads of a system which may be pressurized and for these joints special anchoring arrangements may be necessary.

In all cases environmental considerations applying to the choice of pipe should also apply to the choice of appliances and fittings and of the jointing techniques.

MAJOR COMPONENTS

COMPONENT	DATA SHEET	NOTE
PIPE & FITTINGS		
Cast iron	-	BS416 covers spigot and socket, soil, waste and ventilating pipes and fittings.
		BS437 covers spigot and socket, drain pipes and fittings.
Copper	3.1.2	BS2871:Part 1 covers copper tubes for water, gas and sanitation. Where hard drawn thin walled tube (Table Z) is used it should not be bent or formed.
Carbon steel	3.1.1	BS534 covers seamless and welded carbon steel pipes and specials in sizes 60mm to 2220mm outside diameter, including external and internal protection against the corrosive action of the surrounding medium or conveyed fluid.
		BS3868 covers prefabricated drainage stack units of galvanised steel.
Plastics	3.1.4A	BS4514 covers unplasticized PVC soil and ventilating pipes, fittings and accessories.
		BS5254 covers polypropylene waste pipes and fittings of 25mm to 54mm external diameter.
		BS5255 covers plastics waste pipe and fittings of the following materials: - acrylonitrile butadrene styrene (ABS), - modified unplasticized polyvinyl chloride (MUPVC), - polypropylene (PP), - polyethylene (PE),
		BS5480 covers glass reinforced plastics (GRP) pipes and fittings.
		Additional information may be found in CP312:Part 1 which deals with general principles and choice of material.
		THE FOLLOWING MATERIALS MAY BE EMPLOYED EXTERNALLY OR BELOW GROUND BUT CERTAIN ITEMS MAY SOMETIMES FORM PART OF AN 'INTERNAL' SYSTEM.
Clay	-	BS65 covers vitrified clay pipes, fittings and joints.
		BS1196 covers clayware field drain pipes.
Concrete	-	BS1194 covers concrete porous pipes for under-drainage.
		BS5178 covers prestressed concrete pipes for drainage and sewerage.
		BS5911 covers precast concrete pipes and fittings for drainage and sewerage.

MAJOR COMPONENTS

COMPONENT	DATA SHEET	NOTE
Fibre	–	BS2760 covers pitch-impregnated fibre pipes and fittings over the size range 50mm to 225mm nominal bore.
Asbestos-cement	–	BS3656 covers asbestos-cement pipes, joints and fittings for drainage and sewerage.
Plastics	3.1.4A	BS4660 covers unplasticized PVC underground drain pipes and fittings.
		BS4962 covers plastics pipes for use as light subsoil drains.
Cast iron	–	BS78:Part 2 covers fittings in Grades A, B, C & D with internal diameters from 3" to 48".
		BS1211 covers centrifugally cast (spun) iron pressure pipes for water and sewage.
JOINTING METHODS		
Flanges	3.2.1	Metal flanges to BS10 (imperial) or BS4504 (metric). For galvanised pipe flanges may be of steel and screwed to the pipe. For copper pipe flanges may be of brass, bronze or gunmetal and brazed or bronze welded to the pipe. For plastic pipe flanges shall be welded or screwed to the pipe.
Screwed	3.2.2	Cast bronze or galvanised malleable cast iron fittings to BS143. Galvanised wrought steel fittings to BS1740. Threads should comply with BS21.
Capillary	3.2.3	Capillary fittings to BS864:Part 2 for copper tubes; Part 3 for polyethylene pipes. The solder should comply with BS219. Fittings may be of integral ring or end feed types. These joints are intended to be permanent.
Compression	3.2.4	Compression fittings to BS864:Part 2 for copper tubes; Part 3 for polyethylene pipes. These joints should be used where pipework may require dismantling or where thermal jointing methods may not be practicable or permitted.
Solvent weld	–	Use the solvent cement recommended for the particular plastics material. These joints are intended to be permenent.
Thermofusion weld	–	Use an appropriate technique for the plastics material.
Grooved	3.2.6	May be used for permanent or temporary jointing of steel pipework.
Spigot and socket	–	BS416 covers cast iron, soil, waste and ventilating pipes. BS437 covers cast iron drain pipes. BS6087 covers flexible joints for cast iron piping to BS416 and BS437.

MAJOR COMPONENTS

COMPONENT	DATA SHEET	NOTE
Spigot and socket (rigid, pressure)	-	In cast or spun iron to BS78 and BS1211. Joints: Axially compressed rubber rings (bolted or screwed gland). Fixed in socket groove*
Double spigot (rigid, pressure)	-	In cast or spun iron to BS78 and BS1211. Joints: Axially compressed rubber rings in steel collar with bolted steel glands* In asbestos cement to BS486. Joints: Push-in rubber rings* Axially compressed rubber rings*
Spigot and socket (flexible, pressure)	-	Steel pipe to BS534. Joints: Push-in rubber ring* Ductile iron. Joints: Push-in rubber ring* Axially compressed rubber ring (bolted gland)* Unplasticized PVC to BS3505 and BS3506. Joints: Push-in sliding rubber 'O' ring retained in socket groove produced by heating and shrinking socket*
Double spigot (flexible, pressure)	-	Unplasticized PVC to BS3505 and BS3506. Joints: Push-in rubber rings* Axially compressed rubber ring* * a range of proprietary joints of these types are available.
PUMPS		
Centrifugal	3.4.1	Special consideration should be given to pump
Positive displacement	3.4.3	small solids.
TANKS	3.5.2	Refer to BS CP302 for cesspits, septic and settlement tanks.
SANITARY APPLIANCES	-	BS1125 WC flushing cisterns. BS1184 Copper and copper alloy traps. BS1188 Ceramic wash basins and pedestals. BS1189 Cast iron basins. BS1206 Fireclay sinks. BS1244 Metal sinks. BS1254 WC seats (plastics). BS1329 Metal hand rinse basins. BS1390 Sheet steel baths. BS1876 Automatic flushing cisterns for urinals. BS2745 Bed pan and urine bottle washers.

MAJOR COMPONENTS

COMPONENT	DATA SHEET	NOTE
GENERAL SPECIFICATIONS		BS3380 Wastes and bath overflows. BS3402 Vitreous china sanitary appliances. BS3943 Plastics waste traps. BS4305 Basins (cast acrylic sheet). BS4880 Stainless steel slab urinals. BS5503 Vitreous china WC pans BS5504 Wall hung WC pan. BS5505 Bidets. BS5506 Wash basins. BS5520 Vitreous china bowl urinals. BS5627 Plastic connectors for use with vitreous china WC pans. CP301 Building drainage. CP305 Sanitary appliances. BS497 Manhole covers, road gully gratings and frames. BS1247 Manhole step irons. BS4118 Glossary of sanitation terms. BS6465 Sanitary appliances (scale of provision, etc.).

| FAMILY GROUP | SANITATION | SUB-GROUP | ROOF DRAINAGE |

GENERAL DESCRIPTION

Roof drainage facilitates the removal of water due to rainfall or melting snow. A rainwater pipe is a pipe for conveying rainwater from a roof or other parts of a building.

SERVICE CONDITIONS

FLUID

Surface water collected off roofs and building surfaces generally as a result of rainfall and melting snow. The surface water may contain leaves, small stones, waste paper scraps etc.

TEMPERATURE

At or close to ambient air temperature which may be only just above freezing temperature in winter.

PRESSURE

Systems are open to atmosphere and downpipes normally operate with a core of air. Flooded roofs or blocked downpipes or overflowing drains however may cause vertical pipes to be full of water. The base of the pipe can have a pressure imposed equivalent to the static head due to the column of retained surface water. Horizontal pipes or pipes of shallow slope may run full.

STANDARD PRECAUTIONS SEE SERVICES SECTION APPENDIX 1

A   1, 2, 8

B   1, 2, 3

C   6

D   1, 4

SPECIAL CONSIDERATIONS

Plastics pipes must be carefully stored and handled to avoid damage. In particular the ends of pipe should be protected to avoid the risk of unsatisfactory jointing.

Pipework layouts should incorporate adequate allowances for expansion and contraction since the coefficient of thermal expansion of most thermoplastics pipes is about 5 to 12 times that of traditional metal pipes.

Some plastics materials have reduced impact strength at low temperatures and certain plastics are degraded by exposure to direct sunlight unless their composition includes additives such as carbon black (natural grades of polyethylene or polypropylene are not recommended for outdoor exposure).

A wide variety of jointing methods is available for plastics pipes. Some methods are only applicable to certain materials and the recommendations on jointing for each material, given in Section 4.4 should be studied with care.

service
data sheet

SPECIAL CONSIDERATIONS CONT'D

Many manufacturers of unplasticized PVC pipe offer a range of fittings and accessories but care should be taken to see that compatible fittings and jointing systems are employed, not all manufacturers products are interchangeable.

MAJOR COMPONENTS

COMPONENT	DATA SHEET	NOTE
PIPE & FITTINGS		
Cast iron	-	BS460 covers pipes, fittings and accessories; half-round gutters and O.G. (ogee) gutters and fittings in sizes from 2" to 6".
Asbestos cement	-	BS569 covers pipes, fittings and gutters.
Pressed steel	-	BS1091 covers gutters, rainwater pipes, fittings and accessories.
Wrought copper	-	BS1431 covers half-round, rectangular, ogee gutters, round and rectangular pipes and accessories.
Wrought zinc	-	BS1431 covers half-round, rectangular, ogee gutters, round and rectangular pipes and accessories.
Aluminium	-	BS2997 covers rainwater drainage components in a wide choice of aluminium alloys manufactured by casting, extruding or a wrought process.
Unplasticized PVC	3.1.4A	BS4756 covers rainwater goods. Part 1 applies to half-round gutters and circular pipes.
JOINTING METHOD		
Spigot and socket	-	Refer to 'Special Considerations'.
Solvent welding	-	Use solvent cement recommended for the particular plastics material.
Rubber ring seal joint	-	Refer to manufacturers instructions.
GENERAL SPECIFICATIONS		
		CP301 Building drainage.
		BS1494 Fixing accessories for building purposes.
		BS4118 Glossary of sanitation terms.
		BS6367 Code of practice for drainage of roofs and paved areas.

FAMILY GROUP	SANITATION	SUB-GROUP	WASTE DRAINAGE

GENERAL DESCRIPTION

A laboratory and industrial waste system conveys to a drain the discharge from a laboratory or industrial process. This discharge is classified as being of such a corrosive or dangerous nature that it requires separation from normal waste discharges (unless it can be adequately and safely diluted) and to be conveyed in piping systems resistant to chemical attack or absorption.

SERVICE CONDITIONS

FLUID

Can be numerous liquid substances which may be diluted or flushed when discharged to waste, or may be highly concentrated including chemicals which may be acid or alkaline. For example wastes include chlorides, carbonates, hydroxides, nitrates, sulphates.

TEMPERATURE

Can vary widely often in range 20° to 60°C. For most piping materials, chemical resistance to attack or absorption will decrease with increase in chemical waste temperature.

PRESSURE

Normally open drainage system or atmospheric pressure.

STANDARD PRECAUTIONS SEE SERVICES SECTION APPENDIX 1

A   1, 2, 7, 8

B   1, 2, 3

C   3, 6, 7

D   1, 3, 4

SPECIAL CONSIDERATIONS

Piping, fittings, accessories and jointing methods must be suitable for the chemical waste to be handled, both the degree of concentration and the temperature.

It is essential to ascertain the condition and strength of the effluent before connecting any industrial waste systems to the Local Authority sewers.

Listed categories of the chemical resistances of materials for use in laboratory and industrial waste systems can serve as a guide to material selection. Potential users should satisfy themselves that the chosen material will prove satisfactory under their particular working conditions. Where material properties are listed as subject to limited attack or absorption the material may prove serviceable with good dilution and flushing or may be used where alternative materials are unsatisfactory and where a limited life is permissible.

Additional information is to be found in CP312:Part 1:1973: Code of Practice for plastics pipework (thermoplastics material): Part 1: General principles and choice of materials and in Institute of Plumbing "Plumbing Services Design Guide".

Special Considerations Cont'd

BS CP312 gives the following data on plastics materials and categories of chemical resistance.

Table 1. Physical properties of plastics pipe materials
- unplasticized PVC,
- low density ployethylene,
- high density polyethylene,
- modified (high impact) PVC,
- ABS,
- nylon,
- polypropylene.

Table 2a. Chemical resistance of unplasticized PVC, low-density and high-density polyethylene

This covers a wide range of chemicals, some at different concentrations and at temperatures of 20° and 60°C.

Resistance is rated as follows:
- S- satisfactory,
- U- unsatisfactory. This is because of decomposition, solution, swelling, loss of ductility, etc.
- D- Some attack or absorption. The material may be considered for use when alternative materials are unsatisfactory and where limited life is acceptable. When plastics are to be used with such chemicals, full scale trials under realistic conditions are particularly necessary.
- F- environmental stress cracking hazard. Polyethylenes are subject to this phenomenon if used with certain chemicals, which although chemically inactive produce stress cracks.

Table 2b. Chemical resistance of modified (high impact) PVC, ABS, nylon and polypropylene

Data provided in same format as in Table 2a.

Institute of Plumbing "Plumbing Services Design Guide" (1977) lists the chemical resistance of laboratory and industrial waste systems according to chemical, concentration, temperature (20° and 60°C) for the following piping materials:
- high silicon iron,
- glass,
- polyethylene,
- rigid PVC,
- polypropylene,
- ABS.

Material chemical resistance is classified as follows:
- S- satisfactory.
- U- unsatisfactory.
- L- limited attack or absorption.

MAJOR COMPONENTS

COMPONENT	DATA SHEET	NOTE
PIPE & FITTINGS		
High silicon iron	-	BS1591 covers high silicon iron castings. BS416 & BS437 cover cast iron spigot and socket piping systems.
Glass	-	BS2598 covers glass pipeline and fittings. Part 1 covers borosilicate glass. Part 3 covers pipeline and fittings.
Polyethylene	3.1.4A	BS1973 covers Type 32 pipe for general purposes. BS3976 covers Type 50 pipe. BS5255 covers waste pipe and fittings. See also CP312:Part 1.
PVC	3.1.4A	BS5255 covers modified unplasticized polyvinyl chloride (MUPVC) for waste pipe and fittings. See also CP312:Part 1.
Polypropylene	3.1.4A	BS5254 and BS5255 cover water pipe and fittings. See also CP312:Part 1.
ABS	3.1.4A	BS5254 covers waste pipe and fittings. BS5391:Part 1 covers pipe for industrial uses. BS5391:Part 2 covers fittings for solvent welding. See also CP312:Part 1.
Nylon	-	CP312:Part 1.
JOINTING METHODS		
Flanged	3.2.1	Refer to CP312:Part1:Section II "Jointing methods".
Capillary	3.2.3	BS864:Part 2 covers polyethylene pipes whose joints are intended to be permanent.
Compression	3.2.4	BS864:Part 3 covers polyethylene pipes where pipework may require dismantling or where thermal jointing is not suitable.
Solvent weld	-	Solvent cement is recommended for the particular plastics material. Joints are intended to be permanent.
Thermofusion weld	-	Use appropriate technique for plastics material.
Spigot and socket	-	BS416 and BS437.
Mechanical and combustion joints	-	CP312:Part 1.
GENERAL SPECIFICATIONS		
		BS4118 Glossary of sanitation terms.

| FAMILY GROUP | FIRE PROTECTION | SUB-GROUP | HOSE REEL SYTEMS |

GENERAL DESCRIPTION

Fixed first aid equipment takes the form of metal hose reels permanently connected to a water supply on which is wound flexible tubing having a bore of 19 or 25mm. It is for use by untrained building occupants in containing a fire in its initial stage. Discharge rate of each reel should be not less than 0.4 litre/s.

A hose reel is fire-fighting equipment consisting of a length of tubing fitted with a shut-off nozzle and attached to a reel with a permanent connection to a pressurized water supply. Hose reel installations are normally provided in accordance with statutory regulations including the Factories Act 1961 and the Offices, Shops and Railway Premises Act 1963. British Standards and the recommendations and Rules of the Fire Offices Committee (FOC) provide detailed information on hose reel installations.

It is advisable to consult both the local Fire and the Water Authorities in the early stage of design for the provision needed for particular fire protection systems.

SERVICE CONDITIONS

FLUID

Water: This may be taken direct from the main supply or via a break tank if required by the Water Supply Authority. In some locations water may be taken from a non-portable source which may be brackish or saline.

TEMPERATURE

Ranges from normal mains water temperature up to ambient air temperature, typically 10° to 20°C.

PRESSURE

Typically 200 kN/m^2 to be available at hose reel nozzle.

Allowance must be made for the static height of the hose reel above tap water supply main in assessing the available pressure. If the Supply Authority's water main cannot provide the necessary pressure then pumping equipment (pressure boosting) must be provided.

In tall buildings the reels on lower floors may be supplied by gravity from a break tank providing the required pressure of 200 kN/m^2 is available at the nozzle.

STANDARD PRECAUTIONS SEE SERVICES SECTION APPENDIX 1

A   1, 3, 4, 5, 7, 9, 11, 12

B   1, 2, 3

C   1, 3, 6, 7, 9

D   1, 3, 4, 5

 service data sheet

SPECIAL CONSIDERATIONS

Water in hose reel systems is stagnant except under fire-fighting conditions. For this reason it is best to separate the hose reel system from normal mains water service systems by a break tank. Under some circumstances water treatment may be desirable.

In some areas aggressive water characteristics may require the use of materials to resist attack from specific conditions e.g. dezincification. The local Water Authority should be consulted about water characteristics before selecting materials.

Completed installations are normally required to be tested in the presence and to the satisfaction of the local Fire and the Water authorities.

MAJOR COMPONENTS

COMPONENT	DATA SHEET	NOTE
PIPES		
Carbon steel	3.1.1	BS1387, galvanised medium or heavyweight grades.
Copper	3.1.2	BS2871, Part 1: Tables X,Y or Z.
JOINTING METHOD		
Flanged	3.2.1	Flanges to BS10 (imperial) or BS4504 (metric). Flanges may be of steel and screwed to the pipe.
Screwed	3.2.2	Threads shall comply with BS21. Galvanised screwed fitting shall comply with BS143, BS1256 or BS1740. Sealents may require the approval of local Water Authority.
Capillary	3.2.3	For permanent joints. Fittings shall comply with BS864:Part 2 and solder to BS219.
Compression	3.2.4	Compression joints may be used where pipework requires breaking to facilitate maintenance. Fittings shall comply with BS864:Part 2.
VALVES	3.3	Water Authority may require all valves to be tested and stamped before
Gate	3.3.1	installation. The inlet valve of a normal reel shall be either a
Check	3.3.2	screwdown stop valve to BS1010:Part 2 or a gate valve to BS5154
PUMPS		
Centrifugal	3.4.1	Duplicate pumps required as covered by BS5306:Part 1.

MAJOR COMPONENTS

COMPONENT	DATA SHEET	NOTE
TANKS	3.5.1 3.5.2	Galvanised mild steel cisterns to BS417:Part 2. Pressed steel sectional to BS1564. Cast iron sectional to BS1563. Maximum capacity usually 1125 litres with 50mm minimum size of make-up ball valve.
SPECIFIC ITEMS		
FIRE HOSE REELS	-	BS3169: Specification for first aid reel hoses for fire fighting purposes. Two types of hoses are covered: Type A - Design working pressure 15 bar. Type B - Design working pressure 40 bar. Hose reels should be marked as follows at each end and at intervals not exceeding 10m: (a) Makers name or identification. (b) British Standard number with type letter as suffix, e.g. BS3169/A (c) Nominal bore size, e.g. 19mm. (d) Month and year of manufacture, e.g.10/81. (e) Design working pressure, e.g. 15 bar. BS5274:1985: Fire hose reels for fixed installations Ferrous materials, except stainless steel complying with BS970:Part 1, shall not be used for the waterways of the reel. Hose reels shall be finished in red, preferably No.537 Signal Red as specified in BS3810, and shall be marked with name and address of manufacturer/vendor and name/date of BS, i.e. BS5274:1985. BS5306: Code of practice for fire extinguishing installations and equipment on premises. Part 1: Hydrant systems, hose reels and foam inlets.
GENERAL SPECIFICATIONS	-	BS1625: Graphical symbols and abbreviations for fire protection drawings. BS4922: Glossary of terms associated with fire. Part 4: Fire protection equipment. BS5588: Fire precautions in the design and construction of buildings. Part 1: (Residential) and 3 (office buildings).

service data sheet		SHEET NUMBER	2.4.2.	1
FAMILY GROUP	FIRE PROTECTION	SUB-GROUP	FIRE BRIGADE SYSYTEMS	

GENERAL DESCRIPTION

Fixed equipment for fire brigade use comprises:

(a) Fire hydrants.

(b) Internal fire hydrants fed by,

    (i) dry rising mains,

    (ii) wet rising mains.

(c) Manual foam extinguishing systems.

A <u>fire hydrant</u> (external) is an assembly contained in a box or pit below ground level and comprising a valve and outlet connection from a water supply main.

An <u>internal fire hydrant</u> is an assembly provided inside a building comprising a valve and outlet connection from a water supply main.

A <u>dry riser</u> is a vertical pipe installed in a building for fire-fighting purposes. It is fitted with inlet connections at fire brigade access level and with landing valves at specified points. It is normally dry but capable of being charged with water usually by pumping from fire service appliances.

A <u>wet riser</u> is a vertical pipe installed in a building for fire-fighting purposes and permanently charged with water from a pressurized supply. It is fitted with landing valves at specified points.

A <u>manual foam extinguishing system</u> is a system of pipes connected to a supply of foam and fitted with nozzles at suitable intervals and heights through which foam is discharged by manual operation from a remote point as required. A foam inlet is fixed equipment consisting of an inlet connection, fixed piping and a discharge assembly enabling firemen to introduce foam into an enclosed compartment.

The provision of private external fire hydrants is seldom necessary where an adequate public source of supply exists within 90m of a building, but large complexes, such as factories and hospitals, require special consideration.

Dry risers are normally installed when required by the Local Authority or Insurance company. Most local Fire Brigades publish a standard for dry risers in their area. They are normally limited to buildings up to 60m high, and are installed progressively as the building is constructed in order to provide protection during building operations. In buildings over 30m in height the riser must be installed when the building exceeds 18m in height.

A wet riser is a permanent water supply system which is normally pumped. They are usually required in buildings over 60m high. It is advisable to determine the local Fire Authority requirments for each case.

Internal spaces which contain oil-fired boilers, oil storage tanks or materials or apparatus for which water is not a suitable fire-fighting medium may be fitted with a foam extinguishing system. The pipework should be connected to a point in the open where the fire brigade can connect a foam making branch pipe.

service data sheet		SHEET NUMBER	2.4.2.	2

It is advisable to consult both the local Fire and the Water Authorities in the early stages of design for any provision for fire protection.

SERVICE CONDITIONS

FLUID

External hydrant and internal hydrant systems use water generally derived from mains supply. In some locations water may be taken from a non-portable source and may be brackish or saline.

Foam systems use an aerated foam compound.

TEMPERATURE

Normal mains water temperature up to ambient air temperature. (Hydrant systems equipment is rated for a service temperature between 0°C and 38°C)

PRESSURE

External hydrants operate up to the mains supply pressure.

Dry risers are required to be suitable for working at a pressure of 10 bar.

Wet risers require an outlet pressure not less than 410 kN/m^2. Systems may be classified as:

low pressure (LP): up to 10 bar (1000kN/m^2),
high pressure (HP): up to 20 bar (2000kN/m^2).

To protect hydrant hose connections the outlet valves should incorporate an orifice plate (adjustable butterfly valve). This is to limit the operating outlet pressure on the lower floors of a tall building to 520 kN/m^2. Provision should also be made for a return pipe of not less than 75mm diameter, to connect the landing valves to the supply source so that the static pressure will not exceed 690 kN/m^2.

Foam inlet systems normally have to withstand the small static head imposed on the system when passing foam.

STANDARD PRECAUTIONS SEE SERVICES SECTION APPENDIX 1

Hydrants (external)

A	1, 7, 11, 12
B	1, 2, 3
C	2, 6, 9
D	1, 2, 3, 4

Internal fire hydrants (dry/wet risers)

A	1, 3, 4, 5, 7, 9, 12
B	1, 2, 3
C	1, 2, 3, 4
D	1, 2, 3, 4

91

service data sheet		SHEET NUMBER 2.4.2.	3

Standard Precautions Cont'd

Foam systems

B	1, 3
C	3, 6
D	1, 2

SPECIAL CONSIDERATIONS

Foam systems and dry risers should be efficiently earthed.

Drain pipework from wet risers should should be as short and direct as possible and discharge over a suction tank.

The Fire Authority may require an automatic air vent to be fitted at the top of a dry riser.

High pressures are involved in wet riser systems and direct boosting of the town's mains is not permitted, pumps must be supplied from a suction break tank. The maximum height which is normally permitted to be served from a lower level booster set and break tank is 60m. Higher buildings will therefore require further booster sets and break tanks for each additional 60m or less of height.

For security reasons each hydrant valve should be strapped and padlocked in the closed position.

MAJOR COMPONENTS

COMPONENT	DATA SHEET	NOTE
PIPE		
Carbon steel	3.1.1	BS1387 heavyweight galvanised grade. Pipe fittings tc BS1740. Colour identification as specified in BS1710.
JOINTING METHOD		
Flanged	3.2.1	BS10 for imperial sizes and BS4504 for metric sizes screwed to the pipe.
Screwed	3.2.2	Threads shall comply with BS21.

MAJOR COMPONENTS

COMPONENT	DATA SHEET	NOTE
VALVES	3.3	
Gate	3.3.1	Isolating valves to BS4312. In underground hydrant ring mains isolating valves shall be to BS1218.
Check	3.3.2	
Draw off taps	-	Valves must be accessible for operation and maintenance and located to allow the whole installation to be fully drained.
PUMPS		
Centrifugal	3.4.1	Duplicate pumps. Ensure that pumps are positioned to permanently prime the suction and there is sufficient head to avoid cavitation.
TANKS	3.5.2	Cast iron sectional to BS1563. Pressed steel to BS1564. For wet riser the minimum actual capacity should be 45000 litres. The make-up rate from town's main should be at least 25 litre/s.
FIRE HYDRANTS	-	BS750: Specification for underground fire hydrants and surface box frames and covers. Pillar hydrants should be made of robust material suitably corrosion protected. The hydrant markings should be of gunmetal to BS1400, or other suitable material. Indicator plates for fire hydrants and emergency water supplies to BS3251.
INTERNAL FIRE HYDRANTS	-	BS5041: Fire hydrant systems equipment
DRY RISERS		Part 2: Landing valves for dry risers. Nominal size: 2.5" with instantaneous female outlet to BS336. Inlet: 2.5" male or female threads to BS21, or flanged. Valves shall have solid wedges with inside screw non-rising stems. Materials for components of landing valves shall be in accordance with Table 1 of BS5041:Part 2. Part 4: Boxes for landing valves for dry risers. The boxes shall be made from one of the following materials: - corrosion protected steel, - stainless steel to BS1449:Part 4, - copper alloy to BS2870, 2875, 1400, - aluminium alloy to BS1490 or BS1470-1475. The door, glazing, hinges and pins shall be as specified in BS5041:Part 4.

MAJOR COMPONENTS

COMPONENT	DATA SHEET	NOTE

WET RISERS	-	Part 1: Landing valves for wet risers.
		Types: horizontal, bib-nosed and oblique.
		Valve inlets shall be flanged or screwed.
		   Flanged to BS4504 LP valve table 16/21
		                          HP valve table 25/21
		   Screwed 2.5" male or female to BS21.
		Valve outlet - instantaneous female to BS336.
		Attachements: strap and padlock, blank cap and chain.
		
		Materials for components of landing valves shall be in accordance with Table 3 of BS5041:Part 1.
		
		Part 3: Inlet breeching for dry riser inlets.
		These shall be fitted with male instantaneous connections to BS336, drain valves to BS5154 rating PN16, and non-return valves.
		
		Materials for the components of inlet breeching shall be in accordance with Table 1 of BS5041:Part 3.

FOAM INLETS & DRY RISER INLETS		Part 5: Boxes for foam inlets and dry riser inlets. Materials shall be in accordance with clause 4 of BS5041:Part 5.
<u>GENERAL SPECIFICATIONS</u>	-	BS5306: Code of practice for fire extinguishing installations and equipment on premises. Part 1: Hydrant systems, hose reels and foam inlets. BS1635: Graphical symbols and abbreviations for fire protection drawings. BS4422: Glossary of terms associated with fire. Part 4: Fire protection equipment. BS5588: Fire precautions in the design and construction of buildings. See Part 1 (residential) and 3 (office buildings).

GENERAL DESCRIPTION

An automatic sprinkler system is a system of water pipes fitted with sprinkler heads at suitable intervals and heights. It is designed to control or extinguish a fire by the discharge of water from the heads which open automatically at a specified temperature. The heads can open individually or in groups and can also be activated by a fire detector.

Automatic sprinkler systems in buildings may be designed and installed to suit one or more of the following class of occupancy hazard:

      Extra Light Hazard.

      Ordinary Hazard.

      Extra High Hazard.

These classes depend on the amount and combustibility of the contents.

Sprinkler systems are generally classified under four headings:

      (a) Wet pipe systems.

      (b) Dry pipe systems.

      (c) Alternate systems.

      (d) Pre-action systems.

Specialised automatic systems include deluge and drencher systems.

Sprinkler systems are normally installed in accordance with the Fire Offices Committee (FOC) "Rules for Automatic Sprinkler Installations".

It is advisable to consult the local Fire and Water Authorities in the early stages of the design of automatic sprinkler systems.

This section does not include information on the choice of materials for supply pipelines external to buildings.

SERVICE CONDITIONS

FLUID

Water from mains supply and/or storage.

Acceptable sources of supply are classified as:

      Town mains.

      Elevated private reservoirs.

      Gravity tanks.

      Automatic pumps boosting supplies from reservoirs, rivers, etc.

      Pressure tanks.

TEMPERATURE

Normal mains, tank, reservoir, or river water temperature (normally between 5° and 15°C).

PRESSURE

This depends on the Hazard class:

Hazard class	Running pressure*
Extra Light	2.2 bar
Ordinary	Ranges from 1 to 2 bar
Extra High	Ranges from 1.8 to 8.35 bar depending on the density of discharge, pipe sizing and spacing of sprinklers. Values are tabulated in FOC Rules, Table 233.A.

* Water supply must be capable of providing the running pressure indicated at the installation control valves. Allowance must be made for the difference in height between the highest sprinkler and the valves when water is being discharged at the stipulated rate.

STANDARD PRECAUTIONS SEE SERVICES SECTION APPENDIX 1

A   1, 3, 4, 5, 7, 9, 11, 12

B   1, 2, 3

C   1, 3, 4, 6

D   1, 2

SPECIAL PRECAUTIONS

Water in the system is stagnant except under fire-fighting conditions. For this reason it is best to completely separate it from normal mains water service systems by a break tank/storage tank. Under some circumstances water treatment may be desirable.

In some areas aggressive water characteristics may require the use of materials to resist attack from specific conditions, e.g. dezincification. The local Water Authority should be consulted about water characteristics before selecting materials.

In situations where sprinkler heads are liable to be operated or damaged by accidental blows, they should be protected by stout metal guards, care being taken to see that the normal operation of the sprinkler head by fire is not impeded.

Completed installations are normally required to be tested to the satisfaction of the local Fire Authority and be approved by both the local Fire and Water Authorities.

The FOC Rules provide general information as guidance relating to water suppliers; spacing and location of sprinklers, system components and types of system.

MAJOR COMPONENTS

COMPONENT	DATA SHEET	NOTE
PIPE	-	FOC Para. 4100: Pipework.
Steel	3.1.1	BS1387 preferably heavyweight galvanised. BS3601 for pipework 200mm diameter and over.

MAJOR COMPONENTS

COMPONENT	DATA SHEET	NOTE
JOINTING METHOD		
Flanged	3.2.1	BS10 for imperial sizes, BS4504 for metric sizes.
Screwed	3.2.1	Threads to BS21. Screwed fittings shall be malleable cast iron to BS143, 1256 or wrought steel to BS1740.
VALVES	3.3	FOC Paragraph 4300:Valves. Certain valves may require Water Authority stamping/testing.
PUMPS		
Centrifugal	3.4.1	FOC Paragraph 2540:Automatic pumps.
TANKS	3.5.2	Cast iron sectional to BS1563. Pressed steel to BS1564. FOC: gravity tanks. Paragraph 2530. pressure tanks. Paragraph 2550.
SPECIFIC ITEMS		
SPRINKLER SYSTEMS	-	BS5306: Code of practice for fire extinguishing installations and equipment on premises. Part 2: Sprinkler systems.
	-	FOC Publication: Requirements and testing methods for automatic sprinklers (Jan, 1982).
PRINCIPAL SYSTEM COMPONENTS		FOC Rules (29th Edition)
Wet alarm valve	-	Paragraphs 4331 & 2.
Composite alarm valve	-	Paragraph 4333.
Alarm motor and gong	-	Paragraph 4410.
Location plate	-	Paragraph 4312.3.
Installation test valves	-	Paragraph A1000-1201.
Sprinkler heads	-	FOC documents "Requirements and testing methods for automatic sprinklers", Table 2 (Jan 85).

APPENDIX 1 PRECAUTIONS CHECKLIST

The following list of precautions are referred to in the services sheets by the reference numbers shown below.

PRECAUTION	FURTHER INFORMATION
A. <u>DESIGN AND INSTALLATION</u>	
A1 Make due allowance for thermal expansion including adequate anchoring	Material Data Sheet - Section 4
A2 Make due allowance for the higher coefficients of expansion of plastics materials.	Plastics material text and data sheets - Section 4
A3 Include sufficient air venting devices and ensure that these are properly located.	
A4 Pipework should rise in the direction of flow so that entrained air is propelled to venting points.	
A5 Fit drain points of adequate size to suit both system flushing and emptying at convenient low points in the system.	
A6 Ensure steam lines fall in direction of steam flow.	
A7 System test pressures must not exceed capabilities of components and joints.	Component data sheets - Section 3
A8 Plastics materials are liable to degradation by ultra-violet radiation. Either use an inhibited grade or protect the material.	Plastics materials text and data sheets - Section 4
A9 Flush systems adequately, including deadlegs when commissioning water systems.	
A10 Protect fine gap control valves during flushing by removing or bypassing.	

PRECAUTION	FURTHER INFORMATION
A11 If a water system is not to be used immediately after testing it must be left protected from internal corrosion, either filled with treated water or an inert gas.	
A12 Pumps and fans should be fitted with anti-vibration mountings.	
B <u>OPERATIONAL ABUSE</u>	
B1 A system must not operate beyond its designed limits of pressure, temperature etc.	See limits of particular components in data sheets - Section 3.
B2 Statutory safety requirements must be observed e.g.surface temperature, outlet temperature, pressure limits etc.	Component data sheets - Section 3
B3 Components in the system should be located so that maintenance can be.carried out.	
C <u>CORROSION</u>	
C1 Water treatment - the water composition influences its aggressiveness and treatment may be required. Examine water analysis for aggressive properties.	Corrosion - Section 1 Environment - Section 1
C2 Fluid flow at any point should not exceed the critical velocity for the system materials at the operating temperature. Turbulence created by obstructions results in erosion/corrosion.	Environment - Section 1 Corrosion - Section 1
C3 Flush system adequately to remove deposits in the pipes which may create galvanic corrosion by differential aeration cells.	Corrosion - Section 1
C4 Partial loss of millscale will create areas of different electrical potential and thus form electrolytic potential cells. Chemically clean, flush out, and passivate.	Corrosion - Section 1

PRECAUTION	FURTHER INFORMATION
C5 Internal or external condensation on duct surfaces, due to low temperatures may encourage corrosion. Protect from attack by either vapour barriers or selection of resistant materials.	
C6 Avoid, if possible mixed metal combinations by either direct contact or by metals being deposited out of suspension e.g. copper deposites on zinc or aluminium that may give rise to corrosion due to their relative positions in the galvanic series.	Environment - Section 1 Corrosion - Section 1
C7 Surface coatings must be compatible with the environment and continuous. Small holes may create intensive local attack of the substrate with accelerated perforation. Careful surface preparation for coating and maintenance of the coating in service are essential for satisfactory performance.	Surface coatings - Section 4 Environment - Section 1 Corrosion - Section 1
C8 Insulation must be protected against the ingress of moisture.	Insulation - Section 4
C9 In conditions that promote or support microbiological growth precautions must be taken to limit the consequential contamination. Pipework and fittings in contact with potable water must be made from materials listed by the National Water Council in their Water Fitting Directory.	Components - Section 3 Environment - Section 1 Corrosion - Section 1
D VANDALISM	
D1 Exposed components must be adequately supported and protected from impact. If critical or hazardous, protective casings should be used.	Components - Section 3
D2 Accessible valves and controls should be locked in position or encased.	
D3 Open water surfaces must be protected from contamination.	
D4 Materials liable to rodent attack must be protected	

	PRECAUTION	FURTHER INFORMATION
D5	The removal of expensive components and materials must be discouraged by adequate fixing, inaccessible positioning or detraction from the items value e.g. by permanent marking.	

101

PART 3   COMPONENTS

SCOPE

This Data Sheet covers both carbon and alloy steel pipes (not stainless steel) supplied in seamless or welded forms. Carbon steel may be used up to $480^{o}C$ and alloy steel up to $600^{o}C$, depending on the materials used and the method of manufacture of the pipe providing the specified temperature/pressure relationships are not exceeded.

SPECIFICATIONS

BS1387: 1967 Steel tubes and tubulars for screwing to BS21 threads

Size range	⅛ins to 6ins (6-150mm) nominal bore
Wall thickness	Available in 3 grades; light, medium and heavy.
	Table 1: Dimensions of steel tubes (light)
	Table 2: Dimensions of steel tubes (medium)
	Table 3: Dimensions of steel tubes (heavy)
Manufacture	Light - welded
	Medium and heavy - welded or seamless
Marking	Shall be marked with colour bands at the ends
	Light pipes - brown
	Medium pipes - blue
	Heavy pipes - red
Tests	All tubes tested hydraulically to 700 psi (50 bar); bend test - up to and including 2" (50mm) nominal bore; flattening test - over 2" (50mm) nominal bore.
Other data	Tube can be supplied with either plain ends or with threads conforming to BS 21. BS 1387 allows for tubes to be galvanised prior to thread cutting.

BS3601: 1974 Steel pipes and tubes for pressure purposes: Carbon steel with specified room temperature properties

Size range	Diameters, mm size, and thickness appropriate to this standard, with the exception of butt welded, should be selected from BS3600. Butt welded tubes shall be selected according to Tables 1, 2 or 3 in BS1387.
Manufacture	Tubes may be butt welded (BW), electric resistance and induction welded (ERW), submerged arc welded (SAW) or seamless (S). There are limits on outside diameter and thickness for each process.
	Submerged arc welded tubes can be supplied either longitudinally or spirally welded. Pipe can be prepared with square or bevel ends.
Marking	Tubes shall be legibly marked or the bundle shall be identified with stamped tags.
Heat treatment	The heat treatment of the tube is determined by the method of manufacture.
Tests	Visual, hydraulic, tensile and flattening tests shall be carried out on each batch of tube. Batch size is determined by the size of the tube.
Other data	Table 1: Chemical composition and room temperature mechanical properties.

105

BS3602: Steel pipes and tubes for pressure purposes: Carbon and carbon manganese steel with specified elevated temperature properties

Part 1: 1978 - Seamless, electric resistance welded and induction welded tubes

Size range   Diameters, 10.2-457mm size, and thickness appropriate to this standard shall be selected from BS3600.

Manufacture   Tubes may be seamless, electric resistance welded or induction welded. The tube may be as welded, cold or hot finished.

There are limits on outside diameter and thickness for each process. Tubes shall be tested to category 1 or 2 as requested.

Marking   Tubes shall be legibly marked and colour coded or the bundle shall be identified with stamped tags. The colour coding shall be to BS5383 with types 360 or 410 marked in dark grey and 460 or 490 marked in yellow.

Heat treatment Tube shall be supplied in the condition as shown in Table 1.

Tests   Tubes shall be subjected to the tests applicable to the category of test required. Visual, tensile, flattening and non destructive tests shall be carried out on each batch. Batch size is determined by the size of tube.

Table 1:   Chemical composition, mechanical properties at room temperature. The grade of steel with its method of manufacture are shown against composition, mechanical properties and heat treatment.

Appendix A: Ultrasonic testing of tubes
Appendix B: Minimum 0.2% proof stress values at elevated temperatures up to 450°C.
Appendix C: Verification of elevated temperature values.
Appendix D: Stress rupture values up to 500°C.

Part 2: 1978 - Submerged arc welded tubes

Size range   Diameters, 152-2200mm sizes, and thickness appropriate to this standard shall be selected from BS3600.

Manufacture   Tubes shall be longitudinally welded using a submerged arc welding process. The filler metal used shall be compatible with the parent metal. Tubes may be hot or cold finished.

Heat treatment Tube shall be supplied in the condition as shown in Table 1.

Marking   Tubes shall be legibly marked and colour coded or the bundle shall be identified with stamped tags. The colour coding shall be to BS5383 with grade 410 marked in dark grey and 460 marked in yellow.

Tests   Tubes shall be subjected to the tests applicable to the category of test required. Visual, tensile (both material and weld), bend (weld), hydraulic and non-destructive testing (100% on category 1 and random tests on category 2). A test certificate shall be issued.

Other data   Table 1:   Chemical composition, mechanical properties at room temperature and heat treatment.
Appendix A: Ultrasonic testing of the weld zone of double submerged arc welded tube.
Appendix B: Radiographic acceptance limits.
Appendix C: Minimum 0.2% proof stress at elevated temperatures.
Appendix D: Procedure for verification of elevated temperature valves.
Appendix E: Stress rupture values.

BS3603: 1977 - Steel pipes and tubes for pressure purposes: carbon and alloy steel with specified low temperature properties

Size range	Diameter, 10.2-457 mm sizes, and thickness appropriate to this standard should be selected from BS3600.
Manufacture	Tubes may be seamless electric resistance or induction welded. Welded tube shall not have any filler materials. The tubes may be as welded, cold finished or hot finished.
Heat treatment	Tube shall be supplied in the condition shown in Table 1.
Marking	Tubes shall be legibly marked and colour coded or the bundle shall be identified with stamped tags. The colour coding shall be to BS5383 in light green.
Tests	Tubes shall be subjected to the tests applicable to the category of test required. Visual, tensile, flattening or bend, non destructive test (category 1) and hydraulic (category 2). A test certificate shall be issued.
Other data	Tubes manufactured in accordance with this standard have specified low temperature impact properties.

Table 1:   Chemical composition, room temperature mechanical properties and heat treatment.

Table 2:   Minimum charpy V-notch impact properties at low temperature.

Appendix A :   Ultrasonic testing tubes for longitudinal defects

BS3604: 1978 - Steel pipes and tubes for pressure purposes: Ferritic alloy steel with specified elevated temperature properties

Size range	Diameter, 10.2-457mm sizes, and thickness appropriate to this standard should be selected from BS3600.
Manufacture	Tubes may be seamless, electric resistance welded or induction welded. The tubes may be in the as welded, cold finished or hot finished condition.
Heat treatment	Tube shall be supplied in the condition shown in Table 1.
Marking	Tubes shall be legibly marked and colour coded or the bundle shall be identified with stamped tags. The colour coding shall be to BS5383 identifying the following steel grades as follows: 620 and 621 pink; 660 brown; 622 light blue; 625 and 629 olive; 762 orange.
Tests	Tubes shall be subjected to the tests applicable to the category of test required. Visual, tensile, flattening or bend, non destructive test (category 1) and hydraulic (category 2). A test certificate shall be issued.
Other data	Tubes manufactured to this specification have specified room temperature properties and specified proof stress values at elevated temperatures (up to 550°C).

Table 1 :   Chemical composition, mechanical properties at room temperature and heat treatment.

Appendix A: Ultrasonic testing of tubes for longitudinal defects.

Appendix B: Minimum 0.2% proof stress values at elevated temperatures.

Appendix C: Procedure for verification of elevated temperature values.

Appendix D: Stress rupture values

BS534: 1981 - Specification for steel pipes, and specials for water and sewage

BS1775: 1964 - Steel tubes for mechanical, structural and general engineering purposes

BS3059: 1978 - Specification for steel boiler and superheater tubes

MATERIALS

The above specifications refer to the materials listed below

BS Number	Material/Grade	Data Sheet	Comments
1387	Carbon steel/320	FM11	seamless or welded
	carbon steel/360	FM12	seamless or welded
3601	carbon steel/320	FM11	seamless or welded
	carbon steel/360	FM12	seamless or welded
	carbon steel/410	FM13	seamless or welded
3602/1	carbon steel/360	FM12	seamless or welded
	carbon steel/410	FM13	seamless or welded
	carbon steel/460	FM14	seamless or welded
	carbon steel/490nB	FM15	seamless
3602/2	carbon steel/410	FM13	welded tube
	carbon steel/460	FM14	welded tube
3603	carbon steel/410	FM13	seamless or welded
	low alloy steel/503	FM17	seamless
	low alloy steel/509		seamless
3604	low alloy steel/620	FM18	seamless or welded
	low alloy steel/620	FM19	seamless or welded
	low alloy steel/621	FM20	seamless or welded
	low alloy steel/660	FM22	seamless
	low alloy steel/622	FM21	seamless
	low alloy steel/625		seamless
	low alloy steel/629		seamless
	low alloy steel/629		seamless
	low alloy steel/762	FM23	seamless

CONNECTIONS

The type of connection used must be suitable for the pipe materials, pressure and temperature conditions, the medium handled and the mechanical strength required under the service conditions.

Method	BS Number	Component Data Sheet	Tube	Comments
Screwed	BS143/1256	3.2.2	BS1387	Threads must be tapered conforming to the requirements of BS21. Care should be taken when threading light tube.
Flanged	BS1740			
	BS10	3.2.1	BS1387	Flanges can be attached to BS1387 tube using threads.
			BS3501/4	The ultimate working pressure/ temperature of the system will be determined by the pressure/ temperature limitation of either the flange or the tube, whichever is the lower.
Welded	BS1965	3.2.5	BS3601 BS3602	All welding must be carried out by a competent welder in accordance with an accepted code of practice

Method	BS Number	Component Data Sheet	Tube	Comment
				and may be subjected to a non-destructive test.
Grooved		3.2.6		Grooves can be either formed or machined depending on wall thickness.
Compression	BS4368	3.2.4	BS3601 BS3602 BS3505	Fittings can be either manipulative or non-manipulative.

SERVICE CONSIDERATIONS

1.   When selecting steel pipe the pressure and temperature requirements of BS806: 1975 - Ferrous pipes and piping installations for and in connection with land boilers - must be observed.

BS806 states that pipes manufactured to BS1387 and BS3601/BW320, up to 150mm nominal size, may be used at pressure not exceeding 2.1 N/mm^2 and temperatures not exceeding $260^{o}C$ provided that it is at least of BS1387 medium thickness.

2.   The selection of wall thickness for tubes to BS1387 may be determined by accessibility for future replacement. Accessible tubes for cold water systems, or low temperature, or medium temperature, or domestic hot water systems may be 'medium', while concealed tube should be 'heavy'.

3.   When permitted screwed pipe may be used for accessible joints up to 100mm.

4.   Galvanised pipe should only be used for cold water and domestic hot water systems.

5.   Welded joints should be used on steam systems and medium temperature hot water systems over 50mm, and high temperature hot water systems.

| FAMILY GROUP | PIPE | SUB-GROUP | COPPER AND COPPER ALLOYS |

SCOPE

Copper and copper alloy tubing intended for use in steam, water, gas and sanitation installations. It includes microbore sizes, half hard and annealed tube suitable for use underground, tubes for heat exchangers and hard thin walled tube, unsuitable for bending.

SPECIFICATIONS

BS2871: Copper and copper alloy tubes

Part 1: 1977 - Copper tubes for water, gas and sanitation

Size range	Tube size, outside diameter limits, nominal thickness and maximum working pressure are indicated for tubes in various conditions in Tables W,X,Y,Z. Table W 6-10mm diameter Table X and Z 6-159mm diameter Table Y 6-108mm diameter
Manufacture	Solid drawn tube with ends clean cut and square with the axis of the tube.
Marking	15-42mm diameter inclusive marked at intervals of not more than 500mm with the B.S. number, table designation and manufacturer. Above 42mm at each end with similar information as above.
Heat treatment	The specification includes three conditions of hardness. Tube to table Y only includes a choice to be specified by the customer. Annealed copper tubes in coils Half hard copper tubes in straight length Hard drawn copper tubes in straight lengths.
Tests	Mechanical tests, tensile and drift tests, by agreement between the purchaser and manufacturer. Hydrostatic on pneumatic test to comply with minimum pressure requirements, or tube integrity by eddy current tests.
Other data	Table W: Dimensions and working pressures for annealed copper tubes for use in microbore or minibore. Table X: Dimensions and Working pressures for ½ hard light gauge copper tube. Table Y: Dimensions and working pressures for ½ hard and annealed copper tube. Table Z: Dimensions and working pressures for hard drawn thin wall copper tubes.
NOTE	Tube to BS2871 Part 1 may be obtained with various plastics coverings to provide either thermal insulation or surface protection. PVC, polyethylene and foam plastics coverings are commercially available but are not at present the subject of British Standards.

Part 2: 1972 - Tubes for general purposes

Size range	Tube size range 3-508mm diameter with 0.5-10.5 mm wall thickness Tube size, outside diameter limits and standard thickness (preferred and others) are indicated for tubes used for general purposes. (See also Note on tables 7 to 10) Imperial sizes of tubes listed in tables 7 to 10 are referred to by nominal bore.
Manufacturer	Tubes shall be solid drawn and supplied in straight length and the ends shall be cut clean and square with the axis of the tubes.
Marking	Not indicated.

Heat treatment	Tubes available in the following conditions depending on the material specification used: As drawn - M Temper annealed - TA Annealed - 0 - supplied as coils Half hard - ½H
Tests	Tensile, hardness, flattening, doublebend and drifting tests may be requested. Hydrostatic, pneumatic or eddy current tests may be requested to test the tube integrity.
Other data	Table 3: Preferred sizes (3-508mm) of tubes for shipbuilding and other engineering purposes. Table 4: Preferred sizes (3-50mm) of tubes for purposes other than pipelines. Table 5: Copper tubes (5-219.1mm) for steam services with plain ends (low pressure range - up to and including 7 bar). Table 6: Copper tubes (6-219mm) for steam services with plain ends (high pressure range - over 7 bar and up to 17 bar) Table 7: Copper tubes (⅛"-4") for steam services with screwed ends (low pressure range - up to and including 7 bar) Table 8: Copper tubes (⅛"-4") for steam services with screwed ends (high pressure - up to 17 bar) Table 9: Copper tubes (⅛"-4") for general purposes for pressures up to and including 12 bar. Table 10: Copper tubes (⅛"-4") for general purposes for pressures over 12 bar and up to and including 20 bar.
NOTE:	Tables 7, 8, 9 and 10 list imperial nominal bores as the tube size.

Part 3: 1972 - Tubes for heat exchangers

Size Range	6-50mm diameters
Manufacture	Tubes shall be solid drawn and supplied in straight lengths and the ends shall be cut clean and square with the axis of the tube.
Marking	Not indicated
Heat treatment	Tube available in the following conditions depending on material specification used: As drawn - M Temper annealed - TA Annealed - 0 Half hard - ½H
Tests	Each tube shall be eddy current tested. Hardness, flattening and drift tests may be requested. Hydrostatic or pneumatic tests may be requested. A certificate of compliance may be requested.
Other data	Table 1 Composition and mechanical properties.

MATERIALS

Specification	Material/Grade	Data Sheet	Comment
2871/1	Wrought copper/C106	NF11	Commercially available
	Wrought copper/C107	NF12	
2871/2	Electrolytic / C101 H.C. copper		
	Fire refined / C102 H.C. copper		
	OFHC copper/ C103	NF10	
	Wrought copper/C106	NF11	
	Wrought copper/C107	NF12	
	Brass /CZ110	NF15	
	Brass /CZ119		
	Brass /CZ126	NF21	
	Copper-nickel/CN102		
	Copper-nickel/CN107	NF32	
2871/3	Wrought copper/C106	NF11	
	Brass/CZ110	NF15	
	Brass/CZ111	NF16	
	Brass/CZ126	NF21	
	Copper-nickel/CN102		
	Copper-nickel/CN107	NF32	
	Copper-nickel/CN108		
	Aluminium bronze/CA102	NF28	

CONNECTIONS

The type of connection used must be suitable for the pipe materials, pressure and temperature conditions, the medium handled and the mechanical strength required under the service conditions. Connection methods which are appropriate for different tube types are indicated in the following table.

Method	BS Number	Component Data Sheet	Tube BS Number	Comments
Capillary	864	3.2.3	2871/1	Capillary joints can either have integral solder rings or be end fed. Type of solder limits the service temperature and pressure.
	2051	3.2.3	2871/2	More arduous usage than above. Can either have an integral solder ring or be end fed. Integral braze rings available for high temperature and pressure applications.
Compression	864	3.2.4	2871/1	Type B requiring manipulation of the tube are not to be used on Table Z material.
	2051	3.2.4	2871/2	Not to be used on hard drawn tubes.
Screwed	66/99	3.2.2	2871/2	For use with pressure up to 8.6 bar.
	143/1256	3.2.2.	2871/2	For use with pressures up to 13.6 bar for water and 10.3 bar for steam gas, air and oil.

Method	BS Number	Component Data Sheet	Tube BS Number	Comments
Flanged	10 4504	3.2.1 3.2.1	2871/2))	Fixed by screwing, soldering, or welding to the pipework. BS10 is imperial dimensioning and BS4504 is metric.
Welded	1077	3.2.5	2871/1/2/3	Heat exchanger tubes may be welded or expanded into tube plates.
			2871/3	Tubes may be bronze welded to copper or copper alloy flanges using the techniques outlined in HVCA TR3 - Code of Practice - Brazing and bronze welding of copper pipework.

SERVICE CONSIDERATIONS

1. Copper pipe to the above specifications is also suitable for conveying natural and coal gas, oil products and medical gases but, in the latter case the tube must contain no traces of grease, oil or flux and may require to be provided packaged in a sterile condition.

2. Some soft waters can attack copper tubing and in these localities advice from the local water authority should be sought.

3. Copper to BS2871 Part 1 Tables X and Y can be bent using a machine or an appropriate sized bending spring.
    Copper to BS2871 Part 1 Table Z cannot be readily bent.
    Care must be taken when using imported tube conforming to the dimensions of BS2871 as manipulation by bending may be limited.

4. Excessive water velocities and turbulent conditions can cause impingement attack to the copper tube. The rate of attack is related to the water temperature and the water velocity.

5. Galvanic (bi-metallic) corrosion may occur if dissimiliar metals are joined together in association with an electrolyte e.g. copper/aluminium or copper/galvanised steel.

6. Excess fluxes used for soldering or brazing can be corrosive and must be removed.

7. Solders with a melting point of $183^{o}C$ - tin/lead - are suitable for service up to $100^{o}C$ (integral rings). For higher temperatures a high melting point ($221^{o}C$) tin/silver solder should be used.

8. Copper and stainless steel are comparable in jointing methods. Price relationships between copper and stainless steel fluctuate with metal market trends.

9. Due to its soft condition copper is susceptible to mechanical damage and should not be fixed in a position exposed to impact or abrasion.

FAMILY GROUP	PIPE	SUB-GROUP	STAINLESS STEEL

SCOPE

Stainless steel tube is used where corrosion resistance or appearance are important. Thin wall stainless tube to BS4127 is produced with similar dimensions as copper tube to BS2871 part 1 and can be used as an alternative. The choice may be controlled by economics, conveyed fluid or the environment. Other specifications cover process tubing.

SPECIFICATIONS

BS4127: Light gauge stainless steel tubes
Part 2: 1972 - Metric units

Size range	6-42mm diameter
Manufacture	Welded or seamless
Marking	All tubes over 15mm shall be marked along their length
Tests	Tensile, drift, flattening tests should be performed by the manufacturer. Tube integrity and pressure requirements shall be tested by hydraulic, pneumatic or a non-destructive test.
Other data	Table 1. Dimensions of light gauge stainless steel tube.
	Capillary and compression fittings to BS864 may be used for tube jointing.

BS3605: 1973 - Seamless and welded austenitic stainless steel pipes and tubes for pressure purposes

Size range	Size may be stated as inside or outside diameters as indicated below depending on method of manufacture.
Manufacture	Seamless cold finished pipes (CFS) - up to 219mm outside diameter or 150-600mm inside diameter.
	Seamless hot finished pipes (HFS) 89-355mm outside diameter.
	Seamless hot finished and machined pipes (HFM) 150-750mm inside diameter.
	Longitudinally welded pipe (LW - as welded, LWHT - heat treated, LWCF - cold finished and heat treated) 610mm maximum outside diameter.
	Spirally welded pipe (SW - as welded, SWHT - heat treated, SWCF - cold finished and heat treated), 76.1mm minimum outside diameter.
Marking	At intervals along pipe length indicating pipe designation and manufacturers mark.
Heat treatment	Seamless and cold finished welded pipe shall be solution treated.
Testing	Tensile, flattening or bend, macroscopic, intercrystaline corrosion, hydraulic and non-destructive tests shall be carried out by the manufacturer. The actual combination depends on the pipe category.
	Test certificates shall be supplied.
Other data	Requirements for seamless pipes with specified room temperature properties.

        Table 1   Chemical composition and heat treatment
        Table 2   Mechanical properties

        Requirements for seamless pipes with specified elevated temperatures.

        Table 3   Chemical composition and heat treatment
        Table 4   Room temperature mechanical properties

        Table 5   Minimum 1% proof stress values at elevated temperatures (50-650°C).

        Specific requirements for welded pipes with specific room temperature properties.

Other data - contd.

	Table 6	Chemical composition and heat treatment
	Table 7	Mechanical properties

Specific requirements for welded pipes with specified elevated temperature properties.

	Table 8	Chemical composition and heat treatment
	Table 9	Room temperature mechanical properties
	Table 10	Minimum 1.0% proof stress values at elevated temperatures (50-450°C).

	Appendix B	Ultrasonic testing for longitudinal defects.
	Appendix C	Eddy current testing of longitudinally welded pipes.
	Appendix D	Weld radiography of spirally welded pipes.
	Appendix E	Estimated average stress rupture values for specific steel types.

BS3606: 1978 - Steel tubes for heat exchangers

Size range	16-50mm diameter
Manufacture	Welded or seamless and designated as follows:
	Cold finished seamless (CFS)
	Longitudinally welded and heat treated (LWHT)
	Longitudinally welded, cold finished and heat treated (LWCF).
	Longitudinally welded bead conditioned and heat treated (LWBC).

Marking   Each tube shall be ink marked with designation, specification and manufacturer on each end of the tube and colour coded to BS5383. For small tube the above information may be on attached labels tied to the bundles.

Heat treatment   Shall be supplied in the solution treated condition.

Tests   Visual inspection, tensile, flattening, drift expanding or hydraulic tests shall be executed.
Non-destructive test, as indicated in appendices Band C, may be used.

Other data	Table 1	Chemical composition, mechanical properties at room temperature and heat treatment
		(c) Austenitic stainless steel tube

	Appendix A	Dimensions of welded and seamless tube for heat exchanges
	Appendix B	Ultrasonic testing of tubes for longitudinal defects
	Appendix C	Eddy current testing of tubes for defects
	Appendix E	Designation of steel tube.

MATERIALS

BS Number	Material/Grade	Data Sheet	Comments
4127/2	Austenitic/302	FM24	Water tube for use with capillary or compression fittings to BS864. The solder flux must be suitable for stainless steel.
3605	Austenitic/304	FM24	Includes 304L (304S 22) for reduction of intergranular corrosion (weld decay)
	Austenitic/316	FM25	Includes 316L (316S 22) for reduction of intergranular corrosion (weld decay)
	Austenitic/321	FM26	Used where intergranular corrosion (weld decay) could be a problem.
	Austenitic/347		Similar to 321 but superior for use with nitric acid.
3606	Austenitic/304	FM24	As above
	Austenitic/316	FM25	As above
	Austenitic/321	FM26	As above
	Austenitic/347		As above.

CONNECTION

The type of connection used must be suitable for the pipe material, pressure and temperature conditions, the medium handled and the mechanical strength required under the service conditions.

Method	BS Number	Component Data/Sheet	Tube BS Number	Comment
Capillary	864/2	3.2.3.	4127/2	Copper and copper alloy fittings to BS864 may be used. A special flux must be used (phosphoric acid based). The pressure and temperature limitations of BS864 apply. Stainless steel fittings are available from limited sources.
Compression	864/2	3.2.3.	4172/2	For use where the pipeline may require breaking for maintenance or repair of components. Fittings complying with BS864 may be used.
Screwed		3.2.2.	3605 3606	Screwed fittings are available from specialists and conform to the requirements of the petroleum industry. The material of the fitting should be similar to the pipe material.
Flanged	1560	3.2.1.	3605 3606	Flanges are available from specialists and conform to the requirements of BS1560. The flange should be of the same material as the pipe.

 **component data sheet**

SHEET NUMBER 3.1.3. 4

CONNECTION CONTD.

Method	BS Number	Component Data/Sheet	Tube BS Number	Comment
Welded	1965/2	3.2.4.	3605 3606	Pipe can be butt welded or socket welded. Butt welding shall conform to BS1965 part 2. Sockets are available from specialists and conform to the requirement of the petroleum industry. The welded fitting should be of the same material as the pipe.

SERVICE CONSIDERATIONS

1. Used in conditions that are corrosive to copper or carbon steel.

2. Expensive material and therefore only used when other alternatives have been exhausted for corrosive or economic means.

3. Used for cosmetic reasons where a surface coating would add extra cost to a cheaper material and would have to be periodically refurbished.

4. Austenitic stainless is not as manipulative as copper pipe.

5. Fittings are not readily available and generally conform to petroleum specifications. Therefore they are expensive.

6. Longitudinally welded tube can either be drawn after welding to remove the internal weld bead or it can be rolled out by means of a bead rolling process immediately after welding. The removal of the bead is essential for tube associated with foodstuffs to prevent contamination, to prevent corrosive products lodging in crevices and promoting corrosion and also to reduce conditions for creating turbulant flow. Less expensive than seamless tube.

7. All pipe should be adequately supported.

8. Allowance should be made for expansion and contraction movements by the provision of loops, bellows etc. in the pipe system. Any force created against anchor-blocks should be within the safety factors of the structure.

117

SCOPE

Plastics pipe are made from both thermoplastic and thermosetting plastics. In general plastics pipe is resistant to corrosion, light in weight, easy to join and has a degree of flexibility. The use of plastics pipe in services supplied from the mains of water undertakings is governed by their byelaws. Materials covered are polyvinyl chloride, polyethylene, ABS, and polypropylene. Materials suitable for hot water services are covered in 3.1.4B.

SPECIFICATIONS

Polyvinyl Chloride

BS3505: 1965 - Unplasticized PVC pipe for cold water services

Size range   ⅜" to 24" nominal sizes. The outside diameter limits and wall thickness depend on the class of pipe (see Table 1 or 1A).

Classification   Pipes are classified by maximum sustained working pressure.

Class B   6.0 bar   red marking
Class C   9.0 bar   blue marking
Class D   12.0 bar   green marking
Class E   15.0 bar   brown marking
Class 7   Suitable for screw threading for pressures not exceeding Class C rating.

Marking   All pipe shall be marked at intervals indicating specification, nominal size and manufacturer in the colour appropriate to the class.

Tests   Impact and hydraulic

Other data   Table 1:   Pipe dimensions for classes B,C,D and E.
Table 1A: Dimensions and maximum sustained working pressure for class 7 pipe.

BS3506: 1969 - Unplasticized PVC pipe for industrial use

Size range   ⅜" to 24" norminal size. The outside diameter limits and the wall thickness depend on the class of the pipe (see Table 1).

Classification   Class 0   non pressure
Class B   6.0 bar
Class C   9.0 bar
Class D   12.0 bar
Class E   15.0 bar
Cladd 6
Class 7

Marking   All pipes shall be marked at intervals with specification, class, size and manufacturer.

Tests   Hydraulic

Other data   Table 1:   Pipe Dimensions

BS4515: 1969 - Unplasticized PVC soil and ventilating pipe fittings and accessories.

Size range   82 to 160 mm nominal

Marking   Shall be clearly marked with manufacturer, specification and nominal size.

Tests   Tensile, impact, heat reversion and hydrostatic.

Other data   Table 1:   Dimensions of pipes and fittings
                 Table 10:   Recommended maximum support distances.

BS4576: 1970 - Unplasticized PVC rainwater goods

The pipe specified in this standard is not suitable for soil, waste and ventilation applications.

Size range   63 to 75mm nominal size.

Marking   Shall be clearly marked with manufacturer, specification and nominal size.

Tests   Tensile, heat reversion and impact

Other data   Table 1:   Pipe dimensions.

BS4660: 1973 - Unplasticized PVC underground drain pipe and fittings

Specifies the requirements for unplasticized PVC pipe and fittings suitable for the construction of drains, including foul and surface water sewers.

Size range   110 and 160mm nominal size.

Marking   Shall be clearly marked to show manufacturer, specification and size.

Tests   Tensile, heat reversion and impact.

Other data   Table 1:   Dimensions of pipe and fittings.
                 Appendix M: Notes for guidance on storage, handling and installation.

Polyethylene (low density)

BS1972: 1967 - Polythene pipe (Type 32) for cold water services

Polythene density not greater than 0.93g/ml at 20°C.

Size range $\frac{3}{8}$" to 4" nominal size. The outside diameter limits and wall thickness depend on the class of pipe (Table 1).

Classification   Pipes are classified by maximum sustained working pressure.

Class B   0.6 MN/m^2 red marking
Class C   0.89 MN/m^2 blue marking
Class D   1.20 MN/m^2 green marking
Class C pipes in 1 in. to 3 in. nominal size and class D pipes may be threaded using a taper thread to BS21.

Marking   Shall be marked to show manufacturer specification and size.

Tests   Heat reversion, hydraulic pressure and tensile.

Other data   Table 1:   Pipe dimensions.

Polyethylene (high density).

BS3284:   1967 - Polythene pipes (Type 50) for cold water services

Polyethylene with a density greater than 0.93/ml at 20°C.

Size range   ⅜" to 6" nominal size. The outside diameter limits and wall thickness depend on the class of pipe (Table 1).

Classification   Pipes are classified by maximum sustained working pressure.

Class B	0.60 MN/m^2	red marking
Class C	0.89 MN/m^2	blue marking
Class D	1.20 MN/m^2	green marking

Class C pipes ⅜in to 4in nominal size and class D pipes may be threaded using taper threads to BS21.

Marking   Shall be marked to show manufacturer, specification and size.

Tests   Visual, heat reversion, hydraulic and tensile

Other data   Table 1:   Pipe dimensions

Acrylonitrile-butadiene-styrene copolymer (ABS)

BS5391:   ABS pressure pipe
Part 1:   1976 - Pipe for industrial use

Size range   ¾" to 8" nominal size. The outside diameter limits and wall thickness depend on the class of pipe (Table 1).

Classification   Pipes are classified by maximum sustained working pressure.
                    Unsuitable for threading

Class B	6.0 bar	red marking
Class C	9.0 bar	blue marking
Class D	12.0 bar	green marking
Class E	15.0 bar	brown marking

Suitable for threading in compliance with BS21.

| Class T | 12.0 bar | white marking. |

Marking   Shall be marked to show manufacturer specification, size and class.

Tests   Heat reversion, heat ageing, resistance to weathering, impact and hydrostatic.

Other data   Table 1:   Dimensions.

Polypropylene copolymer

BS4991:   1974 - Propylene copolymer pressure pipe

Specifies requirements for propylene copolymer pressure pipe in two series:-
Series 1 for use with potable water, foodstuffs and pharmacutacals.
Series 2 for use with chemicals, including water at temperatures up to 100°C.

Size range   ¼" to 24" nominal size. The outside diameter limits and wall thickness depend on the class of pipe (Table 2).

Classification   Pipes are classified by maximum sustained working pressure.

Class A	3.0 bar	yellow marking
Class B	6.0 bar	red marking
Class C	9.0 bar	blue marking
Class D	12.0 bar	green marking
Class E	15.0 bar	brown marking.

Marking

Shall be marked to show manufacturer, specification, series number and nominal size.

Tests

Visual, heat reversion, hydrostatic pressure, tensile and impact.

Other data

Table 1:   A guide to working pressures at various temperatures and working life times with water.

Table 2:   Dimensions

Other related specifications:

PVC

BS3505: 1969 - Unplasticized PVC pipe for industrial purposes.

BS 4346: Joints and fittings with unplasticized PVC pressure pipes.

Part 1: 1969 - Injection moulded unplasticized PVC fittings for solvent welding for use with pressure pipes, including potable water.

Part 2: 1970 - Mechanical joints and fittings principally of unplasticized PVC.

Part 3: 1974 - Solvent cements.

BS5255: 1976 - Plastic waste pipe and fittings

BS5481: 1977 - Specification for unplasticized PVC pipe and fittings for gravity sewers.

Polyethylene

BS1973: 1970 - Polythene pipe (Type 32) for general purposes.

BS3796: 1970 - Polythene pipe (Type 50) for general purposes

BS5255: 1976 - Plastic waste pipe and fittings

ABS

BS5255: 1976 - Plastic waste pipe and fittings

BS5392: ABS fittings for use with ABS pressure pipe

Part 1: 1976 - Fittings for use with pipe for industrial uses

Polypropylene

BS5254: 1976 - Polypropylene waste pipe and fittings (external diameter 34.6mm 41.0mm and 54.1mm).

BS5255: 1976 - Plastic waste pipe and fittings

G.R.P

BS5480 - Specification for glass reinforced plastics (GRP) pipes and fittings for use for water supply or sewage.

Part 1: 1977 - Dimensions, materials and classification

General

BS4962: 1973   Performance requirements for plastics pipe for use as light duty sub-soil drains.

A British Standard Code of Practice is available to cover the choice, characteristics and applications of various plastics pipework materials.

CP312 Plastics pipework (thermoplastics)

Part 1: 1973 - General principles and choice of material

This part of the code of practice deals with the selection of thermoplastics pipe systems for particular applications and with general principles applicable to all such systems.

Piping information is included for various applications such as water; soil, waste, rainwater and trade effluents (above ground); gases (gaseous fuels and industrial gases); food and drink other than water; general industrial applications (excluding gases).

Other data
Table 1:   Physical properties of plastics pipe materials.
Table 2a: Chemical resistance of unplasticized PVC, low-density and high density polyethylene.
Table 2b.   Chemical resistance of modified (high impact) PVC, ABS, nylon and polypropylene.
Appendix A   Tests for suitability of soil material (imported or local) for surrounding buried plastic pipes.

Part 2: 1973 - Unplasticized PVC pipework for the conveyance of liquids under pressure

This part of the code gives guidance on the proper applications and installation of UPVC pipe for the conveyance of liquids under pressure. The choice of materials for particular applications is covered in Part 1 of this code.

Working temperatures and pressures are laid down in BS3505 and BS3506.

UPVC pipe should not be used for pressure applications at temperatures exceeding $60^{o}C$. Where piping is required to convey liquids between $20^{o}C$ and $60^{o}C$ the allowable maximum working pressure has to be reduced or alternatively a shorter life expectancy has to be allocated.

Other data   Table 1:   Recommended spacing of support centres for horizontal UPVC pipes.

Part 3: 1973 - Polyethylene pipes for the conveyance of liquids under pressure

This part of the code gives guidance on the proper application and installation of polyethylene pipe for the conveyance of liquids under pressure. The choice of materials for particular applications is covered in Part 1 of this code. This part does not recommend the use of polyethylene pipe for any particular purpose.

Classification   Type 32 with a density less than 0.93 g/ml. This class is not recommended for use at temperatures above $60^{o}C$, except in installations involving no or very low internal pressure. Type 50 with a density greater than a 93g/ml. This class is not recommended for use at temperatures above $70^{o}C$ except in installations involving no or very low internal pressure.

Other data   Table 1:   Reduction in working pressure at elevated temperatures.
Table 2:   Recommended spacing of support centres for horizontal pipes.

MATERIALS

BS Number	Material/Grade	Data Sheet	Comment
3505	Rigid PVC	PL17	Extrusion and moulding compounds
3506			
4346/1			
4514			
4576			
4660			
5255			
5487			
1972	Polyethylene	PL12	
1973	(low density)		

 **component data sheet**

BS Number	Material/Grade	Data Sheet	Comment
3284 3796	Polyethylene (high density)	PL11	
5255 5391 5392	A.B.S.	PL04	Industrial pressure pipe for use between -40°C to +70°C.
4991 5254 5255	Polypropylene	PL14	

CONNECTION

The type of connection used shall be suitable for the pipe materials, pressure and temperature conditions, the medium handled and mechanical strength required under the service conditions.

Method	BS Number	Component Data Sheet	Pipe	Comment
COMPRESSION	864/3	3.2.4.	LDPE HDPE	Compression fittings to BS864/3 use a metallic bore insert to support the tube and prevents collapse when deforming the sealing ring. It may be necessary to protect the metallic insert against corrosion as otherwise the benefits of using plastics pipe may be lost.
SCREWED		3.2.2.	PVC LDPE HDPE	Screwed joints are used on polyethylene pipe and also PVC pipe to BS3606 class 7 for certain wall thicknesses on pipe up to nominal size 2. The thread should be cut with pipe threads conforming to BS21. The thread should be totally enclosed in the fitting. When threaded pipe is used the working pressure must not exceed 9 bar. Sealing shall be with PTFE tape. Metal screwed fittings may be used providing UPVC is the male component.
FLANGE		3.2.1.	PVC LDPE HDPE ABS Polyprop.	Flanges are used for joining pipes and joining pipes to valves and fittings provided with flanges. The flanges may be fixed to the pipe by thermal or solvent welding, or screwed depending on the material. Joint sealing is made by the compression of a gasket or a ring seal set in the face of the flange. A backing ring or wide washers are required to spread the bolt loading.

Method	BS Number	Component Data Sheet	Pipe	Comment
THERMAL WELDED		See Jointing and Bonding	PVC HDPE Polyprop.	The pipe to pipe or flange to pipe connection is made by means of fusing a welding rod of similar material into a prepared chamfer using hot air or inert gas as the heating media, or by heating the faces by hot plattens, removing and instantaneously joining the softened faces by pressure.
SOLVENT		See Jointing and Bonding	PVC ABS	A solvent for the plastics material is applied to the pipe and fitting to soften them, they are placed together and the solvent allowed to evaporate. The joint must be by overlapping.

SERVICES CONSIDERATION

1. The maximum service temperature of plastics pipe is substantially lower than metallic pipes.

2. All plastics have a higher co-efficient of expansion than metallic pipe materials. (See data sheets).

3. The plastics pipe run will have to be supported at shorter intervals than metallic pipes.

4. Unless they have inhibitors deterioration can occur when subjected to ultra violet.

5. The pressure limits of a plastics pipe is temperature dependent. Suppliers data should be consulted.

6. Plastics pipe are poor conductors of electricity and therefore no attempt should be made to use the pipework as a means of earthing electrical equipment.

7. Caution is required in the use of plastics pipes where static electricity may be an important consideration.

8. Plastics pipe have good all round chemical resistance but careful consideration must be taken, concerning the media being conveyed and its temperature, for maximum corrosion protection.

FAMILY GROUP	PIPE	SUB-GROUP	PLASTICS (HOT WATER)

SCOPE

Plastics pipes specially formulated to convey hot water, up to 95°C, for use in central heating systems and hot water services. The plastics developed to withstand hot-water conditions are chlorinated polyvinyl chloride (CPVC), cross linked polyethylene (XLPE) and polybutylene (PB). These materials can be used for either underground heating or above ground.

SPECIFICATIONS

There are as yet, no British Standards available that cover any requirements for plastics pipe for use with water up to 95°C.

The following ASTM specifications apply to plastics materials for hot water pipework.

ASTM D2846: 1973 Chlorinated polyvinyl chloride (CPVC) plastic hot water distribution systems

ASTM D2846 indicates the requirements for CPVC tube and components for use in potable water systems up to a working temperature of 82°C. The requirements include materials, dimensions and tolerances, hydrostatic sustained pressure strength, thermocycling resistance and solvent cement viscosity, joint strength and shelf stability.

Size range	$\frac{3}{8}$"-2" diameter tubing $1\frac{1}{2}$"-2" nominal pipe
Marking	All tube, pipe and fitting shall be marked indicating specification, material designation, pressure rating and nominal size.
Tests	Hydrostatic sustained pressure and thermocycling
Other data	Table 1: Outside dimensions, wall thicknesses and tolerances.

ASTM D3309: 1976 - Polybutylene (PB) plastic hot water distribution systems

ASTM D3309 indicates the requirements for polybutylene tube and components for use in potable water systems up to a working temperature of 82°C. The components comprise of socket type fittings, plastic to metal transition fittings, solvent cements and adhesives. The requirements include materials, dimensions and tolerances, hydrostatic sustained pressure strength, thermocycling resistance and solvent cement viscosity, joint strength and shelf stability.

Size range	$\frac{1}{4}$"-2" diameter tubing $\frac{3}{4}$"-2" nominal pipe
Marking	All tube, pipe and fittings shall be marked indicating specification, material designation, pressure rating and nominal size.
Tests	Thermocycling and hydrostatic burst strength.
Other data	Table 1: Outside dimensions, wall thicknesses and tolerances.

MATERIAL

BS Number	Material/Grade	Data Sheet	Comment
ASTM2846	Chlorinated Polyvinyl Chloride (CPVC)	PL18	Potable water tube available for solvent welding to fittings of same material.
ASTM3309	Polybutylene (PB)	PL10	Potable water tube available for fusion jointing or proprietry fittings
	Crosslinked polyethylene (XLPE)	PL13	Potable water tube available for use with compression fittings, with an insert, for jointing

CONNECTION

The type of connection used shall be suitable for the pipe materials, and the service conditions. Connection methods which are appropriate for different tube types are indicated in the following table:-

Method	BS Number	Component Data Sheet	Tube	Comment
Compression	864/3	3.2.4	XLPE	Compression fittings to BS864 part 3 should be used. A metal insert in the pipe bore shall be used to support the distorted olive.
			PB	Proprietry fittings using 'grab rings' to restrain the tube are available.
Solvent weld			CPVC	CPVC tube may be joined by using CPVC fittings and the correct solvent adhesive recommended by the manufacturer. Time should lapse after welding before the joint is put into service.
Fusion weld			PB	PB tube shall be joined by fusion welding using the method and tools recommended by the manufacturer.
Flange		3.2.1	CPVC) PB) XLPE)	Flanges may be fitted to the pipe, by methods recommended by the pipe manufacturer, for connection to valves, pumps etc.

SERVICE CONSIDERATIONS

1. All plastics materials have a high rate of expansion (approximately 10 x that of metals). This property has to be taken into consideration when planning pipe-runs. Extra stand off clearance, dependent on the material, is required to accommodate expansion.

2. Pipes should not be rigidly supported but allowed freedom of movement to expand and contract. Use the suppliers recommendations for support spacing.

3.   Where sagging of the pipeline is unsightly it should be routed in a duct or under the floor.

4.   Pipe joints should be made to the recommendations of the supplier particularly with reference to preparation, temperature and pressures.

5.   Connections to heat generators should be made with metal pipework.

6.   Soldered joints should not be made closer than 0.5m to an installed plastic to metal adapter in the same pipe-line.

7.   Pipe should be stored away from direct sunlight. Pipe runs should not be exposed to ultra-violet radiation. Under such conditions the pipework should be run in ducts or under floors.

8.   Care should be taken that plastics material pipe runs are protected from unnecessary abuse such as abrasion or crushing.

9.   Problems have been known to exist from the diffusion of oxygen through the plastics material and into the water. This can create corrosion conditions in steel radiators. Consult the manufacturer.

10.   Chlorinated polyvinyl chloride (CPVC) and crosslinked polyethylene (XLPE) are available as straight lengths and changes of direction are made by the use of fittings.

11.   Polybutylene (PB) and crosslinked polyethylene (XLPE) are available in coils and can be bent around corners and obstructions.

SCOPE

Imperial and metric flanges for use over the temperature range $-200^{o}C$ to $+500^{o}C$ and for pressures up to 250 bar in piping systems for water, steam, gas, compressed air or oil. Flanges are available integral with the pipe or the component; slip on plain or boss types for welding, bronze welding or brazing; welding neck flanges for butt welding; screwed boss flanges; or blank and loose flanges for welding on to lapped pipe ends.

SPECIFICATION

BS10: 1962 - Flanges and bolting for pipes, valves and fittings

> Note: this standard is classified as obsolescent but not cancelled.

Range	Pressure, up to and including 2800 lbs/sq.in.
	Temperature, $-200^{o}C$ up to and including $524^{o}C$ (below $-17.8^{o}C$ only after consultation with the manufacturer).
	Size, (nominal bore of pipe) as stated in tables A,D,E,F,H,J,K,R,S and T.
Manufacture	Flanges may be cast or wrought (forged, stamped or plate).
Marking	The system of marking shall be by agreement between purchaser and manufacturer.
Tests	Certification requirements shall be stated on the order to manufacturer.

Other data	Table 1	Application of bolts and stud bolts.
	Table 2	Materials, dimensions and finish of bolts, stud bolts and nuts.
	Table 3	Temperature - pressure ratings for carbon steel flanges.
	Table 4	Temperature - pressure ratings for alloy steel flanges.
	Table 5	Temperature - pressure ratings for cast iron and malleable cast iron flanges
	Table 6a	Temperature - pressure ratings for copper alloy flanges, sizes $\frac{1}{2}$" to 3" (incl).
	Table 6b	Temperature - pressure ratings for copper alloy flanges, sizes over 3".
	Table 7	Flange materials - steel
	Table 8	Bolting - steel
	Table A	Dimensions of plain, boss, integrally cast or forged flanges (for ratings see Tables 3, 5 and 6).
	Table D	Dimensions of plain, boss, integrally cast or forged and welding neck flanges (for ratings see Tables 3, 5 and 6).
	Table E	Dimensions of plain, boss, integrally cast or forged and welding neck flanges (for ratings see Tables 3, 5 and 6).
	Table F	Dimensions of plain, boss, integrally cast or forged and welding neck flanges (for ratings see Tables 3, 5 and 6).
	Table H	Dimensions of plain, boss, integrally cast or forged and welding neck flanges (for ratings see Tables 3, 4, 5 and 6).
	Table J	Dimensions of plain, boss, integrally cast or forged and welding neck flanges (for ratings see Tables 3, 4 and 6).
	Table K	Dimensions of plain, integrally cast or forged and welding neck flanges (for ratings see Tables 3, 4 and 6).
	Table R	Dimensions of plain, integrally cast or forged and welding neck flanges (for ratings see Tables 3 and 4).
	Table S	Dimensions of plain, integrally cast or forged and welding neck flanges (for ratings see Tables 3 and 4).
	Table T	Dimensions of plain, integrally cast or forged and welding neck flanges (for ratings see Tables 3 and 4).

BS4504 - Flanges and bolting for pipes, valves and fitting - Metric series

Part 1: 1969 - Ferrous

Range
Pressure, from 2.5 bar up to and including 400 bar
Temperature, -200°C up to and including +550°C.
Size, 10 to 4000mm nominal bore for integral and loose flanges. The actual range depending on pressure and material designation as indicated in the flange tables. For screw attached flanges range is ⅛" to 6" (6-150mm) nominal bore.

Designation
The flanges shall be designated by the nominal size and flange table reference.
The first part of the table reference is the nominal pressure.
The second part of the table reference indicates the material and type of flange as follows:

1. Steel-integral
2. Steel-welding neck
3. Steel-plate for welding
4. Steel-screwed boss
5. Steel-slip-on boss
6. Steel-loose for welded-on lapped pipe ends
8. Steel plank plate
11. Grey cast iron-integral
12. Malleable cast iron-integral
13. Malleable cast iron-screwed boss

For example 6/4 - steel screwed boss flanges for use up to a nominal pressure of 6 bar.

Manufacture
Flanges may be cast or wrought (plate or forged).

Marking
Flanges made from alloy steel shall be clearly marked to identify the material. Integral flanges need not be marked where the component is marked.

Testing
Certification requirements shall be stated on the order to the manufacturer.

Other data

Table A1   Pressure/temperature rating for steel flanges - indicating material grades for flanges and bolting.

Table A2   Pressure/temperature rating for grey and malleable cast iron-indicating material grades for flanges and bolting).

Table B   Summary of contents of flange tables 2.5/2 to 400/2.

Flange Tables 2.5/2 to 400/2 indicate the dimensions for flanges and bolting for a particular designation over the relevant nominal bore size range.

Part 2: 1974 - Copper alloy and composite flanges

Range
Pressure, up to 40 bar.
Temperature, -200°C up to and including +260°C.
Size, 10 to 1800mm nominal bore. The actual size range depends on the pressure and flange form designation as indicated in the flange tables.

Designation
The flanges shall be designated by the nominal size and flange table reference.
The first part of the table reference is the nominal pressure defined as the maximum permissible working pressure in bar gauge at 20°C.
The second part of the table reference indicates the type of flange as follows:

Type 21. Integral
Type 22. Slip-on boss for brazing or welding
Type 23. Slip-on composite for brazing
Type 24. Slip-on composite for welding
Type 25. Welding neck composite
Type 26. Slip-on composite for welding

For example, 6/22 - slip on flange for brazing or welding: nominal maximum pressure 6 bar.

Manufacture   Flanges may be cast or wrought (forging stock and forgings)
Ferrous parts (composite flanges) are wrought (plate or forgings)

Marking   All slip-on boss flanges and composite flanges suitable for welding shall have marked the appropriate designation letters and numbers indicating material of manufacture.

Other data
Table 1	Summary of flange tables 6/21 to 40/21.
Table 2	Pressure/temperature ratings
Table 3	Materials
Table 4	Jointing surface finish
Table 5	Type of gasket

Indicates the form of gasket for different flange forms and pressure ranges against size range.
(The gasket material must be suitable for fluid at the intended working temperatures and pressures).

Table 6   Bolting material application.
Flange tables 6/21 to 40/21 indicate the dimensions for flanges and bolting for a particular designation over the relevant nominal bore size range.

MATERIALS

BS Number	Material/Grade	Data Sheet	Comment
BS10	Carbon steel/151-23A	FM08	New code 151-360
	Carbon steel/151-23B	FM08	New code 151-360
	Carbon steel/151-26A		
	Carbon steel/151/26B		
	Carbon steel 161A	FM09	New code 161-430
	Carbon steel 161B	FM10	New code 161-480
	Low alloy steel/240	FM16	
	Low alloy steel/620	FM18	
	Low alloy steel/621	FM20	
	Grey cast iron/1452-12	FM01	New code 1452-180
	Grey cast iron/1452-14	FM01	New code 1452-220
	Blackheart iron	FM03	
	Whiteheart iron	FM02	
BS4504	Carbon steel/151-23A	FM08	New code 151-360
Part 1	Carbon steel/151-23B	FM08	New code 151-360
	Carbon steel/151-26A		
	Carbon steel/151-26B		
	Carbon steel/161A	FM09	New code 161-430
	Carbon steel/161B	FM10	New code 161-480
	Carbon steel/161-26A	FM09	New code 161-430
	Carbon steel/161-28A		
	Carbon steel/224-26A		
	Carbon steel/224-28A		

BS Number	Material/Grade	Data Sheet	Comment
	Low alloy steel/240	FM16	
	Low alloy steel/271		
	Low alloy steel/503	FM17	
	Low alloy steel/621	FM20	
	Low alloy steel/622	FM21	
	Grey cast iron/1452-10	FM01	New code 1452-150
	Grey cast iron/1452-12	FM01	New code 1452-180
	Grey cast iron/1452-14	FM01	New code 1452-220
	Blackheart iron	FM03	
	Whiteheart iron	FM02	
BS4504	Brass/CZ110	NF15	
Part 2	Copper-nickel/CN102	NF31	
	Copper-nickel/CN107	NF32	
	Aluminium bronze/CA104		
	Aluminium bronze/AB2		
	Gunmetal/LG2	NF26	
	Gunmetal/LG4	NF27	

SERVICE CONSIDERATIONS

1. Flanges must be selected to suit the temperature and associated maximum working pressure of a system.

2. The pressure/temperature limitations of a component are controlled by the rating of the flange or the component body, whichever is the lower.

3. Flanges must be mounted so that they are parallel to their mating face to ensure a leak tight joint. Welded flanges may require a stress relieving heat treatment.

4. Gaskets must be suitable for the service duty.

5. All bolting must be capable of withstanding the service conditions and be the correct size for the flange as indicated in the flange tables.

6. Requirements for flanges in BS806 shall be adherred to.

7. Some flanges require backing rings to meet operational requirements.

8. The face of the flange may be finished plain or raised and this may determine the type of gasket used.

SCOPE

A threaded, internal or external, tubular fitting for connecting lengths of pipe. The threads may be either parallel or taper. The screwed fittings may be in the form of reducers, elbows, branch connections, sockets, nipples, caps or plugs.

SPECIFICATION

BS66 and 99: 1970 - Cast copper alloy pipe fittings for use with screwed copper tubes.

Note	External threads shall be tapered in accordance with BS21 and internal threads shall be parallel in accordance with BS61. Union threads shall comply with BS2779.
Range	Size range ⅛" to 4" nominal sizes as elbows, tees, crosses, side outlet, sockets, nipples, adaptors, reducers, liners and unions.
	Pressure (a) water - up to 10.3 bar
	(b) steam, air, gas and oil - up to 8.6 bar.
Manufacture	Cast copper alloys
Marking	Manufacturers mark
Other data	Fittings are intended for use with copper tubes to BS61 Table 1 and BS1306 Table 4 with taper screwing of tube to BS61. Tables 1 and 2.
	Pressure tests (a) internal hydraulic test not less than 20.7 bar.
	(b) internal air test not less than 5.2 bar while immersed in water.
	Table 1A Dimensions of ends of fittings, metric
	Table 1B Dimensions of ends of fittings, imperial

BS143 and 1256: 1968 - Malleable cast iron and cast copper alloy screwed pipe fittings for steam, air, water, gas and oil

Note:	BS143 design have BS21 taper internal and taper external pipe threads. BS1256 design have BS21 parallel internal and taper external pipe threads.
Range	Size range, ⅛" to 6" nominal sizes as elbows, tees, crosses, reducers, bends, return bends, sockets, nipples, plugs and caps.
	Pressure, (a) water - up to 13.8 bar
	(b) steam, air, gas and oil - up to 10.3 bar.
Manufacture	Plain and reinforced cast malleable iron or cast copper alloy.
Marking	Manufacturers mark
Other data	Table 1 Ends of fittings for British Standard pipe.

BS1387: 1967 - Steel tube and tubulars

Range	Size range, ⅛" to 6" nominal sizes for sockets, pieces, nipples, long screws, bends, springs and return bends.

Manufacture	Sockets - medium or heavy tubes to BS1387 which may be welded or seamless.
	Tubulars shall be made from tubes which comply with BS1387 as follows.
	Close taper and running nipples - heavy tube.
	Barrel nipples - medium or heavy tube
	Longscrews - heavy tube
	Bends and springs - type 1 bends and type 2, 3, and 4 springs from light tube; type 1A bends from heavy tube.
	Return bends - heavy tube.
	Tubulars and sockets may be galvanised.
	All threads shall be in accordance with BS21.
Marking	Colour bands distinguishing grade.
	(a) Light tubes - brown
	(b) Medium tubes - blue
	(c) Heavy tubes - red
Other data	Table 1: Dimensions of steel tubes - light
	Table 2: Dimensions of steel tubes - medium
	Table 3: Dimensions of steel tubes - heavy
	Table 4: Sockets
	Table 5: Pieces
	Table 6: Running nipples, close taper nipples and barrel nipples
	Table 7: Longscrews
	Table 8: Bends and springs
	Table 9: Return bends.

BS1740: Wrought steel pipe fittings (screwed BSP thread)
Part 1: 1971 - Metric

Range	Size range, 6 to 150mm nominal size for elbows, tees, crosses, reducers, sockets, unions, caps, plugs, bushes and nipples for use with BS1387 tube.
Manufacture	Fittings made from welded and seamless pipe.
	All threads shall be in accordance with BS21.
	Fittings may be galvanised.
Other data	Table 1: Screwed ends of fittings

MATERIALS

BS Number	Material/Grade	Data Sheet	Comments
66 and 99	Gunmetal/LG2-C	NF26	
143	Whiteheart iron/W22-4	FM02	
	Blackheart iron/B18-6	FM03	
1256	Whiteheart iron/W22-4	FM02	
	Gunmetal/LG2-C	NF26	
1387	No specific steel grade quoted		
1740	No specific steel grade quoted		

SERVICE CONSIDERATIONS

1.   Any sealant must be compatible with the system contents and service conditions.

2.   Threads shall be engaged to a degree to provide satisfactory pressure tightness of a joint and suitable alignment of component.

3.   Maximum permissible pressures for screwed joints at temperatures not exceeding $260^{o}C$ are outlined in BS806 Table 3.

SCOPE

Capillary fittings provide a permanent thermal joint between tubes and a component part of a system. A leak tight joint is made by the flow of molten soft solder or braze alloy by capillary action along the annular space between the outside of the tube and the socket of the fitting. The solder or braze alloy may be in the form of an integral ring in the fitting or be applied to the gap between tube and fitting during heating.

SPECIFICATIONS

BS864 - Capillary and compression fittings of copper and copper alloy
Part 2: 1971 - Metric units

These fittings are primarily for use with tube complying with BS2871 part 1, Tables W,X,Y and Z. Solder referred to complies with BS219 grades C and G.

Range	Pressure, maximum working pressure is determined by the working temperature and fitting size - Table 1. Temperature, maximum working temperature 110°C Size, 6mm to 67mm.
Designation	The size by which a fitting is designated shall be the outside diameter of tube with which it is to be used.
Manufacture	Fittings shall be manufactured from drawn tube, pressings or castings.
Marking	Fittings 15mm and over shall be marked 864.
Tests	Internal hydraulic or air pressure tests by the manufacturer for porosity.
Other data	Table 1 Maximum working temperatures and pressures.
	Table 6 Markings for fittings
	Table 7 Capillary fittings
	Appendix A Method of specifying fittings
	Appendix B Fittings for use with copper tubes to be buried underground to BS2871 part 1 Table Y.

BS2051 - Tube and pipe fittings for engineering purposes
Part 1: 1973 - Copper and copper alloy capillary and compression tube fittings for engineering purposes

These are intended primarily for use with tubes of the outside dimensions given in BS2871 part 2.

Range	Pressure, maximum working pressures range from 15 to 210 bar depending on fitting size , mode of manufacture and application medium.
	Temperature, the pressure figures are applicable up to 30°C. For use between 30 and 65°C the maximum permissable working pressures given in Table 3 should be reduced by 40%. Size, 4 to 42mm.
Designation	The size by which a fitting is designated shall be the outside diameter of the tube with which it is to be used.
Manufacture	Fittings shall be manufactured from drawn tube, pressings, stamping rods and castings.
Marking	When specified by purchaser, fittings shall be marked 'ENG'.

135

Tests	Internal hydraulic or air tests by the manufacturer for porosity. When required, a certificate shall be supplied.
Other data	Table 3 Maximum permissable working pressures. Table 6 Dimensions of capillary fittings Appendix A Methods of designating unequal fittings.

MATERIALS

BS Number	Material/Grade	Data Sheet	Comment
864/2	No materials for fitting bodies stated.		
	Soft solder/219 grade G	Table 4.3/4	Integral ring only
	Soft solder/219 grade G	Table 4.3/4	Integral ring only
			Capillary fittings may be supplied with high melting point solder or brazing alloys in the integral ring.
2051/1	Brass/CZ121	NF19	Extruded bars and hollow rods
	Brass/CZ122	NF20	Hot pressings
	Gunmetal/LG2	NF26	Castings
	Wrought copper/C106	NF11	
	Wrought copper/C107	NF12	
	Solder		As recommended by manufacturer
	Braze		As recommended by manufacturer

SERVICE CONSIDERATIONS

1. Fittings to BS864 are intended primarily for use in water or gas piping systems.

2. Sufficient solder should be applied when end filling to fill the gap. Excessive solder will flow into the pipe and cause flow and toxicity problems.

3. All residual flux should be removed to prevent corrosion problems.

4. To obtain a good wetted joint the tube should be free of all dirt and grease.

5. Service temperatures and pressures must be within the capabilities of the jointing material.

6. In conditions where dezincification may be a problem resistant brasses may be used. Consult the manufacturer.

7. Copper fittings can be used for joining stainless steel tube, complying to BS4147, providing an alternative flux is used.

| FAMILY GROUP | PIPE FITTINGS | SUB-GROUP | COMPRESSION |

SCOPE

Compression fittings provide a mechanical joint between tubes or between tubes and a component part of the system in which leak tightness is obtained by the compression of a ring, sleeve or part of the coupling against the outer wall of the tube by means of a securing nut. They can be used for soft thin wall metal tube or plastics tube with a bore insert.

SPECIFICATION

BS864 - Capillary and compression fittings of copper and copper alloy
Part 2: 1971 - Metric units

These fittings are primarily for use with tube complying with BS2871 part 1, Tables W, X, Y and Z.

Two types of compression fittings are indicated:

Type A Fitting: the joint is made by the compression of a ring or sleeve on the outside wall of the tube.

Type B Fitting: the tube is manipulated at or near its end and the joint is made by compressing the manipulated portion of the tube against the face of the body of the fitting or against a loose ring or sleeve within the fitting.

Range   Pressure, maximum working pressure is determined by the working temperature and fitting size - Table 1.

Temperature, maximum working temperature $110^{o}C$.
Size, 6mm to 67mm.

Designation   The size by which a fitting is designated shall be the outside diameter of tube with which it is to be used.

Manufacture   Fittings shall be manufactured from drawn tube, pressings or castings.

Marking   Fittings 15mm and over shall be marked to indicate the fitting type and the tubing grade with which it may be used.

Tests   Internal hydraulic or air pressure tests by the manufacturer for porosity.

Other data   Table 1:   Maximum working temperatures and pressures.
              Table 6:   Markings for fittings
              Table 8:   Compression fittings and union ends
              Appendix A: Methods of specifying fittings
              Appendix B: Fittings for use with copper tubes to be buried underground to BS2871 part 1, Table Y.

BS2051 -Tube and pipe fittings for engineering purposes
Part 1: 1973 - Copper and copper alloy capillary and compression tube fittings for engineering purposes

These are intended primarily for use with tubes of the outside dimensions given in BS2871 part 2.

Two types of compression fittings are indicated.

Type A Fitting: the joint is made by the compression of a ring or sleeve on the outside wall of the tube.

Type B Fitting: the tube is manipulated at or near its end and the joint is made by compressing the manipulated portion of the tube against the face of the body of the fitting or against a loose ring or sleeve within the fitting.

Range   Pressure, maximum working pressures range from 15 to 210 bar depending on fitting size, mode of manufacture and application medium.

	Temperature, up to a temperature of 65°C.
	Size, 4 to 42mm.
Designation	The size by which a fitting is designated shall be the outside diameter of the tube with which it is to be used.
Manufacture	Fittings shall be manufactured from drawn tube, pressings, stamping rods and castings.
Marking	When specified by purchaser, fittings shall be marked 'ENG'.
Tests	Internal hydraulic or air tests by the manufacturer for porosity. When required, a certificate shall be supplied.
	Hydraulic 'type' test for assembled joint, Type A and B, shall withstand an internal hydraulic pressure of 1.5 times the maximum permissible working pressure, Table 3, at normal atmospheric temperature.
Other data	Table 3: Maximum permissible working pressures.
	Table 4: Dimensions of compression fittings
	Appendix A: Methods of designating unequal fittings
	Appendix B: Sizes of copper and copper alloy tubes.

BS4368 - Carbon and stainless steel compression couplings for tubes

Part 1: 1972 - Heavy series (metric)

Equivalent to heavy series couplings of DIN2353

There are three types of couplings:

Type A - the joint is made and the tube is held by the compression of a ring or ferrule, or part of the coupling on the outside surface of the tube.

Type B - the joint is made and the tube is held by the compression of a manipulated portion of the tube at or near its end against the face of the coupling body, or against a loose ring or sleeve within the coupling.

Type C - the joint is made by means of a sealing ring (and retaining washer if required) which does not hold the tube. A second ring is included to hold the tube.

Range	Pressure, pressure/temperature ratings depend on coupling type.
	Type B and C: subject to agreement between purchaser and manufacture.
	Type A: - 10°C to +120°C. At other temperatures the working pressure shall be subject to agreement.
	Size, to suit tubes 6 to 50mm outside diameter.
Manufacture	All carbon steel bodies and nuts shall be cadmium, phosphate or zinc coated.
Marking	Couplings shall be marked with manufacturer, size and series letter H or S.
Tests	Hydraulic test of assembled joint and freedom from porosity.
	Certificate of compliance shall be available when requested.
Other data	Table 1: Nominal working pressure ratings of Type A coupling in accordance with Section 2.
	Table 2: Tube sizes.

Part 3: 1974 - Light series (metric)

Equipment to light series couplings in DIN 2353
There are two types
Type A   up to 15mm-250 bar
            18 to 22mm - 160 bar
            28 to 42mm - 100 bar

Type B   up to 15mm - 260 bar
              18 to 42mm - 160 bar

Range   Size, to suit tubes 6 to 42mm outside diameter

Manufacture   All carbon steel bodies and nuts shall be cadmium, phosphate or zinc coated.

Tests   Hydraulic test of assembled joint and freedom from porosity.
              Certificate of compliance shall be available on request.

Other data   Table 1:   Tube sizes.

MATERIALS

BS Number	Material/Grade	Data Sheet	Comment
864/2			No specific materials quoted
864/3			As above
2051/1	Brass/CZ121	NF19	Extruded bars and hollow rods
	Brass/CZ122	NF20	Hot pressings
	Gunmetal/LG2	NF26	Castings
	Wrought copper/C106	NF11	
	Wrought copper/C107	NF12	
4368/1/3	Carbon steel		Material used to satisfy the pressure/ temperature requirements and for use with the fluid to be contained
	Stainless steel		

Compression fittings made from materials resistant to dezincification are available. They shall comply to the relevant specification for dimensional and test requirements.

SERVICE CONSIDERATIONS

1.   BS864 fittings are intended primarily for use in water and gas piping systems and also engineering purposes where suitable.

2.   Compression fittings, Type B, are not to be used on hard drawn tube equivalent to BS2871 part 1 Table Z.

3.   Compression fittings are used where a pipe run may require breaking for maintenance or replacement of components.

4.   In general it is not recommended to use compression fittings in buried applications.

5.   If de-zincification is a problem then compression fittings should be constructed from resistant materials.

6.   Certain designs of compression fittings are suitable for use at higher temperatures and pressures than are given in the above specifications and also for low pressure steam services. For such applications the manufacturer of the fittings should be consulted.

BSRIA **component data sheet**	SHEET NUMBER 3.2.5	1
FAMILY GROUP PIPE FITTINGS	SUB-GROUP BUTT-WELDED	

SCOPE

Butt-welded fittings form, by welding of prepared ends, a permanent pipe system and are used for medium and high temperature hot water systems, steam systems, and for pipework conveying non corrosive fluids.

SPECIFICATIONS

BS1965 - Butt-welding pipe fittings for pressure purposes
Part 1: 1963 - Carbon steel

Note: Welding neck flanges are covered in the relevant flange specifications. This specification relates to butt-welded fittings for pressure purposes for use with pipe to BS3601 and BS3602.

Range   Size range depends on the fitting form

Elbows	1" to 16" nominal size
Short radius	
elbows	2" to 6" nominal size
Return bends	1" to 12" nominal size
Reducers	1¼" x 1" to 16" x 14" nominal size
Equal tees	1" to 16" nominal size
Cups	1" to 16" nominal size

Note: For 6" nominal size the outside diameter shall also be given.

Pressure   Where pressure/temperature conditions are important the relevant requirements of BS806 shall be observed.

Manufacture   Elbows, return bends and reducers - seamless or electric resistance welded pipe.

Tees   -   seamless pipe or forgings
Caps   -   plate
Fittings over 3/16" thick shall have bevelled ends.

Heat treatment All fittings shall be in the stress relieved condition.

Other data
Table 5	'Off square' tolerances
Table 6	Dimensions of elbows
Table 6a	Dimensions of short radius elbows
Table 7	Dimensions of return bends
Table 8	Dimensions of reducers (concentric and eccentric)
Table 9	Dimensions of equal tees
Table 10	Dimensions of caps
Appendix B	ISO corresponding valves.

Other Specifications

BS3799: 1974 - Steel pipe fittings, screwed and socket welding for the petroleum industry

Substantially agrees with ANSI B16.11, ASTM 234 and ASTM 405.

MATERIALS

BS Number	Material/Grade	Data Sheet	Comment
970	Carbon steel/EN3C		New code 070 M20, forgings
1501	Carbon steel/151-28B		Plate
	Carbon steel/161-28B	FM09	New code 161-430, plate
3602	Carbon steel/27	FM13	New code 410, welded and seamless tube

SERVICE CONSIDERATIONS

1. A permanent pipework system results from welded fittings.
2. Reduced costs compared to a flanged equivalent system.
3. Fittings should fit squarely to pipework ends prior to welding
4. The welding of fittings to pipework shall be carried out by a competent welder in accordance with an accepted code of practice.
5. In particular instances it may be necessary to heat treat the welded joint to prevent distortion.
6. A buried welded pipe may be subject to corrosion due to variations in the soil over long distances.

SCOPE

A pipe jointing system in which a split metal housing, enclosing a sealing joint ring, locates in a formed groove near the pipe ends in order to prevent disengagement of the joint. The grooves are machined or formed in the tube to set parameters. The sealing joint ring is a resilient material and a grade is chosen that will withstand the fluid conditions and system temperature.

SPECIFICATION

Grooved fittings are proprietary items. There is no specification, to date, laid down in British Standards for the requirements of grooved fittings. A reference to them is made in CP2010 part 2.

CP2010 - Pipelines
Part 2: 1970 - Design and construction of steel pipelines inland

Other data   Appendix B: Proprietary types of joint for steel pipes.
                                   B2 Self-sealing joint

MATERIALS

In general the split housing may be constructed from steel or malleable iron with a protective coating. The sealing ring may be made from rubber or an elastomeric material that will withstand the service condtions. When a grooved fitting is used as a joint in a potable water system the seal material and any fitting lubricant must be approved by the relevant authority.

SERVICE CONSIDERATIONS

1.   Groove forming can either be done on site or in a pre-fabrication shop. The groove can either be roller formed or machined. Tools are available to ensure that the correct groove depth is achieved. The groove includes a longitudinal tolerance which allows for a small gap between the pipe ends to accommodate any expansion or contraction.

            Instead of grooves the joint can be made using shoulders on the pipe ends. These shoulders can either be formed by welding on rings or by upsetting the end of the pipe.

2.   The seal consists of a specially shaped ring with inturned lips which bear on the ends of the adjacent pipes when the securing bolts in the housing are tightened. To eliminate leaks the pipe surface must be free of weld spatter, flats, debris etc.

3.   Due to its simple concept the grooved joint finds a use where rapid erection or dismantling is required, or when temporary re-routing of a pipeline is required.

4.   The cost of a joint using a grooved fitting is less than screwing or flanging the joint in both material and labour costs. Lesser skilled operatives can be used for the fittings.

5.   The groove fitting can accommodate realignment of piperuns, particularly rotational for aligning tees, elbows, valves etc.

6.   The correct size fitting must be connected to the pipe to prevent leakage.

7.   Pipe runs can be accommodated at a higher density than with flanged pipes.

FAMILY GROUP	VALVES	SUB-GROUP	GATE

SCOPE

A gate valve operated by a 'gate' constrained within a slide moving across the flowpath. Its characteristics make it unsuitable for throttling or control purposes. The 'gate' and lifting mechanisms come in several forms and can be manual or power actuated. The materials of construction are directly related to the temperature, pressure and fluid content of the service. Various methods of connection to the pipework or system component are available but the most common form of connection are screwed and flanged.

SPECIFICATIONS

BS5150: 1974 - Cast iron wedge and double disk gate valves for general purposes

Size range	Flanged	10 to 1000mm nominal bore
	Screwed	$\frac{1}{2}$" to 6% nominal bore

Type   Shall have rising or non-rising stems to operate:

    (a)   solid or split wedge
    (b)   double disk

Manufacture   Flanged and screwed body end cast iron gate valves, copper alloy faced, resilient seated or all iron valves.

Duty   Pressure, maximum permissible gauge working pressure at $20^{o}C$ as follows 1.6 to 25 bar. Maximum pressure/temperature rating for liquid, gas and steam shall be as detailed in Table 1.
Temperature, all valves shall be suitable for continuous use at their nominal pressure designation within the temperature range of $-10^{o}C$ to $+65^{o}C$.

Restrictions on temperature may be placed by the manufacturer by reason of valve type, trim materials or other factors.

Marking   Markings shall indicate nominal size, nominal pressure rating, body material designation and manufacturer.

Other data	Table 1	Pressure/temperature ratings
	Table 5	Basic materials

BS5151: 1974 - Cast iron gate (parallel slide) valves for general purposes

Size range   40 to 1000mm nominal sizes

Type   Shall have either a rising stem or a non-rising stem.

Manufacture   Flanged body end cast iron parallel slide gate valves which are copper alloy, nickel alloy or stainless steel faced.

Duty   Nominal pressure - maximum permissible gauge working pressure at $20^{o}C$ as follows 10, 16 and 25 bar.

Pressure temperature rating shall be as detailed in Table 1.
All valves shall be suitable for continuous use at their nominal pressure designation within the temperature range of $-10^{o}C$ to $+65^{o}C$.
Restrictions on temperature may be placed by the manufacturer by reason of valve type, trim materials or other factors.

Marking   Markings shall indicate nominal size, nominal pressure rating, body material designation and manufacturer.

Other data   Table 1   Pressure/temperature rating
                  Table 4   Basic materials.

BS5154: 1974 - Copper alloy globe, globe stop and check, check and gate valves for general purposes

Revised version of BS1952.

Size range   Flanged 10 to 80 mm nominal size
                  Screwed $\frac{1}{4}$" to 3" nominal size
                  Capillary or compression (BS864 Part 2) 10 to 54 mm
                  Compression (BS864 Part 3) $\frac{3}{8}$" to 2"
                  Capillary or compression (BS2051 Part 1) 10 to 42 mm

Type   Shall have either rising or non-rising stem (inside or outside) to operate

         (a)   solid or split wedge
         (b)   double-disk
         (c)   parallel slide

Manufacture   Flanged, screwed, capillary or compression body end copper alloy with integral or renewable body seats and screwed, union or bolted bonnets or covers.

Duty   Pressure   maximum permissible gauge working pressure (bar) at $20^{o}C$:-

         Flanged   16, 25 and 40 bar
         Screwed   16, 20, 25, 32 and 40 bar
         Compression and capillary not exceeding those quoted in the respective specifications.

         Temperature, for liquid, gas or steam rating - there are two series of values A and B, differing in their maximum service temperature.
         A   - $260^{o}C$ maximum and, where appropriate, shall have pressure/temperature ratings in accordance with the flange ratings of BS4504.
         B   -   maximum temperature limitation equivalent to the temperature of saturated steam at a pressure of 7, 9, 10.5 and 14 bar for nominal pressures of PN16, PN20, PN25 and PN32 respectively.

         All valves shall be suitable for continual use at their nominal pressure designation within $-10^{o}C$ and $+95^{o}C$.

Marking   Marking shall indicate nominal size, nominal pressure rating, body material designation, manufacturer, flow direction (uni-directional flow values only) trim materials, specification, any limiting temperature and body end threads (if not to BS21).

Other data   Table 1   Pressure/temperature ratings
                  Table 6   Basic materials
                               (a)   Series A
                               (b)   Series B

BS5157: 1974 - Steel Gate (parallel slide) valves for general purposes

Size range   40 to 600 mm nominal bore

Type   Shall have either rising or non-rising stem and of either the full bore or

venturi pattern.

Manufacture — Flanged body end steel gate valves nickel, stainless steel or hard metal faced.

Duty — Nominal pressure - maximum permissible gauge working pressure at 20°C:-
16, 25, 40, 64 and 100 bar.

Pressure/temperature ratings for liquid, gas or steam are dependent on the body material, as indicated in Table 1.

All valves shall be suitable for continuous use at their nominal pressure within the temperature range -10°C to $+120^{o}$C.

Restriction on temperature may be placed by the manufacturer by reason of valve typed trim materials or other factors.

Marking — Markings shall indicate nominal size, nominal pressure rating, body material designation and manufacturer.

Other data — Table 1   Pressure/temperature rating
Table 4   Basic materials.

MATERIALS

BS Number	Material/Grade	Data Sheet	Comments
5150	Cast iron/1452-12	FM01	Body, bonnet, yoke, stuffing box, disk and hand wheel
	Cast iron/1452-14	FM01	Body, bonnet, yoke, disk and stuffing box
	Gunmetal/G1		
	Gunmetal/LG2	NF26	Disk or wedge, disk or wedge facings
	Gunmetal/LG4	NF27	and body seat rings
	Gunmetal/LG2	NF26	Disk stem nut, back seat bushing and gland.
	Aluminium bronze/AB2		Disk or wedge facing ring, body seat ring, disk stem nut, back seat bushing and gland.
	Aluminium bronze/CA103	NF29	Stem, disk stem nut, back seat busing
	Aluminium bronze/CA104		and gland.
	Aluminium bronze/CA106	NF30	
	Brass/CZ116		Stem, disk stem nut, back seat bushing
	Brass/CZ114	NF18	and gland
	Brass/CZ121	NF19	
	Brass/CZ122	NF20	
	Resilient Material		Dependent on temperature range required.
	Stainless steel/410		
	Stainless steel/302	FM24	Stem
	Stainless steel/431		
5151	Cast iron/1452-12	FM01	Gland and handwheel
	Cast iron/1452-14	FM01	Body, bonnet, yoke, stuffing box and disk with separate facing ring.

BS Number	Material/Grade	Data Sheet	Comments
	Gunmetal/ G1		Disk, disk facing ring, body seat
	Gunmetal/LG2	NF26	ring
	Gunmetal/LG4	NF27	
	Gunmetal/LG2	NF26	Stem and gland
	Aluminium bronze/AB2		Disk facing ring and gland
	Aluminium bronze/CA103	NF29	Stem and gland
	Aluminium bronze/CA104		
	Aluminium bronze/CA106	NF30	
	Brass/CZ114	NF18	Gland
	Brass/CZ116	NF19	
	Brass/CZ121	NF20	
	Brass/CZ122		
	Nickel alloy		To suit duty
	Stainless steel/410		Stem
	Stainless steel/302	FM24	
	Stainless steel/413		
	Carbon steel/070M20		To suit duty where grade not detailed
			Stem
5154	Gunmetal/LG2	NF26	Body, bonnet, cover, wedge stem,
Series A			stuffing box and gland
	Gunmetal/LG4	NF27	
	Nickel/copper/NA1		Wedge
	Nickel/copper/NA2		
	Nickel/copper/NA3		
	Stainless steel/1503-713		Wedge, stem, stuffing box and gland
	Stainless steel/1504-845		
	Aluminium bronze/CA103	NF29	Stem
	Aluminium bronze/CA104		
	Aluminium bronze/CA106	NF30	
	Aluminium alloy/LM6	NF05	Handwheel
Series B	Gunmetal/LG2	NF26	Body, bonnet, stuffing box, gland
	Gunmetal/LG4	NF27	and wedge
	Brass/DCB1	NF23	Body, bonnet, stuffing box and wedge
	Brass/DCB3	NF24	
	Brass/PCB1	NF22	
	Brass/CZ121	NF19	As above
	Brass/CZ122	NF20	
	Brass/CZ112	NF17	Stem, stem bush
	Brass/CZ114	NF18	
	Brass/CZ116		
	Brass/CZ121	NF19	
	Brass/CZ122	NF20	
	Alluminium alloy/LM6	NF05	Handwheel
5157	Carbon steel 1503-161	FM10	Body, bonnet, yoke and stuffing box
	Carbon steel 28A or B		
	Carbon steel 1504-161B		

BS Number	Material/Grade	Data Sheet	Comments
	Low alloy steel 1503-240 Low alloy steel 1504-240	FM16	Body, bonnet, yoke and stuffing box
	Low alloy steel 1503-620	FM18/FM19	As above
	Low alloy steel 1503-621 Low alloy steel 1504-621	FM20	As above
	Stainless steel/316 Stainless steel/320 Stainless steel/410 Stainless steel/431	FM25	Stem
	Stainless steel		Disk, body seat - grade suitable for duty
	Stainless steel Nickel alloy Hard facing		Disk facing, body seat facings, and body facings suitable for duty
	Cast iron/1452-12	FM01	Handwheel

CONNECTION

The type of connection may be dictated by the specification. It should be suitable for the pressure and temperature conditions, the medium handled and the mechanical strength required under the service condition.

Method	BS Number	Component Data Sheet	Notes
Flanged	10 4504	3.2.1	Imperial Metric
Screwed	21	3.2.2	Threads conforming to BS21
Capillary	864/2	3.2.3	
Compression	864/2 2051/1	3.2.4.	
Grooved		3.2.6	Flange adapter may be required.

SERVICE CONSIDERATIONS

1. Gate valves can have a variety of different types of closure; wedge type (solid or split), double disk or parallel slide types as laid down by the specifications. A variety of connections may also be available.

2. Gate valves shall be used for isolation only.

3. The stems can either be rising (requiring head-room to accommodate the stem when fully open but can be lubricated) or non-rising. The operating mechanism can be hand operated or driven electrically, hydraulically or pneumatically.

4. Pipework flanges must be aligned and supported as close to the valve as possible to obviate undue stress. Large valves must be supported under the body.

5. Design of the piping system must take account of any pipe movement due to expansion or contraction to ensure no undue stress is imposed on the valve.

6.   Valves must be included in a maintenance programme. Special attention should be paid to ensure there are no leaks via the gland packing as this could promote corrosion of the stem.

7.   Valves that are not used for long periods should be operated periodically. This applies particularly to emergency valves which must function when required.

8.   Undue stress due to excessive vibration or shock loading caused by water hammer could bring about damage or serious failure of the valve. Valve ratings assume non-shock conditions.

9.   Where shock is likely to occur a valve of higher pressure rating should be specified.

10.   In order   to facilitate opening of large valves by reducing the pressure differential, it is advisable to have a small bore bypass.

11.   All gaskets, sealing rings and thread sealing compounds shall be compatible with the fluids, temperatures and pressures. Where potable water is concerned they shall comply with the local water regulations.

12.   The pressure/temperature rating of a valve is determined by either the flange or the valve, whichever is the lower.

SCOPE

A check valve allows flow in one direction only by opening and closing automatically by the hydraulic force of the system contents. Most check valves conform to either a swing or lift concept. The term non-return valve may be used as equivalent.

SPECIFICATION

BS5153: 1974 - Cast iron check valves for general purposes

Size range	Flanged 10 to 1000mm nominal sizes Screwed ½" to 6" nominal sizes.
Type	Swing type are available as: (a) straight (body ports horizontal or vertical) Lift type are available as: (a) straight (body ports horizontal) (b) straight (body ports vertical) (c) angle (body ports at 90°C)
Manufacture	Flanged and screwed end cast iron with either copper alloy, nickel alloy, stainless steel or resilient faced or all iron.
Duty	Pressure, swing valves 6 to 25 bar nominal pressure, lift valves 10 to 25 bar nominal pressure being the maximum working pressure at 20°C. Temperature, the pressure/temperature ratings for use with liquids, gas and saturated steam over a range of -10°C to +220°C are given in Table 1. All valves shall be suitable of operating continuously at the nominal pressure within the temperature range -10°C to +65°C. Restrictions on temperature may be placed by the manufacturer by reason of valve type, trim materials or other factors.
Markings	Markings shall indicate nominal size, nominal pressure rating, body material designation, manufacturer, arrow to indicate flow direction, trim material identification and any limiting temperature.
Other data	Table 1 : Pressure/temperature ratings. Table 5 : Basic materials.

BS5154: 1974 - Copper alloy globe, globe stop and check, check and gate valves for general purposes.

Size range	Flanged 10 to 80mm nominal size Screwed ¼" to 3" nominal size Capillary or compression (BS864/2) 10 to 54mm Compression (BS864/3) ⅜" to 2" Capillary or compression (BS2051/1) 10 to 42mm.
Type	Swing (body end ports horizontal or vertical) Lift (a) piston (horizontal or angle) (b) disk) (horizontal, vertical or body ports at 90°C) (c) ball) (horizontal, vertical or body ports at 90°C) Series A or B valves differing in their maximum service temperatures.

| Manufacture | Flanged, screwed, capillary or compression body end cast copper alloy to suit series A or B conditions. |

| Duty | Pressure, flanged 16, 25 and 40 bar, screwed 16, 20, 25, 32 and 40 bar, capillary and compression to comply with respective specifications requirements. |

Temperature, two series of values.

A: $260^{o}C$ maximum and where appropriate shall have pressure/temperature ratings in accordance with BS4504 flange ratings.

B: maximum temperature limitation equivalent to the temperature of saturated steam at a pressure of 7, 9, 10.5 and 14 bar for nominal pressures of PN15, PN20, PN25 and PN32 respectively.

The pressure/temperature ratings in Table 1 are for liquids, gas and steam.

All valves shall be suitable of continuous use at their nominal pressure designation within the range $-10^{o}C$ to $+95^{o}C$.

| Marking | Marking shall indicate nominal diameter, nominal pressure rating, body material designation, manufacturer, direction of flow specification, trim materials, any limiting temperature and body end threads (other than BS21). |

Other data	Table 1:	Pressure/temperature ratings
	Table 6(a):	Basic materials - series A valves
	Table 6(b)	Basic materials - series B valves.

BS5160: 1977 - Flanged steel globe valves, globe stop and check valves and lift type check valves for general purposes

| Size range | 10 to 450mm nominal sizes. |

Type	Flanged lift type valves shall be:
	(a) straight
	(b) angle
	(c) oblique

| Manufacture | Flanged end cast or forged carbon steel |

| Duty | Pressure, nominal pressure 16, 25 and 40 bar. |

Temperature, up to $475^{o}C$. The pressure/temperature ratings as shown in Table 1. All valves shall be suitable for continuous use at their nominal pressure designation within the temperature range -10 to $+120^{o}C$.

Restrictions may be placed by the manufacturer by reason of valve type, trim materials or other factors.

| Marking | Marking shall show nominal size, nominal pressure rating, body material designation, manufacturer, trim materials, limiting temperature, specification and flow direction. |

| Other data | Table 1: | Pressure/temperature rating |
| | Table 5: | Basic materials |

MATERIALS

BS Number	Material/Grade	Data Sheet	Comments
5153	Grey iron/220	FM01	Body cover, disk (with separate facing ring or all iron) and hinge
	Grey iron/180	FM01	Alternative to 220 where section thickness less than 15mm.

BS Number	Material/Grade	Data Sheet	Comments
	Carbon steel/970-220M07		Hinge pin and hinge to disk connection
	Brass/CZ114	NF18	Hinge pin
	Brass/CZ116		
	Gunmetal/G1)	NF26	Hinge, hinge pin, disk, disk facing
	Gunmetal/LG2)	NF27	ring and body seat
	Gunmetal/LG4)		
	Aluminium bronze/CA103	NF29	Hinge pin
	Aluminium bronze/CA104		
	Aluminium bronze/CA105		
	Aluminium bronze/AB2		Disk with integral face disk facing ring and body seat.
	Stainless steel		Suitable for the service as disk with
	Nickel alloy		integral face, separate facing ring or body seat
	Stainless steel		Hinge pin (all iron valve)
	Resilient material		Disk facing ring
5154 Series A	Gunmetal/LG2	NF26	Body, cover, disk, piston, ball, body seat and disk facing ring where renewable, hinge and hinge pin.
	Gunmetal/LG4		
	Nickel-copper/NA1		Disk, piston, ball, body seat and disk facing ring where renewable.
	Nickel-copper/NA2		
	Nickel-copper/NA3		
	Nickel-copper/NA13		
	Aluminium bronze/CA103	NF29	Hinge and hinge pin
	Aluminium bronze/CA104		
	Aluminium bronze/CA106		
	Stainless steel/1713		Disk, piston, ball, body seat and disk facing ring where renewable, hinge and hinge pin
	Stainless steel/1845		
	Stainless steel/1845		
5154 Series B	Gunmetal/LG2	NF26	Body, cover, disk, piston, ball, body seat where renewable, hinge and hinge pin.
	Gunmetal/LG4	NF27	
	Brass/DCB1	NF23	Body, cover, disk, piston, ball and
	Brass/DCB3	NF24	body seat where renewable
	Brass/PCB1	NF22	
	Brass/CZ121	NF19	CZ122 limited to use below 50mm or 2ins size valves. All components as for gunmetal.
	Brass/CZ122	NF20	
	Brass/CZ112	NF17	Hinge and hinge pin
	Brass/CZ114	NF18	
	Brass/CZ116		
5160	Carbon steel/161-28A		Body, bonnet, yoke and stuffing box
	Carbon steel/161-28B		
	Carbon steel/161-480		
	Low alloy steel/621		Bolting

CONNECTION

The type of connection may be dictated by the specification. It should be suitable for the pressure and temperature, the fluid handled and the mechanical strength required under the service condition.

Method	BS Number	Data Sheet	Notes
Flanged	10	3.2.1	Imperial sizes
	4504	3.2.1	Metric sizes
Screwed		3.2.2	Threads to BS21
Capillary	864/2	3.2.3	
	2051/1	3.2.3	
Compression	864/2	3.2.4	
	864/3	3.2.4	
	2051/1	3.2.4	
Grooved		3.2.6	Flange adaptors may be required

SERVICE CONSIDERATIONS

1. Valves shall be correctly fitted to the pipework using the appropriate connections. They shall be supported as close to the valve as possible to obviate undue stress occurring. Large valves shall also be supported under the body.

2. Lift valves operating in a vertical flow shall have the direction of flow upwards. Swing and lift valves shall be located in an attitude as recommended by the manufacturer.

3. Design of the piping system shall take account of any pipe movement due to expansion or contraction to ensure no undue stress is imposed on the valve.

4. Valves must be incorporated in a maintenance programme for the piping system.

5. Undue stress due to excessive vibration or shock loading caused by water hammer could bring about damage or serious failure of the valve. Valve ratings assume non-shock conditions. Where shock is likely to occur a valve of higher pressure rating should be specified.

6. All gaskets, sealing rings and thread sealing compounds shall be comptaible with the fluids, temperatures and pressures. Where potable water is concerned they shall comply with the local water regulations.

7. The pressure/temperature rating of a valve is determined by either the flange or the valve, whichever is the lower.

8. All excess flux from capillary connections shall be removed to prevent corrosion.

9. Valves shall be sited so that the system is capable of being totally vented or drained.

FAMILY GROUP	VALVES	SUB-GROUP	SCREWDOWN STOP (GLOBE)

SCOPE

Valves used to stop or regulate flow of a liquid or gas. They are operated by means of a screw, actuated
manually or automatically, which lifts or lowers a disk onto a body seat. Globe stop and check valves are of
simular construction except the disk is not attached to the stem. This prevents reversal of flow by the
hydraulic forces of the system closing the disk against the body seat.

SPECIFICATION

BS5152: 1974 - Cast iron globe and globe stop and check valves for general purposes

Size range
:   Flanged 10 to 450mm nominal sizes
    Screwed ½" to 6" nominal sizes

Type
:   Valves shall have a rising stem with inside or outside screw with the following types:

    Globe
    (a)   straight
    (b)   angle
    (c)   oblique (or Y)

    Globe stop and check
    (a)   straight
    (b)   angle

Manufacture
:   Flanged and screwed end cast iron with copper alloy, nickel alloy, stainless steel or
    resilient seated or all iron.

Duty
:   Pressure, maximum permissible gauge working at 20°C shall be 10, 16 and 25 bar (nominal
    pressure).

    Temperature, up to 220°C. The pressure/temperature ratings as shown in Table 1.
    All valves shall be suitable for continuous use at their nominal pressure within the
    temperature range -10°C to +65°C.   Restrictions may be placed by the manufacturer by
    reason of valve type, trim materials or other factors.

Marking
:   Marking shall show nominal diameter, nominal pressure rating, body material designation,
    manufacturer, direction of flow (stop and check valves), trim material, any temperature
    limits, specification, body end threads (other than BS21).

Other data
:   Table 1:   Pressure/temperature ratings
    Table 5:   Basic materials.

BS5154: 1974 - Copper alloy globe, globe stop and check, check and gate valves for general purposes

Size range
:   Flanged 10 to 80mm nominal sizes.
    Screwed ¼" to 3" nominal sizes.
    Capillary or compression (BS864/2) 10 to 54mm
    Compression (BS864/2) ⅜" to 2".
    Capillary or compression (BS2051/1) 10 to 42mm.

Type
:   Valve shall have a rising stem with inside or outside screw with the following types:
    (a)   straight
    (b)   angle
    (c)   oblique (or Y)

Manufacture	Flanged, screwed, capillary or compression body end cast copper alloy to suit series A or B conditions.
Duty	Pressure, flanged 16, 25 and 40 bar, screwed 16, 20, 25, 32 and 40 bar, capillary and compression to comply with respective specification requirements.

Temperature, two series of values

A: 260^oC maximum and where appropriate shall have pressure/temperature ratings in accordance with BS4504 flange ratings.

B: maximum temperature limitation equivalent to the temperatures of saturated steam at a pressure of 7, 9, 10.5 and 14 bar for nominal pressure of PN16, PN20, PN25 and PN32 respectively.

The pressure/temperature ratings in Table 1 are for liquids, gas and steam. All valves shall be suitable of continuous use at their nominal pressure designations within the range -10^oC to $+95^o$C.

Marking	Marking shall indicate nominal diameter, nominal pressure rating, body material designation, manufacture, direction of flow, specification, trim materials, any limiting temperature and body end threads (other than BS21).
Other data	Table 1: Pressure/temperature rating
	Table 6(a) Basic materials, series A.
	Table 6(b) Basic materials, series B.

BS5160: 1977 - Flanged steel globe valves, globe stop and check valves and lift type check valves for general purposes

Size range	10 to 450mm nominal sizes
Type	Valve shall have a rising stem with inside or outside screw with the following types:

Globe or globe stop and check

(a)   straight

(b)   angle

(c)   oblique

Manufacture	Flanged end cast or forged carbon steel
Duty	Pressure, nominal pressure 16, 25 and 40 bar.

Temperature, up to 475^oC. The pressure/temperature ratings as shown in Table 1.

All valves shall be suitable for continuous use at their nominal pressure designation within the temperature range -10^oC to $+120^o$C. Restrictions may be placed by the manufacturer by reason of valve type, trim materials or other factors.

Marking	Marking shall show nominal size, nominal pressure rating, body material designation, manufacturer, trim materials, limiting temperature, specification and flow direction.
Other data	Table 1 : Pressure/temperature rating
	Table 5 : Basic materials.

MATERIALS

BS Number	Material/Grade	Data Sheet	Comments
5152	Grey iron/12 (180)	FM01	Handwheel
	Grey iron/14 (220)	FM01	Body, bonnet. In an all iron valve the disk and disk or body facing shall not be

BS Number	Material/Grade	Data Sheet	Comments
			inferior to the body material.
	Gunmetal/G1 Gunmetal/LG2 Gunmetal/LG3	NF26	Disk and disk facing ring in copper alloy faced valves
	Gunmetal/LG2	NF26	Stem - continuously cast.
	Aluminium bronze/AB2		Cast disk facing or body facing rings.
	Aluminium bronze/CA103 Aluminium bronze/CA104	NF29	Stem, disk stem nut, back seat bushing or gland
	Aluminium bronze/CA106	NF30	
	Brass/CZ114 Brass/CZ116	NF18	Stem, disk stem nut, back seat bushing or gland
	Nickel alloy		Manufacturers option of alloy for disks, disk facing rings and body seat rings.
	Stainless steel		Manufacturers option of alloy for use for disk, disk facing rings, body seat rings, stem, disk stem nut, back seat bushing and gland.
5154 Series A	Gunmetal/LG2 Gunmetal/LG4	NF26 NF27	Used for body, bonnet, disk, body seat ring, stem, stuffing box
	Nickel alloy/NA1 Nickel alloy/NA2 Nickel alloy/NA13		Disk body seat and disk facing ring.
	Stainless steel/713 Stainless steel/845		Disk, body seat and disk facing ring, stem and stuffing box
	Brass/CZ112 Brass/CZ114 Brass/CZ116	NF17 NF18	Stem and stuffing box
	Aluminium bronze/CA103 Aluminium bronze/CA104 Aluminium bronze/CA106	NF29 NF30	Stem and stuffing box
	Phosphor bronze/PB102		Internal fastening
	Aluminium LM6	NF05	Handwheel
5154 Series B	Gunmetal/LG2 Gunmetal/LG4	NF26 NF27	Body, bonnet, disk, renewable body seat and stem
	Nickel alloy		As stainless steel (except stem)
	Grey iron/12 (180)	FM01	Handwheel
5160	Carbon steel/161-28A+B Carbon steel/161-480	FM10 FM10	Body, bonnet, yoke and stuffing box
	Low alloy steel/621	FM20	Bolting
	Stainless steel.		Stem

CONNECTION

The type of connection may be dictated by the specification. It should be suitable for the pressure and temperatures, the fluid handled and the mechanical strength required under the service condition.

Method	BS Number	Data Sheet	Notes
Flanged	10	3.2.1	Imperial sizes
	4504	3.2.1	Metric sizes
Screwed		3.2.2	Threads to BS21
Capillary	864/2	3.2.3	
Compression	864/2	3.2.4	
	864/3	3.2.4	
	2051/1	3.2.4	
Grooved		3.2.6	Flange adaptors may be required.

SERVICE CONSIDERATIONS

1. Screw down valves are used for close regulation or throttling of flow. Fine control can be achieved with needle valve.

2. Due to the sinuous route through the valve the resistance to flow is higher than other valve types. By using an oblique pattern less disruption to the flow pattern is obtained with a smaller loss of pressure across the valve.

3. Valves shall be correctly fitted between piping flanges, which shall be aligned and supported as close to the valve as possible to obviate undue stress occurring. Large valves shall be supported under the body.

4. Design of the piping system shall take account of any pipe movement due to expansion or contraction to ensure no undue stress is imposed on the valve.

5. Valves must be included in any maintenance programme for the piping system. Special attention should be made to ensure there are no leaks via the gland packing as this could promote corrosion with the eventual replacement of the stem.

6. Undue stress due to excessive vibration or shock loading caused by water hammer could bring about damage or serious failure of the valve. Valve ratings assume non-shock conditions. Where shock is likely to occur a valve of higher pressure rating should be specified.

7. The pressure/temperature rating of a valve is determined by either the flange or the valve, whichever is the lower.

8. All gaskets, sealing rings and thread sealing compounds shall be compatible with the fluids, temperatures and pressures. Where potable water is concerned they shall comply with the local water regulations.

9. All excess flux from capillary connectors shall be removed to prevent corrosion.

FAMILY GROUP	VALVES	SUB-GROUP	FLOAT OPERATED

SCOPE

Float operated valves are used principally on the inlets to service tanks for the purpose of maintaining a pre-determined liquid level. A float is generally attached to a lever (metal or plastic) which actuates the valve by following the liquid level, causing the valve to admit more liquid as the float falls and to gradually close as it rises.

Valves are available that operate as the float rises and closes as it drops for the discharge of water accumulating in tanks.

SPECIFICATION

VALVES

BS1212 -Ball valves (excluding floats)
Part 1: 1953 - Piston type

Size range	Bodies available in range $\frac{3}{8}$" to 2" nominal sizes.
Type	Six patterns of body, I to IV
Manufacture	Bodies shall be either sand or die cast or of hot pressing. Levers shall be drawn, extruded or cast.
Duty	Component parts shall be of non-corrodable material.
Marking	Bodies shall be marked with manufacturer and specification. Seats shall be marked with manufacturer and body pattern.

Part 2: 1970 - Diaphragm types (brass body)

Specifies the requirements for a float operated valve in which the flow of water is controlled by the flexing of a diaphragm.

Size range	Available in two nominal sizes, $\frac{3}{8}$" and $\frac{1}{2}$".
Type	Four seat sizes $\frac{1}{8}$", 3/16", $\frac{1}{4}$" and $\frac{3}{8}$" bores.
Manufacture	Metal parts shall be from cast, hot pressed or wrought materials.
Duty	Capable of operating at high (1400kN/m^2), medium (700kN/m^2) and low (300kN/m^2) pressures (maximum) - see Table 1.
Marking	Body shall have the manufacturer and specification. Seat shall have the manufacture (plastic seat size is identified by colour).
Other data	Table 1: Seats and floats.

Part 3: 1979 - Diaphragm type (plastic body) for cold water

Specifies similar requirements to BS1212 part 2 except the body is of plastics material.

Size range	Available $\frac{1}{2}$" nominal bore.
Type	Four seat sizes of $\frac{1}{8}$", 3/16", $\frac{1}{4}$" and $\frac{3}{8}$" bore.
Duty	Capable of operating at high (14 bar), medium (7 bar) and low (3 bar) pressures (maximum) - see Table 1.
Marking	Body shall have manufacturer and specification. Seats shall have manufacturer (size identified by colour).
Other data	Table 1: Seats and floats.

FLOATS

BS1968: 1953 - Floats for ball valves (copper)

    Floats are designed to operate with valves to BS1212.

Size range	Spherical floats of 4½" to 12" nominal diameter.
Type	3 classes, A, B and C
Manufacture	Class A - floats of all sizes with soldered joints Class B - floats of all sizes with solderless joints Class C - floats of all sizes with brazed, welded or silver-soldered joints.
Duty	Temperatures over 37.8^oC (100^oF) floats shall be jointed as for Class C floats.
Marking	Floats shall show manufacturer and specification.
Other data	Lifting effort - the net upward force acting on the float when immersed in water so that half of its volume is below the surface.

        Table 1:   Spherical copper floats

BS2456: 1973 - Floats (plastics) for ball valves for hot and cold water

    Specifies requirements for floats for use in cold water cisterns and expansion systems for hot water suitable for use with valves to BS1212.

Size range	Floats available 102, 114, 127 and 152mm diameter.
Type	Spherical or non-spherical
Duty	Temperature of liquid up to 93^oC.
Marking	Floats shall be marked with manufacture, specification, type. On non-spherical the word UP on intended uppermost surface.
Other data	Lifting effort - the net upward force acting on the float when immersed in water so that half of the volume is below the surface.

        Table 1:   Minimum lifting effort.

MATERIAL

BS Number	Material/Grade	Data Sheet	Comment
1212/1	Brass/SCB1	NF25	Sand or shell castings, excluding seats
	Brass/SCB3		As above
	Brass/DCB3	NF24	Gravity die castings, excluding seats
	Brass/PCB1	NF22	Pressure die castings, excluding seats
	Brass/CZ122	NF20	Hot pressings, excluding seats.
	Brass/CZ121	NF19	Rod for machined components, excluding seats.
	Gunmetal/LG1		Castings, excluding seats
	Gunmetal/LG2	NF26	As above
	Gunmetal/G1		For seats
	Phosphor bronze		Rod for machined seats
	Nylon 6	PL05	For seats
	Nylon 66	PL06	
	Nylon 11	PL07	
	Nylon 12	PL08	
	Ceramic/Agate		Seat tips fixed to the metal by a cement of a fusion mixture inert to the working conditions.

BS Number	Material/Grade	Data Sheet	Comment
1212/2	Rubber		Washers from hard vulcanised rubber
	Rubber		Vulcanised rubber diaphragm complying with BS1154 Group Z14 (hardness Bs degrees 62-70).

All other materials are similar to the requirements for BS1212/1.

BS Number	Material/Grade	Data Sheet	Comment
1212/3	Nylon 6	PL05	Body material not specified
	Nylon 66	PL06	Seat
	Nylon 11	PL07	
	Nylon 12	PL08	
	Acetal copolymer	PL02	Seat, plunger
	Polypropylene	PL14	Seat
	Rubber		As for BS1212 part 2.

All metal materials as specified in BS1212/1.

BS Number	Material/Grade	Data Sheet	Comment
1968	Copper/BS899		
	Brass/SCB1	NF25	Cast boss
	Brass/PCB1	NF22	" "
	Brass/CZ122	NF20	Hot pressed boss
	Gunmetal/1400/LG2	NF26	Hot pressed boss
	Solder/BS219	Jointing & bonding section	Type F
	Braze/BS1845	Jointing & bonding section	
2456	Plastics		Type is not specified but for hot water applications it must be capable of withstanding 100°C.
	Brass/CZ122	NF20	Boss inserts

CONNECTIONS

The type of connection may be dictated by the specification. It should be suitable for the pressure and temperatures, the fluid handled and the mechanical strength required under the service condition.

Method	BS Number	Component Data Sheet	Notes
Compression	864/2	3.2.4.	Hot or cold systems
	864/3		Cold water systems only
Flanged	10	3.2.1	Imperial
	4504		Metric
Screwed	21	3.2.2	Threads conform to BS21.

SERVICE CONSIDERATIONS

1. Valves capable of back-siphonage should not be used.
2. All valve conforming to BS1212 should be securely fixed to the tank wall so as not to place undue stress on the pipe system as the float rises and falls.
3. All valves should be adequately supported. Design of the piping system shall take account of any pipe movement due to expansion or contraction to ensure no undue stress is imposed on the valve.

4. The pressure/temperature rating of a valve is determined by either the flange or the valve, whichever is the lower. Flanges shall be at right angles and concentric to the bore.

5. All gaskets and thread sealing materials shall be compatible with the fluids, temperatures and pressures. Where potable water is concerned they shall comply with the local water regulations.

6. Both angle and in-line types of valve are used in a variety of designs. Some float operated valves are specially suited for high pressure applications.

| FAMILY GROUP | VALVES | SUB-GROUP | BUTTERFLY |

SCOPE

Butterfly valves consists of a circular shaped disk which turns about a diametric axis within the cylindrical bore of the valve body and a quarter rotation of the disk opens or closes the valve quickly. Flow control and a positive shut-off may be achieved depending on the sealing system. In the fully open position the only obstruction to flow is the thickness of the disk.

SPECIFICATION

BS5155: 1974 - Cast iron and carbon steel butterfly valves for general purposes

Size range	40 to 2000mm nominal diameters
Type	Available in the following forms
	(a) double flanged
	(b) wafer
	(1) single flanged
	(2) flangeless
	(c) U-section
Manufacture	Valve bodies shall be cast or wrought material.

Duty   Pressure, the maximum permissible gauge working pressure at $20^{\circ}C$ shall be 2.5, 10, 16 and 25 bar.

Temperature, valves shall be suitable for continuous use at their nominal pressure designation within the temperature range of $-10^{\circ}C$ to $+65^{\circ}C$. Maximum permissible gauge working pressure (bar) and operating temperatures shall be in accordance with BS4504 (flanges), except for restrictions on temperature placed by the manufacturer by reason of the trim materials or other factors.

Application   Valves shall be suitable for the following service application

(a)   tight shut off
(b)   low leakage rate
(c)   regulating

When used with liquids the valve, fully open, shall be suitable for flow velocities of at least 5m/s at the valve inlet.

Marking   Body markings shall show nominal diameter, nominal pressure rating, body material designation, manufacturer and flow direction (uni-directional flow valves only).

Other data   Table 3:   Basic materials.

MATERIALS

BS Number	Material/Grade	Data Sheet	Comments
5155	Grey iron/ 220 Grey iron/ 180	FM01	Body, body with integral seat, disk, disk with integral seat 180 used on sections less than 15mm
	S.G. iron/600/3 S.G. iron/500/7 S.G. iron/420/12 S.G. iron/370/17	FM05	As 1452/220 and rings fitted to body or disk for sealing seating or retaining.

BS Number	Material/Grade	Data Sheet	Comments
	Carbon steel/1501-151 23A	FM08	As grey and S.G. irons
	Carbon steel/1503-151 26A		As S.G. iron
	Carbon steel/1504-161 A	FM09	As grey and S.G. irons
	Carbon steel/1504-161 B	FM10	As grey and S.G. irons
	Stainless steel		Disk, disk with integral seat and rings fitted to body or disk for sealing, seating or retaining.
	Stainless steel/970-316	FM25	Shaft
	Stainless steel/970-320		As 316
	Stainless steel/970-431		As 316
	Gunmetal/LG2	NF26	As stainless steel 845
	Gunmetal/LG4	NF27	As stainless steel 845
	Aluminium bronze/AB2		As stainless steel 845
	Aluminium bronze/CA103	NF29	Internal fastenings
	Aluminium bronze/CA104		Shaft and internal fastenings
	Aluminium bronze/CA106	NF30	As CA103
	Nickel-copper/NA13		Shaft and internal fastenings
	Phosphor bronze/PB102		Internal fastenings
	Resilient material		Rings fitted to body or disk for sealing, seating or retaining. Type depends on service parameters for resilient seated valves.

CONNECTION

The type of connection may be suitable to the contract specification, the pressure/temperature conditions, the medium handled and the mechanical strength required under the service conditions.

Method	BS Number	Component Data Sheet	Comments
Flange	BS10	3.2.1	Imperial sizes
	BS4504	3.2.1	Metric sizes
Welded		3.2.5	Valves designed for welding only.

SERVICE CONSIDERATIONS

1. Valves welded to the pipe are permanent and cannot be replaced or maintained.
2. Flange gasket materials, resilient materials and lining materials must be compatible to the medium and the service conditions.
3. Access must be available for manually activated valves.
4. Large valves must be adequately supported so as to reduce stress on the pipework.
5. In general the disk protudes beyond the valve in the open position. When installing the valve should be shut to prevent damage. Prior to final tightening of the bolts, open the valve to ensure that the valve is central and the disk does not foul the pipework.
6. The system design shall take account of any pipe movement due to expansion or contraction to ensure no undue stress is imposed on the valve.
7. Valve ratings assume non-shock conditions. Where shock loading, due to water hammer, is likely to occur a valve of a higher rating than is required for the stated pressure, should be specified.
8. The pressure/temperature rating of a valve is determined by either the flange or the valve, whichever is the lower.

SCOPE

A plug valve gives a quick and positive open-close operation. They can also be used for coarse throttling on some low flow services. The valve consists of a plug (ball, tapered or cylindrical) which can be rotated to align its ports to those of the body to control the flow. Plug valves can be used for controlling liquids and gases.

SPECIFICATION

BS1552: 1967 - Control plug cocks for low pressure gases

Size range	The size range depends on the type of cock:
Type	Four types of plug cocks

      (a)   Meter control type $\frac{1}{2}$" - $1\frac{1}{4}$" nominal sizes

      (b)   Main type $\frac{1}{2}$" - 2" nominal sizes

      (c)   Union type $\frac{1}{8}$" - 1" nominal sizes

      (d)   Nursery union type $\frac{1}{8}$" - $\frac{1}{2}$" nominal sizes.

Manufacture	Plug cocks shall be cast or hot pressed. All machining shall be free from defects.
Duty	Cocks are primarily intended for use with town gas and also may be used with natural gases and with liquified petroleum gases for certain applications.
	Assembled cock shall withstand a pressure of 5lbs/sq.in in both the ON and OFF positions.
Marking	Marking shall show manufacturer and specification.

BS5158: 1974 - Cast iron and carbon steel plug valves for general purposes

Size range	Flanged:	10-600mm nominal diameters
	Screwed:	$\frac{1}{4}$" - 4" nominal sizes.
Type	Valves shall be of the following patterns	

      (a)   short

      (b)   regular

      (c)   venturi

Manufacture	Flanged and screwed end cast or wrought bodies and plugs.
Duty	Pressure, Nominal pressure (PN), maximum permissible gauge working pressure (bar) at 20°C are PN10, PN16, PN25, PN40, PN64 and PN100.
	Temperature, pressure/temperature ratings apply over the range -10°C to $+400^{o}$C.
	All valves must be capable of continuous use at their nominal pressure designation within the temperature range -10°C to $+65^{o}$C.
	Limitations may be imposed by the manufacturer because of the lubricants and lining materials, seat rings and seals used.
	Application, Table 1 details maximum ratings for liquid, gas and saturated steam use.
Marking	Marking shall show limiting temperature, nominal diameter, nominal pressure rating, body material designation, specification, manufacturer and direction of flow (uni-directional valves only).

Other data   Table 1:   Pressure/temperature ratings
                    Table 5:   Basic materials.

BS5159: 1974 - Cast iron and carbon steel ball valves for general purposes

Size range   Flanged: 10-600mm nominal diameters
                    Screwed: ¼" to 4" nominal sizes

Type   Valves shall be of the following patterns
                    (a)   full bore
                    (b)   reduced bore

Manufacture   Flanged and screwed ends cast or wrought bodies and balls.

Duty   Pressure, Nominal pressure (PN), maximum permissible gauge working pressure
                    (bar) at $20^{o}C$ are PN10, PN16, PN25, PN40, PN64 or PN100.

                    Temperature, pressure/temperature ratings apply over the range $-10^{o}C$ to $+400^{o}C$.
                    All valves must be capable of continuous use at their nominal pressure
                    designation within the temperature range $-10^{o}C$ to $+65^{o}C$.

                    Limitations may be imposed by the manufacturer because of the lubricant and
                    lining materials, seat rings and seals used.

                    Application, Table 1 details maximum ratings for liquid, gas and steam.

Marking   Marking shall show limiting temperature, nominal diameter, nominal pressure
                    rating, body and ball material designations, specification, manufacturer and
                    direction of flow (uni-directional flow valves only).

Other data   Table 1 :   Pressure/temperature ratings
                    Table 5 :   Basic materials.

.MATERIALS

BS Number	Materials/Grade	Data Sheet	Uses
1552	Brass/CZ121	NF19	Machined components rod.
	Brass/CZ122	NF20	Hot pressed components.
	Brass/CZ108		Sheet metal components
	Brass/DCB1-C	NF23	Cast components
	Blackheart iron	FM03	
5158	Grey iron/14 (220)	FM01	Cast iron valves - used for body, plug and gland cover for nominal pressure (PN) valves 10, 16 and 25 up to $300^{o}C$. Steel valves - used for plug only in PN10/16 valves.
	Grey iron/180	FM01	Alternative to 220 where section thickness is less than 15mm.
	Carbon steel/ 161B	FM10	Used for body, plug and gland cover in valves of nominal pressure PN16, PN25, PN40, PN64 and PN100 up to $400^{o}C$.
	Carbon steel/ 161 28	FM09	As 1504/161B.
	Carbon steel/ 151 26	FM08	As 1504/161B
5159	Grey iron/14 (220)	FM01	Body, body connector, cover, ball and insert. Used for nominal pressure valves PN10, PN15 and PN25 up to $300^{o}C$.

SHEET **N**UMBER		3.3.6	3

BS Number	Material/Grade	Data Sheet	Uses
	Grey iron/180		Alternative to 220 where section thickness is less than 15mm.
	Carbon steel/ 161B	FM10	Body, body connector, cover, ball and insert in PN16, PN25, PN40, PN64 and PN100 up to 400°C.
	Carbon steel/ 161 28	FM09	As 1504/161B
	Carbon steel/ 151 26	FM08	As 1504/161B
	Carbon steel/970/1		As 1504/161B in the normalised condition or cold drawn from hot rolled condition.

CONNECTION

The type of connection may be dictated by the specification. It should be suitable for the pressure and temperature, the fluid handled and mechanical strength required under the service conditions.

Method	BS Number	Component Data Sheet	Notes
Flanged	BS10	3.2.1	Imperial sizes
	BS4504	3.2.1	Metric sizes
Screwed	BS21	3.2.2	Threads shall conform to BS21
Welded		3.2.5	Permanent in system
Grooved		3.2.6	Flange adaptors may be required

SERVICE CONSIDERATIONS

1.   Taper or cylindrical plugs can be:

    (a) Non lubricated - with or without soft sleeve between the plug and body. May be used where conventional lubricants are unsuitable. Sleeve or seals on the plug can be PTFE or

    (b) Lubricated - lubricant aids valve operation, perfects the seal between matching faces and reduces erosion/corrosion problems.

2.   Unlubricated plug valves using fluorocarbon sleeves may be used up to 29 bar and 230°C.

3.   Lubricated plug valves are available for pressures up to 690 bar and a working temperature range of -40°C to 325°C depending on materials.

4.   Ball valve body can be of one piece or of multi-piece construction. One piece valves may be welded in line and the ball capable of being removed for maintenance when of the top entry type.

5.   When line pressure is insufficient to ensure a positive leak-tight seal in a ball valve then a valve with an inbuilt seat loading should be used.

6.   All gaskets, sealing rings and thread sealing compounds shall be compatible with the fluids, temperatures and pressures. Where potable water is concerned they shall comply with the local water regulations.

7.   Access must be available for maintenance such as removal of plug or ball, the application of lubricant and repacking of glands.

8.   Design of the piping system shall take account of any pipe movement due to expansion or contraction to ensure no undue stress is imposed on the valve.

9.   Undue stress due to excessive vibration or shock loading caused by water hammer could bring about damage or serious failure of the valve. Valve ratings assume non-shock conditions. Where shock is likely to occur a valve of higher pressure

165

rating should be specified.

10.   Pipework shall be supported close to the valves. Large valves should be individually supported.

component data sheet	SHEET NUMBER 3.4.1.	1

FAMILY GROUP	PUMPS	SUB- GROUP	CENTRIFUGAL

SCOPE

This Data Sheet refers to centrifugal pumps used for water services such as heating and domestic hot water circulation, chilled water circulation, cold water pressure boosting and fire-fighting.

A centrifugal pump uses the action of a rotating bladed impeller to generate centrifugal and other forces to produce a pressure difference between the inlet and outlet connections. The majority of applications in building services involving the use of a centrifugal pump can be dealt with by a single-stage pump which has one impeller with backward curved vanes and is fitted in a casing usually of volute shape to provide maximum conversion of kinetic energy into pressure energy.

When higher pressures are required than can be reasonably obtained by the use of a single impeller several impellers are fitted to a common shaft to form a multi-stage pump. It is usual for multi-stage pumps to incorporate a hydraulic balancing device to relieve the pump bearings from the thrust produced by the high pressure generated at the pump outlet.

Centrifugal pumps may be driven in one of three ways: direct-coupled, V-belt, or close-coupled.

With direct-coupled drive the pump is driven through a flexible coupling from an electric motor with both pump and motor mounted on a common steel or cast-iron baseplate. The pump has its own bearings and the pump duty may be adjusted by changing the impeller diameter.

With V-belt drive the pump is driven by V-belts from an electric motor fitted on the side of the pump on glide rails or sometimes mounted above the pump. The pump has its own bearings.

With close-coupled drive the electric motor has a specially extended shaft which enters the pump casing and to which the impeller is directly fitted. The pump does not have its own bearings and the thrust developed has to be taken up by the bearings in the motor. The pump duty may be adjusted by changing the impeller diameter or by using a multi-speed electric motor.

SPECIFICATIONS

BS1394: - Specification for power driven circulators.

Part 1: 1971 - Glanded and glandless pumps

Size range	200W to 2000W power input at maximum voltage for single and three phase electrical supply.
Type	The types for heating and domestic hot water service circulation are: (a) centrifugal glanded pumps. This pump incorporates a shaft sealing device against leakage to atmosphere, (b) centrifugal glandless pumps. This pump does not incorporate a shaft sealing device against leakage to atmosphere.
Connections	(i) flanged to BS4504, (ii) screwed to BS21.

167

Ratings	All pumps shall be capable of operating satisfactorily at ambient temperatures up to 40°C. These grades of pumps are designated to cover a range of maximum operating conditions.

Grade	Max. Water Temperature	Max. Pressure
1	90°C	3.0 bar
2	120°C	4.5 bar
3 (glanded pumps only)	160°C	10.0 bar

Manufacture	Grade 1 pumps shall be fitted with suitably placed venting devices unless they are of self-purging design. Grade 2 and Grade 3 pumps shall be either self-venting or where a vent is fitted the vented fluid shall be piped away. Stuffing boxes or mechanical seals shall be suitable for the pressure and temperature of the water. Special electrical requirements for glandless pumps are detailed in Section 2 of BS1394.
Marking	These shall indicate: (a) For glandless pumps - BS1394/1, manufacturer, type and serial number, pump grade, rated voltage, frequency, input power and current. (b) For glanded pumps - BS 1394/1, manufacturer, type and serial number, pump grade, quantity, head, speed and brake power required. Direction of impeller rotation shall be indicated by an arrow on the casing.
Tests	Pumps shall be both hydrostatically pressure tested and performance tested. When required by the purchaser a certificate shall be provided.

BS5257: 1975: - Specification for horizontal end-suction centrifugal pumps (16 bar)

Size Range	Inlet 50 to 200mm diameter. Outlet 32 to 150mm diameter. Impeller 125 to 400mm diameter. Pump designation comprises three numbers, the inlet diameter, the outlet diameter and the nominal impeller diameter.
Type	Horizontal end-suction centrifugal pump having a maximum discharge pressure of 16 bar.
Connections	Flanges; preferably to BS4504 class 16.
Ratings	Nominal duty point and pump performance selection information is given in BS5257.
Manufacture	All materials, seals and joints shall be selected with regard to operational temperature requirements.
Tests	Static pressure test of pump casing to 24 bar.

BS4082: - Specification for external dimensions for vertical in-line centrifugal pumps

Part 1: 1969 - 'I' type

Size range   From 40 to 200mm nominal inlet and outlet branch connections.

Type   A single stage pump with the inlet and outlet branches arranged in 'I' configuration and
                  having:
                  - a vertical shaft exit,
                  - a driving unit supported exclusively by the pump casing,
                  - inlet and outlet branch connections, identical in size lying on a common centre line
                    which intersects the vertical pump axis.

Connections   Flanged to BS4504 or BS1560.

Ratings   Pump size for a given duty point and differential head is determined from Fig. 1, and
                  Appendix B gives guidance on selection at other operating speeds (Figs 3, 4 and 5).

                  Casing pressure ratings are:

                  Code   Max. Pressure
                  High pressure series R   60 bar
                  Low pressure series L   25 bar

                  Pumps shall be capable of operating at a temperature up to 175°C.

Designation   This is by a code embodying:
& marking   (a) casing test pressure rating,
                  (b) quantity/differential head code,
                  (c) code letter 'I' configuration.

                  Direction of impeller rotation shall be indicated by an arrow on the casing.

Tests   Casing pressure test to maximum pressure rating (see Ratings above).

Part 2: 1969 - 'U' type

Size range   Inlet connections 40 to 200mm.
                  Outlet connections 40 to 150mm.

Type   A pump with the inlet and outlet branches arranged in 'U' configuration and having:
                  - a vertical shaft axis,
                  - a driving unit supported exclusively by the pump casing,
                  - inlet and outlet branch connections not necessarily identical in size with the flange
                    faces in the same vertical plane. The connection axes parallel in the horizontal plane
                    with the outlet branch located on the horizontal axis of the pump and the inlet branch
                    displaced by dimension 'U' as given in Table 4.

Connections   Flanges to BS4504 or BS1560.

Ratings   Pump size for a given duty point and differential head is determined from Fig 1, and Appendix B gives guidance on selection at other operating speeds (Figs 3, 4 and 5).

Casing pressure ratings are:

Code	Max. Pressure
High pressure series R	60 bar
Low pressure series L	25 bar

Pumps shall be capable of operating at a temperature up to 175°C.

Designation & marking   This is by a code embodying:

(a) casing test pressure rating,

(b) quantity/differential head code,

(c) code letter 'U' configuration.

Direction of impeller rotation shall be indicated by an arrow on the casing.

Tests   Casing pressure test to maximum pressure rating (see Ratings above).

Other Pump Specifications

BS599: 1986: - Methods of testing pumps

Testing performance and efficiency of pumps for liquids which behave as homogeneous liquids. This BS is being progressively replaced by Parts of BS5316.

BS5316: Acceptance tests for centrifugal, mixed flow and axial pumps.
Part 1: 1976: - Class C tests. Part 2: 1977: - Class B tests.

MATERIALS

General   Most British Standards state that pumps shall be constructed of materials appropriate for the application and with the mechanical strength to meet the pressure and temperature ratings. However certain recommendations on materials are made in BS1394: Part 1: Glanded and glandless pumps. These are:

Shafts-   Preferably stainless steel or suitable non-ferrous alloy unless the immersed section is covered by non-corrodible bushes or parts.

Ferrous parts shall be adequately protected against rusting. Pump parts in contact with water of 'zero' hardness or sea water should be of zinc-free bronze.

CONNECTIONS

The type of connection should be suitable for:

(i)   working pressure;

(ii)   temperature conditions;

(iii) the liquid handled;

(iv)   mechanical strength required under service conditions;

(v)   specification requirements.

Method	BS Number	Component Data Sheet	Notes
Flanges	10	3.2.1	Imperial sizes
	4504	3.2.1	Metric sizes
Screwed	21	3.2.2	Threads to BS 21
Grooved	-	3.2.6	Flange adaptor may be required

SELECTION

Pump life is influenced by the resistance of the materials of construction to corrosion, erosion, or a combination of both. Operational factors that lead to a long pump life are:

- pumping neutral liquids at normal ambient temperatures,
- absence of abrasive particles in liquid,
- continuous operation close to point of maximum efficiency,
- an adequate margin of net-positive suction head (NPSH).

Erosion in pumps arises through cavitation and abrasive-wear. Material types in order of increasing cavitation and abrasive-wear resistance are:

Cavitation resistance

1. cast iron
2. bronze
3. cast steel
4. manganese bronze
5. monel
6. 400 series stainless steel
7. 300 series stanless steel
8. nickel-aluminium bronze.

Abrasive-wear resistance

1. cast iron
2. bronze
3. manganese bronze
4. nickel-aluminium bronze
5. cast steel
6. 300 series stainless steel
7. 400 series stainless steel

The following performance criteria should be considered in the selection of pump components:

Impellers: corrosion resistance, abrasive wear resistance, cavitation resistance, casting and machining properties.
Cast iron impellers may be used in small low-cost pumps. For water and non-corrosive services bronze is a widely used impeller material for temperatures up to 120°C. Stainless steel of the 400 series is used where conditions are too arduous for bronze.

Casings: strength, corrosion resistance, abrasive-wear resistance, casting and machining properties.
Cast iron is adequate for most single-stage pumping applications in building services.

Shafts: fatigue strength, corrosion resistance, notch sensitivity.
Shafts are commonly of steel but for arduous conditions either stainless steel or monel should be employed.

Wearing rings: corrosion resistance, abrasive-wear resistance, galling characteristics, casting and machining properties.
Bronze is widely used but for arduous conditions either stainless steel or monel should be employed.

SERVICE CONSIDERATIONS

1.   Isolating valves should be fitted at the inlet and outlet side of pumps for ease of removal and maintenance.

2.   Pumps should be provided with pressure/altitude gauges or suitable tappings at suction and discharge for measurement of operating and static head pressures.

3.   Pumps and other system components may require strainers to be fitted at the pump suction to protect them from particle damage.

4.   Permanent duty changes of direct driven pumps may be achieved by change of impeller diameter and of indirect driven pumps by change of belts and pulleys.

5.   Piping design shall take account of pipe movement due to expansion or contraction to ensure no undue stress is imposed on the pump.

6.   Pumps should be vibration isolated. This may require use of some or all of the following precautions: antivibration mounts, inlet/discharge flexible connections, use of inertia bases, flexible electrical connections, antivibration hangers on adjacent pipework.

7.   System design and pump selection should ensure that any shock loading which could bring about pump failure or damage e.g. water hammer, is avoided.

8.   All gaskets, seals and thread sealing compounds shall be compatible with the liquid handled and with the systems temperatures and pressures. Where potable water is pumped they shall also comply with the local Water Authority requirements.

9.   Pumps should be included in the maintenance programme for the piping system.

10.   Gland seals shall be adequate for the pressure and temperature ratings, shaft speed and liquid conditions.

11.   Pump selection and piping system arrangement shall ensure that when operating the pump has adequate NPSH (net positive suction head) to avoid cavitation or other operational problems.

12.   Pumps for use on open circuits e.g. domestic hot water, cooling tower circuit, must have non-corrosive parts. In typical building services applications this usually means bronze impellers and stainless steel shafts.

| FAMILY GROUP | PUMPS | SUB-GROUP | DOMESTIC |

SCOPE

This Data Sheet covers domestic pumps suitable for operating on single phase electrical supply and used for circulating water in piping systems of domestic heating and domestic hot water supply installations.

A domestic glandless pump does not incorporate a shaft sealing device to prevent liquid leakage to atmosphere. The motor is an integral part of the pump and the power input does not exceed 200 watts at maximum rated voltage. The motor often incorporates a variable speed control.

SPECIFICATIONS

BS1394: - Specification for power driven circulators.
Part 2: 1971 - Domestic glandless pumps

Size range	Power input not exceeding 200W at maximum rated voltage from a single phase electrical supply.
Type	For domestic heating and hot water service circulation.
Connections	Inlet and outlet dimensions of 25, 40, or 50mm nominal bore.
	Screwed connections shall comply with BS21.
	Flanged connections shall comply with BS4504.
Ratings	Two grades of pumps are specified and these shall operate at the following maximum temperature and pressure conditions.

Pump Grade	Maximum Working Temperature	Max. Pressure	Max. Ambient Temperature
1	90°C	3.0 bar	40 °C
2	110°C	3.0 bar	50 °C

Manufacturer's instructions shall state the performance of a pump in terms of quantity and head for water at 80°C. Where the pump is intended for use over a range of voltages, the performance data shall state the voltage at which the specified duty is applicable.

Sound level	The sound level emitted by the pump shall not exceed 32dB(A) when pumping cold water with a background level not exceeding 26dB(A).
Manufacture	Pumps shall be constructed of materials appropriate for the application.

Grade 1 pumps shall be fitted with suitably placed venting devices unless they are of self-purging design.
Grade 2 pumps shall either be self-venting or be fitted with a vent and vent drain pipe.

Electrical requirements shall be as detailed in Section 2 of BS1394.

Marking   These shall indicate - BS1394/2, manufacturer, type and serial numbers, pump grade and
               rated voltage, frequency, input power and current.
               Direction of impeller rotation shall be indicated by an arrow on the casing.

Tests   All pump parts subjected to water pressure shall be hydraulically pressure tested to 1.5
               times the working pressure for a period of 5 minutes. No leakage shall occur during this
               test period.

               Other tests on domestic glandless pumps shall be subject to special agreement between
               the purchaser and manufacturer.

MATERIALS

General   Most British Standards state that pumps shall be constructed of materials appropriate
               for the application and mechanical strength to meet the pressure and temperature
               ratings. Ferrous parts where corrosion could lead to the pump becoming unsafe shall be
               protected against rusting.

CONNECTIONS

The type of connection should be suitable for:
(i)   working pressure,
(ii)   temperature conditions,
(iii) the liquid handled,
(iv)   mechanical strength required under service conditions,
(v)   specification requirements.

Method	BS Number	Component Data Sheet	Notes
Flanges	10	3.2.1	Imperial sizes.
	4504	3.2.1	Metric sizes.
Screwed	21	3.2.2	Threads to BS21.

SERVICE CONSIDERATIONS

1.   Provision should be made for ease of pump removal and maintenance.

2.   Piping design shall take account of any pipe movement to ensure no undue stress is imposed on the pump.

3.   All gaskets, seals and thread sealing compounds shall be compatible with the system temperatures and pressures.

4.   Pumps should be included in a maintenance programme for the piping system.

5.   Changes in duty are usually achievable via the multi-speed motor or variable impeller orifice.

6.   Pump selection and piping system arrangement shall ensure that when operating the pump has adequate NPSH (net positive suction head) to avoid cavitation or other operational problems.

7.   Pumps for use on open circuits should be manufactured from non-corrosive parts usually bronze impellers and stainless steel shafts.

| FAMILY GROUP | PUMPS | SUB-GROUP | POSITIVE DISPLACEMENT |

SCOPE

This Data Sheet covers pumps of the positive displacement type. The two principal classifications are the reciprocating pump and the rotary pump.

A reciprocating pump drives liquid by the movement of a piston within a cylinder. A rotary pump consists of a rotor or similar impeller rotating in a casing with close running clearances. The liquid may be driven by gears, vanes, cams, screws, etc.

SPECIFICATIONS

There are no current British Standards covering size range, type, duty, descriptions, etc.

British Standards relating to the performance of positive displacement pumps are:

BS4617: 1983: - Methods for determining the performance of pumps and motors for hydraulic fluid power transmission

BS5944: Measurement of airborne noise from hydraulic fluid power systems and components
Part 1: 1980 - Method of test for pumps

MATERIALS

General   Most British Standards state that pumps shall be constructed of materials appropriate for the application and mechanical strength to meet the pressure and temperature ratings.

Selection   For reciprocating pumps handling fresh water up to 120°C the following is a general guide:

Pump Component	Material	
	acceptable service	extended life
Valves	steel bronze	400 series stainless steel.
Cylinder	cast iron bronze	steel.
Plungers	400 series stainless steel	hard-faced stainless steel.

Refer also to notes in 3.4.1

CONNECTIONS

The type of connection should be suitable for:

(i)   working pressure,

(ii)   temperature conditions,

(iii)   the liquid handled,

(iv)   mechanical strength required under service conditions,

(v)   specification requirements.

Method	BS Number	Component Data Sheet	Notes
Flanges	10	3.2.1	Imperial sizes.
	4504	3.2.1	Metric sizes.
Screwed	21	3.2.2	Threads to BS21.
Grooved	-	3.2.6	Flange adaptor may be required.

SERVICE CONSIDERATIONS

Note: Positive displacement pumps cover a wide range of types and capacities. The main applications are where a positive displacement rate of liquid is needed independent of the system head or where the head pressure is relatively high for a low pumping rate.

1.   Isolating valves should be incorporated on the inlet and outlet side of pumps for ease of removal and maintenance.

2.   Features of design and the method of liquid movement may present limitations on the pump use. Aspects which should be considered are:

(a) Reciprocating pumps

Piston type   - suitable for lubricating and non-lubricating fluids over wide viscosity range.

Diaphragm type - these provide leak free displacement but diaphragms require periodic replacement,

- diaphragm materials have maximum service temperature limitations e.g. elastomer 100°C, PTFE 200°C

- suitable for a variety of fluids, clean or heavily contaminated, over wide viscosity range.

(b) Rotary pumps

Gear type   - ideal for oils, but not suitable for non-lubricating fluids or those containing solid particles.

Vane type   - suitable for most clean fluids, including those with entrained gases.

Cam/lobe type   - capable of moving fluids with a wide range of viscosities.

Screw type   - suitable for a wide range of viscous fluids including those with abrasive or solid contaminants.

Service Considerations Cont'd

3.   Materials used for bodies, rotors and shafts shall be erosion and corrosion resistant for the liquid being circulated.

4.   All gaskets, seals and thread sealing compounds shall be compatible with the liquids, shaft speeds, temperatures and pressures being used. They shall also comply with local Water Authority requirements where potable water is circulated.

5.   Pumps may be direct or indirect driven. The latter permits the speed and hence the duty to be changed easily.

6.   Design of the piping system shall take account of any pipe movement due to expansion or contraction to ensure no undue stress is imposed on the pump.

7.   Where pumps are required to be vibration isolated then some or all of the following precautions may be necessary: antivibration mounts, inlet/discharge flexible connections, use of inertia bases, flexible electrical connections, antivibration hangers on adjacent pipework.

8.   System design and pump selection should ensure that any shock loading which could bring about pump failure or damage e.g. water hammer, is avoided.

9.   Pumps should be included in a maintenance programme for the piping system.

10.   A pressure relief valve shall be incorporated in all positive displacement pump installations where valved shut-off is possible in order to prevent the pump operating against a closed system.

component data sheet		SHEET NUMBER	3.5.1.	1

FAMILY GROUP	TANKS	SUB-GROUP	CISTERNS

SCOPE

This Data Sheet covers cisterns for the limited storage of cold water or used for feed and expansion purposes in hot or chilled water systems.

A cistern is a rigid open top enclosure for the containment of liquids and it may be provided with a cover to prevent the ingress of debris. Cisterns are also commonly descibed as tanks but in this Handbook the term tank is used to describe bulk storage vessels (see Section 3.5.2).

SPECIFICATIONS

BS417: - Glavanised mild steel cisterns and covers, tanks and cylinders
Part 1: 1964: - Imperial units

Cold and hot water cisterns for domestic purposes

Size range	20 sizes from 4 to 740 gallons capacity, in two grades, with covers.
Manufacture	Materials, workmanship, design and construction, dimensions and tolerances, etc. are described. There is an optional internal coating of bitumen.
Marking	The marking requirements are the test pressure and working head.

Part 2: 1973: - Metric units

Size range	20 sizes of cisterns from 18 to 3364 litres capacity.
Manufacture	Cisterns shall be welded, rivetted or with locked and sealed seams. Cover plate requirements are described and stays and cross-ties shall be in accordance with Table 2. Cisterns shall be constructed of mild steel and galvanised after manufacture.
Marking	Cisterns shall be marked with the BS number, grade, thickness, manufacturer and capacity.
Other data	Table 1 Dimensions of cisterns and covers. Table 2 Types and grades of cisterns to be stayed.

BS2777: 1974: - Asbestos cement cisterns

Size range	12 sizes of cisterns with capacities ranging from 17 to 701 litres.
Manufacture	Material is a mixture of asbestos fibre and cement binder. Cisterns shall be matured to ensure effective hydration of the binder. Internal corners shall be radiused.
Marking	Each cistern shall be marked with the manufacturer, BS number, type reference and capacity.
Tests	Tests for water tightness, water absorption and static strength. A test certificate shall be supplied on request.
Other data	Table 1 Cistern sizes.

BS4213: 1975: - Cold water storage cisterns (polyolefin or olefin copolymers) and cistern covers

These cisterns are generally made from either polyethylene or polypropylene.

Size range	10 sizes of cisterns with capacities ranging from 18 to 455 litres.
Manufacture	This standard specifies requirements for both domestic and industrial applications.
	Cisterns used for expansion in hot water heating systems shall be constructed of materials having a Vicat softening point of not less than 110°C. The Vicat test is described in BS2782:1970: - Method 102D.
	Minimum material thickness ranges from 1.4 to 2.1mm according to cistern capacity. For cisterns above 68 litres capacity manufactured from polyethylene of density not less than 0.94g/ml the minimum thickness may be reduced to 1.6mm.
Marking	Each cistern shall be marked with manufacturer, BS number and type reference. A waterproof label shall be attached indicating that the cistern is either 'for cold water storage only' or the cistern is 'for cold water storage or as an expansion cistern'.
Tests	Type testing shall include tests for deformation, deflection, fatigue and Vicat softening point.
	Routine testing shall include tests for impact resistance, tensile properties, reversion, strain and delamination.
Other data	Table 1 Cistern dimensions and masses.
	Appendix L Notes on installation.

Other Related Specifications

BS1125: 1973: - WC flushing cisterns (including dual flush cisterns and flush pipes)

This covers materials, workmanship, design performance of flushing cisterns of 4, 5 and 9 litres capacity.

BS1876: 1972 (1977): - Automatic flushing cisterns for urinals

This specifies requirements for automatic flushing cisterns in a range of capacities from 4.5 to 27 litres for flushing urinals. It includes materials, design and construction and performance requirements.

CP310: 1965: - Water supply

This deals with the supply of water to houses, schools, offices, public and industrial buildings.

MATERIALS

BS Number	Material/Grade	Data Sheet	Comment
417	Low carbon steel	-	Cisterns shall be galvanised to BS729 after manufacture.
2777	Asbestos cement	-	Cement shall be to BS12.
4213	Polyethylene	PL11	Covers high and low density grades.
	Polyethylene	PL12	With addition of carbon black and antioxidant.
	Polyethylene	PL14	With addition of carbon black and antioxidant.

CONNECTIONS

Connections to mild steel cisterns may be by means of bosses, screwed flanges or pads and studs. Connections on mild steel cisterns should be galvanised. Flanges should comply with BS4504. Openings for connections to other cisterns may be cut on site and the connections made with backnuts and plastics washers.

A special adaptor may be used for the pipe connection. This should be compatible with the pipe and cistern material and also suitable for the operating pressure and temperature conditions. Connections should be selected to avoid galvanic action between dissimilar metals. Jointing materials shall comply with Water Authority requirements.

SERVICE CONSIDERATIONS

1.   Galvanised mild steel, asbestos cement and the listed plastics materials are all suitable for the normal applications of cold water storage and as feed and expansion cisterns. The distinctive individual features are:-

     (a) galvanised mild steel cisterns are rugged and have good corrosion resistance properties,

     (b) asbestos cement cisterns are prone to mechanical damage but have good corrosion resistance properties,

     (c) plastics cisterns can be subject to mechanical damage if abused but they have excellent corrosion resistance properties.

   Where aggressive water or specially conditioned water is stored then protective finishes may be necessary. Specialist advice should be sought in such cases.

2.   All sealing/jointing components and protective surface coatings used on cisterns or connections shall comply with the requirements of the Water Authority.

3.   Plastics cisterns shall be located away from heat sources which could cause damage to the plastics.

4.   Any cut edges or exposed metal surfaces in a galvanised cistern should be protected with cold galvanising paint.

Service Considerations Cont'd

5.   Cisterns exposed to freezing conditions should be protected with thermal insulation. Potable water storage should be protected against heat gain otherwise it can become unpalatable.

6.   Back siphonage from the cistern to the supply main must be prevented.

7.   Cisterns should be located where flooding arising from leaks does not create a hazard.

8.   Ball valves or other high pressure type controls on the water inlet shall comply with Water Authority byelaws.

9.   Sterilization procedures shall be carried out as required by the Water Authority.

component data sheet		SHEET NUMBER 3.5.2.	1
FAMILY GROUP TANKS		SUB-GROUP TANKS	

SCOPE

This Data Sheet covers tanks for the bulk storage of cold and hot water and as hot wells. A hot well is a tank which collects condensate from a steam heating or process system.

SPECIFICATIONS

BS1563: 1949 (1964): - Cast-iron sectional tanks (rectangular)

Size range Tanks up to 40 ft square and 12 ft deep.

Manufacture Sections (unit plates) may be 2, 3 or 4 ft square. Tanks can have internal (Type A) or external (Type B) flanges. Tops may be open or closed. Tanks shall be supported under each transverse joint and at the two ends of the tank. They shall be assembled using appropriate tie rods, bolts etc.

The protection requirements of the internal and external tank surfaces from corrosion will depend on the water and environmental conditions. These requirements are to be agreed with the pruchaser.

Marking Plates shall be marked with manufacturer and BS number.

Temperature range Cold liquids up to 38°C
Hot liquids between 38°C and 150°C.

Other data Typical sizes, approximate weights and nominal capacities of tanks are given in:
Tables 6, 7, 8 and 9 2ft square unit plates.
Table 12 3ft square unit plates.
Tables 15 and 16 4ft square unit plates.

BS1564: 1975 (1983): - Pressed steel sectional rectangular tanks

Size range No limit on cross-sectional area is specified but the maximum recommended depth is 4880mm.

Manufacture Tanks are to be built-up of pressed steel flanged plates 1220mm square. The thickness of plates varies with the tank height, the liquid density and the storage temperature.
Tanks shall be supported at 1220mm centres in one direction under each bottom flange. The sides and ends of the tank shall be supported by stays. The top may be open or closed.
The sectional dimensions are interchangeable with the imperial dimensions of the earlier BS1564: 1949 (1964).

The protection requirements of the internal and external tank surfaces from corrosion will depend on the water and environmental conditions. These requirements are to be agreed with the purchaser.

183

Marking	Tanks shall be marked with manufacturer and BS number.
Pressure range	Up to the static head corresponding to the depth of the tank.
Temperature range	Cold liquids up to 38°C.
	Hot liquids between 38°C and 100°C.
Other data	Typical sizes, approximate weights and nominal capacities of tanks are given in:
	Table 1 1220mm deep, plates 5mm thick.
	Table 2 2440mm deep, plates 5mm thick.
	Table 3 3660mm deep, plates 5mm thick.
	Table 4 4880mm deep, plates 5 & 6mm thick.

Other Related Specifications

BS2594: 1975: - Carbon steel welded horizontal cylindrical storage tanks

This specifies design and construction of carbon steel fusion welded horizontal cylindrical storage tanks for above ground and underground use.

BS4994: 1973: - Vessels and tanks in reinforced plastics

This specifies requirements for design, materials, construction, inspection and testing of vessels for pressure and vacuum service. It also covers tanks in reinforced plastics consisting of a polyester or epoxide resin system reinforced with glass fibres and manufactured by the wet lay-up process. It includes constructions both with and without a lining of thermoplastics. There are pressure and volume limitations for pressure and vacuum vessels but no size limitations for tanks subjected only to the hydrostatic head of liquid contents. It includes examples of design calculations and methods of test.

BS5337: 1976: - Code of practice for the structural use of concrete for retaining aqueous liquids

This specifies design and construction of reinforced and prestressed concrete service reservoirs and tanks.

CP310: 1965: - Water supply

Covers the supply of water to houses, schools, offices, public and industrial buildings.

MATERIALS

BS Number	Material/Grade	Data Sheet	Comment
1563	Grey cast-iron /1452-10(150)	FM01	For sectional plates.
1564	Low carbon steel /4360 grade 43A	-	For sectional plates, stays, cleats and pads.
	Low carbon steel /1449-1 HR14	-	For plates, stays, cleats and pads

Materials Cont'd

BS Number	Material/Grade	Data Sheet	Comment
4994	Glass reinforced plastics	PL38-41	For sectional plates
	Rigid PVC	PL17	-
	PVDF		

CONNECTIONS

Connections to mild steel and cast-iron tanks shall be by means of bosses, screwed flanges or pads and studs. Flanges should comply with BS4504. Openings for connections to other tanks may be cut on site and the connections made with backnuts and plastics washers.

A special pipe connection adaptor may be used. The connection should be suitable for the materials of the pipe and tank and for the operating pressure and temperature conditions.

Connections should be selected to avoid galvanic action between dissimilar metals. Jointing materials shall comply with Water Authority requirements.

SERVICE CONSIDERATIONS

1.   The choice between cast-iron or steel tanks is usually based on initial capital cost. Cast-iron normally has a longer life and lower incidence of maitenance but is heavier than steel. Structural concrete is primarily used for very large reservoirs.

2.   All sealing/jointing compounds and materials used in tanks and connections shall comply with the requirements of the Water Authority.

3.   Tank supports and the associated building structure must be of adequate strength to carry the weight of the tank and its contents.

4.   Internal and external surface coatings will generally be required to protect the tank structure and the internal coating will need to be approved by the Water Authority.

5.   Sectional tanks with internal bottom flanges are suitable for siting on level surfaces. Sectional tanks with external flanges are suitable where there is no restriction to external access or where the exterior of the tank is to be lagged.

6.   Tanks exposed to freezing conditions should be protected with thermal insulation. Potable water storage should be protected against heat gain otherwise the water can become unpalatable.

Service Considerations Cont'd

7.   Tanks should be located where flooding or contamination due to leaks is not a serious hazard.

8.   Ball valves or other high pressure type controls on the water inlet shall comply with Water Authority byelaws.

9.   A washout connection complete with isolating valve may be required.

10   Sterilization procedures shall be carried out as required by the Water Authority.

11.   The interior of tanks and ball valves should be easily accessible through inspection and access covers.

12.   Large tanks may require external and internal access ladders.

FAMILY GROUP	TANKS	SUB-GROUP	CYLINDERS

SCOPE

This Data Sheet covers cylinders used for hot water storage of both the direct and indirect type. Cylinders may be constructed of galvanised mild steel or of copper.

A hot water cylinder is a closed vessel in which domestic hot water is stored. A direct cylinder is a cylinder in which the stored water circulates directly to and from the boiler. An indirect cylinder is a cylinder fitted with a separate internal heat exchanger which is independently supplied by a boiler. In a single-feed indirect cylinder the stored water is heated by the separate internal heater but only one feed cistern is required as the feed water to the internal heater is obtained from within the cylinder. In a double-feed indirect cylinder separate feed cisterns are needed for the hot stored water and the internal heater.

Hot water storage combination units may be of the direct, double-feed indirect and single-feed indirect types. When water is drawn off from the hot water storage vessel there is automatically a replacement from a cold water feed cistern incorporated in the unit. Controlled replacement of the water in the cold water feed cistern is from the water supply. No mixing of primary and secondary water occurs in these units.

SPECIFICATIONS

BS417: - Galvanised mild steel cisterns and covers, tanks and cylinders
Part 1: 1964: - Imperial units

Cold and hot water storage vessels for domestic purposes.

Size range   10 sizes of cylinders from 16 to 97 gallons capacity, in three grades.

Manufacture   The materials, workmanship, design and construction, dimensions and tolerances, etc. are described.

Marking   The marking requirements are the test pressure and working head.

Part 2: 1973: - Metric units

Size range   10 sizes of cylinders from 73 to 441 litres capacity.

Manufacture   Cylinders shall be soundly constructed with domed top and bottom. Seams shall be welded or rivetted. A hand hole and immersion heater access may be provided together with replaceable covers.
Three grades of cylinder are specified with plate thickness varying according to capacity. Cylinders shall be galvanised after manufacture.

Marking   Cylinders shall be marked with BS number, reference, grade, thickness, manufacturer, capacity and maximum working head. Marking shall be near the top of cylinder.

Testing	Cylinders shall be pressure tested in accordance with Table 4 and they shall not show any leakage or appreciable distortion. Cylinders shall be marked 'TESTED'.

Grade	Test pressure, kN/m^2	Maximum working head of water, m
A	483	30
B	276	18
C	138	9

Other data	Table 4 Dimensions of cylinders.

BS699: 1984: - Specification for copper direct cylinders for domestic purposes

Size range	16 sizes of cylinders with capacities from 74 to 450 litres.
Manufacture	Seams shall be either: (i) welded and brazed to give 4 times metal thickness, (ii) overlapped by at least 5mm and brazed, (iii) butt welded. Top and bottom ends shall be domed with the bottom end domed inwards. Note: These cylinders are intended for fixing in a vertical position. Blanked off access for an immersion heater may be provided. Cylinders may be provided with factory applied insulation and protector rods.
Marking	Cylinders shall be permanently marked with the BS number, reference, grade and manufacturer. The following marking may be less permanent: maximum working pressure, capacity, thickness of body and ends.
Pressure range	The maximum working heads are:

Grade	head, m
1	25
2	15
3	10
4	6

Testing	Cylinders shall be pressure tested in accordance with Table 1. Cylinders must not show any leak or appreciable permanent distortion at test pressure. A certificate may be provided on request.
Other data	Table 1 Dimensions and details of copper cylinders.

BS1565: - Galvanised mild steel indirect cylinders, annular or saddle-back type
Part 1: 1949: Imperial units

Size range	7 sizes of cylinders in two grades, maximum working heads 30ft to 60ft.
Manufacture	Included are minimum thickness of material, minimum heating surfaces, methods of manufacture, radius of curvature, bolted ends and handholes, method of galvanising, screwed connections for pipes and for auxillary electric heating.

| Tests | Test requirements specified for primary heaters and complete cylinders. |

| Other data | Dimensions are given in a table and drawings illustrate method of measuring these. Reference is also made to information in BS417, BS699 and BS1566. |

Part 2: 1973: - Metric units

| Size range | 8 sizes of cylinders with capacities from 109 to 455 litres. |

| Manufacture | Cylinders shall be welded or rivetted. Cylinders of 227 litres capacity and greater shall be fitted with detachable tops fixed to external mild steel angles welded to the cylinders. Facilities for an immersion heater shall be provided. Cylinders shall be galvanised after manufacture. Handholes may be included on request.
Note: These cylinders are primarily intended for vertical fixing but may be mounted horizontally when supplied in recommended manner. |

| Marking | Cylinders shall be marked with BS number, size number, class, manufacturer, capacity and working head in metres.
The following may be indicated on a label: function of the various connections, current method of horizontal mounting of cylinder, area of primary heating surface. |

| Pressure range | The maximum permissible working heads are:
　　Class B　　　　18m
　　Class C　　　　9m |

| Testing | Primary heaters. pressure tested as specified by Table 1.
Complete cylinder: pressure tested as specified by Table 1.
A test certificate shall be available on request. |

| Other data | Table 1 Dimensions and details of galvanised and mild steel indirect cylinders. |

BS1566: - Copper indirect cylinders for domestic purposes
Part 1: 1984: - Double-feed indirect cylinders

| Size range | 16 sizes of cylinders with capacities from 72 to 440 litres. |

| Manufacture | All seam joints shall be joined by either:
(i)　welting in a manner to give four times the thickness of metal, and brazing,
(ii)　overlapping by not less than 5mm, and brazing,
(iii)　butt weld.

Optional features may include drain tap bosses, fixing provision for combined immersion heaters and thermostats, fixing provision for gas circulator, additional primary heater, factory applied insulation and protector rods.
Note: These cylinders are intended for fixing in a vertical position. |

| Marking | Cylinders shall be marked with BS number, type, reference, grade and manufacturer. A label shall be applied indicating maximum permissible working head of the cylinder and primary heater, capacity, material thickness, maximum length of immersion heater. |

Pressure range	The maximum working heads are:

Grade	head, m
1	25
2	15
3	10
4	6

Testing Primary heaters: pressure tested as specified by Table 1.

Complete cylinder: pressure tested as specified by Table 1.

No leaks or appreciable permanent distortion shall occur at test pressure. A certificate shall be issued on request.

Other data Table 1 Dimensions and details of copper indirect cylinders (coil type)

Part 2: 1984: - Specification for single-feed indirect cylinders

Size range 7 sizes of cylinders with capacities from 90 to 205 litres.

Manufacture All seam joints shall be joined by either:

(i)   welting in a manner to give four times the thickness of metal, and brazing,

(ii) overlapping by not less than 5mm, and brazing,

(iii) butt welding.

Cylinder bases are domed inwards.

Note: These cylinders are intended for fixing in a vertical position.

Marking Cylinders shall be marked with BS number, type, reference, grade and manufacturer.

A label shall be applied indicating: maximum permissible working head, capacity, quantity of primary water, the metal thickness, maximum cylinder length and location of the primary heater.

Pressure range The maximum working heads are:

Grade	head, m
2	18.3
3	9.1

Testing Primary heater shall be tested to a pressure of 14 kN/m^2 before assembly.

Complete cylinder shall be tested at pressures specified by Table 1.

No leaks or appreciable permanent distortion shall occur during tests. A certificate shall be issued on request.

Other data Table 1 Dimensions and details of single-feed copper indirect cylinders.

Table 2 Metric equivalent dimensions and details of single-feed copper indirect cylinders.

BS3198: 1981: - Specification for copper hot water storage combination units for domestic purposes

Size range	Units with hot water storage capabilities from 65 to 180 litres.
Manufacture	All seams shall be joined by either:

(i) welting in a manner which gives four times the thickness of the metal, and brazing,

(ii) overlapping by not less than 5mm, and brazing,

(iii) butt welding.

Marking

(a) Direct units

Each combination unit shall clearly show the BS number, type, hot water storage capacity and manufacturer.

Other additional markings shall be applied including centre line of float operated valve in feed cistern, centre line of warming pipe, float valve type, sheet metal thickness of hot water storage vessel and feed cistern, maximum length of immersion heater and its location.

(b) Double-feed direct units

As for direct units with additional marking including maximum working pressure of heat exchanger, thickness of sheet metal in primary heater, its surface area and the maximum permissible quantity of primary water if a primary feed and expansion cistern is incorporated.

(c) Single-feed indirect units

As for direct units with additional marking including the maximum permissible quantity of primary water excluding the primary heater contents, thickness of metal in primary heater and its surface area.

Tests

Pressure tests required on the complete combination unit and the primary heaters. Storage vessels and primary heaters shall not show any leak or significant permanent distortion at test pressure.

Other data

Table 1 Minimum area of heating surface of primary heater.

MATERIALS

BS Number	Material/Grade	Data Sheet	Comment
417	Low carbon steel		Cylinders shall be galvanised to BS729 after manufacture.
699	Wrought copper /C106	NF 11	This shall be brazed or welded.
	Aluminium /1050A	NF 01	For protector rods.
1565	Low carbon steel		Galvanised after manufacture.

Materials Cont'd

BS Number	Material/Grade	Data Sheet	Comment
1566/1	Wrought copper /2870-C106 2871-C106	NF 11	For sheet and tubes.
1566/2	Wrought copper /2870-C1096	NF 11	For sheet.
	Aluminium /1050A	NF 01	For protector rods.
3198	Wrought copper /2870-C106 2871-C106	NF 11	For sheet and tubes.

CONNECTIONS

The type of pipe connection on cylinders should be suitable for the materials of the pipe and cylinder and for the operating pressure and temperature conditions. Connections should be selected to avoid galvanic action between dissimilar metals. Jointing materials shall comply with Water Authority requirements.

Cylinders to BS417/2 shall be provided with screwed connections, BSP.F parallel thread.

Copper direct cylinders to BS699 shall be provided with BSP.F screwed thread connections. These are normally internal thread connections but external threads may be supplied if ordered.

Other types of indirect cylinders are normally provided with screwed connections. Connections on the shell have internal threads while primary heater connections have external threads.

SERVICE CONSIDERATIONS

1.   Cylinders shall be capable of operating safely at the system design temperatures and pressures and shall be adequately protected against any abnormal or potentially unsafe situation which could arise. By e.g. safety (relief) valve, open vent, fusible plug.

2.   The location of cylinders shall permit proper access for inspection and maintenance including where appropriate space for withdrawal of the primary heater.

3.   Equipment such as safety (relief) valves, pressure or altitude gauge, immersion heaters, thermostatic control, drain cock, etc. should be fitted as appropriate.

4.   Cylinder and system piping materials should be selected to minimise galvanic action. In waters capable of dezincification brass fittings should be of an inhibited grade.

Service Considerations Cont'd

5.   Water treatment may be required where supplies are aggressive or where scaling of the primary heater is likely to occur.

6.   Insulation should be applied to reduce heat loss from heated cylinders and also where necessary to protect against freezing.

7.   Cylinders should be included in maintenance plans.

 **component
data sheet**

SHEET
NUMBER 3.5.4.

1

FAMILY
GROUP   TANKS

SUB-
GROUP   CALORIFIERS

SCOPE

This Data Sheet covers heating and hot water calorifiers of the non-storage and storage types.

A calorifier is a heat exchanger used for the transfer of heat to water in a vessel by indirect means, the source of heat being contained within a pipe, annular coil or element immersed in the water.

A heating calorifier is used primarily for the transfer of heat to a space heating system, usually in a closed circuit. A hot-water calorifier is for transferring heat to open-circuit domestic hot water systems.

A non-storage calorifier is a calorifier with no storage capacity for the heated water. This is usually a heating calorifier. A storage calorifier is a calorifier incorporating capacity for storing heated water from which hot water can be drawn. This is usually a calorifier for domestic hot water use.

The shell of a calorifier may be copper or carbon steel. The heat exchanger tubes or coils may be of copper/copper alloys, aluminium/aluminium alloys, nickel/nickel alloys or stainless steel.

The primary heating medium used in calorifiers may be low, medium or high temperature hot water, heat transfer fluid, steam or electricity.

SPECIFICATIONS

BS853: 1981: - Specification for calorifiers and storage vessels for central heating and hot water supply

This specification covers calorifiers heated by steam, water, heat transfer fluid or electricity.

Size range	No limits are stated in the specification.
Manufacture	The shell may be carbon steel or copper. There are two grades of calorifier, Grade A which is for higher pressures than Grade B. Grade A calorifiers shall be manufactured in accordance with established welding procedures using approved welders. Grade B calorifiers shall be manufactured using competent welders but specific welding procedures and welder approved tests are not required.
Marking	Calorifiers shall be marked on a metal plate with: manufacturer, shell thickness, design pressures of primary and secondary sides, hydraulic test pressures of both the primary and secondary sides, date of hydraulic test, BS number and grade. If bolts or studs having a tensile strength greater than 392N/mm^2 are used this shall be indicated on a separate adjacent plate.

Pressure range   The working pressures in the shell shall not exceed:

                 Grade A $0.7N/mm^2$

                 Grade B $0.45N/mm^2$

                 The design pressure of the tube battery shall not exceed:

                 Grade A $1.75N/mm^2$

                 Grade B $0.45N/mm^2$

                 For a vessel fitted with an open vent the secondary design pressure shall be equal to
                 the secondary working pressure providing that the working head, including the effect of
                 horizontal vent sections, does not exceed 25m.

Temperature range Shell temperatures shall not exceed:

                 Grade A   120°C

                 Grade B   90°C

                 Tube temperatures shall not exceed:

                 Grade A   300°C

                 Grade B   300°C

Testing   An hydraulic test is required. A test certificate shall be issued with the calorifier to
                 certify that it meets the construction and test requirements.

Other data   Table 1   Material recommended for construction of calorifiers with their stated design
                           stress.

                 Table 2   Filler and brazing materials, forgings and hot pressing stock, bolt and nut
                           materials.

BS3274: 1960: - Tubular heat exchangers for general purposes

Size range   Shell diameters of 6 to 42 inches.

                 Tube lengths of 6 to 16 feet.

                 Tube diameters of 0.5 to 1.5 inches.

Manufacture   For cylindrical shell calorifiers with plain tubes the heat exchangers shall be
                 manufactured in accordance with the relevant clauses and parts of BS5500. These
                 requirements depend on the materials used in the construction. The types of tube battery
                 are:

                     Type 1: fixed tube-plates (non-removable tube bundle),

                     Type 2: U-tube (removable tube bundle),

                     Type 3: floating head (removable tube bundle).

Marking   Nameplates made of corrosion resistant material shall indicate manufacturer, serial
                 number, design pressure and test pressure for both shell and tubes, 'SR' if stress
                 relieved, 'XR' if radiographed, BS number and any additional agreed information.

                 Shell cover, floating head cover and channel shall be marked with the serial number of
                 the heat exchanger.

Testing   Each part shall be hydraulically tested to the pressure specified in Table 9. Test
                 certificates shall be supplied for the hydraulic testing and may be supplied for the
                 materials of construction.

Pressure range   The pressure classification is in 6 steps based on design pressures ranging from 20 to 600 lb/in^2. When a standard heat exchanger is used at temperatures higher or lower than those given for the particular material the design pressure shall be determined from the properties of the material (see BS 5500).

Other data

Table	1	Minimum shell thickness.
Table	2	Standard tube diameters and minimum nominal thickness.
Table	3	Minimum tube plate thickness
Table	10	Testing procedure for basic type of heat exchanger.
Table	11	Design stresses: copper and copper alloys.
Table	12	Design stresses: aluminium and aluminium alloys.
Table	13	Design stresses: nickel and nickel alloys.
Table	14	Design stresses: stainless steel.

Other Related Specifications

BS5500: 1985: - Unfired fusion welded pressure vessels

This contains materials and design stresses, design calculations, manufacturing procedures, tolerances, welding, inspection, non-destructive and pressure testing for pressure vessels and this covers many applications of calorifiers.

MATERIALS

Materials for use in the construction of the components of calorifiers are listed in BS 853 and BS 3274. These standards list the grades and specifications of a wide range of materials which may be used and the reader is referred to these standards for specific selection information.

CONNECTIONS

The pipe connections on calorifiers should be suitable for the material of the pipe and calorifier and also for the operating pressure and temperature conditions, particularly on the primary heating side. Flanges should comply with BS4504.

Connections should be selected to avoid galvanic action between dissimilar metals. Jointing materials shall comply with Water Authority requirements.

SERVICE CONSIDERATIONS

1. The calorifier shall be capable of operating safely at the design temperatures and pressures and shall be adequately protected against any abnormal or potentially unsafe situations which could arise with for example safety (relief) valves, open vents, fusible plugs.

2. The location of calorifiers shall permit proper access for inspection and maintenance including where appropriate space for withdrawal of the primary heater.

3. Equipment such as safety (relief) valves, pressure or altitude gauge, immersion heaters, thermostatic control, drain cock, etc. should be fitted as appropriate.

4. Calorifier and system piping materials should be selected to minimise galvanic action. In waters capable of dezincification inhibited grade brass fittings should be selected.

5. Water treatment may be required where water supplies are aggressive or where scaling of the primary heater is likely to occur.

6. Insulation should be applied to the vessel to reduce heat loss and where necessary it should be protected from the ingress of moisture or freezing.

7. Calorifiers should be included in maintenance schedules.

BSRIA	**component data sheet**		Sheet Number 3.5.5.	1
Family Group	TANKS	Sub-Group	EXPANSION VESSELS	

SCOPE

This Data Sheet covers closed vessels used to accommodate the expansion of water in a closed hot water and chilled water systems.

An expansion vessel is a closed vessel for accommodating the thermal expansion of water in a pressurised hot water heating system or in a chilled water system. A membrane expansion vessel is an expansion vessel in which the expansion of the fluid compresses a membrane against a pre-pressurised volume of gas. The charge of gas may be air, nitrogen or inert gas. The type of expansion vessel where the charge of gas is in direct contact with the fluid without a separating membrane is no longer in common use.

SPECIFICATIONS

BS4814: 1976: - Specification for expansion vessels using an internal diaphragm for sealed hot water heating
        systems

Designation   Expansion vessels are available in two grades, 1 and 2, according to their maximum working pressure and form a construction.

Pressure range   Grade 1 - intended for maximum working pressures up to 7 bar. They have cylindrical or
                             spherical shapes.
                 Grade 2 - intended for maximum working pressures up to 3 bar.

Temperature range All materials of construction must satisfy the working temperature of the system. Membrane materials may have a reduced life at elevated temperatures.

Manufacture   Grade 1 - vessels shall be constructed by welding or mechanical joints, clenched joints
                            are not permitted.
                 Grade 2 - constructed in accordance with BS1500, Part 1.

Marking   Firmly affixed label showing BS number, manufacturer, total vessel volume, manufacturers charging pressure, maximum vessel working pressure, maximum vessel temperature and other relevant information.

BS6144: 1981: - Specification for expansion vessels using an internal diaphragm for unvented hot water supply
        systems

MATERIALS

BS Number	Material/Grade	Data Sheet	Comment
4814	Carbon steel /BS1500-1 /BS1499-1	- -	Plate, sheet and strip with a minimum tensile strength of 275 N/mm^2 and of a welding quality. Rimming steel and grades HR15 or HS15 shall not be used.

198

Materials Cont'd

BS Number	Material/Grade	Data Sheet	Comment
	Elastomeric materials	-	Suitable for the membrane at the stated maximum vessel temperature.
	Butyl	-	Sheet for membrane.

CONNECTIONS

The type of connection on expansion vessels for piping should be suitable for the pressure and temperature condition and the operating conditions in service.

Method	BS Number	Component Data Sheet	Notes
Flanged	10	3.2.1	Imperial sizes.
	4504	3.2.1	Metric sizes.
Screwed	21	3.2.2	Threads to BS21.
Capillary	864/2	3.2.3	
Compression	864/2	3.2.4	
	2051/1		

SERVICE CONSIDERATIONS

1.   Correct sizing of the expansion vessel is very important as it controls the relationship between fill pressure and operating pressure.

2.   Higher system operating pressures allow the use of higher temperatures and smaller pipes and heating surfaces.

3.   Entry of air into the unvented system is limited and some corrosion problems are avoided.

4.   Large systems may require a filling unit comprising a tank with a floor valve and pump to ensure that the system remains pressurised. A pressure switch normally activates the pump to maintain a minimum pressure at the highest point.

SCOPE

This Data Sheet covers column and panel type radiators.

A radiator is a unit supplied with a hot fluid or electricity which provides space heating through warming air by both convection and radiation. Typically about 70% of the heat emission is by convection.

Column radiators are mostly cast iron but are available in cast or extruded aluminium. They are built-up from sections each containing one or more separate fluid passages. Panel radiators are made from sheet indented to form fluid passages. They are usually constructed of pressed steel and may have fins added to increase the surface area.

The heating medium is generally low temperature hot water but suitably constructed radiators may use low pressure steam. Electrically heated radiators are usually oil-filled.

SPECIFICATIONS

BS3528: 1977: - Specification for convection type space heaters operating with steam or hot water.

This defines the equipment and procedure to be used for determining the heat output of convection type space heaters including radiators which operate with steam or hot water.

Other Related Specifications

BS2767: 1972: - Valves and unions for hot water radiators

BS5449: Code of practice for central heating for domestic premises
Part 1: 1977: - Forced circulation hot water systems

BS6284: 1983: - Specification for thermostatic radiator valves

CP341.300-307: 1956: - Central heating by low pressure hot water
        304 - Appliances (column radiators)

MATERIALS

BS Number	Material/Grade	Data Sheet	Comment
1490	Aluminium alloy /LM2	NF04	For cast sections
1474	/6063		For extruded sections
3528	Cast iron /1452-12	FM01	For cast sections
-	Steel /1449-CR1-4	-	For steel sheet for panel radiators

CONNECTIONS

The type of connection should be suitable for:

(1) working pressure,

(ii) operating temperature,

(iii) heating fluid,

(iv) mechanical strength required under service conditions,

(v) specification requirements.

Method	BS Number	Component Data Sheet	Notes
Screwed	21	3.2.2	Threads to BS21

SERVICE CONSIDERATIONS

1. Cast iron radiators are of rugged construction and have established long service life but are more expensive to install than aluminium and steel panel radiators. Some occurances of early failures have occurred with steel panel radiators but most have lives up to 30 years without evidence of deterioration. The long term characteristics of aluminium radiators have not yet been established.

2. Radiators must be capable of operating at the temperature and pressure of the system.

3. Radiators must be mounted so that an adequate air path can pass around them. Entrained dust in the convection currents may cause discolouration to decoration.

4. Radiators shall be supported so that there is no adverse stress on the flow and return pipework.

5. On a two-pipe heating system each radiator should be provided with a lock-shield valve on the return connection for balancing and a control valve on the flow connection. Each radiator should be capable of isolation for maintenance and replacement purposes. An air vent cock should be available at an accessible point on the top of the radiator.

6. Corrosion of radiators should be prevented by chemically treating the water, preventing the ingress of air into the water and taking adequate precautions to prevent dissimilar metal connections that would promote galvanic corrosion. Manufacturers instructions should be followed such as iron nipples between copper pipe and cast aluminium radiators.

7. Deposits in the bottom of steel radiators should be removed as they promote micro-biological attack.

8. Excessive flow rates should be avoided as they may cause an unacceptable noise level and can also promote erosion/corrosion if the metal threshold velocity is exceeded.

9. Radiators have the advantage of being robust, relatively cheap and providing a radiant component of heat emission which can have comfort benefits.

 component
data sheet

SHEET
NUMBER   3.6.2.   1

FAMILY
GROUP   HEAT EMITTERS

SUB-
GROUP   NATURAL CONVECTORS

SCOPE

This Data Sheet covers natural convectors.

A natural convector comprises a heat exchanger normally a finned tube type, which is positioned inside a vented casing. The heat exchanger is supplied with a hot fluid and provides the thermal forces to draw air into the casing and to discharge it into the heated space. Natural convectors include units described as continuous convectors and skirting heaters which provide heating by means of continuous low height heating units sited along the walls near floor level.

The heating medium is generally low temperature hot water but may be medium temperature hot water or low pressure steam. Electrical heating elements can also be used in place of the finned tube heat exchanger.

SPECIFICATIONS

BS3528: 1977: - Specification for convection type space heaters operating with steam or hot water

This defines the equipment and procedure to be used for determining the heat output of convection type space heaters operating with steam or hot water.

Other Related Specifications

BS5449: Code of practice for central heating for domestic premises
Part 1: 1977: - Forced circulation hot water systems

CP341.300-307: 1956: - Central heating by low pressure hot water
        304 - Appliances (convectors)

MATERIALS

BS Number	Materials/Grade	Data Sheet	Comment
-	Aluminium /1050A	NF01	For convector tube fins
	Wrought copper /C106	NF11	For convector tubes
	Steel		For convector tube and fins.

CONNECTIONS

The type of connection should be suitable for:

(i)   working pressure,

(ii) operating temperature,

(iii) heating fluid,

(iv) mechanical strength required under service conditions,

(v)   specification requirements.

Method	BS Number	Component Data Sheet	Notes
Flanged	10	3.2.1	Imperial sizes
	4504	3.2.1	Metric sizes
Screwed	21	3.2.2	Threads to BS21
Capillary	864	3.2.3	
Compression	864	3.2.4	
	2051	3.2.4	

SERVICE CONSIDERATIONS

1.   The particular advantages of convectors are that they can provide long lengths of heat emission under single control. They can also separate at higher fluid pressures than radiators

2.   Continuous convector casings can provide a more pleasing appearaance than radiators or radiant panels but they are generally less rugged.

3.   Natural convectors must be capable of operating at the temperature and pressure of the system.

4.   Natural convectors must be mounted so that an adequate airflow can pass across the heating surfaces to achieve rated output. Entrained dust in the convection currents may cause discolouration to decoration.

5.   Natural convectors shall be supported so that there is no adverse stress on the flow and return pipework.

6.   On a two-pipe heating system each natural convector should be provided with a lock shield valve for balancing on the return connection and a control valve on the flow connection. Each natural convector should be capable of isolation for maintenance and replacement purposes. An air vent cock should be available at an accessible high level point.

7.   Steam convectors should be adequately and correctly trapped.

Service Considerations Cont'd

8.   Enclosures or guards shall be provided to protect people from contact with high temperature surfaces.

9.   Corrosion of heat emitters should be prevented by chemically treating the heating fluid, preventing the ingress of air into the water and taking adequate precautions to prevent dissimilar metal connections that would promote galvanic corrosion.

10.   Excessive flowrates should be avoided as they may cause an unacceptable noise level and can also promote erosion/corrosion if the metal threshold velocity is exceeded.

11.   Provision should be made for expansion/contraction especially when continuous convectors are employed.

| FAMILY GROUP | HEAT EMITTERS | SUB-GROUP | RADIANT HEATERS |

SCOPE

This Data Sheet covers radiant panel, radiant strip and radiant skirting heaters.

A radiant heater is an appliance where the effective heat output is in the form of radiant energy typically about 65% of the total output.

The radiant panel is a substantially flat radiating surface connected to a source of heat. When supplied with hot water or steam it normally consists of steel tube or cast-iron water ways attached to a radiating surface. A radiant strip heater is a radiant panel of elongated form. When supplied with hot water or steam it consists of one or more pipes attached to an emissive radiant surface. A radiant skirting heater provides room heating by means of continuous low height radiant panels sited along the wall near floor level.

The heating medium for radiant panel or strip may be low, medium or high temperature hot water or steam; the medium for radiant skirting is usually low pressure hot water. Electrically heated and gas-fired radiant heaters are also available.

SPECIFICATIONS

None

Related Specifications

CP341.300-307: 1956: - Central heating by low pressure hot water
     304 - Appliances (surface panels)

MATERIALS

BS Number	Material/Grade	Data Sheet	Comment
-	Carbon steel /320	FM11	BS1387 medium grade steel pipe for low and medium temperature hot water systems. Heavy grade should be used for high temperature hot water and for steam systems.
	/360	FM12	As for /320 grade.
	/sheet	-	The grade of sheet steel must satisfy the mechanical requirements of radiant panel and strip heaters.
	Aluminium alloy		Reflectors for strip heaters and for gas and electrical appliances.
-	Wrought copper /C106	NF11	For low temperature hot water radiant curling panels.

CONNECTIONS

The connections for radiant heaters should be suitable for:

(i) working pressure,

(ii) operating temperature,

(iii) heating fluid,

(iv) mechanical strength required under service conditions,

(v) specification requirments.

Method	BS Number	Component Data Sheet	Notes
Flanged	10	3.2.1	Imperial sizes
	4504	3.2.1	Metric sizes
Screwed	21	3.2.2	Threads to BS21
Capillary	864	3.2.3	
Compression	864	3.2.4	
	2051	3.2.4	

SERVICE CONSIDERATIONS

1. Radiant systems provide efficient heating where there are relatively high rates of natural ventilation, e.g. factories and warehouses with outside loading and access doors.

2. High level radiant heaters release the use of valuable floor and wall space for other purposes. The height, spacing and angle of inclination of the panels or strip should be selected to obtain required radiant heat distribution.

3. Radiant heaters must be capable of operating at the temperature and pressure of the heating system.

4. Radiant heaters shall be supported so that there is no adverse stress on the flow and return pipework.

5. On a two-pipe heating system each radiant panel should be provided with a balancing valve on the return connection and a control valve on the flow connection. Each panel should be capable of isolation for maintenance and replacement purposes and provided with facilities for air venting and draining.

6. Steam radiant panels should be adequately and correctly trapped.

7. Panels must be mounted or guarded to protect people from contact with high temperature surfaces.

Service Considerations Cont'd

8.   Internal corrosion of heat emitters should be prevented by chemically treating the
        water, stopping the ingress of air into the water and taking adequate precautions to
        prevent dissimilar metal connections that would promote galvanic corrosion.

9.   Excessive flow rates should be avoided as they may cause an unacceptable noise level and
        can also promote erosion/corrosion if the metal threshold velocity is exceeded.

10.   To reduce losses from radiant heaters the back should be well insulated.

11.   Where multiple pipes are used on radiant strips they should be fed in parallel to avoid
        problems due to differential expansion.

12.   The choice of medium and its temperature is dependent on the mounting location relative
        to the occupants and this will determine the material and method of connection.

FAMILY GROUP	HEAT EMITTERS	SUB-GROUP	FAN CONVECTORS

SCOPE

This Data Sheet covers fan convectors and unit heaters.

A fan convector uses a fan to project air through a casing which contains a heat exchanger which is normally heated by hot water or steam. The range of capacity can vary from that required to heat a small room, to serve a large area, a number of rooms or even a complete building. A unit heater is a forced circulation convector mounted overhead with horizontal or downward discharge. A unit heater uses a large propeller or centrifugal fan to give high air volume flow rates and some control over the direction of the throw of the heated air.

The heating medium for fan convectors and unit heaters may be low, medium or high temperature hot water, steam or electricity. The choice is dependent on location, output and required leaving air temperature.

SPECIFICATIONS

<u>BS4856: - Methods for testing and rating fan coil units, unit heaters and unit coolers</u>
<u>Part 1: 1972: -Thermal and volumetric performance for heating duties; without additional ducting</u>

This Standard deals with methods of carrying out thermal and volumetric flow rate tests on forced convection fluid to air heat exchangers which incorporate their own fans. The units are for heating application and the tests are carried out on units in an essentially clean condition.

<u>Part 3: 1975: - Thermal and volumetric performance for heating and cooling duties; with additional ducting</u>

Similar to Part 1 but relates to units intended for use with additional ducting.

<u>Other Related Standards</u>

<u>BS4856: - Methods for testing and rating fan coil units, unit heaters and unit coolers</u>
<u>Part 4: 1978: - Acoustic performance; without additional ducting</u>
<u>Part 5: 1979: - Acoustic performance; with ducting</u>

<u>CP341.300-307: 1956: - Central heating by low pressure hot water</u>

MATERIALS

BS Number	Material/Grade	Data Sheet	Comment
-	Carbon steel /320	FM11	BS1387 heavyweight pipe for high temperature hot water and steam systems.
	/360	FM12	Same as for grade /320.
1449	-	-	Sheet steel for casings, fan blades and fins. Grade should be selected to suit fabrication techniques, and corrosion resistance requirements.
	Copper /C106	NF11	BS2871, Part 3. Used for heat exchanger pipes, fins and headers for convectors served by high temperature hot water and steam systems.
	Aluminium	NF01	Fins on heat exchangers.

CONNECTIONS

The fan convector connections should be suitable for:

(i)   working pressure,

(ii) operating temperature,

(iii) heating fluid,

(iv) mechanical strength required under service conditions,

(v)   specification requrements.

Method	BS Number	Component Data Sheet	Notes
Flanged	10	3.2.1	Imperial sizes
	4504	3.2.1	Metric sizes
Screwed	21	3.2.2	Threads to BS21

SERVICE CONSIDERATIONS

1.   Fan convectors provide higher intensities of heat output than radiators or natural convectors.

2.   Fan convectors must be capable of operating at the temperature and pressure of the primary heating system.

3.   Fan convectors should be supported so that there is no adverse stress on the flow and return pipework.

Service Considerations Cont'd

4.   The height and spacing of unit heaters should be selected with care to ensure that the required heat distribution is achieved.

5.   On a two-pipe heating system each fan convector should be provided with a balancing valve on the return connection and a control valve on the flow connections. Each fan convector should be capable of isolation for maintenance and replacement purposes and provided with facilities for air venting and draining.

6.   Steam heated fan convectors should be adequately and correctly trapped.

7.   Fan convectors must be mounted or guarded to protect people from contact with high temperature surfaces.

8.   Internal corrosion of heat emitters should be prevented by chemically treating the water, stopping the ingress of air into the water and taking adequate precautions to prevent dissimilar metal connections that would promote galvanic corrosion.

9.   Fan convectors handling dirty or dusty air should be provided with air filters.

10.   Fans should incoporate antivibration mountings.

11.   All fan convectors and associated controls should be included in the plant maintenance programme.

12.   Excessive heating hot water flow rates should be avoided as they may produce noise and can also promote erosion/corrosion if the water threshold velocity is exceeded. Fan and air noise must be considered in locations where there is continuous occupancy.

13.   Thermal cutout should be provided to avoid discharging air at an unaccceptably low temperature.

FAMILY GROUP	HEAT GENERATORS	SUB-GROUP	CAST IRON

SCOPE

The Data Sheet covers cast-iron boilers with a rated output of 44kW and above for central heating and indirect hot water supply.

A cast-iron sectional boiler is a boiler built-up of component sections each having individual integral waterways. The sections are generally produced in several standardised size ranges and the rated output of the boiler is determined by the number of sections incorporated. A cast-iron packaged boiler is a boiler fabricated and delivered in a minimum number of units designed to expedite installation and commissioning. It normally incorporates its ancillary equipment.

SPECIFICATIONS

BS779: 1976: - Cast-iron boilers for central heating and indirect hot water supply (44kW rating and above)

Scope   This Standard applies to cast-iron boilers of the following types:
(a) low pressure steam boilers,
(b) hot water central heating boilers for use in open systems,
(c) hot water central heating boilers for use in pressurised systems.

Size range   44kW output rating and above.

Manufacture   Boilers or boiler sections require the following test procedures to be carried out:

(a) Each type of boiler section type shall be subjected to a hydraulic pressure type test of $1.4N/mm^2$ or four times the maximum operating pressure, whichever is the greater, for a period of thirty minutes. In addition each boiler section shall withstand a pressure test of $0.7N/mm^2$, or twice the maximum operating pressure + $0.35N/mm^2$, whichever is the greater, for one minute plus the time needed for visual inspection.

(b) At least one assembled boiler of each design shall be subjected to a type test which comprises a pressure test of $1.05N/mm^2$ or twice the maximum operating pressure + $0.35N/mm^2$, whichever is the greater, for thirty minutes.

Duty   (a) For steam boilers an operating pressure not exceeding $0.1N/mm^2$ when the safety valve setting does not exceed $0.12N/mm^2$.
Note: Welded steel drums used on cast-iron steam boilers shall comply with BS855 except that the hydraulic test pressure need not exceed $0.24N/mm^2$.

(b) For hot water central heating boilers for use in open systems an operating temperature not exceeding 100°C with the boiler operating pressure not exceeding $0.35N/mm^2$ unless substantiated by approved tests.

(c) For hot water central heating boilers for use in pressurised systems an operating pressure not exceeding $0.35N/mm^2$ unless substantiated by approved test. The flow temperature shall be at least 17°C below the saturated steam temperature equivalent to the minimum system pressure.

Marking   The boiler shall be durably and clearly marked with manufacturer, BS799:1976, rated continuous output with the number of sections to which the output refers, fuel rate and type where applicable.

Steam boilers, boilers for pressurised systems, and open vented boilers designed to operate at pressures over $0.35MN/mm^2$ shall in addition be marked with hydraulic test pressure, date of hydraulic test, design pressure.

Test   Each assembled boiler or boiler section shall be hydraulically tested before despatch in the presence of a representative of the manufacturer or an inspecting authority.
A certificate shall be supplied if required.

Other Data

Table 1	Performance
Table 2	Sizes of safety valves
Table 3	Minimum cross-section of vent pipes
Appendix A	Categories of boilers

Other Related Specifications

BS749: - Underfeed stokers

BS759: - Valves, gauges and other safety fittings for application to boilers and to piping installations for and in connection with boilers

BS799: - Oil burning equipment

BS845: - Acceptance tests for industrial type boilers and steam generators

BS1374: - Recommendations on the use of British Standard log sheets for steam and hot water boiler plant

BS2455: - Methods for sampling and examining deposits from boilers and associated industrial plant

BS2486: - Recommendations for treatment of water for land boilers

BS5978: - Safety and performance of gas-fired hot water boilers (60kW to 2MW input)

BS6644: - Installation of gas-fired hot water boilers of rated inputs between 60kW and 2MW

DD65: - Methods of type testing boilers for thermal performance

 component data sheet

MATERIALS

The quality of material for cast-iron boilers shall be as follows:

(a) The minimum grade of cast-iron used in the manufacture of the boiler pressure bearing parts shall be Grade 12 of BS1452.
Note: In the new version of BS1452 the approximate equivalent of Grade 12 is Grade 180.

(b) Refractory materials used in the construction and assembly of the boiler or boiler components shall be suitable for the operating conditions.

In addition bolts, nuts and set screws shall be of steel having a minimum tensile strength of $430N/mm^2$ and the sulphur or the phosphorous content shall not exceed 0.05%.

Note: The welding of defects shall not be permitted in castings in positions subjected to pressure or of lugs securing sections.

CONNECTIONS

The type of connection must be suitable for the operating pressure and temperature, the hot water or steam conditions and the required mechanical strength.

Method	BS Number	Component Data Sheet	Comment
Flanged	10	3.2.1	Imperial sizes.
	4504		Metric sizes.
Screwed	-	3.2.2	Threads to BS21.

SERVICE CONSIDERATIONS

1. Cast iron boilers have applications for low temperature hot water and low pressure steam heating and hot water services.

2. For the same output sectional boilers are generally larger than other types. However the delivery of such boilers in sections permits installation in boiler rooms offering only limited means of access.

3. Sectional boilers may be extended to cover an increase in output by adding further sections.

4. In the event of a section failure only the failed section needs to be replaced to repair the boiler.

Service Considerations Cont'd

5.   Boiler output should cover the maximum estimated requirements of the system plus the appropriate margin. Consideration should be given to standby requirements and arrangements for operating during winter and summer. Boiler configurations can vary from a single boiler to several smaller boilers that can be fired as load requirements vary.

6.   Adequate air supply is required for efficient boiler operation. This may be by natural vents or forced air supply to the boiler house. Extra ventilating air may be required to maintain the boiler house at a comfortable temperature.

7.   Solid fuel boilers require provision for the removal and disposal of ash.

8.   The boiler and flue materials should be compatible with the products of combustion to minimise corrosion.

9.   Flues and chimneys must satisfy the statutory requirements concerned with the location and discharge of products of combustion.

10.   Access to boiler internals and flues is necessary for cleaning and inspection.

11.   Boilers shall be provided with safety valves or vent pipes, pressure gauge, thermometers and emptying valve. Steam boilers should also have an inspector's test gauge connection, two water gauges with test valves and a stop valve.

12.   Automatic controls shall be suitable for the type of boiler, steam or hot water, the fuel type and method of firing. See also Section 6 of BS779.

13.   Boiler plant together with associated fuel storage and distribution, chimneys and flues, firing equipment and automatic and safety controls shall be included in a comprehensive maintenance programme.

14.   Operating and service manuals should be provided for the particular boiler plant and accessories installed.

FAMILY GROUP	HEAT GENERATORS	SUB-GROUP	WELDED STEEL

SCOPE

This Data Sheet covers welded steel boilers for central heating and indirect hot water supply, with a rated output from 44kW to 3MW.

SPECIFICATIONS

BS855: 1976: - Welded steel boilers for central heating and indirect hot water supply (rated output 44kW to 3MW)

Scope This applies to welded steel boilers for central heating and indirect hot water supply except where the cylindrical shell is over 2m diameter. It also covers boiler mountings and appliances with automatic safety controls which are not necessarily supplied by the boiler manufacturer. Steam boilers are included but hot water boilers pressurised by steam are excluded.

Size range Rated output 44kW to 3MW.

Manufacture The shells shall not be formed from more than two plates bent to cylindrical form. The bending shall be done by machine and local heating or hammering shall not be used. All end plates, crown plates and tube plates shall be of one piece and shall be made from one rolled plate. Plain tubes and stay tubes shall be secured by means of expanding and/or welding. Access shall be by at least one manhole or headhole. Fusion welding process may be used providing that the welds are made in exact conformity with approved procedures by welder or welding machine operators whose competence has been established.

Duty

Type	Output kW min-max	Maximum conditions		
		operating pressure N/mm^2	working temperature °C	design pressure N/mm^2
Steam boilers	45-1500	0.20	132	0.23
Externally pressurised hot water boilers	45-3000	0.45	132	0.52
Vented hot water boilers	45-3000	0.45	100	0.52

Marking The boiler shall be durably and clearly marked with manufacturer, inspecting authority, hydraulic test pressure, date of hydraulic test, design pressure, BS855:1976, and rated continuous output with the number of sections to which the output refers.

Test On the completion of welding each boiler shall be hydraulically tested to 1.5 times the design pressure but with a minimum value of $0.414N/mm^2$.

A certificate shall be supplied if required.

Other data Table 1 Design pressures and flow temperatures.

        Table 2 Design stresses.

        Table 3 & 9 Minimum thickness of shells.

        Table 8 Minimum thickness of plain tubes.

        Table 10 Sizes of safety valves.

        Table 13 Sizes of emptying valves or cocks.

        Table 14 Size of vent pipe connections.

        Appendix B Categories of boilers.

Other Related Specifications

BS749: - Underfeed stokers

BS759: - Valves, gauges and other safety fittings for application to boilers and to piping installations for and in connection with boilers

BS799: - Oil burning equipment

BS1113: - Water tube steam generating plant

BS1501: - Steels for fired and unfired pressure vessels. Plates

BS1502: - Steels for fired and unfired pressure vessels. Sections and bars

BS1971: - Corrugated furnaces for shell boilers

BS2790: - Specification for shell boilers of welded construction

BS3059: - Steel boiler and superheater tubes

BS3602: - Specification for steel pipes and tubes for pressure purposes: carbon and carbon manganese steel with specified elevated temperature properties

BS6644: - Installation of gas-fired hot water boilers of rated inputs between 60kW and 2MW

BS6759: - Safety valves

MATERIALS

Subject to agreement between the purchaser and the manufacturer suitable carbon or carbon manganese steels other than those listed may be used.

Steel bolts, nuts and set screws shall have a minimum tensile strength of $430N/mm^2$. The sulphur or the phospherous content shall not exceed 0.05%

Materials Cont'd

BS Number	Material/Grade	Data Sheet	Comment
855	Carbon steel		
	/1501-151	FM08	For boiler plates. These shall be Class A or B but
	/1501-161	FM09	with minimum grades of 400A or B.
	/1502-151	FM08	For sections and bars.
	/1502-161	FM09	For sections and bars.
BS3059, Part 1		-	For plain tubes and stay tubes. These shall be seamless or electric resistance welded tubes.
BS3601 and BS3602, Part 2	410S 410HFS or CFS	-	For seamless steel cross tubes and uptake tubes.

CONNECTIONS

The type of connection must be suitable for the operating pressure and temperature, the hot water or steam conditions and the required mechanical strength.

Method	BS Number	Component Data Sheet	Comment
Flanged	10	3.2.1	Imperial sizes.
	4504		Metric sizes.
Screwed	-	3.2.2	Threads to BS21.

SERVICE CONSIDERATIONS

1.   These welded steel boilers have applications for low and medium temperature hot water and low pressure steam heating and indirect hot water services.

2.   Boiler output should cover the maximum estimated requirements of the system plus the appropriate margin. Consideration should be given to standby requirements and arrangements for operating during winter and summer. Boiler configurations can vary from a single boiler to several smaller boilers that can be fired as load requirements vary.

3.   Adequate air supply to the boiler house is required for efficient boiler operation. This may be provided by natural or forced air supply means.

4.   The boiler and flue materials should be compatible with the products of combustion to minimize corrosion.

5.   Flues and chimneys must satisfy the statutory requirements concerned with the location and discharge of products of combustion.

6.   Access to tubes and flues is necessary for cleaning, inspection and maintenance.

7.   Sufficient inspection and cleaning holes of adequate size shall be provided.

8.   Boilers shall be provided with safety valves, pressure gauges and emptying valves. Steam boilers shall also have an inspector's test gauge connection, two water gauges with test valves, and a stop valve.

9.   Low temperature open vented hot water boilers should have an opening(s) to which a vent pipe may be fitted.

10.   Pressurised and open vented hot water boilers should be provided with a thermometer.

11.   A low water alarm and where practicable fusible plugs shall be fitted to hand-fired steam boilers.

12.   Automatic controls shall be suitable for the type of boiler, the fuel type and method of firing. See also Section 7 of BS855.

13.   Boiler plant together with associated fuel storage and distribution, chimneys and flues, firing equipment and automatic and safety controls shall be included in a comprehensive maintenance programme.

14.   Operating and service manuals should be provided with the particular boiler plant and accessories installed.

 **component data sheet**

| FAMILY GROUP | HEAT GENERATORS | SUB-GROUP | SHELL |

SCOPE

This Data Sheet covers shell boilers of welded construction to BS2790.

This standard deals with boilers of cylindrical or vertical design constructed by fusion welding which are intended for use to provide steam or hot water above 120°C.

SPECIFICATIONS

BS2790: 1982: - British Standard Specification for shell boilers of welded construction

Scope	This specifies requirements for the materials, design, workmanship, inspection and testing of directly fired and waste heat boilers. The boilers dealt with are of cylindrical or vertical design constructed from carbon or carbon manganese steels by fusion welding to class I, class II or class III requirements. They are intended for land use to provide steam or hot water above 120°C. This standard does not apply to water tube boilers nor to boilers of the locomotive type.
Size range	No size limitations stipulated.
Manufacture	The design shall be in accordance with Section 3 of the Standard. In particular the formulae dealing with the calculation of scantlings shall apply to boilers that are operated under the conditions outlined in Appendix D.
	Note: It is intended that boilers delivered in accordance with this Standard should be operated under conditions free from internal scale. This requires suitable feedwater treatment to be used.
	The workmanship and construction other than welding shall be in accordance with Section 4. The welding shall be in accordance with Section 5; details of requirements for heat treatment are given in clause 5.5.
Marking	Each boiler shall be permanently marked with the name and domicile of the manufacturer, design pressure, year of manufacture, date of hydraulic test and the test pressure, mark of the Inspecting Authority, the British Standard, class of boiler and any other mark required by statute in the country of operation.
Tests	Non-destructive testing requirements are detailed in clause 5.6. These shall be used for acceptance purposes for class I and class II boilers but non-destructive testing is not required for class III boilers. Acceptance criteria for weld defects revealed by visual examination and non-destructive testing shall be as set out in clause 5.7.
	Inspection and pressure testing requirements are given in Section 6. After welding and heat treatment each boiler shall be hydraulically tested to a pressure of 1.5 times the design pressure without any indication of weakness or defect.
Other data	Section 7: Documentation and marking.
	Section 8: Safety valves, fittings and mounting.
	The Standard also contains extensive tabular data and figures with Appendices.

Other Related Specifications

BS18: - Methods for tensile testing of metals

BS131: - Methods for notched bar tests

BS709: - Methods of testing fusion welded joints and weld metal in steel

BS759: - Valves, gauges and other safety fittings for application to boilers and to piping installations for and in connection with boilers

BS806: - Ferrous piping systems for and in connection with land boilers

BS970: - Specifications for wrought steel for mechanical and allied engineering purposes

BS1113: - Water-tube steam generating plant

BS1501: - Steels for fired and unfired pressure vessels. Plates

BS1502: - Steels for fired and unfired pressure vessels. Sections and bars

BS1503: - Steel forgings for pressure purposes

BS3059: - Specification for steel boiler and superheater tubes

BS3601: - Steel pipes and tubes for pressure purposes

BS3602: - Specification for steel pipes and tubes for pressure purposes

BS5500: - Unfired fusion welded pressure vessels

BS6759: - Safety valves

MATERIALS

The boilers are of cylindrical or vertical design and constructed from carbon or carbon manganese steels by fusion welding to class I, II or III requirements. The selection of materials of construction for plate, tube, forging, sections and bars and the property values to be used in design are set out in Section 2, BS2790. The material specifications are listed below.

Product form	BS number/designation	Grade	Comment
Plate	1501:Part 1/151	400B 430B	Minimum temperatures as specified in Table 2.5(1)
	1501:Part 1/161	400B 430B	
	1501:Part 1/164	400B	
	1501:Part 1/223	460B 490B	

Materials Cont'd

Product form	BS number/designation	Grade	Comment
Tube	3059:Part 2/51,52 or ERW	360	
		440	
	3602:Part 1/HFS,CFS,or ERW	360	
		410	
		460	
		490 N6	
Forgings	1503/164	490E	
	1503/221 or 223	410E	
		430E	
		460E	
		490E	
Plate	1501:Part 1/151	400A	Temperature properties as listed in
		430A	Table 2.5(2)
	1501:Part 1/161	400A	
		430A	
	1501:Part 1/164	400A	
	1501:Part 1/223	460A	
		490A	
Tube	3509:Part 1/HFS,CFS or ERW	320	
	3601:/S or ERW	320	
		360	
		410	
Sections and bars	1502/151,161,211 or 221	430	
Forgings	1503/164	490	
	1503/221 or 223	410	
		430	
		460	
		490	

Materials Cont'd

CONNECTIONS

The type of connection must be suitable for the operating pressure and temperature, the hot water or steam conditions and the required mechanical strength.

Method	BS Number	Component Data Sheet	Comment
Flanged	10 4504	3.2.1	Imperial sizes. Metric sizes.
Screwed	-	3.2.2	Threads to BS21.

SERVICE CONSIDERATIONS

1. These boilers have applications for high temperature hot water and steam heating and process systems.

2. Boiler output should cover the maximum estimated requirements of the system plus the appropriate margin. Consideration should be given to standby requirements and the required boiler plant configuration. According to conditions this configuration can vary from a single boiler to several smaller boilers that can be fired as load requirements vary.

3. Adequate air supply to the boiler house is required for efficient boiler operation.

4. The boiler and fire materials should be compatible with the products of combustion to minimise corrosion.

5. Flues and chimneys must satisfy the statutory requirements concerned with the location and discharge of products of combustion.

6. Access to boiler internals and flues is necessary for cleaning, inspection and maintenance.

7. All boilers shall be provided with openings adequate in size and number to allow safe access for fabrication, cleaning, internal inspection and ventilation.

8. Boilers shall be provided with safety valves, pressure gauges, boiler blowdown and drain valves and a stop valve. Steam boilers shall also have two water gauges (unless of less than 145kg/h evaporative capacity), a low water-level alarm, fuel cut-outs or a fusible plug.

9. Automatic controls shall be suitable for the type of boiler, steam or hot water, the fuel type and the method of firing.

10. Boiler plant together with associated fuel storage and distribution, chimneys and flues, firing equipment and automatic and safety controls shall be included in a comprehensive maintenance programme.

11. Operating and service manuals should be provided with the particular boiler plant and accessories installed.

SCOPE

The Data Sheet covers water tube boilers for steam generation. Water tube boilers contain water inside tubes, drums and headers which are heated by combustion and the products of combustion to generate steam.

SPECIFICATIONS

BS1113: 1969: - Water-tube steam generating plant (including super-heaters, reheaters and steel tube economisers)

Scope	This Standard applies solely to water-tube boiler units, normally complete with mountings to BS759.
Size range	No stipulated size limitations.
Manufacture	Construction and workmanship shall be in accordance with Section 3 of the Standard which covers:

A	Drums: general.
B	Rivetted drums.
C	Fusion welded drums.
D	Seamless forged drums.
E	Fitting of tubes.
F	Headers and similar pressure parts.
G	Connection of component parts of boiler units.
H	Welding of non-pressure parts to pressure parts.

Section 4 sets out Rules for Scantlings and deals with thicknesses, design stresses, etc.

Marking	Each boiler shall be clearly marked with name and domicile of manufacturer, manufacturer's serial number, design pressure, year of manufacture, date of hydraulic test and test pressure, the British Standard, mark of Inspecting Authority, and any other mark required by statute in the country of operation.
Tests	Each boiler shall be inspected during the various stages of construction.

Where the construction allows, all components shall be subjected to a hydraulic test pressure. In addition to a range of component tests the completed boiler shall be subjected to a further hydraulic test to the test pressure computed according to the requirements of the Standard.

MATERIALS

Material requirements for the construction of water tube boilers are detailed in Section 2, BS1113.

CONNECTIONS

The type of connection must be suitable for the operating pressure and temperature, the steam conditions and the required mechanical strength.

Method	BS Number	Component Data Sheet	Comment
Flanged	10	3.2.1	Imperial sizes.
	4504		Metric sizes.
Screwed	-	3.2.2	Threads to BS21.

SERVICE CONSIDERATIONS

1. Water tube boilers have applications for high pressure steam systems.

2. Adequate air supply is required for efficient boiler operation.

3. The boiler and flue materials should be compatible with the products of combustion to minimise corrosion.

4. Flues and chimneys must satisfy the statutory requirements concerned with the location and discharge of products of combustion.

5. Access to boiler internals and flues is necessary for cleaning, inspection and maintenace.

6. All boilers shall be provided with openings adequate in size and number to allow safe access for fabrication, cleaning, internal inspection and ventilation.

7. Boilers shall be provided with safety valves, pressure gauges, boiler blowdown and drain valves and a stop valve.

8. Automatic controls shall be suitable for the type of boiler, the fuel type and method of firing.

9. Boiler plant including superheaters, reheaters and economisers, together with associated fuel storage and distribution, chimneys and flues, firing equipment and automatic and safety controls shall be included in a comprehensive maintenance programme.

| FAMILY GROUP | CONTROLS | SUB-GROUP | |

SCOPE

This Data Sheet covers systems of automatic control which are integral with piped heating, hot water, cooling water or chilled water systems. It does not cover control systems for other building services e.g. ventilating and air conditioning systems.

The purpose of a control system may be one or more of the following:

(a) to perform a control function: That is to maintain conditions of temperature, humidity, pressure, fluid flow, liquid level, etc., within predetermined limits of desired levels;

(b) to perform a safety function: That is to prevent conditions of temperature, humidity, pressure, fluid flow, liquid level, etc., from exceeding safe limits and to prevent equipment operating beyond these limits;

(c) to perform an operating function: That is to stop and start plant in a predetermined sequence to provide efficient operating cycles or to match system output to local requirements.

The control system in a piped system comprises a control medium, controller and control valve.

Sensor

A sensor detects and signals a response to changes in the measured temperature, pressure, level, etc.

The application of sensors to piped systems include measuring and signalling changes in:
(a) temperature of the fluid,
(b) pressure of the fluid or the differential pressure across a restriction,
(c) fluid flow rate,
(d) liquid level.
Temperature sensors may be immersed in the pipe fluid, placed in a sensor pocket fitted to the pipe, strapped to the outside surface of the pipe, tanks or calorifiers. Sensor pockets are filled with a conducting fluid.

Control medium

This transmits the sensor signal to the controller. It may be mechanical (including self-acting), electric, electronic, pneumatic, hydraulic or combinations of these.

Controller

This is a device that receives and interprets a signal from the sensor via the control medium and produces a suitable action or impulse for transmission to a control valve. Controllers are frequently mounted inside the control sections of motor-starter panels or are attached to the controlled device.

Control valve

This reacts to the output of the controller and regulates the fluid flowing in the system. It consists of a valve body designed to control the flow of fluid passing through it by positioning a variable orifice in response to the controller signals. The valve operator is usually an electric motor or pneumatic actuator.

SPECIFICATIONS

BS1523: - Glossary of terms used in automatic controlling and regulating systems
Part 1: 1967: - Process and kinetic control

BS5384: 1977: - Guide to the selection and use of control systems for heating, ventilating and air conditioning installations

BS2765: 1969 (1981): - Dimensions of temperature detecting elements and corresponding pockets

BS3955: - Electrical controls for domestic appliances
Part 3: 1979: - General and specific requirements

BS1415: - Mixing valves
Part 1: 1976 - Non-thermostatic, non-compensating mixing valves

BS4740: - Method of evaluating control valve capacity
Part 1: 1971: - Incompressible fluids

MATERIALS

Sensor

Materials should be suitable for the local environment, the control medium and the fluids within pipes or sensor pockets.

(a) Types of temperature sensor

Bimetal, rod and tube	Combination metals with different rates of expansion.
Sealed bellows	Bellows made from copper, stainless steel, cupro-nickel, brass, monel, etc.
Remote bulb	Bulb made from copper, stainless steel, cupro-nickel, brass, monel, etc.
Electrical resistance element	e.g. nickel/chrome wire.
Themocouple	e.g. copper/constantan.

(b) Types of pressure sensor

Bellows	Copper, stainless steel, cupro-nickel, brass, monel, nimonic.
Diaphragms	Stainless steel, brass, fabric reinforced synthetic rubbers, glass fibre reinforced PTFE.
Transducers	Piezo-electric crystals.
Springs	Steel of various grades.

(c) Types of fluid flow

Rotating vane	Stainless steel, gunmetal, manganese bronze, PTFE, glass filled nylon.

(d) Types of liquid level sensor

Float	Brass.

Control medium

This transmits signals around the control system loop either by means of a fluid in a piping network or by electric/electronic signals in cable circuits.

Control medium	Item	Material
Mechanical	Bellows, phial and capillary tubing	Copper, stainless steel.
Pneumatic	Tubing	Copper, nylon, various plastics.
Hydraulic	Tubing	Copper.
Electric/electronic	Cabling	Various types of wiring with coverings/sheathing according to duty and application.

Controller

Housings of controllers are usually of galvanised or painted steel or moulded plastic construction. The casing and internals shall be suitable for the local environmental conditions.

Control valve

Valve bodies are manufactured of iron and bronzes for the less arduous service conditions; for high temperature heating systems they are frequently made of cast carbon steel and for high temperature process work stainless steel or molybdenum based steels are used.
The wearing parts in contact with the fluid are usually made of bronze or stainless steel.
Packing box material is usually moulded PTFE or moulded braided asbestos yarn impregnated with PTFE.
Further details of materials and specifications for control valves are given in the following data sheets.

Screwdown stop (globe) control valves: Data sheet 3.3.3
Float operated control valve: Data sheet 3.3.4
Butterfly control valve: Data sheet 3.3.5
Plug control valve: Data sheet 3.3.6

CONNECTIONS

Sensor and controller systems

Connections should be suitable for the cable entries, control tubing or operating linkages. Small bore control tubing may have capillary, compression, mechanical or other joints according to pipe size, operating pressure, pipe material and fluid handled.

Control valve

The type of connection may be dictated by the piping system specification. It should be suitable for the pressure and temperature conditions and the fluid handled by the valve.

Method	BS Number	Component Data Sheet	Notes
Flanged	10 4504	3.2.1	Imperial sizes. Metric sizes.
Screwed	21	3.2.2	Threads conforming to BS21.
Capillary	864/2	3.2.3	
Compression	864/2 2051/1	3.2.4	
Grooved	-	3.2.6	Flange adaptor may be required.

SERVICE CONSIDERATIONS

General

All materials used must be compatible with the local environment and the temperature, abrasiveness or aggressiveness of the fluid in which they are immersed.

Sensors

1. The selection needs to take into account the setting range, control limits, response time and sensitivity of the sensor.

2. (a) Temperature sensors
    (i) Elements sensing the temperature of a liquid in a pipe should be:
    - capable of being readily withdrawn for servicing or calibration without the need of draining the system,
    - positioned so that the active part of the sensor is wholly immersed in the liquid,
    - positioned so that the sensor is not closer that 12 diameters downstream from a point where fluids at different temperatures are combined unless they are mixed by a pump.

    (ii) Sensors measuring the temperature of a solid surface should be positioned and fixed to ensure effective thermal contact.

    (iii) Sensors measuring the outdoor air temperature as part of the control of a piped service must be positioned to sense a representative ambient temperature which is not influenced by direct solar radiation, abnormal wind conditions or local heat gains. Construction and materials of elements and protective housings must be suitable for local atmospheric and weather conditions and be protected against driving rain, snow, etc.

3. Pressure sensors should be installed and used in accordance with the recommendations in Appendix C of BS1780: Part 2: 1971.

Service Considerations Cont'd

4. Flow measuring sensors such as orifices, venturis and flowmeters should be installed in accordance with the manufacturer's instructions. Installation requirements for differential pressure measurements in pipes are given in BS1042.

5. Liquid level detectors should be positioned away from feed and discharge areas to avoid turbulence and they should be installed in accordance with the manufacturer's instructions.

Control medium

1. The selection of the control medium will depend on: control system design, availability of electrical supply or instrument quality compressed air, relative siting of plant components and the power needed to operate the control valves.

Controllers

1. Controllers should be readily accessible for calibration and servicing and be mounted where they will not be subject to physical damage or abuse.

Control valves

1. The selection of control valves requires consideration of input signal, response time, output, motion and operating power/torque.

2. All control valves should be located in accessible positions to facilitate proper calibration and maintenance.

3. Control valves should generally be provided with isloating valves at each end connection to permit removal from the piping system. Balancing valves/orifices may be required in bypass connections serving three-way valves. The manufacturer/control specialist should be consulted regarding the provision of pipeline strainers at valve inlets.

4. Information on the selection and application of control valves is available in BS5384 (in particular in Figs. 2 to 13 inclusive).

5. See also the service considerations for valves in the following data sheets: 3.3.3, 3.3.4, 3.3.5, 3.3.6.

	component data sheet		SHEET NUMBER	3.9.1.	1
FAMILY GROUP	THERMAL INSULATION	SUB-GROUP			

SCOPE

This Data Sheet deals with the thermal insulation of the following piping, plant and equipment systems:

- Chilled and cold water supplies.
- Central heating, air conditioning and domestic hot and cold water supply installations.
- Steam systems.
- Process pipework and equipment applications.

Thermal insulation materials or systems have the property of resisting the transfer of heat. The purposes of thermal insulation are to restrict heat gains and losses from pipework, plant and equipment and it may also be required for safety reasons or to protect against condensation or freezing.

SPECIFICATIONS

BS5422: 1977: - Specification for the use of thermal insulating materials

This Standard is arranged in the following six sections:

1 General — Scope, definitions and details required to permit correct assessment of work.

2 General use of thermal insulating materials — Physical characteristics of materials and tests.

3 Refrigeration applications — Refers to pipes and equipment containing fluids between 0°C and -40°C.

4 Chilled and cold water supplies: industrial applications — Insulation for industrial pipework, plant and equipment for the following services.
(a) chilled water systems: 0° to 5°C,
(b) cold water systems: about 10°C.
It refers to vapour barriers, prevention of freezing and condensation.

5 Central heating, air conditioning and domestic hot and cold water supply installations — Insulation for pipes and equipment both within and located outside buildings. It refers to insulating materials for:
(a) hot water systems for working temperatures up to 200°C,
(b) cold water systems excluding refrigeration for purposes of protection against condensation and freezing.
It excludes pipework and equipment buried in the ground or located in unventilated ducts.

6 Process pipework and equipment applications — This covers insulating materials on process pipework and equipment for service temperatures between ambient and 650°C excluding pipework and equipment buried in the ground or located in unventilated ducts.

SPECIFICATIONS

BS5970: 1981: - Code of practice for thermal insulation of pipework and equipment (in the temperature range of -100°C to +870°C)

This code recommends the principles to be followed in selecting the most suitable insulating systems for particular requirements of pipework, plant and equipment. It gives guidance on design work on site, application and on the use and choice of finishes.

Other Related Specifications

BS874: 1973 (1980): - Methods for determining thermal insulating properties, with definitions of thermal insulating terms

BS1710: 1984: - Specification for identification of pipelines and services

This Standard specifies colours for identifying pipes conveying fluids in liquid or gaseous condition. The colour specifications are in accordance with BS4800.

BS3533: 1981: - Glossary of thermal insulation terms

BS3958: - Thermal insulating materials
Part 1: 1982: - Magnesia preformed insulation

This Standard deals with properties and dimensions of preformed pipe sections for use up to about 315°C.

Part 2: 1982. - Calcium silicate preformed insulation

This Standard deals with properties and dimensions of two types of preformed insulation for use up to 650°C or 950°C.

Part 3: 1967: - Metal mesh faced mineral mats and mattresses

This sets out the properties and dimensions of insulating mats and mattresses.

Part 4: 1982: - Bonded preformed man-made mineral fibre pipe sections

This Standard specifies physical and chemical requirements, dimensions and finishes for mineral fibre pipe sections, generally for use at elevated temperatures.

Part 5: 1969: - Bonded mineral wool slabs (for use at temperatures above 50°C)

This covers groups of products for hot face temperatures up to limits of 230°C, 540°C and 800°C.

Part 6: 1972 (1980): - Finishing materials: hard setting compositions, self-setting cement and gypsum plaster

This Standard specifies requirements for finishing materials prepared for use by mixing with water which are applied to insulating materials after they have been fixed to piping systems on site.

BS5608: 1978: - Specification for rigid urethane and isocyanurate foam for thermal insulation of pipework and equipment

This Standard sets out classifications, compositions, physical requirements, dimensional tolerances and method of test. It covers cup moulded or continuously formed pipe sections.

BS5615: 1978: - Specification for insulating jackets for domestic hot water storage cylinders

This gives requirements and sets minimum performance for insulating jackets of different sizes. It gives a standard method of test for the determination of the standing heat loss.

CP99: 1972: - Frost precautions for water services

MATERIALS

Thermal insulation material general categories are:

Fibres	- includes mineral wools such as rock, slag, glass, ceramic and hair felt.
Granular	- includes calcium silicate, mangnesia, diatomaceous earth and cork.
Cellular	- includes foamed glass, polyurethane and polystyrene.
Metallic	- includes aluminium foil, dimpled metallic sheets.

Thermal insulating materials for pipework, plant and equipment are:

Aluminium foil	- thin sheets of rolled aluminium.
Aluminium silicate fibre	- filaments or fibres produced from a melt of alumina and silica.
Animal hair	- natural fibre obtained from the coats of animals.
Calcium silicate	- hydrated calcium with added reinforcing fibres.
Cellular glass	- a lightweight expanded glass with small cells, preferably non-intercommunicating, produced by a foaming process.
Cellular plastics (expanded plastics, foamed plastics)	- a generic term for plastics materials when the density is reduced by the presence of numerous small cavities (cells) dispersed throughout the mass. The cells may be open (interconnecting) or closed.
Cellular rubber	- a generic term for vulcanised rubber containing numerous thin-walled cells filled with air or other gas. The walls of the cells may be vulcanised to the soft rubber stage or completely to the hard rubber (ebonite) stage.

Ceramic fibre
- fibrous material, loose or fabricated into convenient forms, mainly intended for use at appropriate elevated temperatures. The fibres may consist of silica or of an appropriate metal silicate, e.g. alumino-silicate.

Diatomite
(kieselguhr,
diatomaceous earth)
- cellular siliceous particles of microscopic size, composed of the skeletons of diatoms.

Felt
- a semi-rigid or flexible sheet consisting of closely interlaced fibres with or without the addition of binders or adhesives.

Foamed-in-situ plastics
- cellular plastics produced in situ and foamed by physical or chemical means.

Glass fibre
(glass wool)
- mineral fibre produced from molten glass.

Loose wool
- mineral wool without a bonding agent although a fibre dressing may be applied to minimise fibre fly and irritation.

Magnesia
- insulating materials containing about 85% by mass of light basic magnesium carbonate the balance being mainly reinforcing fibres.

Man-made fibres
- manufactured fibres as distinct from those that occur naturally e.g. fibres manufactured from glass rock or melted slag.

Mineral fibre
- a generic term for all non-metallic inorganic fibres.

Mineral wool
- a generic term for mineral fibres of a woolly consistency normally made from molten glass, rock or slag.

Plastic composition
- insulating material in loose dry form prepared for application as a paste by mixing with water. They normally set under the influence of heat applied to the internal surface, self-setting grades do not require the application of heat.

Plastics
- a material that contains a polymer as an essential ingredient and which can be shaped by flow.

Rock wool
- mineral wool produced from naturally occurring igneous rock.

Wool
- a generic name used loosly for a random mass of any type of fibre.

INSULATION FIXINGS, FINISHES AND PROTECTIVE COATINGS

These are of considerable importance to the application of insulation. They have the purpose of elimination of ingress of moisture, protection against fire and against mechanical damage and corrosion. The type of finish differs according to operating conditions, the insulating material and its physical form. The methods of fixing insulating materials include adhesives, metal bands, securing pins, staples and wire.

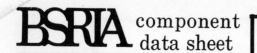

Typical forms of finishes for the exposed surfaces of insulating materials are:

Wire netting and   - galvanised metal with lacing wires of galvanised soft iron or stainless steel.
expanded metal

Self-setting cements   - Portland cement.

Metal bands and wire   - japanned steel, galvanised mild steel, aluminium or stainless steel.

Sheet metal   - aluminium, galvanised mild steel, stainless steel and plastics-coated metal.

Protective tapes   - for example PVC and self-adhesive vinyl.

Protective cloths   - glass fibres, neoprene and other fabrics.

SERVICE CONSIDERATIONS

The choice of thermal insulating methods and finishes involves the following factors:

1.   Form of insulating material. Whether the material is to be provided in preformed,
            flexible or other form and whether any portions are to be fabricated specially for ease
            of removal.

2.   Type of finish. Whether the finish should be sheet metal, wet finish or other form and
            the requirements for vapour barriers, mechanical protection, painting and
            identification.

3.   Items to be insulated. In addition to external surfaces of pipes, plant and equipment
            and fittings whether flanges, brackets, supports etc. are to be insulated.

4.   Nature of surfaces which are to be insulated. Check any specific chemical restrictions
            on insulation and finish where special metal or alloy piping systems or materials are
            involved.

5.   Location of piping and equipment:
            (a) indoors,
            (b) outdoors but protected from the weather,
            (c) outdoors exposed to the weather,
            (d) in ventilated ducts or open trenches.

6.   Temperature conditions:
            (a) normal operating temperature,
            (b) extreme temperature(s)
            (c) fluctuations in temperature.

Service Considerations Cont'd

7.   Ambient atmospheric conditions:

                   (a)   abnormally high or low temperatures,

                   (b)   high humidity,

                   (c)   potentially corrosive atmosphere,

                   (d)   protection against condensation,

                   (e)   protection against freezing.

8.   Special conditions or service requirements:

                   (a)   resistance to compression,

                   (b)   resistance to spread of fire and generation of smoke,

                   (c)   resistance to vibration,

                   (d)   resistance to mechanical damage,

                   (e)   resistance to attack by pests or insects,

                   (f)   presence of corrosive fluids,

                   (g)   resistance of surface to ingress of oils or flammable liquids.

9.   Basis on which thickness and thermal conductivity is determined:

                   (a)   minimum economic thickness, see BS5422,

                   (b)   selection from Tables as included in BS5422,

                   (c)   heat gain or loss per unit dimension or for the complete system,

                   (d)   temperature on the outer surface of the insulation,

                   (e)   conditions of fluid at the point of delivery.

APPLICATION NOTES

The application of insulation and protective coverings is a highly skilled activity. Badly fitted or badly laid material can lead to lower performance than estimated and the need for constant maintenance to deal with problems caused by condensation, water-logging, vibration and mechanical damage.

Well designed and properly applied thermal insulation will give good economic service and should last ten years or more without major difficulty.

The following points relating to application should be considered:

(a) Surfaces must be clean, dry and grease-free before application.

(b) Rigid sections should have 'staggered' joints where more than one layer is involved. Sections should be securely fixed to the pipework or equipment by means of wire, bands or other mechanical fixings.

(c) Mattresses should butt firmly together and be properly secured with wire netting, expanded metal with mechanical fixings, etc.

(d) Where cement or composition finishes are to be applied the outer face of the insulation should be suitably keyed.

APPLICATION NOTES CONT'D

(e) In fire risk areas expanded metal or sheet metal coverings may require to be electrically earthed.

(f) In certain applications e.g. refrigeration and chilled water systems, hangers and supports should be covered or protected in such a way that moisture cannot penetrate the insulation e.g. by using flexible sealants.

(g) When applying several layers of plastic insulation each layer should be allowed to dry out thoroughly before the next layer is applied and before any protective covering is fitted.

(h) Many insulation systems require provision for expansion, particularly on pipes and at pipe connections where movement could otherwise produce cracking in the insulation.

(i) Particular care is needed in the insulation of pipework which is electrically traced.

(j) Insulation thickness on flanges and valves, where specified, should be equal to that on associated pipes.

PART 4 MATERIALS

4.1 FERROUS METALS

The term 'ferrous metals' covers a wide variety of industrially important metals and alloys that contain iron as the major constituant. They can be grouped into wrought iron, cast iron, carbon steel and alloy steel. 'Mild steel' is a term used colloquially for low carbon steel and is not described by any specification and hence is not referred to in this Handbook.

4.1.1 WROUGHT IRON

Commercially pure iron resulting from the reduction of the carbon in cast iron. It is obtained by melting white cast iron and passing an oxidizing flame over it. The iron is left in a pasty condition full of holes, and is then rolled or hammered to unite it into one mass. Wrought iron is a pure iron containing iron-silicate slag. It is not suitable for machine parts requiring strength, but is very ductile and corrosion resistant. It is chiefly for rivets, water pipes, tank plates, and general forged work.

4.1.2 CAST IRON

Data Sheets FM01; FM02; FM03; FM04; FM05; FM06; FM07

The term 'cast iron' does not describe a single material having a particular combination of properties; it covers a wide group of materials with a correspondingly wide range of properties. British Standard specifications cover nearly all general engineering cast irons; they are classified diagramatically in Figure 4.1/1. As an engineering material cast iron offers the following advantages:-

- it can be cast into a wide variety of shapes, including complete internal contours.

- component shape closely related to purpose
- variations can be produced at low cost by simple pattern modifications
- reduced number of parts to assemble
- minimum number of joints, thereby reducing problems of leakage, corrosion, loosening or fretting.

Iron casting can be produced in a very wide range of sizes. Sections down to 3 mm thickness can be readily produced in grey irons, although in common with all gravity castings, difficulties with metal flow make it impracticable to produce large plate areas in very thin section. Thin-walled components, which are consequently better made as pressings, weldments, or non-ferrous die castings, depending on size and operating requirements.

The only upper limit to the size of iron casting is that which can be handled in the foundry.

The dimensional accuracy of iron castings is largely dependent on their size, which usually dictates the method of moulding, and on the numbers produced. Small castings can be produced to accuracies of $\pm$ 0.3mm while castings weighing several tonnes can be produced within a tolerance range of $\pm$ 10mm.

The general-engineering grades of unalloyed grey, malleable, and nodular (spheroidal graphite) cast iron are suitable for the majority of operating requirements, and only when resistance is required to high temperature, corrosion or abrasion does it become necessary to specify alternative types of cast iron.

Cast irons differ from steels in their mechanical properties mainly because of their higher carbon content, which is in the range 3-4 per cent. The carbon can be present either as free graphite or in the combined form as iron carbide, and all the engineering grades of iron are characterised by the presence of at least part of the carbon as free graphite.

The following are the main types of cast iron used in engineering applications.

4.1.2.1 **GREY CAST IRONS**

Grey cast irons, either unalloyed or of low alloy content, cover the tensile strength range 150 to 400 N/mm^2. They account for about 85 per cent of the total production of iron castings in the UK and are used for a wide variety of purposes in motor vehicles, machine tools, power plant, pumps and compressors, and in general mechanical and electrical engineering applications. These materials have good wear resistance and machinability with moderately high tensile and fatigue strength, but they cannot be used under conditions of severe impact loading.

In unalloyed grey irons up to Grade 300 the three basic elements that affect strength and hardness are total carbon, silicon, and phosphorous. Alloy additions, up to 1.5% nickel and 0.5% chromium or molybdenum, are usually made only when strengths above 300 N/mm^2 are required.

The structure and properties of grey irons are particularly influenced by the rate of cooling during solidification, which in turn depends on section thickness. Metal of a given composition may, depending on section thickness of the casting, produce:

- a chilled, white and unmachinable casting;
- a machinable grey casting with unmachinable edges;
- a strong, close-grained, machinable casting;
- a low-strength, open-grained casting on machining.

For this reason specifications for grey iron refer to the properties of the material when cast into a test bar of definite diameter rather than to the properties of the casting itself.

Chilled components must normally be avoided since they are hard and brittle and increase susceptibility to cracking. Many machining operations are difficult or impossible on chilled iron and for general-engineering applications the as-cast edge thickness of grey-iron castings should be above the following minimum values:

Grade (to BS 1452)	Miniumum section thickness for chill-free edge (mm)
150	3-5
180	5-7.5
220	8-10
260	12-16

In grey iron, graphite is present as flake clusters. The strength of grey iron increases as the

242

Figure 4.1/1: British Standards general engineering grades of cast iron.

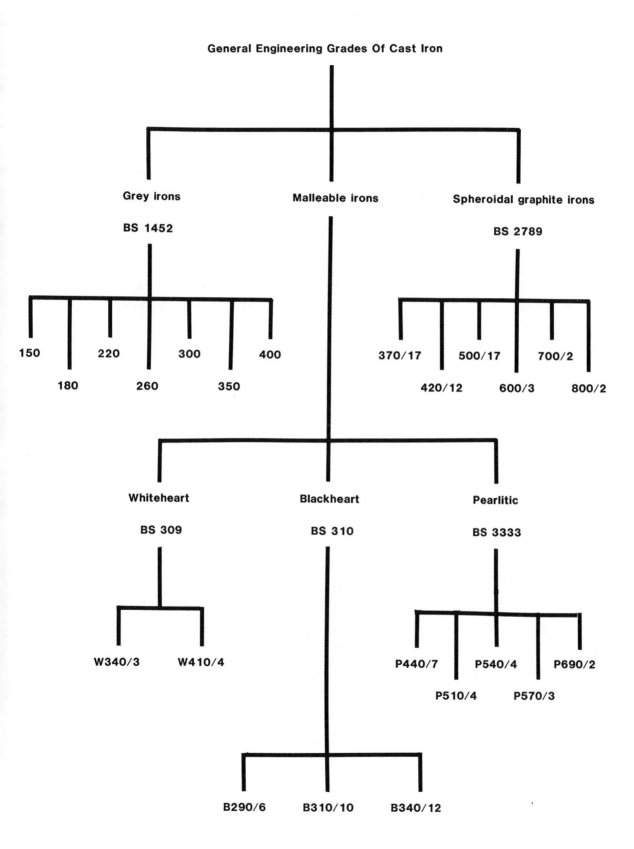

243

amount of free graphite is reduced and as the fineness of the graphite flakes is increased. Strength can also be increased relatively by alloying, but with flake graphite present this increase is small. Alloying is more effective in irons with low graphite content. but even so it is not practicable to achieve tensile strengths much above 400 N/mm^2, and irrespective of strength the elongation is normally less than 1%. Through-hardening heat treatments are not normally applied to grey irons to modify their mechanical properties as is the case with nodular and malleable irons, but grey irons are frequently hardened using flame or induction heating to improve their wear resistance in applications such as gears, cams, and machine tool slides.

4.1.2.2 **NODULAR AND MALLEABLE CAST IRONS.**

These cast irons are produced by metal-treatment processes, which modify the carbon content and its structure, but their mechanical properties are very similar. They have tensile strengths in the range of 300 to 800 N/mm^2 and are used in applications where high fatigue strength or resistance to impact loading is required, for example crankshafts, and vehicle suspension and steering components.

In nodular and malleable irons graphite is present as individual nodules or spheroids. The nodules are extremely small in comparison with the graphite clusters of grey irons and the stress concentrations caused by the presence of nodualar graphite are much smaller than those in flake-grahite irons. Nodular and malleable irons are therefore able to develop the inherent properties of the matrix to a much greater extent than are grey irons, and consequently have higher strength and elongation.

Blackheart malleable iron (BS 310) has a soft ferritic matrix; the tensile strength ranges from approximately 300-375 N/mm^2, with elongations of 6 to 20%, the higher values being obtained at the lower levels.

For some applications a higher tensile strength is required and pearlitic malleable irons (BS 3333) have been developed with harder matrix structures to give greater strength while still retaining some ductility.

The highest strength irons are produced by quenching and tempering, and are still referred to as pearlitic malleable irons although their structures may consist mainly of tempered martensite. Tensile strengths depend on cooling rates and values up to 620,693 and 770 N/mm^2 can be obtained in iron cooled by still air, air blast, and oil quenching respectively, with elongations in the 2 to 11% range.

Whiteheart malleable irons (BS 309) are produced by heat treatment in a decarburizing atmosphere so that a substantial amount of carbon present in the as-cast condition is removed and a carbon gradient exists from edge to centre of the castings. Thin sections can be almost completely decarburized, and they then have properties approximating to those of low carbon steel.

Because of the decarburized skin effect in whiteheart irons lowest strengths are obtained in thinner sections. Tensile properties range from 270 N/mm^2 to almost 500 N/mm^2 with elongations from 4 to 20%.

Nodular irons (BS 2789) in the as-cast condition generally have mainly pearlitic structures, with correspondingly high strength and limited elongation. Normalizing heat treatment can be given to obtain fully pearlitic structure, with increased strength, and nodular irons are often annealed to the ferritic condition when high ductility is required.

Intermediate mechanical properties are obtainable with mixed pearlitic-ferritic structures which can be produced in the ascast condition. Hardening and tempering is not often applied to nodular irons, but there is increasing interest in the use of autempered nodular irons which offer a good combination of high strength, ductility, and toughness.

Tensile properties range from 370 N/mm^2 and 25% elongation in ferritic material to 800 N/mm^2 with 3% elongation in the fully pearlitic grade. By hardening and tempering it is possible to obtain up to 1000 N/mm^2 tensile strength with 2% elongation.

4.1.2.3 HIGH ALLOYED CAST IRONS

These are used to withstand severely abrasive conditions (for example in pulverizing mills), corrosion in chemical plant, and high-temperature stress and oxidation in boiler and furnace installations.

4.1.3 CARBON STEEL

Data Sheets FM08; FM09; FM10; FM11; FM12; FM13; FM14; FM15;

Carbon steels are ferrous alloys that contain essentially only carbon, manganese and silicon, but in which the carbon content is the principle element to control their mechanical properties. These steels can generally be classified into three groups according to their carbon content.

Low Carbon Steel	0.08% - 0.25% Carbon
Medium Carbon Steel	0.25% - 0.50% Carbon
High Carbon Steel	Greater than 0.50% Carbon

Low carbon steel is the most commonly used engineering material because it it cheap, has reasonable mechanical properties and is very ductile. Medium carbon steels are used where higher tensile strengths are required without loss of toughness, e.g. forgings, tools, shafts and gears. High carbon steels are used for withstanding wear, where hardness is necessary at the expense of ductility and toughness e.g. springs, dies and engineering tools.

Carbon steels are made either by continuous casting methods or by the conventional ingot production method. Steels made by the continuous casting method would be almost entirely of the fully killed (i.e. de-oxidised) type, but those made by the ingot method can be produced in three forms as follows:

Fully Killed Steels   -   are fully deoxidised with silicon and/or aluminium, are generally very clean and free from impurities, and are used extensively.

Semi-Killed Steels   -   are partially deoxidised, and although possibly not as clean as killed steels find wide application in structural shapes.

Rimmed Steels   -   are produced with the minimum of deoxidation, and the resultant ingots have a pure iron outer skin which makes them ideal for rolling into strip or plate for use where the ductile properties of the outer skin can be utilised.

The mechanical properties of all carbon steels can be altered either by cold working or by a suitable heat treatment depending on the final properties required. The principle heat treatment processes for carbon steels are:

- annealing, full or process
- normalising
- through thickness hardening and tempering
- case or surface hardening

Full or process annealing is performed to soften the steel, relieve internal stresses and to improve the grain structure. In full annealing of low carbon steel the steel is heated to about 950°C, soaked at temperature for a period depending on section size, and slowly cooled in the furnace. Sub critical or process annealing is extensively used for strip products, but uses a lower treatment temperature in the range 650° to 720°C.

Normalising involves a similar heat treatment, temperature and soaking period to full annealing, but cooling is in air to give a faster cooling rate than for annealing. This results in a finer grain size in the product with consequent improvements in yield strength, tensile strength and impact values.

Through thickness hardening of steel requires the formation of a structure consisting entirely of martensite, and in general is applied more to the medium and higher carbon steel groups. This is achieved by heating to a temperature high enough for the steel to become fully austenitic, then cooling rapidly by quenching either in water or oil to obtain a complete transformation to martensite. The steel composition and design of the component affect the choice of quenching and thus the final properties. Water quenching is rapid giving high hardnesses with the risk of distortion and cracking, whereas oil quenching gives lower hardnesses but less risk of cracking. The martensite formed is very hard and brittle, and thus without some form of tempering the quenched - only product would be useless for engineering purposes.

Tempering is a controlled heat treatment applied to steel components after hardening, and involves reheating to a temperature up to 700°C maximum soaking for a period of time and cooling in air. This process relieves internal stresses from quenching and produces a softer but tougher material more suitable for engineering purposes. An extensive range of properties can be obtained depending upon the chemical composition and the tempering temperature employed.

Medium carbon steels are capable of being through-hardened if the section thickness is small. High carbon steels are almost always used in the fully hardened and tempered state and they are used in many applications in which high hardness is essential. Low carbon steels are generally incapable of being through hardened and can only be improved by case (surface) hardening.

Case hardening may be required where a hard, wear resistant surface has to be combined with adequate core ductility to avoid failure. This can be achieved by enriching the surface with carbon, by heating at 900°C in a solid, liquid or gaseous organic media, until the desired case depth is obtained. The depth of the case obtained is dependent on time at temperature in the media. Further heat-treatment is usually required to refine the core, and to refine and harden the surface layer. Nitrogen, in the form of dissociated ammonia, may also be used to achieve a hard surface layer. The advantages of nitrogen hardening are that the treatment temperature is lower (500°C), with a consequent reduction in distortion and cracking problems and no subsequent heat treatment is required. The nitrided product should retain its surface hardness at a higher service temperature than carburised products.

Carbon steels are not corroded by cold alkaline solutions, but may be attacked by hot alkaline solutions. Mineral acids at most concentrations will corrode carbon steels to some extent at normal ambient temperatures. Chlorinated solvents can cause corrosion problems when heated due to the formation of hydrochloric acid. Carbon steel products will tolerate most other solvents without excessive corrosion. The corrosion rate of carbon steel products conveying or storing water can often be reduced to an acceptable level by adding inhibitors to the water, at a cost far less than using more costly materials with greater corrosion resistance.

Carbon steels containing less than 0.3% Carbon can generally be welded without special requirements. Above 0.3% more care is required, and preheat may be necessary. Choice of welding electrode for the given steel composition is also an important consideration.

4.1.4 ALLOY STEEL

Data Sheets FM16; FM17; FM18; FM19; FM20; FM21; FM22; FM23;

The addition of alloying elements to steel can improve various properties of the steel as compared with carbon steels. Heat treated alloy steels can provide higher strengths combined with appreciable ductility even in large sections. The alloying elements also improve the hardenability of the steel with the result that a quenching media allowing a slower rate of cooling, such as oil, may be used instead of water. The advantage of this is that thinner sections can be treated, and there is less likelihood of distortion and quench cracking. Alloy steels may also be surface hardened by flame or induction hardening techniques.

The most common alloying elements are chromium, cobalt, manganese, molybednum, nickel, niobium and vanadium. Examples of some of the benefits that the elements impart to the steels are:

- stability in the hardened condition to high temperatures such as is required for tool steels is increased by cobalt and vandium additions.
- manganese assists with increase of depth of hardening, and in free cutting steels, i.e. steels with raised sulphur levels, produces a compound (manganese sulphide) which assists machining properties.
- chromium produces an adherent oxide layer and improves the steels resistance to corrosion or oxidation at elevated temperatures. Chromium steels are also used whenever extreme hardness and resistance to wear is required.
- resistance to creep at steam temperatures (400-550°C) is improved by additions of molybdenum and vanadium. Molybdenum is also added to high speed, heat resisting and corrosion resisting steels.
- niobium and vanadium in low carbon steels improve tensile properties due to precipitation of microscopic carbide particles on cooling from hot working temperatures.
- nickel steels are widely used for case hardening applications; as compared with carbon steels the transformation temperatures are lower and thus a lower quenching temperature can be used.

A wide range of properties can be obtained from alloy steels, and thus they are extensively used in a variety of applications. An approximate classification can be made into four general groups as follows:

- structural steels for use in components or machine parts where selection of the steel is

247

made in accordance with the required tensile strength of the finished component.

- tool and die steels
- magnetic alloys for permanent magnets and transformer cores.
- stainless and heat resisting steels.

4.1.5 STAINLESS STEEL

Data Sheets FM24; FM25; FM26

An important division of alloy steels is that concerned with corrosion resistance - stainless steel. It must be noted that under certain conditions, stainless steels will corrode, but in general they are superior in environments where low carbon steel or common structural steels would be attacked. Corrosion resistance is achieved because chromium forms a thin self-healing complex oxide layer on the steel surface under oxidising conditions. If the environment is not an oxidising one then any surface defects will not be repaired and the material will be locally attacked.

Stainless steels can be divided into three types depending on their structure characteristics - ferritic, martensitic and austenitic. The ferritic and martensitic stainless steels are straight chromium steels designated as the type 400 series. The austenitic stainless steels are chromium - nickel alloys designated as the type 300.

The martensitic type stainless steels contain 11.5-18% chromium with 0.15-0.4% carbon, and, like carbon steels, can be hardened and tempered by suitable heat treatments to produce material with a wide range of tensile properties. The strength of these steels is related to the carbon content, and they are used where conditions demand high strength combined with corrosion resistance. Ferritic stainless steels contain 11.5 to 27% chromium with up to 0.2% carbon, and cannot be hardened by heat treatment. Both martensitic and ferritic grades of stainless steel are magnetic. Maximum corrosion resistance is achieved in the hardened state for martensitic types, and in the annealed state for ferritic types.

Austenitic type stainless steels are known under the general title of 18/8, which relates to a chromium content of 16% to 26% and a nickel content of 6% to 12%. The addition of 2% molybdenum to these steels gives increased resistance to pitting, and an improvement in high temperature strength. Other elements such as copper, titanium and niobium are also often added to 18/8 steels in order to improve specific properties. Heating to over 1000°C and cooling rapidly achieves the softest and most malleable condition for austenitic grades, and also ensures that the steel is in the best condition for maximum corrosion resistance.

Austenitic stainless steels are non magnetic, and only hardenable by cold work in which condition they may be weakly magnetic.

If the material is to be welded care must be taken to prevent the conditions which lead to weld decay. This phenomena is an intergranular form of corrosion which can occur in metal adjacent to the weld area where the temperature of the material would be in the range 500 to 800°C. Within this temperature range chromium rich carbide particles can form at the grain boundaries causing a localised depletion of chromium thus lowering the corrosion resistance of the material. Heat treatment after welding at 1000 to 1150°C followed by rapid cooling will overcome the effect. It can also be prevented by selecting a steel composition designed specifically for welded stainless steel components. These steels normally contain a very low carbon content or have small additions of niobium or titanium to prevent the depletion of chromium.

RELATED SPECIFICATIONS

CAST IRON

BOILER & PRESSURE VESSELS

BS 779	: 1976	Cast iron boilers for central heating and indirect hot water supply
BS 853	-	Calorifiers for central heating and hot water supply
Part 1	: 1960	Mild steel and cast iron
BS 1712	: 1951	Cast iron economisers with extended surface horizontal tubes
BS 1713	: 1951	Cast iron smooth tube economisers with pressed socket joints
BS 1894	: 1952	Electrode boilers

PIPES & TUBES

BS 10	: 1962	Flanges and bolting for pipes, valves and fittings
BS 2035	: 1966	Cast iron flanged pipes and flanged fittings.
BS 3974	: 1974	Pipe hangers
Part 1	: 1974	Pipe hangers, slider and roller type supports
BS 4504	-	Flanges and bolting for pipes valves and fittings
Part 1	: 1969	Ferrous
BS 4622	: 1970	Grey iron pipes and fittings
BS 4772	: 1971	Ductile iron pipes and fittings
CP 2010	-	Pipelines
Part 3	: 1972	Design and construction of iron pipelines in land

VALVES & FITTING

BS 143 BS 1256	: 1968	Malleable cast iron screwed fittings for steam, air, water, gas and oil
BS 1641	: 1950	Cast iron pipe fittings for sprinklers and other fire protection installations
BS 3948	: 1965	Cast iron parallel slide valves for general purposes
BS 3952	: 1965	Cast iron butterfly valves for general purposes
BS 3961	: 1965	Cast iron screw-down stop valves and stop and check valves for general purposes
BS 4090	: 1966	Cast iron check valves for general purposes
BS 5150	: 1974	Cast iron wedge and double disk gate valves for general purposes
BS 5151	: 1974	Cast iron gate (parallel slide) valves for general purposes
BS 5151	: 1974	Cast iron globe and globe stop and check valves for general purposes
BS 5153	: 1974	Cast iron check valves for general purposes
BS 5155	: 1974	Cast iron and carbon steel butterfly valves for general purposes
BS 5158	: 1974	Cast iron and carbon steel plug valves for general purposes
BS 5159	: 1974	Cast iron and carbon steel ball valves for general purposes

MATERIALS

BS 309	: 1972	Whiteheart malleable iron castings
BS 310	: 1972	Blackheart malleable iron castings
BS 1452	: 1977	Specification for grey iron castings
BS 1591	: 1975	Corrosion resisting high silicon iron castings

BS 2789	: 1973	Iron castings with spheroidal or nodular graphite
BS 3333	: 1972	Pearlitic malleable iron castings
BS 3468	: 1974	Austenitic cast iron

FLUES & CHIMNEYS

| BS 41 | : 1973 | Cast iron spigots and socket flue or smoke pipes and fittings |
| BS 1563 | : 1949 | Cast iron storage tanks (rectangular) |

HEATING EQUIPMENT

| BS 1252 | : 1957 | Domestic solid fuel cookers with integral boilers |
| BS 3377 | : 1969 | Back boilers for use with domestic solid fuel |

COLD WATER SERVICES AND SANITARY EQUIPMENT

BS 78	-	Cast iron spigot and socket pipes (vertically cast) and spigot and socket
Part 2	: 1965	Fittings
BS 416	: 1973	Cast iron spigot and socket soil, waste and ventilating pipes (sand cast and spun)
BS 437	-	Cast iron spigot and socket drain pipes and fittings
Part 1	: 1970	Pipes bends branches and access fittings
BS 460	: 1964	Cast iron rainwater goods
BS 1211	: 1958	Centrifugally cast (spun) iron pressure pipes for water, gas and sewage

STEEL

BOILER AND PRESSURE VESSELS

BS 853	-	Calorifiers for central heating and hot water supply
Part 1	: 1960	Mild steel and cast iron
BS855	: 1976	Specification for welded steel boilers for central heating and indirect hot water supply (rated output 44kW to 3MW)
BS1501	-	Steel for fired and unfired pressure vessels - plates
Part 1	: 1980	Carbon and carbon manganese steels
Part 2	: 1970	Alloy steels
Part 3	: 1973	Corrosion and heat resisting steels
BS1501-6	: 1958	Steels for use in the chemical, petroleum and allied industries
BS1502	: 1968	Steels for fired and unfired pressure vessels - sections and bars
BS1504	: 1976	Steel castings for pressure purposes
BS1510	: 1958	Steels for use in chemical, petroleum and allied industries (Low temperature supplement to BS1501-6)
BS1894	: 1952	Electrode boilers of rivetted, seamless, welded and cast iron construction for water heating
BS 5500	: 1982	Unfired fusion welded pressure vessels

PIPES AND TUBES

BS10	: 1962	Flanges and bolting for pipes valves and fittings
BS778	: 1966	Steel pipes and joints for hydraulic purposes
BS806	: 1975	Ferrous piping systems for and in connection with land boilers
BS1387	: 1967	Steel tubes and tubulars suitable for screwing to BS21 pipe threads
BS1775	: 1964	Steel tubes for mechanical, structural and engineering purposes
BS3059	-	Steel boiler and superheater tubes
Part 1	: 1978	Low tensile carbon steel tubes without specified elevated temperature properties
Part 2	: 1978	Carbon, alloy and austenitic stainless steel tubes with specified elevated temperature properties
BS3600	: 1976	Specifications for pipes and tubes for pressure purposes
BS3601	: 1974	Steel pipes and tubes for pressure purposes. Carbon steel and specified room temperature properties
BS3602	-	Steel pipes and tubes for pressure purposes. Carbon and carbon manganese steel with specified elevated temperature properties
Part 1	: 1978	Seamless, electric resistance welded and induction welded tubes
Part 2	: 1978	Submerged arc welded tube
BS3603	: 1977	Steel pipes and tubes for pressure purposes. Carbon and carbon manganese steel with specified low temperature duties
BS3604	: 1978	Steel, pipe and tubes for pressure purposes. Low and medium alloy steel
BS3605	: 1975	Seamless and welded austenitic stainless steel pipes
BS 3606	: 1978	Specification for steel tubes for heat exchangers
BS3974	-	Pipe supports
Part 1	: 1974	Pipe hangers, slider and roller type supports
BS4127	-	Light gauge stainless steel tubes
Part 2	: 1972	Metric units
BS4504		Flanges and bolting for pipes, valves and fittings
Part 1	: 1969	Ferrous
BS4508	-	Thermally insulated underground piping systems
Part 1	: 1969	Steel cased systems with air gap

VALVES AND FITTINGS

BS1740	-	Wrought steel pipe fittings (screwed BSP thread)
Part 1	:1971	Metric units
Part 2	: 1971	Imperial units
BS4368	-	Carbon and stainless steel compression couplings for tubes
Part 1	: 1972	Heavy series
BS5155	: 1974	Cast iron and carbon steel butterfly valves for general purposes
BS5157	: 1974	Steel gate (parellel slide) valves for general purposes
BS5158	: 1974	Cast iron and carbon steel plug valves for general purposes
BS5159	: 1974	Cast iron and carbon steel ball valves for general purposes
BS5160	: 1977	Specification for flanged steel globe valves, globe stop and check valves and lift type valves for general purposes

MATERIALS

BS729	: 1971	Hot dip galvanised coatings on iron and steel articles
BS970	-	Wrought steel in the form of blooms, billets, bars and forgings
Part 1	: 1972	Carbon and carbon manganese steels including free cutting steels
Part 2	: 1970	Direct hardening alloy steels including alloy steels capable of surface hardening by nitriding
Part 3	: 1971	Steels for case hardening
Part 4	: 1970	Stainless, heat resisting and valve steels
Part 5	: 1972	Carbon and alloy spring steels for the manufacture of hot formed springs
Part 6	: 1973	Metric values
BS1449	-	Steel plate, sheet and strip
Part 1	: 1972	Carbon steel, plate and sheet and strip
Part 2	: 1975	Stainless and heat resisting steel plate, sheet and strip

CALORIFIERS AND CYLINDERS

BS853	-	Calorifiers for central heating and hot water supply
Part 1	: 1960	Mild steel and cast iron
BS1565	-	Galvanised mild steel indirect cylinders, annular or saddleback
Part 1	: 1949	Imperial units
Part 2	: 1975	Metric

STORAGE TANKS

BS417	-	Galvanised mild steel cisterns and covers, tanks and cylinders
Part 1	: 1964	Imperial units
Part 2	: 1973	Metric units
BS1564	: 1975	Pressed steel sectional rectangular tanks
BS2594	: 1975	Carbon steel welded horizontal cylindrical storage tanks
BS2654	: 1973	Vertical steel welded storage tanks with butt welded sheets for the petroleum industry
BS4741	: 1971	Vertical cylindrical welded steel tanks for low temperature service. Single wall tanks for temperatures down to -50°C

COLD WATER SERVICES

BS534	: 1981	Steel pipes, fittings and specials for water, gas and sewage
BS1091	: 1963 (1980)	Pressed steel gutters, rainwater pipes, fittings and accessories

DATA SHEETS

FERROUS METALS (FM)

CAST IRON

FM01	Grey
FM02	Whiteheart
FM03	Blackheart
FM04	Pearlite
FM05	Spheroidal or nodular graphite
FM06	Austenitic flake alloy
FM07	Austenitic nodular alloy

CARBON STEEL

FM08	Grade 151-360
FM09	Grade 161-430
FM10	Grade 161-480
FM11	Grade 320
FM12	Grade 360
FM13	Grade 410
FM14	Grade 460
FM15	Grade 490 Nb

LOW ALLOY STEEL

FM16	Grade 245/240
FM17	Grade 503
FM18	Grade 620/440
FM19	Grade 620-460
FM20	Grade 621
FM21	Grade 622
FM22	Grade 660
FM23	Grade 762

STAINLESS STEEL

FM 24	Austenitic Type 302/304
FM 25	Austenitic Type 316
FM 26	Austenitic Type 321

| | material data sheet | SHEET NUMBER | FM01 | A |

| FAMILY GROUP | FERROUS | SUB-GROUP | CAST IRON | MATERIAL GREY |

GENERAL DESCRIPTION

General purpose casting material to BS1452 in 7 grades which are required to have a minimum tensile strength corresponding to the grade numbers. Grey cast iron must conform to one of the following tensile range - 150, 180, 220, 260, 300, 350 or 400 N/mm^2. The material is supplied in the as cast condition. Grey cast irons have good wear resistance and machinability with reasonable tensile and fatigue strength but poor impact properties.

CHEMICAL ANALYSIS OR COMPOSITION

No composition requirements except that the phosphorous content may be specified.

Phosphorous limited to reduce the formation of phosphide eutectic which can cause pitting by its loss from the surface during annealing.

PHYSICAL PROPERTIES

PROPERTY	UNITS	VALUES OR RANGE	COMMENTS
DENSITY	kg/m^3	7050-7300	
TENSILE STRENGTH	N/mm^2	150-400	Depending on grade
YIELD STRENGTH	N/mm^2	98-260	Depending on grade
PROOF STRESS ( )	N/mm^2		
ELONGATION	%	0.39-0.75	Unnotched 20mm test
YOUNGS MODULUS	kN/mm^2	100-145	
IMPACT RESISTANCE	J	8-48	
HARDNESS		130-305	Brinell
THERMAL COEFF. OF LINEAR EXPANSION	$^\circ$C^{-1}	10-12.5 x 10^{-6}	
THERMAL CONDUCTIVITY	W/mK	40-52.5	
SPECIFIC HEAT	kJ/kg K	0.265-0.605	
ELECTRICAL RESISTIVITY	ohm m		
ELECTRICAL CONDUCTIVITY	% IACS		

SPECIFICATIONS

STANDARD NUMBER	AUTHORITY	TITLE
BS1452	BSI	Specification for grey iron castings
BS4622	BSI	Grey iron pipes and fittings
BS4504	BSI	Flanges and bolting for pipes and valves

COMPANY SPECIFICATION:

ENVIRONMENT

Service temperature range -50 to +500°C
(grade 220 castings, used in connection with
a loss of ductility at low temperatures.
Above 350°C there is dimensional growth and
scale formation.

Good corrosion resistance in the atmosphere,
concentrated alkalis and soft water.

Poor corrosion resistance to mineral acids,
sea water and dilute alkalis.

JOINTING PROCESS

Fusion welding may be applied for joining and repair.
To obtain optimum results preheating of casting is
required (gas 550-600°C; MIG 200°C).
Bronze welding may be applied for low
temperature, distortion free repairs.

Brazing with BS1845 AG18 alloy produces good
joints without loss of mechanical properties.

SAFETY PRECAUTIONS

Remove any flux to prevent corrosion problems.

PROCESSING AND FORMING TECHNIQUES

Stress relieving - heat slowly to 475-500°C
hold and slow cool to 200°C. Annealing-depend-
ing on section and slow cool to 300-400°C.
Surface and through hardening are readily
achieved. Good castability with excellent
reproduction of detail from sand moulds.
Easily machined.

TYPICAL APPLICATIONS

Pump and valve bodies,
Pipes and fittings
Flanges for pipes, valves and fittings.
Valve trim and handwheels.

YOUR SUPPLIER AND NOTES

 **material data sheet**

FAMILY GROUP	FERROUS	SUB-GROUP	CAST IRON	MATERIAL	WHITEHEART

GENERAL DESCRIPTION

Whiteheart malleable iron conforms to BS309 in the annealed condition. Malleable irons show high ductility, shock resistance, resistance to corrosion and excellent machinability compared to grey iron.

CHEMICAL ANALYSIS OR COMPOSITION

At discretion of manufacturer other than 0.12% maximum for phosphorous

PHYSICAL PROPERTIES

PROPERTY	UNITS	VALUES OR RANGE	COMMENTS
DENSITY	kg/m^3	7400	
TENSILE STRENGTH	N/mm^2	270-410	Dependent on grade and section
YIELD STRENGTH	N/mm^2	150-225	Lower figures for sections under
PROOF STRESS ( )	N/mm^2		15mm
ELONGATION	%	3-10	Lower figures for sections under 15mm
YOUNGS MODULUS	kN/mm^2	176	
IMPACT RESISTANCE	J	2-5	Unnotched 10mm test
HARDNESS		120-180	Brinell
THERMAL COEFF. OF LINEAR EXPANSION	$°C^{-1}$	$10-12.5 \times 10^{-6}$	
THERMAL CONDUCTIVITY	W/mK	41.9 - 45.2	
SPECIFIC HEAT	kJ/kg K	520-665	
ELECTRICAL RESISTIVITY	ohm m		
ELECTRICAL CONDUCTIVITY	% IACS		

BSRIA material data sheet

SPECIFICATIONS

STANDARD NUMBER	AUTHORITY	TITLE
BS309	BSI	Whiteheart malleable iron castings
BS4504	BSI	Flanges and bolting for valves and pipes

COMPANY SPECIFICATION:

ENVIRONMENT

Service temperature range 0 to +500°C with a loss of ductility at low temperatures. Above 350°C there is dimensional growth and scale formation.

Excellent corrosion resistance to hard water and dilute alkalis.

Good corrosion resistance to soft water, the atmosphere and concentrated alkalis.

Poor corrosion resistance to mineral acids (except sulphuric) and sea water.

JOINTING PROCESS

Fusion welding may be used for joining and repair. Optimum results may require the preheating of the casting (gas over 450°C; MIG, 200°C).

Bronze welding may be applied for low temperature, distortion free repairs. Brazing may be used with silver based alloy below 650°C.

SAFETY PRECAUTIONS

Remove any flux to prevent corrosion

PROCESSING AND FORMING TECHNIQUES

Machineability excellent
Thinner sections can be cast than blackheart cast iron.

TYPICAL APPLICATIONS

Malleable iron screwed fittings.
Flanges for piping.

YOUR SUPPLIER AND NOTES

	material data sheet	SHEET NUMBER	FM03	A

FAMILY GROUP	FERROUS	SUB-GROUP	CAST IRON	MATERIAL	BLACKHEART

GENERAL DESCRIPTION

Blackheart malleable cast iron conforms to BS310 for 3 grades in the annealed condition. Created by heat treating white cast iron to produce high fatigue strength and improved impact properties over grey iron.

CHEMICAL ANALYSIS OR COMPOSITION

No composition requirement other than a maximum phoshorous of 12%.

PHYSICAL PROPERTIES

PROPERTY	UNITS	VALUES OR RANGE	COMMENTS
DENSITY	kg/m^3	7350	
TENSILE STRENGTH	N/mm^2	290: 310: 340	Minimum value for each grade
YIELD STRENGTH	N/mm^2	190: 200: 220	Minimum value for each grade
PROOF STRESS ( )	N/mm^2		
ELONGATION	%	6: 10: 12	Minimum value for each grade
YOUNGS MODULUS	kN/mm^2	169	
IMPACT RESISTANCE	J	13-17	Unnotched 10mm
HARDNESS		150 max	Brinell
THERMAL COEFF. OF LINEAR EXPANSION	$^{o}C^{-1}$	$10\text{-}12.5 \times 10^{-6}$	
THERMAL CONDUCTIVITY	W/mK	45.6-49	
SPECIFIC HEAT	kJ/kg K	520-665	
ELECTRICAL RESISTIVITY	ohm m		
ELECTRICAL CONDUCTIVITY	% IACS		

SPECIFICATIONS

STANDARD NUMBER	AUTHORITY	TITLE
BS310	BSI	Blackheart malleable iron castings
BS4504	BSI	Flanges and bolting for valves and pipes

COMPANY SPECIFICATION:

ENVIRONMENT

Service temperature range -40 to +500°C with a loss of ductility at low temperature.
Above 350°C there is a dimensional growth and scale formation.

Excellent corrosion resistance to hard water and dilute alkalis.

Good corrosion resistance to the atmosphere, concentrated alkalis and soft water.

Poor corrosion resistance to mineral acids (except sulphuric) and sea water.

JOINTING PROCESS

Fusion welding may be used for joining and repairs. Optimum results may require pre-heating the casting to prevent chill affects. (gas over 450°C; MIG 200°C).

Bronze welding may be applied for low temperature distortion free repairs.
Brazing may be used with silver based alloys melting below 650°C.

SAFETY PRECAUTIONS

Remove any flux to prevent corrosion.

PROCESSING AND FORMING TECHNIQUES

Good castability with excellent reproduction of detail from sand moulds.

Machinability good providing precautions taken against chilling and surface scale. Heavier sections can be cast than for whiteheart.

TYPICAL APPLICATIONS

Malleable iron screw fittings for pipework.
Flanges for pipes

YOUR SUPPLIER AND NOTES

 **material data sheet**

FAMILY GROUP	FERROUS	SUB-GROUP	CAST IRON	MATERIAL	PEARLITE

GENERAL DESCRIPTION

Pearlitic cast iron conforms to BS3333 for 5 grades either normalised or oil quenched. Improved strength and ductility compared to grey iron together with good wear characteristics. Ideally suited for highly stressed applications.

CHEMICAL ANALYSIS OR COMPOSITION

No composition requirements other than a maximum phosphorous of 0.12%.

PHYSICAL PROPERTIES

PROPERTY	UNITS	VALUES OR RANGE	COMMENTS
DENSITY	kg/m^3	7300	
TENSILE STRENGTH	N/mm^2	440:510:540:570:690	Minimum value for each grade
YIELD STRENGTH	N/mm^2	275:300:320:380:550	Minimum value for each grade
PROOF STRESS ( )	N/mm^2		
ELONGATION	%	7: 4: 5: 3: 2:	Minimum value for each grade
YOUNGS MODULUS	kN/mm^2	172	
IMPACT RESISTANCE	J	2-10	Depending on grade
HARDNESS		140-270	Depending on grade - Brinell.
THERMAL COEFF. OF LINEAR EXPANSION	$°C^{-1}$	$10-12.5 \times 10^{-6}$	
THERMAL CONDUCTIVITY	W/mK	37.5-45.2	
SPECIFIC HEAT	kJ/kg K	520-665	
ELECTRICAL RESISTIVITY	ohm m		
ELECTRICAL CONDUCTIVITY	% IACS		

SPECIFICATIONS

STANDARD NUMBER	AUTHORITY	TITLE
BS3333	BSI	Pearlitic malleable iron castings.

COMPANY SPECIFICATION:

ENVIRONMENT

Service temperature range 0 to +500°C with a loss of ductility at low temperatures. Above 350°C there is a dimensional growth and scale formation.

Excellent corrosion resistance to dilute alkalis and hard water.

Good corrosion resistance to the atmosphere concentrated alkalis and soft water.

Poor corrosion resistance to mineral acids (except sulphuric acid) and sea water.

JOINTING PROCESS

Fusion welding may be used for joining and repairs. Optimum results may require preheating the castings to prevent chill effects (gas over 450°C; MIG 200°C).

Bronze welding may be applied for low temperature distortion free repairs.
Brazing may be used with silver based alloys melting below 650°C.

SAFETY PRECAUTIONS

Remove any flux to prevent corrosion

PROCESSING AND FORMING TECHNIQUES

Heat treated to obtain a pearlite matrix.

Particularly suited to flame and induction hardening.

Good machinability.

TYPICAL APPLICATIONS

Similar to whiteheart and blackheart irons but with increased mechanical strength.

YOUR SUPPLIER AND NOTES

material data sheet		SHEET NUMBER FM05	**A**
FAMILY GROUP FERROUS	SUB-GROUP CAST IRON	MATERIAL SPHEROIDAL OR NODULAR GRAPHITE	

GENERAL DESCRIPTION

Spheroidal graphite (S.G.) cast iron conforming to BS2789. Available in the as-cast or annealed condition in a range of grades corresponding to their minimum tensile strengths / %elongation. Against grey iron there is an improvement in ductility, tensile and impact properties.

CHEMICAL ANALYSIS OR COMPOSITION

The cast material shall conform to the minimum tensile strength and percentage elongation as follows:

As cast or annealed   370/17; 420/12
As cast or normalised 500/7; 600/3; 700/2; 800/2

PHYSICAL PROPERTIES

PROPERTY	UNITS	VALUES OR RANGE	COMMENTS
DENSITY	kg/m^3	7100-7200	
TENSILE STRENGTH	N/mm^2	370-800	Depending on grade
YIELD STRENGTH	N/mm^2	233-471	
PROOF STRESS ( )	N/mm^2		
ELONGATION	%	2-17	Depending on grade
YOUNGS MODULUS	kN/mm^2	169-176	
IMPACT RESISTANCE	J	2-15	Unnotched 10mm test
HARDNESS			
THERMAL COEFF. OF LINEAR EXPANSION	$°C^{-1}$	115-305	Brinell
THERMAL CONDUCTIVITY	W/mK		
SPECIFIC HEAT	kJ/kg K		
ELECTRICAL RESISTIVITY	ohm m		
ELECTRICAL CONDUCTIVITY	% IACS		

SPECIFICATIONS

STANDARD NUMBER	AUTHORITY	TITLE
BS2789	BSI	Iron castings with spheroidal graphite

COMPANY SPECIFICATION:

ENVIRONMENT

Service temperature range -40 to +500°C for 370/17 and 0 to +500°C for the balance. All grades lose ductility at low temperatures. At high temperatures there is a dimensional growth and scale formation.

Excellent corrosion resistance to hard water and dilute alkalis.

Good corrosion resistance to the atmosphere, concentrated alkalis and soft water.

Poor corrosion resistance to mineral acids (except sulphuric acid) and sea water.

JOINTING PROCESS

Fusion welding may be used for joining and repair. Optimum results may require pre-heating of the casting (gas over 450°C; MIG 200°C).

PROCESSING AND FORMING TECHNIQUES

Stress relief - heat slowly to 550-600°C hold and slow cool to 200°C. Annealing - heat slowly to 850-950°C and furnace cool to below 600-500°C. Through harden - heat to 850-950°C oil quench + tempering for wear properties. Surface hardening can be applied by gas flame to obtain a hardness around 700 Brinell. Good castability with excellent re-production of detail from sand and shell moulds, with chills if wear resistance required. Machinability good.

TYPICAL APPLICATIONS

Similar to Grey iron but used where higher operating pressures are encountered for valves, pumps etc.

SAFETY PRECAUTIONS

Remove any flux to prevent corrosion

YOUR SUPPLIER AND NOTES

| FAMILY GROUP | FERROUS | SUB-GROUP | CAST IRON | MATERIAL | AUSTENITIC FLAKE ALLOY |

GENERAL DESCRIPTION

Flake graphite forming austenitic alloys conforming to BS3468. Supplied in the as-cast or annealed condition. Inferior mechanical properties to the nodular alloys. Very low shock resistance. Good resistance to creep and oxidation up to 800-850°C and to many corrosive agents. Non-magnetic grades available.

CHEMICAL ANALYSIS OR COMPOSITION

CARBON (MAX)	2.4-3.0%	NICKEL	12-36%
SILICON	1.0-6.0%	CHROMIUM	5.5%
MANGANESE	0.5-7.0%	COPPER	0.5-70%

The actual composition depends on the grade in BS3468.

PHYSICAL PROPERTIES

PROPERTY	UNITS	VALUES OR RANGE	COMMENTS
DENSITY	kg/m^3	7300	
TENSILE STRENGTH	N/mm^2	120-280	Depending on alloy
YIELD STRENGTH	N/mm^2		
PROOF STRESS ( )	N/mm^2		
ELONGATION	%	1 3	Depending on alloy
YOUNGS MODULUS	kN/mm^2	70-113	Depending on alloy
IMPACT RESISTANCE	J	40-80	
HARDNESS		120-250	Brinell depending on grade
THERMAL COEFF. OF LINEAR EXPANSION	^{o}C^{-1}	5.0-18.7 x 10^{-6}	
THERMAL CONDUCTIVITY	W/mK	37.7-41.9	
SPECIFIC HEAT	kJ/kg K	0.46-0.50	
ELECTRICAL RESISTIVITY	ohm m	1.2-1.6	
ELECTRICAL CONDUCTIVITY	% IACS		

BSRIA material data sheet

SPECIFICATIONS

STANDARD NUMBER	AUTHORITY	TITLE
BS3468	BSI	Austenitic cast iron

COMPANY SPECIFICATION:

ENVIRONMENT

Service temperature range -80 to +800°C depending on grade.
Excellent atmosphere, water and alkali corrosion resistance. Good resistance to dilute acids and fair resistance to concentrated mineral acids.

PROCESSING AND FORMING TECHNIQUES

JOINTING PROCESS

Mechanical fastening by nuts and bolts.

TYPICAL APPLICATIONS

Can be used in aggressive environments and high temperatures for pump components, valves, flue gas dampers, furnace components, compressor components and pressure vessels.

Certain grades can be used for non-magnetic applications.

SAFETY PRECAUTIONS

YOUR SUPPLIER AND NOTES

material data sheet	SHEET NUMBER	FM07	A

FAMILY GROUP	FERROUS	SUB-GROUP	CAST IRON	MATERIAL	AUSTENITIC NODULAR ALLOY

GENERAL DESCRIPTION

Nodular graphite forming austenitic alloy cast iron conforming to BS3468 in the as-cast or annealed condition with good resistance to creep and oxidation up to 800°C and many corrosive medias. Used where high fatigue stress and resistance to impact loading required. Non-magnetic grades available.

CHEMICAL ANALYSIS OR COMPOSITION

CARBON (MAX.)	2.4-3.0%	CHROMIUM	5.5%
SILICON	1.0-6.0%	PHOSPHOROUS	0.08% MAX
MANGANESE	0.5-7.0%	COPPER	0.5% MAX
NICKEL	12-36%		

The actual composition depends on the grade in BS3468.

PHYSICAL PROPERTIES

PROPERTY	UNITS	VALUES OR RANGE	COMMENTS
DENSITY	kg/m^3	7300-7600	
TENSILE STRENGTH	N/mm^2	370-440	Depending on grade
YIELD STRENGTH	N/mm^2		
PROOF STRESS (0.2%)	N/mm^2	170-240	Depending on grade
ELONGATION	%	7-25	Depending on grade
YOUNGS MODULUS	kN/mm^2	85-150	Depending on grade
IMPACT RESISTANCE	J	4-33	Depending on grade
HARDNESS		130-255	
THERMAL COEFF. OF LINEAR EXPANSION	$°C^{-1}$	$5-18.7 \times 10^{-6}$	
THERMAL CONDUCTIVITY	W/mK	12.6	
SPECIFIC HEAT	kJ/kg K		
ELECTRICAL RESISTIVITY	ohm m	1	
ELECTRICAL CONDUCTIVITY	% IACS		

SPECIFICATIONS

STANDARD NUMBER	AUTHORITY	TITLE
BS3468	BSI	Austenitic cast iron

COMPANY SPECIFICATION:

ENVIRONMENT

Service temperature range -190 to +800°C depending on grade.
Excellent atmosphere alkalis and water corrosion resistance. Good resistance to dilute acids and fair resistance to concentrated mineral acids.

PROCESSING AND FORMING TECHNIQUES

JOINTING PROCESS

Mechanical fastening by nuts and bolts.

TYPICAL APPLICATIONS

Suitable for use in aggressive environments and high temperatures for pump component, valves, flue gas dampers, compressor components and refrigeration plant. Certain grades can be used for non-magnetic applications.

SAFETY PRECAUTIONS

YOUR SUPPLIER AND NOTES

material data sheet		SHEET NUMBER	FM08	A

FAMILY GROUP	FERROUS	SUB-GROUP	CARBON STEEL	MATERIAL	GRADE 151-360

GENERAL DESCRIPTION

A semi killed or fully killed carbon steel that achieves a minimum tensile stress of 360 N/mm^2. Available as plate, sections and bars.

CHEMICAL ANALYSIS OR COMPOSITION

CARBON	0.17% MAX	SULPHUR	0.045% MAX
SILICON	0.35% MAX		
MAGANESE	0.40%-1.2%		
PHOSPHOROUS	0.030% MAX		

PHYSICAL PROPERTIES

PROPERTY	UNITS	VALUES OR RANGE	COMMENTS
DENSITY	kg/m^3		
TENSILE STRENGTH	N/mm^2	360-480	
YIELD STRENGTH	N/mm^2	175-205	
PROOF STRESS ( )	N/mm^2		
ELONGATION	%	24-26	
YOUNGS MODULUS	kN/mm^2		
IMPACT RESISTANCE	J		
HARDNESS			
THERMAL COEFF. OF LINEAR EXPANSION	$^{\circ}$C^{-1}		
THERMAL CONDUCTIVITY	W/mK		
SPECIFIC HEAT	kJ/kg K		
ELECTRICAL RESISTIVITY	ohm m		
ELECTRICAL CONDUCTIVITY	% IACS		

BSRIA material data sheet

SPECIFICATIONS

STANDARD NUMBER	AUTHORITY	TITLE
BS 1501	BSI	Steels for pressure vessels - plates

COMPANY SPECIFICATION:

ENVIRONMENT

Flanges for use between -30 and +120°C.
Subject to corrosion in wet conditions such
as rain, condensation, buried and immersed.
Full protection may be achieved by surface
coatings or wrappings.

PROCESSING AND FORMING TECHNIQUES

Manufactured as plate, sections and bar.
Supplied in the normalised condition

JOINTING PROCESS

Weldable
Mechanical fastening by means of nuts and
bolts

TYPICAL APPLICATIONS

Flanges
Boiler plates

SAFETY PRECAUTIONS

YOUR SUPPLIER AND NOTES

 **material data sheet**

SHEET NUMBER	FM09	A

FAMILY GROUP	FERROUS	SUB-GROUP	CARBON STEEL	MATERIAL GRADE	161-430

GENERAL DESCRIPTION

Carbon steel composition that achieves a minimum tensile strength of 430 N/mm^2. It is available as castings, plate, sections and bars. Pressure castings for valves etc.

CHEMICAL ANALYSIS OR COMPOSITION
TYPICAL

CARBON	0.25% max	PHOSPHOROUS	0.050% max
SILICON	0.60% max	SULPHUR	0.050% max
MANAGANESE	0.90% max		

PHYSICAL PROPERTIES

PROPERTY	UNITS	VALUES OR RANGE	COMMENTS
DENSITY	kg/m^3		
TENSILE STRENGTH	N/mm^2	430 min	
YIELD STRENGTH	N/mm^2	230 min	
PROOF STRESS ( )	N/mm^2		
ELONGATION	%	22	
YOUNGS MODULUS	kN/mm^2		
IMPACT RESISTANCE	J	25 min	Charpy V test
HARDNESS			
THERMAL COEFF. OF LINEAR EXPANSION	$^{o}C^{-1}$		
THERMAL CONDUCTIVITY	W/mK		
SPECIFIC HEAT	kJ/kg K		
ELECTRICAL RESISTIVITY	ohm m		
ELECTRICAL CONDUCTIVITY	% IACS		

SPECIFICATIONS

STANDARD NUMBER	AUTHORITY	TITLE
BS 1504	BSI	Steel castings for pressure purposes
BS 4504	BSI	Flanges and bolting - pipes, valves and fittings

COMPANY SPECIFICATION:

ENVIRONMENT

Up to 400°C, at which the yield stress is 139 N/mm^2, for castings for use at pressure. Flange grades may be used down to -50°C.

Subject to corrosion in wet conditions such as rain, condensation, buried and immersed.

Full protection may be achieved by surface coatings or wrappings.

PROCESSING AND FORMING TECHNIQUES

Manufactured into plate, sections and bars. Castings shall be annealed, normalised, or annealed and normalised

JOINTING PROCESS

Weldable
Mechanical by means of nuts and bolts

TYPICAL APPLICATIONS

Valve and pump castings
Flanges

SAFETY PRECAUTIONS

YOUR SUPPLIER AND NOTES

 **material data sheet**

SHEET NUMBER	FM10	**A**

FAMILY GROUP	FERROUS	SUB-GROUP	CARBON STEEL	MATERIAL	GRADE 161-480

GENERAL DESCRIPTION

Carbon steel composition that achieves a minimum tensile strength of 480 N/mm^2. It is available as castings, plate, forgings and bars.

CHEMICAL ANALYSIS OR COMPOSITION

TYPICAL

CARBON	0.30% max	SULPHUR	0.050% max.
SILICON	0.60% max		
MANGANESE	0.90% max		
PHOSPHOROUS	0.050% max		

PHYSICAL PROPERTIES

PROPERTY	UNITS	VALUES OR RANGE	COMMENTS
DENSITY	kg/m^3		
TENSILE STRENGTH	N/mm^2	480 min	
YIELD STRENGTH	N/mm^2	245 min	
PROOF STRESS ( )	N/mm^2		
ELONGATION	%	20 min	
YOUNGS MODULUS	kN/mm^2		
IMPACT RESISTANCE	J	20 min	Charpy V test
HARDNESS			
THERMAL COEFF. OF LINEAR EXPANSION	$^oC^{-1}$		
THERMAL CONDUCTIVITY	W/mK		
SPECIFIC HEAT	kJ/kg K		
ELECTRICAL RESISTIVITY	ohm m		
ELECTRICAL CONDUCTIVITY	% IACS		

BSRIA material data sheet

SPECIFICATIONS

STANDARD NUMBER	AUTHORITY	TITLE
BS 1501	BSI	Steels for pressure vessels - plates
BS 1504	BSI	Steel castings for pressure purposes
BS 4504	BSI	Flanges and bolting - pipes, valves and fittings

COMPANY SPECIFICATION:

ENVIRONMENT

Up to 400°C, at which the yield stress is 161 N/mm^2, for castings for use at pressure.

Subject to corrosion in wet conditions such as rain, condensation, buried or immersed.

Full protection may be achieved by surface coatings or wrappings.

PROCESSING AND FORMING TECHNIQUES

Manufactured as plates, bars, and forgings. Castings supplied in the annealed condition.

JOINTING PROCESS

Weldable
Mechanical fastening by means of nuts and bolts

TYPICAL APPLICATIONS

Valves and pump bodies
Flanges

SAFETY PRECAUTIONS

YOUR SUPPLIER AND NOTES

274

 **material data sheet**

SHEET NUMBER	FM11	A

FAMILY GROUP	FERROUS	SUB-GROUP	CARBON STEEL	MATERIAL	GRADE 320

GENERAL DESCRIPTION

Carbon steel composition that achieves a minimum tensile strength of 320 N/mm^2. It is available as seamless or welded (resistance) pipe with a maximum design stress of 68 N/mm^2 at $400^{o}C$.

CHEMICAL ANALYSIS OR COMPOSITION
TYPICAL

CARBON	0.16% max
MANGANESE	0.3 - 0.7%
PHOSPHOROUS	0.05% max
SULPHUR	0.05% max

PHYSICAL PROPERTIES

PROPERTY	UNITS	VALUES OR RANGE	COMMENTS
DENSITY	kg/m^3	7860	
TENSILE STRENGTH	N/mm^2	320 min 440 max	
YIELD STRENGTH	N/mm^2	195 min	
PROOF STRESS ( )	N/mm^2		
ELONGATION	%	26 min	
YOUNGS MODULUS	kN/mm^2	185-210	Temperature dependent
IMPACT RESISTANCE	J		
HARDNESS		130 max	Brinell
THERMAL COEFF. OF LINEAR EXPANSION	$^{o}C^{-1}$	$12\text{-}13.5 \times 10^{-6}$	
THERMAL CONDUCTIVITY	W/mK	40-50	
SPECIFIC HEAT	kJ/kg K		
ELECTRICAL RESISTIVITY	ohm m		
ELECTRICAL CONDUCTIVITY	% IACS		

BSRIA material data sheet

SPECIFICATIONS

STANDARD NUMBER	AUTHORITY	TITLE
BS 534	BSI	Pipes and specials for water and sewage
BS 806	BSI	Ferrous piping systems - land boilers
BS 1387	BSI	Tubes and tubulars suitable for BS 21 threads
BS 3601	BSI	Pipes and tubes, pressure purposes - room temperature
BS 3606	BSI	Steel tubes for heat exchangers
TR/5	HVCA	Welding of carbon steel pipework

COMPANY SPECIFICATION:

ENVIRONMENT

Maximum design stress of 68 N/mm^2 at 400^oC.
Butt welded (320 BW) pipes with a wall
thickness complying with BS1387-medium
may be used for pressures not exceeding 2.1
N/mm^2 and temperatures not exceeding 260^oC.

Subject to corrosion in wet conditions such
as rain, condensation, buried and immersed.

Full protection may be achieved by surface
coatings or wrappings.

JOINTING PROCESS

Welded joints to requirements of TR/5.
Mechanical fastenings by means of flanges
and bolts.
Screwed joints.

PROCESSING AND FORMING TECHNIQUES

Manufactured by the following methods
Seamless pipe (S)
Electric resistance welded pipes (ERW)
Butt welded pipe (BW)
Normalise temperature 880-940
Non destructive tests may be applied
check the integrity of the pipes.

TYPICAL APPLICATIONS

Pipes for low design stress ($68N/mm^2$ max)
Tubes for heat exchangers up to 50mm dia

SAFETY PRECAUTIONS

YOUR SUPPLIER AND NOTES

 **material data sheet**

SHEET NUMBER	FM12
	A

FAMILY GROUP	FERROUS	SUB-GROUP	CARBON STEEL	MATERIAL	GRADE 360

GENERAL DESCRIPTION

Carbon steel composition that achieves a minimum tensile strength of 320 N/mm^2. It is available as seamless and welded pipe and as plate for flanges.

CHEMICAL ANALYSIS OR COMPOSITION
TYPICAL

CARBON	0.17%	SULPHUR	0.05% max
MANGANESE	0.4-0.8%		
SILICON	0.35% max		
PHOSPHOROUS	0.05% max		

PHYSICAL PROPERTIES

PROPERTY	UNITS	VALUES OR RANGE	COMMENTS
DENSITY	kg/m^3		
TENSILE STRENGTH	N/mm^2	360 min 480 max	
YIELD STRENGTH	N/mm^2	215 min	
PROOF STRESS ( )	N/mm^2		
ELONGATION	%	24	
YOUNGS MODULUS	kN/mm^2	185-210	Temperature dependent
IMPACT RESISTANCE	J		
HARDNESS			
THERMAL COEFF. OF LINEAR EXPANSION	$^{o}C^{-1}$	$12-13.5 \times 10^{-6}$	
THERMAL CONDUCTIVITY	W/mK	40-50	
SPECIFIC HEAT	kJ/kg K		
ELECTRICAL RESISTIVITY	ohm m		
ELECTRICAL CONDUCTIVITY	% IACS		

SPECIFICATIONS

STANDARD NUMBER	AUTHORITY	TITLE
BS 534	BSI	Pipes and specials for water and sewage.
BS 806	BSI	Ferrous piping systems - land boilers.
BS 1387	BSI	Tubes and tubulars suitable for BS 21 threads
BS 1501	BSI	Steels for pressure vessels - plates
BS 3601	BSI	Pipes and tubes, pressure purposes - room temperature
BS 3602 Part 1	BSI	Seamless, electric resistance and induction welded pipes.
BS 4504	BSI	Flanges and bolting - pipes, valves and fittings.
TR/5	HVCA	Welding of carbon steel pipework

COMPANY SPECIFICATION:

ENVIRONMENT

Maximum design stress of 75 N/mm^2 at 400°C (BS806) for ERW and S; 26 N/mm^2 at 480°C (BS806).

Subject to corrosion in wet conditions such as rain, condensation, buried and immersed.

Full protection may be achieved by surface coatings or wrapping.

PROCESSING AND FORMING TECHNIQUES

Manufactured by the following methods:
Seamless (S)
Electric resistance welded (ERW)
Hot formed seamless (HFS)
Cold forms seamless (CFS)
Cold finished electric welded (CEW)
Hot formed or normalised 880-940°C.
Non destructive tests may be applied to check the integrity of the pipes.

JOINTING PROCESS

Welding - to requirements of TR/5
Mechanical fastening by means of flanges and bolts.

Screwed joints.

TYPICAL APPLICATIONS

Pipes for use at elevated temperatures depending on specification applied
Plate for flanges

SAFETY PRECAUTIONS

YOUR SUPPLIER AND NOTES

BSRIA material data sheet

SHEET NUMBER	FM13

A

FAMILY GROUP	FERROUS	SUB-GROUP	CARBON STEEL	MATERIAL	GRADE 410

GENERAL DESCRIPTION

Carbon steel composition that achieves a minimum tensile strength of $410 N/mm^2$. It is available as seamless or welded pipes (fusion and resistance) and plates for flanges (BS 1501-151). Low temperature impact values are quoted in BS3603.

CHEMICAL ANALYSIS OR COMPOSITION
TYPICAL

CARBON	0.2%	SULPHUR	0.045
MANGANESE	0.3-1.3%		
SILICON	0.35%	ALUMINIUM	0.015% (BS3602 PE2 AND 3602 only)
PHOSPHOROUS	0.045		

PHYSICAL PROPERTIES

PROPERTY	UNITS	VALUES OR RANGE	COMMENTS
DENSITY	kg/m^3	7860	
TENSILE STRENGTH	N/mm^2	410 min	
		550 min	
YIELD STRENGTH	N/mm^2	350 min	
PROOF STRESS ( )	N/mm^2		
ELONGATION	%	22-24	
YOUNGS MODULUS	kN/mm^2	185-210	Temperature Dependent
IMPACT RESISTANCE	J	27	
HARDNESS			
THERMAL COEFF. OF LINEAR EXPANSION	$^oC^{-1}$	$12-13.5 \times 10^{-6}$	
THERMAL CONDUCTIVITY	W/mK	40-50	
SPECIFIC HEAT	kJ/kg K		
ELECTRICAL RESISTIVITY	ohm m		
ELECTRICAL CONDUCTIVITY	% IACS		

SPECIFICATIONS

STANDARD NUMBER	AUTHORITY	TITLE
BS 806	BSI	Ferrous piping systems - land boilers
BS 1501	BSI	Steel for pressure vessels - plate
BS 1965 Part 1	BSI	Butt welding pipe fittings - pressure purposes
BS 3601	BSI	Pipes and tubes, pressure purposes - room temperature
BS 3602 part 1 and 2	BSI	Pipes and tubes, pressure purposes - elevated temperatures
BS 3603	BSI	Pipes and tubes, pressure purposes - low temperatures
BS 4504	BSI	Flanges and bolting - pipes, valves and fittings
TR/5	HVCA	Welding of carbon steel pipework

COMPANY SPECIFICATION:

ENVIRONMENT

Maximum working temperature depends on specification, working pressure and method of manufacture.

BS3602 All methods 480°C

BS3601 SAW 260°C with max. permissable design pressure of 2.1 N/mm^2.

Subject to corrosion in wet conditions such as rain, condensation, buried and immersed.

Full protection may be achieved by surface coatings or wrappings.

JOINTING PROCESS

Welded joints

Mechanical fasteners by means of flanges and bolts.

PROCESSING AND FORMING TECHNIQUES

Depending on the specification the grade is available as:-

Hot formed seamless pipe (HFS)

Cold formed seamless pipe (CFS)

Submerged arc welded pipe (SAW)

Electric resistance welded pipe (ERW)

Cold finished electric welded (CEW)

Hot formed or normalised 880-940°C.

Non destructive tests may be applied to check the integrity of the pipes.

TYPICAL APPLICATIONS

Pipe for general purposes.

Plate for flanges

Welding fittings.

SAFETY PRECAUTIONS

YOUR SUPPLIER AND NOTES

BSRIA material data sheet

SHEET NUMBER	FM14
	A

FAMILY GROUP	FERROUS	SUB-GROUP	CARBON STEEL	MATERIAL	GRADE 460

GENERAL DESCRIPTION

Carbon steel composition that achieves a minimum tensile strength of 460 N/mm^2. Available as seamless or welded pipe.

CHEMICAL ANALYSIS OR COMPOSITION

TYPICAL	BS3602Pt 1	BS3602Pt 2		BS 3602 Pt1	BS 3060 Pt2
CARBON	0.22%	0.2%	SULPHUR	0.045%	0.04%
MANGANESE	0.8-1.4%	0.6/1.3%	ALUMINIUM		0.015%
SILICON	0.35%	0.4%			
PHOSPHOROUS	0.045%	0.04%			

PHYSICAL PROPERTIES

PROPERTY	UNITS	VALUES OR RANGE	COMMENTS
DENSITY	kg/m^3		
TENSILE STRENGTH	N/mm^2	460 min 600 max	
YIELD STRENGTH	N/mm^2	280 min	
PROOF STRESS ( )	N/mm^2		
ELONGATION	%	21-22	
YOUNGS MODULUS	kN/mm^2	185-210	Temperature dependent
IMPACT RESISTANCE	J		
HARDNESS			
THERMAL COEFF. OF LINEAR EXPANSION	$^{o}C^{-1}$	$12-13.5 \times 10^{-6}$	
THERMAL CONDUCTIVITY	W/mK	40-50	
SPECIFIC HEAT	kJ/kg K		
ELECTRICAL RESISTIVITY	ohm m		
ELECTRICAL CONDUCTIVITY	% IACS		

SPECIFICATIONS

STANDARD NUMBER	AUTHORITY	TITLE
BS 806	BSI	Ferrous pipe systems - land boilers
BS 3602 Part 1	BSI	Seamless, electric resistance and induction welded pipes
BS 3602 Part 2	BSI	Submerged arc welded tubes

COMPANY SPECIFICATION:

ENVIRONMENT

Maximum permissable temperature 480°C with minimum design stresses of 26N/mm^2

Subject to corrosion in wet conditions such as rain, condensation, buried and immersed. Full protection may be achieved by surface coatings or wrappings.

PROCESSING AND FORMING TECHNIQUES

Manufactured by the following methods:
Hot formed seamless pipe (HFS)
Cold formed seamless pipes (CFS)
Electric resistance welded pipes (ERW)
Cold finished electric welded pipe (CEW)
Submerged arc welded pipe (SAW)
Hot form or normalise 880-940°C.
Non destructive tests may be applied to check the integrity of the pipes.

JOINTING PROCESS

Welding
Mechanical by means of flanges and bolts

TYPICAL APPLICATIONS

Pipes for use at elevated temperatures

SAFETY PRECAUTIONS

YOUR SUPPLIER AND NOTES

 **material data sheet**

| SHEET NUMBER | FM15 | A |

| FAMILY GROUP | FERROUS | SUB-GROUP | CARBON STEEL | MATERIAL | GRADE 490 Nb |

GENERAL DESCRIPTION

Carbon steel composition that achieves a minimum tensile strength of 490 N/mm^2. Available as seamless pipe.

CHEMICAL ANALYSIS OR COMPOSITION

TYPICAL

CARBON	0.23% max	SULPHUR	0.045%
MANGANESE	0.8 - 1.5%	NIOBIUM	0.015-0.10%
SILICON	0.35%		
PHOSPHOROUS	0.45%		

PHYSICAL PROPERTIES

PROPERTY	UNITS	VALUES OR RANGE	COMMENTS
DENSITY	kg/m^3		
TENSILE STRENGTH	N/mm^2	490 min	
		630 max	
YIELD STRENGTH	N/mm^2	340 min	
PROOF STRESS ( )	N/mm^2		
ELONGATION	%	20	
YOUNGS MODULUS	kN/mm^2	185-220	Temperature dependent
IMPACT RESISTANCE	J		
HARDNESS			
THERMAL COEFF. OF LINEAR EXPANSION	$^{o}C^{-1}$	$12-13.5 \times 10^{-6}$	
THERMAL CONDUCTIVITY	W/mK	40-50	
SPECIFIC HEAT	kJ/kg K		
ELECTRICAL RESISTIVITY	ohm m		
ELECTRICAL CONDUCTIVITY	% IACS		

SPECIFICATIONS

STANDARD NUMBER	AUTHORITY	TITLE
BS 806	BSI	Ferrous piping systems - land boilers
BS 3602 Part 1	BSI	Tubes - seamless, electric resistance welded and induction welded

COMPANY SPECIFICATION:

ENVIRONMENT

Up to 480°C with a design stress of 32 N/mm^2. Subject to corrosion in wet conditions such as rain, condensation, buried and immersed. Full protection may be achieved by surface coatings or wrappings.

PROCESSING AND FORMING TECHNIQUES

Manufactured by following methods:
Hot formed seamless pipe (HFS)
Cold formed seamless pipe (CFS)
Non destructive tests may be applied to check the integrity of the pipes.

JOINTING PROCESS

Welded

TYPICAL APPLICATIONS

Pipes for use at elevated temperatures (BS3602 pt 1 gives values at room temperature).

SAFETY PRECAUTIONS

YOUR SUPPLIER AND NOTES

 **material data sheet**

SHEET NUMBER	FM16	A

FAMILY GROUP	FERROUS	SUB-GROUP	LOW ALLOY STEEL	MATERIAL	GRADE 245/240

GENERAL DESCRIPTION

Low alloy composition that achieves a minimum tensile strength of 460 N/mm^2. Available as castings, forgings (420 N/mm^2 minimum tensile) and bars for bolts (up to 610N/mm^2). Castings subjected to stress at elevated temperatures.

CHEMICAL ANALYSIS OR COMPOSITION
TYPICAL

CARBON	0.2% max	SULPHUR	0.040% max
SILICON	0.2 - 0.6%	MOLYBDENUM	0.45 - 0.65%
MANGANESE	0.4 - 1.0%		
PHOSPHOROUS	0.040% max		

PHYSICAL PROPERTIES

PROPERTY	UNITS	VALUES OR RANGE	COMMENTS
DENSITY	kg/m^3		
TENSILE STRENGTH	N/mm^2	460 min	
YIELD STRENGTH	N/mm^2	260 min	
PROOF STRESS ( )	N/mm^2		
ELONGATION	%	18 min	
YOUNGS MODULUS	kN/mm^2		
IMPACT RESISTANCE	J	20 min	Charpy V test
HARDNESS			
THERMAL COEFF. OF LINEAR EXPANSION	$^{\circ}C^{-1}$		
THERMAL CONDUCTIVITY	W/mK		
SPECIFIC HEAT	kJ/kg K		
ELECTRICAL RESISTIVITY	ohm m		
ELECTRICAL CONDUCTIVITY	% IACS		

SPECIFICATIONS

STANDARD NUMBER	AUTHORITY	TITLE
BS 1501	BSI	Steels for pressure vessels - plates
BS 1503	BSI	Steel forgings for pressure purposes
BS 1504	BSI	Steel castings for pressure purposes
BS 1506	BSI	Steels for bolting materials
BS 4504	BSI	Flanges and bolting - pipes, valves and fittings

COMPANY SPECIFICATION:

ENVIRONMENT

Up to 600°C (yield stress 128 N/mm^2 for pressure castings). Nuts can be used down to -100°C

Subject to corrosion in wet conditions such as condensation, rain, immersion, buried.

Full protection may be achieved by surface coatings and wrappings.

PROCESSING AND FORMING TECHNIQUES

Manufactured bars, sections, plate and forgings. Castings supplied in the annealed condition

JOINTING PROCESS

Weldable
Mechanical by means flanges and bolts

TYPICAL APPLICATIONS

Valve and pump bodies, flanges
Bolts (bar stock)
Nuts

SAFETY PRECAUTIONS

YOUR SUPPLIER AND NOTES

286

 **material data sheet**

SHEET NUMBER	FM17

A

| FAMILY GROUP | FERROUS | SUB-GROUP | LOW ALLOY STEEL | MATERIAL | GRADE 503 |

GENERAL DESCRIPTION

Low alloy steel that achieves a minimum tensile strength of 460 N/mm^2. Available as casting, plate, section, bars and forgings. Valves and similar pressure castings for use at low temperatures.

CHEMICAL ANALYSIS OR COMPOSITION
TYPICAL

CARBON	0.12% max	SULPHUR	0.030% max
SILICON	0.60% max	NICKEL	3.0-4.0%
MANGANESE	0.80% max		
PHOSPHOROUS	0.030% max		

PHYSICAL PROPERTIES

PROPERTY	UNITS	VALUES OR RANGE	COMMENTS
DENSITY	kg/m^3		
TENSILE STRENGTH	N/mm^2	460 min	
YIELD STRENGTH	N/mm^2	280 min	
PROOF STRESS ( )	N/mm^2		
ELONGATION	%	20 min	
YOUNGS MODULUS	kN/mm^2		
IMPACT RESISTANCE	J		
HARDNESS			
THERMAL COEFF. OF LINEAR EXPANSION	$^oC^{-1}$		
THERMAL CONDUCTIVITY	W/mK		
SPECIFIC HEAT	kJ/kg K		
ELECTRICAL RESISTIVITY	ohm m		
ELECTRICAL CONDUCTIVITY	% IACS		

SPECIFICATIONS

STANDARD NUMBER	AUTHORITY	TITLE
BS1501	BSI	Steels for pressure vessels - plates
BS1503	BSI	Steel forgings for pressure purposes
BS1504	BSI	Steel castings for pressure purposes
BS3603	BSI	Pipes and tubes, pressure purposes - low temperature
BS4504	BSI	Flanges and bolting - pipes, valves and fittings

COMPANY SPECIFICATION:

ENVIRONMENT

Suitable for use down to $-100^{o}C$ as forgings
and castings.
Subject to corrosion in wet conditions such as
rain, condensation, buried and immersed.

Full protection may be achieved by surface
coatings or wrappings.

PROCESSING AND FORMING TECHNIQUES

Manufactured as plate, section, bars and
forgings.
Castings supplied in the annealed condition.

JOINTING PROCESS

Weldable
Mechanical systems using flanges and bolts

TYPICAL APPLICATIONS

Valve and pump bodies
Flanges

SAFETY PRECAUTIONS

YOUR SUPPLIER AND NOTES

| material data sheet | SHEET NUMBER | FM18 | A |

| FAMILY GROUP | FERROUS | SUB-GROUP | LOW ALLOY STEEL | MATERIAL | GRADE 620/440 |

GENERAL DESCRIPTION

Low alloy steel composition that achieves a minimum tensile strength of 440N/mm^2. Material supplied under normalised and tempered condition as seamless and welded pipe.

CHEMICAL ANALYSIS OR COMPOSITION
TYPICAL

CARBON	0.1-0.18%	SULPHUR	0.04% max	ALUMINIUM	less than 0.02%
MANGANESE	0.4-0.7%	CHROMIUM	0.7-1.1%		
SILICON	0.1-0.35%	MOLYBDENUM	0.45-0.65%		
PHOSPHOROUS	0.04% max				

PHYSICAL PROPERTIES

PROPERTY	UNITS	VALUES OR RANGE	COMMENTS
DENSITY	kg/m^3	7850	
TENSILE STRENGTH	N/mm^2	440 min 590 max	
YIELD STRENGTH	N/mm^2	290 min	
PROOF STRESS ( )	N/mm^2		
ELONGATION	%	22	
YOUNGS MODULUS	kN/mm^2	165-210	Temperature dependent
IMPACT RESISTANCE	J		
HARDNESS			
THERMAL COEFF. OF LINEAR EXPANSION	$^\circ$C^{-1}	$12\text{-}14 \times 10^{-6}$	
THERMAL CONDUCTIVITY	W/mK		
SPECIFIC HEAT	kJ/kg K		
ELECTRICAL RESISTIVITY	ohm m		
ELECTRICAL CONDUCTIVITY	% IACS		

BSRIA material data sheet

B

SPECIFICATIONS

STANDARD NUMBER	AUTHORITY	TITLE
BS 806	BSI	Ferrous piping systems - land boilers
BS 3604	BSI	Pipe and tubes, pressure purposes - elevated temperatures

COMPANY SPECIFICATION:

ENVIRONMENT

Maximum permissable working temperature of $565^{\circ}C$ with a limiting design stress of 25 N/mm^2.

Subject to corrosion in wet conditions such as rain, condensation, buried and immersed.

Full protection may be achieved by surface coatings or wrappings.

PROCESSING AND FORMING TECHNIQUES

Manufactured by the following method:
Hot formed seamless pipe (HFS)
Cold formed seamless pipe (CFS)
Electric resistance welded pipe (ERW)
Cold finished electric welded pipe (CEW)
Normalised at $900 - 960^{\circ}C$
Tempered at $640 - 720^{\circ}C$
Non destructive tests may be applied to check the integrity of the pipe.

JOINTING PROCESS

Welded
Mechanical fasteners using flanges and bolts.

TYPICAL APPLICATIONS

For pipe applications at elevated temperature with pre-calculated design stress limits as indicated in BS3604.

SAFETY PRECAUTIONS

YOUR SUPPLIER AND NOTES

290

 material data sheet

| SHEET NUMBER | FM19 | A |

| FAMILY GROUP | FERROUS | SUB-GROUP | LOW ALLOY STEEL | MATERIAL | GRADE 620: 460 |

GENERAL DESCRIPTION

1 Cr ½Mo low alloy steel composition that achieves a minimum tensile of 460N/mm^2. Available as tube and pipe (seamless and welded) up to 12.5mm wall thickness. Forged flanges with a minimal tensile strength of 480N/mm^2.

CHEMICAL ANALYSIS OR COMPOSITION
TYPICAL

CARBON	0.1-0.15%	SULPHUR	0.04 MAX	ALUMINIUM	Less than 0.02% max.
MANGANESE	0.4-0.7%	CHROMIUM	0.7-1.1%		
SILICON	0.1-0.35%	MOLYBDENUM	0.45-0.65%		
PHOSPHOROUS	0.04 MAX				

PHYSICAL PROPERTIES

PROPERTY	UNITS	VALUES OR RANGE	COMMENTS
DENSITY	kg/m^3		
TENSILE STRENGTH	N/mm^2	460 min 610 max	
YIELD STRENGTH	N/mm^2	180 min	
PROOF STRESS ( )	N/mm^2		
ELONGATION	%	22 min	
YOUNGS MODULUS	kN/mm^2	175-210	Temperature dependent
IMPACT RESISTANCE	J		
HARDNESS		190 max	Brinell
THERMAL COEFF. OF LINEAR EXPANSION	$^\circ$C^{-1}	12-14 x 10^{-6}	
THERMAL CONDUCTIVITY	W/mK		
SPECIFIC HEAT	kJ/kg K		
ELECTRICAL RESISTIVITY	ohm m		
ELECTRICAL CONDUCTIVITY	% IACS		

SPECIFICATIONS

STANDARD NUMBER	AUTHORITY	TITLE
BS 806	BSI	Ferrous piping systems - land boilers
BS 3604	BSI	Pipes and tubes, pressure purposes - elevated temperature
BS 3606	BSI	Steel tubes for heat exchangers

COMPANY SPECIFICATION:

ENVIRONMENT

Maximum permissable working temperature 565°C with a limiting design stress 25N/mm^2.
Subject to corrosion in wet conditions such as rain, condensation, buried and immersed.

Full protection may be achieved by surface coatings or wrappings.

JOINTING PROCESS

Welded
Mechanical fastener using flanges and bolts.

PROCESSING AND FORMING TECHNIQUES

Method of manufacture:
Hot formed seamless pipe (HFS)
Cold formed seamless pipe (CFS)
Electric resistance welded (ERW)
Cold finished electric welded pipe (CEW)
Heat treatment:
Normalised 900 - 960°C
Forgings in the normalised and tempered condition.
Non destructive tests may be applied to check the integrity of pipes.

TYPICAL APPLICATIONS

Pipes for use at pressure at elevated temperature.

Tubes not exceeding 5 mm NB for use in heat exchangers.

Flanges.

SAFETY PRECAUTIONS

YOUR SUPPLIER AND NOTES

material data sheet	SHEET NUMBER FM20	A

FAMILY GROUP	FERROUS	SUB-GROUP	LOW ALLOY STEEL	MATERIAL	GRADE 621

GENERAL DESCRIPTION

Low alloy steel composition that achieves a minimum tensile strength $420N/mm^2$. Available as tube and pipe, castings with a tensile of $480N/mm^2$ minimum and bar stock for bolts (up to $1000N/mm^2$). Pressure castings where good creep strength is required at moderately elevated temperatures.

CHEMICAL ANALYSIS OR COMPOSITION
TYPICAL

CARBON	0.1-0.15%	SULPHUR	0.04 max %	ALUMINIUM	0.02 max %
MANGANESE	0.3-0.6%	CHROMIUM	1.0-1.5%		
SILICON	0.5-1.0%	MOLYBDENUM	0.45-0.65%		
PHOSPHOROUS	0.04 max %				

PHYSICAL PROPERTIES

PROPERTY	UNITS	VALUES OR RANGE (TUBE CAST)		COMMENTS
DENSITY	kg/m^3			
TENSILE STRENGTH	N/mm^2	420 min	480 min	
YIELD STRENGTH	N/mm^2	275 min	280 min	
PROOF STRESS ( )	N/mm^2			
ELONGATION	%	22 min	17 min	
YOUNGS MODULUS	kN/mm^2	175-210		Temperature dependent
IMPACT RESISTANCE	J		30	Charpy V notch
HARDNESS		170		Brinell
THERMAL COEFF. OF LINEAR EXPANSION	$^{o}C^{-1}$	$12-14 \times 10^{-6}$		
THERMAL CONDUCTIVITY	W/mK			
SPECIFIC HEAT	kJ/kg K			
ELECTRICAL RESISTIVITY	ohm m			
ELECTRICAL CONDUCTIVITY	% IACS			

BSRIA material data sheet

SPECIFICATIONS

STANDARD NUMBER	AUTHORITY	TITLE
BS 806	BSI	Ferrous systems - land boilers
BS 1504	BSI	Steel castings for pressure purposes
BS 1506	BSI	Carbon steel bolting material
BS 3604	BSI	Pipes and tubes, pressure purposes - elevated temperatures
BS 3606	BSI	Tubes for heat exchangers
BS 4504	BSI	Flanges and bolting - pipes, valves and fittings

COMPANY SPECIFICATION:

ENVIRONMENT

Maximum permissable working temperature 565°C with a limiting design stress of 25N/mm^2.

Subject to corrosion in wet conditions such as rain, condensation, buried and immersed.

Full protection may be achieved by surface coatings and wrappings.

PROCESSING AND FORMING TECHNIQUES

Method of manufacture for pressure pipes:
Hot formed seamless pipe (HFS)
Cold formed seamless pipe (CFS)
Heat treatment:
Normalised   900 - 960°C
Tempered   640 - 720°C

Also for exchanger tubes: Electric resistance welded tubes ERW
Cold finished electric welded tubes (CEW)
Casting supplied in the normalised and tempered condition

JOINTING PROCESS

Welded
Mechanical fasteners using flanges and bolts.

TYPICAL APPLICATIONS

Pipes for use at pressure at elevated temperature.
Tubes not exceeding 50mm NB for use in heat exchangers.
Flanges
Bar stock for bolts.

SAFETY PRECAUTIONS

YOUR SUPPLIER AND NOTES

| | material data sheet | SHEET NUMBER | FM21 | A |

| FAMILY GROUP | FERROUS | SUB-GROUP LOW ALLOY STEEL | MATERIAL GRADE 622 |

GENERAL DESCRIPTION

Low alloy steel composition that achieves a minimum tensile strength of 490 N/mm^2. Material supplied in the nomalised and tempered condition as seamless pipe for use up to 580°C; for heat exchanger tubes. Cast material supplied with a minimum tensile strength at moderately elevated temperatures.

CHEMICAL ANALYSIS OR COMPOSITION

TYPICAL

CARBON	0.08-0.15%	SULPHUR	0.04 max %	ALUMINIUM	<0.02%
MANGANESE	0.4 -0.7%	CHROMIUM	2.0 - 2.5%		
SILICON	0.5 max %	MOLYBDENUM	0.9 - 1.2%		
PHOSPHOROUS	0.04 max %				

PHYSICAL PROPERTIES

TUBE   CAST

PROPERTY	UNITS	VALUES OR RANGE		COMMENTS
DENSITY	kg/m^3			
TENSILE STRENGTH	N/mm^2	490/640	540 min	
YIELD STRENGTH	N/mm^2	275 min	325 min	
PROOF STRESS ( )	N/mm^2			
ELONGATION	%	20 min	17 min	
YOUNGS MODULUS	kN/mm^2	175-210		Temperature dependent
IMPACT RESISTANCE	J		25 min	Charpy V notch
HARDNESS		170 max		Brinell
THERMAL COEFF. OF LINEAR EXPANSION	°C^{-1}	12-14x10^{-6}		
THERMAL CONDUCTIVITY	W/mK			
SPECIFIC HEAT	kJ/kg K			
ELECTRICAL RESISTIVITY	ohm m			
ELECTRICAL CONDUCTIVITY	% IACS			

SPECIFICATIONS

STANDARD NUMBER	AUTHORITY	TITLE
BS 806	BSI	Ferrous pipe systems - land boilers
BS 1503	BSI	Steel forgings for pressure purposes
BS 1504	BSI	Steel castings for pressure purposes
BS 3604	BSI	Pipes and tubes, pressure purposes - elevated temperature
BS 3606	BSI	Steel tubes for heat exchangers
BS 4504	BSI	Flanges and bolting for pipes, valves and fittings

COMPANY SPECIFICATION:

ENVIRONMENT

Maximum permissable working temperature 580°C with a limiting design stress of 27 N/mm^2.

Castings used up to 600°C (yield stress 180 N/mm^2).

Subject to corrosion in wet conditions such as rain, condensation, buried or immersed. Full protection may be achieved by surface coatings and wrappings.

JOINTING PROCESS

Welded
Mechanical systems using flanges and bolts.

PROCESSING AND FORMING TECHNIQUES

Method of manufacture
Hot formed seamless pipe (HFS)
Cold formed seamless pipe (CFS)
Electric resistance welded tube (ERW)
Cold finished electric welded tube (CEW)
Heat treatment

Normalised @ 900 - 960°C
Tempered @ 650 - 750°C
Non destructive tests may be applied to check the integrity of pipes.

TYPICAL APPLICATIONS

Pipes for use at pressure at elevated temperatures.
Tubes not exceeding 50mm NB for use in heat exchangers.
Flanges.

SAFETY PRECAUTIONS

For welded tubes and pipes a non-destructive test (eddy current, ultrasonic or radiographic) may be used for a continuous examination of the weld area depending on the specification requirements.

YOUR SUPPLIER AND NOTES

 **material data sheet**

| FAMILY GROUP | FERROUS | SUB-GROUP | LOW ALLOY STEEL | MATERIAL | GRADE 660 |

GENERAL DESCRIPTION

Low alloy steel composition that achieves a minimum tensile strength of $460N/mm^2$. Material supplied in the normalised and tempered condition for use up to $580^{o}C$.

CHEMICAL ANALYSIS OR COMPOSITION
TYPICAL

CARBON	0.1 - 0.15%	SULPHUR	0.04% max	VANADIUM	0.22 - 0.28%
MANGANESE	0.4 - 0.7%	CHROMIUM	0.3 - 0.6%	ALUMINIUM	Less than 0.02%
SILICON	0.1 - 0.35%	MOLYBDENUM	0.5 - 0.7%		
PHOSPHOROUS	0.04% max.				

PHYSICAL PROPERTIES

PROPERTY	UNITS	VALUES OR RANGE	COMMENTS
DENSITY	kg/m^3		
TENSILE STRENGTH	N/mm^2	460 min 610 max	
YIELD STRENGTH	N/mm^2	300 min	
PROOF STRESS ( )	N/mm^2		
ELONGATION	%	20	
YOUNGS MODULUS	kN/mm^2	175-210	Temperature dependent
IMPACT RESISTANCE	J		
HARDNESS			
THERMAL COEFF. OF LINEAR EXPANSION	$^{o}C^{-1}$	$12\text{-}14 \times 10^{-6}$	
THERMAL CONDUCTIVITY	W/mK		
SPECIFIC HEAT	kJ/kg K		
ELECTRICAL RESISTIVITY	ohm m		
ELECTRICAL CONDUCTIVITY	% IACS		

SPECIFICATIONS

STANDARD NUMBER	AUTHORITY	TITLE
BS 806	BSI	Ferrous piping systems - land boilers
BS 3604	BSI	Pipes and tubes, pressure purposes - elevated temperatures.

COMPANY SPECIFICATION:

ENVIRONMENT

Maximum permissable working temperature with a limiting design stress of 22 N/mm^2.

Subject to corrosion in wet conditions such as rain, condensation, buried and immersed.

Full protection may be achieved by surface coatings or wrappings.

PROCESSING AND FORMING TECHNIQUES

Method of manufacture:
Hot formed seamless pipes (HSF)
Cold formed seamless pipes (CFS)
Heat treatment:
Normalised @ 930 - 980°C
Tempered @ 640 - 720°C

Non destructive tests may be applied to check the integrity of the pipes.

JOINTING PROCESS

Welded
Mechanical fasteners using flanges and bolts.

TYPICAL APPLICATIONS

Pipes for use at pressure at elevated temperatures.

SAFETY PRECAUTIONS

YOUR SUPPLIER AND NOTES

 material data sheet

SHEET NUMBER	FM23	A

FAMILY GROUP	FERROUS	SUB-GROUP	LOW ALLOY STEEL	MATERIAL	GRADE 762

GENERAL DESCRIPTION

Low alloy steel composition that achieves a minimum tensile strength of 720 N/mm^2. Material supplied in the condition of seamless pipe for use up to 600°C.

CHEMICAL ANALYSIS OR COMPOSITION
TYPICAL

CARBON	0.17 - 0.23%	SULPHUR	0.03% max	NICKEL	0.3-0.8%
MANGANESE	1.0% max	CHROMIUM	10-12.5%	VANADIUM	0.25-0.35%
SILICON	0.5% max	MOLYBDENUM	0.8-1.2%	TUNGSTEN	0.7% max
PHOSPHOROUS	0.03% max				

PHYSICAL PROPERTIES

PROPERTY	UNITS	VALUES OR RANGE	COMMENTS
DENSITY	kg/m^3		
TENSILE STRENGTH	N/mm^2	720 870 max	
YIELD STRENGTH	N/mm^2	470 min	
PROOF STRESS ( )	N/mm^2		
ELONGATION	%	15	
YOUNGS MODULUS	kN/mm^2	165-215	
IMPACT RESISTANCE	J		
HARDNESS			
THERMAL COEFF. OF LINEAR EXPANSION	$°C^{-1}$		
THERMAL CONDUCTIVITY	W/mK		
SPECIFIC HEAT	kJ/kg K		
ELECTRICAL RESISTIVITY	ohm m		
ELECTRICAL CONDUCTIVITY	% IACS		

BSRIA material data sheet

SPECIFICATIONS

STANDARD NUMBER	AUTHORITY	TITLE
BS806	BSI	Ferrous piping systems - land boilers
BS3604	BSI	Pipes and tubes, pressure purposes, elevated temperatures

COMPANY SPECIFICATION:

ENVIRONMENT

Maximum permissable working temperature 600°C with a limiting design stress 38 N/mm^2. Subject to corrosion in wet conditions such as rain, condensation, buried and immersed.

Full protection may be achieved by surface coatings or wrappings.

PROCESSING AND FORMING TECHNIQUES

Method of manufacture:
Hot formed seamless pipe (HFS)
Cold formed seamless pipe (CFS)

Heat treatment:
Normalised @ 1020 - 1070oC
Tempered @ 680 - 780oC

Non destructive tests may be applied to check the integrity of pipe.

JOINTING PROCESS

Welded
Mechanical fasteners using flanges and bolts.

TYPICAL APPLICATIONS

Pipes for use at pressure at elevated temperatures.

SAFETY PRECAUTIONS

YOUR SUPPLIER AND NOTES

 **material data sheet**

| FAMILY GROUP | FERROUS | SUB-GROUP | STAINLESS STEEL | MATERIAL | AUSTENITIC TYPE 302/304 |

GENERAL DESCRIPTION

Type 304 is a non-magnetic corrosion resistant work hardening stainless steel. It can be easily joined by welding or adhesives. Type 304 can only be softened by heat treatment but must be rapidly cooled. It has many outlets in aggressive environments, food, medical and decorative applications.

Type 302 is a cheap version of 304 and is used for thin walled water tube. The properties of 302 are similar to 304.

Type 304L is available with a carbon content of 0.03% max. The low carbon content reduces any tendency to the formation of carbides leading to weld failures

CHEMICAL ANALYSIS OR COMPOSITION

TYPE	302	304	TYPE	302	304
CARBON	0.15 max	0.08 max	CHROMIUM	17.00-19.00	18.00-20.00
MANGANESE	2.00 max	2.00 max	NICKEL	8.00-10.00	8.00-12.00
PHOSPHOROUS	0.045 max	0.045 max	SILICON	1.00 max	1.00 max
SULPHUR	0.030 max	0.030 max			

SYNONYM
18-8 Stainless

PHYSICAL PROPERTIES

PROPERTY	UNITS	VALUES OR RANGE	COMMENTS
DENSITY	kg/m^3	7910	
TENSILE STRENGTH	N/mm^2	515	Annealed minimum
YIELD STRENGTH	N/mm^2	205	Annealed minimum
PROOF STRESS ( )	N/mm^2		
ELONGATION	%	35	Minimum
YOUNGS MODULUS	kN/mm^2	201	
IMPACT RESISTANCE	J	108	
HARDNESS		90	Rockwell B
THERMAL COEFF. OF LINEAR EXPANSION	$^{o}C^{-1}$	$18-19.9 \times 10^{-6}$	
THERMAL CONDUCTIVITY	W/mK	15	
SPECIFIC HEAT	kJ/kg K	0.52	
ELECTRICAL RESISTIVITY	ohm m	7×10^{-8}	
ELECTRICAL CONDUCTIVITY	% IACS		

SPECIFICATIONS

STANDARD NUMBER	AUTHORITY	TITLE
BS 1449 Part 4	BSI	Steel strip and Plate - Stainless
BS 3014	BSI	Welded and Drawn Tube - General Purposes
BS 3605	BSI	Seamless and Welded Tube - Pressure Purposes
BS 4127	BSI	Light gauge stainless steel tubes

COMPANY SPECIFICATION:

ENVIRONMENT

Perform best in oxidising conditions. Liable to stress corrosion in the presence of chlorides. Completely resistant to water. Types 304/302 are attacked by hydrochloric, sulphuric acids and chlorine containing liquids (sodium hydrochlorite). Dry chlorine is accepted. Up to 900°C in steam is tolerated.

PROCESSING AND FORMING TECHNIQUES

Tube formed by seam welding or seamless techniques. Soften at 1000-1100°C - waterquench. Polished finishes obtained by mechanical or electropolishing. Section shapes may be formed by drawing or rolling.

Plate, strip, forgings and castings available in the softened condition.

JOINTING PROCESS

Welding - easily joined using TIG techniques (welded tubes). MMA can give rise to corrosion due to increase in carbon content.
Brazing - easily joined using specially alloyed fillers.
Soldering - using phosphoric acid based fluxes stainless steel can be readily soldered. Good colour match can be obtained from silver bearing solders.

TYPICAL APPLICATIONS

Tube for potable water, heat exchanger, food and beverage trades; dairy equipment and marine applications. Polished finish for decorative architectual applications such as balustrades and cladding, gas flues. Fasteners for aggressive environments. Valve trim.

SAFETY PRECAUTIONS

Solder fluxes must be removed after joining to prevent corrosion.

YOUR SUPPLIER AND NOTES

 **material data sheet**

SHEET NUMBER	FM25

A

FAMILY GROUP	FERROUS	SUB-GROUP	STAINLESS STEEL	MATERIAL	AUSTENITIC TYPE 316

GENERAL DESCRIPTION

Type 316 is a non-magnetic, work hardening, corrosion resistant stainless steel. Superior properties at high temperatures compared to 304. Susceptible to weld decay; but 316L, carbon content 0.03 max, overcomes weld decay failure. Good resistance to attack by most chemicals. The addition of molybdenum increases the price over types 302/304. Available as plate, forgings and castings.

CHEMICAL ANALYSIS OR COMPOSITION

CARBON	0.08% max	CHROMIUM	16.00-18.00	MOLYBDENUM	2.00-3.00
MANGANESE	2.00% max	NICKEL	10.00-14.00		
PHOSPHOROUS	0.045 max	SILICON	1.00 max		
SULPHUR	0.030 max				

SYNONYM
18-8-2 Stainless

PHYSICAL PROPERTIES

PROPERTY	UNITS	VALUES OR RANGE	COMMENTS
DENSITY	kg/m^3	7980	
TENSILE STRENGTH	N/mm^2	515	Annealed minimum
YIELD STRENGTH	N/mm^2	205	Annealed minimum
PROOF STRESS ( )	N/mm^2		
ELONGATION	%	35	Minimum
YOUNGS MODULUS	kN/mm^2		
IMPACT RESISTANCE	J		
HARDNESS		90	Rockwell B
THERMAL COEFF. OF LINEAR EXPANSION	$^oC^{-1}$	$17.3\text{-}19.6 \times 10^{-6}$	
THERMAL CONDUCTIVITY	W/mK	16-22	
SPECIFIC HEAT	kJ/kg K	0.52	
ELECTRICAL RESISTIVITY	ohm m		
ELECTRICAL CONDUCTIVITY	% IACS		

BSRIA material data sheet

SPECIFICATIONS

Standard number	Authority	Title
BS1449 Part 4	BSI	Steel strip and plate - stainless
BS1501 Part 3	BSI	Steel for pressure vessels
BS1503	BSI	Steel forgings for pressure purposes
BS1504	BSI	Steel castings for pressure purposes
BS3014	BSI	Welded and drawn tube, general purposes
BS3605	BSI	Seamless and welded tube, pressure purposes.
BS3606	BSI	Steel tubes for heat exchangers
BS4343	BSI	Factory made insulated metal chimneys

COMPANY SPECIFICATION:

ENVIRONMENT

If held between 450-850°C integranular carbides are formed which result in reduced
corrosion resistance. Prevented by quenching from above 900°C or using 316L. Resistant to low and high concentrations of
sulphuric acid, intermediate concentrations
attack. Resistance to water at all temperatures and pressures. Attacked by
chlorides.

PROCESSING AND FORMING TECHNIQUES

Tubes formed by welding or seamless techniques. Hardened by work hardening.
Softened at 1000 / 1100°C - waterquench.
Polished finishes obtained by mechanical
or electropolishing. Section shapes may
be formed by drawing or rolling. Plate,
forgings and castings supplied in the
softened condition.

JOINTING PROCESS

Welding - easily joined by TIG techniques
(welded tubes) MMA can give rise to reduced
corrosion resistance due to carbide formation.
Brazing - easily joined using special alloy
fillers.
Soldering - using phosphoric acid based fluxes
stainless steel can be readily soldered. Good
colour match can be obtained from silver
bearing solders.

TYPICAL APPLICATIONS

Heat exchange components
Valve bodies and trim
Components for use in corrosive and
high temperature environments
Chimney liners

SAFETY PRECAUTIONS

Phospheric acid solder flux residues must be
totally removed to prevent corrosion.

YOUR SUPPLIER AND NOTES

 material
data sheet

| FAMILY GROUP | FERROUS | SUB-GROUP | STAINLESS STEEL | MATERIAL | AUSTENITIC TYPE 321 |

GENERAL DESCRIPTION

Type 321 is a work hardening stainless steel with titanium as a stabalizing addition. This reduces intergranular corrosion. Good corrosion and high temperature properties.

CHEMICAL ANALYSIS OR COMPOSITION

CARBON	0.08% max	CHROMIUM	17.00-19.00	TITANIUM	5 x C% min
MANGANESE	2.00% max	NICKEL	9.00-12.00		
PHOSPHOROUS	0.045 max	SILICON	1.00 max		
SULPHUR	0.030 max				

PHYSICAL PROPERTIES

PROPERTY	UNITS	VALUES OR RANGE	COMMENTS
DENSITY	kg/m^3	7900	
TENSILE STRENGTH	N/mm^2	515	Annealed Minimum
YIELD STRENGTH	N/mm^2	205	Annealed Minimum
PROOF STRESS ( )	N/mm^2		
ELONGATION	%	35	Minimum
YOUNGS MODULUS	kN/mm^2	207	
IMPACT RESISTANCE	J		
HARDNESS		90	Rockwell B
THERMAL COEFF. OF LINEAR EXPANSION	$^oC^{-1}$	$17.5-19 \times 10^{-6}$	
THERMAL CONDUCTIVITY	W/mK	16-22	
SPECIFIC HEAT	kJ/kg K	0.52	
ELECTRICAL RESISTIVITY	ohm m		
ELECTRICAL CONDUCTIVITY	% IACS		

SPECIFICATIONS

STANDARD NUMBER	AUTHORITY	TITLE
BS 1449 Part 4	BSI	Steel strip and Plate-Stainless
BS 3014	BSI	Welded and Drawn Tube - General Purpose
BS 3605	BSI	Seamless and Welded Tube - Pressure Purpose

COMPANY SPECIFICATION:

ENVIRONMENT

Resistant to attack by intergranular corrosion. Attacked by chlorides. Service temperature up to 800°C in air.

PROCESSING AND FORMING TECHNIQUES

Tube formed by seam welding or seamless techniques. Hardened by work hardening. Softened at 1000 / 1100°C - waterquench. Polished finishes obtained by mechanical or electropolishing but inferior to 304. Section shapes may be formed by drawing or rolling.

JOINTING PROCESS

Welding - easily joined using TIG techniques (welded tubes). MMA can give rise corrosion due to increase carbon content.
Brazing - easily joined using special alloy fillers.
Soldering - using phosphoric acid based fluxes stainless steel can be readily soldered. Good colour match can be obtained from silver bearing solders.

TYPICAL APPLICATIONS

Heat exchanger tubes

SAFETY PRECAUTIONS

Phosphoric acid solder flux must be removed to prevent corrosion.

YOUR SUPPLIER AND NOTES

4.2 NON – FERROUS METALS

Non-ferrous metals and alloys do not contain iron as the major constituent. In this Manual the metals and alloys considered are:

    Aluminium
    Aluminium alloys
    Copper
    Copper alloys
    Lead
    Zinc

During tensile tests non-ferrous metals do not show a sharply defined yield point, as does steel, and it has been necessary to define a stress which corresponds to a definite amount of permanent extension and it is called Proof Stress. The permanent extension specified when testing non-ferrous metals is 0.1% or 0.2% of gauge length.

4.2.1 ALUMINIUM

Data Sheet NF01

Aluminium is available commercially in grades from 99% purity upwards. Pure aluminium has several attributes:

-   lightweight with a density of 2710 kg/m^3 (steel 7800 kg/m^3)
-   high electrical conductivity (60% of copper).
-   high thermal conductivity
-   resistance to corrosion due to a natural surface oxide layer.

It is available as castings or wrought products. Pure aluminium can be used as a cladding to high strength alloys to improve their corrosion resistance, reflectively etc.

Aluminium's main limitations are a relatively low melting point of 660°C and its tendency to creep over 300°C. The oxide layer thickness can be increased by anodising with improved corrosion resistance together with electrical insulation properties. A highly reflective surface as well as a hard wear resistant surface may be obtained by anodising (See Surface Coatings - Inorganic).

The tensile strength of pure aluminium can be improved by cold work (up to 60 N/mm^2, depending on impurities and the degree of work applied).

The elastic modulus of aluminium and its alloys is slightly over one-third that of steel. The elastic deflection under load is correspondingly greater, which allows a better distribution of stress in a composite structure. When an aluminium structure is loaded under shock conditions its greater resiliance enables it to absorb more energy than a corresponding steel structure. The lower value of elastic modulus means that, for equal rigidity, an aluminium alloy beam must have a greater moment of inertia than a steel beam. For long struts or beams the stiffness can be made the same as a steel beam or strut of about twice the weight, provided it is feasible to increase the depth of the beam or the radius of gyration of the strut.

4.2.2 ALUMINIUM ALLOY

The mechanical properties of pure aluminium can be improved by the addition of alloying elements; the principle additions are copper, magnesium and silicon. Aluminium alloys can be split into two distinct groups:

- non heat-treated alloys
- heat-treated alloys

4.2.2.1 NON-HEAT TREATABLE ALLOYS

Data Sheets NF02; NF03; NF04; NF05.

These alloys are stronger than pure aluminium. The wrought alloys can be formed, when in the appropriate temper, without resorting to the necessity of heat treatment, they can only be hardened by cold work. These alloys can be welded but precautions must be taken (see Jointing and Bonding).

Cold work is defined as the reduction in area (RA) caused in a material after an anneal. It is designated as below:

as annealed	- zero cold work	- '0' condition	
quarter hard	- 17% RA	- H2	"
half hard	- 35% RA	- H4	"
three quarter Hard	- 55% RA	- H6	"
hard	- 75% RA	- H8	"

The hardening effects of cold work can be removed by heating to 350-430°C leaving the metal in a stable soft condition capable of further cold work. Castings can be stress relieved by heating in the region of 200°C.

Some significant loss of strength will be noted when the service temperature is in the region of 150 - 200°C.

Aluminium-magnesium alloys possess high resistance to corrosion, especially in marine environments. Aluminium - manganese alloys possess good resistance to corrosion in most atmospheric environments and are used for cladding.

Some useful cast alloys are:-

- aluminium-silicon alloys show great fluidity when cast and can be used for intricate moulds. A vast improvement in the strength can be achieved by modifying the composition with a trace of sodium. These alloys produce pressure tight castings from sand moulds.

- an alloy of aluminium, silicon, copper and iron is suitable for pressure die casting with good fluidity and resistance to atmospheric attack.

   In general, castings cannot be bright anodised as the silicon content tends to give a dark finish.

4.2.2.2 HEAT TREATABLE ALLOYS

Data Sheets NF06; NF07; NF08; NF09

Heat treatment is designed to increase the strength and hardness of an alloy. Its function is to alter the structure of the soluble elements, particularly copper, magnesium, silicon and zinc, which combine to form harder intermetalic compounds. Solution heat-treatment, including quenching, results in the alloy being soft but in an unstable condition. The hard constituents precipitate out thereby improving the mechanical properties of the alloy. The rate of natural ageing varies from alloy to alloy and can take days, but can be accelerated by reheating the alloy (artificial ageing) to cause precipitation to occur within hours. Because of the complex interactions that take place the heat treatment must be rigidly controlled to obtain optimum properties.

A fully heat treated alloy of aluminium, magnesium, manganese and silicon exhibits good electrical properties with excellent welding, anodizing characteristics and high resistance to corrosion.

A similar alloy with the addition of 4% copper is known as Duralumin. This is a high strength alloy but with poor corrosion resistance, welding and anodising properties. It readily responds to age hardening heat treatment.

With the addition of lead and bismuth a free machining heat treatable alloy is formed. However this alloy loses its high strength in operating conditions above 150°C.

A commercial casting alloy of aluminium, silicon and magnesium produces sound castings with good fluidity which responds to a full heat treatment. It has very good resistance to corrosion and anodising characteristics but it exhibits a loss of strength above 150°C.

4.2.3 COPPER

Data Sheets NF10; NF11; NF12

The choice of copper in many applications is associated with its properties:-

- high electrical conductivity
- high thermal conductivity
- resistance to corrosion
- easy working and jointing

Copper is available in a variety of commercial grades dependent on its purity and method of production. Commercially pure copper is highly malleable and ductile but can be hardened by cold work or softened by annealing.

A major output of copper is as tubing for conveying potable water.

Fresh waters generally form protective coatings on copper but high corrosion rates can occur when the layer is either disturbed by high velocity waters or acidic waters. Some types of water continuously dissolve copper due to the presence of high free carbon dioxide, chlorides and sulphates associated with low pH value and low hardness with an increase in attack at higher temperature. The dissolved copper comes out of solution in other parts of the system causing corrosion of components such as zinc coated steel.

Copper tube may suffer intense localised pitting corrosion due to the presence of carbon films if not removed after production.

Corrosion can occur if dirt, debris or rust accumulates on the copper surface.

Copper can be used for underground water and gas pipes due to its corrosion resistance to a wide range of soils. Those soils that are corrosive to copper have a high sulphate and/or chloride content with poor drainage and considerable moisture capacity. Made up ground with a high proportion of cinders is exceptionally corrosive, as is decaying organic matter and sulphate reducing bacteria.

Where it is desirable to use copper pipe in aggressive conditions it should be supplied with a protective covering of polyethylene or a protective coating should be applied using wrapping tapes or a surface coating material.

High purity copper can be divided into:

- oxygen free high conductivity copper which has a very high degree of purity; at least 99.9% copper. It is used for electrical purposes and where high thermal conductivity is important. It is used in general and chemical engineering, and as sheet and strip in buildings. Because it contains oxygen it is not recommended for welding, due to the formation of steam with consequent porosity.

- phosphorous deoxidised copper in which arsenic may or may not be present as a constituant. This type of copper can easily be welded and brazed but there is a reduction in conductivity. Mostly used for the manufacture of tubes.

Under severe conditions of atmospheric corrosion, copper is extremely resistant to attack when compared with ferrous metals. Copper forms a continuous and self-repairing oxide layer on its surface which does not absorb moisture, and offers resistance to further attack. The layer may be converted by the action of air or water to a protective mineral product such as the green patina on roofs. In general copper can be used in dilute reducing acids, caustic alkalis and waters provided that corrosive conditions, such as the presence of air or oxygen, are eliminated.

4.2.4 COPPER ALLOYS

Copper alloys are used for applications requiring increased strength and other special properties. The largest group are the copper-zinc alloys (brasses). Other alloys of importance are the copper-tin alloys (bronzes), the copper-aluminium alloys (aluminiun bronzes) and copper-nickels. These are the major constituents of the alloys, but other elements are added in order to modify the properties and hence extend the range of applications.

Impingement attack in copper and copper alloys may be avoided by limiting fluid flow velocity. A table of recommended flow rates is given in Section 1.4.6.3.

4.2.4.1 COPPER - ZINC (BRASS)

Data Sheets NF13; NF14; NF15; NF16; NF17; NF18; NF19; NF20; NF21; NF22; NF23; NF24; NF25

The zinc content ranges from 0 to 50% for commercially available alloys, which offers the engineer a wide range of mechanical properties e.g. of working, resistance to atmospheric and marine corrosion, and colour.

Brasses can be divided into two types:-

  - single phase (alpha brass)
  - duplex phase (alpha/beta brass)

and they are available in both wrought and cast forms

Corrosion failure of brasses can occur by dezincification, pitting or stress corrosion cracking. Dezincification reduces the strength of a component, by the removal of zinc, and can occur in stagnant or slow moving warm water or hot water relatively high in chlorides and containing little carbonate hardness. Nondezincfiable and dezincification resistant alloys are available to overcome this problem in areas known to have waters that promote this condition. The addition of arsenic in alpha brasses can prevent dezincification and in alpha/beta brasses the addition of 1% tin has been found to be beneficial resulting in a beta free structure.

When there is a combination of a corrosive environment and internal tensile stresses then component failure can occur, particularly in high tensile brasses by stress corrosion or season cracking.

Beta phase brasses cannot be inhibited in this way and must be rendered 'discontinuous' or at a low level alloy by suitable heat-treatment to minimise dezincification.

SINGLE PHASE BRASSES

Alpha brasses, 5 to 37% zinc, are characterised by their ability to be heavily cold worked into sheet, wire, tube and bars. The common brasses in this single phase region are 70/30 and 63/37 copper/zinc alloys. With cold working followed by annealing the as-cast strength can be increasd due to modification of the structure. In some environments the brass may be prone to dezincification which can be prevented by making additions to the alloy as described above. The addition of tin can improve corrosion resistance in marine conditions and lead improves machinability. The above alloys are also available as castings for general engineering with moderate strength and good corrosion properties coupled with economy.

DUPLEX PHASE BRASSES

Copper alloys having over 37% zinc are duplex, alpha/beta, phase brasses. The beta phase in alpha/beta brasses is brittle and consequently these alloys have to be hot worked by rolling, extrusion or hot stamping. The addition of lead ensures good machinability . Castings are also available. The beta phase causes a decrease in elongation and shock resistance and an increase in tensile strength and hardness.

The common alloy in this category is 60/40 brass. By alloying with aluminium, iron, manganese and tin, the tensile strength is increased with little loss of ductility. Such an alloy containing a combination of these elements is called "high tensile brass" and is used in the extruded, forged, stamped, rolled or cast condition.

4.2.4.2 **COPPER - TIN (BRONZE)**

Data Sheets NF26; NF27

Bronzes contain up to 10% tin. In phosphor bronzes the phosphorous acts as a deoxidiser as well as contributing to the alloy's properties, particularly strength under cold work conditions.

Phosphor bronze has improved tensile properties and is resistant to corrosion by sea water. It is available in wrought form as springs and instrument components or as castings for bearings and gears where their capability of carrying heavy loads coupled with a low coefficient of friction is an advantage. The addition of lead improves machinability

Additions of zinc and lead give rise to the range of gunmetal alloys which have good casting and machining properties. Because of the pressure tightness of castings these are of particular use for pump and valve bodies for heating, ventilation and steam applications up to 260°C. Gunmetal castings offer considerable strength with corrosion resistance.

4.2.4.3 COPPER - ALUMINIUM (ALUMINIUM BRONZE)

Data Sheets NF28; NF29; NF30

Despite the absense of tin these alloys are called Aluminium Bronze and contain up to 10% aluminium. They possess high strength, resistance to corrosion and wear, and a colour similar to 18 carat gold. Again there are single and duplex phase alloys. The single phase (5 to 7% aluminium) can be cold or hot worked for decorative purposes. The duplex alloys have 10% aluminium and can only be hot worked and are hardened and tempered similar to steels. The tensile properties can be improved with the addition of iron and nickel. Aluminium bronze is resistant to impingment attack and cavitation erosion as experienced on marine propellers and pump impellors. The wear and abrasion resistance is outstanding. Castings are available in die sand cast forms for pump bodies, marine fitting and non-spark tools. They are used where stainless steel is not suitable because conditions are reducing or because chloride ions are present which cause stress corrosion in stainless steels.

4.2.4.4 COPPER - NICKEL

Data Sheets NF31; NF32.

A range of alloys are available but the most widely used are those containing 10% and 30% nickel. These alloys are resistant stress corrosion and should be used in preference to brasses where such conditions obtain (see Section 1.5.2.4)

4.2.4.5 LOW ALLOY COPPERS

Data Sheet NF33

The properties of copper are influenced by the presence of impurities whether deliberately added as deoxidisers or hardeners, or present as impurities.

For some applications the presence of small quantities of other elements may determine the most suitable type of copper. The addition of up to 0.1% silver can raise the temperature for initial softening of cold worked copper and 0.3 to 0.7% telerium will improve the machinability of copper. High strength and conductivity result from the addition of 0.5 to 1.2% cadmium resulting in it being used for overhead contact conductors.

With heat treatment, improvements in properties can be achieved from other additional elements. A notable example is known as berylium-copper. By using a combination of cold work, solution treatment and precipitation hardening exceptional tensile properties (similar to steel) together with good fatigue and high conductivity is obtained. This alloys principle usage is in springs, electrical contact applications, and non-spark tools.

Copper with an addition of 0.5% chromium can be used for prolonged operation at 300 to 400°C without undue impairment of properties. Fully heat treated, this alloy also retains 85% conductivity of pure copper and hence finds an outlet in welding equipment. These low alloyed coppers are available as cast or wrought products.

4.2.5 LEAD

Data Sheet NF34.

Lead is a heavy, soft, malleable, easily worked and readily cut metal which is highly resistant to corrosion. When freshly cut the metal is bright but it oxidises on exposure to the atmosphere and developes a protective skin. These properties of lead make it a prime choice for weatherings, flashings, cladding and roofing. Lead has been used for pipe in plumbing systems but it can contaminate the water causing a health hazard. For this reason lead has been replaced by copper tubing in general household systems. The health problem arises mainly when the lead pipe is in contact with plumbo-solvent water (soft acidic water with a chemical composition which enhances the ability of water to dissolve lead).

Great care must be taken with lead based soldered joints for pipework destined to carry plumbo solvent waters. A health hazard may be created if solder has flowed excessively into the pipe and the water conditions are such that lead is taken of into solution. This problem may be avoided by using a tin-silver solder.

Lead is a particularly effective sound absorbing material, even in thin sheets. The cost per decibel sound reduction is competitive with many other more rigid panel materials. A lead/steel composite sheet material is available for general engineering and noise control applications where the combined properties have advantages.

The tensile properties of lead can be improved by small additions of alloying elements such as silver (0.004%) and copper (0.004%). An advantage is that thinner sections can be used for components than high purity lead, with an associated reduction in weight without a loss of general characteristics.

Lead sheet made from 'chemical' lead is produced primarily for the fabrication of chemical plant such as liners in electroplating baths.

Other outlets for lead are as free machining agents in steel and copper alloys, a constitutant of low melting solders (Section 4.3.1), electrical battery plates, bearing alloys (white metal) and radiation shields.

4.2.6 ZINC

Data Sheets NF 35; NF 36.

Zinc is a bluish-white metal which is comparitively brittle at normal temperatures, but soft and ductile at 100°C (its annealing temperature). Its main attribute is its ability to protect from corrosion. This property is exhibited whether as an alloy of zinc or as zinc layer. The main outlet for zinc is as a protective coating to steel (galvanising) where it acts as a sacrificial protective layer and is cheap to apply. It can also be applied by electro-plating, by sheradizing, by metal spray, or as a paint. Zinc coatings will be discussed in more detail in

313

Section 4.5.1: Metallic Coatings. Most joining methods can be applied to a zinc coated material. Care must be taken when welding coated components due to the production of toxic fumes.

Zinc of commercial purity is used in the form of sheet and strip for building applications such as roofing, flashings and rainwater goods.

Zinc alloys containing aluminium and magnesium are readily die-cast for low weight and low duty components. They possess dimensional accuracy and corrosion resistance. Typical products are electrical fixtures and lighting components particulary those fixed to brickwork or in cement and plaster such as light switch and socket outlet boxes. These alloys can be readily electroplated or painted, but paint drying equipment must operate well below the melting point of 387°C.

RELATED SPECIFICATIONS

ALUMINIUM AND ALUMINIUM ALLOYS

GENERAL

BS 1470 : 1972   Wrought aluminium and aluminium alloys for general engineering purposes
                   - plate, sheet and strip

BS 1471 : 1972   Wrought aluminium and aluminium alloys for general engineering purposes
                   - drawn tube

BS 1472 : 1972   Wrought aluminium and aluminium alloys for general purposes - forging stock
                   and forgings

BS 1473 : 1973   Wrought aluminium and aluminium alloys for general engineering purposes
                   - rivet, bolt and screw stock

BS 1474 : 1974   Wrought aluminium and aluminium alloys for general engineering purposes
                   - bars, extruded round tubes and sections.

BS 1475 : 1975   Wrought aluminium and aluminium alloys for general engineering purposes - wire

BS 1490 : 1970   Aluminium and aluminium alloy ingots and castings

BS 3660 : 1976   Glossary of terms used in the aluminium industry

BS 3989 : 1966   Aluminium street lighting columns

BS 4300   -   Specifications (supplementary series) for wrought aluminium and aluminium
(1-15)   alloys for general engineering purposes

BS 4868 : 1972   Profiled aluminium sheet for building

BS 4873 : 1972   Aluminium alloy windows

CP 118   : 1969   The structural use of aluminium

CP 143   -   Sheet roof and wall covering

Part 1   : 1958   Aluminium corrugated and troughed

Part 15 : 1973   Aluminium. Metric units

SURFACE COATING

BS 1615 : 1972   Anodic oxidation coatings aluminium

BS 2569 :   -   Sprayed metal coatings

Part 1   : 1964   Protection of iron and steel by aluminium and zinc against atmospheric
                   corrosion

BS 3987 : 1974   Anodic oxide coatings on wrought aluminium for external and architectural
                   applications

BS 5493 : 1977   Code of practice for protection of iron and steel structures against corrosion

ELECTRICAL

BS 2627 : 1970   Wrought aluminium for electrical purposes - wire

BS 2897 : 1970   Wrought aluminium for electrical purposes - strip with drawn or rolled edges

BS 2898 : 1970   Wrought aluminium and aluminium alloys for electrical purposes. Bars,
                   extruded round tube and sections

BS 3988 : 1970   Wrought aluminium for electrical purposes - solid conductors for insulated
                   cables.

BS 6360 : 1981   Specification for conductors in insulated cables and cords

315

RAINWATER GOODS

BS 2997 : 1958 (1980) Aluminium rainwater goods

PIPES AND TUBES

BS 5222   -   Aluminium piping systems

Part 1   : 1975   Dimensions, materials and construction of components

Part 2   : 1976   Design

PRESSURE VESSELS

BS 1500   -   Fusion welded pressure vessels for general purposes

Part 3   : 1965   Aluminium

SOLDERING, BRAZING AND WELDING

BS 219   : 1977   Specification for soft solders

BS 1453 : 1972   Filler materials for gas welding

BS 1723 : 1963   Brazing

BS 1845 : 1977   Specification for filler metals for brazing

BS 2901   -   Filler rods and wires for gas - shielded arc welding

Part 4   : 1970   Aluminium and aluminium alloys and magnesium alloys

BS 3019   -   General recommendations for manual inert-gas tungsten-arc welding

Part 1   : 1958   Wrought aluminium, aluminium alloys and magnesium alloys

BS 3571   -   General recommendations for manual inert-gas metal-arc welding

Part 1   : 1962   Aluminium and aluminium alloys

COPPER AND COPPER ALLOYS

BS 1400 : 1973   Copper alloy ingots and copper and copper alloy castings

BS 2786 : 1963   Brass wire for springs, 2/1 brass

BS 2870 : 1980   Rolled copper and copper alloys. Sheet, strip and foil

BS 2871   -   Copper and copper alloys. Tubes

Part 1   : 1971   Copper tubes for water, gas and sanitation

Part 2   : 1972   Tubes for general purposes

Part 3   : 1972   Tubes for heat exchangers

BS 2872 : 1969   Copper and copper alloys. Forging stock and forgings

BS 2873 : 1969   Copper and copper alloys. Wire

BS 2874 : 1969   Copper and coatings alloys. Rods and sections (other than forgings)

BS 2875 : 1969   Copper and copper alloys. Plate

BS 3885 : 1965   Tolerances for hot brass stampings

CP 143   -   Sheet roof and wall coverings

Part 12 : 1970   Copper. Metric units.

SURFACE COATING

BS 1224 : 1970   Electroplated coatings of nickel and chromium (copper undercoat).

ELECTRICAL

BS 1432	: 1970	Copper for electrical purposes. Strip with drawn or rolled edges
BS 1433	: 1970	Copper for electrical purposes. Rod and bar
BS 1977	: 1976	High conductivity copper tubes for electrical purposes
BS 4109	: 1970	Copper for electrical purposes. Wire for general purposes and for insulated cables and flexible cords
BS 4608	: 1970	Copper for electrical purposes. Rolled sheet, strip and foil.
BS 6360	: 1981	Specification for conductors in insulated cables and cords

CALORIFIERS, HEAT EXCHANGERS AND CYLINDER AND EXPANSION TANKS

BS 853	: 1981	Calorifiers for central heating and hot water supply
BS 1566	-	Copper indirect cylinders for domestic purposes
Part 1	: 1972	Double feed indirect cylinders
Part 2	: 1972	Single feed indirect cylinders
BS 3198	: 1981	Combination hot water storage units (copper) for domestic purposes

PIPES AND TUBES

BS 61	: 1969	Threads for light gauge copper tube
BS 1306	: 1975	Copper and copper alloy pressure piping systems
BS 2579	: 1955	Solid drawn copper alloy tubes for the manufacture of screwed ferrules, and copper alloy screwed ferrules for condenser evaporator, heater and cooler tubes
BS 2871		See Copper and copper alloys - general.

FITTINGS

BS 10	: 1962	Flanges and bolting for pipes, valves and fittings
BS 66 BS 99	: 1970	Cast copper alloy pipe fittings for use with screwed copper tubes.
BS 143	: 1968	Malleable cast iron and cast copper alloy screwed pipe fittings for steam
BS 1256		
BS 864	-	Capillary and compression tube fittings of copper and copper alloy
Part 2	: 1971	Metric units
Part 3	: 1975	Compression fittings for polyethylene pipes
BS 2051	-	Tube fittings for engineering purposes
Part 1	: 1973	Copper and copper alloy capillary and compression tube fittings for engineering purposes.
BS 4504	-	Flanges and bolting for pipes, valves and fittings. Metric series
Part 2:	: 1974	Copper alloy and composite flanges

VALVES

| BS 1010 | - | Draw-off taps and stop valves for water services (screw-down pattern) |
| Part 2 | : 1973 | Draw-off taps and above-ground stop valves |

BS 2767	: 1972	Valves and unions for hot water radiators
BS 2879	: 1980	Draining taps (screw-down pattern)
BS 5154	: 1974	Copper alloy globe, globe stop and check, check gate and gate valves for general purposes

SOLDERING, BRAZING AND WELDING

BS 1453	: 1972	Filler materials for gas welding
BS 1753	: 1977	Brazing
BS 1724	: 1959	Bronze welding by gas
BS 1845	: 1977	Specification for filler metals for brazing
BS 2901	-	Filler rods and wires for gas-shielded metal-arc welding
Part 3:	: 1970	Copper and copper alloys

LEAD

GENERAL

| BS 334 | : 1982 | Specification for compositional requirements of chemical lead |
| BS 1178 | : 1969 | Milled lead sheet and strip for building purposes |

TANKS

| CP 3003 | - | Lining of vessels and equipment for chemical purposes |
| Part 3 | : 1965 | Lead |

PIPES AND TUBES

BS 602	: 1970	Lead and lead alloy pipes for other than chemical purposes
BS 1085		
CP 143	-	Sheet roof and wall coverings
Part 11	: 1970	Lead - metric units

ELECTRICAL

| BS 801 | : 1953 | Lead and lead alloy sheaths of electric cables |

SOLDER AND BRAZING

| BS 219 | : 1977 | Specification for soft solders |
| BS 441 | : 1980 | Resin cored solder wire, 'activated' and 'non-activated' (non-corrosive) |

ZINC

GENERAL

BS 849	: 1939	Plain sheet zinc roofing
BS 1004	: 1972	Zinc alloys for die casting and zinc alloy die casting
CP 143	-	Sheet roof and wall covering
Part 5	: 1964	Zinc
Part 10	: 1973	Galvanised corrugated steel. Metric units

SURFACE COATING

BS 729	: 1971	Hot dip galvanised coatings on iron and steel articles
BS 2569	-	Sprayed metal coatings
Part 1	: 1964	Protection of iron and steel by aluminium and zinc against atmospheric corrosion
BS 2989	: 1982	Hot dip zinc coated steel sheet and coil
BS 3382	-	Electroplated coatings on threaded components
Part 2	: 1961	Zinc on steel components
Part 7	: 1966	Thicker plating on threaded components
BS 5493	: 1977	Code of practice for protective coating of iron and steel structures against corrosion

SOLDERING, BRAZING AND WELDING

| BS 1845 | : 1977 | Specification for filler metals for brazing |

DATA SHEETS

NON-FERROUS METALS (NF)

ALUMINIUM

NF01   Aluminium/1050A/1200

ALUMINIUM ALLOYS

NF02   Aluminim magnesium/5251

NF03   Aluminium manganese/3103

NF04   LM2 casting

NF05   LM6 casting

NF06   Aluminium copper 4 silicon magnesium/2014A

NF07   Aluminium copper/2011

NF09   LM25 casting

COPPER

NF10   Oxygen free high conductivity/C103

NF11   Wrought copper/C106

NF12   Wrought copper/C107

COPPER ALLOYS

NF13   Brass/CZ106

NF14   Brass/CZ105

NF15   Brass/CZ110

NF16   Brass/CZ111

NF17   Brass/CZ112

NF18   Brass/CZ114

NF19   Brass/CZ121

NF20   Brass/CZ122

NF21   Brass/CZ126

NF22   Brass/PCB1

NF23   Brass/DCB1

NF24   Brass/DCB3

NF25   Brass/SCB1

NF26   Gunmetal/LG2

NF27   Gunmetal/LG4

NF28   Aluminium bronze/CA102

NF29   Aluminium bronze/CA103

NF30   Aluminium bronze/CA106

NF31   Cupro-nickel/CN102

NF32   Cupro-nickel/CN107

NF33   Copper-berylium/CB101

320

LEAD

NF34   Lead

ZINC ALLOY

NF35   BS1004A
NF36   BS1004B

	material data sheet		SHEET NUMBER	NF01	A

FAMILY GROUP	NON-FERROUS	SUB-GROUP		MATERIAL	ALUMINIUM 1050A/1200

GENERAL DESCRIPTION

Commercially pure aluminium grades possessing low strength with high ductility. 1050A is marginally more ductile than 1200. These grades are available as sheet, bar, tube and extrusions which have good welding and anodizing characteristics.

CHEMICAL ANALYSIS OR COMPOSITION

1200 - Aluminium 99.0% min.
Cu + Si + Fe + Mn + Zn = 1.0% max
1050A - Aluminium 99.5% min
Cu + Si + Fe + Mn + Zn = 0.5% max

SYNONYM
1B/1C

PHYSICAL PROPERTIES

PROPERTY	UNITS	VALUES OR RANGE	COMMENTS
DENSITY	kg/m^3	2710	
TENSILE STRENGTH	N/mm^2	55-135 (70-150)	Soft-work hardened, 1050A (1200)
YIELD STRENGTH	N/mm^2		
PROOF STRESS	N/mm^2		
ELONGATION	%	32-3 (30-2)	Soft-work hardened, 1050A (1200)
YOUNGS MODULUS	kN/mm^2	69	
IMPACT RESISTANCE	J		Not applicable
HARDNESS		21-40	Brinell
THERMAL COEFF. OF LINEAR EXPANSION	$^{o}C^{-1}$	24×10^{-6}	
THERMAL CONDUCTIVITY	W/mK	226-230	
SPECIFIC HEAT	kJ/kg K		
ELECTRICAL RESISTIVITY	ohm m	$2.8 - 2.9 \times 10^{-8}$	
ELECTRICAL CONDUCTIVITY	% IACS	59.5 - 61.6	

SPECIFICATIONS

STANDARD NUMBER	AUTHORITY	TITLE
BS 1470	BSI	Wrought Aluminium - sheet + plate
BS 1471	BSI	Wrought Aluminium - drawn tubes
BS 1472	BSI	Wrought aluminium - forgings
BS 1474	BSI	Wrought aluminium - bars + sections
DW 142	HVCA	Low, medium and high pressure/velocity air systems

COMPANY SPECIFICATION:

ENVIRONMENT

Resistance to atmospheric attack - excellent

To retain work hardened properties the maximum service should be 100°C.

PROCESSING AND FORMING TECHNIQUES

Formability - Excellent
Machinability - Good
Anodic film   - Clear
Bending radius - annealed, close
(sheet)   - quarter hard, close
              - half hard, $\frac{1}{2}$t
t = thickness - hard, t

JOINTING PROCESS

Brazing	difficult
Welding:	
Oxy-acetylene	good
Gas shielded arc	good
Resistance	good

To prevent galvanic corrosion all bolts etc. for mechanical fixing should be cadmium plated or use a barrier such as jointing compound or insulating washer.

TYPICAL APPLICATIONS

Pipes and fittings
Hollow ware, deep drawn and spun components, cold impact hot forged components, sheet metal fabrications, process equipment for food, petroleum and chemical industries. Flashing and fully supported roof weatherings.

Ducts

SAFETY PRECAUTIONS

YOUR SUPPLIER AND NOTES

material data sheet

| FAMILY GROUP | NON-FERROUS | SUB-GROUP | ALUMINIUM ALLOYS | MATERIAL | ALUMINIUM MAGNESIUM - 5251 |

GENERAL DESCRIPTION

5251 is a non heat treatable alloy and is available as sheet, plate, extrusions, tubes and forgings. It possesses medium strength with high ductility and is hardened by cold work. Good welding and anodizing properties and resistance to marine environments.

CHEMICAL ANALYSIS OR COMPOSITION

Aluminium Balance
Magnesium 1.7 - 2.4%

SYNONYM
N4

PHYSICAL PROPERTIES

PROPERTY	UNITS	VALUES OR RANGE	COMMENTS
DENSITY	kg/m^3	2690	
TENSILE STRENGTH	N/mm^2	160min/275 max	Soft/work hardened
YIELD STRENGTH	N/mm^2		
PROOF STRESS (0.2%)	N/mm^2	60 min/175 max	Soft/work hardened
ELONGATION	%	18 max/3 min	Soft/work hardened
YOUNGS MODULUS	kN/mm^2	70	
IMPACT RESISTANCE	J		Not applicable
HARDNESS		45 - 70	Brinell
THERMAL COEFF. OF LINEAR EXPANSION	$^oC^{-1}$	24×10^{-6}	
THERMAL CONDUCTIVITY	W/mK	155	
SPECIFIC HEAT	kJ/kg K		
ELECTRICAL RESISTIVITY	ohm m	4.7×10^{-8}	
ELECTRICAL CONDUCTIVITY	% IACS	36.7	

material data sheet

SPECIFICATIONS

Standard number	Authority	Title
BS 1470	BSI	Wrought aluminium alloys - sheet plate
BS 1471	BSI	Wrought aluminium alloys - tube
BS 1472	BSI	Wrought aluminium alloys - forgings
BS 1474	BSI	Wrought aluminium alloys - bar
DW 132	HVCA	Low, medium and high pressure/velocity air systems

Company specification:

ENVIRONMENT

Resistance to atmospheric attack - excellent
Subject to attack by alkaline conditions
Generally suitable for building services.

PROCESSING AND FORMING TECHNIQUES

Formability   - excellent
Machinability - good
Anodic film   - clear
Anneal - $\frac{1}{2}$ - 2 hrs @ 360°C, cool in air
Bending radius - annealed, close
(sheet)   - half hard, $\frac{1}{2}$ t
               - hard, t.
(t = thickness)

JOINTING PROCESS

Welding

Oxy-acetylene   good
Gas shielded arc   good
Resistance   excellent

To prevent galvanic corrosion all bolts etc.
for mechanical fixing should be cadmium plated
or use a barrier such as jointing compound or
insulating washer.

TYPICAL APPLICATIONS

Welded structures, sheet metal work containers
General forgings

SAFETY PRECAUTIONS

YOUR SUPPLIER AND NOTES

 **material data sheet**

| FAMILY GROUP | NON FERROUS | SUB-GROUP | ALUMINIUM ALLOY | MATERIAL | ALUMINIUM MANGANESE 3103 |

GENERAL DESCRIPTION

A non-heat treatable aluminium of medium strength, high ductility and excellent formability. It is resistant to atmospheric attack and can be easily welded and anodized. It is available as sheet, plate, welded tube and wire. 3103 is a preferred material for sheet ductwork.

CHEMICAL ANALYSIS OR COMPOSITION

Aluminium	Balance	Silicon	0.6% max
Magnesium	0.1% max	Copper	0.1% max
Manganese	0.8 - 1.5%		
Iron	0.7% max		

SYNONYM

N3

PHYSICAL PROPERTIES

PROPERTY	UNITS	VALUES OR RANGE	COMMENTS
DENSITY	kg/m^3	2730	
TENSILE STRENGTH	N/mm^2	90 min/175 max	Annealed/hard
YIELD STRENGTH	N/mm^2		
PROOF STRESS (0.2%)	N/mm^2	71/185	Annealed/hard
ELONGATION	%	25 max/2 min	Annealed/hard
YOUNGS MODULUS	kN/mm^2	69	
IMPACT RESISTANCE	J		
HARDNESS		29 - 51	Brinell
THERMAL COEFF. OF LINEAR EXPANSION	$^{o}C^{-1}$	23×10^{-6}	
THERMAL CONDUCTIVITY	W/mK	172	
SPECIFIC HEAT	kJ/kg K		
ELECTRICAL RESISTIVITY	ohm m	4.0×10^{-8}	
ELECTRICAL CONDUCTIVITY	% IACS	43.1	

BSRIA material data sheet

SPECIFICATIONS

STANDARD NUMBER	AUTHORITY	TITLE
BS 1470	BSI	Wrought aluminium and alloys - sheet
BS 1475	BSI	Wrought aluminium and alloys - wire
BS 4300/1	BSI	Wrought aluminium and alloys for general engineering purposes - welded tube.
DW 142	HVCA	Low, medium and high pressure/velocity air systems

COMPANY SPECIFICATION:

ENVIRONMENT

Generally suitable for building services.

Resistance to atmospheric attack - very good

Resistance to nitric acid; ammonia; fluorocarbon refrigerants; deionised or soft water. Attacked by dilute acids-alkalines; chlorinated solvents - chloride solutions; lime, mortar and cements; water with Cu ions.

Direct coupling to dissimilar metals can cause galvanic corrosion.

PROCESSING AND FORMING TECHNIQUES

Anneal 350°C	½ - 2 hrs - air cool	
Bend radius	Annealed close	
(Sheet)	Half hard ½t	
(t=thickness)	Hard	
Machinability H4	good	
H8	good	

Anodising - good protection

Plating - good

Vitreous enamel - very good

Formability - good

JOINTING PROCESS

Welding

Oxy-acetylene	good
Gas shielded arc	good
Resistance	excellent

To prevent galvanic corrosion all bolts etc, for mechanical fixing should be cadmium plated or a barrier such as jointing compound or insulating washer used.

TYPICAL APPLICATIONS

Duct work

Sheet metal applications such as covers, supports etc.

SAFETY PRECAUTIONS

YOUR SUPPLIER AND NOTES

material data sheet

SHEET NUMBER	NF04

A

FAMILY GROUP	NON FERROUS	SUB-GROUP ALUMINIUM ALLOY	MATERIAL LM 2 CASTING

GENERAL DESCRIPTION

Alloy for pressure die casting. Medium strength with low shock resistance non heat-treatable alloy.

CHEMICAL ANALYSIS OR COMPOSITION

Aluminium	Balance
Silicon	9.0 - 11.5%
Copper	0.7 - 2.5%
Iron	1.0% max

PHYSICAL PROPERTIES

PROPERTY	UNITS	VALUES OR RANGE	COMMENTS
DENSITY	kg/m^3	2740	
TENSILE STRENGTH	N/mm^2	150 min	Chill cast
YIELD STRENGTH	N/mm^2		
PROOF STRESS (0.2%)	N/mm^2	90 min	Chill cast
ELONGATION	%	1 min	Chill cast
YOUNGS MODULUS	kN/mm^2	71	
IMPACT RESISTANCE	J		
HARDNESS		65-90	Brinell
THERMAL COEFF. OF LINEAR EXPANSION	$^oC^{-1}$	20×10^{-6}	
THERMAL CONDUCTIVITY	W/mK	100	
SPECIFIC HEAT	kJ/kg K		
ELECTRICAL RESISTIVITY	ohm m	6.63×10^{-8}	
ELECTRICAL CONDUCTIVITY	% IACS	26	

SPECIFICATIONS

STANDARD NUMBER	AUTHORITY	TITLE
BS 1490	BSI	Aluminium and aluminium alloys ingots and castings

COMPANY SPECIFICATION:

ENVIRONMENT

Generally suited to building services.
Service temperature - below 150°C. Resistance
to atmospheric attack - fair. Pressure
tightness - good. Resistant to attack by
nitric acid (80+); ammonia; fluorocarbon
refrigerants; deionised and soft water.
Attacked by dilute acids; alkalines;
chlorinated solvents; chloride solutions;
lime, mortar and cements; water with Cu ions.
Direct coupling to dissimilar metals can
cause galvanic corrosion.

JOINTING PROCESS

Welding unsuitable. To prevent galvanic
corrosion all bolts etc. for mechanical
fixing should be cadmium plated or use a
barrier such as jointing compound or insulating material.

PROCESSING AND FORMING TECHNIQUES

Castability - very good
Machinability - fair
Anodic film - grey with fair protection
Resistance to hot tear - excellent
No heat treatment required.

TYPICAL APPLICATIONS

General engineering components that can be
produced by pressure die casting.

SAFETY PRECAUTIONS

YOUR SUPPLIER AND NOTES

SHEET NUMBER	NF 05

A

FAMILY GROUP	NON FERROUS	SUB-GROUP	ALUMINIUM ALLOY	MATERIAL	LM6 CASTING

GENERAL DESCRIPTION

Casting alloy. Medium strength with moderately high shock resistance. High fluidity allowing large intricate castings. Non heat treatable alloy in the as manufactured condition.

CHEMICAL ANALYSIS OR COMPOSITION

Aluminium	Balance
Silicon	10.0 - 13.0%
Iron	0.6% Max
Manganese	0.5% Max

PHYSICAL PROPERTIES

PROPERTY	UNITS	VALUES OR RANGE	COMMENTS
DENSITY	kg/m^3	2650	
TENSILE STRENGTH	N/mm^2	160 min/190 min	Sand cast/chill cast
YIELD STRENGTH	N/mm^2		
PROOF STRESS (0.2%)	N/mm^2	60 min/ 70 min	Sand cast/chill cast
ELONGATION	%	5 min/13 min	Sand cast/chill cast
YOUNGS MODULUS	kN/mm^2	71	
IMPACT RESISTANCE	J		
HARDNESS		55-60	Brinell
THERMAL COEFF. OF LINEAR EXPANSION	$°C^{-1}$	20×10^{-6}	
THERMAL CONDUCTIVITY	W/mK	142	
SPECIFIC HEAT	kJ/kg·K		
ELECTRICAL RESISTIVITY	ohm m	4.65×10^{-8}	
ELECTRICAL CONDUCTIVITY	% IACS	37	

material data sheet

SPECIFICATIONS

STANDARD NUMBER	AUTHORITY	TITLE
BS 1490	BSI	Aluminium and aluminium alloy ingots and castings
BS 5154	BSI	Copper alloy globe check and gate valves

COMPANY SPECIFICATION:

ENVIRONMENT

Generally suitable for building services.
Service temperature - below 150°C. Resistance
to atmospheric attack - good. Pressure tightness
- excellent. Resistant to attack by nitric acid
(80%+); ammonia, fluorocarbon refrigerents; deionised and soft water. Attacked by dilute acids;
alkalines; chlorinated solvents; chloride
solutions; lime, mortar, cements; water with
Cu ions. Direct coupling to dissimilar metal
can cause galvanic corrosion.

PROCESSING AND FORMING TECHNIQUES

Castability - very good
Machinability - fair
Anodic film - grey with fair protection
Resistance to hot tear - excellent.

Anneal 2-4 hrs @ 280 - 350°C to improve
shock resistance.

JOINTING PROCESS

Welding - good
To prevent galvanic corrosion all bolts etc. for
mechanical fixing should be cadmium plated or use
a barrier such as jointing compound or insulating
washer.

TYPICAL APPLICATIONS

Normally used for sand and gravity die
castingwith excellent results. Suitable
for intricate thin walled pressure tight
castings for marine, food industry and
general uses. Valve hand wheels.

SAFETY PRECAUTIONS

YOUR SUPPLIER AND NOTES

| material data sheet | SHEET NUMBER | NF 06 | A |
| FAMILY GROUP NON FERROUS | SUB-GROUP ALUMINIUM ALLOY | MATERIAL ALUMINIUM COPPER 4 SILICON MAGNESIUM-2014A | |

GENERAL DESCRIPTION

Heat treatable alloy for general engineering purposes. Available in sheet, bar, forgings, tube and wire. High strength with medium ductility. Also available as sheet clad with pure aluminium, (CLAD 2014A).

CHEMICAL ANALYSIS OR COMPOSITION

Aluminium	Balance
Copper	3.9 - 5.0%
Silicon	0.5 - 1.0%
Magnesium	0.2 - 0.8%

SYNONYM

H15 , HC15 (clad material)
'Dural'

PHYSICAL PROPERTIES

PROPERTY	UNITS	VALUES OR RANGE	COMMENTS
DENSITY	kg/m^3	2800	
TENSILE STRENGTH	N/mm^2	375 min/440 max	Solution treated/age hardened
YIELD STRENGTH	N/mm^2		
PROOF STRESS (0.2%)	N/mm^2	230 min/380 max	Solution treated/age hardened
ELONGATION	%	10 min/6 min	Solution treated/age hardened
YOUNGS MODULUS	kN/mm^2	74	
IMPACT RESISTANCE	J		Not applicable
HARDNESS		115-145	Brinell
THERMAL COEFF. OF LINEAR EXPANSION	$^oC^{-1}$	22×10^{-6}	
THERMAL CONDUCTIVITY	W/mK	142 - 159	
SPECIFIC HEAT	kJ/kg K		
ELECTRICAL RESISTIVITY	ohm m	$4.5 - 5 \times 10^{-8}$	
ELECTRICAL CONDUCTIVITY	% IACS	32.5 - 38.3	

SPECIFICATIONS

STANDARD NUMBER	AUTHORITY	TITLE
BS 1470	BSI	Wrought aluminium alloys - sheet + plate
BS 1471	BSI	Wrought aluminium alloys - tube
BS 1472	BSI	Wrought aluminium alloys - forgings
BS 1474	BSI	Wrought aluminium alloys - bars

COMPANY SPECIFICATION:

ENVIRONMENT

Unsuitable for use in aggressive conditions due to poor corrosion resistance. Service temperature - up to 200°C Resistance to atmospheric attack - poor. An improvement is achieved by using 2014A clad with high purity aluminium (sheet & plate). Direct coupling to dissimilar metals can cause galvanic corrosion, particularly copper. Liable to stress corrosion. Attacked by lime, mortar and cements. Chlorinated solvents attack. Used for deionised and soft water but not potable water due to attack by Cu ions. Resistant to nitric acid, ammonia and fluorinated refrigerant gases.

JOINTING PROCESS

Welding
  Resistance
  All other methods not recommended. To prevent galvanic corrosion all bolts, etc for mechanical fixing should be cadmium plated or use a barrier such as jointing compound or insulating washers.

PROCESSING AND FORMING TECHNIQUES

Formability - good
Machinability - very good
Anodic film - cloudy
Solution treatment - 2-4 hrs @ 500-510, water quench.
Ageing - 5-20 hrs @ 155-185°C
Anneal - 2 hrs @ 360°C, slow cool
Bending radius - Solution treaded, 3T
(sheet)   - Solution treated + age
                     hardened, 5T
                     (t = thickness)

TYPICAL APPLICATIONS

Low weight, high strength applications

SAFETY PRECAUTIONS

YOUR SUPPLIER AND NOTES

 **material data sheet**

FAMILY GROUP	NON FERROUS	SUB-GROUP	ALUMINIUM ALLOY	MATERIAL	ALUMINIUM SILICON 1 MAGNESIUM MANGANESE - 6082

GENERAL DESCRIPTION

Heat treatable alloy with medium strength and medium ductility. Available in sheet, extrusions, tubes and forgings. Good welding and anodizing properties.

CHEMICAL ANALYSIS OR COMPOSITION

Aluminium	Balance
Silicon	0.7 - 1.3%
Magnesium	0.5 - 1.2%
Manganese	0.4 - 1.0%

SYNONYM

H30

PHYSICAL PROPERTIES

PROPERTY	UNITS	VALUES OR RANGE	COMMENTS
DENSITY	kg/m^3	2700	
TENSILE STRENGTH	N/mm^2	200 min/295 min	Solution treated/age hardened
YIELD STRENGTH	N/mm^2		
PROOF STRESS (0.2%)	N/mm^2	120 min/240 min	Solution treated/age hardened
ELONGATION	%	15 min/8 min	Solution treated/age hardened
YOUNGS MODULUS	kN/mm^2	69	
IMPACT RESISTANCE	J		Not applicable
HARDNESS		60 - 100	Brinell
THERMAL COEFF. OF LINEAR EXPANSION	$^{o}c^{-1}$	23×10^{-6}	
THERMAL CONDUCTIVITY	W/mK	172 - 184	
SPECIFIC HEAT	kJ/kg K		
ELECTRICAL RESISTIVITY	ohm m	$3.7 - 4.1 \times 10^{-8}$	
ELECTRICAL CONDUCTIVITY	% IACS	42.1 - 46.6	

SPECIFICATIONS

STANDARD NUMBER	AUTHORITY	TITLE
BS 1470	BSI	Wrought aluminium alloys - sheet + plate
BS 1471	BSI	Wrought aluminium alloys - tubes
BS 1472	BSI	Wrought aluminium alloys - forgings
BS 1474	BSI	Wrought aluminium alloys - bars

COMPANY SPECIFICATION:

ENVIRONMENT

Generally suitable for building services.
Service temperature - up to 150°C. Resistance
to atmospheric attack - good. Resistant to attack
by nitric acid (80%+); ammonia; fluorocarbon
refrigerants; deionised and soft water. Attacked
by chlorinated solvents; chloride solutions;
lime, mortar and cements; dilute acids; alkaline
solutions; Direct coupling to dissimilar metals
can cause galvanic corrosion.

PROCESSING AND FORMING TECHNIQUES

Formability - good
Anodic film - clear
Machinability - very good
Solution treatment - 4 hours @ 520-540°C
water quench.
Ageing - 5-12 hrs @ 175-185°C
Anneal - ½ - 2 hrs @ 360°C, slow cool
Bending radius - annealed, close
      - solution treated; 2t
      - hardened, 3t
      (t = thickness)
Plating - pretreatment required

JOINTING PROCESS

Welding
    Oxy-acetylene - fair
    Gas shielded arc - good
    Resistance - good
Do not weld in heat treated condition because
weld zone will be softened. To prevent galvanic
corrosion all bolts etc, for mechanical fixing
should be cadmium plated or a barrier such as
jointing compound or insulating washer used.

TYPICAL APPLICATIONS

Cold impact forgings; containers such as
barrels and churns. Pressed and deep drawn
components.
Tube, sections for structural use, pipe,
conduit, structural frames.

SAFETY PRECAUTIONS

YOUR SUPPLIER AND NOTES

 **material data sheet**

	SHEET NUMBER NF08	A

FAMILY GROUP NON FERROUS	SUB-GROUP ALUMINIUM ALLOY	MATERIAL ALUMINIUM COPPER 2011

GENERAL DESCRIPTION

Free machining heat treatable alloy. Available in bar and wire form only. High strength with medium ductility. Subject to stress corrosion.

CHEMICAL ANALYSIS OR COMPOSITION

Aluminium	Balance	Bismuth	0.2 - 0.7%
Copper	5.0 - 6.0%	Lead	0.2 - 0.7%
Iron	0.7 max.		
Silicon	0.4 max		

SYNONYM

FC1

PHYSICAL PROPERTIES

PROPERTY	UNITS	VALUES OR RANGE	COMMENTS
DENSITY	kg/m^3	2830	
TENSILE STRENGTH	N/mm^2	295 - 310 min	Age hardened
YIELD STRENGTH	N/mm^2		
PROOF STRESS (0.2%)	N/mm^2	195 - 230 min	Age hardened
ELONGATION	%	6-5	Age hardened
YOUNGS MODULUS	kN/mm^2	71	
IMPACT RESISTANCE	J		Not applicable
HARDNESS		90 - 100	Brinell
THERMAL COEFF. OF LINEAR EXPANSION	$^{o}C^{-1}$	23×10^{-6}	
THERMAL CONDUCTIVITY	W/mK	163	
SPECIFIC HEAT	kJ/kg K		
ELECTRICAL RESISTIVITY	ohm m	4.4×10^{-8}	
ELECTRICAL CONDUCTIVITY	% IACS	39.2	

material data sheet

SPECIFICATIONS

STANDARD NUMBER	AUTHORITY	TITLE
BS 4300/5	BSI	Aluminium and aluminium alloys for general engineering - free cutting bar and wire.

COMPANY SPECIFICATION:

ENVIRONMENT

Service temperature below 100°C. Resistance to atmospheric attack - fairly good. Resistant to attack by nitric acid; ammonia; fluorocarbon refrigerants; deionised and soft water. Attacked by dilute acids, alkalines; chlorinated solvents; chloride solutions - lime, mortar and cements; water with Cu ions. Direct coupling to dissimilar metals can cause galvanic corrosion. Subject to stress corrosion.

JOINTING PROCESS

(Not suitable for welding) To prevent galvanic corrosion all bolts etc, for mechanical fixing should be cadmium plated or use a barrier such as jointing compound or insulating washer.

PROCESSING AND FORMING TECHNIQUES

Machinability - excellent
Anodic film - cloudy
Formability - fairly good

Solution treatment 6-8 hrs @ 515/525°C, water quench @ 20/30°C.
Age harden 16 hrs @ 160/170°C.

TYPICAL APPLICATIONS

Repetition machined components such as shafts, valve bodies, hydraulic piston and cylinders, screws, nuts, connectors.

SAFETY PRECAUTIONS

YOUR SUPPLIER AND NOTES

| | material data sheet | | SHEET NUMBER | NF09 | A |

| FAMILY GROUP | NON FERROUS | SUB-GROUP | ALUMINIUM ALLOY | MATERIAL | LM25 CASTING |

GENERAL DESCRIPTION

Heat treatable alloy for sand or gravity die castings. Moderately high strength with medium shock resistance to replace M8.

CHEMICAL ANALYSIS OR COMPOSITION

Aluminium	Balance
Silicon	6.5-7.5%
Magnesium	0.2-0.45%
Iron	0.5 max
Manganese	0.3 max

PHYSICAL PROPERTIES

PROPERTY	UNITS	VALUES OR RANGE	COMMENTS
DENSITY	kg/m^3	2680	
TENSILE STRENGTH	N/mm^2	130-230 min/160-290 min	Sand cast/chill cast
YIELD STRENGTH	N/mm^2		
PROOF STRESS (0.2%)	N/mm^2	80-250/80-260	Sand cast/chill cast
ELONGATION	%	1-3/2-10	Sand cast/chill cast
YOUNGS MODULUS	kN/mm^2	71	
IMPACT RESISTANCE	J		
HARDNESS		55-110	Brinell
THERMAL COEFF. OF LINEAR EXPANSION	$^{o}C^{-1}$	22×10^{-6}	
THERMAL CONDUCTIVITY	W/mK		
SPECIFIC HEAT	kJ/kg K		
ELECTRICAL RESISTIVITY	ohm m	4.4×10^{-8}	
ELECTRICAL CONDUCTIVITY	% IACS	39	

 **BSRIA** material
data sheet

SPECIFICATIONS

STANDARD NUMBER	AUTHORITY	TITLE
BS1490	BSI	Aluminium and aluminium alloy ingots and castings

COMPANY SPECIFICATION:

ENVIRONMENT

Service temperature - below 150°C. Resistance to atmospheric attack - Excellent.
Pressure Tightness - Good
Resistant to attack by nitric acid (80%+); deionised and soft water. Attacked by dilute acids; alkalines; chlorinated solvents; chloride solutions; lime mortar and cements; water with Cu ions.
Direct coupling to dissimilar metals can cause galvanic corrosion.

JOINTING PROCESS

Welding - Good
To prevent galvanic corrosion all bolts etc for mechanical fixing should be cadmium plated or use a barrier such as jointing compount or insulating material.
Heat treated components cannot be welded without loss of properties in the heated zone.

PROCESSING AND FORMING TECHNIQUES

Castability - Good
Machinability - Fair
Anodic film - Cloudy with fair protection
                may be dyed with dark colours
Resistance to Hot Tear - Good
Solution Treatment - 4-12 hrs @ 525-545°C, Hot Water Quench
Age Hardening - 8-12 hrs @ 200-210°C slow cool.

TYPICAL APPLICATIONS

Used in as manufactured or heat treated condition. Sand & Gravity die castings for general purposes. Also chemical industry and marine components, door furniture, electrical equipment etc.

SAFETY PRECAUTIONS

YOUR SUPPLIER AND NOTES

material data sheet

SHEET NUMBER	NF10

A

FAMILY GROUP	NON FERROUS	SUB-GROUP	COPPER	MATERIAL	OXYGEN FREE HIGH CONDUCTIVITY - C103

GENERAL DESCRIPTION

Oxygen free high conductivity copper for thermal and electrical purpose. It can be readily brazed and welded and is available as tube, strip, plate, extrusions and bars. Hardness increased by cold work.

CHEMICAL ANALYSIS OR COMPOSITION

Copper 99.95% min

SYNONYM

OFHC - C103

PHYSICAL PROPERTIES

PROPERTY	UNITS	VALUES OR RANGE	COMMENTS
DENSITY	kg/m^3	8940	
TENSILE STRENGTH	N/mm^2	216/317 min	Annealed/Hard
YIELD STRENGTH	N/mm^2		
PROOF STRESS (0.1%)	N/mm^2	46/293 min	Annealed/Hard
ELONGATION	%	55/16 min	Annealed/Hard
YOUNGS MODULUS	kN/mm^2	124	
IMPACT RESISTANCE	J		
HARDNESS		42 - 96	Brinell
THERMAL COEFF. OF LINEAR EXPANSION	$°C^{-1}$	17.7×10^{-6}	
THERMAL CONDUCTIVITY	W/mK	314 - 402	
SPECIFIC HEAT	kJ/kg K		
ELECTRICAL RESISTIVITY	ohm m	$1.74 - 2.15 \times 10^{-8}$	
ELECTRICAL CONDUCTIVITY	% IACS	101.5 - 100	

BSRIA material data sheet

SPECIFICATIONS

STANDARD NUMBER	AUTHORITY	TITLE
BS 1861 in BS 1035	BSI	Oxygen free high conductivity Copper
BS 699	BSI	Copper cylinders - Direct
BS 1566	BSI	Copper cylinders - Indirect
BS 2871 Part 2	BSI	Copper and copper alloy tubes - General

COMPANY SPECIFICATION:

ENVIRONMENT

Withstands reducing atmospheres, such as hydrogen, at elevated temperatures, e.g. during welding. Corrosion resistance good in dilute acids, caustic alkali, sea and other waters. Service temperature range - 200 to +205°C (creep starts at +120°C).

PROCESSING AND FORMING TECHNIQUES

Available in various cold work temper conditions. Sheet and strip easily formed.
Bend radius - annealed, close
(sheet) - hard condition, t
  (t = thickness)
Tube bends can be formed using internal support
Machinability improved with cold work
Annealed 450-650°C

JOINTING PROCESS

Soldering   excellent
Brazing   good
Bronze welding fair
Welding
  Cold pressure good
  Friction   fair
  Induction   fair
  Electron beam excellent
Care must be taken in corrosive media because of possible galvanic action due to contact between dissimilar metals.
Excess flux must be removed to prevent corrosion

TYPICAL APPLICATIONS

Tubes for general purposes. Sheet material for fabrication such as H & C water cylinders High electrical conductivity applications.

SAFETY PRECAUTIONS

YOUR SUPPLIER AND NOTES

341

 **material data sheet**

| FAMILY GROUP | NON FERROUS | SUB-GROUP | COPPER | MATERIAL | WROUGHT COPPER/C106 |

GENERAL DESCRIPTION

Phosphorous deoxidised non-arsenical copper cold worked material with good thermal and electrical conductivity. Can be easily debrazed and welded. Available in many forms particularly tube and extrusions. Preferred material for tubing to BS 2871 Parts 1, 2 and 3.

CHEMICAL ANALYSIS OR COMPOSITION

Copper 99.85% min
Phosphorous 0.013-0.050%

SYNONYM

Phosphorous deoxidized non-arsenical copper

PHYSICAL PROPERTIES

PROPERTY	UNITS	VALUES OR RANGE	COMMENTS
DENSITY	kg/m^3	8940	
TENSILE STRENGTH	N/mm^2	210/340 min	Annealed/Hard
YIELD STRENGTH	N/mm^2		
PROOF STRESS (0.1%)	N/mm^2	46/317 min	Annealed/Hard
ELONGATION	%	58/15 min	Annealed/Hard
YOUNGS MODULUS	kN/mm^2	124	
IMPACT RESISTANCE	J		
HARDNESS		49 - 99	Brinell
THERMAL COEFF. OF LINEAR EXPANSION	$^oC^{-1}$	17.7×10^{-6}	
THERMAL CONDUCTIVITY	W/mK	314-402	
SPECIFIC HEAT	kJ/kg K		
ELECTRICAL RESISTIVITY	ohm m	$1.74 - 2.15 \times 10^{-8}$	
ELECTRICAL CONDUCTIVITY	% IACS	70-90	
HALF HARD CONDITION (BS2871)			
TENSILE STRENGTH	N/mm^2	250 min	
PROOF STRESS (0.2%)	N/mm^2	93 min	
ELONGATION	%	30 min	

material data sheet

SPECIFICATIONS

STANDARD NUMBER	AUTHORITY	TITLE
BS 2871 Parts 1,2 & 3	BSI	Copper and copper alloys - tubes
BS 2051	BSI	Compression and capillary fittings
BS 699/BS 1566	BSI	Copper cylinders
BS 853	BSI	Calorifiers
BS 1306	BSI	Seamless copper for steam services
BS 2051	BSI	Compression and capillary fittings
BS 2871 Parts 1, 2 and 3	BSI	Copper and copper alloys - tubes.

COMPANY SPECIFICATION:

ENVIRONMENT

Corrosion resistance good in dilute acids, caustic alkalis, sea and other waters. Service temperature range - 200 to +205°C (creep starts at +120°C).

Attacked by industrial pollutants (sulphides, ammonia, etc).

PROCESSING AND FORMING TECHNIQUES

Available as annealed and various cold worked tempers. Material easily manipulated

Bend radius - annealed, close

(sheet)   - hard condition, t

Annealed   (t = thickness)

Tube bends can be formed with cold work 450-650°C

JOINTING PROCESS

Soldering	excellent
Brazing	excellent
Bronze welding	good
Welding	
Oxy-acetylene	good
Gas shielded arc	excellent
Resistance	good
Cold pressure	good
Friction	fair
Induction	fair
Electron beam	good

Care must be taken in corrosive media because possible galvanic action due to contact between dissimilar metals such as brazed joints.

Excess flux must be removed to prevent corrosion.

TYPICAL APPLICATIONS

Very popular high purity copper for tubes, cylinders, calorifiers, rain water products, ball valve floats, compression and capillary fittings and heat exchanger tubes.

Seamless tubes for steam services and refrigeration applications.

SAFETY PRECAUTIONS

YOUR SUPPLIER AND NOTES

	material data sheet			SHEET NUMBER	NF12	A
FAMILY GROUP	NON FERROUS	SUB-GROUP	COPPER	MATERIAL	WROUGHT COPPER/C107	

GENERAL DESCRIPTION

Oxygen free copper with good jointing properties. The addition of arsenic improves strength but reduces thermal and electrical conductivities. Strength is retained to slightly higher temperatures than other high purity coppers.

CHEMICAL ANALYSIS OR COMPOSITION

Copper   99.20% min.
Phosphorous 0.015-0.080%
Arsenic   0.30-0.50%

SYNONYM

Phosphorous deoxidial arsenical copper

PHYSICAL PROPERTIES

PROPERTY	UNITS	VALUES OR RANGE	COMMENTS
DENSITY	kg/m^3	8940	
TENSILE STRENGTH	N/mm^2	210/356 min	Annealed/hard
YIELD STRENGTH	N/mm^2		
PROOF STRESS (0.1%)	N/mm^2	46/317 min	Annealed/hard
ELONGATION	%	56/16 min	Annealed/hard
YOUNGS MODULUS	kN/mm^2	124	
IMPACT RESISTANCE	J		
HARDNESS		50-110	Brinell
THERMAL COEFF. OF LINEAR EXPANSION	$^{\circ}$C^{-1}	17.7 x 10^{-6}	
THERMAL CONDUCTIVITY	W/mK	314-402	
SPECIFIC HEAT	kJ/kg K		
ELECTRICAL RESISTIVITY	ohm m	1.74 - 2.15 x 10^{-8}	
ELECTRICAL CONDUCTIVITY	% IACS	35-50	

material data sheet

SPECIFICATIONS

STANDARD NUMBER	AUTHORITY	TITLE
BS 699/BS 1566	BSI	Copper cylinders
BS 853	BSI	Calorifiers
BS 1306	BSI	Seamless copper for steam services
BS 2051	BSI	Compression and capillary fittings
BS 2871 Parts 1 and 2	BSI	Copper and copper alloys - tubes

COMPANY SPECIFICATION:

ENVIRONMENT

Corrosion resistance good in dilute acids, caustic alkali, sea and other waters. Retains cold work characteristics at slightly higher temperature than C103 and C106. Service temperature range - 200 to +120°C (creep starts at 150°C).

Attacked by industrial pollutants (sulphides, ammonia, etc)

PROCESSING AND FORMING TECHNIQUES

Machinability improved with cold work. Available as annealed or various cold work conditions.
Bend radius - annealed, close
(sheet)   hard condition, t
            (t = thickness)
Tubes bends can be formed using internal supports.
Annealed 450-650°C

JOINTING PROCESS

Soldering	excellent
Brazing	excellent
Bronze welding	good
Welding	
Oxy-actylene	good
Gas shielded arc	excellent
Resistance	good
Cold pressure	good
Friction	fair
Induction	fair
Electron beam	good

Care must be taken in corrosive media because of possible galvanic action due to contact between dissimilar metals such as brazed joints.

Excess flux must be removed to prevent corrosion

TYPICAL APPLICATIONS

Tubes for water, gas and sanitation; sheet for water cylinders, calorifiers, ball valve float. Compression and capillary fittings. Seamless tube for steam applications.

SAFETY PRECAUTIONS

YOUR SUPPLIER AND NOTES

	material data sheet		SHEET NUMBER	NF 13	A

FAMILY GROUP	NON FERROUS	SUB-GROUP	COPPER ALLOY	MATERIAL	BRASS/CZ106

GENERAL DESCRIPTION

70/30 possesses the maximum ductility of all Cu/Zn alloys with excellent deep drawing capabilities. Cold worked alloy available in sheet, plate, bar, extrusions. This alloy is prone to dezincification.

CHEMICAL ANALYSIS OR COMPOSITION

Copper 70%
Zinc 30%

SYNONYM

70/30 Brass

PHYSICAL PROPERTIES

PROPERTY	UNITS	VALUES OR RANGE	COMMENTS
DENSITY	kg/m^3	8522	
TENSILE STRENGTH	N/mm^2	278/659	Annealed/hard
YIELD STRENGTH	N/mm^2		
PROOF STRESS (0.1%)	N/mm^2	77/510	Annealed/hard
ELONGATION	%	70/5	Annealed/hard
YOUNGS MODULUS	kN/mm^2	103	
IMPACT RESISTANCE	J		
HARDNESS		65-185	Brinell
THERMAL COEFF. OF LINEAR EXPANSION	$^{o}C^{-1}$	19.9×10^{-6}	
THERMAL CONDUCTIVITY	W/mK	109	
SPECIFIC HEAT	kJ/kg K		
ELECTRICAL RESISTIVITY	ohm m	65×10^{-8}	
ELECTRICAL CONDUCTIVITY	% IACS	27	Soft

SPECIFICATIONS

STANDARD NUMBER	AUTHORITY	TITLE
BS 1184	BSI	Copper and copper alloy traps
BS 2579	BSI	Drawn and screwed copper alloy ferrules
BS 2870	BSI	Copper and copper alloys - sheet
BS 2874	BSI	Copper and copper alloys - rods
BS 2875	BSI	Copper and copper alloys - plate

COMPANY SPECIFICATION:

ENVIRONMENT

CZ106 is prone to dezincification. Service temperature range -250 to +200°C (creep at $<$ +1200°C).

PROCESSING AND FORMING TECHNIQUES

Machinability improved by prior cold work. Annealing temperature critical to prevent 'orange peel' surfaces. Anneal at 500-600°C, too high a temperature can promote dezincification. Alloy has good electro-plating properties.

Bend radius - annealed, close
(sheet)   hard condition, t-2t
                   (t = thickness)

JOINTING PROCESS

Soldering	excellent
Brazing	excellent

Welding
Oxy-acetylene	good
Gas shielded arc	fair
Resistance	good
Cold pressure	fair
Friction	good
Induction	good

Alloy prone to stress cracking - stress relieve at 250°C in stressed components.

Excess flux must be removed to prevent corrosion

TYPICAL APPLICATIONS

Waste traps
Ferrules

SAFETY PRECAUTIONS

Hazardous fumes produced during welding require extraction.

YOUR SUPPLIER AND NOTES

 **material data sheet**

SHEET NUMBER	NF 14	A

FAMILY GROUP	NON FERROUS	SUB-GROUP	COPPER ALLOY	MATERIAL	BRASS/CZ105

GENERAL DESCRIPTION

This alloy is a standard composition for condenser tubes. It is capable of being cold worked to a considerable degree. The addition of arsenics inhibits dezincification. Available as tube and plate.

CHEMICAL ANALYSIS OR COMPOSITION

Copper   70%
Zinc   30%
Arsenic   0.02-0.06%

SYNONYM
Arsenical 70/30 brass

PHYSICAL PROPERTIES

PROPERTY	UNITS	VALUES OR RANGE	COMMENTS
DENSITY	kg/m^3	8938	
TENSILE STRENGTH	N/mm^2	216/250	Annealed/hard (plate)
YIELD STRENGTH	N/mm^2		
PROOF STRESS (0.1%)	N/mm^2	120	Annealed
ELONGATION	%	35/20	Annealed/hard (plate)
YOUNGS MODULUS	kN/mm^2	103	
IMPACT RESISTANCE	J	30-80	
HARDNESS		62-132	Brinell
THERMAL COEFF. OF LINEAR EXPANSION	$^oC^{-1}$	19.9×10^{-6}	
THERMAL CONDUCTIVITY	W/mK	109	
SPECIFIC HEAT	kJ/kg K		
ELECTRICAL RESISTIVITY	ohm m	6.5×10^{-8}	
ELECTRICAL CONDUCTIVITY	% IACS	28	Soft

SPECIFICATIONS

STANDARD NUMBER	AUTHORITY	TITLE
BS 378	BSI	Solid drawn copper alloy tubes for condensers etc.

COMPANY SPECIFICATION:

ENVIRONMENT

Used in conditions where dezincification is critical.

Service temperature range -250 to +200°C

(creep at +200°C)

PROCESSING AND FORMING TECHNIQUES

Machinability improved by cold worked material. Tube available in annealed or as drawn. Plate as annealed, as manufactured and hard temper. Anneal at 500-600°C. Strict temperature control required to prevent grain growth resulting in 'orange peel'.

Good electro-plating material

JOINTING PROCESS

Soldering	excellent
Brazing	good
Welding	
Gas shielded arc	fair
Cold pressure	good
Friction	fair
Induction	fair
Electron beam	fair

Stress relief (@ 250°C) to prevent stress cracking in cold worked components.

Excess flux must be removed to prevent corrosion

TYPICAL APPLICATIONS

Condensers, evaporators, heating and cooling systems.

SAFETY PRECAUTIONS

Fume extraction required, to remove zinc oxide, during welding.

YOUR SUPPLIER AND NOTES

BSRIA

SHEET NUMBER	NF15

A

FAMILY GROUP	NON FERROUS	SUB-GROUP	COPPER ALLOY	MATERIAL	BRASS/CZ 110

GENERAL DESCRIPTION

This is an alpha brass with the characteristics of a 70/30 type. The aluminium improves corrosion resistance and the arsenic inhibits dezincification. Available as plate and tubes for arduous applications.

CHEMICAL ANALYSIS OR COMPOSITION

Copper	76%
Zinc	22%
Aluminium	2%
Arsenic	0.02-0.06%

SYNONYM

Aluminium brass

PHYSICAL PROPERTIES

PROPERTY	UNITS	VALUES OR RANGE	COMMENTS
DENSITY	kg/m^3	8346	
TENSILE STRENGTH	N/mm^2	355/618	Annealed/hard
YIELD STRENGTH	N/mm^2		
PROOF STRESS (0.1%)	N/mm^2	62/463	Annealed/hard
ELONGATION	%	70/8	Annealed/hard
YOUNGS MODULUS	kN/mm^2	103	
IMPACT RESISTANCE	J	60	Soft
HARDNESS		65 - 175	Brinell
THERMAL COEFF. OF LINEAR EXPANSION	$^oC^{-1}$	18.5×10^{-6}	
THERMAL CONDUCTIVITY	W/mK	109	
SPECIFIC HEAT	kJ/kg K		
ELECTRICAL RESISTIVITY	ohm m	6.5×10^{-8}	
ELECTRICAL CONDUCTIVITY	% IACS	23	Soft

SPECIFICATIONS

STANDARD NUMBER	AUTHORITY	TITLE
BS 378	BSI	Drawn tubes for condensers
BS 1184	BSI	Copper and copper alloy traps
BS 2579	BSI	Drawn and screwed copper alloy ferrules
BS 2871 Part 2 and 3	BSI	Copper and copper alloys - tubes
BS 2875	BSI	Copper and copper alloy - plate
BS 1306	BSI	Copper alloys for steam service
BS 4504 Part 2 1974	BSI	Flanges and pipes for pipes and valves

COMPANY SPECIFICATION:

ENVIRONMENT

Good corrosion resistance, and can be used
in conditions where dezincification is
critical.

Service temperature range -200 to +180°C
(creep starts at ≮+180°C)

PROCESSING AND FORMING TECHNIQUES

Machinability improved by prior cold work
Anneal 500-600°C, to prevent 'orange peel'
surfaces use lowest practical temperature.
Electro-plating presents no problems.

JOINTING PROCESS

Soldering	good
Brazing	good
Welding	
Oxy-acetylene	fair
Gas shielded arc	fair
Resistance	good
Friction	good

Stress relieving at 250°C may be required to
prevent stress cracking.
Excess flux must be removed to prevent
corrosion.

TYPICAL APPLICATIONS

Used for condenser tubes and tube plates,
steam pipes, ferrules for plain and screwed
tube and waste traps. General engineering
where corrosion resistance is required.
Used for flanges for pipes, valves and
fittings.

SAFETY PRECAUTIONS

During welding hazardous zinc fume must be extracted.

YOUR SUPPLIER AND NOTES

BSRIA

material data sheet

| FAMILY GROUP | NON FERROUS | SUB-GROUP | COPPER ALLOY | MATERIAL | BRASS/CZ111 |

GENERAL DESCRIPTION

Basically a 70/30 brass with tin to improve corrosion resistance and arsenic to inhibit dezincification. Available as tubes.

CHEMICAL ANALYSIS OR COMPOSITION

Copper   70%
Zinc   29%
Tin   1%
Arsenic   0.02-0.06%

SYNONYM

Admiralty brass

PHYSICAL PROPERTIES

PROPERTY	UNITS	VALUES OR RANGE	COMMENTS
DENSITY	kg/m^3	8520	
TENSILE STRENGTH	N/mm^2	370/587	Annealed/hard
YIELD STRENGTH	N/mm^2		
PROOF STRESS (0.1%)	N/mm^2	154/432	Annealed/hard
ELONGATION	%	60/10	Annealed/hard
YOUNGS MODULUS	kN/mm^2	103	
IMPACT RESISTANCE	J	80-140	
HARDNESS		75-175	Brinell
THERMAL COEFF. OF LINEAR EXPANSION	$^oC^{-1}$	19×10^{-6}	
THERMAL CONDUCTIVITY	W/mK	109	
SPECIFIC HEAT	kJ/kg K		
ELECTRICAL RESISTIVITY	ohm m	6.5×10^{-8}	
ELECTRICAL CONDUCTIVITY	% IACS	25	Drawn

SPECIFICATIONS

STANDARD NUMBER	AUTHORITY	TITLE
BS 378	BSI	Draw copper tubes for condensers
BS 2579	BSI	Drawn copper alloy tubes for ferrules
BS 2871 Part 3	BSI	Copper and copper alloys - exchanger tubes

COMPANY SPECIFICATION:

ENVIRONMENT

Better corrosion resistance than CZ106. Used
in conditions prone to dezincification.
Service temperature range -200 to +180°C
(creep start at <+180°C)

PROCESSING AND FORMING TECHNIQUES

Machinability improved with prior cold work
Material capable of large reductions of
area during drawing. Anneal at 500-600°C.
Use lowest practical temperature to prevent
'orange peel' surfaces. Electro plating
presents no problem.

JOINTING PROCESS

Soldering	excellent
Brazing	excellent

Welding
Oxy-acetylene	good
Gas shielded arc	fair
Resistance	good
Friction	good
Induction	fair

To prevent stress cracking in certain
environments material must be stress
relieved at 250°C.
Excess flux must be removed to prevent
corrosion.

TYPICAL APPLICATIONS

Tubes for heat exchangers, condensers, heaters and coolers. Drawn tube machined into
screwed ferrules.

SAFETY PRECAUTIONS

During welding hazardous zinc fume must be extracted.

YOUR SUPPLIER AND NOTES

| FAMILY GROUP | NON FERROUS | SUB-GROUP | COPPER ALLOY | MATERIAL | BRASS/CZ112 |

GENERAL DESCRIPTION

CZ112 is a hot working brass. It is more corrosion resistant than 60/40 brass with an increase in tensile strength and no reduction in ductility. Available as strip, plate, rod, extruded sections, and forgings in the as manufactured or annealed condition.

CHEMICAL ANALYSIS OR COMPOSITION

Copper	62%
Zinc	37%
Tin	1%

SYNONYM

Naval brass

PHYSICAL PROPERTIES

PROPERTY	UNITS	VALUES OR RANGE	COMMENTS
DENSITY	kg/m^3	8410	
TENSILE STRENGTH	N/mm^2	386 min	
YIELD STRENGTH	N/mm^2		
PROOF STRESS (0.1%)	N/mm^2	124 min	
ELONGATION	%	40 min	
YOUNGS MODULUS	kN/mm^2	103	
IMPACT RESISTANCE	J	24-50	
HARDNESS		80	Brinell
THERMAL COEFF. OF LINEAR EXPANSION	$^\circ C^{-1}$	21.2×10^{-6}	
THERMAL CONDUCTIVITY	W/mK	109	
SPECIFIC HEAT	kJ/kg K		
ELECTRICAL RESISTIVITY	ohm m	$6.2\text{-}6.8 \times 10^{-8}$	
ELECTRICAL CONDUCTIVITY	% IACS	26	Soft

SPECIFICATIONS

STANDARD NUMBER	AUTHORITY	TITLE
BS 853	BSI	Copper calorifiers
BS 1952	BSI	Copper alloy gate valves
BS 1953	BSI	Copper alloy check valves
BS 5154	BSI	Copper alloy globe valves

COMPANY SPECIFICATION:

ENVIRONMENT

CZ112 should be selected for use in conditions prone to corrosion such as fresh water and sea water. Better resistance to corrosion than 60/40 brass. Service temperature range $-200 / +150^{o}C$. (creep starts at $+150^{o}C$).

PROCESSING AND FORMING TECHNIQUES

CZ112 can only be hot worked by extrusion forging, hot rolling etc. Machinability of component good. Alloys are non hardenable by thermal or cold work. Annealing temperature 450-500°C. Alloy readily electro-plated.

JOINTING PROCESS

Soldering	excellent
Brazing	good
Welding	

Oxy-acetylene	good
Gas shielded arc	fair
Resistance	good
Friction	good
Induction	fair

To prevent severe embrittlement all soldering must be carried out on annealed material.

Excess flux must be removed to prevent corrosion.

SAFETY PRECAUTIONS

During welding hazardous zinc fumes must be extracted.

TYPICAL APPLICATIONS

Internal components for gate, check and globe valves such as stems, hinge and hinge pins, stem nuts and bushes, belt ring, stuffing box and gland. Forged components on calorifiers.

YOUR SUPPLIER AND NOTES

355

 **material data sheet**

| FAMILY GROUP | NON FERROUS | SUB-GROUP | COPPER ALLOY | MATERIAL | BRASS/CZ114 |

GENERAL DESCRIPTION

CZ114 is a high strength brass. Tin and aluminium increase strength and corrosion resistance over 60/40 brass. It is available as rods, sections, extrusions and forgings.

CHEMICAL ANALYSIS OR COMPOSITION

Copper	56 - 60%	Iron	0.5 - 1.2%
Zinc	Balance	Tin	0.2 - 1.0%
Manganese	0.3 - 2.0%	Aluminium	1.50% maximum
Lead	0.5 - 1.5%		

SYNONYM

High tensile brass

PHYSICAL PROPERTIES

PROPERTY	UNITS	VALUES OR RANGE	COMMENTS
DENSITY	kg/m^3	8300 - 8400	
TENSILE STRENGTH	N/mm^2	556	
YIELD STRENGTH	N/mm^2		
PROOF STRESS (0.1%)	N/mm^2	309	
ELONGATION	%	35	
YOUNGS MODULUS	kN/mm^2	103	
IMPACT RESISTANCE	J		
HARDNESS		104	Brinell
THERMAL COEFF. OF LINEAR EXPANSION	$^{o}C^{-1}$	20.9×10^{-6}	
THERMAL CONDUCTIVITY	W/mK	109	
SPECIFIC HEAT	kJ/kg K		
ELECTRICAL RESISTIVITY	ohm m	$6.2-6.8 \times 10^{-8}$	
ELECTRICAL CONDUCTIVITY	% IACS		

SPECIFICATIONS

STANDARD NUMBER	AUTHORITY	TITLE
BS 2872	BSI	Copper and copper alloys - forgings
BS 2874	BSI	Copper and copper alloys - rod and sections
BS 5154	BSI	Copper alloy globe valves

COMPANY SPECIFICATION:

ENVIRONMENT

CZ114 should be selected for use in conditions that require fair corrosion resistance combined with high strength.

Service temperature range -180 to +100°C. (creep starts at <100°C).

PROCESSING AND FORMING TECHNIQUES

All forming operations must be performed hot.

Good machinability.

Generally used annealed

Can be electro-plated using standard procedures

Anneal - 450-500°C.

JOINTING PROCESS

Soldering	excellent
Brazing	good
Welding	
Gas shielded arc	fair
Friction	fair

To prevent severe embrittlement all soldering must be carried out on annealed material.

Excess flux must be removed to prevent corrosion.

TYPICAL APPLICATIONS

General engineering applications where a high strength corrosion resisting non magnetic material is required. Used in valves for stems, hinges and pins, stem nuts and bushes, glands, stuffing box and belt ring.

SAFETY PRECAUTIONS

During welding hazardous zinc fumes must be extracted away.

YOUR SUPPLIER AND NOTES

 **material data sheet**

FAMILY GROUP	NON FERROUS	SUB-GROUP	COPPER ALLOY	MATERIAL	BRASS/CZ121

GENERAL DESCRIPTION

Most suitable material for high speed machining. Addition of lead reduces impact properties and corrosion resistance. Welding of components more difficult because of presence of lead. Available as rod,sections and extrusions.

CHEMICAL ANALYSIS OR COMPOSITION

Copper	56-60%
Zinc	Balance
Lead	2.0-3.0%

SYNONYM

Free cutting brass

PHYSICAL PROPERTIES

PROPERTY	UNITS	VALUES OR RANGE	COMMENTS
DENSITY	kg/m^3	8400	
TENSILE STRENGTH	N/mm^2	386-510	
YIELD STRENGTH	N/mm^2		
PROOF STRESS (0.1%)	N/mm^2	108-232	
ELONGATION	%	15-40	
YOUNGS MODULUS	kN/mm^2	103	
IMPACT RESISTANCE	J	40-60	
HARDNESS		80-150	Brinell
THERMAL COEFF. OF LINEAR EXPANSION	$°C^{-1}$	20.9×10^{-6}	
THERMAL CONDUCTIVITY	W/mK	109	
SPECIFIC HEAT	kJ/kg K		
ELECTRICAL RESISTIVITY	ohm m	$6.2-6.8 \times 10^{-8}$	
ELECTRICAL CONDUCTIVITY	% IACS	28	Hard worked

BSRIA material data sheet

SPECIFICATIONS

STANDARD NUMBER	AUTHORITY	TITLE
BS 2874	BSI	Copper and copper alloys - rod and section
BS 2051	BSI	Capillary and compression fittings
BS 1952	BSI	Copper gate valve
BS 1953	BSI	Copper check valve
BS 2867	BSI	Hot water radiator valves
BS 3060	BSI	Screw down valves
BS 2879	BSI	Draining taps
BS 1010 Part 1 and Part 2	BSI	Draw off taps and stop cocks
BS 5154	BSI	Copper alloy valves for general purposes.

COMPANY SPECIFICATION:

ENVIRONMENT

Corrosion resistance is reduced by the lead content compared to non leaded brasses. Maximum water temperature for valve parts 198°C.

PROCESSING AND FORMING TECHNIQUES

Machinability excellent. CZ121 will take limited cold work forming.
It can be electro-plated.
Anneal - 450-500°C.

JOINTING PROCESS

Soldering	excellent
Brazing	good
Welding	
Resistance	fair
Cold pressure	fair
Friction	good
Induction	fair

To prevent severe embrittlement all soldering must be carried out on annealed material.
Excess flux must be removed to prevent corrosion.

TYPICAL APPLICATIONS

Many applications where a machined brass component required. Typical uses compressor fittings; valve components such as body, stem, body seat, hinge etc.; drain taps; stopcocks and radiator components.

SAFETY PRECAUTIONS

During welding hazardous fumes produced which require extraction.

YOUR SUPPLIER AND NOTES

 **material data sheet**

| FAMILY GROUP | NON FERROUS | SUB-GROUP | COPPER ALLOY | MATERIAL | BRASS/CZ122 |

GENERAL DESCRIPTION

CZ122 possesses excellent hot pressing properties. Components so formed can be easily finished by machining. Good extrusion properties. Due to presence of lead the elongation and impact properties are greatly reduced compared to 60/40 brass.

CHEMICAL ANALYSIS OR COMPOSITION

Copper   56.5-60%
Zinc   Balance
Lead   1-2.5%

SYNONYM

PHYSICAL PROPERTIES

Hot stamping brass
BS 218 material

PROPERTY	UNITS	VALUES OR RANGE	COMMENTS
DENSITY	kg/m^3	8410	
TENSILE STRENGTH	N/mm^2	386 minimum	as manufactured
YIELD STRENGTH	N/mm^2		
PROOF STRESS (0.1%)	N/mm^2	308 minimum	as manufactured
ELONGATION	%	25-40	
YOUNGS MODULUS	kN/mm^2	103	
IMPACT RESISTANCE	J	12-20	
HARDNESS		80-120	Brinell
THERMAL COEFF. OF LINEAR EXPANSION	$°C^{-1}$	20.9×10^{-6}	
THERMAL CONDUCTIVITY	W/mK	109	
SPECIFIC HEAT	kJ/kg K		
ELECTRICAL RESISTIVITY	ohm m	$6.2\text{-}6.8 \times 10^{-8}$	
ELECTRICAL CONDUCTIVITY	% IACS	26	Hard worked

 **material
data sheet**

SHEET
NUMBER NF20 B

SPECIFICATIONS

Standard number	Authority	Title
BS 2872	BSI	Copper and copper alloys - forgings
BS 2874	BSI	Copper and copper alloys - rods and sections
BS 1952	BSI	Copper alloy gate valve
BS 1953	BSI	Copper alloy check valve
BS 2051	BSI	Capillary and compression fittings
BS 2767	BSI	Hot water radiator valves
BS 2879	BSI	Draining taps
BS 3060	BSI	Screw down valves

Company specification:

ENVIRONMENT

Valve components limited to service conditions of 198°C. Corrosion resistance good.

PROCESSING AND FORMING TECHNIQUES

Excellent hot pressing and extrusion properties. Formed components possess good machinability. Annealing temperature 450-500°C. A limited amount of cold work can be tolerated. Finish components can be electroplated.

JOINTING PROCESS

Soldering	excellent
Brazing	good
Welding	
Resistance	fair
Cold pressure	fair
Friction	good
Induction	fair

To prevent severe embrittlement all soldering must be carried out on annealed material.

Excess flux must be removed to prevent corrosion

TYPICAL APPLICATIONS

Any forged component can use CZ122. Valve components such as bodies, stems, hinges and hinge pins, wedge or disc, and body seats. Also traps, taps, compression and capillary fittings and ballcock float components.

SAFETY PRECAUTIONS

During welding hazardous fumes produced which require extraction.

YOUR SUPPLIER AND NOTES

material **data sheet**	SHEET NUMBER NF21	**A**

FAMILY GROUP NON FERROUS	SUB- GROUP COPPER ALLOY	MATERIAL BRASS/CZ126

GENERAL DESCRIPTION

Similar characteristics to CZ105. Available as tube.

CHEMICAL ANALYSIS OR COMPOSITION

Copper	69-71%
Zinc	Balance
Arsenic	0.02-0.06%

SYNONYM

Arsenical 70/30 brass

PHYSICAL PROPERTIES

PROPERTY	UNITS	VALUES OR RANGE	COMMENTS
DENSITY	kg/m^3		
TENSILE STRENGTH	N/mm^2	280/465	Annealed/Hard
YIELD STRENGTH	N/mm^2		
PROOF STRESS (0.1%)	N/mm^2	108/385	Annealed/Hard
ELONGATION	%	60/20	Annealed/Hard
YOUNGS MODULUS	kN/mm^2		
IMPACT RESISTANCE	J	30-80	
HARDNESS		70-165	Brinell
THERMAL COEFF. OF LINEAR EXPANSION	$^{o}C^{-1}$	$15\text{-}20 \times 10^{-6}$	
THERMAL CONDUCTIVITY	W/mK	109	
SPECIFIC HEAT	kJ/kg K		
ELECTRICAL RESISTIVITY	ohm m	6.2×10^{-8}	
ELECTRICAL CONDUCTIVITY	% IACS	21-27	

SPECIFICATIONS

STANDARD NUMBER	AUTHORITY	TITLE
BS 1306	BSI	Seamless copper for steam services
BS 2871 Part 2	BSI	Copper and copper alloys – general tubes
BS 2871 Part 3	BSI	Copper and copper alloys – heat exchanger tubes

COMPANY SPECIFICATION:

ENVIRONMENT

Can be used in environments where there is a likelihood
of a problem from dezincification. Corrosion properties
inferior to CZ111.

PROCESSING AND FORMING TECHNIQUES

Drawn or extruded as tubes

JOINTING PROCESS

Soldering	excellent
Brazing	excellent

Welding
Oxy-acetylene	good
Gas shield arc	good
Resistance	good
Friction	good
Induction	fair

Expansion into tube plates

Excess flux must be removed to prevent
corrosion.

TYPICAL APPLICATIONS

Condenser tubes

SAFETY PRECAUTIONS

YOUR SUPPLIER AND NOTES

 **material data sheet**

| FAMILY GROUP | NON FERROUS | SUB-GROUP | COPPER ALLOY | MATERIAL | BRASS/PCB1 |

GENERAL DESCRIPTION

An alpha/beta brass with a low copper content that gives this alloy great plasticity immediately after solidification, thus preventing hot tearing in the die. Reasonably corrosion resistant. Thin sections and holes cast with good finish and accurate dimensions.

CHEMICAL ANALYSIS OR COMPOSITION

Copper	57-60%	Tin	0.5% max
Zinc	Balance	Iron	0.3% max
Lead	0.5-2.0%	Aluminium	0.5% max

SYNONYM
Pressure die cast brass

PHYSICAL PROPERTIES

PROPERTY	UNITS	VALUES OR RANGE	COMMENTS
DENSITY	kg/m^3		
TENSILE STRENGTH	N/mm^2	280-370	
YIELD STRENGTH	N/mm^2		
PROOF STRESS (0.1%)	N/mm^2	90-120	
ELONGATION	%	25-40	
YOUNGS MODULUS	kN/mm^2		
IMPACT RESISTANCE	J		
HARDNESS		60-70	Brinell
THERMAL COEFF. OF LINEAR EXPANSION	$^{o}C^{-1}$	$18-20.5 \times 10^{-6}$	
THERMAL CONDUCTIVITY	W/mK		
SPECIFIC HEAT	kJ/kg K		
ELECTRICAL RESISTIVITY	ohm m		
ELECTRICAL CONDUCTIVITY	% IACS	18	

 **material data sheet**

SPECIFICATIONS

STANDARD NUMBER	AUTHORITY	TITLE
BS 1400	BSI	Copper and copper alloy castings
BS 1010 Part 1 and Part 2	BSI	Draw off taps and stop cocks
BS 1968	BSI	Ballcock floats
BS 2060	BSI	Screw down valves

COMPANY SPECIFICATION:

ENVIRONMENT

Corrosion resistant to normal atmospheric conditions. Prone to dezincification. Service temperature -200 to +120°C (creep start at 150°C).

PROCESSING AND FORMING TECHNIQUES

Pressure die casting. Thick sections give rise to porosity.
Machinability - good.

JOINTING PROCESS

Lead content will give problems during fusion welding and brazing. Inert gas welding and soldering practicable. Excess flux must be removed to prevent corrosion.

TYPICAL APPLICATIONS

Ideal for large production runs which absorb tooling cost such as screwdown valves, ballcock fittings, draw off taps and stop-cocks.

SAFETY PRECAUTIONS

Due to hazardous zinc fume extraction must take place during welding.

YOUR SUPPLIER AND NOTES

SHEET NUMBER	NF23	A

FAMILY GROUP	SUB-GROUP	MATERIAL
NON FERROUS	COPPER ALLOY	BRASS/DCB1

GENERAL DESCRIPTION

Gravity die cast alloy with reasonable corrosion resistance. Accurate quick repeat castings are possible.
Thicker sections possible than for PCB1, relatively good hot shortness properties.

CHEMICAL ANALYSIS OR COMPOSITION

Copper	59-63%
Zinc	Balance
Aluminium	0.5% max
Lead	0.25 max

SYNONYM

Gravity die cast brass

PHYSICAL PROPERTIES

PROPERTY	UNITS	VALUES OR RANGE	COMMENTS
DENSITY	kg/m^3	7800	
TENSILE STRENGTH	N/mm^2	280-370	
YIELD STRENGTH	N/mm^2		
PROOF STRESS (0.1%)	N/mm^2	90-120	
ELONGATION	%	23-50	
YOUNGS MODULUS	kN/mm^2		
IMPACT RESISTANCE	J		
HARDNESS		60-70	Brinell
THERMAL COEFF. OF LINEAR EXPANSION	$^{o}C^{-1}$	$18\text{-}20.5 \times 10^{-6}$	
THERMAL CONDUCTIVITY	W/mK		
SPECIFIC HEAT	kJ/kg K		
ELECTRICAL RESISTIVITY	ohm m		
ELECTRICAL CONDUCTIVITY	% IACS	18	

SPECIFICATIONS

Standard number	Authority	Title
BS 1400	BSI	Copper and copper alloy castings
BS 1010 Part 1 and Part 2	BSI	Draw off taps and stop cocks
BS 1184	BSI	Copper and copper alloy waste traps
BS 1968	BSI	Ballcock floats

Company specification:

ENVIRONMENT

Corrosion resistant to normal atmospheric conditions.
Prone to dezincification
Service temperature range -200 to +120°C
(creep starts at 150°C).

PROCESSING AND FORMING TECHNIQUES

Gravity fed into metal moulds. Large
sections prone to porosity. Cannot
be cold worked.
Machinable.

JOINTING PROCESS

Welding (fusion, and inert gas), brazing
and soft soldering require fluxes. Excess
flux to be removed to prevent corrosion.
Stress relieving to be carried out prior
to soldering.

TYPICAL APPLICATIONS

Ideal for limited repeat low accuracy
production runs such as waste traps, ballcock
float fittings, draw off taps and stop cocks.

SAFETY PRECAUTIONS

Hazardous zinc fume during welding requires
extraction.

YOUR SUPPLIER AND NOTES

 **material data sheet**

| FAMILY GROUP | NON FERROUS | SUB-GROUP | COPPER ALLOY | MATERIAL | BRASS/DCB3 |

GENERAL DESCRIPTION

This alloy is selected when good machining properties are required on a gravity die casting. Medium strength casting with reasonable atmospheric corrosion resistance. Hot shortness properties relatively good.

CHEMICAL ANALYSIS OR COMPOSITION

Copper	58-63%	Aluminium	0.2-0.8
Zinc	Balance	Iron	0.5 max
Lead	0.5-2.5%	Manganese	0.5 max
Nickel	1.0% max	Tin	1.0% max

SYNONYM
Gravity die cast brass

PHYSICAL PROPERTIES

PROPERTY	UNITS	VALUES OR RANGE	COMMENTS
DENSITY	kg/m^3	7900	
TENSILE STRENGTH	N/mm^2	300-340	
YIELD STRENGTH	N/mm^2		
PROOF STRESS (0.1%)	N/mm^2	90-120	
ELONGATION	%	13-40	
YOUNGS MODULUS	kN/mm^2		
IMPACT RESISTANCE	J		
HARDNESS		60-70	Brinell
THERMAL COEFF. OF LINEAR EXPANSION	$°C^{-1}$	$18\text{-}20.5 \times 10^{-6}$	
THERMAL CONDUCTIVITY	W/mK		
SPECIFIC HEAT	kJ/kg K		
ELECTRICAL RESISTIVITY	ohm m		
ELECTRICAL CONDUCTIVITY	% IACS	18	

material
data sheet

SPECIFICATIONS

STANDARD NUMBER	AUTHORITY	TITLE
BS 1400	BSI	Copper and copper alloy castings
BS 2767	BSI	Hot water radiator valves
BS 2879	BSI	Draining taps

COMPANY SPECIFICATION:

ENVIRONMENT

Prone to dezincification. Corrosion resistant to normal atmospheric conditions. Service temperature range -200 to +120°C (creep starts at 150°C).

PROCESSING AND FORMING TECHNIQUES

Gravity fed into metal moulds. Large sections prone to porosity. Good machining properties.

JOINTING PROCESS

Lead content causes problems during fusion welding and brazing. Welding by inert gas acceptable. Soft soldering presents no problems providing any stress relief is done prior to joining.

TYPICAL APPLICATIONS

Ideal for repeat low volume production with reasonable dimensional accuracy and finish machining. Typical usage radiator valves and drain cocks.

SAFETY PRECAUTIONS

Hazardous zinc fumes during welding require extraction.

YOUR SUPPLIER AND NOTES

369

 **material data sheet**

SHEET NUMBER	NF25	**A**

FAMILY GROUP	NON FERROUS	SUB-GROUP	COPPER ALLOY	MATERIAL	BRASS/SCB1

GENERAL DESCRIPTION

Alpha brass casting alloy producing a cheap commercial product from sand moulds. It gives moderate strength castings with good corrosion resistance and pressure tightness. Care on mould design to prevent hot shortness.

CHEMICAL ANALYSIS OR COMPOSITION

Copper	70.0-80.0%	Lead	2.0-5.0%
Zinc	Balance	Nickel	1.0% max
Tin	1.0-3.0%	Iron	0.75% max

SYNONYM
Sand cast brass

PHYSICAL PROPERTIES

PROPERTY	UNITS	VALUES OR RANGE	COMMENTS
DENSITY	kg/m^3	8500-8600	
TENSILE STRENGTH	N/mm^2	170-278	
YIELD STRENGTH	N/mm^2		
PROOF STRESS (0.1%)	N/mm^2	77	
ELONGATION	%	20-45	
YOUNGS MODULUS	kN/mm^2		
IMPACT RESISTANCE	J		
HARDNESS		45-60	Brinell
THERMAL COEFF. OF LINEAR EXPANSION	$^{o}C^{-1}$	$10\text{-}20.5 \times 15^{-6}$	
THERMAL CONDUCTIVITY	W/mK		
SPECIFIC HEAT	kJ/kg K		
ELECTRICAL RESISTIVITY	ohm m		
ELECTRICAL CONDUCTIVITY	% IACS	18	

BSRIA material data sheet

SPECIFICATIONS

STANDARD NUMBER	AUTHORITY	TITLE
BS 1400	BSI	Copper alloy castings
BS 1010 Part 1 and 2	BSI	Draw off taps and stopcocks
BS 1184	BSI	Copper alloy traps
BS 2767	BSI	Hot water radiator valves
BS 2879	BSI	Draining taps

COMPANY SPECIFICATION:

ENVIRONMENT
Used for non critical conditions. Dezincification may occur under certain conditions. Service temperature range -200 to +120°C (creep starts at +150°C)

PROCESSING AND FORMING TECHNIQUES
Cast in sand moulds.
Stress relieve castings at 250-270°C.
Machinability - good

JOINTING PROCESS
Welding is difficult due to hot shortness. Best results from electrical arc and inert gas welding. Castings should be stress relieved before and after welding. Soldering presents no problems. Lead addition causes problems when brazing.

TYPICAL APPLICATIONS
General purpose light duty conditions such as radiator valve bodies, waste traps, draining and draw off taps and stop cocks.

SAFETY PRECAUTIONS

YOUR SUPPLIER AND NOTES

 **material data sheet**

SHEET NUMBER	NF26

A

FAMILY GROUP	NON FERROUS	SUB-GROUP	COPPER ALLOY	MATERIAL	GUNMETAL/LG2

GENERAL DESCRIPTION

A casting material with excellent casting and corrosion resistance used where pressure tightness is required. The lead addition increases fluidity and improves machinability. Mould design critical as alloy hot short. LG2 readily sand, chill and continuously cast with an increase in tensile properties respectively. For heavy sections use LG4.

CHEMICAL ANALYSIS OR COMPOSITION

Copper	Balance	Nickel	2.0% max.
Tin	4.0-6.0%		
Zinc	4.0-6.0%		
Lead	4.0-6.0%		

SYNONYM

Leaded gunmetal

PHYSICAL PROPERTIES

PROPERTY	UNITS	VALUES OR RANGE	COMMENTS
DENSITY	kg/m^3	8990	
TENSILE STRENGTH	N/mm^2	200-270	Sand cast
YIELD STRENGTH	N/mm^2		
PROOF STRESS (0.2%)	N/mm^2	100-130	Sand cast
ELONGATION	%	13-25	Sand cast
YOUNGS MODULUS	kN/mm^2	110	
IMPACT RESISTANCE	J		
HARDNESS		65-75	Brinell
THERMAL COEFF. OF LINEAR EXPANSION	$°C^{-1}$		
THERMAL CONDUCTIVITY	W/mK		
SPECIFIC HEAT	kJ/kg K		
ELECTRICAL RESISTIVITY	ohm m		
ELECTRICAL CONDUCTIVITY	% IACS	10-15	
CONTINUOUSLY CAST PROPERTIES			
TENSILE STRENGTH	N/mm^2	270-340	
PROOF STRENGTH (0.2%)	N/mm^2	100-140	
ELONGATION	%	13-35	
HARDNESS		75-90	Brinell

SPECIFICATIONS

STANDARD NUMBER	AUTHORITY	TITLE
BS 1400 BS 2051 Part 1 1973 BS 853 BS 1010, 1184, 1952, 1953, 1968, 2060, 2767, 5154	BSI BSI BSI BSI	Copper and copper alloy castings Capillary and compression fittings Calorifiers Various valve specifications

COMPANY SPECIFICATION:

ENVIRONMENT

Service temperature range -50 to +180°C. Can be used
in steam environment. Good resistance to corrosion
in marine, atmospheric, buried and immersed conditions.
Used where dezincifiable conditions prevail.

PROCESSING AND FORMING TECHNIQUES

Cast in sand or chill moulds. Liable to
hot shortness. Material cannot be hardened
by heat treatment. Anneal 450-650°C.
Machinability - good with care.
Will electro-plate but care with
preparation required.

JOINTING PROCESS

Welding is possible by electrical arc and inert gas
methods. Brazing is possible but a reduction in
mechanical strength of braze due to presence of lead.
Soldering acceptable after any stress relief operation.

TYPICAL APPLICATIONS

Cast pump components, valve bodies and
components, compression fittings,
calorifier components, radiator and
screwdown valves, draincocks, stopcocks
waste traps.

SAFETY PRECAUTIONS

YOUR SUPPLIER AND NOTES

material data sheet	SHEET NUMBER NF27	**A**
FAMILY GROUP NON FERROUS	SUB-GROUP COPPER ALLOY	MATERIAL GUNMETAL/LG4

GENERAL DESCRIPTION

Alloy ideal for heavy section castings when good pressure tightness and optimum mechanical properties required. Possesses good corrosion resistance. Lead addition improves fluidity and machining properties. Available as sand, chill, and continuously cast material, with an increase in tensile properties respectively. Superior mechanical properties compared to LG2.

CHEMICAL ANALYSIS OR COMPOSITION

Copper	Balance
Tin	6.0-8.0%
Zinc	1.5-3.0%
Lead	2.5-3.5%
Nickel	2.0% max

SYNONYM

Leaded gunmetal

PHYSICAL PROPERTIES

PROPERTY	UNITS	VALUES OR RANGE	COMMENTS
DENSITY	kg/m^3	8800	
TENSILE STRENGTH	N/mm^2	250-320	Sand cast
YIELD STRENGTH	N/mm^2		
PROOF STRESS (0.2%)	N/mm^2	130-140	Sand cast
ELONGATION	%	15-25	Sand cast
YOUNGS MODULUS	kN/mm^2	80	
IMPACT RESISTANCE	J	25-26	
HARDNESS			
THERMAL COEFF. OF LINEAR EXPANSION	$^{\circ}$C^{-1}	70-85	Brinell
THERMAL CONDUCTIVITY	W/mK	18 x 10^{-6}	
SPECIFIC HEAT	kJ/kg K		
ELECTRICAL RESISTIVITY	ohm m		
ELECTRICAL CONDUCTIVITY	% IACS	10-13	
CONTINUOUSLY CAST PROPERTIES			
TENSILE STRENGTH	N/mm^2	300-370	
PROOF STRESS	N/mm^2	130-160	
ELONGATION	%	13-30	
HARDNESS		80-95	Brinell

BSRIA material data sheet

SHEET NUMBER NF27 B

SPECIFICATIONS

Standard number	Authority	Title
BS 1400	BSI	Copper and copper alloy castings
BS 1184, 1952, 1953, 2060, 5154	BSI	Various valve specifications

Company specification:

ENVIRONMENT

Used in steam environment, temperature range
-50 to 180°c.
Reduction im impact properties below -50°C
and creep starts at +180°C.
Good corrosion resistance in marine,
atmospheric, buried and immersed conditions.
Used where dezincification conditions prevail.

PROCESSING AND FORMING TECHNIQUES

Cast in sand or chill moulds, liable to
hot shortness so care in mould design
required. Hardness increased by cold work.
Anneal 450-650°C. Machinability good with
care. Castings can be electroplated but
care with preparation required.

JOINTING PROCESS

Welding is possible by inert gas methods. Brazing
is possible but a reduction in the mechanical
properties of the braze due to presence of lead,
soldering possible after any stress relieving
operations.

TYPICAL APPLICATIONS

Valve bodies and components , cast pump
components and low stress bushings.

SAFETY PRECAUTIONS

YOUR SUPPLIER AND NOTES

material data sheet

SHEET NUMBER	NF28

A

FAMILY GROUP	NON FERROUS	SUB-GROUP	COPPER ALLOY	MATERIAL	ALUMINIUM BRONZE/CA102

GENERAL DESCRIPTION

Aluminium bronze CA102 is capable of cold work to give high strength products of good corrosion and oxidation resistance. Retains tensile properties to high temperatures. Available as tube and plate. Oxide layer can cause joining problems.

CHEMICAL ANALYSIS OR COMPOSITION

Copper	Balance
Aluminium	6.0-7.5%
Iron)	1.0-2.5%
Nickel)	combined
Manganese)	

PHYSICAL PROPERTIES

PROPERTY	UNITS	VALUES OR RANGE	COMMENTS
DENSITY	kg/m^3	7753	
TENSILE STRENGTH	N/mm^2	417/687	Annealed/Hard
YIELD STRENGTH	N/mm^2		
PROOF STRESS (0.1%)	N/mm^2	93/556	Annealed/Hard
ELONGATION	%	69/15	Annealed/Hard
YOUNGS MODULUS	kN/mm^2	103	
IMPACT RESISTANCE	J	11.1-18	
HARDNESS		66-174	Brinell
THERMAL COEFF. OF LINEAR EXPANSION	$°c^{-1}$	$17-18 \times 10^{-6}$	
THERMAL CONDUCTIVITY	W/mK		
SPECIFIC HEAT	kJ/kg K		
ELECTRICAL RESISTIVITY	ohm m	$12-24 \times 10^{-8}$	
ELECTRICAL CONDUCTIVITY	% IACS	13-15	

 **material data sheet**

SPECIFICATIONS

STANDARD NUMBER	AUTHORITY	TITLE
BS 378	BSI	Copper alloy tubes - evaporators etc.
BS 1306	BSI	Seamless copper alloy tubes for steam service.
BS 2871 Part 3	BSI	Copper and copper alloys - heat exchanger tubes
BS 2875	BSI	Copper and copper alloys - plate

COMPANY SPECIFICATION:

ENVIRONMENT

Excellent corrosion resistance due to oxide surface layer. Retention of tensile properties up to 300°C. Withstands steam service provided sulphur dioxide and chlorine not present. Service temperature range -250 to +300°C.

Excellent resistance to impingement and erosion.

PROCESSING AND FORMING TECHNIQUES

CA102 can be cold worked.
Complex shapes may require stress relief -300°C
Annealing 650°C.
Electro-plating may be carried out but complex.
Machinability - good

JOINTING PROCESS

Soldering	good
Brazing	fair
Welding	
Gas shielded arc	good
Manual arc	good
Resistance	good
Friction	fair
Electron beam	fair

Prior to jointing process the protective oxide layer must be removed by active fluxes.

Excess flux must be removed to prevent corrosion.

TYPICAL APPLICATIONS

Used where good strength with corrosion, wear and abrasion resistance required. Tubes in heat exchangers evaporators, heater and coolers particularly in steam service systems. Also tube plates under similar conditions.

SAFETY PRECAUTIONS

YOUR SUPPLIER AND NOTES

material data sheet

| FAMILY GROUP | NON FERROUS | SUB-GROUP | COPPER ALLOY | MATERIAL | ALUMINIUM BRONZE/CA103 |

GENERAL DESCRIPTION

CA103 is a two phase hot working alloy with excellent resistance and strength retention at elevated temperature. Mechanical properties improved slightly by heat treatment with a loss in ductility. After welding/brazing a de-embrittlement operation is required. Available as rod sections and forgings.

CHEMICAL ANALYSIS OR COMPOSITION

Copper	Balance	Manganese	0.5% max
Aluminium	8.8-10.0%		
Iron)	3.0% max		
Nickel)	together		

PHYSICAL PROPERTIES

PROPERTY	UNITS	VALUES OR RANGE	COMMENTS
DENSITY	kg/m^3	7570	
TENSILE STRENGTH	N/mm^2	590	Typical
YIELD STRENGTH	N/mm^2		
PROOF STRESS (0.1%)	N/mm^2	280	Typical
ELONGATION	%	28	Typical
YOUNGS MODULUS	kN/mm^2	121	
IMPACT RESISTANCE	J	11.1-18	
HARDNESS		150-200	Brinell
THERMAL COEFF. OF LINEAR EXPANSION	$^oC^{-1}$	17×10^{-6}	
THERMAL CONDUCTIVITY	W/mK	42-88	
SPECIFIC HEAT	kJ/kg K		
ELECTRICAL RESISTIVITY	ohm m	$12-24 \times 10^{-8}$	
ELECTRICAL CONDUCTIVITY	% IACS	12-14	

SPECIFICATIONS

STANDARD NUMBER	AUTHORITY	TITLE
BS 853	BSI	Copper calorifiers
BS 1952	BSI	Copper valves - gate
BS 2060	BSI	Screw down valves
BS 2872	BSI	Copper and copper alloys - forging
BS 2874	BSI	Copper and copper alloys - rod and sections
BS 5154	BSI	Copper valves - globe

COMPANY SPECIFICATION:

ENVIRONMENT

Excellent corrosion resistance due to oxide layer. Retention of tensile properties to 300°C. Used in valve components up to 260°C. Suitable for steam service providing sulphur dioxide and chlorine not present. Service temperature range -200 to +300°C.

PROCESSING AND FORMING TECHNIQUES

CA103 may be hardened by quenching from 850°C with marginal strength improvement and loss of ductility by tempering at over 400°C. After welding, component should be de-embrittled at above 580°C. Electro-plating may be carried out but complex. Machinable with tool wear.

JOINTING PROCESS

Soldering	good
Brazing	fair

Welding
Gas shielded arc	good
Manual arc	good
Resistance	good
Friction	fair
Electron beam	fair

Prior to jointing process the protective oxide layer must be removed by active flux.
Excess flux must be removed to prevent corrosion.

TYPICAL APPLICATIONS

Used as turned or forged parts where corrosion resistance and strength with abrasion resistance required such as valve stems, hinge stuffing box, gland, and calorifier components.

SAFETY PRECAUTIONS

YOUR SUPPLIER AND NOTES

SHEET NUMBER	NF30		A

FAMILY GROUP	NON FERROUS	SUB-GROUP	COPPER ALLOY	MATERIAL	ALUMINIUM BRONZE/CA106

GENERAL DESCRIPTION

Compared to CA102 the addition of iron strengthens the alloy with no loss of resistance to corrosion. CA106 can be cold worked and is available as plate, forgings, rods and sections. Excellent resistance to impingement and erosion. CA105 preferred for heat exchange tube plate applications.

CHEMICAL ANALYSIS OR COMPOSITION

Copper	Balance
Aluminium	7%
Iron	2.5%

PHYSICAL PROPERTIES

PROPERTY	UNITS	VALUES OR RANGE	COMMENTS
DENSITY	kg/m^3	7753	
TENSILE STRENGTH	N/mm^2	540-570	
YIELD STRENGTH	N/mm^2		
PROOF STRESS (0.1%)	N/mm^2	230-250	
ELONGATION	%	36-40	
YOUNGS MODULUS	kN/mm^2	103	
IMPACT RESISTANCE	J	11.1-18	
HARDNESS		150-160	
THERMAL COEFF. OF LINEAR EXPANSION	$^oC^{-1}$	17×10^{-6}	
THERMAL CONDUCTIVITY	W/mK	42-88	
SPECIFIC HEAT	kJ/kg K		
ELECTRICAL RESISTIVITY	ohm m	$12-24 \times 10^{-8}$	
ELECTRICAL CONDUCTIVITY	% IACS	14-15	

SPECIFICATIONS

STANDARD NUMBER	AUTHORITY	TITLE
BS 853	BSI	Copper calorifier
BS 1952	BSI	Copper valves - gate
BS 2060	BSI	Copper screw down valves
BS 2872	BSI	Copper and copper alloys - forgings
BS 2874	BSI	Copper and copper alloys - rods and sections
BS 2875	BSI	Copper and copper alloys - plate
BS 5154	BSI	Copper valves - Globe

COMPANY SPECIFICATION:

ENVIRONMENT

Excellent corrosion resistance with retention of tensile strength up to 300°C. Withstands steam service provided sulphur dioxide and chlorine not present.

Used in valve components up to 260°C. Service temperature range -250 to +300°C.

PROCESSING AND FORMING TECHNIQUES

Machinability improved by cold work. Bend test for rods and sections -180° with radius of t without cracking. (t = thickness)

Annealing temperature -650°C. De-embrittlement - quenched from 580°C. Stress relieve - 300°C.

CA106 may be electroplated

JOINTING PROCESS

Soldering	good
Brazing	fair
Welding	
Gas shielded arc	good
Manual arc	good
Resistance	good
Friction	fair
Electron beam	fair

Prior to jointing process the protective oxide layer must be removed by active flux.
Excess flux must be removed to prevent corrosion.

TYPICAL APPLICATIONS

Used for components on copper calorifiers, solid ferrules, valve components such as stems, hinges and pin, belt ring, stuffing box and gland.
Tube plates

SAFETY PRECAUTIONS

YOUR SUPPLIER AND NOTES

 **material data sheet**

FAMILY GROUP	NON FERROUS	SUB-GROUP	COPPER ALLOY	MATERIAL	CUPRO-NICKEL/CN102

GENERAL DESCRIPTION

Cold worked alloy offering good corrosion resistance. Iron content inhibits impingement attack. Available as plate, sheet, tubes and extrusions. As the nickel content less than CN107 this alloy will take more cold work.

CHEMICAL ANALYSIS OR COMPOSITION

Copper	Balance
Nickel	10.0-11.0%
Iron	1.0-2.0%
Manganese	0.5-1.0%

SYNONYM

90/10 copper nickel

PHYSICAL PROPERTIES

PROPERTY	UNITS	VALUES OR RANGE	COMMENTS
DENSITY	kg/m^3	8938	
TENSILE STRENGTH	N/mm^2	308/571	Annealed/Hard
YIELD STRENGTH	N/mm^2		
PROOF STRESS (0.2%)	N/mm^2	108/406	Annealed/Hard
ELONGATION	%	45/10	Annealed/Hard
YOUNGS MODULUS	kN/mm^2	242	
IMPACT RESISTANCE	J	155	
HARDNESS		71-137	Brinell
THERMAL COEFF. OF LINEAR EXPANSION	$^{o}C^{-1}$	17.0×10^{-6}	
THERMAL CONDUCTIVITY	W/mK	25-59	
SPECIFIC HEAT	kJ/kg K		
ELECTRICAL RESISTIVITY	ohm m	14.1×10^{-8}	
ELECTRICAL CONDUCTIVITY	% IACS	10	

material data sheet

SPECIFICATIONS

STANDARD NUMBER	AUTHORITY	TITLE
BS 1306	BSI	Drawn copper alloy tubes for steam service
BS 1952	BSI	Copper alloy valves - gate
BS 1953	BSI	Copper alloy valves - check
BS 2870	BSI	Copper and copper alloys - sheet
BS 2871 Part 2 and Part 3	BSI	Copper and copper alloys - tube
BS 2875	BSI	Copper and copper alloys - plate
BS 5154	BSI	Copper alloy valves - globe

COMPANY SPECIFICATION:

ENVIRONMENT

Resistant to marine and sea attack, can withstand
impingement attack from high velocity water.

Service temperature range -200 to +200°C.

Corrosion resistance depends on nickel content -
hence not as good as CN107.

PROCESSING AND FORMING TECHNIQUES

Hardness increased by cold work such as
drawing and rolling.

Annealed at 700°C.

Stress relieved at 250-300°C.

Machinability improved with prior cold work.

Bending radius - annealed, close
(sheet)

JOINTING PROCESS

Soldering	excellent
Brazing	good
Welding	
Gas shielded arc	excellent
Manual arc	good
Resistance	good
Cold pressure	fair
Friction	good
Induction	good
Electron beam	good

Complex welded structures to be stress relieved.

Excess flux must be removed to prevent corrosion.

TYPICAL APPLICATIONS

Condenser, evaporator, heater, cooler tubes
and tube plates. Seamless tubes for steam
service. Valve components such as body seat
and wedge.

SAFETY PRECAUTIONS

YOUR SUPPLIER AND NOTES

| FAMILY GROUP | NON FERROUS | SUB-GROUP | COPPER ALLOY | MATERIAL | CUPRO-NICKEL/CN107 |

GENERAL DESCRIPTION

Corrosion resistant alloy with good mechanical properties. The iron content improves strength and inhibits impingement attack while manganese enhances corrosion resistance. CN107 is hardened by cold work. Available as plate, strip tube and extrusions.

CHEMICAL ANALYSIS OR COMPOSITION

Copper	Balance
Nickel	30-32%
Manganese	0.5-1.5%
Iron	0.4-1.0%

SYNONYM
70/30 copper nickel

PHYSICAL PROPERTIES

PROPERTY	UNITS	VALUES OR RANGE	COMMENTS
DENSITY	kg/m^3	8938	
TENSILE STRENGTH	N/mm^2	355 min/649 min	Annealed/Hard
YIELD STRENGTH	N/mm^2		
PROOF STRESS (0.2%)	N/mm^2	123 min/541 min	Annealed/Hard
ELONGATION	%	45/5	Annealed/Hard
YOUNGS MODULUS	kN/mm^2	158	
IMPACT RESISTANCE	J	150-160	
HARDNESS		80-175	Brinell
THERMAL COEFF. OF LINEAR EXPANSION	$°C^{-1}$	16×10^{-6}	
THERMAL CONDUCTIVITY	W/mK	0.05	
SPECIFIC HEAT	kJ/kg K		
ELECTRICAL RESISTIVITY	ohm m	36.3×10^{-8}	
ELECTRICAL CONDUCTIVITY	% IACS	5	

384

 **BSRIA** material data sheet

SHEET NUMBER	NF32	B

SPECIFICATIONS

STANDARD NUMBER	AUTHORITY	TITLE
BS 378	BSI	Copper alloy tubes for evaporators
BS 1306	BSI	Copper alloy tube for steam service
BS 1952	BSI	Copper alloy valves – gate
BS 1953	BSI	Copper alloy valves – check
BS 2579	BSI	Copper solid ferrules
BS 2870	BSI	Copper and copper alloys – sheet
BS 2871 Part 2 and Part 3	BSI	Copper and copper alloys – tubes
BS 2875	BSI	Copper and copper alloys – plate
BS 5154	BSI	Copper valves – globe

COMPANY SPECIFICATION:

ENVIRONMENT

Particularly resistant to attack by sea water.
Can withstand impingement attack from high
velocity water (up to 4.5m/s). Service
temperature range -200 to +200°C (creep) starts.

PROCESSING AND FORMING TECHNIQUES

Hardness increased by cold work such as
drawing and rolling. Annealed at 700°C.
Machinability improved with prior cold work.

Bending radius – annealed, close.
(sheet)

JOINTING PROCESS

Soldering	excellent
Brazing	excellent
Welding	
Oxy-acetylene	good
Gas Shielded arc	excellent
Manual arc	good
Resistance	good
Cold pressure	fair
Friction	good
Induction	good
Electron beam	good

Complex welded structures to be stress relieved.

Excess flux must be removed to prevent corrosion.

TYPICAL APPLICATIONS

Condensers, evaporator heater and cooler
tubes and tube plates. Tube ferrules and
valve components such as body seat and wedge.
Seamless tube for steam service.

SAFETY PRECAUTIONS

YOUR SUPPLIER AND NOTES

385

SHEET NUMBER NF33	A

FAMILY GROUP NON FERROUS	SUB-GROUP COPPER ALLOY	MATERIAL COPPER BERYLLIUM/CB101

GENERAL DESCRIPTION

Heat treatable alloy combining alloy steel like strength with high electrical and thermal conductivities. Ideal for non magnetic springs in adverse conditions. CB101 may be formed soft and heat treated to obtain design requirements. Available as strip, wire and castings.

CHEMICAL ANALYSIS OR COMPOSITION

Copper   Balance
Beryllium   1.7-1.9%
Nickel)   0.04-0.5%
Cobalt)   Combined

SYNONYM

Beryllium copper

PHYSICAL PROPERTIES

PROPERTY	UNITS	VALUES OR RANGE	COMMENTS
DENSITY	kg/m^3	8250	
TENSILE STRENGTH	N/mm^2	463-540	Solution treated
YIELD STRENGTH	N/mm^2		
PROOF STRESS (0.1%)	N/mm^2	185-247	Solution treated
ELONGATION	%	40-60	Solution treated
YOUNGS MODULUS	kN/mm^2	124-131	
IMPACT RESISTANCE	J		
HARDNESS		85-450	Brinell (condition dependent)
THERMAL COEFF. OF LINEAR EXPANSION	$^{o}C^{-1}$	17×10^{-6}	
THERMAL CONDUCTIVITY	W/mK	0.20-0.25	
SPECIFIC HEAT	kJ/kg K	0.1	
ELECTRICAL RESISTIVITY	ohm m	$4.6-10 \times 10^{-8}$	Heat treatment dependent
ELECTRICAL CONDUCTIVITY	% IACS	16-78	Dependant on condition
COLD WORKED AND AGED PROPERTIES			
TENSILE STRENGTH	N/mm^2	1312-1544	
PROOF STRESS (0.1%)	N/mm^2	1127-1467	
ELONGATION	%	1 - 3	

 **material data sheet**

SHEET NUMBER	NF33	B

SPECIFICATIONS

STANDARD NUMBER	AUTHORITY	TITLE
BS 2870	BSI	Copper and copper alloys - sheet
BS 2873	BSI	Copper and copper alloys - wire

COMPANY SPECIFICATION:

ENVIRONMENT

With high strength and corrosion resistance can be used in conditions detremental to steel. Suitable for non spark conditions such as explosive environment.

PROCESSING AND FORMING TECHNIQUES

Solution treated - quench from 790-820°C.
Cold work temper 1/4 hard, ½ hard or hard.
Precipitation age 335°C for 2 hours.
Max electrical and thermal conductivity achieved by extending ageing time.
All forming completed on solution treated material prior to precipitation aging operations.

JOINTING PROCESS

Soldering	good
Brazing	good

Welding
Gas shielded arc	fair
Manual arc	fair
Resistance	fair
Friction	fair

Welding completed prior to solution treatment.
Brazing completed on solution treated material.
Soldering on finished aged material.
Excess flux must be removed to prevent corrosion.

TYPICAL APPLICATIONS

Springs and contact arms where high strength, corrosion resistance, and electrical conductivity required such as electromagnetic, pressure and temperature responsive instrument using diaphrams, bellows etc. Also non-magnetic applications.
Spark free tools for hazardous or explosive environments.

SAFETY PRECAUTIONS

Due to hazardous fume extraction is required during welding and from heat treatment furnaces.

YOUR SUPPLIER AND NOTES

 **material data sheet**

SHEET NUMBER	NF34

A

FAMILY GROUP	NON FERROUS	SUB-GROUP	LEAD	MATERIAL	LEAD

GENERAL DESCRIPTION

Lead is the heaviest common metal. It can be easily worked but is of low tensile strength with very high creep properties which means that it has to be supported. The addition of antimony improves the mechanical properties without loss of corrosion resistance. It is used as a bearing material with hard particles acting as the load bearing media. Lead is used as the base of many soft solders and fusible alloys as well as an excellent noise dampening media. Lead and its compounds are highly toxic.

CHEMICAL ANALYSIS OR COMPOSITION

Lead   99.25%

Traces of   Antimony
              Copper
              Silver
              Tin

SYNONYM

PHYSICAL PROPERTIES

PROPERTY	UNITS	VALUES OR RANGE	COMMENTS
DENSITY	kg/m^3	11340	
TENSILE STRENGTH	N/mm^2	18	
YIELD STRENGTH	N/mm^2		
PROOF STRESS ( )	N/mm^2		
ELONGATION	%		
YOUNGS MODULUS	kN/mm^2	14	
IMPACT RESISTANCE	J		
HARDNESS		5	Brinell
THERMAL COEFF. OF LINEAR EXPANSION	$^\circ C^{-1}$	29.1×10^{-6}	
THERMAL CONDUCTIVITY	W/mK	17.6	
SPECIFIC HEAT	kJ/kg K	0.013	
ELECTRICAL RESISTIVITY	ohm m		
ELECTRICAL CONDUCTIVITY	% IACS	9.0	

SPECIFICATIONS

Standard number	Authority	Title
BS 219	BSI	Soft solders
BS 334	BSI	Chemical lead (types A and B)
BS 602 and 1085	BSI	Lead and lead alloy pipes for other than chemical purposes.
BS 801	BSI	Lead and lead alloy sheaths of electric cable
BS 1178	BSI	Milled lead sheet and strip for building purposes.
CP 3003 Part 3	BSI	Lining of vessels and equipment for chemical purposes - lead

Company specification:

ENVIRONMENT

Excellent corrosion resistance to the atmosphere and most waters (not soft acidic).

Noise reduction properties.

Attacked by underground backfill of wet clay and cinders.

PROCESSING AND FORMING TECHNIQUES

Lead may be formed by casting, rolling or extruding.

Melting point 327°C.

JOINTING PROCESS

Cold forge welding.

Solder - with care

TYPICAL APPLICATIONS

Flashing for buildings.

Cable sheathing

Chemical tank lining and piping material

Steel cladding for noise reduction

Radiation shielding

Battery plates.

SAFETY PRECAUTIONS

Lead and its compounds are highly toxic.

YOUR SUPPLIER AND NOTES

material data sheet

<table>
<tr><td>SHEET NUMBER</td><td>NF35</td><td>A</td></tr>
</table>

FAMILY GROUP	NON FERROUS	SUB-GROUP	ZINC ALLOY	MATERIAL	BS1004A

GENERAL DESCRIPTION

Die casting characteristics. BS1004A has very good dimension stability and impact values at elevated temperature combined with corrosion resistance. Used for economical mass produced items.

CHEMICAL ANALYSIS OR COMPOSITION

Zinc	Balance
Aluminium	3.9-4.3%
Copper	0.003% Max
Magnesium	0.04-0.06

SYNONYM

Mazak 3

PHYSICAL PROPERTIES

PROPERTY	UNITS	VALUES OR RANGE	COMMENTS
DENSITY	kg/m^3	6700	
TENSILE STRENGTH	N/mm^2	265	
YIELD STRENGTH	N/mm^2		
PROOF STRESS ( )	N/mm^2		
ELONGATION	%	15	
YOUNGS MODULUS	kN/mm^2		
IMPACT RESISTANCE	J	58	
HARDNESS		83	Brinell
THERMAL COEFF. OF LINEAR EXPANSION	$°C^{-1}$	27×10^{-6}	
THERMAL CONDUCTIVITY	W/mK	113	
SPECIFIC HEAT	kJ/kg K	0.1	
ELECTRICAL RESISTIVITY	ohm m		
ELECTRICAL CONDUCTIVITY	% IACS		

BSRIA material data sheet

SPECIFICATIONS

STANDARD NUMBER	AUTHORITY	TITLE
BS 1004	BSI	Zinc alloys for die casting

COMPANY SPECIFICATION:

ENVIRONMENT

Corrosion resistant under atmospheric conditions.
To prevent white corrosion, produced under
prolonged damp conditions, the alloy should be
chromated (DEF Specification 130). No attack from
plaster or cement.

PROCESSING AND FORMING TECHNIQUES

Automatic die casting produced to high
accuracy. Low mould shrinkage (1.2%).
May be electro-plated. A phosphate or
chromate pretreatment required to
obtain maximum paint adhesion.

JOINTING PROCESS

Due to low melting point the alloy can be welded
using alloy as filler material.

Adhesives give a more satisfactory method of non-
mechanical joining.

TYPICAL APPLICATIONS

Produces an economical accurate dimensional
stable product such as electrical switch
and socket boxes.

SAFETY PRECAUTIONS

Welding of alloy can produce zinc fume.

YOUR SUPPLIER AND NOTES

FAMILY GROUP	NON FERROUS	SUB-GROUP	ZINC ALLOY	MATERIAL	BS1004B

GENERAL DESCRIPTION

Good die casting alloy. Alloy B is inferior to alloy A in respect of dimensional stability and impact at elevated temperature. Increased tensile strength and hardness. Used for economical mass-produced items.

CHEMICAL ANALYSIS OR COMPOSITION

Zinc	Balance
Aluminium	3.9-4.3%
Magnesium	0.04-0.06%
Copper	0.75-1.25%

SYNONYM

Mazak 5

PHYSICAL PROPERTIES

PROPERTY	UNITS	VALUES OR RANGE	COMMENTS
DENSITY	kg/m^3	6700	
TENSILE STRENGTH	N/mm^2	315	
YIELD STRENGTH	N/mm^2		
PROOF STRESS ( )	N/mm^2		
ELONGATION	%	9	
YOUNGS MODULUS	kN/mm^2		
IMPACT RESISTANCE	J	57	
HARDNESS		92	Brinell
THERMAL COEFF. OF LINEAR EXPANSION	$^\circ C^{-1}$	27×10^{-6}	
THERMAL CONDUCTIVITY	W/mK	109	
SPECIFIC HEAT	kJ/kg K	0.1	
ELECTRICAL RESISTIVITY	ohm m		
ELECTRICAL CONDUCTIVITY	% IACS		

SPECIFICATIONS

Standard number	Authority	Title
BS 1004	BSI	Zinc alloys for die casting

Company specification:

ENVIRONMENT

Corrosion resistant under atmospheric conditions.
To prevent white corrosion produced under
prolonged damp conditions the alloy should be
chromated (DEF Specification 130).
No attack from cement and plaster.

PROCESSING AND FORMING TECHNIQUES

Automatic die castings produced to high
accuracy.   Low mould shrinkage (1.2%).
May be electro-plated. A phosphate or
chromate pre-treatment required to obtain
maximum paint adhension.

JOINTING PROCESS

Welding possible using similar alloy filler.
Adhesives give a more satisfactory method of
non mechanical joining.

TYPICAL APPLICATIONS

Produces an economical accurate
dimensional stable product such as
electrical switch and socket boxes.

SAFETY PRECAUTIONS

Welding of alloy can produce zinc fume.

YOUR SUPPLIER AND NOTES

4.3 JOINTING AND BONDING

Jointing is the joining of components together to form a structure. Joints can be fabricated by a variety of methods. They can be classified into three types:-

   mechanical - screw connections, clamps flanges and bolts, compression fittings, duct seam interlocks, nuts and bolts, rivets, etc.

   thermal - soldering, brazing, welding.

   bonding - the joining of surfaces of components by means of an adhesive or solvent.

The relationship between different methods of jointing are indicated in Figure 4.3/1.

Soldering and brazing involve the joining of metals by the addition of a molten filler metal of essentially different composition to its parent metal, at temperatures well below the melting points of the metals to be joined. The filler metal must be drawn by capillary force through the mating joint surfaces and not merely be deposited on the surface. It is desirable, though not essential, that there should be some alloying between the filler material and the parent metal. Soft solders cover a melting range 100°C to 400°C and brazing alloys are used between 550°C and 1000°C, depending on the parent metal.

Welding may be defined as the joining of two workpieces of metal by melting adjacent portions so that there is fusion between them to an appreciable depth. The molten parent metal may be supplemented by extra metal, usually containing small amounts of other elements to improve fluidity and deoxidise the melt. For simplicity welding has been sub-divided into Resistance Welding and Fusion Welding.

Bronze welding uses similar techniques to brazing but the filler metal, usually copper rich, does not fill the gap by capillary action and relies on the fillet formed for joint strength.

4.3.1 SOFT SOLDERING

Soft-soldering is distinguished from other hot-joining processes which employ metalic bonding materials in that parent metals are not melted and that the intermediate film of filler metal is a low melting point alloy (usually tin and lead). In the majority of soft solders the active constituent is tin which promotes wetting of the substrate metals. The lead acts as a diluent and has the beneficial effect of producing low melting point alloys. During the soldering process the liquid solder wets the surface; a reaction at the interface between the solder and the parent metal occurs. A flux is normally required to assist wetting by the removal of surface dirt and oxides.

A soldered joint comprises the parent metal components, the soft solder alloy and a flux to assist wetting.

The parent metal and the end use of the soldered joint determine the selection of both the solder alloy and the type of flux used.

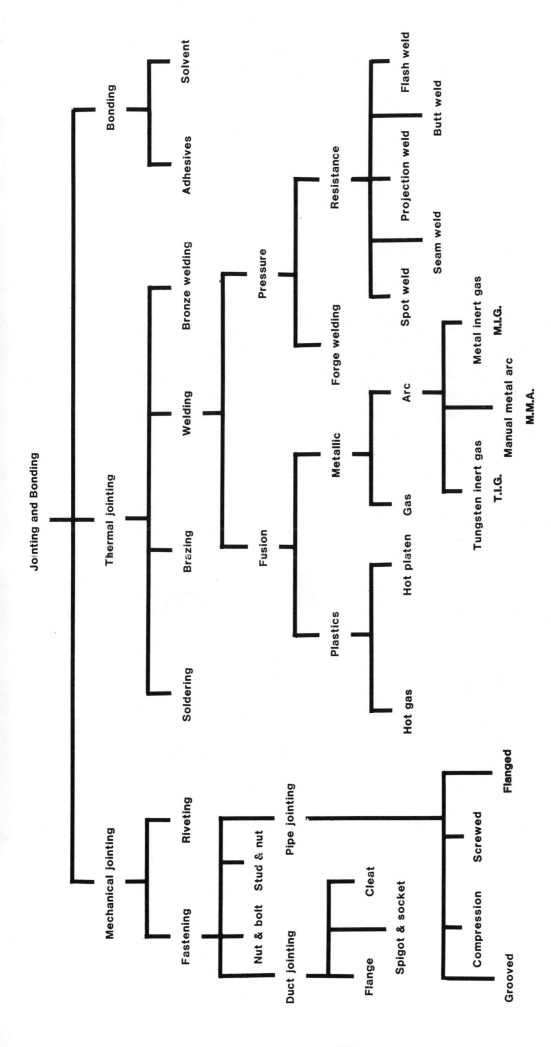

Figure 4.3/1: Jointing and bonding systems.

395

4.3.1.2 SOLDERING METHODS

There are several methods of applying heat, solder and flux. The important systems are:

- dip or mass soldering, whereby there is direct contact with molten solder in a bath, which also acts as heat source.
- conduction heating by a solid heat source such as soldering irons, hotplates and resistance elements for re-flow soldering.
- non-contact heating techniques employing gas-air burners, jets of hot gas, focussed light soldering and electrical heating using high frequency induction techniques and ovens.

Which ever of the above methods is used, it is of vital importance that the surfaces to be joined be correctly prepared. Two stages of preparation are necessary:

- cleaning to remove all traces of oil or grease.
- treatment to remove oxide and tarnish. The process varies with the parent metals to be joined and invariably involves an acidic solution.

Joint design should allow the capillary penetration of solder into an overlapped area of the two surfaces. The preferred range of joint gap is from 0.08 mm to 0.18 mm. With small gaps there is a strong possibility of entrapment of air and flux with resultant weak joints or the promotion of corrosive conditions. With large clearances the joint becomes mechanically weaker as there is less support from the parent metal. The influence of thermal expansion during heating on joint clearance must also be considered. The quoted joint gaps are at soldering temperature. Joints should be designed so that shrinkage on cooling results in the solder being under compression rather than tension.

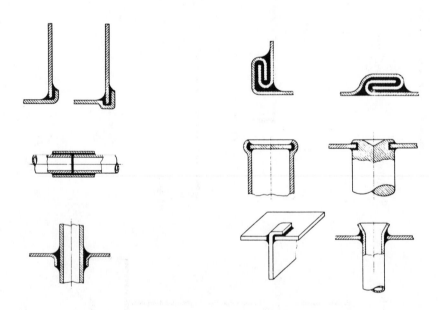

Figure 4.3/2: Soldered Joint Design   Figure 4.3/3: Soldered Joint Design:
                                                            Improved strength.

396

Solders are weak compared with the metals they join. Applied stresses should be in a direction parallel to the plane of the solder film i.e. loading in shear, so that the required joint strength can be obtained by using an appropriate area of overlap (Figure 4.3/2). A way to introduce extra strength to a solder joint is to shape the surfaces so that they engage or interlock mechanically such as clinching, knurling, lock seam jointing etc. (Figure 4.3/3).

Where a sequence of hot jointing processes is to be applied to a component, soft soldering would be the last operation owing to the low melting-point of solder alloys.

HEALTH AND SAFETY

Certain fluxes for soft soldering and solders containing lead and cadmium can be detrimental to health. Users of soft solders and soft soldering fluxes should determine whether their soldering procedures create a hazard for their operators or the users of their product and take suitable action to contain any hazard.

4.3.1.3 PARENT METALS

Some metals are more readily soldered than others, however, it is possible to improve solderability by coating one metal with a more solderable one. Soft soldering is most easily carried out on metals which do not oxidize so readily such as tin, copper, low carbon steel, nickel, gold and silver. On other materials with tenacious oxide films soldering is virtually impossible. The following commonly used materials can be soldered.

STEEL

Low carbon and low alloy steels are readily soldered providing a corrosive flux is used. The normal soldering temperatures do not affect the properties of the steel. There are few limitations to the solder alloy, but higher tin content increase the ease of wetting.

Once the steel surface has been cleaned it is important to prevent its reoxidation prior to jointing. This can be overcome by use of temporary protection or by coating with a solderable layer.

The most common layers are:

-   tinplate - extremely easy to solder, using mild non-corrosive fluxes.
-   terne plate - a coating of a lead/tin alloy. This is not quite so easy to solder as tinplate, though easier than uncoated steel, and does not have as good storage properties either. A non-corrosive flux may be used.
-   galvanising - a zinc coating is not easily melted by tin/lead solders but by using a corrosive flux and a solder containing 50% tin good soldered joints can be achieved. The joint is dull in appearance due to the presence of zinc but this does not indicate a poor joint.

COPPER AND COPPER ALLOYS

Copper is by far the most common metal that is soldered, and when freshly cleaned it has excellant solderability using a non-corrosive flux. Because copper readily oxidizes soldering should be carried out immediately following the application of the flux otherwise reoxidisation will occur. Failing this, and unless corrosive fluxes can be accepted, it is advisable to coat the surface by 'tinning' to retain the soldering properties.

Tin bronzes, including phosphor bronze, are easily soldered with tin/lead solders. Surface preparation is the same as for copper and activated resin fluxes are adequate. Gunmetal is similar to tin bronzes in solderability.

For aluminium bronze, silicon bronze and beryllium-copper, which oxidize very rapidly, the use of a strongly corrosive flux is recommended. High tensile manganese bronze requires to be pre-plated with nickel or copper to ensure reliable soldering.

Alloys such as nickel-silver tarnish less than copper and therefore retain a good solderable surface using a mild activated flux. Nickel-silver may show a tendency to de-wet.

Brass is commonly soldered with a corrosive flux. Should a less corrosive flux be desirable then the metal must be clean and pickled prior to soldering. Solders of low antimony content should be specified, as the presence of more than 0.25 to 0.5% can result in brittle joints. Molten solder induces stress corrosion cracking in susceptible stressed brass components.

STAINLESS AND ALLOY STEELS

Certain alloy steels with a high chromium content undergo rapid oxidation and the layer formed is a barrier to wetting by solder. By using a strongly corrosive flux, orthophosphoric acid based, soldering can be achieved. After soldering, residual flux must be totally removed to prevent corrosion. High tensile steels are not recommended for soldering because of their tendency to fail if high stresses are imposed. High carbon and alloy steel subjected to external stress may fracture catastrophically during contact with liquid solder, the tendency increasing with the applied stress and the strength of the steel. Good results and colour match are obtained on stainless steel by soldering with an alloy containing silver.

CAST IRON

Soldering of cast iron is difficult due to the presence of graphite; flake is more difficult than nodular graphite. Providing the casting skin is removed cast iron can be electro-plated with iron, copper and nickel to improve solderability. Localised heating of the casting may cause cracking and distortion. Immersion or oven soldering is preferred.

NICKEL AND NICKEL ALLOYS

Nickel has good solderability and is frequently used as a solderable coating. Nickel alloys also readily respond if carefully prepared. A mildly activated resin flux is normal but in high chromium alloys a more active flux is required. Where nickel and its alloys are chosen for their corrosion resistance the solder must be compatible with the environment.

ALUMINIUM AND ALUMINIUM ALLOYS

Aluminium and its alloys can be soldered using tin-zinc based alloys. Because of the tenacious oxide layers a very corrosive flux must be used to obtain wettable conditions. All traces of the flux must be removed to prevent corrosion.

4.3.1.4 SOLDER ALLOYS

The choice of solder for a particular application is determined by several factors. These include parent materials, working environment, alloy corrosion resistance, electro-chemical potential (galvanic effect) of the filler material with respect to other parts of the assembly and any toxicological considerations. See Table 4.3/4 for a range of commercially available solders as specified in BS 219 and typical uses.

TIN-LEAD

Data Sheets JB01; JB02

The most commonly used soft solders are based on a tin-lead combination. An alloy of 62% tin, 38% lead produces an instantaneous solidification eutectic at 183°C. All other tin-lead alloys produce a pasty state between totally liquid and completely solid. This can be used to advantage for wiped joints but generally while in the pasty state the joint has no strength. Because of this a maximum working temperature of 100°C is imposed on tin-lead joints. Low temperature applications must retain joint ductility and impact stength; an alloy of 90% tin, 10% lead satisfies these requirements. Antimony is added to tin-lead solders to increase strength but when brass or zinc based alloys are soldered a detrimental brittle compound is formed.

TIN-SILVER

Data Sheet JB03

The eutectic alloy 95.5% tin, 3.5% silver has a melting point of 221°C. These alloys possess retention of strength at higher temperatures and freedom from toxicity problems compared with tin-lead solders. They are free flowing and have high penetration abilities in the molten state with good wetting properties.

Tin-silver alloys should be used when plumbo solvency is a problem. These alloys can be used for soldering stainless steel with good colour matching.

TIN-ZINC

Soft soldering of aluminium and its alloys with tin-zinc alloys offers the possibilities of joints with less distortion than occurs with brazing or welding and less loss of strength because of the lower melting temperature. Because of the strong oxides formed by the tin-zinc solder and the aluminium the use of very corrosive fluxes is required to allow the solder to flow.

4.3.1.5 FLUXES

To assist in the wetting of component surfaces by molten solder, a flux is used to dissolve any thin oxide film and prevent further oxidation. A flux is acidic in nature or yields an acid when heated. It must be easily displaced by the solder as it wets and spreads over the surface. Fluxes can be classified into three groups.

Corrosive: these are inorganic salts or acids and are used where conditions require a rapid working and highly active flux. Zinc chloride is a common flux, while phosphoric acid is used when soldering stainless steel. Flux residues that remain after soldering are very active and promote corrosion unless totally removed.

BS 219 GRADE	CONTENT %	MELTING RANGE °C		TYPICAL USES
Tin T1 T2	min. 99.90 99.75		232 232	Certain food handling equipment, special can soldering, step soldering and other special applications
T3	99.00		232	Step soldering
Tin/lead A AP K	max. 64/36 64/36 60/40	183 183 183	185) 185) 188)	Soldering of electrical connections to copper Soldering of brass and zinc Hand soldering of electronic assemblies. Hot-dip coating of ferrous and non-ferrous metals. High quality sheet metal work. Capillary joints including light gauge tubes in copper and stainless steel. Manufacture of electronic components. Machine soldering of printed circuits. Use at less than 100°C.
KP	60/40	183	188	Hand and machine soldering of electronic components. Can soldering
F R G	50/50 45/55 40/60	183 183 183	212) 224) 234)	General engineering work on copper, brass and zinc. Can soldering Services below 100°C. Capillary joints.
H J	35/65 30/70	183 183	244) 255)	Jointing of electrical cable sheaths.
V W	20/80 15/85	183 227	276) 288)	Lamp solder. Dip soldering. For service at very low temperatures (e.g. less than -60°C)
Tin/lead/antimony B M	50/BAL/3 45/BAL/2.7	185 185	204) 215)	Hot-dip coating and soldering of ferrous metals. High quality engineering. Capillary joints of ferrous metals. Jointing of copper conductors
C	40/BAL/2.4	185	227	General engineering. Heat exchangers. General dip soldering. Jointing of copper conductors
L D	32/BAL/1.9 30/BAL/1.8	185 185	243) 248)	Plumbing, wiping of lead and lead alloy cable sheathing. Dip soldering
N	18.5/BAL/1.1	185	275	Dip soldering
Tin/antimony 95A	95/5	236	243	High service temperatures (e.g. greater than 100°C) and refrigeration equipment. Step soldering
Tin/silver 96S	96/4		221	Non-toxic solder. Resistance to creep. High service temperature (e.g. greater than 100°C).
Tin/lead/silver 5S	5.25/BAL/1.6	296	301	For service both at high (e.g. greater than 100°C) and very low (e.g. less than -60°C) temperatures
62S	62.5/BAL/2.2		178	Soldering of silver coated substrates
Tin/lead/cadmium T	50/BAL/18.5		145	Low melting point solder for assemblies that could be damaged by normal soldering temperatures. Step soldering. For thermal cut outs.

Table 4.3/4: Solder alloys.

Intermediate: these fluxes become active at soldering temperatures but the period of activity may be short as they volatilize rather readily. Hydrazine based fluxes require sufficient heat (200°C) to decompose and volatalize the constituents. Undecomposed flux may creep giving corrosive deposits remote from the joint.

Non-corrosive: these are of particular use in applications where residual flux cannot be removed, such as in electrical equipment. They are based on rosin activated by small additives. They should be hard, non-hygroscopic, electrically non-conducting and the amount of additive should not cause corrosion.

The quantity of flux used should be sufficient to promote wetting. Excessive quantities may become trapped and cause corrosion. For a particular application one should select the mildest flux that will produce an adequate joint.

4.3.2 BRAZING

This is a process for joining metals in which molten filler metal is drawn by capillary attraction into the space between closely adjacent surfaces of the parts to be joined. In general, the melting point of the filler metal is above 600°C but always below the melting temperature of the parent metal. The strength of a joint depends to a major extent on the effectiveness of the surface bond and to a much lesser extent on the actual tensile strength of the brazing filler material. When, as is recommended practice, such a joint is designed so the loading is largely in shear, the actual "pull off" strength of the brazed joint far exceeds the as cast strength of the bulk filler metal (see Figure 4.3/5).

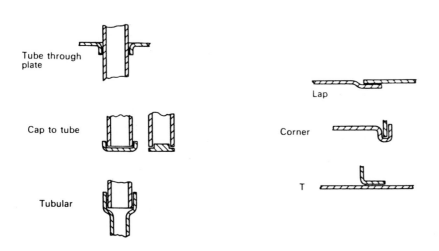

Figure 4.3/5: Brazed joint design.

To achieve good penetration and to minimise voids, and flux and gas entrapment it is necessary to ensure that:

-   the gap lies in the dimension range in which capillary action fills it and keeps it filled. See Table 4.3/6.
-   the surfaces to be joined are parallel to each other;
-   the surface condition of the parent metal is capable of wetting and spreading the molten filler.

Alloy system	Parent metals			
	Copper	Copper-base alloys	Ferrous metals	Aluminium and its alloys
Copper			Interference to 0·075	
Silver	0·025–0·10	0·025–0·10	rarely used	
Copper–zinc Bronze-welding type	0·075–0·40	0·075–0·40	0·05–0·25	
Copper–phosphorus	0·075–0·40	0·075–0·40		
Silver–copper	0·025–0·20	0·025–0·20	0·05–0·20	
Copper–silver–zinc Copper–silver–phosphorus Copper–silver–tin Copper–silver–zinc–cadmium–nickel Copper–silver–zinc–cadmium	0·025–0·20		0·05–0·20	
Cobalt–chromium–boron Nickel–chromium–boron Nickel–chromium–silicon–boron Nickel–silicon–boron Nickel–phosphorus			0·025–0·15	
Silver–palladium–manganese Nickel–palladium–manganese Copper–palladium–nickel–manganese			0·025–0·15	
Palladium–nickel Copper–nickel Copper–palladium			0·025–0·15	
Silver–palladium			0·025–0·10	
Silver–copper–palladium	0·025–0·10	0·025–0·10	0·025–0·10	
Gold–nickel Gold–copper	0·05–0·20	0·05–0·20	0·05–0·20	
Aluminium–silver–nickel (or manganese) Aluminium–silicon Aluminium–silicon–copper				0·10–0·60

Table 4.3/6:   Recommended joint-clearances (mm).

If the gap is too small the brazing alloy will not penetrate. Large clearances are wasteful of filler metal, they present a risk that the filler might run completely through, and are conducive to flux traps and shrinkage cavities. The assembly may be one of different metals having substantially different expansion characteristics and it is the gap at brazing temperature that matters. Even if components of the same material are being joined the assembly may be such as to make it difficult to contrive that one component is not hotter than the other at the time when the braze runs into the joint. If the assembly is of materials with different expansion rates, and if one part fits inside the other, suitable clearances at room temperature might provide too tight or too loose a fit at brazing temperature. It may be possible to reverse the fitting of the parts to correct such an occurrence. It is advantageous to compress the brazing material during cooling.

It is easier to braze joints where the components are self-locating.

Surface preparation is important. The surface should be grease, oil and scale free to facilitate good wetting of the parent metals.
The basic characteristics of the various methods are as follows:

hand and torch	–	very flexible allowing a wide range of joints to be produced. The standard of joint depends on operator skill.
mechanised torch	–	requires less operator skill.
high frequency electric	–	rapid and reproducible heating cycle. Clean and fairly flexible with high initial cost.
furnace	–	continuous furnance ideal for large runs. A protective atmosphere eliminates the need for flux.
electric resistance	–	rapid and clean but restricted to a limited range of shapes and sizes.

4.3.2.2 PARENT METALS

Most standard engineering metals can be joined by brazing.

COPPER AND COPPER ALLOYS

As indicated in the HVCA Code of Practice on Brazing and Bronze Welding, providing the correct filler metal and flux are used, copper and its alloys can be brazed easily. The main problem with copper is the production of steam when brazing oxygen bearing tough pitch grades (C101 and C102: BS2870 - 2875 Wrought Copper and Copper Alloys). Steam can seriously disrupt the structure and cause embrittlement. It can be overcome by not using hydrogen and to use oxygen free or phosphorous deoxidised copper (C103 or C106: BS2870-2875). Copper-phosphorous filler alloys are primarily used for the brazing of copper without the use of flux. They are basically copper, with varying amounts of phosphorous and silver. Where service conditions require the joint to resist torsional stresses, flexing or shock loading then the use of the 15% silver alloy, CP1, is recommended.

Silver brazing is the preferred method of producing assemblies with strong ductile joints where one or both components are brass or bronze. Torch heating or excess flux may cause surface discolouration.

Alloys in a highly stressed or cold worked condition, such as cupro-nickels, may crack during brazing due to braze penetration along the grain boundaries of the parent metal. Where there is a risk of this failure, consideration should be given to:

- use of annealed rather than cold worked material
- annealing prior to brazing
- heating at a slow rate to prevent large thermal gradients
- redesign of the joint to avoid external stresses

As the fabrication is in the annealed condition, design calculations must take this into account.

Alloys such as copper-beryllium or copper-chromium, when fully hardened, should be held for the minimum time at elevated temperature. Due to the oxide layer, good precleaning and fluxing is essential to obtain good wetting of the parent material.

Alloys containing aluminium e.g. aluminium-brass and aluminium-bronze, have a tenacious oxide and an active flux must be used. The time of contact between the molten braze metal must be as short as possible in order to minimise the solution of the aluminium into the braze metal. When brasses and bronzes containing aluminium are brazed to ferrous materials a diffusion of aluminium through the braze may combine with iron to form a brittle compound. This may be overcome by plating the copper alloy with copper or nickel or by using proprietary materials comprising a layer of copper or copper-nickel alloy sandwiched between two layers of braze; the layer remains solid during brazing operations.

Copper alloys containing lead, to promote free machining produce brazed joints of reduced mechanical strength. The use of such alloys should be avoided if they are to be subjected to high stresses or impact in service. Alloys with lead in excess of 1.5% should not be brazed.

Copper alloys containing iron and nickel must not be joined with copper-phosphorous or copper silver phosphorus brazing alloys due to the formation of brittle nickel and iron phosphide phases in the joint.

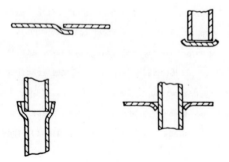

Figure 4.3/7: Brazed joint design for aluminium.

ALUMINIUM AND ALUMINIUM ALLOYS

An aluminium alloy, of the high silicon type and of slightly lower melting point than the parent material, is melted into the joint by furnace or torch heating. A special flux is needed and, because of the close proximity to the melting point of the parent material, accurate temperature control is required. Brazing is not recommended for alloys containing more than 2% magnesium because the oxide film is difficult to remove with ordinary fluxes and the joints tend to be brittle. For aluminium brazing the design of the joint is modified, see Figure 4.3/7 to provide some degree of lapping because of the inability of the molten filler metal to flow freely.

STEEL

Low carbon steel may be brazed by means of any of the conventional heating methods.

Any of the standard brazing alloys may be used, except copper - phosphorous due to the formation of a brittle phosphide in the braze.

When low carbon steel is brazed to metals containing aluminium, beryllium or similar metals diffusion of these metals can result in the formation of a brittle oxide film at the low carbon steel/brazing alloy interface. Electro-plating the components can prevent this forming. A sandwich braze alloy, as described in the copper section, will also prevent the diffusion. Steel components may be furnace brazzed using copper as the filler metal. Providing air is eliminated no flux is required.

Alloy steel responds in a similar manner to low carbon steel but appropriate fluxes must be used to remove oxide films to promote wetting by the molten braze metal. Copper-phosphorous braze metals must not be used because of the formation of a brittle phase.

Providing the temperatures do not exceed the lower melting points of the filler metal, steel assemblies may be hardened and tempered after brazing.

STAINLESS STEEL

Strong ductile joints may easily be made on stainless steel. Care must be taken as brazing will involve heating the steel to a temperature where carbide precipitation (weld decay) would take place. If this is to be avoided it is essential that the steel be stabilised or be of a low carbon type (304L/316L). When the component is to be exposed to water or humidity in service a galvanic action between the braze material and the steel results in crevice corrosion. This is rare in 18/8 austenitic steels, but is more likely in nickel free chromium steels of the ferritic or martensitic type. Special filler metals have been developed to overcome this problem. Due to the oxide layer, fluxes have to be used when brazing. Stainless steel is prone to stress cracking by penetration attack of the molten braze. This can be overcome by annealing the components before joining.

Where stainless steel is used in highly corrosive environments, or at elevated temperatures likely to cause oxidation, the choice of brazing alloy is important and a noble metal brazing alloy should be used; the choice of alloy will depend on the degree of corrosion resistance required.

CAST IRON

The engineering grades of cast iron can be joined to most metals and alloys by conventional brazing techniques.

BS 1845 GRADE	TRADE NAME	MELTING RANGE °C	TENSILE STRENGTH N/mm²	% ELONGA- TIONS	HARD- NESS HV	ELECT. COND. % IACS	REMARKS	PRINCIPAL USE
AG1	EASYFLO MX20	620-640	450	35	131	22	Used for max duct- ility & smooth joints. Require well fitted joints with small gaps.	General purpose low melting point alloys for brazing ferrous & non ferrous materials.
AG2	EASYFLO 2 MX12	610-620	450	30	135	20		
AG11	MATTEBRAZE 34	612-668	320	20		20	Used where wide joint gaps arise with pronounced fillets. Not recomm- ended where slow heating may produce liquation	As above
AG12	ARGOSWIFT	607-655	472	24	140			
CP1	SIL-FOS PHOS 15	644-700	650	10	187		Rough textured braze fillets spoil aesthetic appearance	Fluxless brazing of copper water cylinders, sheet metal fabrications etc.
CP2	SILBRALLOY PHOS 2	644-740	500	5	195		Brittle phase formed with nickel & ferrous base materials. Joint tols.0.05mm-0.12mm.	
CP3	PHOS 0	705-800	504	2		8	Joint tols.0.025mm- 0.08mm. High fluidity.	As above but with smaller joint gaps.
CP4	PHOS 5	640-740	472	6		10		
	ARGOBRAZE 56	600-711	331	15		10.5	Care to prevent liqua- tion during slow heating. Special flux to be used on stainless steel. Gap filling prop- erties.	Stainless steel (austenitic) fabrications with no crevice corrosion attack.
	H7TN	728-762						
	COPPER	1083					Close fitting steel parts up to 0.075mm joint gap.	Steel fabrications no flux if furnace brazed. Air brazing using flux.
	JMM'B' BRONZE	1081-1101	240				Joint gaps up to 0.5mm	Furnace brazed steel parts including austenitic & ferritic stainless. Air brazing using flux.
PD1	PALLABRAZE 810	807-810					Joint gap 0.025 - 0.1mm	Oxidation resistant to 500°C.
PD14	PALLABRAZE 1237	1237					Ditto / Better strength at eleviated temper- atures than Au alloys.	Retention of mechanical properties & oxidation resistant to 700°C. All stainless steel fabrications without crevice corrosion for use at elevated temperatures.
AU 5V	OROBRAZE 950	950					Joint gaps as PD1. Gives smooth fillets of good strength at elevated temperatures.	More corrosion resistant than PD alloys. Used for fabrications of stainless steel without crevice corrosion for applications at 500°C max.
	OROBRAZE 980	950-980					Cheaper alloy than AU 5V but with all its characteristics.	

Table 4.3/8: Braze alloys.

Lap joints, stressed in shear are generally used; it is important that the recommended joint gap for the braze material is not exceeded. To obtain the necessary close dimensions the faces may be machined before brazing. To prevent oxidation, unless brazing is performed in a controlled atmosphere, and to reduce the surface tension of the filler a flux is used. Many fluxes are corrosive and must be removed immediately after brazing.

Silver brazing alloys melting below 650°C are preferred for cast irons since there is then no risk of modifying the structure or properties of the casting during the brazing operation.

4.3.2.3 BRAZING ALLOYS

Filler alloys for brazing are designated in BS1845 - Filler Metals for Brazing. There are other commercial alloys for special applications that are not within the scope of this specification, see Table 4.3/8. It is essential that the filler selection takes into account the metallurgical compatibility between parent metal and filler alloy i.e. no brittle or undesirable phases or compounds should be formed during brazing.

ALUMINIUM BRAZING ALLOYS

Melting range of 535 to 630°C. They are used only for brazing aluminium and aluminium alloys and basically consist of an aluminium-silicon alloy.

SILVER BRAZING ALLOYS

Data Sheet JB04

Melting range of 600 to 800°C. They are basically a silver-copper-zinc alloy, some with an addition of cadmium. They can be sub-divided into two groups depending on whether they contain cadmium or not:

The alloys with cadmium possess relatively low melting points combined with excellent fluidity and mechanical properties. There is little restriction on the range of parent metals that may be joined, although care must be taken when alloys containing aluminium, beryllium and phosphorous are involved. The wide melting range alloys should not be specified where slow heating rates can be achieved because of the danger of liquation (separation of liquid from solid during fusion). The toxicity of cadmium may restrict the use of this braze filler material.

Cadmium free alloys are used in applications where the toxicity of cadmium may be a problem and a higher temperature environment is encountered. Parent metal choice is wide. These alloys have better strength at temperature than alloys containing cadmium.

COPPER-PHOSPHOROUS BRAZING ALLOYS

Data Sheet JB05

Melting range of 640 to 800°C. Copper-phosphorous alloys are commonly used as they are cheaper than silver brazing alloys and require no flux when brazing copper to copper and copper to copper alloys (the latter providing that they have less than 10% alloying elements and are free of strong oxide forming metals such as aluminium) . For lower copper content alloys a flux is used.

Though the mechanical properties appear similar to low melting point silver brazing alloys they are somewhat inferior in that they are stiff and lack ductility. As these alloys contain no zinc they cannot suffer from dezincification and have very good overall corrosion resistance. These alloys should not be used in hot sulphur bearing environments and should never be used on ferrous metals or nickel bearing alloys owing to the formation of brittle compounds.

COPPER BRAZING ALLOYS

These are mainly used for brazing ferrous parts, particularly in controlled atmosphere furnaces without the use of flux. High penetration powers mean that very small gaps of 0.25 mm will produce strong brazed joints.

NOBLE METAL BRAZING ALLOYS

These are based on palladium, with a melting range of 805 to 1235°C, and gold with a range of 905 to 1020°C. These alloys have high corrosion resistance and are suitable for elevated temperature applications. Gold alloys have excellent flow properties and resultant joints are neat and smooth. Palladium based alloys are particuarly resistant to crevice corrosion associated with stainless steel fabrications.

4.3.2.4 **FLUXES**

The function of a brazing flux is to prepare the surface of the joint so that the molten brazing alloy will wet and form a bond with the parent metal by diffusion at the interface. Fluxes are compounded normally from alkali halide mixtures and borax, and vary in composition so that they are only active over the particular brazing temperature range involved. Suppliers of brazing alloys have available proprietary fluxes to match filler metals. They may be supplied as powder to be mixed or as paste and applied over all the joint surfaces prior to heating.

4.3.3 BRONZE WELDING

Bronze welding is a process in which the filler metal is basically a copper-zinc alloy (with some additions to improve strength and help deoxidation), applied in such a way that, although some of the filler metal may penetrate into capillary gaps between the components being joined, the main objective is to obtain strength in the joint by building up a fillet of the deposited metal.

The copper-zinc filler metal finds general application in the bronze welding of copper and ferrous metals. However, its use on copper based fittings, particularly brasses and gunmetals, is not recommended, because the melting points of the filler metals and the parent metals are too close to avoid melting the parent metal. Like all brass alloys, the copper-zinc filler metal can suffer from dezincification.

General design concepts for bronze welding, particularly the type of joint or edge preparation are similar to those applied in fusion welding (see Figure 4.3/8). By designing the joint to give a fairly large area of contact between filler alloy and parent metal and by introducing a shear stress component as well as the tensile stress placed upon the filler material, optimum strength is obtained.

The strength of a bronze welded joint is reduced by the lack of proper wetting or excessive penetration of the filler alloy into the parent metal. A porous deposit will have poor mechanical characteristics similar to a bad casting.

The main applications of bronze welding are as follows:-

Bronze welding of copper - both the tough-pitch coppers (BS1036-1040) and deoxidised copper (BS1172-1174) are suitable for bronze welding. The difficulty encountered when gas welding tough-pitch copper i.e. creation of 'steam porosity', does not arise because the parent metal is not melted. There is no risk of gassing provided that an oxidising flame is used.

Bronze welding of ferrous materials - the main virtue on ferrous materials is that bronze welding is a lower temperature process when compared with fusion welding resulting in less distortion and less metallurgical disturbance. Care must be taken when joining heat-treated steels to apply only minimal heat for the shortest time to prevent any softening.

Repair of ferrous components - iron castings can be repaired by bronze welding providing the fault is well prepared so that the contact between parent metal and filler is as large as possible. Bronze welding can be used to reface worn components such as valve seats, pumps impellers, etc. using a high tensile brass filler metal.

Dissimilar metals - the jointing of dissimilar metals is possible with bronze welding, particualarly between copper and steel.

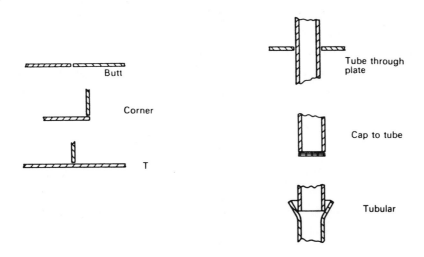

Figure 4.3/9: Bronze welded joint design.

4.3.4 RESISTANCE WELDING

Resistance welding differs from most other forms of welding in that no filler metal or flux is added at the weld, and the weld is invariably consoldiated under pressure. It derives its name from the fact that heat for welding is produced by the resistance of the gap between the work pieces to an electric current. The main applications for this process are as spot welds or seam welds of lap and butt joints. The most important properties which influence weldability, and, therefore, the selection of suitable welding conditions are:

- thermal conductivity; metals with high thermal conductivity (copper or aluminium) readily conduct heat away from the weld point and more current is required to maintain an adequate welding temperature.

- expansion; coefficient of thermal expansion and shrinkage/contraction on solidification are important. In materials of high thermal expansion and high thermal conductivity where shrinkage takes place rapidly, it is necessary to maintain sufficient electrode force to prevent shrinkage cavities and cracks.
- surface condition; rust, paint, grease, etc. must be removed prior to welding. The surface must be clean and the oxide layers reduced to a minimum. Metallic coatings do not seriously reduce weldability.
- high temperature strength; materials with high strength when hot require higher electrode pressures in order to maintain a seal around the molten weld metal.
- metal structure; it is important that the metallurgical structure of both the weld and the heat affected zone should be adequate to withstand the demands made upon the joint in service.

Resistance welding includes the following processes:-

- spot welding where pressure and electrical current are applied at discrete points along the lapped joint; extensively used in sheet metal fabrication.
- seam welding uses wheels as electrodes and the current is pulsed as the joint progresses giving a continuous weld with minimal heating; used extensively in sheet metal fabrication.
- projection welding of studs, nuts, collars and discs to sheet metal.
- tube welding where the strip edges are heated continuously by high frequency current through sliding contacts. Pressure rolls then force the edges together.
- butt welding where component ends are held under pressure before power is applied so that heat is generated at and behind the interface so that the metal softens and welding occurs.
- flash welding describes the procedure in which two clamped components are energised and brought close together so that arcing occurs. This condition is allowed to continue until insufficient heat is developed to cause welding when the gap is closed under high pressure.
- friction welding is achieved by rubbing two abutting surfaces together, usually by rotation, until enough heat is generated to weld them together.

4.3.4.1 **WELDABLE METALS AND ALLOYS**

STEEL

Low carbon steels may be readily resistance welded by all processes, deep drawing grades are excellent.

Medium carbon and alloy steels may be welded but high electrode pressure must be maintained after the current pulse to prevent cracking and this is normally followed by post weld heat treatment.

Austenitic stainless steels, compared with low carbon steels, require lower currents and high electrode pressures in spot and projection welding. It is important to keep the heating times to a minimum to reduce the tendency for carbide formation in the range 600 to 900°C, thus minimising corrosion attack at the weld.

410

ALUMINIUM AND ALUMINIUM ALLOYS

Resistance weldability is governed mainly by their relatively high condictivity and the presence of a tenacious high resistance oxide layer. Surface preparation is of the utmost importance. Pure aluminium is the most difficult to spot weld and easiest to butt weld, however strong alloys clad with pure aluminium are more easily spot welded due to their total lower conductivity. Flash butt welding may be applied to all aluminium alloys providing rapid heating and careful control of time and speed of application of the upset force is applied.

COPPER AND COPPER ALLOYS

Due to its extremely high electrical and thermal conductivity copper is not normally regarded as weldable by spot or projection welding. It may be satisfactorily butt and flash butt welded.

Brasses increase in weldability with increase in zinc content. Resistance butt welding is frequently used for brass wire but flash butt welding is not suitable due to the volatilization of zinc. Brass should be annealed after welding to render it immune from cracking.

Tin bronzes have relatively low conductivity and can be readily joined by all resistance welding methods. Phosphor bronzes may tend to stick to the electrodes.

Aluminium bronzes are possible to weld providing they are single phase types.

Silicon bronzes have low conductivity and may be satisfactorily spot and resistance butt welded. Weld time and electrode pressures are lower than low carbon steel and current higher.

Cupro-nickels and nickel silvers react similarly to silicon bronzes.

NICKEL AND NICKEL ALLOYS

Nickel, Monel, Inconel and the Nimonic alloys may be satisfactorily spot, projection and flash butt welded. Nimonics, Monel and Inconel react similarly to austenitic stainless steel but with higher pressure. Nickel requires higher currents and, being softer, requires lower forces.

DISSIMILAR METALS

It is normally easier to make satisfactory joints between dissimilar metals by resistance welding than by fusion welding or brazing, since the problem of fluxing does not arise and techniques may be chosen to minimize the danger of brittle phases. When spot welding dissimilar metals it may be necessary to use electrodes of differing conductivity against the different parts, i.e. a higher conductivity electrode against the lower conductivity material.

4.3.5 FUSION WELDING

This is a welding process in which the weld is made by fusion of the parent meal by means of externally applied heat but without pressure. Filler wire may or may not be used. The heat may originate from an electric arc or from the combustion of gases.

QUALITY CONTROL

For the most part welded joints are examined non-destructively. These include visual

411

examination, crack detection (penetrant, magnetic or eddy current), radiographical, ultra-sonic or by pressure tests (hydrostatic or pneumatic). The nature and extent of testing depends upon a number of factors, including the nature of the welding process, design of the joint, metal thickness, requirements of the relevant construction code and the severity of service.

HEALTH AND SAFETY

Under the requirements of the Health and Safety at Work Act adequate precautions must be taken. These include recommended eye shields and curtains against radiation, protective clothing and fume extraction.

4.3.5.1 **FUSION WELDING METHODS**

There are many methods of fusion welding but the following are the most important.

MANUAL METAL ARC (MMA)

An arc welding process (AC or DC) in which the metal electrode forms the filler metal. The filler metal may be coated with a flux which consists of bonded mineral, metal and organic powders. This coating stabilises the arc, gives off protective gases, melts to form a protective and refining slag for the weld pool, and provides alloying elements for the weld metal. This method is widely used for the welding of various types of steel. The major precaution that must be taken with coated electrodes is that they must be dry to prevent embrittlement in the weld due to the absorbtion of moisture in the coating.

TUNGSTEN INERT GAS (TIG)

This is a method in which an electric arc is maintained between a non-consumable electrode of tungsten and the work, in an inert gas atmosphere. Contamination of the weld pool by atmospheric oxygen and nitrogen is prevented by the gas shroud. Whether an autogenous weld, using molten parent metal alone to fill the weld gap, or filler metal is used normally depends on the thickness of material. The electrical supply (A.C. or D.C.) is normally determined by the materials to be welded (aluminium and its alloys generally require an A.C. supply).

The most common cover gas is argon and because it is inert fluxes are not required. The addition of hydrogen to the argon will increase the weld pool temperature which in turn allows gas to escape with the result that porosity is reduced.

METAL INERT GAS (MIG)

This is a method of welding in which the source of heat is an electric arc, invariably D.C., struck between the work and welding electrode, in an inert gas shield, using a continuous consumable wire which acts as filler metal. A variety of gases and gas mixtures are used from argon, which is expensive, to carbon dioxide, which is comparatively cheap. Process factors that are affected by gas composition include spatter bead shape and weld profile. Some gases are better used with certain parent metals than others. The choice of filler wire is dependent on the parent metals.

GAS WELDING

The process involves the melting of the parent metal and filler metal, if used, by means of a flame using a fuel gas combined with oxygen. Acetylene is normally employed because the oxyacetylene flame provides the highest temperature of all the commonly used fuel gases. Arc welding is replacing gas welding but it does have uses in the fields of maintenance and repair or in isolated areas where no electrical service is available. Flux residue, which is a potential source of corrosion or of defects in multi-pass welds, must be removed after the deposition of each pass. The process is applicable to practically all commercial ferrous and non-ferrous materials.

OTHER WELDING METHODS

Electron beam welding may be used for production runs where the metals have to be joined with virtually no distortion. The narrow penetrating weld can be achieved in or out of a vacuum. Although capital cost is high, the process may be economic where justified by high throughput.

Laser beam welding is another method of jointing giving a high intensity narrow beam without the use of a vacuum chamber. Use is restricted to the joining of thin sections which are normally inaccessible, require a limited heat affected zone and a precise location.

4.3.5.2 **WELDABLE METALS AND ALLOYS**

CARBON STEEL

The welding of carbon steel may be accomplished by the majority of processes, the choice of method being dependent upon thickness, type and position of joint and to some extent type of steel. Thin steel is best welded using one of the inert gas methods. Fillet joints may be made using manual welding with prefluxed rods or CO_2 shielded metal inert gas. Butt joints in thick sheet and plate requires manual metal or metal inert gas. Problems may exist in various steels when welding, for example gas shield welding of rimming steel can produce porous welds, killed steels give better results with welding and high sulphur content steels must use the correct electrode to avoid hot cracking.

Gas welding is best accomplished using a neutral flame and no flux with the filler metal copper coated to ensure freedom from rust.

Electrodes for carbon steel are laid down in BS 1453 for gas welding and BS 639 for manual metal arc welding.

HVCA TR/5, Carbon Steel Welding Practice, deals with pipework for water, steam and gas pressures up to and including 17.0 bar and/or temperatures from -220°C up to and including 220°C and with wall thicknesses not exceeding 20mm.

LOW ALLOY STEEL

There are two main problems in welding this type of steel - the avoidance of hardened zone cracking and the provision of weld metal of adequate tensile strength to match the parent material. The latter is overcome by special electrodes with alloy additions in the flux coating and by the provision of alloy steel filler wires in gas-shielded arc welding. Hardened zone cracking is influenced by cooling conditions, steel composition, electrodes and component restraint. Heating up to around 200°C and hold after welding will help overcome the problem in steels of high hardenability and will reduce residual stresses. The rate at which any filler rod is laid will also influence any possibility of cracking.

Alloy steels can be welded by similar processes to low carbon steel. Special electrodes are

413

available for gas welding. Filler wires are defined in BS 2901 and MMA electrodes in BS 639, 2926 and 2493.

HIGH ALLOY HEAT RESISTANT AND STAINLESS STEELS.

These fall into three catagories, martensitic chromium steels, higher chromium ferritic steels and nickel-chromium austenitic steels.

The martensitic steels require conditions similar to low alloy and carbon steels: preheat to at least 200°C followed by slow cooling or post-weld heat treatment at 650-750°C (the latter being essential if matching low hydrogen electrodes or filler rods are used). Austenitic electrodes or filler rods are preferred.

The ferritic alloys suffer from serious embrittlement. Welding with matching filler rods is possible and preheating to 200°C followed by slow post-weld cooling is advisable. In some instances the structure should be post-annealed at 850°C.

The austenitic steels are preferably welded by either the manual arc or inert gas methods. Gas welding tends to give rise to increases in carbon with resulting corrosion problems.
There are three main problems which may arise when welding austentic steels:-

Weld Decay: CO_2 gas can be used as a cover gas but care must be taken to prevent carbide pickup with a resulting loss of corrosion resistance in the weld area. This arises through the formation of chromium rich carbides when the material is heated in the temperature range 550 to 850°C as in parts of the heat affected zone of a weld. These chromium rich carbides reduce the chromium content of the surrounding areas and therefore reduce the materials resistance to corrosion and stress corrosion attack.

Methods of protection are:-

heat treatment after welding by heating to 1000 to 1150°C followed by rapid cooling.
-   use of very low carbon contents, 0.3% max.
-   use of stabilised alloys which contain preferential acrbide formers such as niobium or titanium.

Hot Cracking: hot cracks may form in the weld metal but can be controlled by a variety of means such as weld metal analysis and minimising the stress on the weld as it cools.

Heat Affected Zone (or Underbead Cracking): this occurs when welding stabilised steels and is caused by the combination of high weld restraint and liquidation at the toe of the weld. It may also occur during subsequent stress relief. Prevention is by reducing weld restraint particularly when welding thick sections and by dressing welds prior to stress relief.

Filler wires for stainless steel welding are specified in BS 1453 and BS 2901. MMA electrodes are specified in BS 2926.

CAST IRON

Cast irons may be welded provided suitable precautions are taken. Difficulties arise due to lack of ductility in the parent material to accomodate weld shrinkage stresses; formation of hard brittle phases, hardening in the heat affected zone and high sulphur content may cause cracking

414

in the weld. Due to their graphite form spheroidal graphite and other ductile irons are more weldable than grey iron. The choice of process depends on the type of component and its composition. Gas welding is suitable for light components and MMA for heavier ones. To accomodate shrinkage stresses and to minimise hardening, pre-heating to 550°C and slow cooling is essential. If preheating is not possible apply the minimum heat input and use small diameter electrodes. Also bronze welding may be employed with a resultant lower working temperature.

Recommended filler wires are specified in BS 1453.

ALUMINIUM AND ALUMINIUM ALLOYS

Aluminium and many of its alloys are readily welded by inert gas methods using a flux. The inert gas cover prevents the formation of oxide in the molten pool. MIG welding is faster than TIG and is used mainly for joints in material over 6 mm thick.
When gas welding, all traces of flux must be removed to prevent subsequent corrosion. Cracking due to restraint can occur in certain alloys because of the high contraction rate during cooling of weld metal. High strength alloys are prone to cracking if welded with parent metal filler material.

The strength and ductility of wrought materials will be reduced by fusion welding. Alloys which depend on cold work for strength will be locally annealed in the weld area and since they do not respond to heat treatment, no recovery of strength is possible without subsequent cold work. The properties of heat treatable alloys may be restored by heat treatment after welding. Distortion can be a problem but can be overcome by correct design and welding technique. The resistance to corrosion may be altered in the region of the weld. Where a strong alloy has been clad with pure aluminium for corrosion protection no cladding will be present in the weld bead.

Cast aluminium and alloys are welded in a similar manner to wrought material with similar precautions. Castings may be welded to wrought aluminium and its alloys.

Careful choice of filler metal must be made if the fabrication has to be anodised because different alloys have differing appearances.

Filler wires are defined in BS 1453 and BS 2901.

COPPER AND COPPER ALLOYS

The welding of tough-pitch copper, with residual oxygen, using oxyacetylene is not recommended due to the risk of gassing. It can be welded using an inert gas shielded process with a boron-copper filler.

Oxygen free and deoxidised copper may be welded by gas, TIG and MIG methods. There are no problems from gassing but care must be taken that porosity does not result from the argon cover gas. The use of filler wires to BS 1453 and BS 2901 is recommended. Recommended procedures for fusion welding copper are found in BS 1077.

Copper-aluminiums cannot be gas welded but MMA or preferably TIG and MIG methods may be used. Most alloys are welded with fillers of matching composition. Where non-parent filler materials are used care must be taken that corrosion resistance properties are not impaired.

Copper-nickel alloys can suffer from problems of embrittlement and porosity. These can be overcome using filler wires containing titanium as a deoxidant. Filler wires are available for

90/10, and 70/30 cupro-nickels, to BS 2901. Either TIG or MIG methods are normally used.

Copper-tin alloys can cause difficulties during welding. Tin bronzes ususally contain phosphorous and both oxyacetylene and TIG welds tend to be porous. A bronze welding technique is preferable. Gunmetal may produce better welds. Both types of bronze are prone to hot shortness and shrinkage porosity. Leaded gunmetals are difficult to weld.

Copper-zinc welding is not easy due to excessive zinc fume formation. Gas welding using an oxidising flame and parent filler or silicon brass filler is possible. TIG and MIG welding systems both use non zinc filler alloys in preference to brass although various brass fillers are available for TIG welding. MMA and MIG welding use silicon bronze or aluminium bronze alloys. The susceptibility of brass for season cracking should be born in mind.
Stress relief of brass components is desirable.

Filler wires for copper and its alloys are defined in BS1453 and BS2901.

LEAD AND LEAD ALLOYS

Lead and its alloys may be welded by gas methods using a neutral flame and without flux. The edges should be cleaned before welding and parent metal filler is used.

NICKEL AND NICKEL ALLOYS

The materials are divided into two groups, non-heat treatable (pure nickel, Monel, Inconel, Nimonic 75) and the heat treatable (K Monel, Nimonic 80 and 90). For welding, all materials must be stress free, i.e. annealed or solution treated. Heat treated alloys are artificially aged after welding. Nickel alloys are susceptible to hot weld cracking and therefore great care must be taken to cool slowly.

Gas welding is suitable for all non-heat treated alloys with pure and K Monel not requiring flux. Fluxes are available for other alloys but must be removed after welding. Nickel and Monel require a slightly reducing flame, Inconel and Nimonic 75 require a distinctly reducing flame while a strongly reducing flame is required for K Monel.

TIG welding is used for sheetwork using argon. A patchy tenacious oxide film is formed by nickel alloys and can cause welding problems.

For heavier gauges MMA using flux-coated electrodes and MIG methods are adopted. Special filler wires for nickel alloys have been developed and are defined in BS 2901.

4.3.6 PLASTICS WELDING

Only thermoplastics can be welded, but the welding technique is quite different from that of metals because of low heat resistance of plastics compared to metals. Welding is especially useful in the case of plastics such as polyethylene, polypropylene, and polyfluorocarbons, which are difficult to join by adhesives.

Most frequently, welding is accomplished by electrically heated inert gas or air at temperatures of 190 to 260°C, depending on the thermal stability of the plastic; a suitable filler rod is used to fill the joint. Intimate fusion between the surfaces and the weld takes place, resulting in a weldment nearly as strong as the parent material. The welding of plastics is much slower than of metals.

An alternative is an adaptation of butt welding. In this method the plastic components to be welded together are held by pressure against a heated platen. When the softening temperature is reached the platen is removed and the gap speedily closed under pressure causing the components to fuse. This method is used for the welding of plastic pipes, both for above and underground systems.

Ultrasonic welding has recently found favour for joining plastics together and for joining plastics and metals. More rigid plastics such as ABS are better suited for ultrasonic welding than the softer ones.

Other methods are electrical induction and dielectric heating. The latter is especially suitable for ABS, acetals, and acrylic polymers with a high dissipation factor, usually 0.01 or greater.

Directly related to welding is heat sealing of thermoplastic film and fabrics. For this purpose the heat may be generated by thermal, dielectric, or ultrasonic methods; some moderate pressure is required to produce a strong joint.

4.3.7 ADHESIVE BONDING

An adhesive can be defined as any substance capable of holding materials together by surface attachment. Adhesives have an advantage over other joining methods in that they can be applied to the surfaces of material combinations such as metal/metal, glass/metal, metal/plastic, plastic/plastic and ceramic/ceramic providing there is compatibility between all elements. Structural members joined by adhesives are notably free from residual stress. A serious disadvantage of adhesives is that their strength decreases as the temperature increases.

There are various types of adhesives:-

- those involving a solvent, which evaporates during the process of bonding (solvent loss).
- those that use a catalyst or accelerator to harden the adhesive (chemical reaction).
- those that comprise thermoplastic material heated to above its melting point, wetting the surfaces to be joined (hot melt).

For maximum adhesion between the parent materials and the adhesive the surfaces must be properly prepared. All oil, grease and dirt must be removed and, where required, the surfaces abraded and degreased. Bonded joints perform best under tension, compression or shear loading, less well under cleavage and relatively poorly under peel loading.

The properties of adhesives can be modified, by the addition of filler materials, thereby changing the expansion rate to make it compatible with the parent materials or to make it thixotropic to improve its gap filling properties.

Care must be taken in the choice of an adhesive, particularly if it requires a hot curing cycle. It may be impossible to heat the assembly to temperature because its bulk may preclude the use of simple heating arrangements or the curing temperature may destroy the assembly.

The pot life of the adhesive must be long enough to complete the application and the assembly process. Adequate adhesive should be mixed to complete the assembly. In some systems the larger the bulk of mixed adhesive material the faster the curing occurs. Poor adhesion will result if partially cured adhesive is applied.

A guide to some of the engineering adhesives is given below; for more detailed information the manufacturer should be consulted.

ACRYLIC

The maximum service temperature is 50°C. It has good strength, excellent resistance to sunlight, good moisture resistance and resistant to some oils. Acrylics have been used for bonding acrylic (Perspex), glass, metals and leather. It is transparent after curing.

BITUMENS

Data Sheet JB06

Under this title all asphalt based adhesives are included. Bitumens are low-cost thermoplastic materials of mineral origin. They are dark in colour with poor strength. At room temperature they may be soft and sticky or hard and brittle depending on the compound used. Bitumens will adhere to many types of surface including concrete, glass and metal and are used in applications where low stress are encountered e.g. floor laying, attaching tiles to walls etc. They are available as water emulsions, hot melts and in solvent solution. Bitumen based adhesives have good resistance to water and alkali but oils and solvents cause softening.

CYANOACRYLATE

Data Sheet JB07

A general purpose, transparent structural adhesive which will bond most materials producing high strength joints (up to $20N/mm^2$). It is resistant to oils and some solvents and to water but not to steam. The adhesives sets in seconds by pressure being applied to the film between the two surfaces to be bonded. Optimum strength is obtained from thin glue lines. Its advantage is that it sets rapidly while its disadvantage is its expense; it is therefore only used where its particular properties are valuable. Maximum continuous service temperature is 80°C.

EPOXY

Data Sheet JB08

Thermoset resin adhesives are available as two-part systems with hardeners or one-part hot curing systems. They are primarily metal/metal structural adhesives but can also be used for bonding glass, ceramics, wood, some rubbers and most plastics, but unsuitable for polyethylene and PTFE. With unmodified systems high strength bonds ($30 N/mm^2$ in shear) are obtained with low flexibility and impact strength. Additives can improve these properties. A maximum service temperature of 90°C is recommended. Cured epoxy resins have excellent resistance to oils, water, solvents and mould growth.

Their great advantages are low shrinkage, no volatiles released during curing and only pressure contact required. They are good insulators and gap fillers (0.025 to 0.3 mm).

EPOXY - PHENOLIC

Data Sheet JB09

An epoxy modified with phenolic produces a structural adhesive for bonding metals for service up to 260°C (shear strengths are reduced from $20 N/mm^2$ 20°C to 6.5 N/mm^2 at 260°C). They offer good resistance to water, oils, chemicals and mould.   Epoxy-Phenolics can be used to bond stainless steels.

EPOXY-POLYAMIDE

Data Sheet JB10

Polyamides, when combined with epoxy resins, function as a curing agent resulting in a more flexible bond.   By varying the proportion of polyamide the flexibility can be increased or decreased, with shear strengths of 21 to 28 N/mm^2.   As the proportion of polyamide is increased so the bond strength decreases.   This form of adhesive is resistant to water, oils and chemicals but this property decreases with increase of polyamide.   It will bond most rigid and flexible materials including metals, rubbers, glass, ceramics and most plastics, including nylon.   It is not suitable for polyethelene or PTFE.

EPOXY-POLYSULPHIDE

Data Sheet JB11

Polysulphide improves the elasticity and peel strength of an epoxy bond.   The combination has a shear strength of 30 to 35 N/mm^2 and can be used up to 90°C.   Epoxy-polysulphide has good solvent resistance and is used for bonding metal, in particular steel, to concrete.

NATURAL RUBBER

Data Sheet JB12

Natural rubber based adhesives set by solvent or water evaporation and/or by vulcanisation with the aid of heat or at room temperature with an accelerator.   Vulcanised bonds can be used up to 90°C whilst unvulcanised bonds are limited to less than 65°C.   Low strength and the thermoplastic nature of natural rubber excludes it from structural applications.   Natural rubber has good resistance to water and mould growth but is adversly affected by oils, solvents and many chemicals, particularly oxidising agents.

NEOPRENE RUBBER

Data Sheet JB13

Neoprene based adhesives are generally suitable where the maximum service temperature is less than 90°C.   They have good resistance to water, some oils, most chemicals, including weak acids, and some solvents, with the exception of aromatic hydrocarbons and strong oxidising agents.   These adhesives are not suitable for structural applications due to their tendency to cold flow under low loads.

Neoprenes may be used for bonding natural and synthetic rubbers, some plastics (not polyethylene or PTFE), timber and metal.   Neoprene rubber is resistant to sunlight.

NITRILE RUBBER

Data Sheet JB14

Nitrile rubber adhesives can achieve a shear strength 6.5N/mm^2 and can be used over a range of -50 to + 150°C. They are not recommended for structural purposes.   Nitrile rubber is resistant to oils, mould growth, water, many solvents and most acids (but not strongly oxidising acids).

Nitrile rubber is used for bonding timber, metal, plastics (especially PVC) and rubber.

PHENOL FORMALDEHYDE

This is a thermosetting resin which forms the basis of many structural adhesives in combination with epoxy or nitrile rubber. It has a maximum service temperture of 100°C and is used to bond wood to preprimed metal and phenolic and melamine plastics to either wood or metal. It is resistant to oils, water (including boiling water), solvents and mould growth.

PHENOLIC - NEOPRENE

Data Sheet JB15

This is an ideal adhesive for low temperature and vibration applications. After heat curing it can achieve a shear strength of up to 20 N/mm^2. The low temperature limit is -55°C. It has excellent resistance to water, most oils and solvents, and mould growth. Phenolic-neoprene may be used to bond metals, rubbers, plastics, timber, glass and ceramics.

PHENOLIC-NITRILE

Data Sheet JB16

Phenolic-nitrile adhesive has a shear strength of 25 N/mm^2, reducing to 12N/mm^2 at 175°C, with good impact strength and resistance to cold flow. The minimum operating temperature is -50°C. Phenolic-nitrile is resistant to water, oils, salt spray, many solvents and mould growth and may be used to bond metals, plastics, timber, glass and ceramics.

PHENOLIC-POLYAMIDE

A combination of thermosetting phenolic and thermoplastic polyamide bonding preprimed metals to give a joint of high strength. It has a shear strength of 35 N/mm^2 at room temperature, 20 N/mm^2 at 150°C and 16 N/mm^2 at -55°C. The adhesive is in the form of phenolic resin bonded to a polyamide film with the application of heat and pressure.

PHENOLIC VINYL

This adhesive has a shear strength of 35N/mm^2 up to 80°C with a rapid reduction up to 100°C. The minimum service temperature is -50°C. It is an excellent adhesive for bonding metal, pre-treated rubber, plastics and timber. Adhesives of this type are resistant to water, oils, mould growth and some solvents. Bonding is by heat curing.

POLYESTER-ACRYLIC

Data Sheet JB17

Polyester acrylic cures by the exclusion of air (anaerobic) without shrinkage or evaporation. It will bond metals, glass and thermosetting plastics with an invisible bond line. Several formulations are available to suit a variety of conditions within a temperture range of -50°C to +200°C. Shear stresses of 15 to 24 N/mm^2 may be obtained. All forms are resistant to oils, acids, water and certain solvents. In the liquid state there will be some attack on thermoplastics.

POLYURETHANES

Data Sheet JB18

Polyurethane adhesive is flexible, has good peel strength and resistance to shock and vibration. It is resistant to acids, alkalis, oils and fuels but is affected by water. It can be used for bonding metals, rubbers, foams, plastics and glass. A maximum temperature of +95°C is recommended.

ACRYLIC ACID DIESTERS

This is a liquid which cures in the absence of air (anaerobic) under the catalytic action of the abutting surfaces. It is thermoplastic and softens over 250°C; the normal service temperature range is -50°C to +150°C. It exhibits a shear strength of up to 48 N/mm^2.

A typical application for this adhesive is the locking of close-tolerance components for engineering purposes.

POLYAMIDE

Polyamides have good adhesion to metals, many plastics and leather. They are resistant to water, oils, mould growth and certain solvents. This adhesive is hot cured at between 100-170°C and sets immediately on cooling. It is not regarded as a structural adhesive.

POLYESTER

Polyester adhesives have gap filling properties with very small (in the order of 1%) shrinkage. They are also capable of withstanding mechanical and thermal movement due to their flexible properties. Polyesters are resistant to water, oils and mould growth. They are used for bonding metals, concrete, PVC, glass and ceramics.

POLYVINYL ACETATE (PVA)

Data Sheet JB 19

A versatile non-structural adhesive used to bond timber, leather, metal, glass, ceramics and many plastics (not PVC or polyethylene). It has a low heat resistance with a maximum service temperature of +50°C. Because of cold flow characteristics at low stress it is not a structural adhesive. Polyvinyl acetates have good resistance to oils, mould growth and sunlight, fair water resistance but liable to damage by freezing.

421

RELATED SPECIFICATIONS

SOFT SOLDERING

BS 91	: 1954	Electrical cable soldering sockets
BS 219	: 1959	Soft solders
BS 441	: 1954	Resin cored solder wire activated and non-activated (non-corrosive)
BS 5245	: 1975	Phosporic acid based flux for soldering stainless steel
BS AU90	: 1965	Soft solders for automobile use
DTD 599A	: 1961	Non-corrosive flux for soft soldering

BRAZING

BS 449	: 1965	Glossary of terms
BS 1723	: 1963	Brazing
BS 1845	: 1977	Specification for filler metals for brazing
BS 4416	: 1969	Methods for penetrant testing of welded or brazed joints in metals
HVCA TR/3		Brazing and bronze welding of copper pipework and sheet

BRONZE WELDING

BS 1453	: 1972	Filler rods and wires for gas welding
BS 1724	: 1959	Bronze welding
BS 1845	: 1977	Filler metals for brazing - group CZ brazing brasses
HVCA TR/3		Brazing and bronze welding of copper pipework and sheet

RESISTANCE AND FUSION WELDING

GENERAL

BS 499	–	Welding terms and symbols
Part 1	: 1965	Welding, brazing and thermal cutting glossary
Part 2	: 1980	Symbols for welding
Part 3	:	Terminology of and abbreviations for fusion weld imperfections as revealed by radiography
		Chart of British Standard welding symbols (based on BS 499, Part 2)
BS 679	: 1959	Filters for use during welding and similar industrial operations
BS 1542	: 1960	Equipment for eye, face and neck protection against radiation arising during welding and similar opertions
BS 2653	: 1955	Protective clothing for welders
BS 5044	: 1973 (1982)	Specification for contrast aid paints used in magnetic particle flaw detection

PROCESSES

BS 693	: 1960	General requirements for oxy-acetylene welding of mild steel
BS 1077	: 1963	Fusion-welded joints in copper
BS 1453	: 1972	Filler materials for gas welding

BS 4206	:	1967	Methods of testing fusion welds in copper and copper alloys
BS 4360	:	1979	Weldable structual steels
BS 1140	:	1980	General requirements for spot welding of light assemblies in mild steel
BS 1821	:	1982	Class 1 oxy-acetylene welding of steel pipelines and pipe assemblies for carrying fluids
BS 2630	:	1982	Projection welding of uncoated low carbon steel sheet and strip using embossed projections
BS 2633	:	1973 (1981)	Class I arc welding of ferritic steel pipework for carrying fluids
BS 2640	:	1982	Class II oxy-acetylene welding of steel pipelines and pipe assemblies for carrying fluids
BS 2971	:	1977 (1982)	Class II arc welding of carbon steel pipework for carrying fluids
BS 2996	:	1958	Projection welding of low carbon wrought steel studs, bosses, bolts, nuts and annular rings
BS 3019		-	General recommedations for manual inert-gas tungsten-arc welding
Part 1	:	1958	Wrought aluminium, aluminium alloys and magnesium alloys
Part 2	:	1960	Austenitic stainless and heat-resisting steels
BS 3571		-	General recommendations for manual inert-gas metal-arc welding
Part 1	:	1962	Aluminium and aluminium alloys
BS 4204			Specification for flash welding of steel tubes for pressure applications
BS 4515	:	1969	Field welding of carbon steel pipelines
BS 4570		-	Fusion welding of steel castings
Part 1	:	1970	Production, rectification and repair
Part 2	:	1972	Fabrication welding
BS 4677	:	1971	Class I arc welding of austenitic stainless steel pipeline for carrying fluids
BS 5135	:	1974	Metal-arc welding of carbon and carbon manganese steels
BS 6265	:	1982	Specification for resistance seam welding of uncoated and coated low carbon steel
DD 39	:	1974	Welding on steel pipelines under pressure
CDA TN2			Gas shielded arc welding of copper and copper alloys
HVCA:TR5			Welding of carbon steel pipework

EQUIPMENT

BS 638		-	Arc welding plant, equipment and accessories
BS 807	:	1955	Spot welding electrodes
BS 1389	:	1960	Dimensions of hose connections for welding and cutting equipment
BS 3065	:	1965	The rating of resistance welding and resistance heating machines
BS 3067	:	1959	Dimensions of blanks for seam welding wheels
BS 3856	:	1965	Platens for projection welding machines
BS 4215	:	1967	Spot welding electrodes and electrode holders
BS 4577	:	1970	Materials for resistance welding electrodes and ancillary equipment
BS 4819	:	1972	Resistance welding water-cooled transformers of the press-package and portable types

WELDING CONSUMABLES

BS 639	:	1976	Covered electrodes for the manual metal-arc welding of carbon and carbon-manganese steels
BS 2493	:	1971	Low alloy steel electrodes for manual metal-arc welding
BS 2901		-	Filler rods and wires for gas-shielded arc-welding
Part 1	:	1970	Ferritic steels
Part 2	:	1970	Austenitic stainless steels
Part 3	:	1970	Copper and copper alloys
Part 4	:	1970	Aluminium and aluminium alloys and magnesium alloys
Part 5	:	1970	Nickel and nickel alloys
BS 2926	:	1970	Chromium-nickel austenitic and chromium steel electrodes for manual metal-arc welding
BS 4165	:	1971	Electrodes wires and fluxes for the submerged-arc welding of carbon steel and medium tensile steel

TESTING AND INSPECTION

BS 709	:	1971	Methods of testing fusion welded joints and weld metal in steel-metric units
BS 1295	:	1969	Tests for use in the training of welders. Manual metal-arc and oxy-acetylene welding of mild steel
BS 2600		-	Methods for the radiographic examination of fusion welded butt joints in steel
Part 1	:	1973	5mm up to and including 50mm thick
Part 2	:	1973	Over 50mm up to and including 200mm thick
BS2704	:	1978	Calibration blocks and recommendations for their use in ultrasonic flaw detection
BS 2910	:	1973	Methods for the radiographic examination of fusion welded circumferential butt joints in steel pipes
BS 3451	:	1973 (1981)	Methods of testing fusion welds in aluminium and aluminium alloys
BS 3923		-	Methods for ultrasonic examination of welds
Part 1	:	1978	Manual examination of fusion welded butt joints in ferritic steels
Part 2	:	1972	Automatic examination of fusion welded butt joints in ferritic steels
Part 3	:	1972	Manual examination of nozzle welds
BS 3971	:	1980	Image quality indicators for radiography and recommendations for their use
BS 4069	:	1982	Magnetic flaw detection inks and powders
BS 4129	:	1967	Resistance welding properties of welding primers and weld-through sealers
BS 4397	:	1967	Methods for magnetic particle testing of welds
BS 4416	:	1969	Methods for penetrant testing of welded or brazed joints in metals
BS 4870		-	Approval testing of welding procedures
Part 1	:	1981	Fusion welding of steel
Part 2	:	1982	TIG or MIG welding of aluminium and its alloys
BS 4871		-	Approval testing of welders working to approved welding procedures
Part 1	:	1982	Fusion welding of steel
Part 2	:	1982	TIG or MIG welding of aluminium and its alloys
BS 4872			Approval testing of welders when welding procedure approval is not required
Part 1	:	1972	Fusion welding of steel

| Part 2 | : | 1976 | TIG or MIG welding of aluminium and its alloys |
| PD 6493 | : | 1980 | Guidance on some methods for derivation of acceptance levels for defects in fusion welded joints |

ADHESIVE BONDING

BS 647	:	1969	Methods of sampling and testing glues (bone skin and fish glues)
BS 1203	:	1963	Synthetic resin adhesives (phenolic and amino plastics) for plywood.
BS 1204		-	Synthetic resin adhesives (phenolic and amino plastics)
Part 1	:	1979	Gap filling adhesives
Part 2	:	1979	Close contact adhesives
BS 1444	:	1970	Cold setting case in adhesive powders for wood
BS 3544	:	1962	Methods of testing P.V.A. adhesives for wood
BS 3940	:	1965	Adhesives based on bitumen or coal tar
BS 4071	:	1966	P.V.A. emulsion adhesives for wood
BS 5407	:	1976	Classification of adhesives
BS 5442	:		Classificaton of adhesives in construction
Part 1	:	1977	Adhesives for use with flooring materials
Part 2	:	1978	Adhesives for use with interior wall and ceiling coverings
Part 3	:	1979	Adhesives for use with wood

Ministry of Supply Standards

DTD 775B	Adhesives suitable for joining metals
DTD 861A	Adhesives for metals (low pressure type)
DTD 5577	Heat stable structural adhesives

425

DATA SHEETS

JOINTING AND BONDING (JB)

THERMAL

JB01	Soft solder	40/60
JB02	Soft solder	60/40
JB03	Soft solder	96/4
JB04	Silver based brazing alloy	
JB05	Copper phosphorous brazing alloys	

ADHESIVES

JB06	Bitumen
JB07	Cyanoacrylate
JB08	Epoxy
JB09	Epoxy-phenolic
JB10	Epoxy-polyamide
JB11	Epoxy-polysulphide
JB12	Natural rubber
JB13	Neoprene
JB14	Nitrile rubber
JB15	Phenolic-neoprene
JB16	Phenolic-nitrile
JB17	Polyester-acrylics
JB18	Polyurethane
JB19	Poly-vinyl acetate

| FAMILY GROUP | JOINING AND BONDING | SUB-GROUP | THERMAL | MATERIAL | SOFT SOLDER 40/60 |

GENERAL DESCRIPTION

40/60 tin/lead solder is a low temperature solder with a melting range of 183-234°C. The tin content ensures that it will readily wet a wide range of substrates, provided that suitable flux is used. This alloy has a 'pasty' range during solidification and care should be taken not to stress joints.

CHEMICAL ANALYSIS OR COMPOSITION

Tin   40%
Lead   Remainder
Antimony 0.4% max.

PHYSICAL PROPERTIES

PROPERTY	UNITS	VALUES OR RANGE	COMMENTS
DENSITY	kg/m^3	9300	
TENSILE STRENGTH	N/mm^2	43	Typical bulk solder
YIELD STRENGTH	N/mm^2		
PROOF STRESS ( )	N/mm^2		
ELONGATION	%	30-120	Typical bulk solder depending on extension rate
YOUNGS MODULUS	kN/mm^2		
IMPACT RESISTANCE	J		
HARDNESS			
THERMAL COEFF. OF LINEAR EXPANSION	$^\circ$C^{-1}		
THERMAL CONDUCTIVITY	W/mK		
SPECIFIC HEAT	kJ/kg K		
ELECTRICAL RESISTIVITY	ohm m		
ELECTRICAL CONDUCTIVITY	% IACS	10.2	
SHEAR STRENGTH	N/mm^2	40	Copper joint - typical
		31	Brass joint - typical
		35.5	Steel joint - typical

427

SPECIFICATIONS

STANDARD NUMBER	AUTHORITY	TITLE
BS219	BSI	Specification for soft solders

COMPANY SPECIFICATION:

ENVIRONMENT

Mechanical properties fall away rapidly at temperatures over 100°C.
Lead based solders are liable to attack by 'plumbosolvent' waters.

PROCESSING AND FORMING TECHNIQUES

Maximum strength obtained when parallel joint gaps of 0.08-0.18mm are used. Joint has greater strength for 'peel'.
Solder can be hand fed into the joint or pipe fittings are available with solder in place. Preforms are also available. Melting may be achieved by a variety of heat sources.

JOINTING PROCESS

Heat applied by:-
  gas torch,
  electric soldering bit,
or electrical induction.
Assembly should be prefluxed, appropriate to the metals being joined, to improve wetting conditions.
Lead is a toxic material.
Fluxes are corrosive and excess must be removed.

TYPICAL APPLICATIONS

General engineering joining of copper, brass and zinc. Pipe jointing using end feed fittings or with integral solder rings.
Can soldering.

SAFETY PRECAUTIONS

Lead is a toxic material.

YOUR SUPPLIER AND NOTES

| material data sheet | | SHEET NUMBER | JB02 | A |

| FAMILY GROUP | JOINING AND BONDING | SUB-GROUP | THERMAL | MATERIAL | SOFT SOLDER 60/40 |

GENERAL DESCRIPTION

60/40 tin/lead solder is a low temperature solder with a narrow melting range of 183-188°C. The high tin content ensures that it will readily wet a wide range of substrates, provided that a suitable flux is used. Solder is available as ingots, wire or prefluxed cored wire.

CHEMICAL ANALYSIS OR COMPOSITION

Tin	60%
Lead	Remainder
Antimony	0.5% max

PHYSICAL PROPERTIES

PROPERTY	UNITS	VALUES OR RANGE	COMMENTS
DENSITY	kg/m^3	8550	
TENSILE STRENGTH	N/mm^2	59	Typical bulk solder
YIELD STRENGTH	N/mm^2		
PROOF STRESS ( )	N/mm^2		
ELONGATION	%	30-60	Typical bulk solder depending on extension rate
YOUNGS MODULUS	kN/mm^2		
IMPACT RESISTANCE	J		
HARDNESS			
THERMAL COEFF. OF LINEAR EXPANSION	$°C^{-1}$		
THERMAL CONDUCTIVITY	W/mK		
SPECIFIC HEAT	kJ/kg K		
ELECTRICAL RESISTIVITY	ohm m		
ELECTRICAL CONDUCTIVITY	% IACS	11.5	
SHEAR STRENGTH	N/mm^2	45	Copper joint - typical
		34	Brass joint - typical
		35.5	Steel joint - typical

SPECIFICATIONS

STANDARD NUMBER	AUTHORITY	TITLE
BS219	BSI	Specification for soft solders

COMPANY SPECIFICATION:

ENVIRONMENT

Mechanical properties fall away rapidly at temperatures over 100°C.

Lead based solders are liable to attack by 'plumbosolvent' waters.

PROCESSING AND FORMING TECHNIQUES

Maximum strength obtained when parallel joint gaps of 0.08-0.18mm are used.
Joint has greater strength in shear and minimum for 'peel'.
Solder can be hand fed into the joint or pipe fittings are available with solder in place. Melting may be achieved by a variety of heat sources.

JOINTING PROCESS

Heat applied by:-
    gas torch,
    electric soldering bit,
or   electrical induction.
Assembly should be pre-fluxed, appropriate to the metals being joined, to improve wetting conditions.

Fluxes are corrosive and excess must be removed.

TYPICAL APPLICATIONS

Capillary pipe fittings for jointing copper and stainless steel tubes.

Electronic assembly and machine soldering of printed circuits.
Hot dip coating of ferrous and non-ferrous metals.

SAFETY PRECAUTIONS

Lead is a toxic material

YOUR SUPPLIER AND NOTES

| | material data sheet | | SHEET NUMBER | JB03 | A |

| FAMILY GROUP | JOINING AND BONDING | SUB-GROUP | THERMAL | MATERIAL | SOFT SOLDER 96/4 |

GENERAL DESCRIPTION

96/4 tin/silver solder melts at 221°C. It is an ideal low temperature jointing material in service applications above 100°C. At 100°C the tensile strength is four times that of 60/40 tin/lead solders with a vastly improved creep resistance. 96/4 is non-toxic and not attacked by 'plumbosolvent' water conditions but it is more expensive.

CHEMICAL ANALYSIS OR COMPOSITION

Tin   96%
Silver   4%

PHYSICAL PROPERTIES

PROPERTY	UNITS	VALUES OR RANGE	COMMENTS
DENSITY	kg/m^3		
TENSILE STRENGTH	N/mm^2	37-55	Typical bulk solder
YIELD STRENGTH	N/mm^2		
PROOF STRESS ( )	N/mm^2		
ELONGATION	%	30-40	Typical bulk solder depending on extension rate
YOUNGS MODULUS	kN/mm^2		
IMPACT RESISTANCE	J		
HARDNESS			
THERMAL COEFF. OF LINEAR EXPANSION	$^{\circ}$C^{-1}		
THERMAL CONDUCTIVITY	W/mK		
SPECIFIC HEAT	kJ/kg K		
ELECTRICAL RESISTIVITY	ohm m		
ELECTRICAL CONDUCTIVITY	% IACS		
SHEAR STRENGTH	N/mm^2	74	Copper joint-typical
		39	Brass joint-typical

BSRIA material data sheet

SPECIFICATIONS

Standard number	Authority	Title
BS219	BSI	Specification for soft solder

Company specification:

ENVIRONMENT

Mechanical properties retained at temperatures above 100°C.
Resistant to 'plumbosolvent' waters.

PROCESSING AND FORMING TECHNIQUES

Maximum strength obtained when parallel joint gaps 0.08-0.18mm are used.
Joint has greater strength in shear and minimum for 'peel'.
Solder can be hand fed into the joint or pipe fittings are available with solder in place.
Melting may be achieved by a variety of heat sources.

JOINTING PROCESS

Heat applied by:-
    gas torch
    electric solder bit
or   electrical induction.

Assembly should be prefluxed appropriate to the metals being joined.
Some fluxes are corrosive and excess flux must be removed to prevent corrosion.

TYPICAL APPLICATIONS

Capillary fittings for joining copper tubing at service temperatures above 100°C. Pipe jointing in 'plumbosolvent' waters. Applications where non-toxic materials required.

SAFETY PRECAUTIONS

YOUR SUPPLIER AND NOTES

 material
data sheet

SHEET NUMBER	JB04	**A**

FAMILY GROUP	JOINING AND BONDING	SUB-GROUP	THERMAL	MATERIAL	SILVER BASED BRAZING ALLOY

GENERAL DESCRIPTION

This alloy melts between 600-750°C. The inclusion of cadmium improves fluidity and lowers the melting temperature. A flux is required. Most materials can be joined, including joints of dissimilar metals providing their melting points are above 750°C. Such joints are strong, ductile and have good resistance to corrosion. A range of alloys are described in BS1845. Brazed joints can be electroplated.

CHEMICAL ANALYSIS OR COMPOSITION

Silver	25-60%
Copper	15-40%
Zinc	10-34%
Cadmium	0-25%

PHYSICAL PROPERTIES

PROPERTY	UNITS	VALUES OR RANGE	COMMENTS
DENSITY	kg/m^3		
TENSILE STRENGTH	N/mm^2	345-500	Typical
YIELD STRENGTH	N/mm^2		
PROOF STRESS ( )	N/mm^2		
ELONGATION	%	20-35	Typical
YOUNGS MODULUS	kN/mm^2		
IMPACT RESISTANCE	J		
HARDNESS		130-140	Vickers pyramid no.
THERMAL COEFF. OF LINEAR EXPANSION	$°C^{-1}$		
THERMAL CONDUCTIVITY	W/mK		
SPECIFIC HEAT	kJ/kg K		
ELECTRICAL RESISTIVITY	ohm m		
ELECTRICAL CONDUCTIVITY	% IACS	20-23	Typical

SPECIFICATIONS

STANDARD NUMBER	AUTHORITY	TITLE
BS 1723	BSI	Brazing
BS 1845 (Type AG)	BSI	Filler alloys for brazing

COMPANY SPECIFICATION:

ENVIRONMENT

Brazing alloys containing cadmium are undesirable for use in potable water systems due to health problems.

Joints between dissimilar metals may be subject to galvanic attack.

Generally brazing alloys are corrosion resistant but conditions can prevail where stress corrosion may occur.

JOINTING PROCESS

Heat applied by:-
    gas torch
    furnace
    electrical induction
or electric resistance

Assembly should be pre-fluxed, appropriate to the metals being joined.
Brazing alloy may be used in wire, strip or pre-forms.
Fluxes are corrosive and excess must be removed.

SAFETY PRECAUTIONS

Brazing alloys with cadmium must not be used where contact with foodstuffs is possible.

PROCESSING AND FORMING TECHNIQUES

Maximum strength obtained when parallel joint gaps 0.05-0.25mm are used. Maximum mechanical properties are obtained when the joint has greatest strength in shear and minimum where 'peel' conditions prevail.

Braze alloy can be hand fed into the joint or pipe fitting. Integral braze alloys are available in pipe fittings to BS864.

TYPICAL APPLICATIONS

Jointing of assemblies or pipework that require moderate strength and operate at temperatures above the limits of soft solder.

Assemblies that require electroplating.

YOUR SUPPLIER AND NOTES

BSRIA material data sheet	SHEET NUMBER JB05	**A**
FAMILY GROUP JOINING AND BONDING	SUB-GROUP THERMAL	MATERIAL COPPER-PHOSPHOROUS BRAZING ALLOYS

GENERAL DESCRIPTION

Copper based alloys of silver, phosphorous and copper with a melting range of 640-700°C. Their outstanding feature is their ability to braze copper in air without the use of flux. When flux is used the alloys are suitable for brazing all copper based alloys. Parent metals containing nickel, cobalt or iron should not be brazed with these alloys as a brittle joint is formed. Maximum service temperature is about 200°C   The braze alloys produce a rough surface.

CHEMICAL ANALYSIS OR COMPOSITION

Copper	81-92.5%
Silver	0-14.5%
Phosphorous	4.5-7.5%

PHYSICAL PROPERTIES

PROPERTY	UNITS	VALUES OR RANGE	COMMENTS
DENSITY	kg/m^3		
TENSILE STRENGTH	N/mm^2	430-660	Typical
YIELD STRENGTH	N/mm^2		
PROOF STRESS ( )	N/mm^2		
ELONGATION	%	5-10	Typical
YOUNGS MODULUS	kN/mm^2		
IMPACT RESISTANCE	J		
HARDNESS		185-195	Vickers pryramid no.
THERMAL COEFF. OF LINEAR EXPANSION	°C^{-1}		
THERMAL CONDUCTIVITY	W/mK		
SPECIFIC HEAT	kJ/kg K		
ELECTRICAL RESISTIVITY	ohm m		
ELECTRICAL CONDUCTIVITY	% IACS		

SPECIFICATIONS

STANDARD NUMBER	AUTHORITY	TITLE
BS1723	BSI	Brazing
BS1845 (Type CP)	BSI	Filler alloys for brazing

COMPANY SPECIFICATION:

ENVIRONMENT

These alloys must not be exposed to
hot sulphurous gases or to air at a
temperature in excess of 200°C.

PROCESSING AND FORMING TECHNIQUES

Maximum strength obtained when joint gaps of
0.04-0.2mm are used.
Joint has greatest strength in shear and
minimum for 'peel'.
Braze alloy can be hand fed into the joint
or pre-forms may be used.
Melting may be achieved by a variety of
heat sources.

JOINTING PROCESS

Heat must be applied rapidly, by gas torch
methods to prevent liquation. When required,
for copper based alloy jointing a flux should
be used.
Copper may be joined without flux.

Some fluxes are corrosive and excess fluxes must
be removed to prevent corrosion. Copper, silver
and phosphorous alloys should not be used on
nickel and cobalt base alloys, ferrous materials
or copper alloys with significant nickel, cobalt
and iron additions due to the formation of
brittle compounds at the interface between the
braze metal and the parent metal.

TYPICAL APPLICATIONS

Copper cyclinders and pipework.
Refrigeration components
Medical gas components
Electrical assemblies
Any copper application where
a flux residue is undersirable.

YOUR SUPPLIER AND NOTES

SAFETY PRECAUTIONS

436

FAMILY GROUP	JOINTING AND BONDING	SUB-GROUP	ADHESIVES	MATERIAL	BITUMEN

GENERAL DESCRIPTION

A non-structural adhesive of mineral origin. May be applied hot or cold.   Good resistance to water but oil and solvents attack. Bitumen adhesives may include fibrous fillers or rubber additions. Slight increase in temperature reduces adhesive properties (e.g) sunlight.

CHEMICAL ANALYSIS OR COMPOSITION

PHYSICAL PROPERTIES

PROPERTY	UNITS	VALUE OR RANGE	COMMENTS
DENSITY	kg/m^3		
SHEAR STRENGTH	N/mm^2		
TENSILE STRENGTH	N/mm^2		
ELONGATION	%		
COMPRESSIVE STRENGTH	N/mm^2		
FLEXURAL STRENGTH	N/mm^2		
IMPACT STRENGTH	J		
TENSILE MODULUS	N/mm^2		
HARDNESS			
THERMAL COEFF. OF LINEAR EXPANSION	$^oC^{-1}$		
MIN./MAX. SERVICE TEMPERATURE	^oC	-2/	
DEFLECTION TEMPERATURE	^oC		
THERMAL CONDUCTIVITY	W/mK		
FLAMMABILITY			
DIELECTRIC STRENGTH	kV/mm		
VOLUME RESISTIVITY	ohm cm		
PERMITIVITY	ohm cm		
ARC RESISTANCE	secs		
NUMBER OF PARTS		1	
CURING METHOD		Cold	
OPTICAL PROPERTIES			
FRICTION			
MOULD SHRINKAGE			
WATER ABSORPTION			

BSRIA material data sheet

SPECIFICATIONS

STANDARD NUMBER	AUTHORITY	TITLE
BS 3940	BSI	Adhesives based on bitumen or coal tar

COMPANY SPECIFICATION:

ENVIRONMENT

RESISTANCE TO ATTACK FROM:

ORGANIC OILS	No
MINERAL OILS	No
ORGANIC SOLVENTS	No
ACIDS	
ALKALIS	Yes
SALT WATER	
WATER IMMERSION	Yes
STEAM	
SUNLIGHT	Softened
MOULD	

PROCESSING AND FORMING TECHNIQUES

1 part system applied direct from container. Cured by solvent evaporation

TYPICAL APPLICATIONS

Non-structural
Bonds to concrete, glass, metal, felt paper and foils.

JOINTING PROCESS

Remove all surface contamination and apply evenly to one or both surfaces.

YOUR SUPPLIER AND NOTES

SAFETY PRECAUTIONS

| material data sheet | | SHEET NUMBER | JB07 | A |

| FAMILY GROUP | JOINTING AND BONDING | SUB-GROUP | ADHESIVES | MATERIAL | CYANOACRYLATE |

GENERAL DESCRIPTION

Cyanaocrylate gives a fast cure with high strength. It will bond many materials without prolonged surface treatment, clamps or heat treatment. No volatile solvents are involved and hence bond shrinkage is negligible. The bond line is thin and colourless. The bond is achieved by reacting with surface moisture. Expensive compared to other adhesives but small quantities are required. Poor impact and gap filling properties (o.25mm max gap).

CHEMICAL ANALYSIS OR COMPOSITION

PHYSICAL PROPERTIES

PROPERTY	UNITS	VALUE OR RANGE	COMMENTS
DENSITY	kg/m^3		
SHEAR STRENGTH	N/mm^2	12.5-22.5	Depending on grade
TENSILE STRENGTH	N/mm^2		
ELONGATION	%		
COMPRESSIVE STRENGTH	N/mm^2		
FLEXURAL STRENGTH	N/mm^2		
IMPACT STRENGTH	J		
TENSILE MODULUS	N/mm^2		
HARDNESS			
THERMAL COEFF. OF LINEAR EXPANSION	$^oC^{-1}$		
MIN./MAX. SERVICE TEMPERATURE	^oC	-60/+80	
DEFLECTION TEMPERATURE	^oC		at 1.81 N/mm^2
THERMAL CONDUCTIVITY	W/mK		
FLAMMABILITY			
DIELECTRIC STRENGTH	kV/mm		
VOLUME RESISTIVITY	ohm cm		
PERMITIVITY	ohm cm		
ARC RESISTANCE	secs		
NUMBER OF PARTS		1	
CURING METHOD		Cold	
OPTICAL PROPERTIES			
FRICTION			
MOULD SHRINKAGE			
WATER ABSORPTION			

SPECIFICATIONS

STANDARD NUMBER	AUTHORITY	TITLE

COMPANY SPECIFICATION:

ENVIRONMENT

RESISTANCE TO ATTACK FROM:

ORGANIC OILS	Yes
MINERAL OILS	Yes
ORGANIC SOLVENTS	Yes
ACIDS	Slight
ALKALIS	No
SALT WATER	
WATER IMMERSION	Slight
STEAM	No
SUNLIGHT	
MOULD	

PROCESSING AND FORMING TECHNIQUES

The minium to fill gap which must be 0.25mm maximum. Apply adhesive to components and lightly press together. Fast cure means no repositioning possible. The cure time is dependent on humidity, material and thickness of bondline.

TYPICAL APPLICATIONS

Structural adhesive with a rigid bond. Used for bonding metals, rubbers, ceramics, glass and wood.

JOINTING PROCESS

Remove all surface contamination, oil, grease, rust, oxides etc. Abrade the surface and degrease.

YOUR SUPPLIER AND NOTES

SAFETY PRECAUTIONS

Fumes cause irritation - well ventilated conditions required. Care must be taken on spillage on skin as bonding can take place if brought into contact with other material. All spillages should be wiped up.

SHEET NUMBER	JB08	**A**

FAMILY GROUP	SUB-GROUP	MATERIAL
JOINTING AND BONDING	ADHESIVES	EPOXY

GENERAL DESCRIPTION

Epoxy resins exhibit high strength with low flexibility and impact strength. Additives improve its properties. Epoxies are non-volatile adhesives, with low volume shrinkage and only pressure contact required. Excellent insulating properties. A hardener is required for the reaction to commence. Properties depend on the resin/ hardener combination.

CHEMICAL ANALYSIS OR COMPOSITION

Epoxide resin + hardener.

PHYSICAL PROPERTIES

PROPERTY	UNITS	VALUE OR RANGE	COMMENTS
DENSITY	kg/m^3	116 - 1200	
SHEAR STRENGTH	N/mm^2	30	
TENSILE STRENGTH	N/mm^2		
ELONGATION	%		
COMPRESSIVE STRENGTH	N/mm^2		
FLEXURAL STRENGTH	N/mm^2		
IMPACT STRENGTH	J		
TENSILE MODULUS	N/mm^2		
HARDNESS			
THERMAL COEFF. OF LINEAR EXPANSION	$^oC^{-1}$		
MIN./MAX. SERVICE TEMPERATURE	^oC	/+100	
DEFLECTION TEMPERATURE	^oC		
THERMAL CONDUCTIVITY	W/mK		
FLAMMABILITY			
DIELECTRIC STRENGTH	kV/mm		
VOLUME RESISTIVITY	ohm cm		
PERMITIVITY	ohm cm		
ARC RESISTANCE	secs		
NUMBER OF PARTS		1 or 2	
CURING METHOD		Hot or cold	
OPTICAL PROPERTIES			
FRICTION			
MOULD SHRINKAGE			
WATER ABSORPTION			

SPECIFICATIONS

STANDARD NUMBER	AUTHORITY	TITLE

COMPANY SPECIFICATION:

ENVIRONMENT

RESISTANCE TO ATTACK FROM:

ORGANIC OILS	Yes
MINERAL OILS	Yes
ORGANIC SOLVENTS	Yes
ACIDS	Yes
ALKALIS	Yes
SALT WATER	Yes
WATER IMMERSION	Yes
STEAM	Yes
SUNLIGHT	
MOULD	Yes

PROCESSING AND FORMING TECHNIQUES

1 part system - hardener premixed in and activated by hot cure.
2 part system - resin and hardener mixed in strict proportions and activated by cold or hot cure.
Mixing in of moisture may impair the cured properties. Cure times are dependent on temperature

TYPICAL APPLICATIONS

Structural applications. Epoxy adhesives will adhere to metals, nylon, polystyrene rubber and thermosetting plastics.

JOINTING PROCESS

All surfaces must be grease and oil free, and abraded if practical. Mixing in of moisture may impair the cured properties.

YOUR SUPPLIER AND NOTES

SAFETY PRECAUTIONS

Epoxy adhesives may cause skin problems and barrier creams or gloves should be used for protection.

FAMILY GROUP	JOINTING AND BONDING	SUB-GROUP	ADHESIVES	MATERIAL	EPOXY - PHENOLIC

GENERAL DESCRIPTION

An epoxy modified with phenolic extends the service range of epoxy resins to $+260^{\circ}C$. This adhesive is used in structural applications. Epoxides are a non-volatile system with a low volume shrinkage.

CHEMICAL ANALYSIS OR COMPOSITION

PHYSICAL PROPERTIES

PROPERTY	UNITS	VALUE OR RANGE	COMMENTS
DENSITY	kg/m^3		
SHEAR STRENGTH	N/mm^2	20 (6.5)	Room temperature (260ºC)
TENSILE STRENGTH	N/mm^2		
ELONGATION	%		
COMPRESSIVE STRENGTH	N/mm^2		
FLEXURAL STRENGTH	N/mm^2		
IMPACT STRENGTH	J		
TENSILE MODULUS	N/mm^2		
HARDNESS			
THERMAL COEFF. OF LINEAR EXPANSION	$^{\circ}C^{-1}$		
MIN./MAX. SERVICE TEMPERATURE	$^{\circ}C$	-240/+260	
DEFLECTION TEMPERATURE	$^{\circ}C$		
THERMAL CONDUCTIVITY	W/mK		
FLAMMABILITY			
DIELECTRIC STRENGTH	kV/mm		
VOLUME RESISTIVITY	ohm cm		
PERMITIVITY	ohm cm		
ARC RESISTANCE	secs		
NUMBER OF PARTS		1 or 2	
CURING METHOD		Hot or cold	
OPTICAL PROPERTIES			
FRICTION			
MOULD SHRINKAGE			
WATER ABSORPTION			

SPECIFICATIONS

STANDARD NUMBER	AUTHORITY	TITLE

COMPANY SPECIFICATION:

ENVIRONMENT

RESISTANCE TO ATTACK FROM:

ORGANIC OILS	Yes
MINERAL OILS	Yes
ORGANIC SOLVENTS	Yes
ACIDS	Yes
ALKALIS	Yes
SALT WATER	Yes
WATER IMMERSION	Yes
STEAM	Yes
SUNLIGHT	Yes
MOULD	Yes

PROCESSING AND FORMING TECHNIQUES

Adhesive cold applied and either hot or cold cured. Cure time is dependent on the temperature. Applied to one surface and components held together with light pressure.

The mixing in of moisture will impair the cured properties.

TYPICAL APPLICATIONS

For use in applications up to $260^{\circ}C$.

JOINTING PROCESS

Surfaces should be lightly abraded and degreased prior to the adhesive application.

YOUR SUPPLIER AND NOTES

SAFETY PRECAUTIONS

Some hardeners may cause skin complaints and barrier creams or gloves should be used.

BSRIA material data sheet

| FAMILY GROUP JOINTING AND BONDING | SUB-GROUP ADHESIVES | MATERIAL EPOXY – POLYAMIDE |

GENERAL DESCRIPTION

The addition of polyamide to epoxy provides a flexible adhesive curing at room temperature. The flexibility varies with the polyamide proportion. The shear strength drops to a very low value at 100°C.   It has a longer pot life than unmodified epoxy adhesives. Epoxides are a non-volatile system with a low volume shrinkage and only pressure contact required.

CHEMICAL ANALYSIS OR COMPOSITION

PHYSICAL PROPERTIES

PROPERTY	UNITS	VALUE OR RANGE	COMMENTS
DENSITY	kg/m^3		
SHEAR STRENGTH	N/mm^2	21-28	Room temperature
TENSILE STRENGTH	N/mm^2		
ELONGATION	%		
COMPRESSIVE STRENGTH	N/mm^2		
FLEXURAL STRENGTH	N/mm^2		
IMPACT STRENGTH	J		
TENSILE MODULUS	N/mm^2		
HARDNESS			
THERMAL COEFF. OF LINEAR EXPANSION	$°C^{-1}$		
MIN./MAX. SERVICE TEMPERATURE	°C	-40 / +90	
DEFLECTION TEMPERATURE	°C		
THERMAL CONDUCTIVITY	W/mK		
FLAMMABILITY			
DIELECTRIC STRENGTH	kV/mm		
VOLUME RESISTIVITY	ohm cm		
PERMITIVITY	ohm cm		
ARC RESISTANCE	secs		
NUMBER OF PARTS		2	
CURING METHOD		Cold	
OPTICAL PROPERTIES			
FRICTION			
MOULD SHRINKAGE			
WATER ABSORPTION			

SPECIFICATIONS

STANDARD NUMBER	AUTHORITY	TITLE

COMPANY SPECIFICATION:

ENVIRONMENT

RESISTANCE TO ATTACK FROM:

ORGANIC OILS	Yes
MINERAL OILS	Yes
ORGANIC SOLVENTS	Yes
ACIDS	Yes
ALKALIS	Yes
SALT WATER	Yes
WATER IMMERSION	Yes
STEAM	Yes
SUNLIGHT	Yes
MOULD	Yes

JOINTING PROCESS

Surfaces should be abraded and degreased.

SAFETY PRECAUTIONS

Some hardeners may cause skin complaints
and barrier creams or gloves should be
used.

PROCESSING AND FORMING TECHNIQUES

Parts mixed in the proportions stated by
manufacturer. The mix is applied to one
component and they are brought together
with pressure applied.

The mixing in of moisture may impair the
cured properties. The cure time is
dependent on the temperature.

TYPICAL APPLICATIONS

Structural applications using a range of
rigid and flexible materials such as metal
glass, rubbers, ceramics and nylons.

YOUR SUPPLIER AND NOTES

	material data sheet	SHEET NUMBER	JB11	A

FAMILY GROUP	JOINTING AND BONDING	SUB-GROUP	ADHESIVES	MATERIAL	EPOXY-POLYSULPHIDE

GENERAL DESCRIPTION

Epoxy - polysulphide is used for bonding metal to concrete. An improvement in peel strength and elasticity are achieved over unmodified epoxy. Epoxides are a non-volatile system wtih low volume shrinkage.

CHEMICAL ANALYSIS OR COMPOSITION

PHYSICAL PROPERTIES

PROPERTY	UNITS	VALUE OR RANGE	COMMENTS
DENSITY	kg/m^3		
SHEAR STRENGTH	N/mm^2	21-28	
TENSILE STRENGTH	N/mm^2		
ELONGATION	%		
COMPRESSIVE STRENGTH	N/mm^2		
FLEXURAL STRENGTH	N/mm^2		
IMPACT STRENGTH	J		
TENSILE MODULUS	N/mm^2		
HARDNESS			
THERMAL COEFF. OF LINEAR EXPANSION	$°C^{-1}$		
MIN./MAX. SERVICE TEMPERATURE	$°C$	-50/+70	
DEFLECTION TEMPERATURE	$°C$		
THERMAL CONDUCTIVITY	W/mK		
FLAMMABILITY			
DIELECTRIC STRENGTH	kV/mm		
VOLUME RESISTIVITY	ohm cm		
PERMITIVITY	ohm cm		
ARC RESISTANCE	secs		
NUMBER OF PARTS		2	
CURING METHOD		Cold	
OPTICAL PROPERTIES			
FRICTION			
MOULD SHRINKAGE			
WATER ABSORPTION			

SPECIFICATIONS

STANDARD NUMBER	AUTHORITY	TITLE

COMPANY SPECIFICATION:

ENVIRONMENT

RESISTANCE TO ATTACK FROM:

ORGANIC OILS	Yes
MINERAL OILS	Yes
ORGANIC SOLVENTS	Yes
ACIDS	Yes
ALKALIS	Yes
SALT WATER	Yes
WATER IMMERSION	Yes
STEAM	Yes
SUNLIGHT	Yes
MOULD	Yes

PROCESSING AND FORMING TECHNIQUES

Mix components in the proportions indicated by the manufacturer. Apply to one surface to be bonded and join surfaces together by applying light pressure until cured.

Mixing in of moisture may impair the cured properties. Cure time is dependent on the temperature.

TYPICAL APPLICATIONS

Structural applications. Bonding of steel plates and beams to concrete.

JOINTING PROCESS

Lightly abrade components and degrease.

YOUR SUPPLIER AND NOTES

SAFETY PRECAUTIONS

Some hardeners can cause skin complaints and precautions such as gloves or barrier creams should be used.

| | material data sheet | SHEET NUMBER | JB12 | A |

| FAMILY GROUP | JOINTING AND BONDING | SUB-GROUP | ADHESIVES | MATERIAL | NATURAL RUBBER |

GENERAL DESCRIPTION

Natural rubber based adhesives set by solvent or water evaporation and/or by vulcanisation. They are used for non-structural purposes due to its cold flow characteristics. Rubber adhesives have limited resistance to many chemicals, oils or solvents. The solvent may be inflammable.

CHEMICAL ANALYSIS OR COMPOSITION

Natural rubber + volatile solvent or water.

PHYSICAL PROPERTIES

PROPERTY	UNITS	VALUE OR RANGE	COMMENTS
DENSITY	kg/m^3		
SHEAR STRENGTH	N/mm^2		
TENSILE STRENGTH	N/mm^2		
ELONGATION	%		
COMPRESSIVE STRENGTH	N/mm^2		
FLEXURAL STRENGTH	N/mm^2		
IMPACT STRENGTH	J		
TENSILE MODULUS	N/mm^2		
HARDNESS			
THERMAL COEFF. OF LINEAR EXPANSION	$^oC^{-1}$		
MIN./MAX. SERVICE TEMPERATURE	^oC	-30 / +60 (+90)	(vulcanised)
DEFLECTION TEMPERATURE	^oC		
THERMAL CONDUCTIVITY	W/mK		
FLAMMABILITY			
DIELECTRIC STRENGTH	kV/mm		
VOLUME RESISTIVITY	ohm cm		
PERMITIVITY	ohm cm		
ARC RESISTANCE	secs		
NUMBER OF PARTS		1	
CURING METHOD		Cold (Hot)	(Vulcanisation)
OPTICAL PROPERTIES			
FRICTION			
MOULD SHRINKAGE			
WATER ABSORPTION			

SPECIFICATIONS

STANDARD NUMBER	AUTHORITY	TITLE

COMPANY SPECIFICATION:

ENVIRONMENT

RESISTANCE TO ATTACK FROM:

ORGANIC OILS	Limited resistance
MINERAL OILS	Limited resistance
ORGANIC SOLVENTS	Limited resistance
ACIDS	
ALKALIS	
SALT WATER	Yes
WATER IMMERSION	Yes
STEAM	
SUNLIGHT	
MOULD	Yes

PROCESSING AND FORMING TECHNIQUES

Generally 1 part system applied to surfaces, left until tacky and the parts placed together. Vulcanisation can improve strength and heat resistance by either heat curing or by the addition of an accelerator.

TYPICAL APPLICATIONS

Non-structural applications. Suitable for bonding leather, fabric and rubber to themselves and to timber and metal, to attach metal foil to wood and paper and sponge rubber to itself or to metal and wood.

JOINTING PROCESS

Degrease and lightly abrade components.

YOUR SUPPLIER AND NOTES

SAFETY PRECAUTIONS

Fire risk with the solvents.

| SHEET NUMBER | JB13 | **A** |

| FAMILY GROUP | JOINTING AND BONDING | SUB-GROUP | ADHESIVES | MATERIAL | NEOPRENE |

GENERAL DESCRIPTION

A synthetic rubber adhesive used where the maximum temperature is 90°C. Not resistant to aromatic hydrocarbons such as petrol, or strong oxidising agents. Due to their cold flow characteristics they cannot be used in structural applications. Normally associated with an inflamable solvent.

CHEMICAL ANALYSIS OR COMPOSITION

Neoprene rubber combined with a volatile solvent.

PHYSICAL PROPERTIES

PROPERTY	UNITS	VALUE OR RANGE	COMMENTS
DENSITY	kg/m^3		
SHEAR STRENGTH	N/mm^2		
TENSILE STRENGTH	N/mm^2		
ELONGATION	%		
COMPRESSIVE STRENGTH	N/mm^2		
FLEXURAL STRENGTH	N/mm^2		
IMPACT STRENGTH	J		
TENSILE MODULUS	N/mm^2		
HARDNESS			
THERMAL COEFF. OF LINEAR EXPANSION	$°C^{-1}$		
MIN./MAX. SERVICE TEMPERATURE	°C	-50/+90	
DEFLECTION TEMPERATURE	°C		
THERMAL CONDUCTIVITY	W/mK		
FLAMMABILITY			
DIELECTRIC STRENGTH	kV/mm		
VOLUME RESISTIVITY	ohm cm		
PERMITIVITY	ohm cm		
ARC RESISTANCE	secs		
NUMBER OF PARTS		1	
CURING METHOD		Cold	
OPTICAL PROPERTIES			
FRICTION			
MOULD SHRINKAGE			
WATER ABSORPTION			

SPECIFICATIONS

STANDARD NUMBER	AUTHORITY	TITLE

COMPANY SPECIFICATION:

ENVIRONMENT

RESISTANCE TO ATTACK FROM:

ORGANIC OILS }
MINERAL OILS }   Some oils

ORGANIC SOLVENTS   Aliphatic but not aromatic

ACIDS   Weak acids

ALKALIS   Weak alkalis

SALT WATER

WATER IMMERSION   Yes

STEAM

SUNLIGHT   Yes

MOULD   Yes

PROCESSING AND FORMING TECHNIQUES

Generally 1 part system applied to both
surfaces, left until tacky and
the placing of parts together.
Vulcanisation can improve strength and
heat resistance by either heat curing
or by the addition of a catalyst.

TYPICAL APPLICATIONS

Non structural applications. Neoprene
adhesives will bond timber, metal,
natural and synthetic rubbers, PVC,
phenolic laminate and leather to each
other or themselves.

JOINTING PROCESS

Degrease and lightly abrade components. When
bonding vulcanised rubber to metal a chlorinated rubber primer must be applied to the
metal.

YOUR SUPPLIER AND NOTES

SAFETY PRECAUTIONS

Fire risk with the solvent.

| FAMILY GROUP | JOINTING AND BONDING | SUB-GROUP | ADHESIVES | MATERIAL | NITRILE RUBBER |

GENERAL DESCRIPTION

Nitrile rubber adhesives are not recommended for structural purposes due to their cold flow characteristics. They have a higher service temperature than neoprene rubber. Temperature range and strength can be improved by vulcanisation.

CHEMICAL ANALYSIS OR COMPOSITION

Nitrile rubber + volatile solvent

PHYSICAL PROPERTIES

PROPERTY	UNITS	VALUE OR RANGE	COMMENTS
DENSITY	kg/m^3		
SHEAR STRENGTH	N/mm^2	6.5	Typical
TENSILE STRENGTH	N/mm^2		
ELONGATION	%		
COMPRESSIVE STRENGTH	N/mm^2		
FLEXURAL STRENGTH	N/mm^2		
IMPACT STRENGTH	J		
TENSILE MODULUS	N/mm^2		
HARDNESS			
THERMAL COEFF. OF LINEAR EXPANSION	$^oC^{-1}$		
MIN./MAX. SERVICE TEMPERATURE	^oC	-50/+150	
DEFLECTION TEMPERATURE	^oC		
THERMAL CONDUCTIVITY	W/mK		
FLAMMABILITY			
DIELECTRIC STRENGTH	kV/mm		
VOLUME RESISTIVITY	ohm cm		
PERMITIVITY	ohm cm		
ARC RESISTANCE	secs		
NUMBER OF PARTS		1	
CURING METHOD		Cold	
OPTICAL PROPERTIES			
FRICTION			
MOULD SHRINKAGE			
WATER ABSORPTION			

SPECIFICATIONS

STANDARD NUMBER	AUTHORITY	TITLE

COMPANY SPECIFICATION:

ENVIRONMENT

RESISTANCE TO ATTACK FROM:

ORGANIC OILS	Yes
MINERAL OILS	Yes
ORGANIC SOLVENTS	Most
ACIDS	Yes (not oxidising acids)
ALKALIS	Yes
SALT WATER	Yes
WATER IMMERSION	Yes
STEAM	
SUNLIGHT	
MOULD	Yes

JOINTING PROCESS

Degrease and lightly abrade components.
When bonding vulcanised rubber to metal a
chlorinated rubber primer must be applied
to the metal.

SAFETY PRECAUTIONS

Fire risk with the solvent.

PROCESSING AND FORMING TECHNIQUES

Generally 1 part system applied to both
surfaces, soft until tacky and placing
the parts together. Vulcanisation can
improve strength and heat properties by
either heat curing or by the addition
of a catalyst.

TYPICAL APPLICATIONS

Non structural applications. Nitrile
adhesives will adhere timber, leather,
rubber, fabric, paper, plastics
(including PVC) to themselves and to
metal and glass.

YOUR SUPPLIER AND NOTES

 **material data sheet**

SHEET NUMBER	JB15

A

FAMILY GROUP	JOINTING AND BONDING	SUB-GROUP	ADHESIVES	MATERIAL	PHENOLIC - NEOPRENE

GENERAL DESCRIPTION

Phenolic - neoprene adhesives are used where resistance to vibration or low temperatures are important. The adhesive is used in both structural and non-structural applications. This system is heat cured and maintains room temperature tensile strength up to 120°C.

CHEMICAL ANALYSIS OR COMPOSITION

PHYSICAL PROPERTIES

PROPERTY	UNITS	VALUE OR RANGE	COMMENTS
DENSITY	kg/m^3		
SHEAR STRENGTH	N/mm^2	17-21	
TENSILE STRENGTH	N/mm^2		
ELONGATION	%		
COMPRESSIVE STRENGTH	N/mm^2		
FLEXURAL STRENGTH	N/mm^2		
IMPACT STRENGTH	J		
TENSILE MODULUS	N/mm^2		
HARDNESS			
THERMAL COEFF. OF LINEAR EXPANSION	°C^{-1}		
MIN./MAX. SERVICE TEMPERATURE	°C	-55/+120	
DEFLECTION TEMPERATURE	°C		
THERMAL CONDUCTIVITY	W/mK		
FLAMMABILITY			
DIELECTRIC STRENGTH	kV/mm		
VOLUME RESISTIVITY	ohm cm		
PERMITIVITY	ohm cm		
ARC RESISTANCE	secs		
NUMBER OF PARTS		1	
CURING METHOD		Hot	
OPTICAL PROPERTIES			
FRICTION			
MOULD SHRINKAGE			
WATER ABSORPTION			

SPECIFICATIONS

STANDARD NUMBER	AUTHORITY	TITLE

COMPANY SPECIFICATION:

ENVIRONMENT

RESISTANCE TO ATTACK FROM:

ORGANIC OILS	Partial
MINERAL OILS	Partial
ORGANIC SOLVENTS	Yes
ACIDS	
ALKALIS	
SALT WATER	
WATER IMMERSION	Yes
STEAM	
SUNLIGHT	Yes
MOULD	Yes

JOINTING PROCESS

Abrade and degrease components.

PROCESSING AND FORMING TECHNIQUES

Apply adhesive to components. Place components together with pressure and heat cure (care must be taken that all components can withstand the temperature without failing).

TYPICAL APPLICATIONS

Applicable for non-structural and structural uses.
Bonds metals, rubbers, wood, glass ceramics and thermoset plastics to themselves and each other.

YOUR SUPPLIER AND NOTES

SAFETY PRECAUTIONS

FAMILY GROUP	JOINTING AND BONDING	SUB-GROUP	ADHESIVES	MATERIAL	PHENOLIC - NITRILE

GENERAL DESCRIPTION

Phenolic - nitrile has good resistance to heat and chemicals. The high strength is obtained by hot curing. It has good impact strength and resistance to cold flow.

CHEMICAL ANALYSIS OR COMPOSITION

PHYSICAL PROPERTIES

PROPERTY	UNITS	VALUE OR RANGE	COMMENTS
DENSITY	kg/m^3		
SHEAR STRENGTH	N/mm^2	25	
TENSILE STRENGTH	N/mm^2		
ELONGATION	%		
COMPRESSIVE STRENGTH	N/mm^2		
FLEXURAL STRENGTH	N/mm^2		
IMPACT STRENGTH	J		
TENSILE MODULUS	N/mm^2		
HARDNESS			
THERMAL COEFF. OF LINEAR EXPANSION	$^oC^{-1}$		
MIN./MAX. SERVICE TEMPERATURE	^oC	-50/+175	
DEFLECTION TEMPERATURE	^oC		
THERMAL CONDUCTIVITY	W/mK		
FLAMMABILITY			
DIELECTRIC STRENGTH	kV/mm		
VOLUME RESISTIVITY	ohm cm		
PERMITIVITY	ohm cm		
ARC RESISTANCE	secs		
NUMBER OF PARTS		1	
CURING METHOD		Cold/Hot	
OPTICAL PROPERTIES			
FRICTION			
MOULD SHRINKAGE			
WATER ABSORPTION			

BSRIA material data sheet

SPECIFICATIONS

Standard Number	Authority	Title

Company Specification:

ENVIRONMENT

Resistance to Attack From:

Organic oils	Yes
Mineral Oils	Yes
Organic Solvents	Some
Acids	
Alkalis	
Salt Water	Yes
Water Immersion	Yes
Steam	Yes
Sunlight	
Mould	Yes

JOINTING PROCESS

Abrade and degrease components

SAFETY PRECAUTIONS

PROCESSING AND FORMING TECHNIQUES

Apply adhesive to component. Place components together with pressure.

TYPICAL APPLICATIONS

Structural adhesive used for bonding metals, plastics, wood, ceramics, glass and rubbers to themselves and each other

YOUR SUPPLIER AND NOTES

material data sheet	SHEET NUMBER JB17		**A**

FAMILY GROUP JOINTING AND BONDING	SUB-GROUP ADHESIVES	MATERIAL POLYESTER-ACRYLICS

GENERAL DESCRIPTION

A single constituent liquid which cures in the absence of air under the catalytic action of a surface. Some materials require priming. Typical applications are the locking of engineering components with close tolerances

CHEMICAL ANALYSIS OR COMPOSITION

PHYSICAL PROPERTIES

PROPERTY	UNITS	VALUE OR RANGE	COMMENTS
DENSITY	kg/m^3		
SHEAR STRENGTH	N/mm^2	Up to 48	
TENSILE STRENGTH	N/mm^2		
ELONGATION	%		
COMPRESSIVE STRENGTH	N/mm^2		
FLEXURAL STRENGTH	N/mm^2		
IMPACT STRENGTH	J		
TENSILE MODULUS	N/mm^2		
HARDNESS			
THERMAL COEFF. OF LINEAR EXPANSION	$^oC^{-1}$		
MIN./MAX. SERVICE TEMPERATURE	^oC	-50/+150	
DEFLECTION TEMPERATURE	^oC		
THERMAL CONDUCTIVITY	W/mK		
FLAMMABILITY			
DIELECTRIC STRENGTH	kV/mm		
VOLUME RESISTIVITY	ohm cm		
PERMITIVITY	ohm cm		
ARC RESISTANCE	secs		
NUMBER OF PARTS		1	
CURING METHOD		Cold or hot	
OPTICAL PROPERTIES			
FRICTION			
MOULD SHRINKAGE			
WATER ABSORPTION			

BSRIA material data sheet

SPECIFICATIONS

STANDARD NUMBER	AUTHORITY	TITLE

COMPANY SPECIFICATION:

ENVIRONMENT

RESISTANCE TO ATTACK FROM:

ORGANIC OILS

MINERAL OILS

ORGANIC SOLVENTS

ACIDS

ALKALIS

SALT WATER

WATER IMMERSION

STEAM

SUNLIGHT

MOULD

PROCESSING AND FORMING TECHNIQUES

Liquid adhesive is applied to one face
and the components are placed together
with pressure. Cure time dependent on
adhesive. Some materials such as
aluminium, stainless steel and plastics
require priming prior to assembly. Only
one component need be primed.

TYPICAL APPLICATIONS

Structural adhesive for the locking of
components. Will bond metals, most
plastics (not PVC, polycarbonate or
acrylic), glass and ceramics.

JOINTING PROCESS

Lightly abrade and degrease components

YOUR SUPPLIER AND NOTES

SAFETY PRECAUTIONS

Precautions to be taken to avoid contact with
eyes.

material data sheet		SHEET NUMBER JB18	A

FAMILY GROUP JOINTING AND BONDING	SUB-GROUP ADHESIVES	MATERIAL POLYURETHANE

GENERAL DESCRIPTION

Bonds made with polyurethane adhesives are flexible, have good peel strength and resistant to shock and vibration. Due to their sensitivity to moisture they cannot be used in humid environments. May be used in cryogenic applications with an increase in shear strengths.

CHEMICAL ANALYSIS OR COMPOSITION

PHYSICAL PROPERTIES

PROPERTY	UNITS	VALUE OR RANGE	COMMENTS
DENSITY	kg/m^3		
SHEAR STRENGTH	N/mm^2	7.6	at 20°C
TENSILE STRENGTH	N/mm^2		
ELONGATION	%		
COMPRESSIVE STRENGTH	N/mm^2		
FLEXURAL STRENGTH	N/mm^2		
IMPACT STRENGTH	J		
TENSILE MODULUS	N/mm^2		
HARDNESS			
THERMAL COEFF. OF LINEAR EXPANSION	$°C^{-1}$		
MIN./MAX. SERVICE TEMPERATURE	°C	-250/+95	
DEFLECTION TEMPERATURE	°C		
THERMAL CONDUCTIVITY	W/mK		
FLAMMABILITY			
DIELECTRIC STRENGTH	kV/mm		
VOLUME RESISTIVITY	ohm cm		
PERMITIVITY	ohm cm		
ARC RESISTANCE	secs		
NUMBER OF PARTS		2	
CURING METHOD		Hot	
OPTICAL PROPERTIES			
FRICTION			
MOULD SHRINKAGE			
WATER ABSORPTION			

SPECIFICATIONS

STANDARD NUMBER	AUTHORITY	TITLE

COMPANY SPECIFICATION:

ENVIRONMENT

RESISTANCE TO ATTACK FROM:

ORGANIC OILS	Yes
MINERAL OILS	Yes
ORGANIC SOLVENTS	
ACIDS	Yes
ALKALIS	Yes
SALT WATER)	Adhesive moisture
WATER IMMERSION)	sensitive
)	
STEAM	
SUNLIGHT	
MOULD	

ND = No Data

JOINTING PROCESS

Lightly abrasive and degrease components
Unsuitable for bonding in highly humid atmospheres.

PROCESSING AND FORMING TECHNIQUES

Mix the adhesive components as directed by the manufacturer

TYPICAL APPLICATIONS

Structural adhesive. Capable of operating at cryogenic temperatures. Polyurethane bonds metals, rubbers, foams, plastics, glass and wood to themselves and each other.

YOUR SUPPLIER AND NOTES

SAFETY PRECAUTIONS

material data sheet		SHEET NUMBER JB19	**A**

FAMILY GROUP JOINTING AND BONDING	SUB-GROUP ADHESIVES	MATERIAL POLY-VINYL ACETATE

GENERAL DESCRIPTION

A non-structural adhesive with a low maximum service temperature. PVC is clean to use. It has poor resistance to heat and freezing conditions. Normally cold cured but can be hot cured with increase in tensile strength. It is unsuitable for bonding rubbers, PVC or polyethylene.

CHEMICAL ANALYSIS OR COMPOSITION

SYNONYM

PVA

PHYSICAL PROPERTIES

PROPERTY	UNITS	VALUE OR RANGE	COMMENTS
DENSITY	kg/m^3		
SHEAR STRENGTH	N/mm^2	20	Hot cured
TENSILE STRENGTH	N/mm^2		
ELONGATION	%		
COMPRESSIVE STRENGTH	N/mm^2		
FLEXURAL STRENGTH	N/mm^2		
IMPACT STRENGTH	J		
TENSILE MODULUS	N/mm^2		
HARDNESS			
THERMAL COEFF. OF LINEAR EXPANSION	$°C^{-1}$		
MIN./MAX. SERVICE TEMPERATURE	$°C$	0/+50	
DEFLECTION TEMPERATURE	$°C$		
THERMAL CONDUCTIVITY	W/mK		
FLAMMABILITY			
DIELECTRIC STRENGTH	kV/mm		
VOLUME RESISTIVITY	ohm cm		
PERMITIVITY	ohm cm		
ARC RESISTANCE	secs		
NUMBER OF PARTS		1	
CURING METHOD		Cold or Hot	
OPTICAL PROPERTIES			
FRICTION			
MOULD SHRINKAGE			
WATER ABSORPTION			

BSRIA material data sheet

SPECIFICATIONS

STANDARD NUMBER	AUTHORITY	TITLE
BS 3544	BSI	Method of testing PVA adhesives for wood
BS 4071	BSI	PVA adhesives for wood

COMPANY SPECIFICATION:

ENVIRONMENT

RESISTANCE TO ATTACK FROM:

ORGANIC OILS	Yes
MINERAL OILS	Yes
ORGANIC SOLVENTS	No
ACIDS	
ALKALIS	
SALT WATER	
WATER IMMERSION	Moderate
STEAM	No
SUNLIGHT	Yes
MOULD	Yes

PROCESSING AND FORMING TECHNIQUES

Apply to surface of one component bring together and cure under pressure. Excess adhesive should be wiped away.

TYPICAL APPLICATIONS

Non structural applications. PVA bonds metal, wood products, leather, glass, most plastics, paper and cloth and asbestos to themselves and each other.

JOINTING PROCESS

Lightly abrade and degrease components

YOUR SUPPLIER AND NOTES

SAFETY PRECAUTIONS

4.4 PLASTICS

Plastics differ from all traditional materials in that made they are produced by chemical synthesis. They are now well established as materials for use in many fields and are finding increasing application in engineering. Rubbers and elastomers in general have some common features with plastics but are essentially different in their engineering characteristics. They are dealt with separately in Section 4.6.

STRUCTURE OF PLASTICS

As an aid to the better appreciation of the characteristics of plastics, some understanding is required of the composition and structural features of the polymers that form their basis. These polymers, which are almost all organic in nature, are among the synthetic products of the petrochemical industry and all contain carbon. They are made by polymerisation whereby many small molecules combine to form a more complex large molecule. The large molecules so formed have a chain-like structure with inumerable identical groups of atoms. Substances composed of such large molecules are called polymers and the simpler substances from which they are derived are known as monomers; if only one species of monomer is present the product is known as a homopolymer and if two a copolymer. Whether they are formed from one or more monomers, materials that are formed of chain-like molecules are called polymers.

For one group of polymers, cohesion depends on the relative weak forces of attraction between the molecules. When these molecules are heated the intermolecular forces are weakened with the result that they soften and eventually become viscous liquids which, however, solidify on cooling as the polymers return to their former state. This process of softening and hardening can be repeated indefinitely; polymers that can permit such a cyclic process are called thermoplastics.

During the production of some polymers, chemical reactions do not stop at the formulation of the long molecular chains, but continue to link the molecules to each other by chemical bonds. These bonds are in all directions and the molecules are said to be cross-linked. Once these strong chemical cross-links have formed, the resulting polymers cannot be remelted by subsequent heating and materials based on them are called Thermosetting plastics (thermosets for short).

Typical examples of thermoplastics and thermosets used in engineering are shown in Figure 4.4/1.

RELATIVE CHARACTERISTICS OF PLASTICS

Thermoplastics and thermosetting polymers possess certain common characteristics because of their organic nature and molecular structure. Because of the relatively loose packing of the molecule chains they all have relatively low densities. All unfilled plastics have densities ranging from 830 to 2200 kg/m^3 compared with aluminium at 2700 kg/m^3 and stainless steel at 7900 kg/m^3.

Owing to the weak intermolecular forces their stiffness and strength are relatively low (10 to 100 N/mm^2 compared with at least 200 N/mm^2 for steel or aluminium) on a cross-sectional area basis but, on a weight for weight basis, stiffness and strength are more favourable and can be

465

increased by the orientation of the molecular chains during processing. As the intermolecular forces decrease rapidly with increasing temperature, there is a corresponding loss in stiffness and strength.

Polymers have very low electrical and thermal conductivities low coefficients of friction and high coefficients of thermal expansion. They are degraded, or oxidised, at quite moderate temperatures and, since most contain a large proportion of carbon and often also hydrogen, they burn.

The terms polymer and plastics are not synonymous. Polymers are idealised substances that consist of long chain molecules, whereas plastics are industrial materials containing, in addition to the base polymer, impurities arising from their production process or deliberately added to achieve specific properties.

Additives to the base material can act in many ways such as heat stabilizers or lubricants, which aid the flow of plastic melts during processing. Some thermoplastics also contain varying amounts of plasticizers which are incorporated to make them more flexible.

Both thermosets and thermoplastics may also contain pigments and fillers. Some inexpensive fillers, known as extenders, serve to reduce the amount of the base polymer in a given plastic and therefore reduce the cost. Other fillers are added to improve the mechanical, electrical or thermal properties of the plastic. Plasticizers and fillers in plastics can amount to more than half the weight or volume but even in small quantities, they can have a significant influence on the properties of base plastics.

Plastic composites with extra stiffness and a modest improvement in strength can be produced by the incorporation of high modulus fibrous fillers. Glass fibres can extend the range of tensile strength to an upper limit of about 200 N/mm^2 and of Youngs modulus values to 10 GN/mm^2 (unfilled thermoplastics are usually 0.3 to 3.0 GN/mm^2 compared with 70 GN/mm^2 for aluminium and 200 GN/mm^2 for steel). It is also possible to produce foamed thermoplastics, the foam can offer high stiffness per unit weight although at the expense of some loss of tensile strength.

All plastics can be destroyed by flame or excessive heat. The rate of destruction depends on the type of plastic, the temperature and the duration of exposure to heat. In general, thermoplastics are more readily destroyed than thermosets. Plastics burn with differing characteristics - polyethylenes burn like hard wax, polypropylene like soft wood, acrylic like hardwood, PVC decomposes rapidly but is self-extinguishing. PTFE will not burn in air below 300°C. The burning of plastics may generate toxic or dense fumes.

The chemical resistance of plastics is complementary to that of metals in that most plastics resist aqueous solutions of weak acid bases and salts but some organic solvents may cause swelling in thermoplastics and even dissolution. Strong oxidising acids may also attack, possibly causing embrittlement. In general an increase in temperatures causes a deterioration in chemical resistance.

The resistance to weathering and to ultra violet (UV) exposure depends on the type of plastic and on its composition. Acrylic is exceptional with its long term durability. PVC and thermoset polyesters have good UV resistance with the result that they have been used out of doors for some time. Many other plastics in their natural state are degraded when left exposed to UV although their useful life can be extended by incorporating UV absorbers.

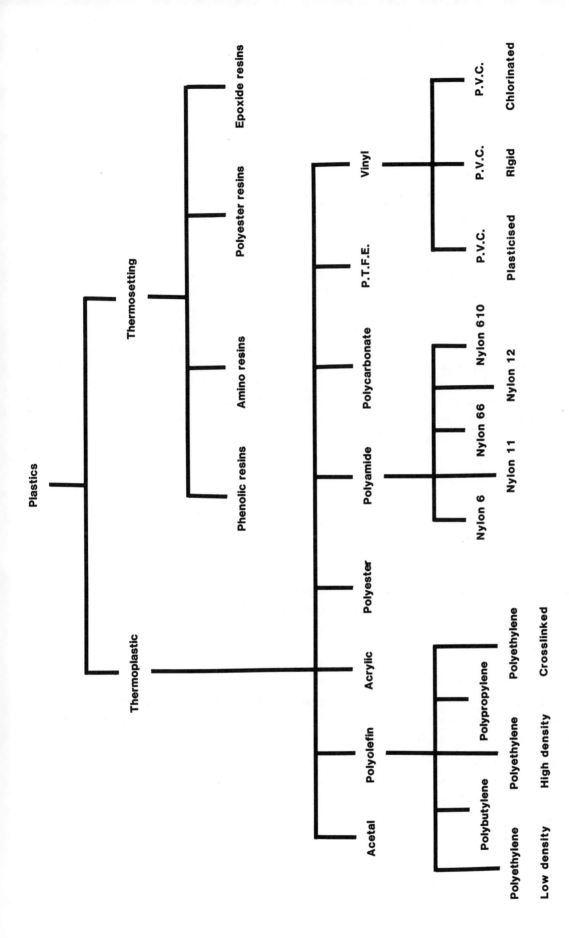

Figure 4.4/1: Plastics materials.

467

Some plastics are extremely resistant to damage by impact such as ABS, polyethylene and nylon. The thermosets are usually more brittle than thermoplastics. However, reinforcement, with fillers such as long glass fibres in polyesters and epoxies and cotton cloth in phenolics, confers an improvement in impact resistance.

The coefficient of friction for unlubricated plastics spans an extremely wide range. The coefficient of friction of PTFE is extremely low whilst, generally, a figure between 0.3 to 0.5 is obtained for a plastic rubbing against a metal. These values can be decreased by adding a lubricant filler to the plastic (such as molybdenum disulphide in nylon, PTFE in polyacetal or graphite in phenolic) or by lubrication. At the other extreme some plastics surfaces can be so soft that they tend to stick under light compression.

Plastics are good thermal insulators and can have outstanding electrical insulation properties. Values of thermal conductivities of plastics are much less than those of metals. Unfilled plastics have values at 20°C in the range of 0.2 to 0.5 W/mK and foams can have values down to 0.03 W/mK (whereas copper is 385 W/mK and aluminium 240 W/mK). These low values can be a mixed blessing; and while they are of importance for the reduction of heat losses in buildings they are a hindrance when trying to dissipate heat from a bearing.

Most unfilled plastics have extremely high volume resistivities. Many thermoset plastics are used in electrical applications such as lamp-holders, plugs, sockets, switches, etc. Domestic wiring is frequently insulated with plasticized PVC. In contrast high surface resistivities prevent the dissipation of electrostatic charge from the surface of plastic articles. This can vary in its effect from dust accumulation, to the point where electrical discharge in some atmospheres could spark off an explosion. The resistivities of plastics can be reduced by incorporating conducting fillers or antistatic agents, or by washing the surface with a surface active agent.

Variation in temperature and absorption of liquids are factors affecting dimensional stability. The linear thermal expansion coefficient of unfilled plastics is between 3 to 10 times that of metals and therefore an expansion of about 0.1% for each 100°C change in temperature must be allowed. Expansion can be reduced by adding fillers to the plastics and they thereby become similar to metals in this respect.

Some thermoplastics swell as the result of absorbing small quantities of liquid and this can be a reversible process. Nylon is one of the worst absorbers and can produce dimensional changes of the order of 1% between wet and dry conditions. Other liquids such as oils and industrial solvents can also cause swelling in plastic materials.

A variety of automatic and semi-automatic techniques allow easy economical and reproducible manufacture of components. Many of the techniques used have been adapted from the processing of other materials and include extrusion, injection moulding, transfer moulding, blow moulding, vacuum forming and callendering. The methods available allow the design and manufacture of complicated shapes often without the need for assembly. Surface effects and texture can also be obtained as an integral part of processing. There are technqiues for joining most plastics to themselves and other materials. Adhesives are widely used and articles made from some thermoplastics can be welded (thermally or ultrasonically). To obtain optimum results the correct jointing method must be chosen.

4.4.1 THERMOPLASTICS

4.4.1.1 ACETAL

Data Sheets PL01, PL02

Acetal homopolymer resins are polymers of formaldehyde. Acetal copolymers are based on formaldehyde with the addition of a copolymer. Acetal resins offer a range of properties unequalled by other thermoplastics, combining high strength with good temperature resistance, good abrasion resistance, exceptional dimensional stability and with low thermal expansion. Tensile strength can be in the order of 100 N/mm^2 at room temperature, reducing to about half this value at 66°C.

Both homopolymer and copolymer resins may be considered competitive with nylon (polyamides) with improved heat resistance, better dimensional stability, creep characteristics, load carrying capacity and lower co-efficient of expansion. Acetal resins are considered as engineering plastics and have found application in the replacement of steel, zinc, aluminium, copper and their alloys. One advantage is the reduction in weight achieved by using acetal resin components (45% lighter than zinc).

Acetal resins are resistant to most organic chemicals, including alcohols, but are attacked by moderately strong acids and oxidising agents. Acetal homopolymer resin is attacked by strong alkalis but the copolymer is normally resistant. Resistance to outdoor exposure is moderate to poor, unless the resin is stabilised or suitably pigmented (black being the most effective colour).

Melting points for the resin and polyacetal are 175°C and 163°C respectively. Heat distortion temperatures are some 50°C lower in both cases.

Acetal resins can be readily injection moulded and extruded. The addition of colour pigments is not detrimental to their properties. All the standard metal working techniques can be used to machine acetal resins. It is important that the tools are sharp, have chip clearance and the workpiece is well supported and cooled.

All usual joining systems may be used including thermal and ultrasonic welding. Acetal components may be bonded by means of adhesives, such as epoxides, providing that the surfaces are prepared and abraded. Mechanical assembly can be achieved by using thread inserts.

The outlets for acetal resins are legion, including gears, bearings, plumbing components, pump components etc.

4.4.1.2 ACRYLIC

Data Sheet PL03

There are two completely different acrylic materials;
-   thermoplastic moulding materials
-   cast acrylic sheet and mouldings which resemble crosslinked thermosets (perspex).

The combination of the following properties differentiates acrylic plastics from other materials:

- completely transparent with optical clarity

- exceptional stability to outdoor weathering and absence of discolouration or degradation from ultra-violet radiation

- outstanding acceptance of suitable decorative paints, lacquers and metallic deposition.

These properties have lead to their wide use in the appliance, automotive, industrial and architectural fields.

Besides being optically transparent, acrylics are available with an opaque finish and are used for sanitary ware products (baths and basins).

Acrylic materials are brittle when compared to other plastics. They are notch sensitive, and sharp corners or sudden changes in section are sources of weakness which may lead to splitting. Therefore, well radiused corners are required. The impact strength of acrylic materials is maintained down to -40°C.

Acrylic materials have a high strength/weight ratio with a stress in the region of 68 N/mm^2 at room temperature, reducing to zero at 95°C.

They are stable up to 90°C Above this temperature they begin to soften and, at 150°C, become flexible and can be formed. On cooling the formed shape is retained and is quite stable. On heating acrylic sheet for the first time to forming temperature and then cooling there is a permanent shrinkage of about 2% on linear measurements with a corresponding increase in thickness. On subsequent heating no further shrinkage occurs. Water absorption is fairly low.

Surface hardness is comparable to aluminium. Light scratches and blemishes can be removed by grinding and polishing.

Thermal expansion is high, approximately seven times that of steel.

The burning characteristics are comparable to hardwood and are classified as burning readily. Acrylic materials do not continue to burn after the source of ignition has been removed.

Acrylic materials exhibit good electrical insulation properties and can be used satisfactorily over a wide range of frequencies; they are non-tracking. Coloured grades have similar electrical properties to the clear material.

Chemical resistance of acrylic materials are similar to other thermoplastics. They are resistant to dilute acids (except hydrofluoric or hydrocyanic) and alkali solutions. They are also resistant to many organic solvents, fats, mineral oils, aqueous solutions of inorganic salts and most common gases. Chlorinated aliphatic hydrocarbons (chloroform, trichloroethylene) aromatic hydrocarbons (benzene, toluene, petrol), acetone, alcohols, ethers and esters cause swelling, crazing and weakening of the material.

Acrylic materials can be used in contact with foodstuffs.
The optical characteristics of transparent acrylics are exceptional. The overall light transmission for normally incident light is about 92%. The apparent loss being due to reflection at each surface. It has a refractive index of 1.49.

Acrylic material has excellent weathering characteristics. It is known to have an ability to maintain its physical and optical properties for up to 20 years in adverse conditions. These excellent outdoor characteristics have lead to the material being used for glazing, illuminated

470

panels, and lighting globes. The breakage resistance of acrylic is between 6-17 times greater than window glass. It will not yellow when in close proximity to fluorescent light sources.

Of all the transparent plastics, acylics are by far the most suitable for the production of decorative components. The materials can be spray painted, silk screened, hot stamped, roller coated and vacuum metalised.

Acrylic materials are available as cast sheet and rod, moulding and powders.

Acrylic sheet, rod and tube are easy to machine using normal engineering methods. However heat created during machining must be kept to a minimum to prevent melting of the acrylic material. There is little difference in machining cast and extruded forms, however care must be taken with extruded acrylic as its breakage, craze resistance and notch sensitivity are all inferior to those of cast acrylic sheet. Powders may be used for injection or blow moulding.

Acrylic materials may be fabricated using cements or ultrasonic welding. When ultrasonically welded poor bond strengths will result if the jointing faces are incorrectly designed. Solvents such as chloroform may be used as an adhesive but the joints have poor resistance to weathering and water. The Tensol range of cements provide a high joint strength.

4.4.1.3 ACRYLONITRILE BUTADIENE STYRENE (ABS)

Data Sheet PL04

ABS is part of a range of copolymers based on styrene. They possess outstanding resistance to fracture by impact over a wide temperature range as well as a good strength/weight ratio. They are notch sensitive and care must be taken in the design to avoid sudden changes in section and sharp corners. ABS is hygroscopic with a water absorption of about 0.4% and precautions must be taken to prevent surface imperfections appearing as a result of high moisture content.

ABS material is rigid, tough, temperature resistant, and has high impact strength down to -40°C. It also possesses a high gloss finish and can be metal plated to provide a decorative finish. In the form of pipes it is used for the conveyance of soil, waste, rainwater and trade effluent above ground, transmission of gaseous fuel below ground and nonflammable industrial gases above and below ground.

ABS materials have very few limitations, but are affected by chlorinated hydrocarbons, ketones, concentrated acids and alkalis. Special grades may be formulated to suit food applications.

The weathering of ABS is not very good. Under normal exposure in temperate climates there is an appreciable reduction in strength after 12 months exposure. Changes brought about by ultraviolet light can be minimised by painting.

The electrical properties are not outstanding but are adequate for use in many general purpose electrical applications.

Normal engineering practices may be employed for machining ABS materials.

ABS is easily solvent cemented to itself to provide bonds with strengths of the order of 75% of the parent material. Solvent solutions of dissolved ABS can be used; solvents alone give a weak bond. Solvent cemented bonds should be thoroughly dried before applying any external load. Epoxy adhesives may be used where solvent cement bonding is impracticable, i.e. in confined

471

spaces where solvent fumes may be dangerous. Components must be dry, clean and grease free. Hot gas welding may be applied to joining ABS materials. Hot nitrogen or inert gas is used at 250-310°C with a filler rod.

ABS burns readily with a black sooty flame.

4.4.1.4 POLYAMIDE (NYLON)

Data Sheets PL05, PL06, PL07, PL08

The outstanding properties of polyamides (nylons) are high mechanical strength, good creep resistance, excellent low friction properties, toughness, light weight, good rigidity, high shock resistance, high fatigue resistance, high chemical and hydrocarbon resistance, good electrical properties (particularly in low moisture absorption grades) high softening point, good heat resistance and excellent surface finish.

Although many of these properties may be found in other plastics materials, it is their combination in one product that make polyamides such excellent plastics. Normal plastic design rules apply to nylon but careful consideration must be given to the working environment in respect of humidity and temperature.

Nylon can be copolymerised to produce materials with properties differing from those of the base polymers and can be further modified by the inclusion of additives to improve certain properties.

Five types of nylon are available: 6.6, 6, 6.10, 11 and 12. The number signifies the number of carbon atoms contained in the materials from which they are made. They can be produced with varying melt viscosities to best suit the method of fabrication from low viscosity for complex injection moulding to very high viscosities for extrusion or blow moulding.

Each nylon type possesses common properties as well as some unique ones. Nylon 6.6 has the highest melting-point and is the stiffest and strongest, but it can absorb a considerable amount of moisture. Nylon 6 has a lower melting point, better impact strength and absorbs more moisture than nylon 6.6 with the result that they are less stable. Nylon 11 and 12 are expensive versions but due to lower water absorption compared to nylon 6 (saturation values of 2.6% for nylon 12, 2.9% for nylon 11 and 10% for nylon 6) they show better dimensional stability and minimal variation of properties with changing humidity. They are also more flexible than nylon 6 or nylon 6.6 Nylon 6.10 properties fall between nylon 6.6 and nylon 11.

Other properties, such as heat and light ageing, mould release and antistatic can be improved by additions. Flexibility can be improved with the use of plasticizers. Graphite and molybdenum disulphide will improve frictional characterisitics. The addition of glass fibre makes a vast improvement in mechanical properties.

Unfilled nylons exhibit good rigidity, but they are particularly sensitive to deformation at elevated temperatures and have a high coefficient of thermal expansion. These properties can preclude them from replacing metal components. Glass fibre reinforcement has gone a long way to overcome these shortcomings as well as reducing moisture absorption and improving the life at elevated (100°C) temperature. The reinforcement provides increased tensile, shear and compressive strength and flexural modulus.

472

The most important technical drawback is that nylons are hygroscopic. This affects their dimensional stability, mechanical strength and electrical properties.

At temperatures above 70°C oxidative degradation occurs. This affects their mechanical properties, causes embrittlement and reduces wear resistance. There are additions that can improve the upper limit to 100-120°C. Nylons are also subject to hydrolytic degradation and this, allied to the oxidative degradation, has limited their use in hot water systems.

Nylon is attacked by concentrated mineral acids, hot dilute mineral acids, oxidising agents, halogens (including bleaching agents, containing chlorine) and hot concentrated alkalis. It is unaffected by hydrocarbon and chlorinated hydrocarbon solvents, oils, many organic liquids, detergents, concentrated alkalis and dilute acids.

As about 80% of total deformation on a loaded component occurs in the first 48 hours the long term effects can be fairly accurately predicted.

Nylon components can be produced by most normal plastic manufacturing methods. The most widely used is injection moulding. In the moulded form nylon 6 and 6.6 are particularly rigid. By using nylon 11 and 12, which are more flexible, the ejection of components with relatively severe undercuts becomes a practical proposition, such as snap fittings. Nylon granules must be thoroughly dry before use or this can lead to poor finish, voids and degradation.

Tubes, profiles, films and coatings for wire and cable can be extruded. Small fluid reservoirs and other vessels requiring good chemical resistance are made by blow moulding.

Nylon may be applied directly to metal components as a protective coating by fluidised bed techniques, flame spraying or electrostatic deposition. Another method of coating is by applying nylon powder to a component and rotating it in a suitably heated environment to melt the nylon. Nylon is a relatively expensive plastic but the cost can be kept down by using the nylon as a thin lining or covering for an item made from a material that would not be suitable for an application otherwise.

Machining, such as turning, milling, drilling, thread cutting, sawing etc can all be carried out with little difficulty.

Nylon assemblies may be constructed by welding (induction, hot gas or ultrasonically), or use of adhesives, moulded-in thread inserts should be used.

Nylon components can be finished by polishing, vacuum metallising and painting.

Nylon finds many applications. In light to medium engineering it is used for gears, bearings and slides; in the automotive and domestic appliance industries its uses are legion. Since it is non-toxic it can be used in direct contact with food stuffs. It is resistant to fungi and mould growth and, because it can be sterilised by boiling water, steam or gamma radiation it is suitable for many medical applications.

Though the electrical properties of nylon are not outstanding they are adequate for many applications such as terminal blocks, power tool mouldings, switch components etc.

Weatherability and ultra-violet resistance are good if the nylon is UV stabilised.

4.4.1.5 POLYCARBONATE

Data Sheet PL09

Polycarbonate has similar light transmission properties to acrylic and glass. Its high impact properties at low temperature, good optical characteristics, ability to withstand high temperatures, good UV properties all make polycarbonate an ideal candidate for street lamp covers for high output lights. Its good impact properties are of particular interest where anti-vandal considerations are paramount.

Polycarbonate has good weatherability. When the material is ultra-violet stabilised it can be exposed to light sources without undue loss of properties.

Polycarbonate has an excellent retention of stability over a wide range of temperatures and humidities. Moisture absorption and coefficient of thermal expansion are low, enabling the material to be used in electrical and optical applications. The creep resistance of polycarbonate is high, even more than some thermoset materials. The heat distortion temperature is high and it will not deflect under its own weight at temperatures up to 130°C#, with a retention of its mechanical properties to very near this temperature.
The ability of polycarbonate to retain its electrical properties through a wide temperature and humidity range makes it a unique insulating material for many electrical applications. Since polycarbonate has also a high degree of dimensional stability it is used as insulators, meter covers and connectors.

At room temperature and 60% relative humidity polycarbonate absorbs up to 0.19% water. When immersed in water the value increases to a maximum of 0.58% with rising temperature. However, it is not recommended for permanent immersion at temperatures greater than 60°C otherwise there can be a loss of impact properties.

Polycarbonates are resistant to acids, and many fats and oils. Chemical decomposition can be caused by alkaline solutions and ammonia (gas and solutions). Swelling is caused by benzene, acetone and carbontetrachloride.

All mechanical properties, except impact resistance, can be improved by the addition of 30% glass fibre.

Polycarbonate is classified as self extinguishing. It is available in a wide range of colours and can also be coated with various metallic finishes using the vacuum metallisation technique.

Due to high heat distortion temperature polycarbonate does not tend to 'stick' during machining. Normal engineering techniques are employed.

Polycarbonate may be joined to itself by solvent welding, using methylene chloride, or ultrasonic welding methods will join polycarbonate. The latter is preferred as it can be closely controlled and is more economical. Epoxy or other adhesives are suitable for fixing this material to itself or dissimilar materials.

Polycarbonate may be processed by injection moulding, extrusion, blow moulding and vacuum forming.

4.4.1.6 **POLYBUTYLENE**

Data Sheet PL10

Polybutylene is a member of the polyolefin group of plastics, along with polyethylene and polypropylene, and is generally available only in the forms of tube or film. Polybutylene has excellent resistance to creep at room and elevated temperature. It will retain useful strength within a service temperture range of -20°C to +82°C. The material exhibits good flexibility and tube, which is available in long lengths, may be continuously run without the necessity of using fittings at corners and bends (particulary useful when laying heating systems below ground or under floors). Good tensile and yield stresses are available together with high impact properties.

The National Water Council (NWC) has approved the use of polybutylene tube above ground only and for operation within pressure and temperature limitations of 12 bar at 20°C and 2 bar at 82°C. NWC approval extends to both cold water use and for continual use in contact with hot water. Its light weight enhances its ease of handling and long lengths can be used with few joints. Polybutylene tube is joined by fusion welding by proprietary compression fittings using metal 'grab' rings or by flanges.

The abrasion resistance of polybutylene is excellent, resulting in its use for conveying abrasive slurries such as fly-ash and gypsum, to settling tanks and shows savings in cost and an extended life over lined steel pipe.

Polybutylene is not recommended for extended outdoor exposure unless stabilised for ultraviolet resistance by use of a special additive or carbon black.

The material is resistant to most chemicals but is attacked by nitric acid, concentrated sulphuric acid, chlorine gas, fuel oil and petrol. Some solvents also attack polybutylene including benzene, carbon-tetrachloride. Polybutylene tube is suitable for use in hot or cold water systems. In hot water systems pipe sag between supports is a minimum.

In film form it possesses high tear strength and high puncture resistance. Its permeability to oxygen is superior to polyethylene resulting in better storage life of packaged products.

Because polybutylenes are superior to other polyolefins, (e.g. yield strength twice polyethylene; impact strength three times low density polyethylene). Any product can be made thinner, lighter, and easier to handle than with the other materials.

4.4.1.7 **POLYETHYLENE (POLYTHENE)**

Data Sheets PL11, PL12

Polyethylene is the most significant member of the polyolefin group of plastics which includes polybutylene and polypropylene.

Polyethylene can be divided into three types - low density (918 to 930 Kg/m^3), medium density (930 to 950 kg/m^3) and high (950 to 965 kg/m^3) density.

Low density polyethylenes are characterised by their low cost, flexibility, translucency, toughness and impact strength whereas the chief merits of high density materials are higher service temperatures, improved chemical resistance, greater rigidity and better resistance to permeation of gases. Medium density polyethylene is easiest to weld and is used for gas

475

pipelines. Pipe and a full range of fittings are available.

All polyethylenes have good resistance to impact over a wide temperature range and are better than many other thermoplastics. The higher densities, having higher softening points, find uses in applications which have to hold hot water without becoming limp. The maximum service temperature for low density pressure pipes is 40°C and for high density, 60°C.

Polyethylenes are tough at low temperatures and have excellent electrical insulation properties and chemical resistance. They can be extruded and moulded. Metal can be coated with polyethylene but care is required in the selection of density as the higher densities tend to be brittle.

Polyethylene pipes intended for the conveyance of gas below ground should have a density greater than 930 kg/m^3.

Strong oxidising agents (fuming nitric and concentrated sulphuric acid) can decompose polyethylene, but it is relatively unaffected by most organic solvents, vegetable oils, water, alkalis, most concentrated acids (including hydrofluoric) and ozone (away from ultra-violet radiation) at room temperature.

Polyethylene does not taint items that come into contact with it and hence is used for food containers.

Polyethylenes have limitations, particularly in respect of permeation of gases. High density grades have better barrier properties than low densities and are also superior to polypropylene.

Continuous exposure to outside weather has a detrimental effect on polyethylene. A maximum period of 6 months is recommended, but, with the addition of carbon black, a life in excess of 10 years can be expected, and at least 8 years with other colour pigments.

Stress-cracking can occur when in contact with certain liquids, such as detergents.

Polyethylenes are not self-extinguishing and burn slowly with a yellow tipped blue flame and little smoke. The burning material may drip with a continuation of burning.

Normal plastics design rules apply to polyethylene such as the elimination of stress raisers to reduce impact and stress cracking failures. Since polyethylene is a crystalline polymer there is a fairly high mould shrinkage along the line of flow and therefore tight tolerances are difficult to maintain.

Polyethylene materials can be welded providing that adequate pressure and temperatures are used but the maximum temperature must be controlled to prevent oxidation. It is difficult to weld differing density materials.

Both low-density and high-density polyethylenes have a high degree of flexibility and this permits manufacture of long length coils of pipe. Therefore they can be laid underground in long continuous lengths by mole ploughing.

The low-density material has a relatively low tensile strength and pressure pipes made from it are therefore generally restricted to those of smaller bore. High-density polyethylene is a rather stiffer and stronger material and, consequently larger bore pipes, up to 1600 mm diameter, are available. Polyethylene tube and pipe and ballfloats of high, low and medium densities, have been approved by the National Water Council.

4.4.2 THERMOSETTING PLASTICS

4.4.2.1 AMINO RESINS

Amino resins are thermosetting materials made by condensing formaldehyde with compounds such as urea or melamine. When compounded with suitable fillers, pigments, etc, they can be moulded into hard infusible products.

Urea-formaldehyde (UF) mouldings are self extinguishing and they also possess moderate heat resistance. Good mechanical properties are associated with hardness and abrasion resistance. UF exhibits moderate resistance to weak acids and alkalis, and high resistance to oil, grease and solvents. Due to its freedom from odour and taste it is suitable for foodstuff containers. UF has good electrical properties including a high resistance to tracking leading to their use for electrical fittings, where good heat resistance is also a requirement.

Melamine formaldehyde (MF) has similar properties to UF but has, in addition, an improved resistance to boiling water, weak acids and alkalis. Due to these advantages MF is used for the manufacture of table-ware.

Amino resin products possess a very high gloss finish. Mouldings are not generally used in continuous load bearing applications since they are brittle and notch sensitive at all reasonable service temperatures. The temperature which amino plastics material will withstand without serious degradation depends both on the resin and the filler. Cellulose filled UF mouldings will discolour and degrade if maintained at temperatures above 80°C. MF resins are more resistant and can withstand continuous exposure without degradation up to 120°C. Amino resin products may be produced by compression, transfer or injection moulding.

Unfilled amino resins are used as adhesives for wood, coating resins, laminating resins, wet strength paper resins and for the treatment of textiles.

4.4.2.2 EPOXIDE RESINS

Data Sheet PL19

Epoxides (also known as epoxy) are a highly versatile class of thermosetting plastics springing from a large variety of possible starting materials which provide a wide range of properties and are presented to the user in many different forms; liquids, pastes and solids; one part, two part and three part systems.

Epoxy resin systems comprise one or more parts. The one part systems normally used for adhesives, contain resin and hardener in a mixture. An acceptable shelf life for one part systems is obtained by using hardeners that only react at elevated temperatures, normally in excess of 90°C. Systems containing two parts or more, used for adhesives, impregnation or moulding, can either cure at room temperature or at an elevated temperature depending on the type of hardener used. The time for cure of the low temperature systems can be shortened by applying heat. The pot life of these systems is limited, particularly where large quantities are involved, as curing is by an exothermic reaction. The proportions of the mix are tolerant but care must be taken not to mix in moisture as there can be a loss of properties.

Epoxides require little or no pressure while they cure. Despite their classification as thermosetting, the cure does not necessarily demand the use of heat. The top curing temperature is about 180°C but some can cure slowly at 5°C. They do not release volatiles during cure and hence shrinkage is low.

Epoxy resin systems wet and adhere to a wide variety of surfaces, which are fundemental requirements not only for adhesives and coatings but also when impregnation, lamination or casting and when a filler is used in a formulation.

Epoxy resin adhesives form strong and permanent joints between a wide variety of materials. They are used for bonding metals, stone, concrete, ceramics, glass, plastics and other organic materials. The properties of the bonds are such that primary load bearing structures can be safely built using epoxy adhesive joints only.

Mechanical properties are good for an amorphous non-crystalline polymer, having toughness and reasonable impact strength. Being a thermosetting material epoxies are not susceptible to plastic flow under stress.

Many properties can be improved by reinforcing the epoxy formulation with fibre or powder. Tensile properties can be increased and thermal expansion and shrinkage reduced for example, depending on the proportions of the reinforcing agent.

A paint finish based on epoxy system can be designed to resist foods, drinks, cosmetics, hot detergent solutions, be hard wearing and colour stable. These finishes are used in aggressive environments without deterioration. They often possess high build properties with no solvent loss.

The epoxies used for floor applications are cold curing. As they can withstand attack from corrosive chemicals and most solvents they are ideal materials for places such as the metal finishing industry. In addition they will withstand heavy abrasion and mechanical shock. Compared to concrete they have about twice the strength in tensile, compressive and flexural loading conditions. The epoxy floor toppings, which are a thin layer, can be laid as a continuous joint free layer which readily flow around machinary or shaped into gulleys or skirtings.

Electrical properties of epoxy systems are outstanding. Insulation, power factor and dielectric constant are excellent over a wide range of frequencies and temperatures. Certain of the systems are resistant to nuclear radiation. Epoxy systems have repaced ceramics as an insulating material because they are cheap, robust and capable of being cast into more intricate forms. The impregnation of glass fibre material for printed circuit boards is a major appplication. As liquid impregnation material, in rotor and stator manufacture, the important characteristic is that, at room temperature, the formulation has a long pot life while its heat curing time is short.

The maximum service temperature may vary from 60°C to 200°C depending on formulation. All may be used at cryogenic temperatures but within the usable range mechanical and electrial properties will change. Formulations that cure at room temperatures will seldom have useful mechanical properties above 80°C. For higher working temperatures a hot curing systems should be used.

Due to the large range of formulations manufacturers recommendations should be sought for specific applications.

It must be noted that uncured epoxy systems are active organic materials and can present dermatitic hazards. Some formulations produce strong smells. Work areas have to be well ventilated and have facilites for personal hygiene and barrier creams available.

4.4.2.3 PHENOLIC

Data Sheet PL20

The principle uses of phenolic are as surface coatings i.e. wire enamels and storing lacquers, adhesives and impregnation agents.

Their important properties are rigidity, electrical insulation, chemical resistance and thermal and dimensional stability. The principal filler is wood flour producing a grade suitable for a range of small components such as handles and knobs, domestic electric fittings and mechanical components subjected to low working stresses such as fan blades and castors. High temperature grades are available for valve wheels, etc. Chemical resistant grades are available for pump components working in corrosive liquids and shock resistant grades for impellors where mechanical strength and dimensional stability are required.

Electrical applications are best served by grades with low loss and high dielectric strength humidity resisting compounds such as tropical environment switchgear and encapsulation materials.

Modification is achieved by the choice of filler material; heat resistance comes from using asbestos; shock and chemical resistance from using cotton and mineral; low loss electric from using mica or nylon, depending upon water absorption limits.

Glass filled phenolics are the strongest and basically obey Hookes Law under tension. They suffer little from creep and impact strengths vary with the filler. Phenolics are good electrical insulators and give dielectric strengths in oil at 90°C of up to 350V/mil.

The resistance of phenolics to water, acids and most organic solvents is good. However, strong alkalis and oxidising agents will destroy them.

Phenolic resins are basically brown in colour and darken under the influence of light. Coloured grades can be obtained using a melamine/phenolic combination.

Phenolics reinforced with glass, cloth, paper or asbestos fabric are available as laminates.

Phenolics have low thermal conductivities, depending upon the filler used and are therefore commonly used for heat insulation applications. The coefficients of linear expansion are also dependent on the filler. Mineral fillers like asbestos, glass and mica give the lowest dimensional variation and organic fillers such as wood flour give the highest. Depending on the grade the coefficient of linear expansion can vary between 8 and 60 x 10^{-6}/°C. The normal operating temperature limit for phenolic mouldings is about 150°C but grades are available which can operate up to 220°C for restricted periods. Phenolics are not easily set alight and are self-extinguishing but will support combustion. At high operating temperatures mouldings decompose and char.

483

4.4.2.4 POLYESTER

Data Sheet PL21

Thermosetting polyesters are unsaturated liquid polyester resins normally containing a peroxide catalyst which can be activated by an accelerator or hardener to produce curing at normal ambient temperatures. In the absence of an accelerator, curing can be produced at temperatures of 70 to 150°C.

The unsaturated resins are dissolved in a monomer that is capable of crosslinking with the polyester to form a copolymer. Styrene is the monomer most commonly used for this purpose.

The cure is exothermic and can generate high internal temperatures in a large mass of resin. Temperatures should normally be kept to below 140°C to prevent internal cracking. Control in this respect is possible by formulation and restricting the amount of resin cured at any one time. During curing shrinkage of up to about 8% may occur.

Unfilled polyester resins are normally used as surface coatings, for potting and encapsulation, thread locking compounds and casting. Filled resins are used for body repairs, castings and industrial mouldings. The filled mixture has relatively good flexibility, gives good adhesion and cures at ambient temperatures.

An activated polyester resin can be centrifugally cast around the inside of a concrete pipe to provide a smooth durable chemical resisting lining. This results in smoother finish and reduced frictional resistance.

Cured polyester resins can be transparent or coloured, glossy or matt. They have good mar and stain resistance, withstanding contact with such commodities as coffee, beer, water, detergents, spirits, oils, fats, and other other chemicals. They are affected by alkalis and some solvents. Polyester resins have excellent weather resistance and are good thermal and electrical insulators. Their thermosetting nature also ensures good chemical, electrical and mechanical properties at elevated temperatures.

The most widespread use of polyester resins is as glass fibre reinforced plastics (GRP) mouldings.

4.4.2.5 POLYIMIDE

Mechanical, thermal and electrical properties surpass those of most other rigid plastics. Though polyimide is expensive its use is justified by the economic advantage derived from such factors as increased durability, reliability and safety, decreased down time due to repairs and replacement.

Polyimide parts can be used continuously at 250°C with an undectectable loss in weight. In environments containing no free oxygen the continuous service temperature is even higher, above 300°C with intermittent exposures up to 480°C. Tests indicate that polyimide has a good potential for cryogenic applications. The coefficient of thermal expansion is lower than most plastics; similar to alumimium.

About 50% of its tensile strength and stiffness properties at room temperature are retained at 250°C. Impact and creep are better than for phenolics and melamines.

484

Polyimide polymers offer excellent performances in applications involving sliding friction contact as a result of their low coefficient of friction and excellent abrasion resistance. These properties have led to their use as non-lubricated bearings in environments where conventional lubricants would fail (high pressure low speed, high temperature, vacuum). Polyimide does not melt and rubbing surfaces can be allowed to reach a temperature of 395°C.

Solid polyimides possess a good combination of high dielectric strength, low dielectric constant and low dissipation factor.

Polyimides are insoluble in organic solvents and resistant to most acids. They are not attacked by aliphatic or aromatic solvents, ethers, esters, alcohols or hydraulic fluids. They are attacked by strong alkalis and aqueous ammonia. Polyimides are not suitable for prolonged exposure to hydrazine, boiling water or steam.

By using a variety of adhesives, such as epoxy or phenolic systems, polyimide parts can be cemented to themselves or other plastics, metals and rubber.

Polyimide finds uses in insulation of electrical components exposed to high temperatures. Mechanical applications include balls of check valves, bearing components, seals on compressors and piston rings. In many mechanical and electrical applications, thermal insulation characteristics and dimensional stability at high temperature plus abrasion and creep resistance are important reasons for using polyimide.

4.4.3 CELLULAR PLASTICS

Cellular plastics or foams may be produced in a variety of ways, such as 'gassing' the liquid plastic, vaporising a volatile liquid content (such as Freon), heating with air to form a liquid foam which is subsequently cured, by fusion with a fully dispersed soluble medium such as starch which is subsequently leached out by a washing process, or by the addition of a substance which decomposes during processing, dispersing a gas throughout the matrix. There is also the possibility of producing the resin in the form of bubbles of minute size and cementing them together to yield a cellular structure.

The method used is significant mainly in controlling production cost and suitability for in-situ foaming when this is required. It is more useful to classify cellular plastics by their general physical characteristics as this will also affect their specific physical properties. Density is a variable factor since specific weight of cellular plastics can range from as little as 16 kg/m^3 upwards in the same polymer.

The cells produced may be closed, interconnecting open cells (like a sponge), or a mixture of both. Closed cell structures will be non-absorbent and non-permeable, and open cell structures absorbent or permeable. The cell form will also affect the physical properties. Deformation under load will depend upon whether it is an open or closed cell structure. Resin properties are more significant in the case of rigid foams and open cell flexible foams.

The type of resin has a significant effect on the behaviour of the material at elevated temperatures. In the case of thermoplastic foams approaching the softening temperature plastic 'memory' effect is initiated, leading to shrinkage and partial collapse of the cells with marked loss of compressive strength. Thermoset foams, on the other hand, will retain their cellular form although they may suffer a loss of load carrying capacity.

4.4.3.1 POLYURETHANE FOAMS

Data Sheets PL22, PL23

Polyurethanes are particularly suitable for foaming in-situ and exhibit good adhesion to most surfaces, e.g. as a lightweight solid 'filler', insulant or core material. Its thermal insulation value is extremely good. Flexible polyurethane foams represent the bulk of the production (exceeding all other types of cellular plastics) for upholstery, underlays, lightweight insulation for clothing, protetive packing, buoyance, vibration insulation, etc. These are open cell foams exhibiting high resilience.

Rigid closed cell polyurethane foams of low density (38 kg/m^3) are widely produced in sheet form for sandwich constructions, insulation, etc. and in a variety of laminates.

The requirements for the use of polyurethane foam as an insulating medium for buried pipes are laid down in CP 3009. It is stated that if the maximum fluid temperature in the pipe exceeds 95°C then polyurethane, or any other foamed plastic, must not be used as the insulating media.

4.4.3.2 CELLULAR PVC

Cellular or foamed PVC is produced in a variety of forms:-

- flexible open cell foams of moderate to high density, which have similar characteristic to latex rubber and are mainly used as synthetic leathercloth.

- flexible closed cell foams of low density for gaskets, trim, backing, buoyancy and insulation in clothing, etc. as well as general industrial purposes where dimensional stability is not important.

- rigid closed cell foam with densities from about 32 kg/m^3 upwards for structural, sandwich, insulation, buoyancy, and general industrial purposes.

- rigid open cell foams (microporous PVC), mainly for use as separators in accumulators, but also for filters.

The particular attractions of rigid PVC foams are high strength and good fire resistance. The material is also easy to work with woodworking tools.

4.4.3.3 POLYETHYLENE FOAM

Flexible, closed cell polyethylene foams are used for cushioning, vibration damping, packaging and gaskets, although its price is not strictly competitive with other materials in these fields. It may be chosen for such duties where superior chemical resistance is required, or where a coloured expanded lightweight material is advantageous (e.g. for display packaging). Polyethylene foams are relatively poor as heat insulators.

Rigid polyethylene foams are of high density, a microporous foam being used as a filter. Another high density foam is used as a cable insulation. Structural foams are also produced with a solid skin over a low density core.

4.4.3.4 EXPANDED POLYSTYRENE

Polystyrene foams are known as expanded polystyrene. They are produced only in the rigid form

486

which has a closed cell structure. It is another foam readily expanded in-situ, or relatively simply produced in heated moulds. Density can be as low as 28 kg/m^3. Expanded polystyrene finds particular application as a packaging material, for thermal and acoustic insulation, and flotation gear. It also has the particular advantage of being a low cost material although its mechanical properties, chemical resistance and temperature resistance are all poor. Resilience is also low. It is readily attacked by most solvents and hydrocarbons, and has maximum service temperature of about 70°C.

4.4.3.5 EVA MICROCELLULAR FOAM

Ethylene vinyl acetate (EVA) copoylmers are tough, rubbery, thermoplastic materials. They are similar to microcellular rubber foam in many ways, having equivalent physical properties at a much lower density, including almost unlimited colour possibilities and greatly improved resistance to chemicals, oils and greases.

4.4.3.6 THERMOSET FOAM

Data Sheet PL 24

Amongst the cellular thermoset resins, only phenolic, urea formaldehyde, epoxy and silicone have made any appreciable mark in the commercial field.

Phenolic is attractive because it can be rapidly and readily foamed in-situ, but it is less suitable for foaming in contact with metal surfaces because of the acid residues produced. The main advantages of the foam are rigidity, thermal insulation and a high maximum service temperature. Mechanically, however, the rigid foam material is brittle.

Urea formaldehyde (UF) is readily foamed in-situ and has good thermal insulation, making it attractive for cavity wall filling. The foam does not support combustion. The structure, however, is mostly open pore. Physically the rigid foam is light and friable.

Expanded epoxides are limited to more specialised applications because of high cost. They have a uniform texture with good dimensional stability. More commonly, epoxide resins are used in the production of composite foams, e.g. containing polystyrene beads expanded by the exothermic heat of the resin during setting. Such a composite foam normally has an increasing density from the centre outwards.

Rigid silicone foams are brittle and costly to produce. They offer a high temperature resistance (300°C for continuous exposure and 400°C for intermittent exposure) but suffer a marked loss in compressive strength above 180°C. They are cured mainly in a sandwich construction for use at elevated temperatures.

Flexible silicone foams are more readily available, although costly. They are of closed cell type of moderate density and have a maximum service temperature of the order of 200°C. They are used mainly for gaskets and static seals subject to extremes of temperatures.

4.4.4 LAMINATED PLASTICS

Laminated plastics comprise layers of fibrous material impregnated with, and bonded together by, a thermosetting resin to form a rigid solid material. They are most commonly available in sheet form but are also produced in bars, rods, tubes and sections. The properties of the resulting material depend on the type and proportions of resin used and the type of fibrous reinforcement employed.

They can be classifed generally as either decorative or industrial laminate; industrial laminates may be sub-divided into mechanical and electrical grades.

4.4.4.1 FIBROUS REINFORCEMENT

In general the reinforcement materials are used in the form of papers or thin fabric, although there is also a more limited application of felted materials. In manufacture these are preimpregnated with a predetermined quantity of resin and part cured. They are then stacked in layers after cutting to suitable shapes and fully cured under heat and pressure in high pressure moulds. Certain sections, e.g. wrapped tubes, may be oven cured on a mandrel without pressure, although moulded tubes are generally preferred. General characteristics of reinforcement materials are set out below.

PAPER REINFORCEMENT

Data Sheet PL25

This is the cheapest type for any resin system, yeilding a lightweight material with good mechanical strength and easily cut, drilled and machined. It also has excellent electrical properties.

COTTON FABRIC REINFORCEMENT

Data Sheet PL26

This offers superior mechanical but inferior electrical properties, although electrical grades may be used where high wear resistance is required (e.g. for contact breaker rotor arms) and the electrical voltages involved are low.

Weaves used range from coarse (30 threads) to very fine (120 threads); the finer the weave the better the machined finish and the dimensional stability and the closer the tolerance possible. As far as electrical grades are concerned, the finer the weave the lower the water absorption and the better the electrical properties.

ASBESTOS REINFORCEMENT

Data Sheet PL27

Asbestos reinforcement is used where increased resistance to heat is rquired, particularly for mechanical applications. Other properties improved are rigidity, dimensional stability and, to a lesser degree, chemical resistance. The asbestos may be in the form of paper, woven fabric or felt. Paper reinforcement has the disadvantage of being prone to edge chipping but gives a finer finish than fabric or felt. In all cases, machining is rather difficult because of the abrasive nature of the reinforcement.

Electrical grades of asbestos reinforced laminates are less attractive because of low insulation resistance and electrical strength but they may be used for low voltage applications where their mechancial properties are advantageous.

The resin used with asbestos reinforcement is normally phenolic.

GLASS FABRIC REINFORCEMENT

Data Sheet PL 28

Glass fabric gives greatly increased strength, rigidity and dimensional stability, with high resistance to heat. Water absorption is low and electrical and dielectric properties are good under both dry and humid conditions. Cost is relatively high, particularly as it is normally used with epoxide or polyamide resins for maximum benefit. Glass fabric reinforcement may, however, be used with any of the resin systems to establish particular requirements.

NYLON FABRIC REINFORCEMENT

This material offers certain advantages for electrical grades because of its very low water absorption, even under long exposure to extreme humidity. Its mechanical applications are limited by a low service temperature and a tendency to cold flow under stress. Mechanical properties are only moderate and flexural strength is low.

WOOD VENEER REINFORCEMENT

This reinforcement material is very attractive for decorative laminates although it may also have some structural applications. Its general properties are broadly similar to cotton fabric reinforcement.

4.4.4.2 RESINS

PHENOLIC RESIN

Data Sheets PL25, PL26, PL27

Phenolic resin is the 'traditional', and still the most widely used, type for general purpose, mechanical and electrical laminates, with all types of reinforcement. Maximum operating temperature varies quite widely with the type of fibrous reinforcement used. Phenolic laminates have the particular advantage of good machining properties.

EPOXIDE RESINS

Data Sheet PL28

Epoxide resins are now very widely used for high performance grades of laminates for both mechanical and electrical duties. Cost and performance are directly related to the epoxide resin system used, as well as to the reinforcement. Thus, modified epoxide laminates with paper reinforcement have exceptionally high resistance to tracking as well as high service tempertures. Flame retardant resin systems are also available.

In general modified epoxide cotton fabric laminates offer the superior electrical properties of paper or glass fabric epoxide laminates together with the mechanical strength and good machining qualities of phenolic cotton fabric laminates.

POLYESTER RESINS

Polyester resins are normally associated with glass fabric reinforcement and are the cheapest type of glass laminate. Again flame retardant resin systems are available. Mechanical and electric properties are inferior to epoxide glass fabric laminates

MELAMINE RESINS

Melamine resins have the advantage of providing a hard, scratch-resistant surface and superior electrical properties (particularly in resistance to arcing and tracking). They are thus particularly useful for their insulating properties in duties involving high humidity and/or a dirty environment. Their hard surface makes them attractive as decorative structural laminates, mechanical strength being comparable with polyester laminates.

SILICONE RESINS

Silicone resins have the highest resistance to heat. Electrical properties are also excellent and maintained over a wide temperature range. Their high cost otherwise limits their application and their mechanical properties are generally inferior to other resin system laminates.

POLYAMIDE RESINS

Polyamide resins have superior mechanical, thermal and electrical properties under severe environmental conditions and with glass fabric reinforcement have a maximum service temperature of the same order as a glass reinforced silicone laminate but with superior mechanical properties (e.g. two to three times the flexural strength at both room and elevated temperatures).

OTHER MATERIALS

PTFE is used as a filler or impregnant to impart self-lubricating low-friction characteristics to a mechanical grade of laminate for use as a dry bearing material. To realise these properties fully the PTFE must be uniformly disposed through the laminate so that, regardless of the machined shape, the PTFE is present at the bearing surface.

Graphite filling is also used as an alternative to PTFE for self-lubricating low-friction laminate materials.

4.4.5 FILLED PLASTICS

The filling or loading of thermoplastic injection moulding resins with short fibres of inorganic reinforcing material is now well established. The reinforcement mainly used is glass fibre, although asbestos fibre may be used for higher service temperatures, and carbon fibres when greater stiffness is required. The general effect is an improvement of all the mechanical properties of the composite, as compared with those of the resin system.

The main requirements are that the type of fibre used must have a substantially higher modulus of elasticity and tensile strength than the resin to effect such improvements; it should be readily wetted by the resin; it should not deteriorate, corrode or react with the resin. The higher modulus and higher strength requirements are obvious, but unless it is uniformly disposed and effectively bonded, the potential of the reinforcement may not be realised in the composite

490

because of lack of transfer of loading from the matrix to the reinforcement.   To achieve satisfactory wetting and bonding, coupling agents may have to be incorporated (e.g. silicons).

Non-fibrous reinforcements used with thermoplastics include both powders and microballoons or glass spheres.   Powders may be used to impart hardness, rigidity and wear resistance and may not have a marked effect on other properties (in some cases these effects can be adverse).   Other solids, notably molybdenum disulphide or graphite, may be added purely as lubricants. Microballoons may be used to produce bulk without any market increase in density, and glass spheres to improve the compressive strength of the resin.

Commercially available filled resins are described below.

4.4.5.1   FILLED NYLONS

Data Sheet PL 29

The proportion of glass fibre used in filling nylons may range from 10 to 55% by weight, with the specific gravity of the composite ranging from about 1.15 to 1.5.   A particularly significant feature is that, in addition to improving strength, the maximum service temperature is raised and low temperature mechanical strength improved.   Heat stabilised nylon 6 with about 30% glass filling may be used at a maximum service temperature of 100 to 120°C, or up to 150°C if not stressed.   The maximum service temperature for short term exposure may be as high as 200°C.

The characteristics of other glass filled grades of nylon, may be favourable for specific applications.   All show an improvement in strength and mechanical properties.   Glass filled nylon 6.6 has excellent resistance to cyclic stress and higher strength than the unfilled resin, although it tends to be more brittle.   Nylons loaded with glass spheres show particularly good impact resistance.

4.4.5.2   FILLED ACETAL

Data Sheet PL 30

Acetal resins are a major group of glass filled thermoplastics, the filler normally amounting to 20% to 30% by weight and specific gravities up to 1.65.   With 30% filler, tensile strength is approximately doubled and the modulus of elasticity and hardness substantially improved. Particularly significant are the improvement in dimensional stability and the reduction in the thermal coefficient of expansion.

The emergence of glass filled acetal resins as commercial materials has largely depended on the development of suitable coupling agents and improved fibre geometry.   Numerous commercial grades are now available for injection moulding.

4.4.5.3   FILLED ABS

Data Sheet PL 31

Glass filled ABS for injection moulding contains about 20% glass by weight, resulting in a specific gravity of 1.16 to 1.23.   Its mechanical properties are substantially improved (particularly impact strength), and thermal expansion roughly halved so that mould shrinkage is very low.   Some electrical characteristics are also improved, notably the dielectric strength and power factor.

491

4.4.5.4 FILLED PTFE

Data Sheet PL32, PL33

Considerable development has taken place in the field of filled polytetrafluorethylene (PTFE) to improve mechanical and thermal properties (particularly when used as a bearing material) and electrical properties. Glass filling is used to improve mechanical properties, but bronze powder filling, graphite filling, or a mixture of both, can develop superior bearing properties.

The addition of bronze improves the thermal conductivity of the material, making it more suitable for high speed bearings. Graphite filling gives a very low coefficient of friction with good resistance to wear and deformation under load.

With normal sintering, glass filling is limited to 15% by weight and yields a non-porous composite but the permitted filling may be increased to up 40% by inert gas sintering. A 28% glass content is generally considered the optimum for bearing applications, wear resistance and chemical resistance.

4.4.5.5 FILLED POLYCARBONATES

Data Sheet PL34

The main advantages offered by glass filled polycarbonates are substantial improvements in rigidity, dimensional and temperature stability with heat deflection temperatures up to 20% higher than for unfilled grades. Glass content from 20 to 40% by weight is commonly used. All grades show good flame resistance characteristics.

4.4.5.6 FILLED POLYSTYRENE

Glass filling, with a glass content up to 20-30% by weight, results in a marked improvements in all mechanical properties. Asbestos filling (up to 25%) improves flexural strength and impact resistance, and may be used with or without glass reinforcement. Both types show a substantial reduction in mould shrinkage, asbestos filling being superior to glass filling

4.4.5.7 FILLED POLYETHYLENE

Glass filled polyethylene, with a glass content of up to 30% by weight, is a comparatively recent development with, as yet, relatively little industrial or commerical application. The main advantage offered is greater rigidity compared with the unfilled resin, but only slight elevation of the heat deflection temperature.

4.4.5.8 FILLED POLYPROPYLENE

Data Sheets PL35, PL36, PL37

Unfilled polypropylene is classified as an 'engineering' plastic and also finds considerable application in 'domestic' industries via injection moulding or blow moulding. Filling enables the main limitations of the basic resin (mainly lack of rigidity, low temperature impact strength and relatively poor creep characteristics) to be countered, and also the more favourable characteristics (e.g. reasonably high softening point) to be enhanced.

Both glass and asbestos filling may be employed. Glass filling materially improves all the mechanical strength figures and gives a substantial reduction in the thermal expansion coefficient. The strength of 25% glass filled at 135°C is the same as unfilled at 20°C. Asbestos filling substantially increases rigidity and improves heat stability but has less favourable effects on other mechanical strength (strength at 70°C similar to unfilled at 20°C) with a loss of surface gloss. Talc is also used as a filler to improve rigidity and provide other favourable characteristics for injection moulding, notably good flow characteristics and low mould shrinkage. A disadvantage of talc is that it is hygroscopic.

4.4.5.9 FILLED POLYESTER

Glass filled thermoplastic polyester resins have excellent injection moulding characteristics with good strength, a high heat distortion and a high finish.

Their electrical properties are also attractive. The proportion of glass used may range up to 30%.

4.4.5.10 FILLED POLYSULPHONES

Unfilled polysulphones are high strength thermoplastics noted for their ability to retain their mechanical properties and dimensional stability at comparatively elevated temperatures - up to 150°C for continuous duty. The mechanical properties, thermal expansion characteristics and stability and particularly creep resistance can be enhanced by glass filling with up to about 30% glass by weight. Filled polysulphones are now sufficiently developed to be considered as alternatives for light metals in many applications.

4.4.5.11 FILLED PPO

Glass filled polyphenylene oxide (PPO) has come to be considered as an alternative to light metals, particularly as it is relatively cheap. The unfilled resins are noted for their exceptional dimensional stability and have excellent rigidity and creep resistance for a thermoplastics material. Electrical properties are also generally excellent.

Commerical grades contain 20% to 30% glass. The latter exhibits less than 1% creep at 30 N/mm^2 stress maintained for 500 hours at a temperature of 80°C as well as showing a substantial improvement in flexural endurance. The tensile strength is approximately the same as nylon in both filled and unfilled versions.

4.4.6 GLASS REINFORCED PLASTICS

The production of GRP has become an industry of its own within the plastics industry by virtue of the excellent combinations of properties, their wide range of applications and their remarkable growth in commercial importance.

The strength to weight ratio is high and they can be used to replace metals such as steel and aluminium in applications where saving in weight is advantageous (see Table 4.4/2). The mechanical properties of GRP are excellent but depend largely on the type of reinforcement used.

Resistance to weather and marine conditions is very good and, because of its resistance to marine organisms, GRP is used in boat building.

It is difficult to generalise about properties for these glass reinforced materials, mainly due to the very wide range of resin filler and reinforcement types available.

493

The most widely used combinations are polyester or epoxy with glass fibre, but carbon fibres in resins have been developed for special purposes. Only the polyester/glass fibre system will be considered in this section.

It is the resin content which determines the thermal properties, chemical resistance, water absorption and some of the electrical properties.

To obtain the optimum properties of the system the resin mix must totally wet the glass reinforcement. Non-wetting will produce spots which are mechanically weak or a path for a fluid to escape along the reinforcing fibre. There are several methods for making articles in these materials:-

- hand lay-up - the mould is covered with successive layers of resin and reinforcement and compacted by hand tools into a homogenous mass. The laminate is built up until the thickness is achieved, after which the resin is cured. This is the lowest cost method but slow.

- spray up - reinforcement, in the form of chopped strands and resin are sprayed onto the moulding. Compared with hand lay-up, the production rate is increased, but operator skill is still important.

- filament winding - the reinforcement, as a continuous filament, is wound onto a rotating mandrel. The filament is coated with resin immediately prior to winding. The direction of the reinforcement can be aligned with the direction of the principle stresses which occur in the moulding under service conditions. This process is limited to the production of hollow articles such as pipes and duct sections.

Table 4.4/2: Glass reinforced plastics compared with other materials.

Metal	Timber	Concrete
Compared with metals GRP has:	Compared with timber GRP has:	Compared with concrete GRP has:
1. Higher strength/weight ratio	1. Much higher strength	1. Considerable weight saving
2. Easier and cheaper manufacture of complex shapes	2. Greatly increased strength/ weight ratio.	2. Excellent design potential
3. Good corrosion resistance	3. Improved dimensional stability	3. Better chemical resistance
4. Ability to incorporate self colours.	4. Better weathering properties.	4. Superior weathering properties
	5. Higher water resistance	5. Higher strength/weight ratio
	6. Ease of fabricating complete structure.	

To obtain a smooth surface the first coat on the mould, the gel coat, may not have any reinforcement and could contain colouring agents. There are methods to mass produce articles using presses and moulds which will give a smooth finish on all surfaces.

Pigments may be used for through colouring (added to the resin), or more usually, for colouring the gel coat.

There are two main types of glass used in reinforcement:-

- low alkali, which is essential for electrical applications and it is desirable where good weathering and water resistance properties are required.

- high alkali, which has better resistance to mineral acid attack and is usually used in the chemical and nuclear industries.

Choice of reinforcement material for GRP laminates depends on the particular requirements of the job, cost, ease of working, and other factors. The following is a general guide.

4.4.6.1 GLASS FIBRE MAT

Data Sheet PL38

This is the usual material employed for GRP laminates since it is easy to shape, costs considerably less than glass cloth and, with modern soluble binders, is readily wetted.

4.4.6.2 WOVEN GLASS CLOTH

Data Sheet PL39

This generally produces the strongest laminates, but is not always easy to wet thoroughly. The greatest tensile strength is obtained by using the thinnest cloths with the closest weave, which can aggravate the problem of wetting. As a consequence, interlaminar adhesion can be poor locally.

4.4.6.3 WOVEN GLASS ROVINGS

Data Sheet PL40

These cloths are obtainable in various thicknesses with weights from about $0.3kg/m^2$ upwards. They do not have the same strength as woven cloths but drape well and are wetted out fairly easily. Since they cost less than woven cloths they are often used as a reinforcement layer, perhaps in conjunction with glass fibre mat, or as a simple means of adding bulk to increase stiffness.

4.4.6.4. ROVINGS

Data Sheet PL41

These are normally used for reinforcing glass mat layers, and also to add to bulk and improve stiffness. They are widely used to increase strength in boat hull construction.

4.4.6.5. GLASS FIBRE TISSUE

This was originally developed to hide the pattern of glass cloths but is also used as a 'cushioning' layer between the gel coat and the main reinforcement layers in a female mould.

4.4.6.6. GLASS FIBRE TAPE

This is simply woven cloth in tape form, and is the most convenient material to use where narrow strips of reinforcement are required. It is a strong material, readily handled, and easy to use for small repair jobs.

RELATED SPECIFICATIONS

GENERAL

<u>PIPE AND TUBES</u>

BS 4728	: 1971	Determination of the resistance to constant internal pressure of thermoplastic pipe
BS 4962	: 1982	Performance requirements for plastics pipes for use as light duty sub-soil drains
BS 5255	: 1976	Plastics waste pipe and fittings
BS 5556	: 1978	Specification for general requirements for dimensions and pressure ratings for pipe of thermoplastics materials
BS 5955	-	Code of practice for plastics pipework (thermoplastics materials).
CP 312	-	Plastics pipework (thermoplastics materials)
Part 1	: 1973	General principles and choice of material.
Part 2	: 1973	Unplasticized PVC pipework for the conveyance of liquids under pressure
Part 3	: 1973	Polyethylene pipes for conveyance of liquids under pressure

<u>VALVES</u>

BS 1212	-	Specification for float operated valves (excluding floats)
Part 3	: 1979	Diaphragm type (plastics body) for cold water services).

<u>TANKS AND CISTERNS</u>

BS 4213	: 1975	Cold water storage cisterns (polyolefin or olefin copolymer) and cisterns covers
BS 4994	: 1973	Vessels and tanks in reinforced plastics
PD 6480	: 1977	Explanatory supplement to BS 4994

<u>VESSEL LININGS</u>

CP 3003	-	Lining of vessels and equipment for chemical purposes.
Part 4	: 1965	Plasticized PVC sheet
Part 5	: 1966	Epoxy resin
Part 6	: 1966	Phenolic resin

<u>FLOATS</u>

BS 2456	: 1973	Floats (plastics) for ball valves for hot and cold water

ABS

BS 5391	-	Specification for ABS pressure pipe
Part 1	: 1976	Pipes for industrial use
BS 5392		Specification for ABS fittings for use with ABS pressure pipe
Part 1	: 1976	Fittings for use with pipe for industrial uses

POLYETHYLENE

BS 1972	: 1967	Polythene pipe (Type 32) for cold water services

BS 1973	: 1970 (1982)	Polythene pipe (Type 32) for general purposes including chemical and food industry uses
BS 3284	: 1967	Polythene pipe (Type 50) for cold water services
BS 3796	: 1970	Polythene pipe (Type 50) for general purposes including chemical and food industry uses
BS 5114	: 1975 (1980)	Performance requirements for joints and compression fittings foruse with polyethylene pipes
CP 312		Part 3 - see Pipes and Tubes general

POLYPROPYLENE

| BS 4991 | : 1974 (1982) | Propylene copolymer pressure pipe |
| BS 5254 | : 1976 | Polypropylene waste pipes and fittings (O.D.s 34.6, 41 and 54.1mm). |

PVC

BS 3505	: 1968 (1982)	Unplasticized PVC pipe for cold water services
BS 3506	: 1969	Unplasticized PVC pipe for industrial purposes
BS 4514	: 1969	Unplasticized PVC soil and ventilating pipe, fittings and accesories
BS 4576	-	Unplasticized PVC rainwater goods
Part 1	: 1970 (1982)	Half round gutters and circular pipes
BS 4660	: 1970 (1982)	Unplasticized PVC underground drainpipe and fittings
BS 5481	: 1977	Specification for unplasticized PVC pipe and fittings for gravity sewers
BS 5955		Part 6 - see Pipes and Tubes general
CP 312		Part 2 - see Pipes and Tubes general

PTFE

| BS 4375 | : 1968 | Unsintered PTFE tape for thread sealing applications |

POLYVINYL CHLORIDE

| BS 5955 | - | Code of practice for plastics pipework (thermoplastics materials) |
| Part 6 | : 1980 | Installation of unplasticized PVC pipework for gravity drains and sewers |

PHENOLIC

| PL2 | : 1969 | Phenolic resin-bonded cotton fabric round tube (maximum ID 75mm). |

CELLULAR

BS 3927	: 1965	Phenolic foam materials for thermal insulation and building applications.
BS 4841	-	Rigid urethane foams for building applications.
Part 1	: 1975	Laminated board for general purposes.
Part 2	: 1975	Laminated board for use as a wall and ceiling insulation
BS 5241	: 1975	Rigid urethane foam when dispensed or sprayed on a construction site.
BS 5608	: 1978	Specification for preformed rigid urethane and isocyanurate foam for thermal insulation of pipework and equipment

LAMINATES

Epoxide

BS 4045   : 1966   Epoxide resin pre-impregnated glass fibre fabrics.

Phenolic

BS 771   –   Phenolic moulding materials
Part 1   : 1980   Specification for physical properties (excluding type 1.2 material)
Part 2   : 1980   Specification for physical properties of type 1.2 material.
BS 2572   : 1976   Specification for phenolic laminated sheet.
BS 5102   : 1974   Phenolic resin bonded paper laminated sheets for electrical purposes.

GRP

BS 5480   –   Specification for glass reinforced plastics (GRP) pipes and fittings for use
                    for water supply and sewerage.
Part 1   : 1977   Dimensions, materials and classification.

DATA SHEETS

PLASTICS (PL)

<u>THERMOPLASTICS</u>

PL01	Acetal homopolymer resin
PL02	Acetal copolomer resin
P103	Acrylic
PL04	Acrylonitrile-butadiene-styrene
PL05	Polyamide-nylon 6
PL06	Polyamide-nylon 66
PL07	Polyamide-nylon 11
PL08	Polyamide-nylon 12
PL09	Polycarbonate
PL10	Polybutylene
PL11	High density polyethylene
PL12	Low density polyethylene
PL13	Crosslinked polyethylene
PL14	Polypropylene
PL15	P.T.F.E.
PL16	Polyvinyl chloride-plasticised
PL17	Polyvinyl chloride-rigid
PL18	Chlorinated PVC

<u>THERMSETS</u>

PL19	Epoxide resins
PL20	Phenolic
PL21	Polyester

<u>CELLULAR</u>

PL22	Polyurethane - flexible
PL23	Polyurethane - rigid
PL24	Phenolic

<u>LAMINATES</u>

PL25	Phenolic/paper
PL26	Phenolic/cotton
PL27	Phenolic/asbestos
PL28	Epoxy/cotton

FILLED

PL29	Nylon 66 + glass filling
PL30	Acetal + glass filling
PL31	ABS + glass filling
PL32	PTFE + glass filling
PL33	PTFE + bronze filling
PL34	Polycarbonate + glass filling
PL35	Polypropylene + asbestos filling
PL36	Polypropylene + talc filling
PL37	Polypropylene + glass filling

REINFORCED

PL38	Polyester + glass fibre mat
PL39	Polyester + glass fibre cloth
PL40	Polyester + glass fibre rovings

| FAMILY GROUP | PLASTICS | SUB-GROUP | THERMOPLASTICS | MATERIAL | ACETAL HOMOPOLYMER RESIN |

GENERAL DESCRIPTION

Acetal homopolymer resin is termed an engineering plastic and as such finds many applications as metal component replacements. It possesses high strength and rigidity excellent dimensional stability, and resilience. These properties are retained over a wide range of temperature, humidity and solvent exposure. Behaviour under cyclic or impact loading is outstanding. Suitable for use with potable water.

CHEMICAL ANALYSIS OR COMPOSITION

SYNONYM

Delrin

PHYSICAL PROPERTIES

PROPERTY	UNITS	VALUE OR RANGE	COMMENTS
DENSITY	kg/m^3	1425	
SHEAR STRENGTH	N/mm^2	69	
TENSILE STRENGTH	N/mm^2	25-75	
ELONGATION	%	124	10% Deflection
COMPRESSIVE STRENGTH	N/mm^2		
FLEXURAL STRENGTH	N/mm^2		
IMPACT STRENGTH	J	1.9	Izod
TENSILE MODULUS	N/mm^2	3500	
HARDNESS		M94, R120	
THERMAL COEFF. OF LINEAR EXPANSION	$^{o}C^{-1}$	8.1×10^{-5}	
MIN./MAX. SERVICE TEMPERATURE	^{o}C	$-40/^{+}120$	
DEFLECTION TEMPERATURE	^{o}C	124	at 1.81 N/mm^2
THERMAL CONDUCTIVITY	W/mK	0.23	
FLAMMABILITY	mm/min	-25	
DIELECTRIC STRENGTH	kV/mm		
VOLUME RESISTIVITY	ohm cm	10^{15}	
PERMITIVITY	ohm cm		
ARC RESISTANCE	secs	125	
NUMBER OF PARTS			
CURING METHOD			
OPTICAL PROPERTIES		Translucent to opaque	
FRICTION		0.05-0.3	
MOULD SHRINKAGE	mm/mm	0.5	
WATER ABSORPTION	%	0.25	

SPECIFICATIONS

STANDARD NUMBER	AUTHORITY	TITLE

COMPANY SPECIFICATION:

ENVIRONMENT

RESISTANCE TO ATTACK FROM:

MINERAL ACIDS (WEAK)	Resists some
MINERAL ACIDS (STRONG)	Attacked
ALKALIS (WEAK)	Resist some
ALKALIS (STRONG)	Attacked
SOLVENTS (CHLORINATED)	Resistant
OILS AND GREASES	Resistant
DETERGENTS	Resistant
U.V. RESISTANCE	Chalks slightly
WEATHERABILITY	Improved with inhibitors

OXYGEN PERMEABILITY

NITROGEN PERMEABILITY

CARBON DIOXIDE PERMEABILITY

JOINTING PROCESS

Welded by thermal, ultra-sonic or spin
techniques. Adhesive bonding following
surface pretreatment by etching. Mechanical
systems by moulded inserts

SAFETY PRECAUTIONS

PROCESSING AND FORMING TECHNIQUES

Injection moulding and extrusion
Excellent machinability
Components can be painted and printed

TYPICAL APPLICATIONS

General engineering such as gears, bearings,
ball race cages, light duty springs, valve
components, snap assemblies, pump components, automobile components, fuel
tanks
Ball valves, stop cocks and taps

YOUR SUPPLIER AND NOTES

| SHEET NUMBER | PL02 | A |

| FAMILY GROUP | PLASTICS | SUB-GROUP | THERMOPLASTICS | MATERIAL | ACETAL COPOLYMER RESIN |

GENERAL DESCRIPTION

Acetal copolymer combines high strength, good fatigue strength and good resistance to high temperatures with rigidity. These properties favour its use as a replacement for metals. Polyacetal has slightly superior properties to acetal resin. Suitable for use with potable water.

CHEMICAL ANALYSIS OR COMPOSITION

SYNONYM

Kemetal

PHYSICAL PROPERTIES

PROPERTY	UNITS	VALUE OR RANGE	COMMENTS
DENSITY	kg/m^3	1410-1425	
SHEAR STRENGTH	N/mm^2		
TENSILE STRENGTH	N/mm^2	60-72	
ELONGATION	%	60-75	
COMPRESSIVE STRENGTH	N/mm^2	110	
FLEXURAL STRENGTH	N/mm^2		
IMPACT STRENGTH	J	1.6-2.2	Izod
TENSILE MODULUS	N/mm^2	2830	
HARDNESS	mm/min	M78-M80	Rockwell
THERMAL COEFF. OF LINEAR EXPANSION	$^{o}C^{-1}$	8.5-9.7x10^{-5}	
MIN./MAX. SERVICE TEMPERATURE	^{o}C	/100	
DEFLECTION TEMPERATURE	^{o}C	110	at 1.81 N/mm^2
THERMAL CONDUCTIVITY	W/mK	0.23	
FLAMMABILITY	mm/min	25	
POWER FACTOR			
DIELECTRIC STRENGTH	kV/mm		
VOLUME RESISTIVITY	ohm cm	10^{14}	
PERMITIVITY	ohm cm		
ARC RESISTANCE	secs	240	
NUMBER OF PARTS			
CURING METHOD			
OPTICAL PROPERTIES		Translucent to opaque	
FRICTION			
MOULD SHRINKAGE			
WATER ABSORPTION	%	0.22	

SPECIFICATIONS

STANDARD NUMBER	AUTHORITY	TITLE

COMPANY SPECIFICATION:

ENVIRONMENT

RESISTANCE TO ATTACK FROM:

MINERAL ACIDS (WEAK)	Resists some
MINERAL ACIDS (STRONG)	Attacked
ALKALIS (WEAK)	Resistant
ALKALIS (STRONG)	Resistant
SOLVENTS (CHLORINATED)	
OILS AND GREASES	
DETERGENTS	

U.V. RESISTANCE	Chalks slightly
WEATHERABILITY	

OXYGEN PERMEABILITY
NITROGEN PERMEABILITY
CARBON DIOXIDE PERMEABILITY

JOINTING PROCESS

Welded by thermal, ultrasonic and spin
techniques. Adhesive bonding is suitable
providing a pretreatment etch has been applied.

SAFETY PRECAUTIONS

PROCESSING AND FORMING TECHNIQUES

Injection moulding and extrusion
characteristics are excellent.
Excellent machinability

TYPICAL APPLICATIONS

Hot water components, fan components,
lubricated   bearings and gears, automobile components and precision engineering
components. Solar heating systems -
taps and valves.

YOUR SUPPLIER AND NOTES

material data sheet

SHEET NUMBER	PL03

A

FAMILY GROUP	PLASTICS	SUB-GROUP	THERMOPLASTICS	MATERIAL	ACRYLIC

GENERAL DESCRIPTION

Acrylics are completely transparent and optically clear, they are exceptionally stable to outdoor weathering and do not discolour or degrade under U.V. radiation. They are stiff, strong and do not shatter. Some solvents can cause stress cracking. May be coloured. Impact strength is maintained down to -40°C. Heat distortion temperature is similar to ABS but below nylon and polycarbonate. Acrylic is less abrasion resistant than glass.

CHEMICAL ANALYSIS OR COMPOSITION

SYNONYM

Perspex

PHYSICAL PROPERTIES

PROPERTY	UNITS	VALUE OR RANGE	COMMENTS
DENSITY	kg/m^3	1190	
SHEAR STRENGTH	N/mm^2		
TENSILE STRENGTH	N/mm^2	54.5-76	
ELONGATION	%	4-5	
COMPRESSIVE STRENGTH	N/mm^2	27.6-124	
FLEXURAL STRENGTH	N/mm^2	55 131	
IMPACT STRENGTH	J	0.4-3.1	Izod
TENSILE MODULUS	N/mm^2	$2.8-3.1 \times 10^3$	
HARDNESS		M85-M100	Rockwell
THERMAL COEFF. OF LINEAR EXPANSION	$^{o}C^{-1}$	$5-9 \times 10^{-5}$	
MIN./MAX. SERVICE TEMPERATURE	^{o}C	$/90^{o}$	
DEFLECTION TEMPERATURE	^{o}C	74-104	at 1.81 N/mm^2
THERMAL CONDUCTIVITY	W/mK	0.17-0.25	
FLAMMABILITY		Burns readily	
POWER FACTOR		0.02-0.03	At 1MHz
DIELECTRIC STRENGTH	kV/mm	0.45-0.55	
VOLUME RESISTIVITY	ohm cm	less than 10^{14}	
PERMITIVITY	ohm cm	2.2-3.2	At 1MHz
ARC RESISTANCE	secs	No tracking	
NUMBER OF PARTS			
CURING METHOD			
OPTICAL PROPERTIES		Transparent	
FRICTION			
MOULD SHRINKAGE	%	0.2-1.0	
WATER ABSORPTION	%	0.2-0.4	

SPECIFICATIONS

STANDARD NUMBER	AUTHORITY	TITLE

COMPANY SPECIFICATION:

ENVIRONMENT

RESISTANCE TO ATTACK FROM:

MINERAL ACIDS (WEAK)	Resistant
MINERAL ACIDS (STRONG)	Attack by oxidising acids
ALKALIS (WEAK)	Resistant
ALKALIS (STRONG)	Slight attack
SOLVENTS (CHLORINATED)	Soluble
OILS AND GREASES	Resistant
DETERGENTS	Resistant
U.V. RESISTANCE	Unaffected
WEATHERABILITY	Good

OXYGEN PERMEABILITY	1×10^{-11} cm^3/cm^2 sec cm Hg/cm
NITROGEN PERMEABILITY	1×10^{-11} cm^3/cm^2 sec cm Hg/cm
CARBON DIOXIDE PERMEABILITY	1×10^{-11} cm^3/cm^2 sec cm Hg/cm

JOINTING PROCESS

Ultrasonic welding
Solvent welding
Mechanical fasteners
Adhesive - acrylics in solution, rubber base

SAFETY PRECAUTIONS

PROCESSING AND FORMING TECHNIQUES

Acrylics can be cast, extruded, injection moulded and thermoformed
Normal engineering machining techniques may be employed.

TYPICAL APPLICATIONS

Sanitary ware such as baths and basins. Glazing. Lighting fixtures
Illuminated building panel and advertisement signs. Automobile light trim.
Textiles and fibres
Lenses

YOUR SUPPLIER AND NOTES

| | | SHEET NUMBER | PL04 | A |

| FAMILY GROUP | PLASTICS | SUB-GROUP | THERMOPLASTICS | MATERIAL | ACRYLONITRILE - BUTADIENE-STYRENE |

GENERAL DESCRIPTION

ABS materials are tough, stiff, resist abrasion and are readily metal plated. The properties of ABS depend on the relative properties of the constituents. They have good stain resistance but are attacked by strong acids and alkalis, chlorinated solvents, esters and ketones. Some greases can present a stress cracking hazard. ABS is capable of working in aggressive environments at high temperatures. Suitable for use with potable water.

CHEMICAL ANALYSIS OR COMPOSITION

SYNONYM

ABS

PHYSICAL PROPERTIES

PROPERTY	UNITS	VALUE OR RANGE	COMMENTS
DENSITY	kg/m^3	1020-1180	
SHEAR STRENGTH	N/mm^2		
TENSILE STRENGTH	N/mm^2	20-60	
ELONGATION	%	3-80	Depending on supplier
COMPRESSIVE STRENGTH	N/mm^2	31-86	
FLEXURAL STRENGTH	N/mm^2	45-90	
IMPACT STRENGTH	J	3-10	Izod
TENSILE MODULUS	N/mm^2	1380-2900	
HARDNESS		R75-115	Rockwell
THERMAL COEFF. OF LINEAR EXPANSION	$^oC^{-1}$	$7\text{-}13\times10^{-5}$	
MIN./MAX. SERVICE TEMPERATURE	^oC	-30/+80	
DEFLECTION TEMPERATURE	^oC		
THERMAL CONDUCTIVITY	W/mK	0.16-0.22	
FLAMMABILITY		Burns readily	
POWER FACTOR		0.007-0.026	
DIELECTRIC STRENGTH	kV/mm	0.31-0.41	
VOLUME RESISTIVITY	ohm cm	$10^{13}\text{-}10^{16}$	
PERMITIVITY	ohm cm		
ARC RESISTANCE	secs	50-85	
NUMBER OF PARTS			
CURING METHOD			
OPTICAL PROPERTIES		Translucent to opaque	
FRICTION		0.21	
MOULD SHRINKAGE	%	0.4-0.7	
WATER ABSORPTION	%	0.2-0.45	

 **material data sheet**

SPECIFICATIONS

STANDARD NUMBER	AUTHORITY	TITLE
CP 312: Part 1	BSI	Plastics pipework (thermoplastic)
BS 5255	BSI	Plastic waste pipe and fittings
BS 5391 Part 1	BSI	ABS pressure pipe - pipe for industrial use
BS 5392 Part 1	BSI	ABS fittings for use with ABS pressure pipe - fittings for use with pipe for industrial use.

COMPANY SPECIFICATION:

ENVIRONMENT

RESISTANCE TO ATTACK FROM:

MINERAL ACIDS (WEAK)	Resistant
MINERAL ACIDS (STRONG)	Attacked by oxidising acids
ALKALIS (WEAK)	Resistant
ALKALIS (STRONG)	Resistant
SOLVENTS (CHLORINATED)	Soluble
OILS AND GREASES	Some cause crazing
DETERGENTS	Resistant

U.V. RESISTANCE	Slight yellowing
WEATHERABILITY	Improved with black additive

OXYGEN PERMEABILITY	0.92×10^{-9} cm^3/cm^2 sec cm Hg/cm
NITROGEN PERMEABILITY	0.86×10^{-9} cm^3/cm^2 sec cm Hg/cm
CARBON DIOXIDE PERMEABILITY	

JOINTING PROCESS

Joined by solvent bonding
Hot gas welding with the use of filler rods
Adhesives - epoxy

PROCESSING AND FORMING TECHNIQUES

ABS can be injection moulded, extruded, rotationary moulded and thermoformed. Good machinery properties

TYPICAL APPLICATIONS

Pipes, fittings and valves for non-potable water. Housing for domestic durable goods Internal sink and bath wastes. Inspection chambers, access systems. Ventilator pipes and grills. Solar heating systems Telephone handsets

YOUR SUPPLIER AND NOTES

SAFETY PRECAUTIONS

material data sheet	**SHEET NUMBER** PL05	**A**

FAMILY GROUP PLASTICS	**SUB-GROUP** THERMOPLASTICS	**MATERIAL** POLYAMIDE - NYLON 6

GENERAL DESCRIPTION

Nylon materials are stiff, strong, tough and abrasion resistant. All types of nylon are hygroscopic which affects the properties, particularly dimensional stability. Strong mineral acids attack nylon.

The basic type, Nylon 6, has low dimensional stability and a very high moisture absorption factor. Compared to other types it has higher impact resistance and lower melting point than nylon 66. Water absorption impairs its electrical properties. Suitable for use with potable water.

CHEMICAL ANALYSIS OR COMPOSITION

PHYSICAL PROPERTIES

PROPERTY	UNITS	VALUE OR RANGE	COMMENTS
DENSITY	kg/m^3	1120-1150	
SHEAR STRENGTH	N/mm^2		
TENSILE STRENGTH	N/mm^2	44-86	
ELONGATION	%	10-300	
COMPRESSIVE STRENGTH	N/mm^2	46-110	
FLEXURAL STRENGTH	N/mm^2		
IMPACT STRENGTH	J	1.6	Izod
TENSILE MODULUS	N/mm^2		
HARDNESS		R95-R120	Rockwell
THERMAL COEFF. OF LINEAR EXPANSION	$^{o}C^{-1}$	8.9×10^{-5}	
MIN./MAX. SERVICE TEMPERATURE	^{o}C	/90	
DEFLECTION TEMPERATURE	^{o}C	60-88	at 1.81 N/mm^2
THERMAL CONDUCTIVITY	W/mK	0.25	
FLAMMABILITY		Self Extinguishing	
POWER FACTOR		0.023-0.18	10^3 Hz
DIELECTRIC STRENGTH	kV/mm	11-50	
VOLUME RESISTIVITY	ohm cm	$10^{12}-10^{15}$	
PERMITIVITY	ohm cm		
ARC RESISTANCE	secs		
NUMBER OF PARTS			
CURING METHOD			
OPTICAL PROPERTIES		Translucent to opaque	
FRICTION			
MOULD SHRINKAGE	%	0.7-1.5	
WATER ABSORPTION	%	8.5-11.8	

SPECIFICATIONS

STANDARD NUMBER	AUTHORITY	TITLE

COMPANY SPECIFICATION:

ENVIRONMENT

RESISTANCE TO ATTACK FROM:

MINERAL ACIDS (WEAK)	Resistant (hot, attacked)
MINERAL ACIDS (STRONG)	Attacked
ALKALIS (WEAK)	Resistant
ALKALIS (STRONG)	Resistant (hot, attacked)
SOLVENTS (CHLORINATED)	Resistant
OILS AND GREASES	Resistant
DETERGENTS	Resistant

U.V. RESISTANCE	Discolours slightly
WEATHERABILITY	No loss of properties

OXYGEN PERMEABILITY

NITROGEN PERMEABILITY

CARBON DIOXIDE PERMEABILITY

PROCESSING AND FORMING TECHNIQUES

Excellent injection moulding characteristics

Also available as castings extrusions and blown sheet

Machinability - excellent

TYPICAL APPLICATIONS

Used for gears, cams, bushes and bearings where its high lubricity can be exploited

Chemical plant components

JOINTING PROCESS

Adhesives - epoxy, pherlics, rubber base.

Welding by induction, hot gas or ultrasonics

Mechanical by moulded in inserts

YOUR SUPPLIER AND NOTES

SAFETY PRECAUTIONS

material data sheet	SHEET NUMBER	PL06	A

FAMILY GROUP	PLASTICS	SUB-GROUP	THERMOPLASTICS	MATERIAL	POLYAMIDE-NYLON 66

GENERAL DESCRIPTION

Nylon 66 has a high module of elasticity and a high melting point. Its water and moisture absorption is high, but less than nylon 6. Suitable for use with potable water.

CHEMICAL ANALYSIS OR COMPOSITION

PHYSICAL PROPERTIES

PROPERTY	UNITS	VALUE OR RANGE	COMMENTS
DENSITY	kg/m^3	1130-1160	
SHEAR STRENGTH	N/mm^2		
TENSILE STRENGTH	N/mm^2	62-83	
ELONGATION	%	40-300	
COMPRESSIVE STRENGTH	N/mm^2	46-86	
FLEXURAL STRENGTH	N/mm^2		
IMPACT STRENGTH	J	2.7	Izod
TENSILE MODULUS	N/mm^2	1206-2862	
HARDNESS		R108,R120	Rockwell
THERMAL COEFF. OF LINEAR EXPANSION	$^oC^{-1}$	8×10^{-5}	
MIN./MAX. SERVICE TEMPERATURE	^oC	/90-150	
DEFLECTION TEMPERATURE	^oC	75-105	at 1.81 N/mm^2
THERMAL CONDUCTIVITY	W/mK	0.25	
FLAMMABILITY		Self-extinguishing	
POWER FACTOR		0.04	10^3 Hz
DIELECTRIC STRENGTH	kV/mm	15-40	
VOLUME RESISTIVITY	ohm cm	$10^{14}-10^{15}$	
PERMITIVITY	ohm cm		
ARC RESISTANCE	secs	130-140	
NUMBER OF PARTS			
CURING METHOD			
OPTICAL PROPERTIES		Translucent to opaque	
FRICTION			
MOULD SHRINKAGE	%	1.0-2.5	
WATER ABSORPTION	%	7.5-9.0	

SPECIFICATIONS

STANDARD NUMBER	AUTHORITY	TITLE

COMPANY SPECIFICATION:

ENVIRONMENT

RESISTANCE TO ATTACK FROM:

MINERAL ACIDS (WEAK)	Resistant (hot, attacked)
MINERAL ACIDS (STRONG)	Attacked
ALKALIS (WEAK)	Resistant
ALKALIS (STRONG)	Resistant (hot, attacked)
SOLVENTS (CHLORINATED)	Resistant
OILS AND GREASES	Resistant
DETERGENTS	Slight attack
U.V. RESISTANCE	Discolours slightly
WEATHERABILITY	Black improves properties

OXYGEN PERMEABILITY
NITROGEN PERMEABILITY
CARBON DIOXIDE PERMEABILITY

JOINTING PROCESS

Adhesives - epoxy, phenolics and rubber
base.
Welding by induction, hot gas or ultrasonic
Mechanical by moulded in inserts

SAFETY PRECAUTIONS

PROCESSING AND FORMING TECHNIQUES

Excellent injection moulding characteristics
Also supplied as extruded rods and tubes

TYPICAL APPLICATIONS

Engineering mouldings and extrusions for
gear wheels, pinions, bearing pads etc.

YOUR SUPPLIER AND NOTES

| FAMILY GROUP | PLASTICS | SUB-GROUP | THERMOPLASTICS | MATERIAL | POLYAMIDE-NYLON 11 |

GENERAL DESCRIPTION

Nylon 11 has a very low moisture and water absorption factor with a resulting good dimensional stability. It possesses high impact strength, low melting point and a low module of elasticity. Electrical properties are retained under humid conditions. Nylon 11 is expensive when compared to nylon 6 but has superior chemical, abrasion and weathering resistance. Suitable for use with potable water.

CHEMICAL ANALYSIS OR COMPOSITION

PHYSICAL PROPERTIES

PROPERTY	UNITS	VALUE OR RANGE	COMMENTS
DENSITY	kg/m^3	1040-1060	
SHEAR STRENGTH	N/mm^2		
TENSILE STRENGTH	N/mm^2	49-57	
ELONGATION	%	300	
COMPRESSIVE STRENGTH	N/mm^2	54	
FLEXURAL STRENGTH	N/mm^2		
IMPACT STRENGTH	J		
TENSILE MODULUS	N/mm^2	1275	
HARDNESS		R108	Rockwell
THERMAL COEFF. OF LINEAR EXPANSION	$°C^{-1}$	15×10^{-5}	
MIN./MAX. SERVICE TEMPERATURE	$°C$	/90	
DEFLECTION TEMPERATURE	$°C$	48-55	at 1.81 N/mm^2
THERMAL CONDUCTIVITY	W/mK		
FLAMMABILITY	mm/min	0.7	
POWER FACTOR			
DIELECTRIC STRENGTH	kV/mm	17	
VOLUME RESISTIVITY	ohm cm	$10^{11}-10^{14}$	
PERMITIVITY	ohm cm		
ARC RESISTANCE	secs		
NUMBER OF PARTS			
CURING METHOD			
OPTICAL PROPERTIES		Translucent	
FRICTION			
MOULD SHRINKAGE	%	1.0-2.5	
WATER ABSORPTION	%	2.9	

BSRIA material data sheet

SPECIFICATIONS

STANDARD NUMBER	AUTHORITY	TITLE

COMPANY SPECIFICATION:

ENVIRONMENT

RESISTANCE TO ATTACK FROM:

MINERAL ACIDS (WEAK)	Resistant (hot attack)
MINERAL ACIDS (STRONG)	Attacked
ALKALIS (WEAK)	Resistant
ALKALIS (STRONG) (hot attack)	Resistant
SOLVENTS (CHLORINATED)	Resistant
OILS AND GREASES	Resistant
DETERGENTS	Resistant
WATER ABSORBTION %	2.9
U.V. RESISTANCE	Discolours slightly
WEATHERABILITY	Good

OXYGEN PERMEABILITY 0.02×10^{-9} cm^3/cm^2 sec cm Hg/cm

NITROGEN PERMEABILITY 0.09×10^{-9} cm^3/cm^2 sec cm Hg/cm

CARBON DIOXIDE PERMEABILITY 0.002×10^{-9} cm^3/cm^2 sec cm Hg/cm

PROCESSING AND FORMING TECHNIQUES

Excellent inection moulding characteristics

Machinability - excellent

Coatings applied by fluidised bed method

TYPICAL APPLICATIONS

Coatings for decoration, electrical insulation and protection from corrosion such as power tools, hand rails, automobile trim, valve trim

JOINTING PROCESS

Adhesives - epoxy, phenolics and rubber based.
Welding by induction, hot gas or ultrasonic.
Mechanical by means of moulded in inserts and snap fittings

YOUR SUPPLIER AND NOTES

SAFETY PRECAUTIONS

| FAMILY GROUP | PLASTICS | SUB-GROUP | THERMOPLASTICS | MATERIAL | POLYAMIDE - NYLON 12 |

GENERAL DESCRIPTION

Nylon 12 and nylon 11 are similar materials but nylon 12 has slightly lower moisture absorption, lower density and better mould flow properties. Its low temperature impact resistance is inferior. Both nylon 12 and 11 are expensive compared to nylon 6 but have better chemical resistance compared to nylon 6 and 66. Suitable for use with potable water.

CHEMICAL ANALYSIS OR COMPOSITION

PHYSICAL PROPERTIES

PROPERTY	UNITS	VALUE OR RANGE	COMMENTS
DENSITY	kg/m^3	1010-1020	
SHEAR STRENGTH	N/mm^2		
TENSILE STRENGTH	N/mm^2	39-64	
ELONGATION	%	150-400	
COMPRESSIVE STRENGTH	N/mm^2		
FLEXURAL STRENGTH	N/mm^2		
IMPACT STRENGTH	J	1.6-5.7	Izod
TENSILE MODULUS	N/mm^2	1270-1325	
HARDNESS		M31,R106	Rockwell
THERMAL COEFF. OF LINEAR EXPANSION	$^oC^{-1}$	$10.4x10^{-5}$	
MIN./MAX. SERVICE TEMPERATURE	^oC	/90	
DEFLECTION TEMPERATURE	^oC	50-60	at 1.81 N/mm^2
THERMAL CONDUCTIVITY	W/mK		
FLAMMABILITY	mm/min	15-20	
POWER FACTOR			
DIELECTRIC STRENGTH	kV/mm	25-60	
VOLUME RESISTIVITY	ohm cm	$10^{10}-10^{14}$	
PERMITIVITY	ohm cm		
ARC RESISTANCE	secs	109	
NUMBER OF PARTS			
CURING METHOD			
OPTICAL PROPERTIES		Transparent to translucent	
FRICTION			
MOULD SHRINKAGE	%	0.8-2.0	
WATER ABSORPTION	%	2.6	

515

SPECIFICATIONS

STANDARD NUMBER	AUTHORITY	TITLE

COMPANY SPECIFICATION:

ENVIRONMENT

RESISTANCE TO ATTACK FROM:

MINERAL ACIDS (WEAK)	Fairly resistant
MINERAL ACIDS (STRONG)	Attacked
ALKALIS (WEAK)	Fairly resistant
ALKALIS (STRONG)	Fairly resistant
SOLVENTS (CHLORINATED)	Poor resistance
OILS AND GREASES	Resistant
DETERGENTS	Resistant

U.V. RESISTANCE	Discolours slightly
WEATHERABILITY	

OXYGEN PERMEABILITY

NITROGEN PERMEABILITY

CARBON DIOXIDE PERMEABILITY

JOINTING PROCESS

Adhesive bonding with epoxy, phenolic or
rubber based adhesives. Welding by induction, hot gas or ultrasonic.
Mechanical by means of moulded in inserts
or snap fittings.

SAFETY PRECAUTIONS

PROCESSING AND FORMING TECHNIQUES

Excellent injection moulding characteristics
Machinability - good

TYPICAL APPLICATIONS

Abrasion resistant gears and pinions
Electrical wire insulation
Regulating valves for central heating
Corrosion resistant applications

YOUR SUPPLIER AND NOTES

| | material data sheet | | SHEET NUMBER PL09 | A |

| FAMILY GROUP | PLASTICS | SUB-GROUP | THERMOPLASTICS | MATERIAL | POLYCARBONATE |

GENERAL DESCRIPTION

Polycarbonates are tough, transparent, stiff and strong, and they have moderate outdoor weathering resistance, and good electrical insulation properties. Mechanical properties well maintained with increasing temperature. May be used at temperatures down to $-100^{\circ}C$. Suitable for use with potable water.

CHEMICAL ANALYSIS OR COMPOSITION

PHYSICAL PROPERTIES

PROPERTY	UNITS	VALUE OR RANGE	COMMENTS
DENSITY	kg/m^3	1200	
SHEAR STRENGTH	N/mm^2		
TENSILE STRENGTH	N/mm^2	55-65	
ELONGATION	%	80-130	
COMPRESSIVE STRENGTH	N/mm^2	86	
FLEXURAL STRENGTH	N/mm^2	90 100	
IMPACT STRENGTH	J	16-22	Izod
TENSILE MODULUS	N/mm^2	2413	
HARDNESS		M70,R118	Rockwell
THERMAL COEFF. OF LINEAR EXPANSION	$^{\circ}C^{-1}$	6.6	
MIN./MAX. SERVICE TEMPERATURE	$^{\circ}C$	/135	
DEFLECTION TEMPERATURE	$^{\circ}C$	130-140	at 1.81 N/mm^2
THERMAL CONDUCTIVITY	W/mK	0.19	
FLAMMABILITY		Self-extinguishing	
POWER FACTOR			
DIELECTRIC STRENGTH	kV/mm	32-35	
VOLUME RESISTIVITY	ohm cm	$2.1-2.5 \times 10^{16}$	
PERMITIVITY	ohm cm	10-120	
ARC RESISTANCE	secs		
NUMBER OF PARTS			
CURING METHOD			
OPTICAL PROPERTIES		Transparent	
FRICTION			
MOULD SHRINKAGE	%	0.5-0.7	
WATER ABSORPTION	%	0.15	

SPECIFICATIONS

STANDARD NUMBER	AUTHORITY	TITLE

COMPANY SPECIFICATION:

ENVIRONMENT

RESISTANCE TO ATTACK FROM:

MINERAL ACIDS (WEAK)	Resistant
MINERAL ACIDS (STRONG)	Slow attack
ALKALIS (WEAK)	Limited resistance
ALKALIS (STRONG)	Attacked
SOLVENTS (CHLORINATED)	Soluble
OILS AND GREASES	Resistant
DETERGENTS	Fairly resistant
U.V. RESISTANCE	Stabalized grades
WEATHERABILITY	Slight discolour

OXYGEN PERMEABILITY $\quad$ 0.03 x 10^{-9} cm^3/cm^2 sec cm Hg/cm

NITROGEN PERMEABILITY $\quad$ 0.17 x 10^{-9} cm^3/cm^2 sec cm Hg/cm

CARBON DIOXIDE PERMEABILITY $\quad$ 1.04 x 10^{-9} cm^3/cm^2 sec cm Hg/cm

PROCESSING AND FORMING TECHNIQUES

Polycarbonates can be injection moulded, blow moulded, extruded and vacuum formed. Due to its high heat distortion temperature polycarbonate does not stick during normal machining

TYPICAL APPLICATIONS

Non breakable glazing material such as street lamp covers. Solar heating glazing Electrical capacitor dielectric, PCB connectors, electrical component covers. Safety helmets

JOINTING PROCESS

Adhesive bonding using epoxies. Welding by thermal or ultrasonic methods

YOUR SUPPLIER AND NOTES

SAFETY PRECAUTIONS

Impact properties of polycarbonate can be dramatically reduced by attack from some paint coatings and label adhesives

| | material data sheet | SHEET NUMBER | PL10 | A |

| FAMILY GROUP | PLASTICS | SUB-GROUP | THERMOPLASTICS | MATERIAL | POLYBUTYLENE |

GENERAL DESCRIPTION

Polybutylene is a polyolefin plastic which can withstand high temperatures. Possesses good toughness, high yield strength, high impact properties, high tear and puncture resistance. It has exceptional resistance to stress cracking. As pipe it is used in hot and cold water systems. Suitable for use with potable water with N.W.C. approval for pipe and fittings for hot and cold water applications.

CHEMICAL ANALYSIS OR COMPOSITION

PHYSICAL PROPERTIES

PROPERTY	UNITS	VALUE OR RANGE	COMMENTS
DENSITY	kg/m^3	910-930	
SHEAR STRENGTH	N/mm^2		
TENSILE STRENGTH	N/mm^2	23-34	
ELONGATION	%	300-380	
COMPRESSIVE STRENGTH	N/mm^2		
FLEXURAL STRENGTH	N/mm^2		
IMPACT STRENGTH	J		
TENSILE MODULUS	N/mm^2	180	
HARDNESS		60D	Shore
THERMAL COEFF. OF LINEAR EXPANSION	$°C^{-1}$	1.3×10^{-4}	
MIN./MAX. SERVICE TEMPERATURE	$°C$	-20/+104	
DEFLECTION TEMPERATURE	$°C$	55	at 1.81 N/mm^2
THERMAL CONDUCTIVITY	W/mK		
FLAMMABILITY	mm/min	25	
POWER FACTOR			
DIELECTRIC STRENGTH	kV/mm		
VOLUME RESISTIVITY	ohm cm		
PERMITIVITY	ohm cm		
ARC RESISTANCE	secs		
NUMBER OF PARTS			
CURING METHOD			
OPTICAL PROPERTIES		Translucent	
FRICTION			
MOULD SHRINKAGE	mm/mm	0.075/0.065	Unaged(mm) /Aged(mm)
WATER ABSORPTION	%	0.01-0.026	

SPECIFICATIONS

STANDARD NUMBER	AUTHORITY	TITLE
D3309	ASTM	Polybutylene plastic hot water distribution systems

COMPANY SPECIFICATION:

ENVIRONMENT

RESISTANCE TO ATTACK FROM:

MINERAL ACIDS (WEAK)	Resistant
MINERAL ACIDS (STRONG)	Attacked by oxidising acids
ALKALIS (WEAK)	Resistant
ALKALIS (STRONG)	Resistant
SOLVENTS (CHLORINATED)	Depends on solvent
OILS AND GREASES	Attacked
DETERGENTS	

U.V. RESISTANCE	Crazes
WEATHERABILITY	Improved with stabilisers

OXYGEN PERMEABILITY

NITROGEN PERMEABILITY

CARBON DIOXIDE PERMEABILITY

JOINTING PROCESS

Welded using hot plate system. Mechanically
gripping fittings used for pipe joints.
Adhesive bonding

SAFETY PRECAUTIONS

PROCESSING AND FORMING TECHNIQUES

Extrusion similar to polyethylene
but with modified dies
Machinability poor

TYPICAL APPLICATIONS

Hot and cold water pipes (up to 50mm)
Pipe fittings. Solar heating systems.
Film for containers and pallet wrapping.
Slurry conveyance in pipes.

YOUR SUPPLIER AND NOTES

BSRIA material data sheet

| FAMILY GROUP | PLASTICS | SUB-GROUP | THERMOPLASTICS | MATERIAL | HIGH DENSITY POLYETHYLENE (HDPE) |

GENERAL DESCRIPTION

HDPE has a density range 950/965 kg/m^3.   It is much stronger and stiffer than LDPE and can be used at higher temperatures. HDPE is not as tough at low temperatures but chemical resistance is improved. Gas permeability is less than compared to LDPE. HDPE has low water absorption and density together with high resistance to stress cracking. Suitable for use with potable water.

CHEMICAL ANALYSIS OR COMPOSITION

SYNONYM

Polythene, HDPE

PHYSICAL PROPERTIES

PROPERTY	UNITS	VALUE OR RANGE	COMMENTS
DENSITY	kg/m^3	950-965	
SHEAR STRENGTH	N/mm^2		
TENSILE STRENGTH	N/mm^2	21.4-38	
ELONGATION	%	20-1000	
COMPRESSIVE STRENGTH	N/mm^2	18.6-25	
FLEXURAL STRENGTH	N/mm^2		
IMPACT STRENGTH	J	0.5-19	Izod
TENSILE MODULUS	N/mm^2		
HARDNESS		D60-70	Shore
THERMAL COEFF. OF LINEAR EXPANSION	$^\circ$C^{-1}	11-13x10^{-5}	
MIN./MAX. SERVICE TEMPERATURE	$^\circ$C	-40/+100	
DEFLECTION TEMPERATURE	$^\circ$C	45-55	at 1.81 N/mm^2
THERMAL CONDUCTIVITY	W/mK	0.45-0.52	
FLAMMABILITY		Very slow	
POWER FACTOR		<0.0003	10^6 Hz
DIELECTRIC STRENGTH	kV/mm	>0.8	
VOLUME RESISTIVITY	ohm cm	10^{16}	
PERMITIVITY	ohm cm		
ARC RESISTANCE	secs		
NUMBER OF PARTS			
CURING METHOD			
OPTICAL PROPERTIES		Transparent to opaque	
FRICTION		0.2	
MOULD SHRINKAGE	%	1.5-3.0	
WATER ABSORPTION	%	<0.01	

SPECIFICATIONS

STANDARD NUMBER	AUTHORITY	TITLE
CP 312: Part 3	BSI	Plastic pipework (thermoplastic)
BS 3284	BSI	Cold water purposes
BS 3796	BSI	General purposes including chemical and food applications

COMPANY SPECIFICATION:

ENVIRONMENT

RESISTANCE TO ATTACK FROM:

MINERAL ACIDS (WEAK)	Resistant
MINERAL ACIDS (STRONG)	Slow attack by oxidising acids
ALKALIS (WEAK)	Resistant
ALKALIS (STRONG)	Resistant
SOLVENTS (CHLORINATED)	Swelling
OILS AND GREASES	Resistant
DETERGENTS	Resistant depends on grade

U.V. RESISTANCE	Crazes rapidly
WEATHERABILITY	Depends on grade

OXYGEN PERMEABILITY

NITROGEN PERMEABILITY

CARBON DIOXIDE PERMEABILITY

JOINTING PROCESS

Adhesive bonding using phenolic and silicone
adhesives
Welding

SAFETY PRECAUTIONS

To improve UV resistance use a black grade
or a weather inhibited grade in other colours

PROCESSING AND FORMING TECHNIQUES

Excellent processing by injection moulding, extrusion, blow moulding, rotational
moulding and thermoforming

Machinability - excellent

TYPICAL APPLICATIONS

Water and waste pipes and fittings.
Gas service pipework. Rainwater products.
Tanks. Corrosion protection cladding
for insulated buried mains. Blow moulded
containers. Solar heating - glazing,
pipes and fittings and flat plate collectors.

YOUR SUPPLIER AND NOTES

material data sheet	SHEET NUMBER	PL12	**A**

FAMILY GROUP	PLASTICS	SUB-GROUP	THERMOPLASTICS	MATERIAL	LOW DENSITY POLYETHYLENE LDPE

GENERAL DESCRIPTION

LDPE has a density range 918/930/kg/m³. It has good low temperature toughness, flexibility, high coefficient of expansion(10xABS) and good chemical resistance, though detergents can cause stress cracking. Max service temperature for LDPE is lower than HDPE. Suitable for use with potable water.

CHEMICAL ANALYSIS OR COMPOSITION

SYNONYM

Polythene, LDPE

PHYSICAL PROPERTIES

PROPERTY	UNITS	VALUE OR RANGE	COMMENTS
DENSITY	kg/m^3	918-930	
SHEAR STRENGTH	N/mm^2		
TENSILE STRENGTH	N/mm^2	4-16	
ELONGATION	%	90-800	
COMPRESSIVE STRENGTH	N/mm^2	-	
FLEXURAL STRENGTH	N/mm^2		
IMPACT STRENGTH	J	No break	Izod
TENSILE MODULUS	N/mm^2	140-190	
HARDNESS		41-46	Shore
THERMAL COEFF. OF LINEAR EXPANSION	$°C^{-1}$	$16-18 \times 10^{-5}$	
MIN./MAX. SERVICE TEMPERATURE	$°C$	-40/+90	
DEFLECTION TEMPERATURE	$°C$	30-40	at 1.81 N/mm^2
THERMAL CONDUCTIVITY	W/mK	0.33	
FLAMMABILITY		Very slow	
POWER FACTOR		0.0005	10^6 Hz
DIELECTRIC STRENGTH	kV/mm	0.46-0.70	
VOLUME RESISTIVITY	ohm cm	10^{16}	
PERMITIVITY	ohm cm		
ARC RESISTANCE	secs	135-160	
NUMBER OF PARTS			
CURING METHOD			
OPTICAL PROPERTIES		Transparent to opaque	
FRICTION			
MOULD SHRINKAGE	%	1.5-3.5	
WATER ABSORPTION	%	0.015	

 **BSRIA** material
data sheet

SPECIFICATIONS

STANDARD NUMBER	AUTHORITY	TITLE
CP312: Part 3	BSI	Plastic pipework (thermoplastic)
BS 1972	BSI	Cold water services
BS 1973	BSI	General purposes including chemical and food industries applications

COMPANY SPECIFICATION:

ENVIRONMENT

RESISTANCE TO ATTACK FROM:

MINERAL ACIDS (WEAK)	Resistant
MINERAL ACIDS (STRONG)	Attacked by oxidising acids
ALKALIS (WEAK)	Resistant
ALKALIS (STRONG)	Resistant
SOLVENTS (CHLORINATED)	Resistant below 60°C
OILS AND GREASES	Resistant
DETERGENTS	Fairly resistant

U.V. RESISTANCE	Crazes rapidly
WEATHERABILITY	Depends on grade

OXYGEN PERMEABILITY 9×10^{-11} cm^3/cm^2 sec cm Hg/cm

NITROGEN PERMEABILITY 24×10^{-11} cm^3/cm^2 sec cm Hg/cm

CARBON DIOXIDE PERMEABILITY 130×10^{-11} cm^3/cm^2 sec cm Hg/cm

JOINTING PROCESS

Adhesive bonding using phenolic adhesives.

Welding

PROCESSING AND FORMING TECHNIQUES

Excellent processing by injection moulding, extrusion, blow moulding, rotational moulding and thermoforming

Machinability - good

TYPICAL APPLICATIONS

Pipes and pipe fittings for water and waste disposal. Low loss electrical wire covering. Blow and rotational moulded containers.

Temporary drainage hose

Solar heating systems - pipes and fittings and cold water storage

YOUR SUPPLIER AND NOTES

SAFETY PRECAUTIONS

BSRIA material data sheet

| FAMILY GROUP | PLASTICS | SUB-GROUP | THERMOPLASTICS | MATERIAL | CROSSLINKED POLYETHYLENE (XLP) |

GENERAL DESCRIPTION

XLP is a modified polyethylene with improved mechanical and thermal properties. XLP tubing has NWC approval for use up to 90°C at 2 bar for hot water services in specific sizes.

CHEMICAL ANALYSIS OR COMPOSITION

Polyethylene compounds with modifications.

SYNONYM

XLP, PEX

PHYSICAL PROPERTIES

PROPERTY	UNITS	VALUE OR RANGE	COMMENTS
DENSITY	kg/m^3	936-955	
SHEAR STRENGTH	N/mm^2		
TENSILE STRENGTH	N/mm^2	16-30 min	
ELONGATION	%	300 min	At break 20°C
COMPRESSIVE STRENGTH	N/mm^2	15-38 min	
FLEXURAL STRENGTH	N/mm^2		
IMPACT STRENGTH	J		No fracture
TENSILE MODULUS	N/mm^2	1700 min	
HARDNESS			
THERMAL COEFF. OF LINEAR EXPANSION	$°C^{-1}$	17×10^{-5}	
MIN./MAX. SERVICE TEMPERATURE	°C	-100/95	Intermittant
DEFLECTION TEMPERATURE	°C		
THERMAL CONDUCTIVITY	W/mK	0.38	
FLAMMABILITY			
POWER FACTOR			
DIELECTRIC STRENGTH	kV/mm	21-23	
VOLUME RESISTIVITY	ohm cm		
PERMITIVITY	ohm cm		
ARC RESISTANCE	secs		
NUMBER OF PARTS			
CURING METHOD			
OPTICAL PROPERTIES			
FRICTION		0.08-0.1	
MOULD SHRINKAGE			
WATER ABSORPTION	mg/4d	0.01	

SPECIFICATIONS

STANDARD NUMBER	AUTHORITY	TITLE

COMPANY SPECIFICATION:

ENVIRONMENT

RESISTANCE TO ATTACK FROM:

MINERAL ACIDS (WEAK)

MINERAL ACIDS (STRONG)

ALKALIS (WEAK)

ALKALIS (STRONG)

SOLVENTS (CHLORINATED)

OILS AND GREASES

DETERGENTS

U.V. RESISTANCE   Poor

WEATHERABILITY

OXYGEN PERMEABILITY $0.8\text{-}3.0 \times 10^{-13}$ gm/m^{2}s bar

NITROGEN PERMEABILITY

CARBON DIOXIDE PERMEABILITY

PROCESSING AND FORMING TECHNIQUES

Extrusion + modification process

TYPICAL APPLICATIONS

Tubing for:-
Cold and hot water services
Heating systems (radiator and underfloor)
Electrical cable covering

JOINTING PROCESS

Pipes joined using compression fittings to
BS 864 part 2 incorporating internal support
liners.

YOUR SUPPLIER AND NOTES

SAFETY PRECAUTIONS

Known to absorb oxygen into the system
with possible corrosion of ferrous components in a system.

 **material data sheet**

SHEET NUMBER	PL14	A

FAMILY GROUP	PLASTICS	SUB-GROUP	THERMOPLASTICS	MATERIAL	POLYPROPYLENE

GENERAL DESCRIPTION

Polypropylene combines excellent chemical resistance, fatigue resistance and electrical insulation properties with good temperature resistance and useful values of strength and stiffness and impact resistance at low temperatures. It is attacked by strong oxidising agents.

Available as a high impact plastics material. Suitable for use with potable water.

CHEMICAL ANALYSIS OR COMPOSITION

PHYSICAL PROPERTIES

PROPERTY	UNITS	VALUE OR RANGE	COMMENTS
DENSITY	kg/m^3	902-906	
SHEAR STRENGTH	N/mm^2		
TENSILE STRENGTH	N/mm^2	20-38	
ELONGATION	%	700-1100	
COMPRESSIVE STRENGTH	N/mm^2	31-55	
FLEXURAL STRENGTH	N/mm^2	34.5-55	
IMPACT STRENGTH	J	0.5-16	Izod
TENSILE MODULUS	N/mm^2	1170-1550	
HARDNESS		R50-110	Rockwell
THERMAL COEFF. OF LINEAR EXPANSION	$^oC^{-1}$	11×10^{-5}	
MIN./MAX. SERVICE TEMPERATURE	^oC	-10/+80	
DEFLECTION TEMPERATURE	^oC	55-60	at 1.81 N/mm^2
THERMAL CONDUCTIVITY	W/mK	0.12	
FLAMMABILITY		Slowly with flaring drops	
ELECTRICAL POWER FACTOR	$10^6 H_2$	$< 0.0002-0.0004$	
DIELECTRIC STRENGTH	kV/mm	> 0.80	
VOLUME RESISTIVITY	ohm cm	$> 10^{16}$	
PERMITIVITY	ohm cm	2.0	At 1M Hz
ARC RESISTANCE	secs	136-185	
NUMBER OF PARTS			
CURING METHOD			
OPTICAL PROPERTIES		Opaque	
FRICTION			
MOULD SHRINKAGE		1.0-3.0	
WATER ABSORPTION	%	0.02	

SPECIFICATIONS

STANDARD NUMBER	AUTHORITY	TITLE
CP 312 Part 1	BSI	Plastics pipework (thermoplastic)
BS 4991	BSI	Propylene copolymer pressure pipe
BS 5254	BSI	Polypropylene waste pipe and fittings (external diameter 34.6 mm, 41.0 mm 54.1 mm)
BS 5255	BSI	Plastic waste pipes and fittings

COMPANY SPECIFICATION:

ENVIRONMENT

RESISTANCE TO ATTACK FROM:

MINERAL ACIDS (WEAK)	Resistant
MINERAL ACIDS (STRONG)	Slow attack by Oxidising acids
ALKALIS (WEAK)	Resistant
ALKALIS (STRONG)	Resistant
SOLVENTS (CHLORINATED)	Resistant below 80ºC
OILS AND GREASES	Resistant below 60ºC
DETERGENTS	Resistant

U.V. RESISTANCE	Poor
WEATHERABILITY	Improved with black additive

OXYGEN PERMEABILITY

NITROGEN PERMEABILITY

CARBON DIOXIDE PERMEABILITY

JOINTING PROCESS

Hot gas welding with filler rod

Hot tool welded

Induction welded

SAFETY PRECAUTIONS

PROCESSING AND FORMING TECHNIQUES

Polypropylene can be injection moulded, extruded, blow moulded and thermoformed.

TYPICAL APPLICATIONS

Pressure pipes for water and gas.

Valve trim.

Plastic radiators.

Tanks, W.C. cisterns and ball floats

Capacitor dielectrics and cable insulation.

Thin wall containers. Blow moulded components. Textile and carpeting materials. Consumer goods and appliance components.

Hinges

Solar heating

Snap fitting pipe supports

YOUR SUPPLIER AND NOTES

 **material data sheet**

SHEET NUMBER	PL15	**A**

FAMILY GROUP	PLASTICS	SUB-GROUP	THERMOPLASTICS	MATERIAL	P.T.F.E.

GENERAL DESCRIPTION

The properties of PTFE are unique. PTFE resists all common aggressive environments, has an exceptionally low coefficient of friction, has first class electrical properties, can be used continuously at $250^{\circ}C$ and is tough. It can be processed by sintering techniques with complicated shapes machined. Suitable for use with potable water.

CHEMICAL ANALYSIS OR COMPOSITION

PHYSICAL PROPERTIES

PROPERTY	UNITS	VALUE OR RANGE	COMMENTS
DENSITY	kg/m^3	2140-2200	
SHEAR STRENGTH	N/mm^2		
TENSILE STRENGTH	N/mm^2	17-34	
ELONGATION	%	200-600	
COMPRESSIVE STRENGTH	N/mm^2	11.7	
FLEXURAL STRENGTH	N/mm^2		
IMPACT STRENGTH	J	3.4-5.4	Izod
TENSILE MODULUS	N/mm^2	400	
HARDNESS			
THERMAL COEFF. OF LINEAR EXPANSION	$^{\circ}C^{-1}$	10×10^{-5}	
MIN./MAX. SERVICE TEMPERATURE	$^{\circ}C$	-260/+250	
DEFLECTION TEMPERATURE	$^{\circ}C$	120-140	at 1.81 N/mm^2
THERMAL CONDUCTIVITY	W/mK	0.25	
FLAMMABILITY		None	
ELECTRICAL POWER FACTOR		0.002	10^6 Hz
DIELECTRIC STRENGTH	kV/mm	0.40-0.60	
VOLUME RESISTIVITY	ohm cm	10^{19}	
PERMITIVITY	ohm cm	2.0	At 1M Hz
ARC RESISTANCE	secs	200	
NUMBER OF PARTS			
CURING METHOD			
OPTICAL PROPERTIES		Opaque	
FRICTION		0.02-0.15	
MOULD SHRINKAGE		5.0-10.0	
WATER ABSORPTION		None	

SPECIFICATIONS

STANDARD NUMBER	AUTHORITY	TITLE

COMPANY SPECIFICATION:

ENVIRONMENT

RESISTANCE TO ATTACK FROM:

MINERAL ACIDS (WEAK)	Resistant
MINERAL ACIDS (STRONG)	Resistant
ALKALIS (WEAK)	Resistant
ALKALIS (STRONG)	Resistant
SOLVENTS (CHLORINATED)	Resistant
OILS AND GREASES	Resistant
DETERGENTS	Resistant

U.V. RESISTANCE	Good
WEATHERABILITY	Good

OXYGEN PERMEABILITY

NITROGEN PERMEABILITY

CARBON DIOXIDE PERMEABILITY

JOINTING PROCESS

Adhesive bonding following pretreatment by etching.

SAFETY PRECAUTIONS

During machining operators must not smoke.

PROCESSING AND FORMING TECHNIQUES

PTFE is formed by sintering into finished articles or simple shapes and then finished by machining. Tape can be manufacturered by non-sintering techniques

TYPICAL APPLICATIONS

Gaskets seals, thread sealing tapes and flexible bellows in pipe runs. Dry bearing materials such as sliding pipe supports. High frequency and high temperature insulation of electrical cables.

Coatings and linings for hoppers and chutes to reduce friction. Non stick applications. Tube for aggressive fluids. Heat exchanger bundles.

YOUR SUPPLIER AND NOTES

| material data sheet | | SHEET NUMBER | PL16 | A |

| FAMILY GROUP | PLASTICS | SUB-GROUP | THERMOPLASTIC | MATERIAL | POLYVINYL CHLORIDE PLASTICISED |

GENERAL DESCRIPTION

Plasticised PVC compounds are usually much more flexible than rigid compounds. The degree of flexibility and changes in other properties depend markedly on the nature and concentration of the plasticiser used. Suitable for use with potable water.

CHEMICAL ANALYSIS OR COMPOSITION

SYNONYM

PVC

PHYSICAL PROPERTIES

PROPERTY	UNITS	VALUE OR RANGE	COMMENTS
DENSITY	kg/m^3	1200-1700	
SHEAR STRENGTH	N/mm^2		
TENSILE STRENGTH	N/mm^2	10-24	
ELONGATION	%	105-400	
COMPRESSIVE STRENGTH	N/mm^2	6.2-11.7	
FLEXURAL STRENGTH	N/mm^2		
IMPACT STRENGTH	J		Varies depending on % of plasticiser
TENSILE MODULUS	N/mm^2		
HARDNESS		30-90R	Rockwell
THERMAL COEFF. OF LINEAR EXPANSION	$°C^{-1}$	$7-25 \times 10^{-5}$	
MIN./MAX. SERVICE TEMPERATURE	$°C$	-260/+70	
DEFLECTION TEMPERATURE	$°C$		
THERMAL CONDUCTIVITY	W/mK	0.12-0.17	
FLAMMABILITY		Self-extinguishing	
ELECTRICAL POWER FACTOR			
DIELECTRIC STRENGTH	kV/mm	14-18	
VOLUME RESISTIVITY	ohm cm	$10^{11}-10^{15}$	
PERMITIVITY	ohm cm		
ARC RESISTANCE	secs		
NUMBER OF PARTS			
CURING METHOD			
OPTICAL PROPERTIES		Transparent to opaque	
FRICTION			
MOULD SHRINKAGE	%	1.5-3.0	
WATER ABSORPTION	%	0.15-0.75	

531

SPECIFICATIONS

STANDARD NUMBER	AUTHORITY	TITLE

COMPANY SPECIFICATION:

ENVIRONMENT

RESISTANCE TO ATTACK FROM:

MINERAL ACIDS (WEAK)	Resistant
MINERAL ACIDS (STRONG)	Slight attack
ALKALIS (WEAK)	Resistant
ALKALIS (STRONG)	Resistant
SOLVENTS (CHLORINATED)	Soluble
OILS AND GREASES	Resistant
DETERGENTS	Slight attack

U.V. RESISTANCE	Slight
WEATHERABILITY	Good

OXYGEN PERMEABILITY
NITROGEN PERMEABILITY
CARBON DIOXIDE PERMEABILITY

JOINTING PROCESS

Solvent welding
Adhesive bonding using acrylic, neoprene
rubber, phenolic neoprene, phenolic-
nitrile and phenolic-vinyl.
Thermal bonding using hot gas welding
and filler rods. Mechanical jointing.

SAFETY PRECAUTIONS

Migration of plasticiser could result
in brittle failure of electrical cable
insulation

PROCESSING AND FORMING TECHNIQUES

Flexible PVC may be callendered,
extruded, blow moulded, injection
moulded and vacuum formed

Moulding quality - good

TYPICAL APPLICATIONS

Insulation and sheathing of cables and
wires.
Grommets and end connectors. Floor
covering materials. Adhesives and
pressure sensitive tapes. Flexible
duct connectors. Handwheels. Sheathed
metal tube. Tank linings

YOUR SUPPLIER AND NOTES

SHEET NUMBER	PL17		**A**

FAMILY GROUP	PLASTICS	SUB-GROUP	THERMOPLASTICS	MATERIAL	POLYVINYL CHLORIDE RIGID

GENERAL DESCRIPTION

Rigid (unplasticised) PVC is hard, tough, strong and stiff, has good chemical and weathering resistance, is self extinguishing, and can be highly transparent. The surface is scuff and abrasion resistant. Rigid PVC is resistant to most inorganic chemicals in solution. Can be used with potable water.

CHEMICAL ANALYSIS OR COMPOSITION

SYNONYM

UPVC

PHYSICAL PROPERTIES

PROPERTY	UNITS	VALUE OR RANGE	COMMENTS
DENSITY	kg/m^3	1200-1500	
SHEAR STRENGTH	N/mm^2		
TENSILE STRENGTH	N/mm^2	35-62	
ELONGATION	%	2-140	
COMPRESSIVE STRENGTH	N/mm^2	55-90	
FLEXURAL STRENGTH	N/mm^2		
IMPACT STRENGTH	J	0.7-27	Izod
TENSILE MODULUS	N/mm^2	2513-4140	
HARDNESS		115R	Rockwell
THERMAL COEFF. OF LINEAR EXPANSION	$°C^{-1}$	$5-18.5 \times 10^{-5}$	
MIN./MAX. SERVICE TEMPERATURE	$°C$	0/+60	
DEFLECTION TEMPERATURE	$°C$	57-64	at 1.81 N/mm^2
THERMAL CONDUCTIVITY	W/mK	0.12-0.17	
FLAMMABILITY		Self-extinguishing	
ELECTRICAL POWER FACTOR		0.006-0.02	10^6Hz
DIELECTRIC STRENGTH	kV/mm	$>10^{14}$	
VOLUME RESISTIVITY	ohm cm		
PERMITIVITY	ohm cm		
ARC RESISTANCE	secs	60-80	
NUMBER OF PARTS			
CURING METHOD			
OPTICAL PROPERTIES		Transparent to opaque	
FRICTION			
MOULD SHRINKAGE	%	0.2-0.4	
WATER ABSORPTION	%	0.04-0.4	

SPECIFICATIONS

STANDARD NUMBER	AUTHORITY	TITLE
CP312: Part 1	BSI	Plastics pipework (thermoplastic)
BS3168	BSI	Rigid PVC extrusion and moulding components
BS3505	BSI	Unplastized PVC for cold water service
BS3506	BSI	Unplastized PVC for industrial purposes
BS4346	BSI	Joints for unplastized PVC pressure pipes
BS4514	BSI	Unplasticized PVC soil and ventilating pipes
BS4576	BSI	Rain water goods
BS4660	BSI	PVC underground drainpipe and fittings
BS5255	BSI	Plastic waste pipe and fittings
BS5481	BSI	PVC pipe and fittings for gravity sewers

COMPANY SPECIFICATION:

ENVIRONMENT

RESISTANCE TO ATTACK FROM:

MINERAL ACIDS (WEAK)	Resistant
MINERAL ACIDS (STRONG)	Slight attack
ALKALIS (WEAK)	Resistant
ALKALIS (STRONG)	Resistant
SOLVENTS (CHLORINATED)	Soluble
OILS AND GREASES	Resistant
DETERGENTS	Resistant

U.V. RESISTANCE	Adversely affected
WEATHERABILITY	Excellent

OXYGEN PERMEABILITY $3.4.10^{-11}$ cm^3/cm^2 sec cm Hg/cm

NITROGEN PERMEABILITY $1.2.10^{-11}$ cm^3/cm^2 sec cm Hg/cm

CARBON DIOXIDE PERMEABILITY $1.6.10^{-11}$ cm^3/cm^2 sec cm Hg/cm

JOINTING PROCESS

Solvent welding
Mechanical systems
Adhesive bonding using acrylic, neoprene rubber,
phenolic - neoprene, phenolic-nitrile, and
phenolic-vinyl. Thermal bonding using hot gas
welding and filler rods

SAFETY PRECAUTIONS

PROCESSING AND FORMING TECHNIQUES

Rigid PVC can be formed by extrusion,
injection mould, blow moulding, compression moulding and vacuum forming
Machinability - excellent
Moulding quality - fair to good

TYPICAL APPLICATIONS

Pipes, pipe fittings and valves for water
and gas services and mains, drains, waste
vent, house sewer, solar systems and
conduit piping. Industrial process piping
and irrigation systems. Wall cladding.
Fume extraction ducting. Electrical
conduit. Rainwater systems. Cold water
storage tanks.

YOUR SUPPLIER AND NOTES

material data sheet		SHEET NUMBER PL18	A

FAMILY GROUP	PLASTICS	SUB-GROUP THERMOPLASTICS	MATERIAL CHLORINATED P.V.C.

GENERAL DESCRIPTION

CPVC is a modified rigid PVC compound with improved mechanical and thermal properties. Pipe can be used for hot and cold water services. CPVC provides a corrosion resistant pipe with little scale build up.

CHEMICAL ANALYSIS OR COMPOSITION

SYNONYM

CPVC

PHYSICAL PROPERTIES

PROPERTY	UNITS	VALUE OR RANGE	COMMENTS
DENSITY	kg/m^3	1540	
SHEAR STRENGTH	N/mm^2		
TENSILE STRENGTH	N/mm^2	34.5 min	ASTMD1784
ELONGATION	%	8	
COMPRESSIVE STRENGTH	N/mm^2	107 min	
FLEXURAL STRENGTH	N/mm^2	100 min	
IMPACT STRENGTH	J	34.7	J/m of notch
TENSILE MODULUS	N/mm^2	1930 min	ASTMD1784
HARDNESS		117-119	Rockwell R
THERMAL COEFF. OF LINEAR EXPANSION	$^oC^{-1}$	$8x10^{-5}$	
MIN./MAX. SERVICE TEMPERATURE	^oC		
DEFLECTION TEMPERATURE	^oC	55	at 1.81 N/mm^2
THERMAL CONDUCTIVITY	W/mK	$16.76x10^{-2}$	
FLAMMABILITY		Self-extinguishing	
DIELECTRIC STRENGTH	kV/mm	39	25^oC @ 65% RH
VOLUME RESISTIVITY	ohm cm	$6x10^{15}$	20^oC @ 65% RH
PERMITIVITY	ohm cm		
ARC RESISTANCE	secs		
NUMBER OF PARTS			
CURING METHOD			
OPTICAL PROPERTIES			
FRICTION			
MOULD SHRINKAGE			
WATER ABSORPTION	%	0.11	24 hours

SPECIFICATIONS

STANDARD NUMBER	AUTHORITY	TITLE
D 1784 - 75	ASTM	Chlorinated PVC compounds
D 2846 - 73	ASTM	CPVC Plastic hot water distribution

COMPANY SPECIFICATION:

ENVIRONMENT

RESISTANCE TO ATTACK FROM:

MINERAL ACIDS (WEAK)	Resistant
MINERAL ACIDS (STRONG)	Attacked by nitric & sulphuric acids
ALKALIS (WEAK)	Resistant
ALKALIS (STRONG)	Resistant
SOLVENTS (CHLORINATED)	Soluble in some solvents
OILS AND GREASES	Resistant
DETERGENTS	Resistant

U.V. RESISTANCE

WEATHERABILITY

OXYGEN PERMEABILITY

NITROGEN PERMEABILITY

CARBON DIOXIDE PERMEABILITY

JOINTING PROCESS

Solvent welding of socket fittings to pipe
using suppliers recommended materials.
Do not remove surplus cement
Hot air welding

SAFETY PRECAUTIONS

Do not use solvent solutions in restricted
spaces

PROCESSING AND FORMING TECHNIQUES

Extrusion
Moulding
Thermoforming
Calendering

TYPICAL APPLICATIONS

Pipes and fittings used for hot and
cold water services

Valves

YOUR SUPPLIER AND NOTES

material data sheet		SHEET NUMBER	PL19	A

FAMILY GROUP	PLASTICS	SUB-GROUP	THERMOSETS	MATERIAL	EPOXIDE RESINS

GENERAL DESCRIPTION

Epoxides are more expensive than unsaturated polyesters and are tough, have extremely good resistance to alkalis, adhere well to many materials and shrink little during curing at ambient temperature without pressure. Electrical properties are excellent with good mechanical properties. Epoxides are a versatile material capable of meeting requirements for structural and coating applications. On curing no volatiles are released.

CHEMICAL ANALYSIS OR COMPOSITION

PHYSICAL PROPERTIES

PROPERTY	UNITS	VALUE OR RANGE	COMMENTS
DENSITY	kg/m^3	1110-1400	
SHEAR STRENGTH	N/mm^2		
TENSILE STRENGTH	N/mm^2	27-90	
ELONGATION	%	2-6	
COMPRESSIVE STRENGTH	N/mm^2	103-172	
FLEXURAL STRENGTH	N/mm^2	82-110	
IMPACT STRENGTH	J	0.4-0.9	
TENSILE MODULUS	N/mm^2	1500-3600	
HARDNESS		M100-M120	Rockwell
THERMAL COEFF. OF LINEAR EXPANSION	$°C^{-1}$	$4.5-6.5 \times 10^{-5}$	
MIN./MAX. SERVICE TEMPERATURE	$°C$	/140(200)	Continuous (intermittant)
DEFLECTION TEMPERATURE	$°C$	45	at 1.81 N/mm^2
THERMAL CONDUCTIVITY	W/mK	0.17-0.21	
FLAMMABILITY		Slow	
POWER FACTOR			
DIELECTRIC STRENGTH	kV/mm		
VOLUME RESISTIVITY	ohm cm	$10^{12}-10^{17}$	
PERMITIVITY	ohm cm		
ARC RESISTANCE	secs	45-120	
NUMBER OF PARTS			
CURING METHOD			
OPTICAL PROPERTIES		Transparent	
FRICTION			
MOULD SHRINKAGE			
WATER ABSORPTION	%	0.08-0.15	

SPECIFICATIONS

STANDARD NUMBER	AUTHORITY	TITLE

COMPANY SPECIFICATION:

ENVIRONMENT

RESISTANCE TO ATTACK FROM:

MINERAL ACIDS (WEAK)	Resistant
MINERAL ACIDS (STRONG)	Attacked
ALKALIS (WEAK)	Resistant
ALKALIS (STRONG)	Slight attack
SOLVENTS (CHLORINATED)	Fairly resistant
OILS AND GREASES	Resistant
DETERGENTS	Resistant

U.V. RESISTANCE	Good - slight chalking
WEATHERABILITY	

OXYGEN PERMEABILITY

NITROGEN PERMEABILITY

CARBON DIOXIDE PERMEABILITY

JOINTING PROCESS

Adhesive bonding difficult. Some success can be obtained by abrading the surfaces.

SAFETY PRECAUTIONS

Hardeners can be dermetitic

PROCESSING AND FORMING TECHNIQUES

Epoxides are used as castings or as a potting media.

For other systems see Reinforced Plastics

TYPICAL APPLICATIONS

Many adhesive types based on epoxides Seamless floor covering. Anti-corrosion protection of concrete, wood and metals. High grade electrical insulators. Impregnating and potting agent. Resin base for impregnated glass fibre materials.

YOUR SUPPLIER AND NOTES

 **material data sheet**

| FAMILY GROUP | PLASTICS | SUB-GROUP | THERMOSETS | MATERIAL | PHENOLIC |

GENERAL DESCRIPTION

Phenolics are strong but brittle, good electrical insulators and have a maximum normal service temperature around
+150°C. Phenolics are destroyed by strong alkalis and oxidising agents. Dark colours are supplied. Fibrous
fillers can be incorporated to reduce costs and improve impact strength and electrical properties.

CHEMICAL ANALYSIS OR COMPOSITION

PHYSICAL PROPERTIES

PROPERTY	UNITS	VALUE OR RANGE	COMMENTS
DENSITY	kg/m^3	1240-1320	
SHEAR STRENGTH	N/mm^2		
TENSILE STRENGTH	N/mm^2	48-55	
ELONGATION	%	1.0-1.5	
COMPRESSIVE STRENGTH	N/mm^2	69-207	
FLEXURAL STRENGTH	N/mm^2		
IMPACT STRENGTH	J		
TENSILE MODULUS	N/mm^2		
HARDNESS		M-24-M128	Rockwell
THERMAL COEFF. OF LINEAR EXPANSION	$°C^{-1}$	$2.5-6.0 \ 10^{-5}$	
MIN./MAX. SERVICE TEMPERATURE	°C	/150	
DEFLECTION TEMPERATURE	°C	115-126	at 1.81 N/mm^2
THERMAL CONDUCTIVITY	W/mK	0.15	
FLAMMABILITY		Very low	
POWER FACTOR			
DIELECTRIC STRENGTH	kV/mm		
VOLUME RESISTIVITY	ohm cm	$10^{11}-10^{12}$	
PERMITIVITY	ohm cm		
ARC RESISTANCE		Tracks	
NUMBER OF PARTS			
CURING METHOD			
OPTICAL PROPERTIES			
FRICTION			
MOULD SHRINKAGE			
WATER ABSORPTION	%	0.1-0.2	

SPECIFICATIONS

STANDARD NUMBER	AUTHORITY	TITLE

COMPANY SPECIFICATION:

ENVIRONMENT

RESISTANCE TO ATTACK FROM:

MINERAL ACIDS (WEAK)	Slight attack
MINERAL ACIDS (STRONG)	Attacked
ALKALIS (WEAK)	Slight attack
ALKALIS (STRONG)	Decomposes
SOLVENTS (CHLORINATED)	
OILS AND GREASES	
DETERGENTS	

U.V. RESISTANCE	Surface darkens
WEATHERABILITY	

OXYGEN PERMEABILITY	
NITROGEN PERMEABILITY	9.5×10^{-12} cm^3/cm^2 sec cm Hg/cm
CARBON DIOXIDE PERMEABILITY	

JOINTING PROCESS

Adhesive bonding after abrading the surface

PROCESSING AND FORMING TECHNIQUES

See Reinforced Plastics for more general processing and usage

TYPICAL APPLICATIONS

Adhesives

Laminations and impregnations.
Electrical plugs and sockets
Moulded handles, knobs etc
Bottle tops and closures
Baked enamels.

YOUR SUPPLIER AND NOTES

SAFETY PRECAUTIONS

| | | SHEET NUMBER | PL21 | A |

| FAMILY GROUP | PLASTICS | SUB-GROUP | THERMOSETS | MATERIAL | POLYESTER |

GENERAL DESCRIPTION

Unsaturated polyesters offer good resistance to U.V., water, acids, alkalis and many organic solvents and they are fairly good electrical insulators. The cure is exothermic with the generation of high internal temperatures in large masses causing cracking. Polyesters are mainly used as the resin in glass reinforced plastics.

CHEMICAL ANALYSIS OR COMPOSITION

PHYSICAL PROPERTIES

PROPERTY	UNITS	VALUE OR RANGE	COMMENTS
DENSITY	kg/m^3	1100-1460	
SHEAR STRENGTH	N/mm^2		
TENSILE STRENGTH	N/mm^2	5.5-90	
ELONGATION	%	2	At break
COMPRESSIVE STRENGTH	N/mm^2	90-250	
FLEXURAL STRENGTH	N/mm^2	88	
IMPACT STRENGTH	J		
TENSILE MODULUS	N/mm^2	2070-4413	
HARDNESS			
THERMAL COEFF. OF LINEAR EXPANSION	$^oC^{-1}$	$5.5-10 \times 10^{-5}$	
MIN./MAX. SERVICE TEMPERATURE	^oC		
DEFLECTION TEMPERATURE	^oC	45-78	at 1.81 N/mm^2
THERMAL CONDUCTIVITY	W/mK	0.19	
FLAMMABILITY		17-50	Retardant additives 5 mm/min
POWER FACTOR			
DIELECTRIC STRENGTH	kV/mm		
VOLUME RESISTIVITY	ohm cm	10^{15}	
PERMITIVITY	ohm cm		
ARC RESISTANCE	secs	125	
NUMBER OF PARTS			
CURING METHOD			
OPTICAL PROPERTIES		Transparent to opaque	
FRICTION			
MOULD SHRINKAGE	in/in		
WATER ABSORPTION	%	0.15-0.6	

SPECIFICATIONS

STANDARD NUMBER	AUTHORITY	TITLE

COMPANY SPECIFICATION:

ENVIRONMENT

RESISTANCE TO ATTACK FROM:

MINERAL ACIDS (WEAK)	Resistant
MINERAL ACIDS (STRONG)	Fairly resistant
ALKALIS (WEAK)	Attacked
ALKALIS (STRONG)	Attacked
SOLVENTS (CHLORINATED)	Attacked
OILS AND GREASES	Resistant
DETERGENTS	Resistant

U.V. RESISTANCE	Yellows slightly
WEATHERABILITY	Good

OXYGEN PERMEABILITY

NITROGEN PERMEABILITY

CARBON DIOXIDE PERMEABILITY

PROCESSING AND FORMING TECHNIQUES

Polyester resins are cast or coated.
For other methods, see Reinforced Plastics.

TYPICAL APPLICATIONS

Coating materials such as floors
Potting and encapsulation
Thread locking compounds

JOINTING PROCESS

Adhesive bonding after abrading the surface

YOUR SUPPLIER AND NOTES

SAFETY PRECAUTIONS

Hardeners can be dermetitic

	material data sheet	SHEET NUMBER	PL22	A

FAMILY GROUP	PLASTICS	SUB-GROUP	CELLULAR	MATERIAL	POLYURETHANE-FLEXIBLE

GENERAL DESCRIPTION

Flexible polyurethanes are open cell foams. Their flexible and load bearing properties are exploited in such industries as upholstery. They exhibit high water absorption.

CHEMICAL ANALYSIS OR COMPOSITION

PHYSICAL PROPERTIES

PROPERTY	UNITS	VALUE OR RANGE	COMMENTS
DENSITY	kg/m^3	12-50	
SHEAR STRENGTH	N/mm^2		
TENSILE STRENGTH	N/mm^2	1.3×10^{-1}	
ELONGATION	%	400	At break
COMPRESSIVE STRENGTH	N/mm^2	2.1×10^{-1}	
FLEXURAL STRENGTH	N/mm^2		
IMPACT STRENGTH	J		
TENSILE MODULUS	N/mm^2		
HARDNESS			
THERMAL COEFF. OF LINEAR EXPANSION	$^oC^{-1}$		
MIN./MAX. SERVICE TEMPERATURE	^oC	/110	
DEFLECTION TEMPERATURE	^oC		
THERMAL CONDUCTIVITY	W/mK		
FLAMMABILITY			
DIELECTRIC STRENGTH	kV/mm		
VOLUME RESISTIVITY	ohm cm		
PERMITIVITY	ohm cm		
ARC RESISTANCE	secs		
NUMBER OF PARTS			
CURING METHOD			
OPTICAL PROPERTIES			
FRICTION			
MOULD SHRINKAGE			
WATER ABSORPTION	%	90	By volume

543

BSRIA material data sheet

SPECIFICATIONS

STANDARD NUMBER	AUTHORITY	TITLE

COMPANY SPECIFICATION:

ENVIRONMENT

RESISTANCE TO ATTACK FROM:

MINERAL ACIDS (WEAK)

MINERAL ACIDS (STRONG)

ALKALIS (WEAK)

ALKALIS (STRONG)

SOLVENTS (CHLORINATED)

OILS AND GREASES

DETERGENTS

U.V. RESISTANCE   Yellowing occurs

WEATHERABILITY

OXYGEN PERMEABILITY

NITROGEN PERMEABILITY

CARBON DIOXIDE PERMEABILITY

JOINTING PROCESS
   Thermal methods
   Adhesive bonding

SAFETY PRECAUTIONS

PROCESSING AND FORMING TECHNIQUES

Foamed to required shape and varying density. Foam are formed by mixing two components which create a chemical reaction. The exothermic reaction aids curing.

TYPICAL APPLICATIONS

Cushioning, upholstery, underlays light weight insulation for clothing, protective packing and vibration insulation

YOUR SUPPLIER AND NOTES

material data sheet

| FAMILY GROUP | PLASTICS | SUB-GROUP | CELLULAR | MATERIAL | POLYURETHANE - RIGID |

GENERAL DESCRIPTION

Rigid polyurethane are produced over a range of densities with mechanical properties increasing with density. The foam is produced by a chemical in the presence of water forming closed cells in which is trapped the blowing agent. Its principle use is in thermal insulation. Exhibits low water absorption.

CHEMICAL ANALYSIS OR COMPOSITION

SYNONYM

PHYSICAL PROPERTIES

PROPERTY	UNITS	VALUE OR RANGE	COMMENTS
DENSITY	kg/m^3	38	
SHEAR STRENGTH	N/mm^2		
TENSILE STRENGTH	N/mm^2	$3.4-25 \times 10^{-1}$	
ELONGATION	%		
COMPRESSIVE STRENGTH	N/mm^2	$2.1-23 \times 10^{-1}$	
FLEXURAL STRENGTH	N/mm^2		
IMPACT STRENGTH	J		
TENSILE MODULUS	N/mm^2		
HARDNESS			
THERMAL COEFF. OF LINEAR EXPANSION	$^oC^{-1}$	$2.2-4.0 \times 10^{-5}$	
MIN./MAX. SERVICE TEMPERATURE	^oC	$/100^oC$	
DEFLECTION TEMPERATURE	^oC		
THERMAL CONDUCTIVITY	W/mK		
FLAMMABILITY			
DIELECTRIC STRENGTH	kV/mm		
VOLUME RESISTIVITY	ohm cm		
PERMITIVITY	ohm cm		
ARC RESISTANCE	secs		
NUMBER OF PARTS			
CURING METHOD			
OPTICAL PROPERTIES			
FRICTION			
MOULD SHRINKAGE			
WATER ABSORPTION	%	2	By volume

SPECIFICATIONS

STANDARD NUMBER	AUTHORITY	TITLE

COMPANY SPECIFICATION:

ENVIRONMENT

RESISTANCE TO ATTACK FROM:

MINERAL ACIDS (WEAK)	
MINERAL ACIDS (STRONG)	Attacked
ALKALIS (WEAK)	
ALKALIS (STRONG)	Attacked
SOLVENTS (CHLORINATED)	Swelling
OILS AND GREASES	
DETERGENTS	

U.V. RESISTANCE

WEATHERABILITY

OXYGEN PERMEABILITY

NITROGEN PERMEABILITY

CARBON DIOXIDE PERMEABILITY

JOINTING PROCESS

SAFETY PRECAUTIONS

Allow fumes to escape before enclosing newly formed foam

PROCESSING AND FORMING TECHNIQUES

Intimate mixing of components chemically forms foam. The exothermic reaction aids curing

TYPICAL APPLICATIONS

Thermal insulation of buildings, refrigerators, freezers and insulated transport containers

Bouyancy systems

Mould components

In situ foamed packaging support material

YOUR SUPPLIER AND NOTES

material data sheet		SHEET NUMBER	PL24	A

FAMILY GROUP	PLASTICS	SUB-GROUP	CELLULAR	MATERIAL	PHENOLIC

GENERAL DESCRIPTION

Rigid thermoset closed cell structure resulting in low water vapour transmission properties, thus reducing corrosion problems of substrates. Stress corrosion of substrate reduced due to the absence of chlorides.

Good fire retarding performance and limited formation of fume and smoke. Low density packaging or cavity filling agent can be foamed insitu with good adhesion to wood and ceramic materials. Mechanical strength is density and direction related.

CHEMICAL ANALYSIS OR COMPOSITION

PHYSICAL PROPERTIES

PROPERTY	UNITS	VALUE OR RANGE	COMMENTS
DENSITY	kg/m^3	35 (60)	Low (high)
SHEAR STRENGTH	N/mm^2	0.12 (0.25)	Low (high)
TENSILE STRENGTH	N/mm^2		
ELONGATION	%		
COMPRESSIVE STRENGTH	N/mm^2	0.16 (0.4)	Depending on density & direction
FLEXURAL STRENGTH	N/mm^2		
IMPACT STRENGTH	J		
TENSILE MODULUS	N/mm^2		
HARDNESS			
THERMAL COEFF. OF LINEAR EXPANSION	$°C^{-1}$	35×10^{-6}	
MIN./MAX. SERVICE TEMPERATURE	$°C$	-200/130(190)	Continuous (intermittant)
DEFLECTION TEMPERATURE	$°C$		
THERMAL CONDUCTIVITY	W/mK	0.029-0.032	Depends on density
FLAMMABILITY			
DIELECTRIC STRENGTH	kV/mm		
VOLUME RESISTIVITY	ohm cm		
PERMITIVITY	ohm cm		
ARC RESISTANCE	secs		
NUMBER OF PARTS			
CURING METHOD			
OPTICAL PROPERTIES			
FRICTION			
MOULD SHRINKAGE			
WATER ABSORPTION	%	6	

SPECIFICATIONS

STANDARD NUMBER	AUTHORITY	TITLE

COMPANY SPECIFICATION:

ENVIRONMENT

RESISTANCE TO ATTACK FROM:

MINERAL ACIDS (WEAK)	Resistant
MINERAL ACIDS (STRONG)	
ALKALIS (WEAK)	Resistant
ALKALIS (STRONG)	
SOLVENTS (CHLORINATED)	Resistant
OILS AND GREASES	
DETERGENTS	

U.V. RESISTANCE

WEATHERABILITY

OXYGEN PERMEABILITY

NITROGEN PERMEABILITY

CARBON DIOXIDE PERMEABILITY

JOINTING PROCESS

SAFETY PRECAUTIONS

In situ foaming - protection of eyes from
chemical splashes

PROCESSING AND FORMING TECHNIQUES

Supplied in preformed slabs or purpose
built forms.
Also available to be foamed in situ as
a packaging media.

TYPICAL APPLICATIONS

Insulation applications on roofs, walls,
profile pipe sections, cold storage,
ductwork.
Packaging and cavity filling media.

YOUR SUPPLIER AND NOTES

| FAMILY GROUP | PLASTICS | SUB-GROUP | LAMINATES | MATERIAL | PHENOLIC/PAPER |

GENERAL DESCRIPTION

Phenolic/paper laminates primarily designed as electrical insulating materials. They also possess good mechanical features but impact and wear properties are inferior to other types.

Available as sheet, round tube and rectangular tube, angle and bar. Low water absorption particularly in high humidity and tropical conditions, in which its electrical properties are retained to a high degree.

CHEMICAL ANALYSIS OR COMPOSITION

Phenolic resin with paper reinforced laminations.

SYNONYM

Tufnol-swan, heron or kite grades

PHYSICAL PROPERTIES

PROPERTY	UNITS	VALUE OR RANGE	COMMENTS
DENSITY	kg/m^3	1360	
SHEAR STRENGTH	N/mm^2	105-110	Flatwise
TENSILE STRENGTH	N/mm^2		
ELONGATION	%		
COMPRESSIVE STRENGTH	N/mm^2	350/215	Flatwise/Edgewise
FLEXURAL STRENGTH	N/mm^2		
IMPACT STRENGTH	J	2.6-3.9	
TENSILE MODULUS	N/mm^2		
HARDNESS			
THERMAL COEFF. OF LINEAR EXPANSION	$^oC^{-1}$		
MIN./MAX. SERVICE TEMPERATURE	^oC	/90(120)	Continuous (intermittant)
DEFLECTION TEMPERATURE	^oC		
THERMAL CONDUCTIVITY	W/mK		
FLAMMABILITY			
POWER FACTOR			
DIELECTRIC STRENGTH	kV/mm	2.5-19	
VOLUME RESISTIVITY	ohm cm		
PERMITIVITY	ohm cm	4.5-5.4	At 1MHz
ARC RESISTANCE	secs		
NUMBER OF PARTS			
CURING METHOD			
OPTICAL PROPERTIES			
FRICTION			
MOULD SHRINKAGE			
WATER ABSORPTION	mg	20-150	
THERMAL CLASSIFICATION		E	BS 2757

SPECIFICATIONS

STANDARD NUMBER	AUTHORITY	TITLE
BS 1314	BSI	Phenolic resin bonded tubes.
BS 1885	BSI	Phenolic resin bonded rectangular tubes
BS 1951	BSI	Thermosetting resin bonded paper tubes
BS 2572	BSI	Phenolic laminated sheet
BS 5102	BSI	Phenolic resin bonded sheet-electrical

COMPANY SPECIFICATION:

ENVIRONMENT

RESISTANCE TO ATTACK FROM:

MINERAL ACIDS (WEAK)	Resistant
MINERAL ACIDS (STRONG)	Attack
ALKALIS (WEAK))	Caustic soda attacks,
ALKALIS (STRONG))	resistant to others
SOLVENTS (CHLORINATED)	Resistant
OILS AND GREASES	Resistant
DETERGENTS	Resistant

U.V. RESISTANCE

WEATHERABILITY

OXYGEN PERMEABILITY

NITROGEN PERMEABILITY

CARBON DIOXIDE PERMEABILITY

JOINTING PROCESS

Mechanical jointing
Bonded by epoxy adhesives with correct preparation

SAFETY PRECAUTIONS

PROCESSING AND FORMING TECHNIQUES

Machined dry so as not to impair electrical insulation properties. All normal machining processes may be used.

TYPICAL APPLICATIONS

Components for corrosive conditions
Electrical insulants, jigs and fixtures.
High voltage insulation

YOUR SUPPLIER AND NOTES

BSRIA material data sheet

SHEET NUMBER	PL26	**A**

FAMILY GROUP	PLASTICS	SUB-GROUP	LAMINATES	MATERIAL	PHENOLIC/COTTON

GENERAL DESCRIPTION

Cotton fabric laminates are well known for their toughness, resilience, mechanical strength, wear resistance and electrical insulation properties. The finess of the weave is reflected in the level of the properties. The finer the weave the more intricate the component e.g. fine weaves - fine threads, medium weaves - coarse threads.

CHEMICAL ANALYSIS OR COMPOSITION

Phenolic resin + cotton fabric of fine, medium or coarse weave.

SYNONYM

Tufnol - lynx, vole carp, whale or crow
         grades

PHYSICAL PROPERTIES

PROPERTY	UNITS	VALUE OR RANGE	COMMENTS
DENSITY	kg/m^3	1320-1360	
SHEAR STRENGTH	N/mm^2		
TENSILE STRENGTH	N/mm^2		
ELONGATION	%		
COMPRESSIVE STRENGTH	N/mm^2	290-325/185-215	Flatwise/Edgewise
FLEXURAL STRENGTH	N/mm^2		
IMPACT STRENGTH	J	7.0-13.6	kJ/m^2
TENSILE MODULUS	N/mm^2		
HARDNESS			
THERMAL COEFF. OF LINEAR EXPANSION	$^{o}C^{-1}$		
MIN./MAX. SERVICE TEMPERATURE	^{o}C	/120 (130)	Continuous (Intermittant)
DEFLECTION TEMPERATURE	^{o}C		
THERMAL CONDUCTIVITY	W/mK		
FLAMMABILITY			
DIELECTRIC STRENGTH	kV/mm		
VOLUME RESISTIVITY	ohm cm		
PERMITIVITY	ohm cm	4.6	Medium weave
ARC RESISTANCE	secs		
NUMBER OF PARTS			
CURING METHOD			
OPTICAL PROPERTIES			
FRICTION			
MOULD SHRINKAGE			
WATER ABSORPTION	mg	45-150	
THERMAL CLASSIFICATION		E	BS 2757

BSRIA material data sheet

SPECIFICATIONS

STANDARD NUMBER	AUTHORITY	TITLE
BS 2572	BSI	Phenolic laminated sheet
BS PL2	BSI	Phenolic/cotton fabric round tube (up to 75mm)
BS PL3	BSI	Phenolic/cotton fabric round rod (up to 75mm)

COMPANY SPECIFICATION:

ENVIRONMENT

RESISTANCE TO ATTACK FROM:

MINERAL ACIDS (WEAK)	Resistant
MINERAL ACIDS (STRONG)	Attacked
ALKALIS (WEAK))	Caustic soda attacks
ALKALIS (STRONG))	Resistant to others
SOLVENTS (CHLORINATED)	Resistant
OILS AND GREASES	Resistant
DETERGENTS	Resistant

U.V. RESISTANCE

WEATHERABILITY

OXYGEN PERMEABILITY

NITROGEN PERMEABILITY

CARBON DIOXIDE PERMEABILITY

JOINTING PROCESS

Mechanical jointing
Bonded by epoxy adhesives with correct preparation

SAFETY PRECAUTIONS

PROCESSING AND FORMING TECHNIQUES

Readily machined using conventional engineering practices
Fine weave - fine detail.
Medium weave - standard detail
Coarse weave - large sections
No cutting fluids to be used during machining. Care required to prevent burning

TYPICAL APPLICATIONS

Fine Weave - high precision turned and machined parts for fine gears, insulation boards, fine threads.
Medium Weave - shock loading, wide faced gears, low tension electrical applications

YOUR SUPPLIER AND NOTES

SHEET NUMBER	PL27		**A**

FAMILY GROUP	PLASTICS	**SUB-GROUP**	LAMINATES	**MATERIAL**	PHENOLIC/ASBESTOS

GENERAL DESCRIPTION

The addition of asbestos (as a paper or a fabric) to phenolic resin produces a laminate able to operate at higher temperatures than paper or cotton based laminates and have better electrical properties. Asbestos fabric laminate has good mechanical wear resistance and dimensional stability.

Available as sheet, tube rod and sections.
Fabric laminate has good mechanical wear resistance and dimensional stability.

CHEMICAL ANALYSIS OR COMPOSITION

Phenolic resin
a. asbestos paper reinforced
b. asbestos fabric reinforced

SYNONYM

Tufnol - asp or adder grades

PHYSICAL PROPERTIES

PROPERTY	UNITS	VALUE OR RANGE	COMMENTS
DENSITY	kg/m^3	1640 (1820)	Fabric (paper)
SHEAR STRENGTH	N/mm^2	110 (85)	Flatwise - fabric (paper)
TENSILE STRENGTH	N/mm^2		
ELONGATION	%		
COMPRESSIVE STRENGTH	N/mm^2	160 (310)	Edgewise (flatwise)
FLEXURAL STRENGTH	N/mm^2		
IMPACT STRENGTH	J	24 (4.8)	Fabric (paper) kJ/m^2
TENSILE MODULUS	N/mm^2		
HARDNESS			
THERMAL COEFF. OF LINEAR EXPANSION	$°C^{-1}$		
MIN./MAX. SERVICE TEMPERATURE	$°C$	/165 (185)	Continuous (intermittant)
DEFLECTION TEMPERATURE	$°C$		
THERMAL CONDUCTIVITY	W/mK		
FLAMMABILITY			
POWER FACTOR			
DIELECTRIC STRENGTH	kV/mm		
VOLUME RESISTIVITY	ohm cm		
PERMITIVITY	ohm cm		
ARC RESISTANCE	secs		
NUMBER OF PARTS			
CURING METHOD			
OPTICAL PROPERTIES			
FRICTION			
MOULD SHRINKAGE			
WATER ABSORPTION	mg	55-280	
THERMAL CLASSIFICATION		F	BS 2757

SPECIFICATIONS

STANDARD NUMBER	AUTHORITY	TITLE
BS 2572	BSI	Phenolic laminated sheet

COMPANY SPECIFICATION:

ENVIRONMENT

RESISTANCE TO ATTACK FROM:

MINERAL ACIDS (WEAK)	Resistant
MINERAL ACIDS (STRONG)	Attack
ALKALIS (WEAK))	(Caustic soda attacks
ALKALIS (STRONG))	(Others Resistant
SOLVENTS (CHLORINATED)	Resistant
OILS AND GREASES	Resistant
DETERGENTS	Resistant

U.V. RESISTANCE

WEATHERABILITY

OXYGEN PERMEABILITY

NITROGEN PERMEABILITY

CARBON DIOXIDE PERMEABILITY

JOINTING PROCESS

Mechanical jointing
Bonded by epoxy adhesives with correct
preparation

SAFETY PRECAUTIONS

Dust should be removed by extraction or
damped down as asbestos is a hazardous
material

PROCESSING AND FORMING TECHNIQUES

Readily machined using normal engineering
practices. Not suitable for gear cutting

TYPICAL APPLICATIONS

Components subject to high temperature,
gears (coarse tooth)
Bearings and wear resistant components.
Chemical resistant components.
Low voltage insulants.

YOUR SUPPLIER AND NOTES

SHEET NUMBER	PL28		**A**

FAMILY GROUP	PLASTICS	SUB-GROUP	LAMINATES	MATERIAL	EPOXY/ COTTON

GENERAL DESCRIPTION

Epoxy/cotton fabric laminate, with a fine weave, have good mechanical properties, good wear resistance and low water absorption, resulting in good dimensional stability, and excellent resistance to electrical tracking.

CHEMICAL ANALYSIS OR COMPOSITION

Epoxide resin with cotton cloth reinforcement.

PHYSICAL PROPERTIES

PROPERTY	UNITS	VALUE OR RANGE	COMMENTS
DENSITY	kg/m^3	1360	
SHEAR STRENGTH	N/mm^2		
TENSILE STRENGTH	N/mm^2		
ELONGATION	%		
COMPRESSIVE STRENGTH	N/mm^2	290/190	Flatwise/Edgewise
FLEXURAL STRENGTH	N/mm^2		
IMPACT STRENGTH	J	4.6	kJ/m^2
TENSILE MODULUS	N/mm^2		
HARDNESS			
THERMAL COEFF. OF LINEAR EXPANSION	$°C^{-1}$		
MIN./MAX. SERVICE TEMPERATURE	$°C$	/130 (150)	Continuous (intermittant)
DEFLECTION TEMPERATURE	$°C$		at 1.81 N/mm^2
THERMAL CONDUCTIVITY	W/mK		
FLAMMABILITY			
POWER FACTOR			
DIELECTRIC STRENGTH	kV/mm		
VOLUME RESISTIVITY	ohm cm	4.3	At 1M Hz
PERMITIVITY	ohm cm		
ARC RESISTANCE	secs		
NUMBER OF PARTS			
CURING METHOD			
OPTICAL PROPERTIES			
FRICTION			
MOULD SHRINKAGE			
WATER ABSORPTION	mg	5-15	
THERMAL CLASSIFICATION		B	BS2757

BSRIA material data sheet

SPECIFICATIONS

STANDARD NUMBER	AUTHORITY	TITLE
BS 3953	BSI	Resin bonded woven glass fabric laminates sheet

COMPANY SPECIFICATION:

ENVIRONMENT

RESISTANCE TO ATTACK FROM:

MINERAL ACIDS (WEAK)	Resistant
MINERAL ACIDS (STRONG)	Attacked
ALKALIS (WEAK)	Resistant
ALKALIS (STRONG)	Slight attack
SOLVENTS (CHLORINATED)	Fairly resistant
OILS AND GREASES	Resistant
DETERGENTS	Resistant

U.V. RESISTANCE

WEATHERABILITY

OXYGEN PERMEABILITY

NITROGEN PERMEABILITY

CARBON DIOXIDE PERMEABILITY

JOINTING PROCESS

Mechanical jointing
Bonded by epoxy adhesives with correct
preparation

SAFETY PRECAUTIONS

PROCESSING AND FORMING TECHNIQUES

Readily machined using conventional
engineering processes. Not suitable for
gear cutting

TYPICAL APPLICATIONS

Similar applications to phenolic based
laminate but with superior electrical and
mechanical properties such as insulants,
high precision machined components,
chemical resistant components, high
temperature components.

YOUR SUPPLIER AND NOTES

FAMILY GROUP	PLASTICS	SUB-GROUP	FILLED	MATERIAL	NYLON 66 + GLASS FILLING

GENERAL DESCRIPTION

Glass fibre reinforced nylon 66 is anisotropic in their strength properties. The properties, even in the weak plane exceed those of unfilled nylon 66.

CHEMICAL ANALYSIS OR COMPOSITION

Nylon 66 + 30% glass filling.

SYNONYM

PHYSICAL PROPERTIES

PROPERTY	UNITS	VALUE OR RANGE	COMMENTS
DENSITY	kg/m^3	1340-1370	
SHEAR STRENGTH	N/mm^2		
TENSILE STRENGTH	N/mm^2	134-193	
ELONGATION	%	5-10	
COMPRESSIVE STRENGTH	N/mm^2	127-138	
FLEXURAL STRENGTH	N/mm^2		
IMPACT STRENGTH	J	210	Notched Izod
TENSILE MODULUS	N/mm^2	6900-8620	
HARDNESS		R118-R120	Rockwell
THERMAL COEFF. OF LINEAR EXPANSION	$^oC^{-1}$	$1.5-2.0 \times 10^{-5}$	
MIN./MAX. SERVICE TEMPERATURE	^oC	/120	
DEFLECTION TEMPERATURE	^oC		
THERMAL CONDUCTIVITY	W/mK		
FLAMMABILITY		Slow	
POWER FACTOR			
DIELECTRIC STRENGTH	kV/mm		
VOLUME RESISTIVITY	ohm cm	10^{14}	
PERMITIVITY	ohm cm		
ARC RESISTANCE	secs		
NUMBER OF PARTS			
CURING METHOD			
OPTICAL PROPERTIES		Translucent to opaque	
FRICTION			
MOULD SHRINKAGE			
WATER ABSORPTION	%	0.65-0.75	

SPECIFICATIONS

STANDARD NUMBER	AUTHORITY	TITLE

COMPANY SPECIFICATION:

ENVIRONMENT

RESISTANCE TO ATTACK FROM:

MINERAL ACIDS (WEAK)	Resistant
MINERAL ACIDS (STRONG)	Attacks
ALKALIS (WEAK)	Resistant
ALKALIS (STRONG)	Resistant
SOLVENTS (CHLORINATED)	Resistant
OILS AND GREASES	
DETERGENTS	

U.V. RESISTANCE

WEATHERABILITY

OXYGEN PERMEABILITY
NITROGEN PERMEABILITY
CARBON DIOXIDE PERMEABILITY

JOINTING PROCESS

Mechanical
Adhesive

SAFETY PRECAUTIONS

PROCESSING AND FORMING TECHNIQUES

Injection moulding

TYPICAL APPLICATIONS

Replacement of light metal castings.
Similar applications to unfilled nylon
66 but where greater mechanical properties
are required

YOUR SUPPLIER AND NOTES

FAMILY GROUP	PLASTICS	SUB-GROUP	FILLED	MATERIAL	ACETAL + GLASS FIBRE

GENERAL DESCRIPTION

Glass reinforced acetal is used where high stiffness and creep resistance is required. It is a strong competitor to die cast metals. The majority of mechanical properties are improved while thermal expansion and mould shrinkage are reduced compared to unfilled acetal.

CHEMICAL ANALYSIS OR COMPOSITION

Acetal + 30% glass fibre

PHYSICAL PROPERTIES

PROPERTY	UNITS	VALUE OR RANGE	COMMENTS
DENSITY	kg/m^3	1600-1630	
SHEAR STRENGTH	N/mm^2		
TENSILE STRENGTH	N/mm^2	80-120	
ELONGATION	%	3-6	
COMPRESSIVE STRENGTH	N/mm^2		
FLEXURAL STRENGTH	N/mm^2		
IMPACT STRENGTH	J	50	Notched Izod
TENSILE MODULUS	N/mm^2		
HARDNESS		M75-90	Rockwell
THERMAL COEFF. OF LINEAR EXPANSION	$^{\circ}$C^{-1}	3.6-8.1x10^{-5}	
MIN./MAX. SERVICE TEMPERATURE	$^{\circ}$C		
DEFLECTION TEMPERATURE	$^{\circ}$C	157-170	at 1.81 N/mm^2
THERMAL CONDUCTIVITY	W/mK		
FLAMMABILITY		0.8-1.0	
POWER FACTOR			
DIELECTRIC STRENGTH	kV/mm	4.6	
VOLUME RESISTIVITY	ohm cm	10^{14}	
PERMITIVITY	ohm cm		
ARC RESISTANCE	secs	136	
NUMBER OF PARTS			
CURING METHOD			
OPTICAL PROPERTIES		Opaque	
FRICTION			
MOULD SHRINKAGE			
WATER ABSORPTION			

BSRIA material data sheet

SPECIFICATIONS

STANDARD NUMBER	AUTHORITY	TITLE

COMPANY SPECIFICATION:

ENVIRONMENT

RESISTANCE TO ATTACK FROM:

MINERAL ACIDS (WEAK)	Slight resistance
MINERAL ACIDS (STRONG)	Attacked
ALKALIS (WEAK)	Copolymer base attacked
ALKALIS (STRONG)	Copolymer base attacked
SOLVENTS (CHLORINATED)	Resistant
OILS AND GREASES	
DETERGENTS	

U.V. RESISTANCE	Chalks slightly
WEATHERABILITY	

OXYGEN PERMEABILITY

NITROGEN PERMEABILITY

CARBON DIOXIDE PERMEABILITY

JOINTING PROCESS

Mechanical

Adhesives

SAFETY PRECAUTIONS

PROCESSING AND FORMING TECHNIQUES

Injection moulded

TYPICAL APPLICATIONS

Replacement for metal diecastings. Engineering components such as gears, pinions and bearings

YOUR SUPPLIER AND NOTES

| | | SHEET NUMBER | PL31 | A |

| FAMILY GROUP | PLASTICS | SUB-GROUP | FILLED | MATERIAL | ABS + GLASS FILLED |

GENERAL DESCRIPTION

Compared to ABS, reinforcement raises the heat deflection temperature, impact values and tensile strength. The thermal expansion is dramatically reduced while maintaining its ability to be decoratively metalised.

CHEMICAL ANALYSIS OR COMPOSITION

ABS + 20% glass.

PHYSICAL PROPERTIES

PROPERTY	UNITS	VALUE OR RANGE	COMMENTS
DENSITY	kg/m^3	1160-1230	
SHEAR STRENGTH	N/mm^2		
TENSILE STRENGTH	N/mm^2	58.6-100	
ELONGATION	%	2.5-3.0	
COMPRESSIVE STRENGTH	N/mm^2	82-151	
FLEXURAL STRENGTH	N/mm^2		
IMPACT STRENGTH	J	110	notched Izod
TENSILE MODULUS	N/mm^2		
HARDNESS		M65-100	Rockwell
THERMAL COEFF. OF LINEAR EXPANSION	$^{\circ}C^{-1}$	$2.9-3.6\times10^{-5}$	
MIN./MAX. SERVICE TEMPERATURE	$^{\circ}C$		
DEFLECTION TEMPERATURE	$^{\circ}C$	98-110	at 1.81 N/mm^2
THERMAL CONDUCTIVITY	W/mK		
FLAMMABILITY		Slow	
POWER FACTOR			
DIELECTRIC STRENGTH	kV/mm	30	
VOLUME RESISTIVITY	ohm cm		
PERMITIVITY	ohm cm		
ARC RESISTANCE	secs		
NUMBER OF PARTS			
CURING METHOD			
OPTICAL PROPERTIES		Translucent to opaque	
FRICTION			
MOULD SHRINKAGE	%	0.2-0.3	
WATER ABSORPTION	%	0.18-0.2	

SPECIFICATIONS

STANDARD NUMBER	AUTHORITY	TITLE

COMPANY SPECIFICATION:

ENVIRONMENT

RESISTANCE TO ATTACK FROM:

MINERAL ACIDS (WEAK)	Resistant
MINERAL ACIDS (STRONG)	Attack by oxidising acids
ALKALIS (WEAK)	Resistant
ALKALIS (STRONG)	Resistant
SOLVENTS (CHLORINATED)	Soluble
OILS AND GREASES	
DETERGENTS	
U.V. RESISTANCE	Slight yellowing
WEATHERABILITY	Slight embrittlement

OXYGEN PERMEABILITY

NITROGEN PERMEABILITY

CARBON DIOXIDE PERMEABILITY

PROCESSING AND FORMING TECHNIQUES

Injection moulding

TYPICAL APPLICATIONS

Similar to ABS. but where more stringent mechanical properties are required

JOINTING PROCESS

YOUR SUPPLIER AND NOTES

SAFETY PRECAUTIONS

 **material data sheet**

SHEET NUMBER	PL32	**A**

FAMILY GROUP	PLASTICS	SUB-GROUP	FILLED	MATERIAL	PTFE + GLASS FILLING

GENERAL DESCRIPTION

Glass filled PTFE shows good wear and chemical resistance. It has good bearing properties but may promote shaft scoring with high loads and speeds. Special sintering (inert gas) processes produce non-porous mouldings with improved creep resistance.

CHEMICAL ANALYSIS OR COMPOSITION

PTFE + 25% glass fibre.

PHYSICAL PROPERTIES

PROPERTY	UNITS	VALUE OR RANGE	COMMENTS
DENSITY	kg/m^3	2230-2250	
SHEAR STRENGTH	N/mm^2		
TENSILE STRENGTH	N/mm^2	14.5-18.5	
ELONGATION	%	280	
COMPRESSIVE STRENGTH	N/mm^2		
FLEXURAL STRENGTH	N/mm^2		
IMPACT STRENGTH	J	48	
TENSILE MODULUS	N/mm^2		
HARDNESS		D55-D57	Rockwell
THERMAL COEFF. OF LINEAR EXPANSION	$^oC^{-1}$		
MIN./MAX. SERVICE TEMPERATURE	^oC		
DEFLECTION TEMPERATURE	^oC		at 1.81 N/mm^2
THERMAL CONDUCTIVITY	W/mK		
FLAMMABILITY		Non burning	
POWER FACTOR			
DIELECTRIC STRENGTH	kV/mm	2.6-2.9	
VOLUME RESISTIVITY	ohm cm	10^{13}	
PERMITIVITY	ohm cm		
ARC RESISTANCE	secs		
NUMBER OF PARTS			
CURING METHOD			
OPTICAL PROPERTIES			
FRICTION			
MOULD SHRINKAGE			
WATER ABSORPTION	%	0.013	

563

BSRIA material data sheet

SPECIFICATIONS

STANDARD NUMBER	AUTHORITY	TITLE

COMPANY SPECIFICATION:

ENVIRONMENT

RESISTANCE TO ATTACK FROM:

MINERAL ACIDS (WEAK)
MINERAL ACIDS (STRONG)
ALKALIS (WEAK)
ALKALIS (STRONG)
SOLVENTS (CHLORINATED)
OILS AND GREASES
DETERGENTS

U.V. RESISTANCE
WEATHERABILITY

OXYGEN PERMEABILITY
NITROGEN PERMEABILITY
CARBON DIOXIDE PERMEABILITY

JOINTING PROCESS

Mechanical
Adhesive after surface preparation by
specialist etching solutions

SAFETY PRECAUTIONS

Smoking during machining may
cause health problems.

PROCESSING AND FORMING TECHNIQUES

Compression moulding and sintering

TYPICAL APPLICATIONS

Valve seats, gaskets, seals and components requiring resistance to creep
and chemical attack.
Bearings with low PV values

YOUR SUPPLIER AND NOTES

material data sheet		SHEET NUMBER PL33	A

FAMILY GROUP PLASTICS	SUB-GROUP FILLED	MATERIAL PTFE + BRONZE FILLING

GENERAL DESCRIPTION

PTFE filled with bronze powder is a very good bearing material and is preferable to glass filled PTFE for high speed applications. It possesses superior thermal conductivity to unfilled PTFE and can therefore disapate generated heat. The addition of graphite to the bronze improves low speed wear rates.

CHEMICAL ANALYSIS OR COMPOSITION

PTFE + 60% Bronze

PHYSICAL PROPERTIES

PROPERTY	UNITS	VALUE OR RANGE	COMMENTS
DENSITY	kg/m^3	3800	
SHEAR STRENGTH	N/mm^2		
TENSILE STRENGTH	N/mm^2	12-13.8	
ELONGATION	%	80	
COMPRESSIVE STRENGTH	N/mm^2		
FLEXURAL STRENGTH	N/mm^2		
IMPACT STRENGTH	J		
TENSILE MODULUS	N/mm^2		
HARDNESS		D64-D65	Rockwell
THERMAL COEFF. OF LINEAR EXPANSION	$^oC^{-1}$		
MIN./MAX. SERVICE TEMPERATURE	^oC		
DEFLECTION TEMPERATURE	^oC		at 1.81 N/mm^2
THERMAL CONDUCTIVITY	W/mK		
FLAMMABILITY		Non burning	
POWER FACTOR			
DIELECTRIC STRENGTH	kV/mm		
VOLUME RESISTIVITY	ohm cm		
PERMITIVITY	ohm cm		
ARC RESISTANCE	secs		
NUMBER OF PARTS			
CURING METHOD			
OPTICAL PROPERTIES			
FRICTION			
MOULD SHRINKAGE			
WATER ABSORPTION	%	0.019	

BSRIA material data sheet

SPECIFICATIONS

STANDARD NUMBER	AUTHORITY	TITLE

COMPANY SPECIFICATION:

ENVIRONMENT

RESISTANCE TO ATTACK FROM:

MINERAL ACIDS (WEAK)
MINERAL ACIDS (STRONG)
ALKALIS (WEAK)
ALKALIS (STRONG)
SOLVENTS (CHLORINATED)
OILS AND GREASES
DETERGENTS

U.V. RESISTANCE
WEATHERABILITY

OXYGEN PERMEABILITY
NITROGEN PERMEABILITY
CARBON DIOXIDE PERMEABILITY

JOINTING PROCESS

Mechanical
Adhesive after surface preparation by specialist
etching solutions

SAFETY PRECAUTIONS

Health Hazard
During machining no smoking should be
enforced

PROCESSING AND FORMING TECHNIQUES

Compression moulding followed by
sintering

TYPICAL APPLICATIONS

Bearing applications and applications in
chemical environments where a dissapation
of heat is required.

YOUR SUPPLIER AND NOTES

BSRIA material data sheet

FAMILY GROUP	PLASTICS	SUB-GROUP	FILLED	MATERIAL	POLYCARBONATE AND GLASS FILLING

GENERAL DESCRIPTION

Glass fibre reinforced polycarbonate shows improvements over unfilled material in rigidity, dimensional stability with temperature increase and fatigue endurance. Thermal expansion is similar to that of light metals and together with faster production cycles, lower density and elimination of finishing processes it becomes very competitive. Compared with unreinforced polycarbonate, tensile strength is higher, elongation lower and impact properties reduced.

CHEMICAL ANALYSIS OR COMPOSITION

Polycarbonate + 10-40% glass fibre

PHYSICAL PROPERTIES

PROPERTY	UNITS	VALUE OR RANGE	COMMENTS
DENSITY	kg/m^3	1350-1520	
SHEAR STRENGTH	N/mm^2		
TENSILE STRENGTH	N/mm^2	82-172	
ELONGATION	%	0.9-5.0	
COMPRESSIVE STRENGTH	N/mm^2	90-149	
FLEXURAL STRENGTH	N/mm^2		
IMPACT STRENGTH	J	1.0-2.0	
TENSILE MODULUS	N/mm^2	3450-11700	
HARDNESS		M88-M97	Rockwell
THERMAL COEFF. OF LINEAR EXPANSION	$^oC^{-1}$	$1.7-5.0 \times 10^{-5}$	
MIN./MAX. SERVICE TEMPERATURE	^oC		
DEFLECTION TEMPERATURE	^oC	145-150	at 1.81 N/mm^2
THERMAL CONDUCTIVITY	W/mK		
FLAMMABILITY		Self-extinguishing	
POWER FACTOR			
DIELECTRIC STRENGTH	kV/mm	18-19.5	
VOLUME RESISTIVITY	ohm cm	$4-5 \times 10^{16}$	
PERMITIVITY	ohm cm		
ARC RESISTANCE	secs	5-120	
NUMBER OF PARTS			
CURING METHOD			
OPTICAL PROPERTIES		Translucent to opaque	
FRICTION			
MOULD SHRINKAGE	mm/mm	0.025-0.075	
WATER ABSORPTION	%	0.07-0.2	

SPECIFICATIONS

STANDARD NUMBER	AUTHORITY	TITLE

COMPANY SPECIFICATION:

ENVIRONMENT

RESISTANCE TO ATTACK FROM:

MINERAL ACIDS (WEAK)	Resistant
MINERAL ACIDS (STRONG)	Attacked by oxidising acids
ALKALIS (WEAK)	Limited resistance
ALKALIS (STRONG)	Attacked
SOLVENTS (CHLORINATED)	Soluble
OILS AND GREASES	
DETERGENTS	
U.V. RESISTANCE	Colour change
WEATHERABILITY	Slight embrittlement

OXYGEN PERMEABILITY

NITROGEN PERMEABILITY

CARBON DIOXIDE PERMEABILITY

JOINTING PROCESS
  Mechanical
  Adhesive
  Solvent welding

SAFETY PRECAUTIONS

PROCESSING AND FORMING TECHNIQUES

Injection moulding

TYPICAL APPLICATIONS

Injection moulded components

YOUR SUPPLIER AND NOTES

material data sheet		SHEET NUMBER	PL35	A

| FAMILY GROUP | PLASTICS | SUB-GROUP | FILLED | MATERIAL | POLYPROPYLENE + ASBESTOS FILLING |

GENERAL DESCRIPTION

Asbestos filled polypropylene is used where higher rigidity is required than can be obtained in unfilled polypropylene. It is more rigid than other unfilled thermoplastic materials at 20°C. Its stiffness at 70°C is similar to unfilled polypropylene at 20°C. It has a reduction in linear thermal expansion and mould shrinkage with a loss of surface gloss. Asbestos filled polypropylene has improved heat stability properties. In general properties are inferior to glass filled material.

CHEMICAL ANALYSIS OR COMPOSITION

Polypropylene + 40% asbestos.

PHYSICAL PROPERTIES

PROPERTY	UNITS	VALUE OR RANGE	COMMENTS
DENSITY	kg/m^3	1280-1370	
SHEAR STRENGTH	N/mm^2		
TENSILE STRENGTH	N/mm^2	39-40	
ELONGATION	%	3	At break
COMPRESSIVE STRENGTH	N/mm^2		
FLEXURAL STRENGTH	N/mm^2		
IMPACT STRENGTH	J	81	
TENSILE MODULUS	N/mm^2		
HARDNESS			
THERMAL COEFF. OF LINEAR EXPANSION	$°C^{-1}$	2.6×10^{-5}	
MIN./MAX. SERVICE TEMPERATURE	°C		
DEFLECTION TEMPERATURE	°C	85-117	at $1.81 \ N/mm^2$
THERMAL CONDUCTIVITY	W/mK	0.49	
FLAMMABILITY		Slow burning	
POWER FACTOR DIELECTRIC STRENGTH	kV/mm		
VOLUME RESISTIVITY	ohm cm	10^{16}	
PERMITIVITY	ohm cm		
ARC RESISTANCE	secs		
NUMBER OF PARTS			
CURING METHOD			
OPTICAL PROPERTIES			
FRICTION			
MOULD SHRINKAGE			
WATER ABSORPTION	%	0.04	

SPECIFICATIONS

STANDARD NUMBER	AUTHORITY	TITLE

COMPANY SPECIFICATION:

ENVIRONMENT

RESISTANCE TO ATTACK FROM:

MINERAL ACIDS (WEAK)	Resistant
MINERAL ACIDS (STRONG)	Attacked by oxidising acids
ALKALIS (WEAK)	Resistant
ALKALIS (STRONG)	Resistant
SOLVENTS (CHLORINATED)	Swells
OILS AND GREASES	
DETERGENTS	

U.V. RESISTANCE	Loss of properties
WEATHERABILITY	Improved with inhibitors

OXYGEN PERMEABILITY

NITROGEN PERMEABILITY

CARBON DIOXIDE PERMEABILITY

JOINTING PROCESS

Welding using hot gas and filler rods. Pressure
sensitive adhesives
Mechanical systems

Snap fittings

SAFETY PRECAUTIONS

PROCESSING AND FORMING TECHNIQUES

Injection moulding

TYPICAL APPLICATIONS

Applications where strength is to be
retained at high temperature such as
engine components (air filter holders
heat mouldings and electrical connectors)

YOUR SUPPLIER AND NOTES

FAMILY GROUP	PLASTICS	SUB-GROUP	FILLED	MATERIAL POLYPROPYLENE + TALC FILLING

GENERAL DESCRIPTION

Compared to unfilled polypropylene a talc filler will improve rigidity with a reduction in linear thermal expansion and mould shrinkage though it is inferior to asbestos or glass filled. Talc has the disadvantage of being hygroscopic. It shows good flow characteristics during injection moulding. Resists most chemicals except oxidising acids at high concentrations.

CHEMICAL ANALYSIS OR COMPOSITION

PHYSICAL PROPERTIES

PROPERTY	UNITS	VALUE OR RANGE	COMMENTS
DENSITY	kg/m^3	1040-1210	
SHEAR STRENGTH	N/mm^2		
TENSILE STRENGTH	N/mm^2	26-29	
ELONGATION	%	8-20	At break
COMPRESSIVE STRENGTH	N/mm^2		
FLEXURAL STRENGTH	N/mm^2		
IMPACT STRENGTH	J	4-5	
TENSILE MODULUS	N/mm^2		
HARDNESS			
THERMAL COEFF. OF LINEAR EXPANSION	$^oC^{-1}$	$7-15 \times 10^{-5}$	
MIN./MAX. SERVICE TEMPERATURE	^oC		
DEFLECTION TEMPERATURE	^oC		
THERMAL CONDUCTIVITY	W/mK		
FLAMMABILITY			
POWER FACTOR			
DIELECTRIC STRENGTH	kV/mm		
VOLUME RESISTIVITY	ohm cm	$> 10^{16}$	
PERMITIVITY	ohm cm		
ARC RESISTANCE	secs		
NUMBER OF PARTS			
CURING METHOD			
OPTICAL PROPERTIES		Translucent to opaque	
FRICTION			
MOULD SHRINKAGE			
WATER ABSORPTION	%	0.02	

SPECIFICATIONS

STANDARD NUMBER	AUTHORITY	TITLE

COMPANY SPECIFICATION:

ENVIRONMENT

RESISTANCE TO ATTACK FROM:

MINERAL ACIDS (WEAK)	Resistant
MINERAL ACIDS (STRONG)	Attacked by oxidising acids
ALKALIS (WEAK)	Resistant
ALKALIS (STRONG)	Resistant
SOLVENTS (CHLORINATED)	Swells
OILS AND GREASES	
DETERGENTS	Resistant

U.V. RESISTANCE

WEATHERABILITY

OXYGEN PERMEABILITY

NITROGEN PERMEABILITY

CARBON DIOXIDE PERMEABILITY

JOINTING PROCESS

Welding using hot gas and filler rods
Pressure sensitive adhesives after surface
pretreatment
Snap fittings
Mechanical systems

SAFETY PRECAUTIONS

PROCESSING AND FORMING TECHNIQUES

Injection moulding

TYPICAL APPLICATIONS

Washing machine components
Fans and cowls
Drains and gratings

YOUR SUPPLIER AND NOTES

| FAMILY GROUP | PLASTICS | SUB-GROUP | FILLED | MATERIAL | POLYPROPYLENE + GLASS FILLING |

GENERAL DESCRIPTION

With the addition of 25-30% glass filling the room temperature tensile properties of unfilled polypropylene are retained up to 135°C. Compared with asbestos filled polypropylene there is an improvement in tensile strength and rigidity, and a marked reduction in linear thermal expansion.

CHEMICAL ANALYSIS OR COMPOSITION

Polypropylene + 25-30% Glass fibre.

PHYSICAL PROPERTIES

PROPERTY	UNITS	VALUE OR RANGE	COMMENTS
DENSITY	kg/m^3	1050-1240	
SHEAR STRENGTH	N/mm^2		
TENSILE STRENGTH	N/mm^2	40-62	
ELONGATION	%	5-50	At break
COMPRESSIVE STRENGTH	N/mm^2	38-48	
FLEXURAL STRENGTH	N/mm^2		
IMPACT STRENGTH	J	0.8-2.0	
TENSILE MODULUS	N/mm^2	3100-6200	
HARDNESS		R90-R110	Rockwell
THERMAL COEFF. OF LINEAR EXPANSION	$°C^{-1}$	$2.9-5.2 \times 10^{-5}$	
MIN./MAX. SERVICE TEMPERATURE	$°C$		
DEFLECTION TEMPERATURE	$°C$	130-152	at 1.81 N/mm^2
THERMAL CONDUCTIVITY	W/mK		
FLAMMABILITY		Slow burning	
POWER FACTOR			
DIELECTRIC STRENGTH	kV/mm	16-19	
VOLUME RESISTIVITY	ohm cm	10^{16}	
PERMITIVITY	ohm cm		
ARC RESISTANCE	secs	74	
NUMBER OF PARTS			
CURING METHOD			
OPTICAL PROPERTIES		Opaque	
FRICTION			
MOULD SHRINKAGE	mm/mm	0.1-0.2	
WATER ABSORPTION	%	0.01-0.05	

SPECIFICATIONS

STANDARD NUMBER	AUTHORITY	TITLE

COMPANY SPECIFICATION:

ENVIRONMENT

RESISTANCE TO ATTACK FROM:

MINERAL ACIDS (WEAK)	Resistant
MINERAL ACIDS (STRONG)	Attacked by oxidising acids
ALKALIS (WEAK)	Resistant
ALKALIS (STRONG)	Resistant
SOLVENTS (CHLORINATED)	Swells
OILS AND GREASES	
DETERGENTS	Resistant

U.V. RESISTANCE

WEATHERABILITY	Improved with inhibitors

OXYGEN PERMEABILITY

NITROGEN PERMEABILITY

CARBON DIOXIDE PERMEABILITY

JOINTING PROCESS

Welding using hot gas and filler rods
Pressure sensitive adhesives
after surface pre-treatment

Snap fittings
Mechanical systems

SAFETY PRECAUTIONS

PROCESSING AND FORMING TECHNIQUES

Injection moulding
Compression moulding

TYPICAL APPLICATIONS

Housing for motor switch gear and lighting fittings exposed to high temperature (100°C+). Computer and telephone exchange equipment. Any application that is run at a sustained high temperature where retention of strengths is required.

YOUR SUPPLIER AND NOTES

| | | | SHEET NUMBER | PL38 | A |

| FAMILY GROUP | PLASTICS | SUB- GROUP | REINFORCED | MATERIAL | POLYESTER + GLASS FIBRE MAT |

GENERAL DESCRIPTION

The glass fibre mat is used for quick easy shaping and costs less than other forms of glass fibre. This form is easily wetted by the resin. The glass weight normally ranges over 30-55% with improved properties as the glass content increases. Mechanical properties are roughly equal in all planes.

CHEMICAL ANALYSIS OR COMPOSITION

Polyester + 30-55% glass fibre mat

SYNONYM

GRP

PHYSICAL PROPERTIES

PROPERTY	UNITS	VALUE OR RANGE	COMMENTS
DENSITY	kg/m^3	1500-1700	
SHEAR STRENGTH	N/mm^2		
TENSILE STRENGTH	N/mm^2	12-18	
ELONGATION	%	2.4-3.5	
COMPRESSIVE STRENGTH	N/mm^2	15-17	
FLEXURAL STRENGTH	N/mm^2	20-27	
IMPACT STRENGTH	J		
TENSILE MODULUS	N/mm^2	$1.1-1.6x10^4$	
HARDNESS			
THERMAL COEFF. OF LINEAR EXPANSION	$°C^{-1}$	$20-28x10^{-6}$	
MIN./MAX. SERVICE TEMPERATURE	$°C$		
DEFLECTION TEMPERATURE	$°C$		
THERMAL CONDUCTIVITY	W/mK	0.19-0.24	
FLAMMABILITY		Burns	
DIELECTRIC STRENGTH	kV/mm	25-37	
VOLUME RESISTIVITY	ohm cm	$10^{15}-10^{16}(10^{12}-10^{13})$	Dry (wet)
PERMITIVITY	ohm cm		
ARC RESISTANCE	secs		
NUMBER OF PARTS			
CURING METHOD			
OPTICAL PROPERTIES			
FRICTION			
MOULD SHRINKAGE			
WATER ABSORPTION	%	0.8-1.4	

SPECIFICATIONS

STANDARD NUMBER	AUTHORITY	TITLE
BS 3496:	BSI	E glass fibre chopped strand mat for reinforced polyester resin system
BS 3532:	BSI	Unsaturated polyester resin systems for fibre reinforcement
BS 5480 Pt 1	BSI	G.R.P. pipes and fittings for water supply or sewage

COMPANY SPECIFICATION:

ENVIRONMENT

RESISTANCE TO ATTACK FROM:

MINERAL ACIDS (WEAK)	Resistant
MINERAL ACIDS (STRONG)	
ALKALIS (WEAK)	Resistant
ALKALIS (STRONG)	
SOLVENTS (CHLORINATED)	
OILS AND GREASES	Resistant
DETERGENTS	

U.V. RESISTANCE	Inhibitors added
WEATHERABILITY	Good

OXYGEN PERMEABILITY
NITROGEN PERMEABILITY
CARBON DIOXIDE PERMEABILITY

JOINTING PROCESS

Adhesive bonding using epoxy systems after
an abrasive pretreatment
Mechanical fixing

SAFETY PRECAUTIONS

Precautions to be taken over fumes
during moulding

PROCESSING AND FORMING TECHNIQUES

The glass fibre mat is laid over the
mould surface and the resin sprayed
or stippled in. This is repeated until
the desired thickness is obtained. To
ensure maximum properties the glass must
be totally wetted.

TYPICAL APPLICATIONS

Pipes and fittings
Water tanks
Boats
Automobile body shells
Component covers
Duct work
Roof panels

YOUR SUPPLIER AND NOTES

 **material data sheet**

FAMILY GROUP	PLASTICS	SUB-GROUP	REINFORCED	MATERIAL	POLYESTER + GLASS FIBRE CLOTH

GENERAL DESCRIPTION

Higher strength is obtained with glass cloth than with mat. The finer the weave the greater the strength. Care must be taken that all the fibres are wetted by the resin or inferior properties will result. Leak paths for liquids or gases can result if the fibres are not wetted.

CHEMICAL ANALYSIS OR COMPOSITION

Polyester + 60-70% glass fibre cloth

SYNONYM

GRP

PHYSICAL PROPERTIES

PROPERTY	UNITS	VALUE OR RANGE	COMMENTS
DENSITY	kg/m^3	1880	
SHEAR STRENGTH	N/mm^2		
TENSILE STRENGTH	N/mm^2	34	
ELONGATION	%	3.4	
COMPRESSIVE STRENGTH	N/mm^2	29	
FLEXURAL STRENGTH	N/mm^2	12	
IMPACT STRENGTH	J	7-41	Notched
TENSILE MODULUS	N/mm^2	2.6×10^4	
HARDNESS			
THERMAL COEFF. OF LINEAR EXPANSION	$°C^{-1}$	$12 \cdot 10^{-6}$	
MIN./MAX. SERVICE TEMPERATURE	$°C$	/150-180	No load
DEFLECTION TEMPERATURE	$°C$	200-230	at 1.81 N/mm^2
THERMAL CONDUCTIVITY	W/mK	0.29	
FLAMMABILITY		Burns	
DIELECTRIC STRENGTH	kV/mm	28	
VOLUME RESISTIVITY	ohm cm	10^{16} (10^{11})	Dry (wet)
PERMITIVITY	ohm cm		
ARC RESISTANCE	secs		
NUMBER OF PARTS			
CURING METHOD			
OPTICAL PROPERTIES			
FRICTION			
MOULD SHRINKAGE			
WATER ABSORPTION	%	0.45	

SPECIFICATIONS

STANDARD NUMBER	AUTHORITY	TITLE
BS 3396 Pt 3:	BSI	Glass fibre fabric for use with polyester resin systems
BS 3532:	BSI	Unsaturated polyester resin systems for fibre reinforcement
BS 5480 Pt. 1	BSI	GRP pipes and fittings for water supply or sewage

COMPANY SPECIFICATION:

ENVIRONMENT

RESISTANCE TO ATTACK FROM:

MINERAL ACIDS (WEAK)	Resistant
MINERAL ACIDS (STRONG)	Slight effect
ALKALIS (WEAK)	Resistant
ALKALIS (STRONG)	Decomposed
SOLVENTS (CHLORINATED)	
OILS AND GREASES	Resistant
DETERGENTS	
U.V. RESISTANCE	Improved with inhibitors
WEATHERABILITY	Good
OXYGEN PERMEABILITY	
NITROGEN PERMEABILITY	
CARBON DIOXIDE PERMEABILITY	

JOINTING PROCESS

Adhesive bonding using epoxy systems after an abrasive pretreatment. Mechanical fixing.

SAFETY PRECAUTIONS

Precautions to be taken over fumes during moulding

PROCESSING AND FORMING TECHNIQUES

Glass fibre cloth is laid over the mould surface and the resin is sprayed or stippled into the weave. This is repeated by layering until the required thickness is obtained.

TYPICAL APPLICATIONS

Pipes required for pressure or high temperature work. Applications where higher strength and rigidity is required than provided by glass fibre mat Solar heating systems enclosing boxes and glazing

YOUR SUPPLIER AND NOTES

BSRIA material data sheet

SHEET NUMBER	PL40 **A**

FAMILY GROUP	PLASTICS	SUB-GROUP	REINFORCED	MATERIAL	POLYESTER & GLASS FIBRE ROVING (WOVEN)

GENERAL DESCRIPTION

Undirectional glass roving reinforcement gives maximum mechanical properties along the roving direction. This fibre reinforcement gives the strongest mechanical properties.

CHEMICAL ANALYSIS OR COMPOSITION

Polyester + 70-75% undirectional.

SYNONYM

GRP

SYNONYM

PHYSICAL PROPERTIES

PROPERTY	UNITS	VALUE OR RANGE	COMMENTS
DENSITY	kg/m^3	1980	
SHEAR STRENGTH	N/mm^2		
TENSILE STRENGTH	N/mm^2	63	
ELONGATION	%	2.7	
COMPRESSIVE STRENGTH	N/mm^2	23	
FLEXURAL STRENGTH	N/mm^2	42	
IMPACT STRENGTH	J		
TENSILE MODULUS	N/mm^2	3.3×10^{-4}	
HARDNESS			
THERMAL COEFF. OF LINEAR EXPANSION	$^o C^{-1}$	8×10^{-6}	
MIN./MAX. SERVICE TEMPERATURE	$^o C$		
DEFLECTION TEMPERATURE	$^o C$		
THERMAL CONDUCTIVITY	W/mK	0.43	
FLAMMABILITY		Burns	
DIELECTRIC STRENGTH	kV/mm		
VOLUME RESISTIVITY	ohm cm	10^{16} (10^{16})	Dry (wet)
PERMITIVITY	ohm cm		
ARC RESISTANCE	secs		
NUMBER OF PARTS			
CURING METHOD			
OPTICAL PROPERTIES			
FRICTION			
MOULD SHRINKAGE			
WATER ABSORPTION	%	0.5	

 **material data sheet**

SPECIFICATIONS

STANDARD NUMBER	AUTHORITY	TITLE
BS 3522:	BSI	Unsaturated polyester resin systems for fibre reinforcement
BS 3691:	BSI	Glass fibre rovings for the reinforcement of polyester resin systems
BS 3749:	BSI	Woven roving fabrics for reinforcement of polyester resins
BS 5480 Pt 1:	BSI	GRP pipes and fittings for water supply or sewage

COMPANY SPECIFICATION:

ENVIRONMENT

RESISTANCE TO ATTACK FROM:

MINERAL ACIDS (WEAK)	Resistant
MINERAL ACIDS (STRONG)	
ALKALIS (WEAK)	Resistant
ALKALIS (STRONG)	
SOLVENTS (CHLORINATED)	
OILS AND GREASES	Resistant
DETERGENTS	
U.V. RESISTANCE	Inhibitors added
WEATHERABILITY	Good

OXYGEN PERMEABILITY
NITROGEN PERMEABILITY
CARBON DIOXIDE PERMEABILITY

JOINTING PROCESS

SAFETY PRECAUTIONS

Precautions to be taken over fumes during moulding

PROCESSING AND FORMING TECHNIQUES

Drapes more easily than glass fibre cloth Resin is sprayed or stippled in the roving. This is repeated until the required thickness is obtained. To ensure maximum properties the glass must be totally wetted

TYPICAL APPLICATIONS

Similar applications as other reinforced polyester but where improved mechanical properties are required.

YOUR SUPPLIER AND NOTES

BSRIA **material data sheet**		SHEET NUMBER PL41	**A**
FAMILY GROUP PLASTICS	SUB-GROUP REINFORCED	MATERIAL POLYESTER + GLASS FIBRE ROVINGS	

GENERAL DESCRIPTION

Mechanical properties obtained with rovings is superior to those from glass fibre mat.

CHEMICAL ANALYSIS OR COMPOSITION

SYNONYM

GRP

SYNONYM

PHYSICAL PROPERTIES

PROPERTY	UNITS	VALUE OR RANGE	COMMENTS
DENSITY	kg/m^3	1760	
SHEAR STRENGTH	N/mm^2		
TENSILE STRENGTH	N/mm^2	32	
ELONGATION	%	3.7	
COMPRESSIVE STRENGTH	N/mm^2	17	
FLEXURAL STRENGTH	N/mm^2	32	
IMPACT STRENGTH	J		
TENSILE MODULUS	N/mm^2	2×10^{-4}	
HARDNESS			
THERMAL COEFF. OF LINEAR EXPANSION	$^{\circ}C^{-1}$	15.10^{-6}	
MIN./MAX. SERVICE TEMPERATURE	$^{\circ}C$		
DEFLECTION TEMPERATURE	$^{\circ}C$		
THERMAL CONDUCTIVITY	W/mK	0.28	
FLAMMABILITY		Burns	
DIELECTRIC STRENGTH	kV/mm		
VOLUME RESISTIVITY	ohm cm	10^{16} (10^7)	Dry (wet)
PERMITIVITY	ohm cm		
ARC RESISTANCE	secs		
NUMBER OF PARTS			
CURING METHOD			
OPTICAL PROPERTIES			
FRICTION			
MOULD SHRINKAGE			
WATER ABSORPTION			

 **material data sheet**

SPECIFICATIONS

STANDARD NUMBER	AUTHORITY	TITLE
BS 3522:	BSI	Unsaturated polyesters resins for fibre reinforcement
BS 3691:	BSI	Glass fibre rovings for the reinforecement of polyester resin system
BS 3749:	BSI	Woven roving fabrics fibre for reinforcement of polyester resin
BS 5480 Pt 1	BSI	GRP pipes and fittings for water supply or sewage

COMPANY SPECIFICATION:

ENVIRONMENT

RESISTANCE TO ATTACK FROM:

MINERAL ACIDS (WEAK)	Resistant
MINERAL ACIDS (STRONG)	
ALKALIS (WEAK)	Resistant
ALKALIS (STRONG)	
SOLVENTS (CHLORINATED)	
OILS AND GREASES	Resistant
DETERGENTS	

U.V. RESISTANCE

WEATHERABILITY

OXYGEN PERMEABILITY

NITROGEN PERMEABILITY

CARBON DIOXIDE PERMEABILITY

PROCESSING AND FORMING TECHNIQUES

Forms easily over the mould during (easier than fabric). Resin/roving system manufactured with resin applied by spray or stippled by hand. Maximum properties obtained after glass totally wetted.

TYPICAL APPLICATIONS

Reinforced pipes and fittings. Tanks and insulation
Ductwork
Expansion tanks
Electrical component covers

JOINTING PROCESS

Adhesive bonding using epoxy systems after an abrasive pretreatment:
Mechanical fixing

YOUR SUPPLIER AND NOTES

SAFETY PRECAUTIONS

Precautions to be taken over fumes during moulding

4.5 SURFACE PROTECTION

The functions of a surface coating are:-

- prevention of corrosion
- decorative finish
- to impart special properties

A single type of coating may fulfil one, two or all functions.

The range of surface coatings is shown in Figure 4.5/1. Surface coatings provide an economical means for combining the properties of the substrate and the coating to give a composite material that has both good mechanical properties and good corrosion resistance in the working environment. Ideally, a surface coating should form a continuous barrier that completely isolates the substrate from the environment. Unfortunately, this is seldom achieved, since the method of application of the coating can give rise to discontinuties such as pores, pits and cracks. Discontinuities can be produced by subsequent production operations or by mechanical damage. Under such conditions it is necessary to consider not only the corrosion resistance of the coating and the substrate but their effect when in contact with each other and the environment, particularly for metallic coatings.

One of the most important factors when choosing a protective coating is the environment, which is fully discussed in Section 1.4.

SURFACE PREPARATION

To achieve maximum protection from the surface coating it is essential that the substrate is in suitable condition to receive the coating.

Surface contamination due to handling, production processes, oil, or atmospheric dirt must be removed by solvent or chemical cleaning, possibly assisted by ultrasonics or electrolytic action.

Superficial corrosion, oxidation resulting from hot working, and scale must be removed by abrasion or immersion in acid or alkali pickling solutions. The solution used and the time of immersion are dependent on material and severity of corrosion. Table 4.5/2 gives a summary of pickling methods for different metal substrates.

Should the surface coating be required to have a particular finish such as satin, polished etc. then the substrate surface must be pretreated by grit blasting, abrading, polishing or etching.

4.5.1 METALLIC COATINGS

When Choosing a metallic coating the parameters that must be considered are:-

- the environment

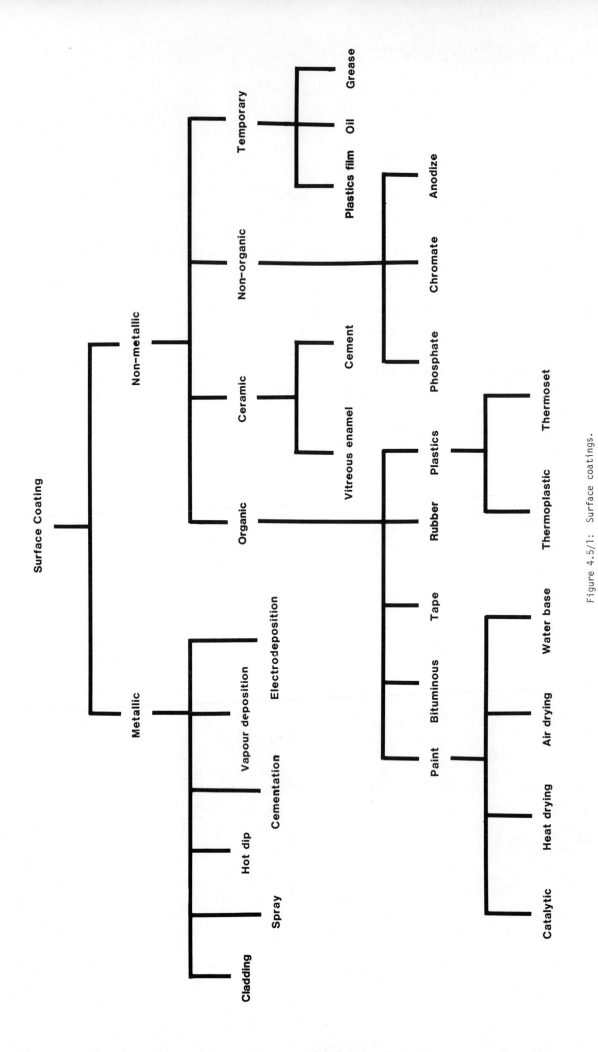

Figure 4.5/1: Surface coatings.

584

Metal	Soak cleaning	Immersion pickling	Electrolytic pickling	Salt-bath descaling
Iron or steel	Dilute acids used for removing light corrosion only. Pitting can occur with cast iron	Simple acid solutions used for removing rust or scale from plain carbon steels or cast irons. Stronger acid mixtures used for alloy steel. High-strength steels may suffer hydrogen embrittlement. Cast irons may become pitted	Anodic or cathodic treatment in acids used for steels especially prior to electroplating. Alkaline processes suitable for treating cast iron.	Mainly used for removing heavy scales from alloy steels and for removing siliceous scales from cast iron
Copper-base alloys	Dilute sulphuric acid used for removing light tarnish	Dilute mineral acids, often in mixtures or with addition of dichromate salts, used for removing heavier oxide scales	Mild cathodic alkali processes used for removal of light tarnish	Mainly used to remove very tough scales or adherent siliceous scales
Zinc and its alloys	Very dilute acids only used with short duration treatments		Not used	Not used
Tin and lead	Dilute acids used for removing light tarnish	Fluoboric acid solutions used for general pickling	Not used	Not used
Aluminium and its alloys	Dilute acid or alkali solutions used for light etching only. Smut deposits removed by subsequent nitric acid dipping	Nitric/hydro-fluoric acid mixtures and hot chromic/sulphuric acid mixtures used for general pickling. Hydrofluoric acid or caustic alkali mixtures used for etching	Not used	Sodium hydride used for removing adherent siliceous scales
Magnesium and its alloys	Not often used	Chromic/hydro-fluoric, nitric, phosphoric, acetic and sulphuric acids all used in combinations for general pickling and etching	Not used	Not used
Nickel and its alloys	Not used	Sulphuric and hydrofluoric acids used for general pickling	Cathodic treatment in acids	Little used except for heat-resisting high-nickel alloys

Table 4.5/2: Pickling methods for different metals.

- the substrate to which the coating is being applied
- the coating metal
- the type of coating, as controlled by its method of application
- the need for an under-coat or other surface preparation

Metallic coatings can be divided into anodic and cathodic types:-

Anodic Coatings

Anodic coating metals (i.e metals that are anodic to the substrate) include, for steel zinc, aluminium and cadmium. If any discontinuities, pores or breaks exist in the anodic film a galvanic cell is formed between coating and substrate such that the substrate will be protected by a sacrificial anode until all the coating material in the vicinity has been corroded. The area of substrate protected after a break depends on the electrical conductivity of the corrosive environment. In solutions of low conductivity, (e.g. potable water), iron is readily attacked if the break in a zinc coating is larger than 3 to 12mm. In sea water the protection may extend over 100mm or more.

Cathodic Coatings

Cathodic coatings include, for steel and iron, tin, lead, copper, nickel and chromium, and give effective protection to the substrate only when they are continuous and free from pores. They offer protection because they have higher corrosion resistance than the substrate, but if a break occurs then intense local corrosion of the substrate will take place.

A variety of processes exist for applying metal coatings. They use different techniques and produce coatings with differing characteristics.

MOLTEN APPLICATIONS

In molten applications the surface coating metal is heated to the molten state and the substrate material is either immersed in the molten bath (hot dip) or has the molten coating metal flowed or otherwise transferred on to its surface (soldering). The molten coating metal may react with the solid substrate metal to produce an alloy by diffusion. To ensure that the molten metal totally wets the substrate a flux is used to remove any oxide layer. Hot dipped coatings are normally specified by their weight rather than thickness. The thickness of coating is dependent on time in the bath. Hot dipping tends to produce rather thick coatings and it is not easy to control uniformity with irregularly shaped objects. Zinc, aluminium and lead are the only commercially important coating metals in this category.

SPRAY APPLICATIONS

Spray application is widely applied to the protection of large structures against corrosion. Aluminium and zinc are the most commonly applied coatings by this technique, using an oxy-acetylene spray gun and metal in the form of powder or wire. During the spraying process the globules of molten metal flatten out against the surface; there is some flow into pores and irregularities which locks the coating together. Unlike hot dipping there is usually little alloying between the substrate and coating. The coating can be porous and therefore, for total protection, a further surface coating, such as paint, may be required. Zinc and aluminium and their alloys are used as sprayed coatings for the protection of steel against atmospheric corrosion in thicknesses in the range of 50-150mm, while thicker coatings are used for immersion applications. These coatings provide sacrificial protection to the steel substrate. The stiffling action of the corrosion products is greater than with hot dip or electrodeposited coatings and consequently longer lifes may be obtained in service. When spraying steel the surface remains cool and no distortion is created.

ELECTRODEPOSITION

Electrodepostion produces purer and more even coatings than other techniques and enables better control to be achieved. The method used (such as bath or barrel plating) depends on the shape and size of component. It is of vital importance that the component to be processed is free of grease and oxides. The principal metals electrodeposited are copper, cadmium, chromium, gold, lead, nickel, silver, tin and zinc. As some metals do not produce a fault free surface (e.g. micro-cracking in chromium deposits) another material must be pre-plated as an undercoat and this material must also be able to cope with the environment for the total protection of the substrate. The use of plastics materials as a substrate can offer advantages over the use of metals. With the development of 'electroless' coating techniques and special surface pre-treatment it is now possible to coat plastics materials, notably ABS and polyproylene, with most standard electrodeposited metals.

CEMENTATION

Cementation is the process by which the metal substrate is heated while in contact with a powder of the coating metal to a temperature somewhat below the melting point of either. The 'Sherardising Process' uses this principle by coating steel with zinc to form a surface alloy between the steel and the zinc. Other coating materials are aluminium (calorising) and chromium (chromising). Although cementation coated surfaces are not as corrosion resistant as coatings applied by other methods they have the advantage that thin controlled coatings can be applied.

CLADDING

Metal cladding is carried out by sandwiching the base metal between two layers of coating metal and then rolling the composite to produce firm adhesion. The base material can have inferior properties compared to the skin material for the appearance or environmental considerations, e.g. pure aluminium cladding of poor corrosion resistant high strength aluminium alloy for use in corrosive environments. Similarly steel plate can be clad in stainless steel, nickel or nickel alloys. There is no protection of the base metal from edge attack.

VAPOUR DEPOSITION

The deposition of metals from the vapour phase is a method of producing a coating having properties that differ from those of coatings produced by other means. It is possible to obtain coatings that have an extremely high degree of purity and freedom from oxides, extremely thin and bright, and can be deposited directly onto either metallic or non-metallic substrates. A typical metal used is pore free aluminium for decorative, protective and reflective applications. Precious metal deposits can be applied by vapour deposition with the advantage that thin film deposits result in low costs for the deposited material. This operation must be performed under a vacuum.

4.5.1.1 Aluminium

Its value lies in the relative inertness of the coating itself, caused by the stability and coherence of the surface oxide film. However, the surface is soft and must be protected from abrasion. Aluminium coatings may be applied by dipping, spraying or vacuum deposition. Aluminium is anodic to steel but large discontinuities can lead to local attack. Reaction at high temperatures converts aluminium coat to alumina. Tenacious natural oxide layer gives high level of protection. Aluminium alloys can be coated with aluminium by spraying and hot dip coating. Hot dipped coatings, with fluxing, produces a coating of the order of 150 g/m^2 on steel (about 25 microns). Sprayed metal coatings on steel produce thicknesses in the range of 50 - 150 microns.

High strength aluminium alloys and steel clad with high purity aluminium is commercially available. Protection of raw edges is required.

An aluminium coating provides good atmospheric protection, with firm adhesion to the substrate, up to a relatively high temperature (900°C). Less corrosion resistant aluminium alloy should be protected by aluminium cladding if immersed or buried.

Cementation by the Calorizing method produces coatings of 0.5-1 mm thick. Calorised material must not be severely deformed (a maximum of 5% elongation) otherwise the coating cracks.

Vacuum vapour deposition is used for decorative and protective applications.

4.5.1.2. Cadmium

Cadmium resembles zinc in being anodic to steel but its protective power is not as good. It is superior to zinc for very humid internal atmospheres but not for external use. Cadmium plating is more expensive than zinc and about 25 microns thick.

In exposure to industrial atmospheres the sulphates formed are water soluble and hence the coating is rapidly washed away by rainwater; in a marine atmosphere the chlorides formed are insoluble resulting in an extended coating life. Cadmium can be soldered with activated resin flux; welding cadmium plated components produces toxic fumes. The formation of toxic compounds precludes the use of cadmium coated materials with foodstuffs.
Cadmium provides good protection in stagnant or soft water but poor resistance to acidic conditions. It can be used as a protective layer between copper and steel to prevent galvanic action. Added protection is given by chromate passivation of coating. Commonly used for coatings on electronic components and fasteners.

Cadmium coatings are also produced by vapour deposition.

4.5.1.3 Chromium

The commonest use of chromium as a coating material is in the form of an electrodeposit, which remains virtually inert on exposure to the atmosphere or when immersed in water. Because of its high degree of resistance to corrosion and tarnishing, together with its colour and high lustre, it is mainly used as a decorative finish, high temperature oxidation protection and aggressive environment protection. Its hardness of 800-900HV also makes it suitable for wear resistant coatings.

Thin decorative deposits of chromium (0.3 to 1.0 microns) are always porous due to micro-cracks leading to corrosion of the underlying metal. Since chromium provides a large cathodic area, rapid localised attack occurs. Chromium is almost always used in conjunction with suitably corrosion resistant undercoats such as nickel and copper for complete protection should have thicknesses of 25 - 125 microns. Decorative electrodeposited coatings are usually about 0.3 microns thick whereas hard chromium for wear protection should have thicknesses of 25-125 microns.

Chromium coatings are produced by electro-deposition, cementation and spraying. Steel, aluminium, zinc, copper and their alloys can be coated.

Chromium, in the form of a diffusion coating for steel, leads to improved oxidation resistance, surface hardness and wear resistance. Chromised steel has equivalent corrosion resistance properties to high chromium stainless steel up to 750°C provided the surface layer is not damaged. Since chromium relies on its oxide layer for corrosion resistance it must not be used in reducing conditions such as hydrochloric or sulphuric acid.

4.5.1.4 **Copper**

Copper can be applied to steel, zinc alloys, aluminium or plastics. Coats may be applied by electrodeposition, electroless plating or cladding. Copper up to 15 micron thick is used as a precoat leveler prior to nickel plating. Prior to case hardening of steel, parts required soft areas are copper plated to prevent carbon diffusion.

Copper coatings offer a very high degree of corrosion resistance when exposed to the atmosphere. Its high ductility and good electrical and thermal conductivity enhance its value as a coating material. When used as an electrodeposit the high degree of levelling obtained can reduce the amount of pre-plate polishing required for highly decorative finishes. Copper coatings tarnish quickly and if a bright finish is required then it must be protected by a clear lacquer. Copper is widely used as undercoat for more noble metals, e.g. nickel. Plastics can be electrolessly plated after the substrate has been correctly prepared. Steel can be clad by immersion in molten copper. However, since copper is cathodic to steel coating integrity is of prime importance.

Copper can be buried in soil providing that it is not acidic.

4.5.1.5 **Lead**

Lead is applied to steel or copper by hot dipping, cladding or electrodeposition. Pure lead tends to produce pin holes which could result in localised attack and equally does not form a compound or combine with the steel. By adding up to 20% tin the porosity problem can be overcome. A hot-dip coating of 80% lead and 20% tin, called Terne Plate, can be used where resistance to acid fumes is required. A thickness of up to 25 microns can be achieved.

Lead protects ferrous and copper based alloys from corrosion in acidic environments. Coatings are applied by hot-dipping, electrodeposition and cladding. The coating is very soft and ductile, and can be formed without failure. As lead is cathodic to steel attack is accelerated at pinholes in the coating.

4.5.1.6 **Nickel**

Nickel is one of the most important of the common coating materials because it has virtually the

589

same strength, hardness and ductility as steel yet it is corrosion resistant to the atmosphere and water. The ductility of the coating is dependent on the method of production and its purity. Nickel coatings, with a copper precoat, are used as an underlay for chromium coatings. When coating steel, a copper coat is often electrodeposited first in order to render the nickel coat more adherent and to make the total coating more corrosion resistant by making it more impervious.

Nickel plating (in the range of 5 to 60 microns thick) is applied to steel, copper and zinc and their alloys, and aluminium. It provides resistance to high temperature oxidation and to corrosion when immersed in sea and potable water.

The natural oxide layer will break down with a lack of oxygen such as in crevices and buried in the soil. Nickel coats have a good resistance to alkalis and sulphur but are attacked by hydrochloric acid, strong oxidising acids and salts. Polishing improves corrosion protection. Nickel can be soldered using an activated resin flux. Bright electrodeposits may cause the solder to dewet and result in poor joints.

Steel can be protected by cladding with nickel sheet and welding the edges to form an envelope. This enables the steel to be used in hostile environments.

4.5.1.7 Silver

Silver is one of the noble metals and is generally resistant to corrosion. However, it is prone to tarnish by traces of sulphur in contaminated atmospheres. Silver is the best conductor of electricity and therefore finds many outlets as an electrical contact material. To improve its wear and tarnish problems a thin electrodeposit of corrosion resistant rhodium is applied (0.4 to 5.0 microns).

Sulphur tarnish prevents soldering but clean silver presents no problems. The oxide layer on rhodium can cause problems if not soldered quickly.

Silver coatings may be applied by electrodeposition, vacuum deposition and electroless plating of plastics.

4.5.1.8 Tin

Typical coating thicknesses vary from 0.5 to 5 microns. Tin is applied to steel or copper and its alloys by hot dipping or electrodeposition. Tin is cathodic with respect to steel and no protection is offered if there are any breaks in the coating. In contact with organic acids, such as fruit juices, the tin acts as a sacrificial anode. Tin is a non-toxic material and possesses excellent solderability and electrical conductivity.

Hot dipped coatings on steel and copper are usually in the range 25-75 g/m^2.

Tin exhibits poor resistance to alkalis, sea water and marine environments but resists attack by potable water. Tinned coatings are readily soldered. Long term contact with food products requires a vinyl, phenolic or wax coating for complete protection.

4.5.1.9 Zinc

Zinc is a soft metal of low strength that corrodes freely, but relatively slowly, in the atmosphere at a constant rate. The rate of corrosion in marine and rural atmospheres is one

590

fifth that of industrial environments. In conditions of high humidity a white corrosion product is formed (white rust) but it can be avoided by passivating the zinc surface by a chromate treatment. Protection is improved by painting.

Zinc coatings may be applied by hot dipping, metal spraying, electro-deposition or cementation (Sheradizing).

Hot dipping can produce films up to 75 micron, electrodeposition up to 25 micron and metal sprayed coatings up to 300 micron.

The weight of coating must relate to the severity of the environment and length of time between maintenance, see Figure 4.5/3.

Zinc provides a very good anode when coupled to steel and so gives efficient sacrificial protection. Protection can be maintained over quite large areas of exposed substrate.

The alloy layer is harder than mild steel but the zinc layer is comparitively soft. If abraded the hard alloy layer protects the base metal.

Galvanizing by hot dip in molten zinc is carried out at 450°C. At this temperature there will be no effect on the mechanical properties of the substrate but there could be some stress relief which may cause distorton. Components should be stress relieved prior to coating application.

The galvanized coating consists of a layer of zinc/iron alloy covered by pure zinc. The extent of the zinc/iron layer is dependent on the reactivity of the steel. The most reactive are steels with a silicon content of about 0.25%.

Sheradising is used for the surface protection of small objects, both steel and non-ferrous, by coating them with a thin layer of zinc rich alloy while heating in a drum of zinc powder. Close toleranced articles can be protected because of the control over the process.

Zinc can be electroplated onto steel to give a fine and smooth finish. It is used to protect delicate objects where rough or uneven finishes cannot be tolerated (i.e. instrument parts) and for articles that cannot withstand the pre-treatment and temperatures in the other coating processes. The zinc coating is very ductile and can be applied to components that may subsequently be formed. Zinc plated coatings are usually passivated to prevent 'wet storage' staining; the most usual treatment is a simple chromate dip.

Zinc-rich paints may be used alone for protection or as a primer followed by conventional overcoats. They are formulated either in synthetic organic media, such as epoxy resins, chlorinated rubber, or in silicate media which has the advantage of withstanding up to 500°C, such as would be required for chimneys. In order to obtain the effect of a true zinc coating from such paints it is essential that the dry paint film should be capable of conducting electricity and should be in contact with the base metal. To ensure good contact the steel must be abraded (e.g. shot or grit blasted) before application. Zinc-rich paint should conform with BS 4652 and contain 90% metallic zinc in the dry film. Zinc-rich paints are also used to repair damage in other types of zinc coatings caused by corrosion, welding or mechanical damage.

Good sacrificial protection is given by zinc coatings applied to aluminium alloys, the coatings being applied by metal spraying. The sprayed coating is porous and therefore only suitable for applications where zinc is anodic with respect to the substrate.

591

Figure 4.5/3: Typical lives of zinc coatings in selected environments.

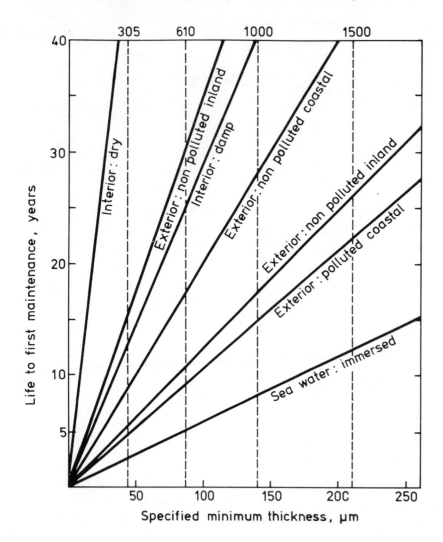

4.5.2 INORGANIC COATINGS

(See also Ceramic Coatings - Section 4.5.7.)

Inorganic coatings are produced by treating the metal chemically in such a way that an appropriate compound is formed. Such coatings applied to steel are not good enough to protect on their own and are used as pre-treatments for the applications of paint and plastics. The common inorganic coating methods are phosphating, chromating and anodising.

4.5.2.1 PHOSPHATING

A Surface conversion process of iron and steel produces a coating with limited corrosion protection. It is primarily used as a pretreatment for painting. Zinc may also be phosphate treated.

The process produces a coating containing phosphate and other desirable elements; the type of coating depends on the bath composition.

These coatings have excellent adhesion to the substrate but provide little corrosion resistance on their own and would normally be covered with another finish. Alternatively, these coatings will hold a layer of grease or oil which will improve their protection capacity. A phospate coating would normally be about 1 to 2 g/m^2, though heavier coating can be produced.

4.5.2.2 CHROMATE

Chromate coatings are usually applied to zinc, aluminium and their alloys, and cadmium. They are normally chemically produced with a coating thickness of the order of 1 micron or less. The chromate treatment of zinc and cadmium is also referred to as passivation. The coating on aluminium produces an irradescent colouring and provides a small measure of protection against corrosion; it is electronically conducting. All chromate surface treatment form an excellent base for paint. Chromate treatments should not be applied to components which are to be used in contact with explosives. Chromate treatment may be applied to phosphate finishes to improve paint adhesion. Provides some resistance to corrosion compared with non-chromated articles. Corrosion protection breaks down at 65°C.

4.5.2.3 ANODISING

This is an electrolytic process in which the component is made anodic in a suitable electrolyte. The coating consists of the oxide of the base metal, the most common being aluminium. The coating produced on aluminium and its alloys is hard, refractory, electrically insulating, and can be coloured. It provides protection against atmospheric corrosion and is an excellent pre-treatment for painting.

The electrolytic process is carried out with various electrolytes:-

- sulphuric acid
- chromic acid
- hard anodising version of the sulphuric system.

The sulphuric method is most appropriate for decorative finishes; hard anodic surfaces provide good wear resistance.

593

The chromic method is used for castings

Sulphuric acid methods produce thicker films than those with chromic acid as the electrolyte. The coatings produced by the sulphuric acid process should be sealed by immersion in hot water for optimum protection. Where wear resistance is required components should be hard anodized by a variation of the sulphuric acid method. The chromic acid process, which is less corrosive, is preferred for the anodizing of castings and components where entrapped electrolyte may be a hazard.

There may be a slight dimensional increase during the anodizing process but the effect is negligible for most purposes.

Aluminium alloys containing silicon produce dark coatings.

4.5.3 PAINTS

The term 'paint' will be assumed to include varnishes and lacquers. These coatings have the following properties in varying degrees depending on the composition of the coating: good flowing and levelling, satisfactory spreading rate and film thickness, fast drying, impermeability, good adhesion, flexibility, hardness, abrasion resistance and durability.
A paint consists of:-

- medium (vehicle) - a clear varnish or gum that attaches itself to the surface of the object to be coated and solidifies there.
- solvent - provides the surface coating material in a form in which it can be readily applied and evaporates after application.
- pigment - these are materials chosen for their opaqueness and colouring capacity.
- extenders - increase the body of the paint and so improve abrasion resistance.
- driers - catalysts to improve the rate of setting and final strength.

When an organic coating consists of a medium and solvent only, it is termed a varnish. Paints are varnishes that have pigments and/or extenders.

Painting usually consists of primer, undercoat and finish. Priming paint is formulated to secure maximum adhesion and often contains, as pigments, substances which have corrosion inhibiting properties such as red lead and zinc chromate. In some cases the adhesion is improved by the primer mildly attacking the metal substrate (etch primer) such as on aluminium. The undercoat is essentially used to build up thickness. The finishing paint is designed to provide maximum weather resistance and imparts the final colour and texture. The three coats should be compatible with each other and therefore should come from the same source.

Paints are categorised by their drying method and by their major constituants. A summary of the properties of paints is in Table 4.5/4.

594

Table 4.5/4: Summary of paint properties.

COATING	Short Oil Alkyd	Long Oil Alkyd	Silicone Alkyd	PVC Acetate Copolymer	Vinyl Acrylic	Resin Modified Chlorinated Rubber
PROPERTY						
Physical Property	Hard	Flexible	Tough	Tough	Tough	Hard
Water Resistance	Fair	Fair	Good	Very Good	Good	Very Good
Acid Resistance	Fair	Poor	Fair	Excellent	Very Good	Very Good
Alkali Resistance	Poor	Poor	Poor	Excellent	Very Good	Very Good
Solvent Resistance	Fair	Poor	Fair	Aliphatic Hydrocarbon Good / Aromatic Hydrocarbon Poor	Aliphatic Hydrocarbon Good / Aromatic Hydrocarbon Poor	Aliphatic Hydrocarbon Good / Aromatic Hydrocarbon Poor
Temperature Resistance	Good	Good	Best of Group	Fair (65°C)	Fair (65°C)	Fair
Weathering	Fair	Good	Very Good	Very Good	Excellent	Good
Recoating	Easy	Easy	Fair	Easy	Easy	Easy

COATING	Water Base Acrylic Polymers	Water Base Polyvinyl Acetate	Epoxy Amine	Epoxy Polyamide	Epoxy Coal tar	Epoxy Ester
PROPERTY						
Physical Property	Scrub Resistant	Scrub Resistant	Hard	Tough	Hard	Flexible
Water Resistance	Poor	Poor	Good	Very Good	Excellent	Good
Acid Resistance	Poor	Poor	Good	Fair	Good	Fair
Alkali Resistance	Poor	Poor	Good	Excellent	Good	Poor
Solvent Resistance	Poor	Poor	Very Good	Fair	Poor	Fair
Temperature Resistance	Fair	Fair	Very Good	Good	Good	Good
Weathering	Excellent	Very Good	Fair-Chalks	Good-Chalks	Poor	Good-Chalks
Recoating	Easy	Easy	Difficult	Difficult	Difficult	Reasonable

COATING	Polyurethane Air Drying Varnish	Polyurethane Two Pack System	Polyurethane Moisture Reactive	Polyurethane Non-Yellowing	Zinc-Water Base	Zinc-Organic Base
PROPERTY						
Physical Property	Very Tough	Tough Hard	Very Tough Abrasion Resistant	Fairly Hard To Rubbery	Tough Abrasion Resistance. Excellent Chemical Bond	Tough-Hard Excellent Bond
Water Resistance	Fair	Good	Fair	Good	Good	Good
Acid Resistance	Fair	Fair	Fair	Fair	Poor	Poor
Alkali Resistance	Fair	Fair	Fair	Fair	Poor	Poor
Solvent Resistance	Fair	Good	Good	Good	Excellent	Good
Temperature Resistance	Good	Good	Good	Good	Excellent	Excellent
Weathering	Yellowing	Some Yellowing and Chalking	Fades in light Yellows in Shade	Very Good	Excellent	Excellent
Recoating	Requires Care	Difficult	Difficult	Difficult	Easy	Easy

4.5.3.1   **AIR DRYING PAINTS**

OLEORESINOUS

These are developed from a linseed oil based coating. By replacing a portion of the linseed oil with tung oil a brushable paint with improved weathering and water resistance is produced that dries in 12 to 16 hours. The higher the proportion of oil the better the weathering characteristics.

ALKYD RESINS

These are the most widely used air drying resins.   As with oleoresinous varnishes, the properties depend on the percentage of oil (or oil 'length'), viz:-

-   long oil alkyd resins (60 to 80% oil) are normally used to produce glossy finishes with brush application.
-   medium oil alkyd resins (40 to 60% oil) are used in undercoats or in quick drying finishes where appearance and flexibility are of less importance.
-   short oil alkyd resins (less than 40% oil) are very quick drying and only usable in strong solvents. They are not brushing paints.

Alkyds are susceptible to degradation by acids and alkalis (lime plaster or new concrete) and are not suitable for total immersion. With the addition of polyamides a gel is produced, then referred to as a thixotropic paint.

Coats are touch dry after about 4 hours when white spirit is the solvent.

EPOXY-ESTERS

They are sometimes called one-pack epoxies (see Section 4.5.1.2. for two-part epoxcies) but they closely resemble alkyds. Compared with alkyds, epoxy-esters have better chemical resistance but poorer weathering properties. They tend to degrade under ultra-violet light, resulting in 'chalking' and 'yellowing'. They show very good adhesion to the substrate.

CHLORINATED RUBBER

Chlorinated rubbers on their own produce brittle coatings but are improved with the addition of a plasticiser, normally chlorinated paraffin. Chlorinated rubbers have very good water and chemical resistance (including acids, alkalis, moist gases, oxidising agents, etc) but poor resistance to aromatic solvents (the common paint solvents), animal fats and oils. Inter-coat adhesion is achieved by solvent fusion. It can be applied by brush, but previous coats may be picked up, or by spray. They are particularly useful in aggressive, highly corrosive environments. A high build can be achieved with a total protective coating of around 300 microns. Due to their thermoplastic nature, chlorinated rubbers cannot be used over 80°C.

ALKYD SILICONE

A mixture of alkyd and a silicone resins produces a high gloss paint for use where long durability is required under severe conditions. This has good temperature resistance but, due to the use of silicone, the cost is approximately four times that of alkyd resins alone.

4.5.3.2 PAINT CURED BY CATALYTIC ACTION

EPOXY

Paints based on epoxy resins can be cured at ambient temperatures by the addition of a catalyst. The proportion of catalyst is critical and the pot life of the mix is dependent on the ambient temperature; indefinite at 4°C, 12 to 16 hours at 20°C. The minimum working temperature should be 10°C. By means of the catalyst it is possible to obtain finishes which approach the toughness and abrasion resistance of vitreous enamel without the tendency to chip and with better adhesion. The curing can be speeded up by the use of heat. At temperatures above 120-150°C the finishes yellow, as they do slightly in sunlight. Ultra-violet radiation degrades the outer skin and forms 'chalking'. Although this is cosmetically detrimental it does not affect the protective properties of the coating. Epoxy systems are expensive but the cost can be reduced by adding cheaper materials. By adding tar, a surface coating with increased water resistance and good durability is produced which is appreciably cheaper than the unmodified epoxy.

POLYURETHANES

Compared with epoxies, two part polyurethanes show slightly lower chemical and solvent resistance but higher water resistance. They dry to a higher gloss with a more flexible film. The catalyst used is moisture sensitive so that great care must be taken during mixing. Because of the high gloss, overcoating can be difficult unless the previous coating is abraded.

One pack polyurethane systems are based on a resin where a partial reaction has occurred to give a prepolymer and reaction with atmospheric moisture gives polymerisation and film formation. They dry to very hard films and are used on metal surfaces liable to impact. The chemical and solvent resistance is inferior to that of the two pack systems and durability is not as good as some alkyd systems. Clear solutions are ideal for floors but a poor finish will be obtained if conditions are humid at the time of application.

4.5.3.3 PAINTS DRIED BY HEAT

In factory applied surface coatings it is necessary to obtain a quick curing paint system. This can be achieved by raising the temperature of the film in order that the chemical reaction may be speeded up. This is called 'stoving'. By adjusting the composition, some air drying paints, such as alkyd and epoxy, may be force dried.

ACRYLIC

Paints based on acrylic resins are used widely in the motor industry and are cured by the application of heat. Their advantages are speed of drying to give a tough and mar-resistant film with excellent durability and colour retention.

WATER BASED PRIMERS

With the introduction of electro-painting systems, surface coatings consisting of water soluble resins were developed. These are used in the car industry by totally immersing the body in a tank of paint, applying an electric current to attract the paint, removing and then stoving at 160°C for 1 hour. This system ensures that paint is applied to all external and internal faces of box sections to give complete coverage. This system is also applied to window frames for complete protection.

597

4.5.3.4 WATER BASED PAINTS

The air drying types consist of the polymer emulsion paints in which the polymer together with thickeners and pigment are in suspension in an aqueous solution. Film formation takes place by the evaporation of the water and the coalescence of the polymer with the pigment.

VINYL EMULSIONS

They contain polymers of vinyl acetate together with a monomer. The copolymers can be produced in a range of finishes, matt for inside and semi-gloss or egg shell for either internal or external applications. External finishes may also have additions of fibres or grit for a rough cast appearance.

ACRYLIC EMULSIONS

The hardness and flexibility of acrylic emulsions can be controlled by the proportion of monomer added. The range of finishes available are gloss, semi-gloss, eggshell and matt which are characterised by their good adhesion to most surfaces together with lasting elasticity. In addition to being used for internal or external walls they may be used as primers for wood, hardboard and other absorbent surfaces.

4.5.4 BITUMINOUS COATINGS

Bituminous coatings are low cost coatings, whose protection properties depend on film thickness. There is a wide range of materials based on either mineral bitumen or coal tar fractions applied as unheated solutions, hot solutions, or hot melts; bituminous emulsions are little used. Specially developed materials, based on powdered coal dispersed in pitch, are widely used for the protection of underground pipes.

Blast cleaning before coating gives the best performance but is not essential for many uses. The materials are heated as needed in boilers near the point of application. For vertical surfaces the materials is daubed on with a stiff brush, covering small rectangular areas with short strokes and overlapping to form a continuous coating. In weld areas the brush strokes should be in the direction of the weld; a second coat should then be applied in the opposite direction. For horizontal surfaces the material can be poured on and trowelled-out and, if unevenness occurs where a smooth surface is required, it may be permissible to play a blow-lamp on to the surface and finish by trowelling.

Bitumen solutions and emulsions are readily applied by brush or spray and are often used as priming coats for heavy-duty finishes. The specifier should consider inhibitive oleo-resin-based primers for heavy-duty bitmen provided that sufficient drying time (several weeks) can be allowed before overcoating.

In general, only bituminous material should be used for overcoating bituminous materials. It is, however, possible to overcoat with some emulsion paints or cement paints and these may be desirable to reduce surface heating in sunlight.

Bituminous coatings have good resistance to dilute acids and alkalis, salt solutions and water, but are not resistant to vegatable oils, hydrocarbons and other solvents. They may become brittle in cold weather and soften in hot weather. Bitumen-coated articles should not be stacked.

4.5.4.1 COAL TAR PITCHES AND BITUMENS

Coal tar pitches have high resistance to moisture and good adhesion to steel, so they are very suitable for structures that are immersed in water (especially foul water) or buried in the ground. The appropriate water supply authority should be consulted before coal-tar-based material is used in conjunction with potable water. Coal tar pitch is less readily softened by hydrocarbon oils.

Prolonged exposure to weather and sunlight cause surface chalking because of oxidation and loss of plasticizing components, so coal-tar pitches and bitumens should never be specified for such conditions (unless they are overcoated with asphaltic material in solutions or emulsion form), nor should they be used in very hot conditions (such as may arise in a pipeline downstream of a compressor).

The coatings may be reinforced with glass fibre especially for the protection of pipelines. Wrappings made from vegetable fibres such as cotton or hessian are liable to microbiological attack.

4.5.4.2 ASPHALT COATINGS

Asphalt coatings have much better resistance than coal tar pitches to sunlight, weather and exposure to the direct heat of the sun. Resistance to breakdown under sunlight can be improved with flake aluminium. Asphalt coatings are recommended for buried or submerged conditions and they are best used with inhibitive primers.

4.5.5 WRAPPING TAPES

Wrapping with adhesive tape protects ferrous metals, particularly pipelines, joints, valves, and other fittings by excluding the environment from the substrate. To improve adhesion of the wrapping tape, any corrosion products should be removed and the substrate primed.

Buried pipelines are often supplied wrapped at works with bitumen or coal tar reinforced by glass fibre and only the joints require wrapping at site.

When applying wrapping tape an overlap of at least half the width of the tape is recommended and for coating pipes of up to 300mm diameter it is good practice to use a tape of width matching approximately the diameter of the pipe. Application by hand is satisfactory for small jobs but for large installations, such as long pipelines, fully automatic or semi-automatic methods are used. The skill lies in applying consistent tension throughout the operation, uniform bonding and the avoidance of air pockets.

Three types of wrapping are commonly available.

4.5.5.1 PETROLEUM-JELLY TAPES

These consist of fabric of natural or synthetic fibre or glass cloth impregnated with petroleum jelly. The coating is permanently plastic; it is suitable for application to irregular profiles and should be smoothed by hand, taking care to avoid any air pockets. When used above ground, these tapes should be protected by a bituminous-tape overwrap in situations where they may be subject to damage. They are also suitable for insulation between metallic components to avoid bimetallic contacts which could promote corrosion.

599

4.5.5.2 **SYNTHETIC RESIN OR PLASTIC TAPES**

The most readily available synthetic tapes are polyvinyl chloride and polyethylene tapes. These polymer strips, usually 125 micron to 250 micron thick, with a fabric core, are coated on one side with an impact adhesive, normally of synthetic rubber base. They are usually available in a range of colours if pipe identification is required.

Synthetic resin or plastic tapes are suitable as insulation to avoid bimetallic contacts, particularly in damp or dirty conditions.

Best protection is obtained if the steel is first cleaned and coated with a conventional rust inhibitive primer. For exterior exposure black polyethylene tape is preferred to polyvinyl chloride because its surface degrades much less on exposure to sunlight and weather.
A thermosetting plastic coating can be applied to protect substrates from the environment by using two pack taping. In this method of high-duty protection a woven tape is impregnated, after wrapping, with a two-pack composition, normally a polyester or two-pack epoxy. The technique used is similar to that used in the preparation of glass fibre moulding, except that the resin-impregnated glass cloth is intended to adhere to the metal substrate. This method is used especially for shafting exposed to marine conditions and for surfaces which may be subject to cavitation.

4.5.5.3 **COAL TAR AND BITUMEN TAPE**

These tapes are used mainly for buried pipelines. They have a high resistance to moisture and good adhesion to steel. The fabric reinforcement is usually made from glass fibre. The steel should first be cleaned and given a coating of coal tar or bitumen primer. According to the temperture expected in service the low temperature properties of the tape can be varied. For some high temperatures and especially for high duty requirements, the grade of coal tar or bitumen used is such that it is necessary to heat the tape to soften it sufficiently for good application and bonding, and to heat the overlap when applied in order to obtain the best seal.

4.5.6 PLASTIC AND RUBBER COATINGS

Plastic coatings give a much thicker coating than organic films and consequently give better protection to the underlying material. They can be applied by dipping into a melt or into a fluidised bed of powder or by spraying onto the surface. So that the plastic material will adhere the substrate must be free of oxidation, which is removed chemically or by grit blast. The substrate is then primed to give a satisfactory bond with the plastic coating.

The metal is pre-heated so that when it is dipped there is sufficient heat to gelate the plastic onto the metal or to melt the particles so that they flow and form a coherent film.

The following plastics materials are available as surface coatings.

4.5.6.1 **POLYETHYLENE**

This is the cheapest of the thermoplastic coatings. The low density grade is normally used since it has better melt flow characteristics. It is not as durable as other coatings and is susceptable to stress cracking, particularly on flat surfaces. Polyethylene is usually applied by hot dipping, dusting or spraying of polymer dissolved in a solvent. The coating thickness can vary from 0.3 to 3 mm. For maximum adhesion to steel or cast iron a primer must be applied. Low density polyethylene service temperature range is -70 to +95°C.

4.5.6.2 POLYVINYLCHLORIDE (PVC)

PVC is one of the most widely used plastics coating. It is available in hardnesses ranging from soft and rubbery to very hard. These coatings are generally applied by dipping and achieve film thickness of 1.0 to 2.5mm. Coated substrates can be formed without failure. PVC cannot be applied to zinc or soft soldered assemblies as they will melt at the application temperatures. Service temperatures range from -50 to +70°C.

4.5.6.3 POLYAMIDE (NYLON)

Nylon coatings have outstanding adhesion and attractive glossy tough surfaces as well as electrical insulating and corrosion resistant properties. They are applied as powders by spraying or dipping. Nylon II is the normal grade used for surface coating. Coatings of 0.2 to 1.0mm can be applied. The adhesion to steel and aluminium is outstanding but to copper and brass is poor due to the oxide layer. Smooth nylon coatings can be produced on comparatively rough coasting, such as handwheels. Nylon coatings will not withstand mineral acids. Nylon coated steel pipe hangers are satisfactory in arduous off-shore environments and chemical works. Service temperatures range from -50 to 120°C.

4.5.6.4. CHLORINATED POLYETHYLENE

Penton, a chlorinated polyethylene, offers excellent resistance to acids, alkalis and solvents between -60 and +120°C although it is an expensive material. Pipes, valves and tanks may be supplied coated for use in corrosive environments. Coatings of 0.2 to 1.0mm can be obtained.

4.5.6.5 EPOXY

Fully cured epoxy coatings are thermoset materials. They are applied by fluidised bed or electrostatic spray methods in a partially cured form so that they are sufficiently thermoplastic to form a continuous film. Coatings applied by electrostatic spraying are thinner than those produced in a fluidised bed and hence produce a more flexible film. Thick coatings are required for edge protection. Epoxy coatings have a service temperature range of -50 to +150°C with good acid and alkaline resistance and fair solvent resistance. The cured film is non-toxic and non-flammable.

4.5.6.6 PTFE

PTFE is applied as a dispersion. Since it cannot be obtained as a continuous film it does not offer very much protection against corrosion. Its major usage has been in the fields of non-stick applications. PTFE has a service temperature range of -80 to +250°C. Coatings of 0.01 to 0.1mm thick can be obtained.

4.5.6.7 RUBBER

Rubber lined pipe can be used where temperatures or pressure are higher than can be safely handled by an all rubber pipe. Working pressures are then only limited by the pressures that the pipe will withstand. Two types of rubber may be specified, and are equally useful in corrosive conditions. Hard rubber is the most commonly used although soft rubber is the more appropriate for dealing with abrasive slurries and the like. Both types may operate up to 80°C. Special compounds have been developed to withstand attack by oils and petrol. Besides lining pipes various valve components are supplied rubber coated as well as the body.

4.5.7 CERAMIC COATINGS

Ceramics as a surface coating offer high hardness, resistance to abrasion and corrosion protection as well as high temperature properties considerably superior to those of other materials. Their main disadvantages are their liability to crack under conditions of mechanical and thermal shock and their cost.

4.5.7.1 VITREOUS ENAMEL

The constituants are metallic oxides, the exact composition depends on the application. For acidic conditions the major constituant is silica while for basic conditions it is alumina and zirconia. The normal substrates are steel or iron but vitreous enamelling may be applied to any base providing it can withstand the firing temperature. When enamelling steel its carbon content must be very low so as to prevent the formation of bubbles in the coatings. Highly refined iron must have a carbon content of below 0.06%. Grey cast iron can only be vitreous enamelled with a low melting point frit.

To promote adhesion of the ceramic coating the steel or iron must be cleaned and may be pretreated with a nickel coating.

There are two methods of applying vitreous enamel coatings:-

Wet Process - the powdered frit is suspended in water, with clay, and is applied to the substrate by spray or dip. The coating is heated gently to dry the coat and is then fired at 850°C. This is repeated until the required thickness is achieved. The composition of the coats varies, with the top coat containing various metallic oxides to achieve the colour.

Dry process - This method achieves better adhesion, and hence better corrosion resistance, than the wet process. The dry frit is dusted over the substrate and the whole is fired. The firing temperature depends on the frit composition and the base material (iron and steel 700°C and aluminium about 500°C). This is repeated until the required thickness is obtained.

Both methods produce a coat thickness of between 0.08 and 0.12mm. The thinner the film the more flexible it is and hence is less liable to damage from thermal shock. Thick films give longer life when exposed to corrosive media and do not suffer porosity.

Vitreous enamelling is used in sanitary ware, flues, road signs, decorative enamelled nameplates, culinary ware, etc.

4.5.7.2 CEMENT

Cement coatings are generally applied internally to steel and cast iron pipes by centrifugal casting. Temperature changes have little effect on the pipe or lining as their coefficients of expansion are very similar. The lined pipe can be cut and fitted just as ordinary pipe. Pipe complying with BS534, with an outside diameter between 60.3 mm and 2220 mm should have a lining of between 6mm and 23mm, depending upon the pipe size.

Cement lined pipes are used in cold water lines or in the transfer of corrosive media such as oil field flow lines, brine, dilute acids or where liquids must be kept iron or rust free.

Cement lined pipe is generally joined with screwed seal rings or flanges. Coated pipe may be welded but precautions must be taken. The lining must be clear of the welding or cutting areas. After the opertion this lining should be made continuous by hand rendering.

Old pipelines that have shown evidence of corrosion have been renovated in situ and had their life extended by coating the inside with cement. Even after 30 years the coating has revealed no evidence of lining deterioration or corrosion of the substrate.

4.5.8 TEMPORARY PROTECTION

The term temporary relates to the fact that the protective is easily removable and does not imply lack of durability as a corrosion preventative. These materials should be used for the protection of finished surfaces where easy removal is required after a period of storage.

4.5.8.1 STRIPPABLE FILMS

Strippable surface coatings of plastics materials are often used to protect objects during storage and transit to prevent attack by corrosion or impact damage on fine finish material such as stainles steel or plastic panels. They can be applied by spray or dip methods. Latex rubber can be used but steel and iron surfaces must be pretreated to prevent attack by its constituants.

4.5.8.2 OILS AND GREASE

Oils and greases used for rust protection normally need a corrosion inhibitor and in addition it is necessary that they themselves are entirely non-corrosive, i.e. there is no active acid component. Mineral oils on their own are not good as they do not attach themselves to metal without the addition of activated compounds such as stearates.

Lanolin can be applied to steel by brush, spray or dip techniques and gives protection against corrosion of several years in indoor environments.

Preservation oils are generally applied in much thinner layers than greases. Hence these coatings, rarely over 6 micron, are normally used for the protection of components during manufacturing operations or for finished parts that have been phosphated. The oils used are specially formulated to adhere to metal surfaces even if they are damp, and must include rust inhibiters.

4.5.8.3 WAX

Wax films are normally applied by hot dipping and are much thicker than grease and oils and hence offer better protection. Wax films give steel objects a complete protection of three years indoors and up to two years outdoors. Coatings can be in the region of 50 micron thick. This method is most appropriate for small components.

4.5.8.4 PACKAGING

Components can be packaged to give them protection from the environment during storage. Changes of relative humidity can lead to condensation in the sealed package resulting in corroson. This

603

can be overcome by placing silica gel in the package to absorb any resulting moisture or by including a volatile corrosion inhibitor

4.5.8.5 **VOLATILE CORROSION INHIBITOR (VCI)**

VCI papers are special types of wrapping developed to prevent corrosion of iron, steel and aluminium without the use of rust preventative coatings. They can be harmful to cadmium, magnesium and zinc and should not be used when these metals are present.

The chemicals in the paper volatilize. The vapour completely surrounds and protects the metal surfaces but leaves no deposit on the metal. The chemicals inactiviate the moisture in the air and render it non-corrosive. It is not necessary to have the metal parts in contact with VCI papers; a simple closed package is all that is required.

Protection from VCI can fail for any of the following: inadequate sealing of package, prior presence of corrodents on the steel surface, volatile acids within the package and too remote from the surface being protected.

RELATED SPECIFICATIONS

METALLIC COATINGS

GENERAL

BS 1391	: 1952	Performance tests for protective schemes used in the protection of light gauge steel and wrought iron against corrosion
BS 3745	: 1970 (1979)	Evaluation of results of accelerated corrosion tests on metallic coatings
BS 4479	: 1969 (1979)	Recommendations for the design of metal articles that are to be coated
BS 5493	: 1977	Protective coating of iron and steel structures against corrosion
CP 3012	: 1972	Cleaning and preparation of metal surfaces

MOLTEN APPLICATIONS

BS 417	-	Galvanised mild steel cisterns and covers, tanks and cylinders
Part 1	: 1964	Imperial units
Part 2	: 1973	Metric units
BS 443	: 1969	Galvanised coatings on wire
BS 729	: 1971	Hot-dip galvanised coatings on iron and steel articles
BS 1565	-	Galvanised mild steel indirect cylinders, annular or saddle-back type
Part 1	: 1949	Imperial units
Part 2	: 1973	Metric units
BS 2920	: 1973	Cold-reduced tinplate and cold-reduced blackplate
BS 2989	: 1975	Hot-dip galvanised plain steel sheet and coil
BS 3083	: 1980	Hot-dipped galvanised corrugated steel sheets for general purposes

SPRAY APPLICATIONS

BS 2569	-	Sprayed metal coating
Part 1	: 1964	Protection of iron and steel by aluminium and zinc against atmospheric corrosion
Part 2	: 1965	Protection of iron and steel against corrosion and oxidation at elevated temperatures
BS 4161	: 1971	Sprayed unfused metal coatings for engineering purposes
BS 4950	: 1973	Sprayed and fused metal coatings for engineering
ISO 2063		Metallic coatings. Protection of iron and steel against corrosion. Metal spraying of zinc and aluminium

ELECTRODEPOSITION

BS 1224	: 1970	Electroplated coatings of nickel and chromium
BS 1706	: 1960	Electroplated coatings of cadmium and zinc on iron and steel
BS 1872	: 1964	Electroplated coatings of tin
BS 2816	: 1973	Electroplated coatings of silver for engineering purposes
BS 3382	-	Electroplated coatings on threaded components
BS 3597	: 1963	Electroplated coatings of 65/35 tin-nickel alloy
BS 4292	: 1982	Electroplated coatings of gold and gold alloy
BS 4601	: 1970	Electroplated coatings of nickel plus chromium on plastics materials
BS 4641	: 1970	Electroplated coatings of chromium for engineering purposes
BS 4758	: 1971	Electroplated coatings of nickel for engineering purposes

CEMENTATION

BS 4921	: 1973	Sheradised coatings on iron and steel articles

CLADDING

BS 1822	: 1952	Nickel clad steel plate
BS 3740	: 1964	Steel plate clad with corrosion-resisting steel

INORGANIC COATINGS

BS 1615	: 1972	Anodic oxidation coatings on aluminium
BS 3189	: 1973	Phosphate treatment of iron and steel
BS 3987	: 1974	Anodic oxide coatings on wrought aluminium for external architectural applications
BS 5599	: 1978	Specification for hard anodic oxide coatings on aluminium for engineering purposes

PAINTS

GENERAL

BS 2015	: 1965 (1979)	Glossary of paint terms
BS 3900	-	Methods of test for paints
BS 4800	: 1981	Specification for paint colours for building purposes
BS 5493	: 1977	Code of practice for protective coatings of iron and steel structures against corrosion
PAS 32	: 1980	Specification for a paint system comprising an undercoat and gloss finish
CP 231	: 1966	Painting of buildings
CP 3012	: 1972	Cleaning and preparation of metal surfaces

TYPES AND COMPONENT PARTS

BS 245	: 1976	Specification for mineral solvents (white spirit and related hydrocarbon solvents) for paints and other purposes
BS 332	: 1956	Liquid driers for oil paints
BS 1070	: 1973 (1979)	Black paint (tar based)
BS 1795	: 1976	Specification for extenders for paints
BS 2521 BS 2528	: 1966 (1979)	Lead based priming paints
BS 3698	: 1964 (1979)	Calcium plumbate priming paint
BS 3761	: 1970	Non-flammable solvent-based paint remover
BS 4310	: 1968 (1979)	Permissible limit of lead in low-lead paints and similar materials
BS 4652	: 1971 (1979)	Metallic zinc-rich priming paint (organic media)
BS 4756	: 1971	Ready mixed aluminim priming paints for woodwork
BS 4764	: 1971 (1979)	Powder cement paints
BS 5082	: 1974	Water thinned priming paints for wood

BITUMINOUS COATINGS

BS 1070 : 1973 (1979) Black paint (tar based)

BS 3416 : 1975   Black bitumen coating solutions for cold application

BS 4147 : 1980   Hot applied bitumen based coatings for ferrous products

BS 4164 : 1980   Specification for coal tar based hot applied coating materials for protecting
                        iron and steel including suitable primers where required

BS 5493 : 1977   Code of practice for protective coatings of iron and steel structures against
                        corrosion

CERAMIC COATINGS

BS 1344 -   Methods of testing vitreous enamel finishes - Parts 1 to 17

BS 3830 : 1973   Vitreous enamelled steel building components

BS 4495 : 1969   Recommendations for the flame spraying of ceramic and cermet coatings

BS 4900 : 1976   Specification for vitreous enamelling colours for building purposes

 **material data sheet**

SHEET NUMBER	SC01

A

FAMILY GROUP	SURFACE COATING	SUB-GROUP	METALLIC	MATERIAL	ALUMINIUM

GENERAL DESCRIPTION

Aluminium coatings may be applied by dipping, spraying or vacuum deposition. Aluminium is anodic to steel but large discontinuities can lead to local attack. Reaction at high temperatures converts aluminium coat to alumina. Tenacious natural oxide layer give high level of protection. Aluminium alloys can be coated with aluminium by spraying and cladding. Hot dip coating of 50 μm obtained.

CHEMICAL ANALYSIS OR COMPOSITION

Aluminium   100%

SYNONYM

Calorizing (cementation)

PHYSICAL PROPERTIES

PROPERTY	UNITS	VALUES OR RANGE	COMMENTS
DENSITY	kg/m^3		
TENSILE STRENGTH	N/mm^2		
YIELD STRENGTH	N/mm^2		
PROOF STRESS ( )	N/mm^2		
ELONGATION	%		
YOUNGS MODULUS	kN/mm^2		
IMPACT RESISTANCE	J		
HARDNESS			
THERMAL COEFF. OF LINEAR EXPANSION	$°C^{-1}$		
THERMAL CONDUCTIVITY	W/mK		
SPECIFIC HEAT	kJ/kg K		
ELECTRICAL RESISTIVITY	ohm m		
ELECTRICAL CONDUCTIVITY	% IACS		

 **BSRIA** material data sheet

SPECIFICATIONS

STANDARD NUMBER	AUTHORITY	TITLE
BS 2569 Parts 1 & 2	BSI	Sprayed metal coatings
DEF STAN 03 - 3	MOD	Protection of aluminium and alloys spray coatings

COMPANY SPECIFICATION:

ENVIRONMENT

Good atmospheric protection with good adhesion to substrate, providing the coat is thick. Good high temperature (up to 900°C) resistance. Protect less corrosion resistant aluminium alloys by cladding to protect from water, buried or aggressive conditions. Not considered a wear resistant coating.

PROCESSING AND FORMING TECHNIQUES

Dipping - Prefluxed steel passed through aluminium at 700°C
Spraying - coats 50 - 150 μm applied followed by anneal
Vaccuum deposition
Cladding - applied by rolling. Surface prepared by mechanical cleaning or pickling.

JOINTING PROCESS

TYPICAL APPLICATIONS

Steel structural components
Coated steel flue liners
Friction grip bolts
Clad sheet and strip
Decorative reflective finishes on metals and plastics

SAFETY PRECAUTIONS

Edges of clad sheet vulnerable to environmental attack.

YOUR SUPPLIER AND NOTES

 **material data sheet**

SHEET NUMBER	SC 02

A

FAMILY GROUP	SURFACE COATING	SUB-GROUP	METALLIC	MATERIAL	CADMIUM

GENERAL DESCRIPTION

Usually applied by electrodeposition. Cadmium is anodic to iron and so gives excellent corrosion protection to steel. More expensive than zinc. Ideal for use in enclosed humid applications. Excellent corrosion resistance. Coatings of 4-8 μm depending on requirements. Less abrasion resistant than zinc.
Highly toxic material and not to be used in contact with foodstuffs.

CHEMICAL ANALYSIS OR COMPOSITION

Cadmium   100%

SYNONYM

PHYSICAL PROPERTIES

PROPERTY	UNITS	VALUE OR RANGE	COMMENTS
DENSITY	kg/m^3		
SHEAR STRENGTH	N/mm^2		
TENSILE STRENGTH	N/mm^2		
ELONGATION	%		
COMPRESSIVE STRENGTH	N/mm^2		
FLEXURAL STRENGTH	N/mm^2		
IMPACT STRENGTH	J		
TENSILE MODULUS	N/mm^2		
HARDNESS			
THERMAL COEFF. OF LINEAR EXPANSION	$°C^{-1}$		
MIN./MAX. SERVICE TEMPERATURE	$°C$		
DEFLECTION TEMPERATURE	$°C$		at 1.81 N/mm
THERMAL CONDUCTIVITY	W/mK		
FLAMMABILITY			
DIELECTRIC STRENGTH	kV/mm		
VOLUME RESISTIVITY	ohm cm		
PERMITIVITY	ohm cm		
ARC RESISTANCE	secs		
NUMBER OF PARTS			
CURING METHOD			
OPTICAL PROPERTIES			
FRICTION			
MOULD SHRINKAGE			
WATER ABSORPTION			

 **material data sheet**

SPECIFICATIONS

STANDARD NUMBER	AUTHORITY	TITLE
BS1706	BSI	Electroplated coatings of cadmium on steel
BS 3382 Part 1	BSI	Threaded components - cadmium on steel

COMPANY SPECIFICATION:

ENVIRONMENT

Good protection in stagnant or soft water. Poor resistance to acidic conditions. Good resistance to humid conditions. Protective layer between copper and steel to prevent galvanic action. Good resistance to atmospheric but not as good as zinc. Cadmium anodic to steel. Added protection given by chromate passivation of coating.

PROCESSING AND FORMING TECHNIQUES

Electrodeposition - Cyanide electrolyte with current at 5A/dm. Surface preparation by sandblast and alkaline clean.

JOINTING PROCESS

Good solderability of cadmium coats using activated resin flux. Passivated coatings require a corrosive (acid) flux which must be removed

TYPICAL APPLICATIONS

Coated fastener for protection and low torque. Electronic chassis and metalwork. Improves adhesion when used as undercoat for zinc.

SAFETY PRECAUTIONS

Welded components must not be made from cadmium because of toxic fumes. Toxisity of cadmium precludes it from contact with foodstuff.

YOUR SUPPLIER AND NOTES

 **material
data sheet**

SHEET NUMBER	SC 03

A

FAMILY GROUP	SUB-GROUP	MATERIAL
SURFACE COATINGS	METALLIC	CHROMIUM

GENERAL DESCRIPTION

Chromium coatings produced by electro-deposition, diffusion and spraying. Steel, aluminium, zinc and copper, and their alloys normally coated. Used as a decorative finish, for high temperature oxidation protection or aggressive environment protection. Plated surface forms micro cracks which require nickel and copper under-lays for complete protection. Chromium coatings used for wear protection with a thickness of 25-125 μm Decorative finishes require 0.25 - 0.5 μm thickness.

CHEMICAL ANALYSIS OR COMPOSITION

Chromium   100%

SYNONYM

PHYSICAL PROPERTIES

PROPERTY	UNITS	VALUES OR RANGE	COMMENTS
DENSITY	kg/m^3		
TENSILE STRENGTH	N/mm^2		
YIELD STRENGTH	N/mm^2		
PROOF STRESS ( )	N/mm^2		
ELONGATION	%		
YOUNGS MODULUS	kN/mm^2		
IMPACT RESISTANCE	J		
HARDNESS			
THERMAL COEFF. OF LINEAR EXPANSION	$^{\circ}C^{-1}$		
THERMAL CONDUCTIVITY	W/mK		
SPECIFIC HEAT	kJ/kg K		
ELECTRICAL RESISTIVITY	ohm m		
ELECTRICAL CONDUCTIVITY	% IACS		

SPECIFICATIONS

STANDARD NUMBER	AUTHORITY	TITLE
BS 1224:	BSI	Electroplating nickel and chromium
BS 3382: Part 3	BSI	Threaded components - nickel & chromium on steel
BS 3382: Part 4	BSI	Threaded components - nickel on copper and alloys

COMPANY SPECIFICATION:

ENVIRONMENT

Good corrosion resistance in acidic conditions; high temperature oxidation conditions. Good resistance to water.

Due to micro-cracking, for full protection of substrate, precoats required. Attacked by sulphuric acid, reducing solutions and halogens. Good resistance to atmosphere.

PROCESSING AND FORMING TECHNIQUES

Electrodeposition - Precoats of copper and nickel - acid electrolyte
Diffusion - heat in powder at 1350°C
Spray

JOINTING PROCESS

TYPICAL APPLICATIONS

Decorative finish
Hard chromium deposits for wear resistance which will retain lubricants and decrease friction.

SAFETY PRECAUTIONS

YOUR SUPPLIER AND NOTES

BSRIA

material data sheet

SHEET NUMBER SC04	A

FAMILY GROUP SURFACE COATINGS	SUB-GROUP METALLIC	MATERIAL COPPER

GENERAL DESCRIPTION

Copper plate applied to steel, zinc alloys, aluminium or plastics. Coat applied by electrodeposition, electro less plating and cladding. Copper up to 15 μm used as a precoat leveler to nickel plating. During case hardening of steel, parts required with a soft area are copper plated to prevent carbon diffusion.

CHEMICAL ANALYSIS OR COMPOSITION

Copper   100%

SYNONYM

PHYSICAL PROPERTIES

PROPERTY	UNITS	VALUES OR RANGE	COMMENTS
DENSITY	kg/m^3		
TENSILE STRENGTH	N/mm^2		
YIELD STRENGTH	N/mm^2		
PROOF STRESS ( )	N/mm^2		
ELONGATION	%		
YOUNGS MODULUS	kN/mm^2		
IMPACT RESISTANCE	J		
HARDNESS			
THERMAL COEFF. OF LINEAR EXPANSION	$^{o}C^{-1}$		
THERMAL CONDUCTIVITY	W/mK		
SPECIFIC HEAT	kJ/kg K		
ELECTRICAL RESISTIVITY	ohm m		
ELECTRICAL CONDUCTIVITY	% IACS		

SPECIFICATIONS

STANDARD NUMBER	AUTHORITY	TITLE
BS 1224:	BSI	Electroplated coatings of nickel and chromium
DEF 5000 Part VII	MOD	Requirements for service telecommunication equipment
BS 3382 Part 3	BSI	Thread components - nickel on steel
BS 3382 Part 4	BSI	Thread components - nickel on copper and alloys

COMPANY SPECIFICATION:

ENVIRONMENT

Bright surface lost by tarnishing in atmosphere, protection by a lacquer film.

Good resistance to buried in soil providing not acidic.

Cathodic to steel so coating integrity is of prime importance.

PROCESSING AND FORMING TECHNIQUES

Electrodeposition - Acid or alkaline electrolytes at current of $10A/dm^2$.

Cladding - Immersion in molten copper and hot rolling at 950^oC.

Surface prepared by sandblasting or tumbling followed by acid dip.

Electroless plating of plastics.

JOINTING PROCESS

Good solderability

TYPICAL APPLICATIONS

Decorative finish. Coating to steel grounded rods.

Precoat for nickel or chromium/nickel coatings.

Electrical components e.g. PCEs

Masking stop coat for hardening processes.

Coating on steel improves rubber bonding.

SAFETY PRECAUTIONS

YOUR SUPPLIER AND NOTES

material data sheet

SHEET NUMBER	SC05

A

FAMILY GROUP	SURFACE COATING	SUB-GROUP	METALLIC	MATERIAL	LEAD

GENERAL DESCRIPTION

Lead protects ferrous and copper base alloys from corrosion in acidic environments. Coatings applied by hot-dipping, electrodeposition and cladding. Coating is very soft and ductile enabling forming without failure. Hot dipped coatings on steel are applied as Terne Coat (up to 12.5μm). Lead coatings can be used for noise reduction applications. As lead is cathodic to steel attack is accelarated at pinholes produced in the coating.

CHEMICAL ANALYSIS OR COMPOSITION

1. Lead   100%
2. Terne coat 80%
            20 tin

SYNONYM

Terne coat

PHYSICAL PROPERTIES

PROPERTY	UNITS	VALUES OR RANGE	COMMENTS
DENSITY	kg/m^3		
TENSILE STRENGTH	N/mm^2		
YIELD STRENGTH	N/mm^2		
PROOF STRESS ( )	N/mm^2		
ELONGATION	%		
YOUNGS MODULUS	kN/mm^2		
IMPACT RESISTANCE	J		
HARDNESS			
THERMAL COEFF. OF LINEAR EXPANSION	$^oC^{-1}$		
THERMAL CONDUCTIVITY	W/mK		
SPECIFIC HEAT	kJ/kg K		
ELECTRICAL RESISTIVITY	ohm m		
ELECTRICAL CONDUCTIVITY	% IACS		

616

SPECIFICATIONS

STANDARD NUMBER	AUTHORITY	TITLE
DEF 5000 Part VII	M.O.D.	Requirements for service telecommunication equipment
ISO 4999	ISO	Continuous hot dipped terne plate
A309/54	ASTM	Long terne sheet steel

COMPANY SPECIFICATION:

ENVIRONMENT

Very good corrosion properties except in high chloride environments. Good resistance to oxidising acids up to 125 μm for steel protection form sulphuric acid. Good resistance to atmospheric, water and buried conditions. Lead is cathodic to steel. Tern coat gives better protection than lead due to its better adherance properties and lack of pinholes.

JOINTING PROCESS

Terne coat - solders easily

SAFETY PRECAUTIONS

Lead is a toxic material

PROCESSING AND FORMING TECHNIQUES

Hot dip - Substrate immersed in molten bath at 350°C

Surface prepared by mechanical cleaning and sulphuric acid pickle.

TYPICAL APPLICATIONS

Acid resistance - coatings for chemical plant, particularly involving sulphuric acid.
Sound damping
Terne coat steel used for deep-drawn components and roofing material.

YOUR SUPPLIER AND NOTES

BSRIA material data sheet

SHEET NUMBER	SC06

A

FAMILY GROUP	SURFACE COATINGS	SUB-GROUP	METALLIC	MATERIAL	NICKEL

GENERAL DESCRIPTION

Nickel plating is applied to steel (7.5-40µm), copper and zinc and their alloys (5-12.5µm), and aluminium. Offers resistance to high temperature oxidation and to corrosion when immersed in water. Used as an undercoat to chromium coating. Nickel is normally plated on to a copper pre-coat. Substrates may be clad by nickel sheet.

CHEMICAL ANALYSIS OR COMPOSITION

Nickel   100%

SYNONYM

PHYSICAL PROPERTIES

PROPERTY	UNITS	VALUES OR RANGE	COMMENTS
DENSITY	kg/m^3		
TENSILE STRENGTH	N/mm^2		
YIELD STRENGTH	N/mm^2		
PROOF STRESS ( )	N/mm^2		
ELONGATION	%		
YOUNGS MODULUS	kN/mm^2		
IMPACT RESISTANCE	J		
HARDNESS			
THERMAL COEFF. OF LINEAR EXPANSION	$^\circ C^{-1}$		
THERMAL CONDUCTIVITY	W/mK		
SPECIFIC HEAT	kJ/kg K		
ELECTRICAL RESISTIVITY	ohm m		
ELECTRICAL CONDUCTIVITY	% IACS		

618

material data sheet

SPECIFICATIONS

STANDARD NUMBER	AUTHORITY	TITLE
BS 1224	BSI	Electroplated coating of nickel
BS 3382 Part 3	BSI	Threaded components - nickel or nickel + chromium on steel
BS 3382 Part 4	BSI	Threaded components - nickel or nickel + chromium on copper and its alloys
BS 4601	BSI	Nickel plating on plastics materials

COMPANY SPECIFICATION:

ENVIRONMENT

High temperature oxidation resistant. Corrosion resistance to sea and potable water. Natural oxide layer will break down with a lack of oxygen such as crevices and buried in the soil. Good resistance to alkalis and sulphur. Attacked by hydrochloric acid, strong oxidising acids and salts. Polishing improves corrosion protection.

PROCESSING AND FORMING TECHNIQUES

Electro-deposition - For maximum protection a duplex system of bright and semi-bright layers recommended

Metal spray

Cladding - welded envelope oversteel roll bonded at 1200°C.

Electroless plating of plastics

Surface prepared by mechanical clean, degrease or pickled.

JOINTING PROCESS

Nickel can be soldered using an activated resin flux. Bright electrodeposits may cause the solder to dewet and result in poor joints.

TYPICAL APPLICATIONS

Precoat for chromium plating coatings for protection from high temperature oxidation and chemical attack.

Wear resistant coatings for engineering.

SAFETY PRECAUTIONS

YOUR SUPPLIER AND NOTES

material data sheet

SHEET NUMBER	SC07

A

FAMILY GROUP	SURFACE COATING	SUB-GROUP	METALLIC	MATERIAL	SILVER

GENERAL DESCRIPTION

Silver is applied to copper and nickel and their alloys by electrodeposition or vaccuum deposition. Plastics are electroless plated. Highest electrical conductivity of all metals and used as a contact material. Wear is improved with a rhodium coating. Tends to tarnish unless protected.

CHEMICAL ANALYSIS OR COMPOSITION

Silver plus rhodium flash finish if required

SYNONYM

PHYSICAL PROPERTIES

PROPERTY	UNITS	VALUES OR RANGE	COMMENTS
DENSITY	kg/m^3		
TENSILE STRENGTH	N/mm^2		
YIELD STRENGTH	N/mm^2		
PROOF STRESS ( )	N/mm^2		
ELONGATION	%		
YOUNGS MODULUS	kN/mm^2		
IMPACT RESISTANCE	J		
HARDNESS			
THERMAL COEFF. OF LINEAR EXPANSION	$°C^{-1}$		
THERMAL CONDUCTIVITY	W/mK		
SPECIFIC HEAT	kJ/kg K		
ELECTRICAL RESISTIVITY	ohm m		
ELECTRICAL CONDUCTIVITY	% IACS		

SPECIFICATIONS

STANDARD NUMBER	AUTHORITY	TITLE
BS 2816	BSI	Electroplated coatings of silver
BS 3382 Part 6	BSI	Threaded components - silver on copper and its alloys

COMPANY SPECIFICATION:

ENVIRONMENT

Tarnish due to sulphur in atmosphere
Rhodium plating freshly plated articles prevents
tarnishing.

PROCESSING AND FORMING TECHNIQUES

Electrodeposition - Cyanide electrolyte
using current density $10A/dm^2$
Electroless plating of plastics

Vapour deposition.

JOINTING PROCESS

Sulphur tarnish prevents soldering. Clean
silver no problems. Oxide layer on rhodium
can cause problems if not soldered quickly.

TYPICAL APPLICATIONS

Sliding and spring electric contacts

Plating of plastics for electrical and
decorative purpose.

SAFETY PRECAUTIONS

YOUR SUPPLIER AND NOTES

		SHEET NUMBER	SC 08	A

FAMILY GROUP	SURFACE COATING	SUB-GROUP	METALLIC	MATERIAL	TIN

GENERAL DESCRIPTION

Tin produces a tough adherent coating to substrates and tolerates extensive forming. It is produced by hotdipping, or electrodeposition. It is corrosion resistant to the atmosphere and many corrosive agents such as fruit juice. It is a non-toxic material. Tin is cathodic to iron so any coating failure would promote localised attack. Tin coating is applied to steel and copper and its alloys with plated thicknesses of 2.5 - 12.5 μm depending on function and 12.5-25 μm for hotdipped.

CHEMICAL ANALYSIS OR COMPOSITION

Tin   100%

SYNONYM

Tin plate (on steel)

PHYSICAL PROPERTIES

PROPERTY	UNITS	VALUES OR RANGE	COMMENTS
DENSITY	kg/m^3		
TENSILE STRENGTH	N/mm^2		
YIELD STRENGTH	N/mm^2		
PROOF STRESS ( )	N/mm^2		
ELONGATION	%		
YOUNGS MODULUS	kN/mm^2		
IMPACT RESISTANCE	J		
HARDNESS			
THERMAL COEFF. OF LINEAR EXPANSION	$°C^{-1}$		
THERMAL CONDUCTIVITY	W/mK		
SPECIFIC HEAT	kJ/kg K		
ELECTRICAL RESISTIVITY	ohm m		
ELECTRICAL CONDUCTIVITY	% IACS		

BSRIA material data sheet

SPECIFICATIONS

STANDARD NUMBER	AUTHORITY	TITLE
BS 1872	BSI	Electroplated coatings of tin
BS 2920	BSI	Cold reduced tinplate
BS 3382 Part 5	BSI	Threaded Components - tin on copper and its alloys

COMPANY SPECIFICATION:

ENVIRONMENT

Poor resistance to alkalis. Good resistance to organic acids (fruit juices). Good resistance to attack by potable water and attacked by sea water and marine environments. Cathodic to iron

PROCESSING AND FORMING TECHNIQUES

Hot dip - Pre-fluxed and dipped in molten tin at 320°C. Electrodeposition - electrolytic bath, acid or alkaline, at 2-25 A/dm^2 produces dull coating. Bright coating produced by remelt process. Surface prepared by mechanical and alkali cleaning.

JOINTING PROCESS

Tinned coatings are readily soldered with 4 pm thickness

TYPICAL APPLICATIONS

Tin plate steel strip and sheet. Electrical applications for solderability and electrical conductivity. Can making industry.

SAFETY PRECAUTIONS

Long term attack by food products require a vinyl, phenolic or wax coating inside the enclosure for complete protection.

YOUR SUPPLIER AND NOTES

BSRIA material data sheet

FAMILY GROUP	SURFACE COATING	SUB-GROUP	METALLIC	MATERIAL	ZINC

GENERAL DESCRIPTION

Applied to metal surfaces by sheradising, hot dip galvanising, electrodeposition or spraying. Acts as sacrificial coating in the protection of steel substrate. Care to be taken from direct or indirect contact with copper due to rapid attack on zinc coating. Coating thicknesses of 7.5 - 125 µm for electrodeposits and dependent on steel reactivity and time in the bath for hot dipped. The thicker the coat the better the protection.

CHEMICAL ANALYSIS OR COMPOSITION

Zinc or zinc alloys depending on method and substrate.

SYNONYM

PHYSICAL PROPERTIES

PROPERTY	UNITS	VALUES OR RANGE	COMMENTS
DENSITY	kg/m^3		
TENSILE STRENGTH	N/mm^2		
YIELD STRENGTH	N/mm^2		
PROOF STRESS ( )	N/mm^2		
ELONGATION	%		
YOUNGS MODULUS	kN/mm^2		
IMPACT RESISTANCE	J		
HARDNESS			
THERMAL COEFF. OF LINEAR EXPANSION	$°C^{-1}$		
THERMAL CONDUCTIVITY	W/mK		
SPECIFIC HEAT	kJ/kg K		
ELECTRICAL RESISTIVITY	ohm m		
ELECTRICAL CONDUCTIVITY	% IACS		

SPECIFICATIONS

STANDARD NUMBER	AUTHORITY	TITLE
BS 729 Part 1	BSI	Hotdip galvanised iron and steel
BS 2569 Part 1	BSI	Sprayed metal coatings - zinc
BS 2989	BSI	Hot dip galvanised sheet and coil
BS 3083	BSI	Hot dip galvanised corrogated sheet
BS 3382 Part 2	BSI	Threaded components - zinc on steel
BS 5493	BSI	Protective coatings of iron and steel
BS 4921:	BSI	Sherardizing

COMPANY SPECIFICATION:

ENVIRONMENT

Rate of protection dependent on thickness, service life and environment. Use in potable water, seawater and underground. Soft water attacks zinc. Contact with copper and copper solutions can promote attack. Dark in colour and attacked by alkalis, acids and steam. Limiting temperature 200°C.

PROCESSING AND FORMING TECHNIQUES

Sheradising - Heat to 260-320°C in zinc powder.

Hotdip - Prefluxed and dipped in zinc at 450°C.

Spray - zinc wire or powder fed into oxy-gas torch.

Electrodeposition - Electrolyte acid (dull) or alkaline (bright) operated at 2-10 A/dm^2. Surface mechanically cleaned and pickled.

JOINTING PROCESS

Soldered with difficulty after passivation. Untreated coating is somewhat less difficult. Coated steel may be welded but weld area must be protected by a zinc rich finish.

TYPICAL APPLICATIONS

Protective coatings for pipework, water tanks, rain products, roofing materials, fixings (nails etc), pressed steel lintels, window frame. Pre-coated steel sheet and strip is available.

SAFETY PRECAUTIONS

Zinc is toxic and must not come into contact with food stuffs. Extraction of weld fumes required as they are toxic.

YOUR SUPPLIER AND NOTES

FAMILY GROUP	SURFACE COATINGS	SUB-GROUP	INORGANIC	MATERIAL	PHOSPHATING

GENERAL DESCRIPTION

Surface conversion process of iron and steel presenting a coating with limited corrosion protection. Primarily used as a pretreatment for painting. The surface will readily absorb oil and grease to prolong corrosion prevention in non-arduous environments. Zinc may also be phosphate treated.

CHEMICAL ANALYSIS OR COMPOSITION

Solution contains phosphoric acid and metal phosphates.

SYNONYM

PHYSICAL PROPERTIES

PROPERTY	UNITS	VALUES OR RANGE	COMMENTS
DENSITY	kg/m^3		
TENSILE STRENGTH	N/mm^2		
YIELD STRENGTH	N/mm^2		
PROOF STRESS ( )	N/mm^2		
ELONGATION	%		
YOUNGS MODULUS	kN/mm^2		
IMPACT RESISTANCE	J		
HARDNESS			
THERMAL COEFF. OF LINEAR EXPANSION	$^{\circ}C^{-1}$		
THERMAL CONDUCTIVITY	W/mK		
SPECIFIC HEAT	kJ/kg K		
ELECTRICAL RESISTIVITY	ohm m		
ELECTRICAL CONDUCTIVITY	% IACS		

BSRIA material data sheet

SPECIFICATIONS

STANDARD NUMBER	AUTHORITY	TITLE
BS 3189	BSI	Phosphate treatment of iron and steel

COMPANY SPECIFICATION:

ENVIRONMENT

Little corrosion resistance unless the surface is oiled. Coating soft and easily broken.

PROCESSING AND FORMING TECHNIQUES

Immersion - articles immersed at temperature, left for required time, washed, dried and oiled if applicable. Surface prepared by degrease in alkali solution.

JOINTING PROCESS

TYPICAL APPLICATIONS

Paint and organic coating pre-treatment for steel and cast iron. Oiled phosphate finish for articles in non-arduous situations.

SAFETY PRECAUTIONS

YOUR SUPPLIER AND NOTES

627

	material data sheet		SHEET NUMBER	SC11	A

FAMILY GROUP	SURFACE COATINGS	SUB-GROUP	INORGANIC	MATERIAL	CHROMATE

GENERAL DESCRIPTION

Chromate is mainly applied to zinc, cadmium (also called passivation) and aluminium. Very thin films are formed which act as a barrier to the environment. Acts as a pretreatment for an organic coating system. Chromate treatment may be applied to phosphate finishes to improve paint adhesion

CHEMICAL ANALYSIS OR COMPOSITION

Solution of sodium dichromate acidified with sulphuric acid.

SYNONYM

PHYSICAL PROPERTIES

PROPERTY	UNITS	VALUES OR RANGE	COMMENTS
DENSITY	kg/m^3		
TENSILE STRENGTH	N/mm^2		
YIELD STRENGTH	N/mm^2		
PROOF STRESS ( )	N/mm^2		
ELONGATION	%		
YOUNGS MODULUS	kN/mm^2		
IMPACT RESISTANCE	J		
HARDNESS			
THERMAL COEFF. OF LINEAR EXPANSION	$°C^{-1}$		
THERMAL CONDUCTIVITY	W/mK		
SPECIFIC HEAT	kJ/kg K		
ELECTRICAL RESISTIVITY	ohm m		
ELECTRICAL CONDUCTIVITY	% IACS		

BSRIA material data sheet

SHEET NUMBER SC11   B

SPECIFICATIONS

STANDARD NUMBER	AUTHORITY	TITLE
BS 1706: 1960	BSI	Electroplated cadmium and zinc on iron and steel
BS 3382 Part 1	BSI	Threaded components - cadmium on steel
BS 3382 Part 2	BSI	Threaded components - zinc on steel

COMPANY SPECIFICATION:

ENVIRONMENT

Presents some resistance to corrosion compared with non-chromated articles. Corrosion protection breaks down at 65°C

PROCESSING AND FORMING TECHNIQUES

Immersion - clean, immerse for required time, wash and dry.

JOINTING PROCESS

TYPICAL APPLICATIONS

Pre-paint treatment for zinc and cadmium plated articles
Pre-paint treatment of aluminium components.

SAFETY PRECAUTIONS

YOUR SUPPLIER AND NOTES

FAMILY GROUP	SURFACE COATINGS	SUB-GROUP	INORGANIC	MATERIAL	ANODISING

GENERAL DESCRIPTION

An anodic oxide surface coating produced electrolytically in an acid electrolyte. The most common material commercially anodised is aluminium and its alloys. The thickness, colour and properties depend on composition and electrolyte. The coating affords corrosion protection, electrical insulation, pretreatment for painting and decorative finishes. Hard anodising can be applied for wear resistance.

CHEMICAL ANALYSIS OR COMPOSITION

Metallic oxide surface layer.

SYNONYM

PHYSICAL PROPERTIES

PROPERTY	UNITS	VALUES OR RANGE	COMMENTS
DENSITY	kg/m^3		
TENSILE STRENGTH	N/mm^2		
YIELD STRENGTH	N/mm^2		
PROOF STRESS ( )	N/mm^2		
ELONGATION	%		
YOUNGS MODULUS	kN/mm^2		
IMPACT RESISTANCE	J		
HARDNESS			
THERMAL COEFF. OF LINEAR EXPANSION	$°C^{-1}$		
THERMAL CONDUCTIVITY	W/mK		
SPECIFIC HEAT	kJ/kg K		
ELECTRICAL RESISTIVITY	ohm m		
ELECTRICAL CONDUCTIVITY	% IACS		

SPECIFICATIONS

STANDARD NUMBER	AUTHORITY	TITLE
BS 1615: DEF 151	BSI M.O.D.	Anodic oxidation coatings on aluminium Anodizing of aluminium and its alloys

COMPANY SPECIFICATION:

ENVIRONMENT

The acids and alkalines that heavily attack
aluminium will attack anodic coatings.
Good resistance to atmospheric and marine
attack. Chromic acid process is less
corrosion resistant compared to sulphuric
processed articles.

Sealed sulphuric processed components have
good corrosion resistance.

PROCESSING AND FORMING TECHNIQUES

Electrolytic process with various
electrolytes -

1. Sulphuric acid
2. Chromic acid
3. Hard anodising version of sulphuric
   system.

JOINTING PROCESS

TYPICAL APPLICATIONS

Sulphuric - decorative finishes with sealed
dyes paint pretreatment. Hard anodic films
for wear resistance. General anodic film
on wrought products - result depending on
composition. Chromic - used for castings
or components where entrappment may occur.
Pretreatment for vitreous enamelling of
aluminium.

SAFETY PRECAUTIONS

YOUR SUPPLIER AND NOTES

4.6 RUBBERS AND ELASTOMERS

A rubber is a natural polymeric material with long flexible molecule chains and the ability to deform elastically when vulcanised. During the vulcanisation process, rubber molecules are linked with adjacent rubber molecules at intervals along their length, usually using sulphur, to form a crosslinked elastic material which is stable over a wide range of temperature. The term 'rubber' is applied to the raw material, but more generally to the vulcanised material.

An elastomer is a polymer possessing elastic properties and is an alternative term for synthetic rubber. It is produced by the synthesis of monomers, invariably petro-chemicals, followed by polymerisation to form long chain molecules. Catalysts are required to initiate polymerisation and, after initiation, polymerisation takes place continuously.

Some of the properties of rubber and elastomers that influence their selection are indicated below:-

TEMPERATURE LIMITS

All rubbers and elastomers deteriorate over a period at high temperatures, especially in air. They become brittle or resinous and lose their elastomeric properties. This affect is time-dependent and varies from one compound to another. At temperatures below 0°C rubbers and elastomers progressively stiffen and lose their resilience as the temperature falls until brittleness occurs, and cracks appear if the rubber is flexed. This brittleness and stiffness is reversable as the temperature rises. Special elastomer compounds are available for extreme temperature limits but they may alter other elastomeric characteristics. Any decision on the appropriate rubber or elastomer for the temperature range must also take into consideration the environment.

AGEING

Ageing covers the progressive deterioration of a rubber or elastomer with time. This characteristic can be controlled to some extent by compounding and by the life history of the material. A compound prone to oxidation would age rapidly if, while in store or in service, it is subjected to hot conditions, sunlight or other unfavourable environments but if the conditions are favourable the material could be free from ageing for long periods. Ageing affects tensile strength, hardness and reduces elongation.

ABRASION RESISTANCE

The abrasion resistance of a material improves with increasing hardness and may be further improved by compounding. Good abrasion resistance is often allied to high tear resistance. This is a particularly important property when considering dynamic seals.

TEAR RESISTANCE

The higher the tear resistance the less likelihood of a material failing should it be accidently cut. Rubbers and elastomers with a low tear resistance require careful hándling to avoid the possibility of damage occuring. The inclusion of fibres in the rubber or elastomer greatly improves tear resistance.

PERMEABILITY

This is important when considering a rubber or elastomer for sealing gases or for vacuum work. Permeability varies considerably with different rubbers and elastomers, their compounds, hardness and temperature. A further consideration for vacuum work is that absorbed gases may outgas and volatile constituents may evaporate from the material at low pressures.

A summary of the physical properties are indicated in Table 4.6/1.

ENVIRONMENT

The life expectancy of a rubber or elastomer is influenced by the environment in which it functions. A material in contact, or immersed, in a fluid will normally tend to absorb a certain amount of that fluid, and the material will swell or increase in volume. This will tend to alter the properties of the rubber or elastomer particularly hardness, strength, resilience and abrasion resistance. These conditions may be tolerated, depending on the materials function, provided there is no chemical attack. If continuously immersed the material has a limit to the quantity of fluid that can be absorbed and the volumetric expansion will remain constant. This is temperature dependent with higher the temperature the greater amount of fluid absorbed. Water, oils and solvents tend to swell rubbers and elastomers, the degree depending on the compound of fluid absorbed.

Conversely if the material is dried out it will shrink and this could result in a loose seal and leakage at a joint. Shrinkage can leave the material harder and less flexible.

In situations where electrical arcing occurs ozone is produced which can attack materials differently.

RESILIENCE

Resilience or elastic recovery is a measure of the ability of a rubber or elastomer to return to its original shape when a compression load is removed. The resilience for rubbers and elastomers will vary with temperature. Resilience may be referred to in property tables as compression or tensile set. Compression set is significant as rubbers and elastomers used as seals are loaded in compression and some permanent reduction in dimensions or shrinkage may occur. Tension set can influence the selection where a material is stretched and fails to return to its original form.

FLEXIBILITY

The flexibility of a rubber or elastomer can be modified by the working temperature, pressure of any fluid in contact and any other factor which affects the compound and its hardness. By compounding or selecting a filler material the flexibility can be predicted.

HARDNESS

In general rubbers and elastomers with low hardness are more flexible and therefore more applicable for sealing on rough surfaces. The hardness of any material can be modified by compounding and is normally expressed as a number of degrees. Hardness values used range from 40-45 degrees for soft compounds up to 90-95 degrees for hard compounds. The actual hardness figure is difficult to measure and so the figures quoted are just an indication. Hardness is affected by swelling. Swelling reduces the hardness as does an increase in temperature.

4.6.1 RUBBER

4.6.1.1 NATURAL RUBBER

Data Sheet RE01

Natural rubber is highly deformable and will undergo essentially full recovery. They show marked changes in tensile properties with temperature changes. As the temperature increases their stiffness is lost but as temperatures decrease the strength increases with a loss of elongation until it becomes brittle below -73°C. When vulcanised rubber becomes susceptible to oxidation. Antioxidants are usually added but natural rubber still shows properties inferior to those of most elastomers. Similarly natural rubber is inferior to elastomers in oil and solvent resistance showing a tendency to swell. When stretched natural rubber is subject to attack by ozone.

The properties of vulcanised natural rubber are greatly influenced by the degree of vulcanisation and the filler materials. The inclusion of carbon black greatly improves the majority of its mechanical properties. Its tensile strength increases as does its modulus of elasticity, hardness, abrasion resistance and electrical conductivity but its elongation is decreased. The hardness of rubber can vary from very soft to solid ebonite.

Natural rubber finds applications in springs, energy absorbers, vibration isolators and noise suppression materials. They are also found in adhesives. The majority of applications are found as additions to elastomers, cork etc. to extend the property ranges of other materials.

4.6.2 ELASTOMERS

4.6.2.1 BUTADIENE ACRYLONITRILE
Data Sheet RE02

Butadiene acrylonitrile is commonly known as 'nitrile' rubber or NBR.

'Nitrile' rubbers have excellent resistance to fuels and oils, even at elevated temperatures. The higher the acrylonitrile content the better the resistance but at the expense of resilience and low temperature resistance. They exhibit excellent resistance to acids and good oxidation, sunlight ageing, heat ageing and water absorption.

The mechanical properties indicate that 'nitrile' rubbers possess excellent abrasion properties and good tensile, compression set and creep properties. Resistance to degreasing solvents and ketones is poor.

With a service temperature range of between -20°C to 120°C and its oil and fuel resistance 'nitrile' rubbers are ideal for applications involving 'O' rings, seals, gaskets and diaphragms. Where low temperature flexibility is required at the expense of oil resistance compounds with low acrylonitrile content should be used. Medium content of acrylonitrile compound find uses in conveyor belt covers, hose, valves and bearings.

4.6.2.2 BUTADIENE-STYRENE
Data Sheet RE03

Butadiene-styrene (SBR) is an important elastomer as it is cheap and more readily available than natural rubber, of which it is considered a synthetic substitute. SBR is available as an oil extended elastomer. Up to 35% of oil is added to the compound prior to vulcanising which tends to swell and soften the elastomer leading to improved properties. Compounds of SBR display good wear and weather resistance, excellent low temperature characteristics, low gas permeability and good tensile properties. It has a tendency to have, depending on composition, poor resilience, large heat build-up, low resistance to oils and fuels and poor fatigue resistance. The service temperature ranges from -60°C to +70°C.

They are chemically resistant to alkalis, most dilute mineral acids but are attacked by concentrated nitric, sulphuric and chromic acids.

Their major application is for automobile tyre carcases but they find utilisation in conveyor belts, drive belts, sound and shock absorption, hoses and air seals.

4.6.2.3 BUTYL

Data Sheet RE04

Butyl rubber has good ozone, weathering, heat and chemical resistance but hydrocarbon solutions tend to cause swelling. These rubbers are highly impervious to gases and therefore find applications as inflated components and diaphragms. The service temperature range for butyl rubber is wide, -50°C to +125°C, and it retains good tear resistance at elevated temperatures. At room temperature they are less resilient than vulcanised natural rubber and other elastomers and hence have useful damping and sound or shock absorbing properties but mechanical vibration can lead to a build up of heat.

Unlike other rubbers and elastomers the inclusion of carbon black does not improve its tensile properties.

Butyl rubbers are attacked by concentrated solutions of nitric, sulphuric and chromic acids. They possess good electrical properties.

Other applications for butyl rubber include gaskets and seals, steam hoses, electrical insulation and coated fabrics for water-proof articles subject to weathering.

4.6.2.4 CHLOROPRENE

Data Sheet RE05

Chloroprene elastomers are commonly named 'Neoprene'. The most outstanding characteristic of 'neoprene' is its resistance to deterioration. It is resistant to oils, ozone, light and various chemicals. Neoprene is attacked by concentrated nitric, suphuric and chromic acids, pickling solutions especially nitric-hydrofluoric acid mixes, sodium hypochlorite and liquid chlorine. Aromatic and chlorinated hydrocarbons swell 'neoprene' but it can be reduced by the addition of fillers. The resistance to oils is not as good as 'nitrile' or polysulphide rubbers. They are fairly impermeable to gases, better than natural rubber but inferior to butyl. 'Neoprene' has good flame resistance and is self-extinguishing. Its electrical properties are inferior to natural rubber, styrene-butadiene, butyl and silicone but because of its good flame and weather resistance it is used for cable sheathing. The service temperature ranges from -30°C to +130°C.

The abrasion, tear and crack resistance are good and wear resistance very good, especially when filled with carbon black.

As with other rubbers and elastomers the mechanical properties vary depending on the filler materials and their quantity. It possesses good elasticity and its hardness and creep characteristics are similar to natural rubber.

Because of its outstanding oil and chemical resistance 'neoprene' is used for gaskets, seals, 'O' rings, diaphragms, hoses, tank liners and cable insulation. Its ozone resistance gives it uses in electrical systems where there is a possibility of arcing or electrical discharge. Other applications are conveyor belts - particularly in fire hazard applications, bridge bearings, adhesives and extruded forms for various sealing applications.

4.6.2.5 CHLOROSULFONATED POLYETHYLENE

Chlorosulfonated polyethylene is commonly called 'Hypalon'. 'Hypalon' is unsurpassed in its resistance to ozone. Its ageing properties, compression recovery and low temperature properties are good. The service temperature ranges from -40°C to +120°C. Abrasion, wear, fatigue, impact, cutting and cracking resistance are good. The elastomer is resistant to ultraviolet degradation as well as possessing high resistance to damage by oxidation, water, oil and weathering.

'Hypalon' has good resistance to chemicals, oils and greases, and particularly to oxidising agents such as concentrated sulphuric acid, hypochlorite solutions, and to alkalis. Like other chlorine containing polymers it is immune to bacteria and mico-organism attack. 'Hypalon' can be coloured and the addition of pigment does not affect its properties, indoors or outdoors. It possesses good gas permeability properties.

'Hypalon' has moderate mechanical properties with its tensile strength and elasticity inferior to 'neoprene'. The tensile strength is not affected by fillers. Electrical properties make it appropriate for low voltage insulations and its electrical properties are not adversely affected by long term weathering, water immersion or underground exposure.

'O' rings, seals and gaskets, transmission belts, high temperature conveyor belts, flexible hose pipes, cable covering and mountings are typical component products. Also 'hypalon' is used as a coating for pumps, tank linings and tubes where chemical resistance is required.

4.6.2.6 ETHYLENE-PROPYLENE
Data Sheet RE06

Commercial products consist of two types:-

    a.   Saturated copolymer, designated EPM,

    b.   terpolymer, designated EPDM.

Ethylene-propylene is exceptionally resistant to heat, oxygen, ozone as well as chemicals and weathering. Service temperature is in the range of -40°C to +150°C. As rubber is generally sold by volume rather than by weight its low specific gravity gives it a price advantage. Ethylene-propylene rubbers possess good mechanical and electrical properties, and resilience.

Applications include seals and gaskets, hose and cable coverings.

4.6.2.7 SILICONE

Data Sheet RE07

They are expensive compared with other rubbers. Silicone rubbers have a long service life at elevated temperatures varying from 10 to 20 years at 120°C to 0.5 to 2 years at 230°C. The service temperature ranges from -60°C to +230°C. They offer good resistance to attack from chemicals, ozone and weathering. Silicone rubbers are attacked by cold concentrated nitric, sulphuric and hydrochloric acids, hot diluted acids and alkalis and high pressure steam. It is swollen by some solvents.

The mechanical properties of silicone rubbers are moderate in comparison with other elastomers particularly in tensile and tear strengths and extensibility. Compression set at room temperature is comparable but there is less change with variation in service temperature. Flexibility is retained to lower temperatures than most elastomers.

Silicone rubbers are used where their exceptional properties justify the relatively increased cost. They are considered to be resistant to fungal and bacterial attack, tasteless, odourless and physiologically inert and therefore find applications in contact with foodstuffs, beverages and medical products.

Products include 'O' rings, gaskets and cable sheaths.

4.6.3 CELLULAR RUBBERS

Vulcanised rubbers, natural and elastomers, can be made in cellular form by the addition of a blowing agent which evolves gas during vulcanisation, saturating the unvulcanised mix with nitrogen or aerating the composition prior to vulcanisation. According to the method of manufacture and after-treatment, the cells in cellular rubber may be either closed or open. Closed cellular material possess good thermal properties. The size of the cells may also be controlled which will vary the physical properties of the material.

Cellular rubbers have good elastic properties (even under severe loading), cushioning, acoustic properties.

Property		Rubber and Elastomers										
	NR	NBR	SBR	IR	CR	CSM	EP	SI	PS	PU	ACM	FC
Tensile stress	E	G	G	G	G	G	G	F	P	E	G	E
Compression set	E	G/E	G	G	G	G	G	F	P	E	G	E
Resilience	E	F/G	G	P	G	F	G	G	G	G	F	F
Impermeability	F	G	F	E	G	G	G	P	G	F	G	G
Electrical resistivity	E	P/F	E	E	F	G	E	E	F	G	P	F
Service max	+100	+120	+70	+125	+130	+120	+150	+230	+90	+100	+130	+175
temperature °C min	-50	-20	-60	-50	-20	-40	-40	-60	-50	-50	-40	-20
Abrasion resistance	E	G	G	F/G	G	G	G/E	P	P	E	G	G
Tear resistance	G/E	F	F	G	G	G	G/E	P	P	G/E	F/G	F/G
Flame resistance	P	P	P	P	G	G	P	F	P	P	P	E
Water resistance	E	E	G/E	E	G	G	E	E	F	G	P	E

NR = Natural rubber   NBR = Acrylontrile Butadiene   SBR = Butadiene styrene

IR = Butyl   CR = Chloroprene   CSM = Chlorosulphanted polyethylene

EP = Ethylene/propylene   SI = Silicone   PS = Polysulphide

PU = Polyurethane   ACM = Acrylic   FC = Fluorocarbon

Their relative performance is indicated by:-

E = excellent   G = good   F = fair   P = poor

Table 4.6/1 Summary of rubber and elastomer physical properties.

RELATED SPECIFICATIONS

HOSE

BS1435	: 1975	Rubber hose assemblies for oil suction and discharge services.
BS2952	: 1958	Rubber hose for internal combustion engine cooling systems.
BS3165	: -	Rubber suction hose for fire-fighting purposes.
Part 1	: 1959	Type A hose with partially embedded wire.
BS3169	: 1970	Rubber reel hose for fire-fighting purposes.
BS3212	: 1975	Flexible rubber tube and hose for use in LPG vapour phase and LPG/air installations.
BS3716	: 1964	General purpose rubber water hose.
BS3832	: 1971	Wire braid reinforced rubber hose, Type B, and hose assemblies fitted with end couplings.
BS4089	: 1966	Rubber hose and hose assemblies for LPG lines.
BS4221	: 1973	Spiral/braid wire reinforced rubber hose and hose assemblies fitted with end couplings.
BS4586	: 1970	Spiral wire reinforced rubber hose and hose assemblies with end couplings.
BS4749	: 1971	Textile reinforced rubber covered hydraulic hose, types 1 and 2, and hose assemblies fitted with end couplings.
BS5118	: 1975	Rubber air hose.
BS5119	: 1975	Low pressure rubber water hose.
BS5120	: 1975	Rubber hose for gas welding and allied processes.
BS5121	: 1975	Rubber sandblast hose.
DS5122	: 1975	Rubber hose for saturated steam.
BS5173	: -	Methods of test for hoses. (Parts 1-6).
BS5244	: 1976	Recommendations for application, storage and life expiry of hydraulic rubber hose and assemblies.
BS5342	: 1977	Specification for rubber hose for high pressure saturated steam.

BELTING AND TRANSMISSION DRIVES

BS351	: 1976	Specification for rubber, balata or plastics flat transmission belting of textile construction for general use.
BS1440	: 1971	Endless V-belt drives, sections Y, Z, A, B, C, and D.
BS2890	: 1973	Troughed belt conveyors.
BS3289	: 1960	Conveyor belting for underground use in coal mines.
BS3733	: 1974	Endless V-belts for agriculture purposes.
BS3790	: 1973	Endless wedge belt drives of SPZ, SPA, SPB and SPC sections.

SEALS, GASKETS ETC.

BS1399	: 1970	Rotary shaft lip seals.
BS1806	: 1962	Dimensions of toroidal sealing rings ('O' seals and their housings).
BS2494	: 1976	Materials for elastomeric joint rings for pipework and pipelines.
BS3063	: 1965	Dimensions of gaskets for pipe flanges.
BS4255	: -	Preformed rubber gaskets for weather exclusion from buildings.
Part 1	: 1967	Non-cellular gaskets.
Part 2	: 1975	Cellular gaskets.
BS4518	: 1974	Metric dimensions of toroidal sealing rings ('O' rings) and their housings.
BS4865	: -	Dimensions of gaskets for flanges to BS4504.
Part 1	: 1972	Dimensions of non-metallic gaskets for pressures up to 64 bar.
BS5292	: 1980	Specification for jointing materials and compounds for installations using water, low pressure steam or 1st, 2nd and 3rd family gases.

MATERIALS

BS1154	: 1978	Specification for natural rubber compounds (high quality).
BS1155	: 1979	Specification for natural rubber compounds (high quality) for extrusion.
BS3472	: 1974	Styrene-butadiene rubber (SBR) - non pigmented, emulsion polymerised, general purpose types.
BS3650	: 1976	Specification for oil extended styrene-butadiene rubbers (SBR). Non pigmented, emulsion polymerised, general purpose types.
BS4355	: 1968	Centrifuged ammonia-preserved natural rubber lattices.
BS4396	: 1976	Raw natural rubber.
BS4661	: 1971	Emulsion polymerised anionic styrene-butadiene rubber lattices.
BS5047	: 1974	Butadiene rubber (BR) - solution polymerised types.
BS5375	: 1976	Methods of test for raw general purpose chloroprene rubbers.
BS5474	: 1977	Test recipe and evaluation of vulcanisation characteristics for raw non oil extended isoprene rubbers.

METHODS OF TEST

BS903	: -	Methods of testing vulcanised rubber (Parts A1-A33, B1-B19, C1-C4, D1-D7, E1-E9 and F1-F9).
BS1672	: 1972	Methods of testing natural rubber lattices.
BS1673	: -	Methods of testing raw rubber and unvulcanised compounded rubber (Parts 1-10).
BS2044	: 1953	Laboratory tests for resistivity of conductive and anti-static rubbers.
BS2719	: 1975	Methods of use and calibration of pocket type rubber hardness meters.

TANKS AND VESSELS

CP3003	: -	Linings of vessels and equipment for chemical purposes.
Part 1	: 1967	Rubber.

DATA SHEETS

RUBBER AND ELASTOMERS (RE)

RUBBER

RE01   Natural rubber

ELASTOMERS

RE02   Butadiene-acrylonitrile
RE03   Butadiene-styrene
RE04   Butyl
RE05   Chloroprene
RE06   Ethylene/propylene
RE07   Silicone
RE08   Polysulphide

material data sheet	SHEET NUMBER	RE01	A

FAMILY GROUP	RUBBER AND ELASTOMERS	SUB-GROUP	RUBBER	MATERIAL	NATURAL RUBBER

GENERAL DESCRIPTION

A good general purpose rubber with high resistance to tearing and abrasion. High resilience at room temperature and therefore low heat build-up under the action with metals and fabrics. Mechanical properties improved by vulcanisation and the inclusion of carbon black. Natural rubber is moderately resistant to acids and alkalis but has poor resistance to oils, some solvents, weathering, ageing, oxidizing agents and ozone cracking. Natural rubber can be vulcanised to the hard or ebonite state. Natural rubber properties depend on the filler material and their proportions.

CHEMICAL ANALYSIS OR COMPOSITION

Compounds of natural rubber are formulated with a variety of fillers (carbon black, china clay, rutile, talc) in a range of proportions giving a variety of properties.

PHYSICAL PROPERTIES

PROPERTY	UNITS	VALUE OR RANGE	COMMENTS
DENSITY	kg/m^3	930	Typical
SHEAR STRENGTH	N/mm^2		
TENSILE STRENGTH	N/mm^2	7-2	BS1154 and BS1155
ELONGATION	%	500-800	BS1154 and BS1155 - at break
COMPRESSIVE STRENGTH	N/mm^2		
TEAR STRENGTH	N/mm^2	70-140	50% carbon black filler
IMPACT STRENGTH	J		
TENSILE MODULUS	N/mm^2	2-6	50% carbon black filler
HARDNESS		30-95	Durometer (Shore A)
COMPRESSION SET	%	25-45	BS1154 and BS1155
THERMAL COEFF. OF LINEAR EXPANSION	$°C^{-1}$	$1.5-1.8 \times 10^{-4}$	
MIN./MAX. SERVICE TEMPERATURE	°C	-50/+100	
DEFLECTION TEMPERATURE	°C		
THERMAL CONDUCTIVITY	W/mK	$2.8-4.2 \times 10^{-1}$	Filler dependent
FLAMMABILITY			
DIELECTRIC STRENGTH	kV/mm	12-20	Filler dependent
VOLUME RESISTIVITY	ohm cm	$1.0-600 \times 10^{-15}$	Filler dependent
PERMITIVITY	ohm cm		
ARC RESISTANCE	secs		
RESILIENCE	%	15-80	Temperature dependent
FRICTION		0.4-1.1	
MOULD SHRINKAGE			
WATER ABSORPTION		0.1-3.0	Filler dependent

BSRIA material data sheet

SPECIFICATIONS

STANDARD NUMBER	AUTHORITY	TITLE
BS1154	BSI	Specification for natural rubber compounds (high quality)
BS1155	BSI	Specification for natural rubber compounds (high quality) for extrusion
BS2494	BSI	Materials for elastomeric joint rings for pipework and pipelines
BS4396	BSI	Raw natural rubber
BS6057	BSI	Rubber lattices
CP3003 Part 1	BSI	Lining of vessels and equipment for chemical pruposes - rubber

COMPANY SPECIFICATION:

ENVIRONMENT

RESISTANCE TO ATTACK FROM:

MINERAL ACIDS (WEAK)	Excellent
MINERAL ACIDS (STRONG)	Good - except nitric & sulphuric
ALKALIS (WEAK)	Excellent
ALKALIS (STRONG)	Good
SOLVENTS (CHLORINATED)	Attacked - swelling
HYDROCARBONS (ALIPHATIC)	Attacked - swelling
HYDROCARBONS (AROMATIC)	Attacked - swelling
HEAT AGEING	Good
WEATHERABILITY	Fair - poor
OZONE	Attacked
OXIDATION	Good
OXYGEN PERMEABILITY	$18\text{-}19.5\times10^{-8}cm^3/cm^2/sec/cm$
NITROGEN PERMEABILITY	$6.6\text{-}22.5\times10^{-8}cm^3/cm^2/sec/cm$
CARBON DIOXIDE PERMEABILITY	$102\text{-}220\times10^{-8}cm^3/cm^2/sec/cm$

JOINTING PROCESS

Adhesives suited to the environment

PROCESSING AND FORMING TECHNIQUES

Natural rubber is usually vulcanised and mixed with fillers and other ingredients.

Rubber produced by mastication, compounding and processed (extrusion, calendering or moulding)

TYPICAL APPLICATIONS

Contact adhesives
Conveyer and transmission belting.
Shock absorbers, seals, packings and weather strips.
Tyre covers for low heat build applications.
Electrical insulation
Hoses and tubing
Vessel linings

YOUR SUPPLIER AND NOTES

SAFETY PRECAUTIONS

material data sheet

SHEET NUMBER	RE02

A

FAMILY GROUP	RUBBER AND ELASTOMERS	SUB-GROUP	ELASTOMERS	MATERIAL	BUTADIENE - ACRYLONITRILE

GENERAL DESCRIPTION

Butadiene-Acrylonitrile (Nitrile) elastomer has moderate mechanical properties. The elastomer has good resistance to oil and solvent attack, particularly with high acrylonitrile content, which is better than natural rubber and butadiene-styrene. Similarly it has better heat ageing and light properties. The low temperature performance of nitrile is poor. The mechanical properties of nitrile elastomers can be improved by the addition of carbon black. Fair to good resistance to acids and alkalis and very good resistance to water.

CHEMICAL ANALYSIS OR COMPOSITION

Compounds of butadiene-acrylonitrile elastomers are formulated with a carbon black filler in a range of proportions.

SYNONYM
Nitrile

PHYSICAL PROPERTIES

PROPERTY	UNITS	VALUE OR RANGE	COMMENTS
DENSITY	kg/m^3	950-1020	Varies with acrylonitrile content
SHEAR STRENGTH	N/mm^2		
TENSILE STRENGTH	N/mm^2	7.7-12.6	BS2751
ELONGATION	%	150-600	BS2751 - at break
COMPRESSIVE STRENGTH	N/mm^2		
TEAR STRENGTH	N/mm^2	10-32	50% carbon black filler
IMPACT STRENGTH	J		
TENSILE MODULUS	N/mm^2	7-15	50% carbon black filler
HARDNESS			
COMPRESSION SET	%	17-30	BS2751
THERMAL COEFF. OF LINEAR EXPANSION	$°C^{-1}$	$0.65-2.3 \times 10^{-4}$	
MIN./MAX. SERVICE TEMPERATURE	$°C$	-20/+120	
DEFLECTION TEMPERATURE	$°C$		
THERMAL CONDUCTIVITY	W/mK		
FLAMMABILITY			
DIELECTRIC STRENGTH	kV/mm	2	BS3222
VOLUME RESISTIVITY	ohm cm	10^9-10^{12}	
PERMITIVITY	ohm cm		
ARC RESISTANCE	secs		
RESILIENCE	%	20-55	Temperature and filler dependent
FRICTION			
MOULD SHRINKAGE			
WATER ABSORPTION	%	0.4	Carbon black filler

 **material data sheet**

SPECIFICATIONS

STANDARD NUMBER	AUTHORITY	TITLE
BS2494	BSI	Materials for elastomeric joint rings for pipework and pipelines
CP3003 Part 1	BSI	Lining of vessels and equipment for chemical purposes - rubber

COMPANY SPECIFICATION:

ENVIRONMENT

RESISTANCE TO ATTACK FROM:

MINERAL ACIDS (WEAK)	Good
MINERAL ACIDS (STRONG)	Fair
ALKALIS (WEAK)	Good
ALKALIS (STRONG)	Good
SOLVENTS (CHLORINATED)	Good - fair
HYDROCARBONS (ALIPHATIC)	Excellent
HYDROCARBONS (AROMATIC)	Excellent - good
HEAT AGEING	Fair
WEATHERABILITY	Poor
OZONE	Fair
OXIDATION	Good
OXYGEN PERMEABILITY	$3.2\text{-}10.5 \times 10^{-8} cm^3/cm^2/sec/cm$
NITROGEN PERMEABILITY	$0.9\text{-}3.7 \times 10^{-8} cm^3/cm^2/sec/cm$
CARBON DIOXIDE PERMEABILITY	$23\text{-}66 \times 10^{-8} cm^3/cm^2/sec/cm$

JOINTING PROCESS
Nitrile can be bonded to metals during processing.
Adhesives suited to the environment.

PROCESSING AND FORMING TECHNIQUES

Nitrile elastomer is usually vulcanised with the addition of plasticisers, especially aromatic oils, to help processing and improve resilience and low temperature properties. The addition of carbon blacks may improve mechanical properties.

Elastomer produced by mastication, compounding and processed (extrusion, calendering or moulding)

TYPICAL APPLICATIONS
Products in contact with hydrocarbons, oils or greases such as hose, gaskets, oil seals.

Cable covers
Sealing strips
Belting covers
Vessel linings

YOUR SUPPLIER AND NOTES

SAFETY PRECAUTIONS

material data sheet

SHEET NUMBER	RE03

A

FAMILY GROUP	RUBBER AND ELASTOMERS	SUB-GROUP	ELASTOMER	MATERIAL	BUTADIENE - STYRENE

GENERAL DESCRIPTION

A synthetic version of natural rubber. With the addition of carbon black the mechanical properties are similar but it is inferior in resilience, tear and temperature resistance. Relatively unaffected by alkalines, most dilute mineral acids and ethylene glycol but attacked by concentrated acids. At elevated temperatures tensile strength, breaking elongation and resistance to tearing decrease markedly and more so than natural rubber.

CHEMICAL ANALYSIS OR COMPOSITION

Compounds of butadiene-styrene elastomers are formulated with a variety of fillers (carbon black, silica) in a range of proportions to give a variety of properties

SYNONYM

SBR

PHYSICAL PROPERTIES

PROPERTY	UNITS	VALUE OR RANGE	COMMENTS
DENSITY	kg/m^3	940	Typical
SHEAR STRENGTH	N/mm^2		
TENSILE STRENGTH	N/mm^2	12-28	Filler dependent
ELONGATION	%	300-650	At break
COMPRESSIVE STRENGTH	N/mm^2		
TEAR STRENGTH	N/mm^2	25-60	50% carbon black filler
IMPACT STRENGTH	J		
TENSILE MODULUS	N/mm^2	5-7.5	Filler dependent
HARDNESS		40-88	BS3351 and BS3629
COMPRESSION SET	%	25-30	BS3351 and BS3629
THERMAL COEFF. OF LINEAR EXPANSION	$^oC^{-1}$	2.3×10^{-4}	Typical
MIN./MAX. SERVICE TEMPERATURE	^oC	-60/70	Typical
DEFLECTION TEMPERATURE	^oC		
THERMAL CONDUCTIVITY	W/mK	$1.7-2.5 \times 10^{-1}$	Unfilled vulcanised elastomer
FLAMMABILITY			
DIELECTRIC STRENGTH	kV/mm	15-25	Filler dependent
VOLUME RESISTIVITY	ohm cm	$10^{-2}-10^{15}$	Filler dependent
PERMITIVITY	ohm cm		
ARC RESISTANCE	secs		
RESILIENCE	%	6-59	Temperature dependent
FRICTION			
MOULD SHRINKAGE			
WATER ABSORPTION	%	1-2	Filler dependent

 **material
data sheet**

SPECIFICATIONS

STANDARD NUMBER	AUTHORITY	TITLE
BS2494	BSI	Materials for elastomeric joint rings for pipework and pipelines.
BS3472	BSI	Styrene-butadiene rubber.
BS3650	BSI	Specification for oil extended styrene-butadiene rubbers.
BS4661	BSI	Emulsion polymerised anionic styrene-butadiene rubber latices.
CP3003 Part 1	BSI	Lining of vessels and equipment for chemical purposes - rubber

COMPANY SPECIFICATION:

ENVIRONMENT

RESISTANCE TO ATTACK FROM:

MINERAL ACIDS (WEAK)	Good
MINERAL ACIDS (STRONG)	Good
ALKALIS (WEAK)	Good
ALKALIS (STRONG)	Good
SOLVENTS (CHLORINATED)	Attacked - swollen
HYDROCARBONS (ALIPHATIC)	Attacked - swollen
HYDROCARBONS (AROMATIC)	Attacked - softened
HEAT AGEING	Fair
WEATHERABILITY	Fair - poor
OZONE	Attacked
OXIDATION	Fair
OXYGEN PERMEABILITY	$13\text{-}34 \times 10^{-8} cm^3/cm^2/sec/cm$
NITROGEN PERMEABILITY	$5\text{-}14.5 \times 10^{-8} cm^2/cm^2/sec/cm$
CARBON DIOXIDE PERMEABILITY	$95\text{-}195 \times 10^{-8} cm^3/cm^2/sec/cm$

JOINTING PROCESS

Bonded to steel and other metals
during processing.
Adhesives suited to the
environment.

PROCESSING AND FORMING TECHNIQUES

Butadiene-styrene rubbers are usually
vulcanised with the addition of a
variety of filler materials.

Elastomer produced by mastication,
compounding and processed (extrusion,
calendering or moulding).

TYPICAL APPLICATIONS

Bulk of use as tyres.
Sound and shock absorption
Power transmission belts
Hoses
Conveyor belting
Pipework joints and seals
Vessel linings

YOUR SUPPLIER AND NOTES

SAFETY PRECAUTIONS

| | material data sheet | | SHEET NUMBER | RE04 | A |

| FAMILY GROUP | RUBBER AND ELASTOMER | SUB-GROUP | ELASTOMER | MATERIAL | BUTYL |

GENERAL DESCRIPTION

Butyl elastomer is a general purpose material with fairly good mechanical properties. Low resilience at room temperature can lead to considerable heat build-up under the action of mechanical vibration. It has good resistance to oil and most solvents. Butyl rubber is highly impervious to gases. Butyl also has good tear resistance at elevated temperature.

CHEMICAL ANALYSIS OR COMPOSITION

Compounds of butyl elastomer are formulated with a variety of fillers, (carbon black, clay and silica) in a range of proportions giving a variety of properties.

PHYSICAL PROPERTIES

PROPERTY	UNITS	VALUE OR RANGE	COMMENTS
DENSITY	kg/m^3	920	Typical
SHEAR STRENGTH	N/mm^2		
TENSILE STRENGTH	N/mm^2	9-21	BS 3227
ELONGATION	%	300-700	BS 3227
COMPRESSIVE STRENGTH	N/mm^2		
TEAR STRENGTH	N/mm^2	45-60	BS 3227
IMPACT STRENGTH	J		
TENSILE MODULUS	N/mm^2		
HARDNESS	%	40	
COMPRESSION SET		$1.1-1.8 \times 10^{-4}$	Typical
THERMAL COEFF. OF LINEAR EXPANSION	$^{o}C^{-1}$	-50/+125	Typical
MIN./MAX. SERVICE TEMPERATURE	^{o}C		
DEFLECTION TEMPERATURE	^{o}C		
THERMAL CONDUCTIVITY	W/mK		
FLAMMABILITY			
DIELECTRIC STRENGTH	kV/mm	22-35	Filler dependent
VOLUME RESISTIVITY	ohm cm	$12.2-4 \times 10^{15}$	Filler dependent
PERMITIVITY	ohm cm		
ARC RESISTANCE	secs		
RESILIENCE	%	7-76	Temperature dependent
FRICTION			
MOULD SHRINKAGE			
WATER ABSORPTION	%	3	Filler dependent

SPECIFICATIONS

STANDARD NUMBER	AUTHORITY	TITLE
BS 2494	BSI	Materials for elastomeric joint rings for pipework and pipelines
BS 3227	BSI	Specification for butyl rubber compounds
BS 3003 Part 1	BSI	Lining of vessels and equipment for chemical purposes - rubber

COMPANY SPECIFICATION:

ENVIRONMENT

RESISTANCE TO ATTACK FROM:

MINERAL ACIDS (WEAK)	Excellent) except nitric
MINERAL ACIDS (STRONG)	Excellent) and sulphuric
ALKALIS (WEAK)	Excellent
ALKALIS (STRONG)	Excellent
SOLVENTS (CHLORINATED)	Attacked - swollen
HYDROCARBONS (ALIPHATIC)	Attacked - swollen
HYDROCARBONS (AROMATIC)	Attacked - swollen
HEAT AGEING	Good
WEATHERABILITY	Excellent
OZONE	Excellent
OXIDATION	Excellent
OXYGEN PERMEABILITY	$0.3\text{-}1.0 \times 10^{-8} cm^3/cm^2/sec/cm$
NITROGEN PERMEABILITY	$0.1\text{-}0.35 \times 10^{-8} cm^3/cm^2/sec/cm$
CARBON DIOXIDE PERMEABILITY	$0.03\text{-}0.1 \times 10^{-8} cm^3/cm^2/sec/cm$

JOINTING PROCESS

Butyl rubber can be bonded to metals during vulcanisation.
Adhesives suited to the environment.

SAFETY PRECAUTIONS

PROCESSING AND FORMING TECHNIQUES

Butyl elastomer are usually vulcanised with a variety of fillers. Various vulcanising agents impart different properties.

Elastomer produced by mastication, compounded and processed (extrusion, calendering or moulding).

TYPICAL APPLICATIONS

Products that depend on low gas permeability such as tyre inner tubes, steam hoses, diaphragms.

Shock and vibration absorption
Flexible electrical insulants
Fabric coating
Joint rings in pipework
Vessel linings
Sealant for caulking expansion and contraction joints, metal/glass seals, metal/metal seal for separation of dissimilar metals, electrial conduiting sealing.

YOUR SUPPLIER AND NOTES

| | material data sheet | SHEET NUMBER RE05 | A |

| FAMILY GROUP | RUBBER AND ELASTOMER | SUB-GROUP | ELASTOMER | MATERIAL | CHLOROPRENE |

GENERAL DESCRIPTION

Chloroprene (Neoprene) has very good resistance to ozone attack. It possesses good mechanical and electrial properties and resistance to heat and flame. Chemical resistance to aromatic solvents is excellent with filled compounds but poor to halogenated solvents. Neoprene has good resistance to water, weathering, gas permeability and compression set. Resistance to oils is not as good as nitrile.

CHEMICAL ANALYSIS OR COMPOSITION

Compounds of neoprene are formulated with a variety of fillers (carbon black, clay, silica, whiting) and softeners in a range of proportions giving a variety of properties.

SYNONYM
Neoprene

PHYSICAL PROPERTIES

PROPERTY	UNITS	VALUE OR RANGE	COMMENTS
DENSITY	kg/m^3	1200	Typical
SHEAR STRENGTH	N/mm^2		
TENSILE STRENGTH	N/mm^2	11-15.5	BS 2752
ELONGATION	%	100-550	BS 2752 - at break
COMPRESSIVE STRENGTH	N/mm^2		
TEAR STRENGTH	N/mm^2	25-65	Compound dependent
IMPACT STRENGTH	J		
TENSILE MODULUS	N/mm^2	3-5	Typical
HARDNESS		40-88	Durometer (Shore A)
COMPRESSION SET	%	25-30	BS 2752
THERMAL COEFF. OF LINEAR EXPANSION	$^{o}C^{-1}$	2×10^{-4}	Typical
MIN./MAX. SERVICE TEMPERATURE	^{o}C	-20/+130	
DEFLECTION TEMPERATURE	^{o}C		
THERMAL CONDUCTIVITY	W/mK	2.1×10^{-1}	Typical
FLAMMABILITY		Self extinguishing	
DIELECTRIC STRENGTH	kV/mm	1.2-29	Compound dependent
VOLUME RESISTIVITY	ohm cm	$10^8 - 10^{13}$	Compound dependent
PERMITIVITY	ohm cm		
ARC RESISTANCE	secs		
RESILIENCE	%	29-66	Compound dependent
FRICTION			
MOULD SHRINKAGE			
WATER ABSORPTION			

SPECIFICATIONS

STANDARD NUMBER	AUTHORITY	TITLE
BS 2494	BSI	Materials for elastomeric jointings for pipework and pipelines.
BS 5375	BSI	Methods of test for raw general purpose chloroprene rubbers
CP 3003 Part 1	BSI	Lining of vessels and equipment for chemical purposes - rubber

COMPANY SPECIFICATION:

ENVIRONMENT

RESISTANCE TO ATTACK FROM:

MINERAL ACIDS (WEAK)	Excellent) except nitric
MINERAL ACIDS (STRONG)	Excellent) and sulphuric
ALKALIS (WEAK)	Excellent
ALKALIS (STRONG)	Excellent
SOLVENTS (CHLORINATED)	Poor
HYDROCARBONS (ALIPHATIC)	Fair
HYDROCARBONS (AROMATIC)	Good
HEAT AGEING	Good
WEATHERABILITY	Good
OZONE	Excellent
OXIDATION	Excellent
OXYGEN PERMEABILITY	$3-10 \times 10^{-8} cm^3/cm^2/sec/cm$
NITROGEN PERMEABILITY	$0.9-3.5 \times 10^{-8} cm^3/cm^2/sec/cm$
CARBON DIOXIDE PERMEABILITY	$19.5-56.5 \times 10^{-8} cm^3/cm^2/sec/cm$

JOINTING PROCESS

Bond to metals is improved with a priming
coat of chlorinated rubber.
Adhesives suited to the environment.

PROCESSING AND FORMING TECHNIQUES

Neoprene is usually vulcanised with
a variety of fillers, antioxidants
and plasticisers. Elastomer
produced by mastication, compounding
and processed (extrusion, calendering
or moulding).

TYPICAL APPLICATIONS

Products in contact with oils and
solvents such as seals, gaskets, hoses
and automobile components.
Products requiring resistance to
weathering and corrosion such as cable
sheaths, vessel linings, marine
applications and glazing strips.
Interlayer between copper and natural
rubber.
Conveyor belts
Industrial clothing

YOUR SUPPLIER AND NOTES

SAFETY PRECAUTIONS

 **material data sheet**

FAMILY GROUP	RUBBER AND ELASTOMER	SUB-GROUP	ELASTOMER	MATERIAL	ETHYLENE/PROPYLENE

GENERAL DESCRIPTION

Ethylene propylene copolymers (EPM) and terpolymer (EPDM) with good resistance to ozone, oxidation, weathering, and heat and light-ageing superior to natural rubber. Because of their amorphous structure good flexibility is retained at low temperatures. They possess poor resistance to most electrical properties and can accept high loadings of oil and fillers. EPM is slightly superior to EPDM in resistance to heat-ageing oxidation and chemical attack.

CHEMICAL ANALYSIS OR COMPOSITION

Compounds of ethylene/propylene are formulated with a variety of fillers (carbon black, silica, calcium carbonate, hard clay) and oils in a range of proportions giving a variety of properties.

SYNONYM
EPM
EPDM

PHYSICAL PROPERTIES

PROPERTY	UNITS	VALUE OR RANGE	COMMENTS
DENSITY	kg/m^3	850	Typical
SHEAR STRENGTH	N/mm^2		
TENSILE STRENGTH	N/mm^2	10-16	Typical
ELONGATION	%	250-750	Typical
COMPRESSIVE STRENGTH	N/mm^2		
TEAR STRENGTH	N/mm^2	25-40	Typical
IMPACT STRENGTH	J		
TENSILE MODULUS	N/mm^2	5	Typical
HARDNESS		40-75	Typical - Durometer (Shore A)
COMPRESSION SET	%	5-20	Typical
THERMAL COEFF. OF LINEAR EXPANSION	$^oC^{-1}$	$1.8-2.3 \times 10^{-4}$	Typical
MIN./MAX. SERVICE TEMPERATURE	^oC	-40/+150	Typical
DEFLECTION TEMPERATURE	^oC		
THERMAL CONDUCTIVITY	W/mK	3.6×10^{-1}	EPM Compounds
FLAMMABILITY			
DIELECTRIC STRENGTH	kV/mm	28-40	EPM Compounds
VOLUME RESISTIVITY	ohm cm	$10^{14}-10^{16}$	EPM Compounds
PERMITIVITY	ohm cm		
ARC RESISTANCE	secs		
RESILIENCE	%	40-50	Typical
FRICTION			
MOULD SHRINKAGE			
WATER ABSORPTION	%	0.7-2.0	Typical

SPECIFICATIONS

STANDARD NUMBER	AUTHORITY	TITLE
BS 2494	BSI	Materials for elastomeric jointings for pipework and pipelines.
BS 6063	BSI	Methods of test for non-oil extended raw general purpose ethylene-propylene-diene rubbers (EPDM).

COMPANY SPECIFICATION:

ENVIRONMENT

RESISTANCE TO ATTACK FROM:

MINERAL ACIDS (WEAK)	Excellent) except nitric
MINERAL ACIDS (STRONG)	Excellent) and sulphuric
ALKALIS (WEAK)	Excellent
ALKALIS (STRONG)	Excellent
SOLVENTS (CHLORINATED)	Attacked - swollen
HYDROCARBONS (ALIPHATIC)	Attacked
HYDROCARBONS (AROMATIC)	Attacked - softened
HEAT AGEING	Good
WEATHERABILITY	Excellent
OZONE	Excellent
OXIDATION	Excellent
OXYGEN PERMEABILITY	
NITROGEN PERMEABILITY	
CARBON DIOXIDE PERMEABILITY	

JOINTING PROCESS

Bonded to metal during vulcanisation with the aid of special cements.
Adhesives suited to the environment.

PROCESSING AND FORMING TECHNIQUES

Ethylene/propylene elastomers are vulcanised by the addition of cross linking agents, depending whether it is a copolymer or terpolymer, and a variety of filler additions and oil extenders.
Elastomer produced by mastication, compounding and processed (extrusion, calendering or moulding).

TYPICAL APPLICATIONS

Jointings for pipework, seals and gaskets.
Hoses
Conveyor belts
Cable coverings.

YOUR SUPPLIER AND NOTES

SAFETY PRECAUTIONS

 **material data sheet**

| FAMILY GROUP RUBBER AND ELASTOMER | SUB-GROUP ELASTOMER | MATERIAL SILICONE |

GENERAL DESCRIPTION

Silicone elastomers have a wide service temperature range and good resistance weathering, oxidation, ozone and water. The mechanical properties vary from poor to moderate depending on the compound. Silicone has reasonable resistance to acids and akalis but shows poor resistance to most solvents and oils. Silicone elastomers are more permeable to gas than other elastomers.

CHEMICAL ANALYSIS OR COMPOSITION

Compounds of silicone elastomer are formulated with a variety of fillers (silica, ferric oxide, carbon black, cadmium oxide, kaolin, calcium carbonate) in a range of proportions giving a variety of properties.

PHYSICAL PROPERTIES

PROPERTY	UNITS	VALUE OR RANGE	COMMENTS
DENSITY	kg/m^3	1000-1600	Typical
SHEAR STRENGTH	N/mm^2		
TENSILE STRENGTH	N/mm^2	3.5-15	At break
ELONGATION	%	40-800	Compound dependent
COMPRESSIVE STRENGTH	N/mm^2		
TEAR STRENGTH	N/mm^2	5-4	Compound dependent
IMPACT STRENGTH	J		
TENSILE MODULUS	N/mm^2	1-3	
HARDNESS		35-90	Durometer (Shore A)
COMPRESSION SET	%	10-70	
THERMAL COEFF. OF LINEAR EXPANSION	$°C^{-1}$	$2.5-4.0 \times 10^{-4}$	Typical
MIN./MAX. SERVICE TEMPERATURE	$°C$	-60/+230	
DEFLECTION TEMPERATURE	$°C$		
THERMAL CONDUCTIVITY	W/mK	$1.6-4.2 \times 10^{-1}$	Typical
FLAMMABILITY			
DIELECTRIC STRENGTH	kV/mm	16-22	Temperature dependent
VOLUME RESISTIVITY	ohm cm	$10^{11}-10^{16}$	Temperature dependent
PERMITIVITY	ohm cm		
ARC RESISTANCE	secs		
RESILIENCE	%	46-54	Compound dependent
FRICTION			
MOULD SHRINKAGE			
WATER ABSORPTION	%	0.2	Typical

 **material data sheet**

SPECIFICATIONS

STANDARD NUMBER	AUTHORITY	TITLE
BS 2494	BSI	Materials for elastomeric jointings for pipework and pipelines.

COMPANY SPECIFICATION:

ENVIRONMENT

RESISTANCE TO ATTACK FROM:

MINERAL ACIDS (WEAK)	Good ⎫ except nitric
MINERAL ACIDS (STRONG)	Fair ⎭ and sulphuric
ALKALIS (WEAK)	Excellent
ALKALIS (STRONG)	Excellent
SOLVENTS (CHLORINATED)	Attacked - swollen
HYDROCARBONS (ALIPHATIC)	Fair
HYDROCARBONS (AROMATIC)	Attacked - slight swelling
HEAT AGEING	Excellent
WEATHERABILITY	Excellent
OZONE	Excellent
OXIDATION	Excellent
OXYGEN PERMEABILITY	
NITROGEN PERMEABILITY	
CARBON DIOXIDE PERMEABILITY	

JOINTING PROCESS

Sealants require thorough cleaning of substrates and surface priming as directed.

PROCESSING AND FORMING TECHNIQUES

Silicone elastomers are usually vulcanised and have a variety of filler additions.
Elastomer produced by mastication, compounding and processed (extrusion, calendering or moulding).

TYPICAL APPLICATIONS

Used where their high cost can be justified due to their properties such as seals, gaskets and diaphragms.
Non-stick belts and rollers
Electrical insulation and cable covers
Impregnated fabric laminates
Sealant for general sealing, caulking and glazing
Potting and moulding

YOUR SUPPLIER AND NOTES

SAFETY PRECAUTIONS

| FAMILY GROUP | RUBBER AND ELASTOMER | SUB-GROUP | ELASTOMER | MATERIAL | POLYSULPHIDE |

GENERAL DESCRIPTION

Polysulphides have excellent resistance to oils and solvents but possess poor mechanical properties. They show high resistance to ozone, weather and gas permeability but their heat resistance and low temperature characteristics are relatively poor. In the liquid state they act as sealing compounds. Two part sealants are converted to the solid state by the addition of catalysts while single part polysulphides cure by moisture absorption.

CHEMICAL ANALYSIS OR COMPOSITION

Compounds of polysulphide elastomer are formulated with a variety of fillers (carbon black, silica, titanium dioxide) in a range of proportions to give a variety of properties.

PHYSICAL PROPERTIES

PROPERTY	UNITS	VALUE OR RANGE	COMMENTS
DENSITY	kg/m^3	1600 (1130-1300)	Solid (cured liquid) - typical
SHEAR STRENGTH	N/mm^2		
TENSILE STRENGTH	N/mm^2	4-11 (1.4-6)	Solid (cured liquid) -filler dependent
ELONGATION	%	300-700 (450-950)	Solid (cured liquid) -filler dependent
COMPRESSIVE STRENGTH	N/mm^2		
TEAR STRENGTH	N/mm^2		
IMPACT STRENGTH	J		
TENSILE MODULUS	N/mm^2		
HARDNESS		70-78 (45-60)	Solid (cured liquid) -Durometer (Shore)
COMPRESSION SET	%	37-100	Solid
THERMAL COEFF. OF LINEAR EXPANSION	$°C^{-1}$		
MIN./MAX. SERVICE TEMPERATURE	$°C$	-50/+90	
DEFLECTION TEMPERATURE	$°C$		
THERMAL CONDUCTIVITY	W/mK		
FLAMMABILITY			
DIELECTRIC STRENGTH	kV/mm		
VOLUME RESISTIVITY	ohm cm	$8 \times 10^6 - 7 \times 10^{12}$ ($3 \times 10^9 - 4 \times 10^{11}$)	Solid (cured liquid) - filler dependent
PERMITIVITY	ohm cm		
ARC RESISTANCE	secs		
NUMBER OF PARTS		1 or 2	
RESILIENCE	%	15-25	
FRICTION			
MOULD SHRINKAGE			
WATER ABSORPTION			

BSRIA material data sheet

SPECIFICATIONS

STANDARD NUMBER	AUTHORITY	TITLE

COMPANY SPECIFICATION:

ENVIRONMENT

RESISTANCE TO ATTACK FROM:

MINERAL ACIDS (WEAK)	Good
MINERAL ACIDS (STRONG)	Attacked
ALKALIS (WEAK)	
ALKALIS (STRONG)	Attacked
SOLVENTS (CHLORINATED)	Good
HYDROCARBONS (ALIPHATIC)	Excellent
HYDROCARBONS (AROMATIC)	Good
HEAT AGEING	Fair
WEATHERABILITY	Very good
OZONE	Very good
OXIDATION	Very good
OXYGEN PERMEABILITY	
NITROGEN PERMEABILITY	
CARBON DIOXIDE PERMEABILITY	

JOINTING PROCESS

Thoroughly clean substrates and
prime as required

SAFETY PRECAUTIONS

PROCESSING AND FORMING TECHNIQUES

Polysulphide elastomer is usually
vulcanised with the addition of
fillers and plasticisers.
Elastomer produced by mastication
and compounding.

Liquid forms are processed.

TYPICAL APPLICATIONS

Solid
Seals, hose linings, cable covers
Liquid
General sealing and caulking between
metal, wood and masonry joints.
Sealing between dissimilar metals.
Fire barrier sealant.

YOUR SUPPLIER AND NOTES

4.7 SEALING MATERIALS

A sealing material maintains a seal between the surfaces of a joint which may be subject to some degree of movement. Its function is to resist the passage of heat, light, sound, fluids, gas, odour, dust etc. through the joint. It does not contribute to the structural properties of the joint. Sealing materials must also accommodate continuing changes in gap geometry due to thermal expansion and contraction, or moisture flexing in the system, component vibration and tolerance variations. As well as being able to perform its functions sealants must have an acceptable appearance, durability and be cost effective.

Sealing materials have some flexibility and typical materials are mastics, rubbers, elastomers (Section 4.6), plastics (Section 4.4), cork, asbestos, fibres, paper, metals etc. They are used where the system cannot be permanently sealed by soldering, brazing, welding or adhesive bonding. Types of sealing materials available are listed in Table 4.7/1.

Sealing materials may function in either static or dynamic situations.

Static applications:-

    Seals between flanges on pipes, ducts and components.

    Thread filling compounds on screwed joints.

    External seals on pipes and ducts such as grooved joints, heat shrunk materials and tapes.

Dynamic applications:-

    Valve stem packing.

    Pump and compressor shaft seals.

Static applications rely on the compression load on the sealing material to cause it to flow into imperfections and overcome surface irregularities. This loading should overcome the effects of any hydrostatic and fluid pressures within the system.

Dynamic applications, such as valve spindle seals, rely on an external pressure compressing packing rings so that they fill the space between the valve body and spindle. This pressure leads to a reaction which must exceed the operating system pressures. Another dynamic method is to activate the seal by the system pressure to overcome leakage, such as the deformation of an elastomeric lip or 'O' ring to seal against the shaft and housing. 'O' rings can also be used in static situations.

Joint preparation is important when applying sealing materials. All loose material such as dust, dirt, rust, scale etc. should be removed. Any solvents used should be totally removed so that they do not affect the sealing materials. At all times the manufacturers recommendations should be sought particularly where protective coatings have been applied to the joint surfaces.

Application	Materials	Types
Gaskets and Jointing	Rubbers and elastomers	See Section 4.6
	Cork	
	Rubber bonded cork	
	Asbestos	Compressed asbestos fibre
		Woven asbestos
		Asbestos millboard
	Asbestos substitutes	Glassfibre
		Mineral wool
	Paper	Impregnated paper
	Plastics	PTFE and composites
	Vulcanised fibre	
	Metal	Metal clad fibre
		Spiral wound and filler
		Corrugated metal
Gland Packing	See Table 4.7/2	
Seal Rings	Rubbers and elastomers	See Section 4.6
	Metal	Range of metals
Tapes (pressure sensitive)	See Table 4.7/3	
Tapes (thread sealing)	PTFE	
Heat shrink seals	Plastics	Irradiated plastics

Flexible Compounds

Mastics	Bituminous	
	Butyl	
	Oil based compounds	
Sealants	Polysulphide	
	Silicone	
	Polyurethane	
	Acrylic	
	Anaerobic sealant	

Table 4.7/1 List of Sealing Materials

All sealing materials must be compatible with the environment and also any material that will be in contact with potable water or food-stuffs must be approved by the relavent authority such as the National Water Council.

4.7.1. SOLID SEALING MATERIALS

Solid sealing materials may be used for either static or dynamic applications and they generally rely on externally applied compression of the material to generate a sealing force. They are typically gaskets (ready made), jointings (supplied in sheet form to be cut to shape) or ring seals ('O' or 'U' rings). They are supplied in a variety of materials and conditions depending on the operating parameters of a system such as pressures (or vacuum), operating temperatures, nature of fluid, contamination of fluid, mechanical and thermal cycling, available joint loading etc.

Some of the considerations to be taken into account in selecting sealing materials are:-

a. Thickness - It is preferable to opt for as thin a gasket as possible. The seal must be capable of deforming enough to take up any surface irregularities of the mating surfaces. The surface finish, seating stress and material compressibility affect the selection of the thickness.

b. Shape - For example circular bolted flanges with flat or raised faces should have gaskets designed to fit between the flange bore and the bolt circle, alternatively the gasket may incorporate the holes and extend over the complete face. The former are called ring gaskets and the latter full face gaskets. The ring type require less compressive loading by virtue of their restricted area but care is needed with hard materials, particularly when thick, in case the flanges are deformed when bolted. For non-circular flanges, such as ducts, it is more usual for the gasket to be full face. Grooves for seal rings must be machined to close tolerances.

c. Clearances - Clearances are necessary to prevent a gasket protruding into the bore when compressed but too large a clearance could cause a gap. In either case turbulant conditions, with associated erosion or corrosion problems could occur.

Several materials are available for solid seals. Prime attributes are resilience and elasticity associated with reasonable tensile strength. Many materials are suitable for low temperature and pressure applications but harder and more incompressible compositions are required at higher temperatures and pressures. For these circumstances rubbers and elastomers are generally replaced by fibre and metalic materials.

662

4.7.1.1   GASKETS AND JOINTINGS

RUBBER AND ELASTOMERS

These are an important range of materials used for gaskets, jointing and moulded sealing rings. These materials are dealt with in detail in Section 4.6, Rubber and Elastomers.

Rubbers spread laterally when a compressive load is imposed. It is essential that a limit to the degree of compression is imposed, particularly on thick sections. The addition of woven materials, cloth or metallic, between plies of the rubber restricts the tendency to spread.

Sealing rings are used for both static and dynamic sealing applications. The most common are 'O' section rings and lip seals, see Section 4.7.1.3. They both respond to system pressure by deforming and sealing any gap present. In most cases the seals are located in a premachined groove which allows for movement and deformation to complete the sealing action on assembly of the joint.

CORK

Because of its ease of compressibility cork readily acts as a seal on rough and uneven surfaces. Unfortunately cork is not very easily manipulated since it crumbles and breaks and will only tolerate slight distortion or stretching. Cork can be used up to 150°C but at temperatures above 70°C compressive set is likely to be encountered.

It is a low cost sealing material with a resistance to oils and solvents but is affected by acids, alkalis and prolonged water immersion.

RUBBER BONDED CORK

Cork/rubber compositions offer a range of seal materials for moderate pressure and temperature (-30°C to +150°C) applications, with a wide range of properties controlled by the choice of elastomer. The combination enables bonded cork to affect a tight seal under light loads and allows the seal to undergo distortion without failure. The spreading associated with rubber seals is markedly reduced thus eliminating the requirement for a clearance factor. Complicated shaped seals are more easily made from rubber bonded cork than from plain cork. Depending on the elastomer they can be compatible with lubricating oils, fuels, coolants and water.

Asbestos fibre seals extend the range for sealing materials beyond the limits of elastomers. There are three types of sealing material using asbestos:-

Compressed fibre and mixtures of polymer and fibre,

Woven asbestos fibre often impregnated with elastomer and metal reinforced,

Asbestos millboard.

Compressed Asbestos Fibre

This sealing material has many uses as a flange seal for low, medium and high pressure applications. The asbestos fibre and the polymer, reduced to a thick solution by a solvent, are mixed together and hot callender rolled to the desired thickness and the solvent removed. The variety of fibre length and polymer additions enable compressed asbestos fibre to be offered for a variety of applications. They can be reinforced with brass and steel mesh. Compressed asbestos products are capable of operating at temperatures up to 540°C but there is an associated drop-off in tensile strength. Because the material is relatively hard, compared to other solid sealing materials, the associated compressive load is greater and therefore the residual stress is much higher. For a liquid seal the residual stress is 15 to 30 N/mm^2 but for a searching gas it could be up to 45 N/mm^2. The range of impregnants and associated properties are wide rangeing and the manufacturer should be consulted to ensure correct selection. Some grades of compressed asbestos fibre have National Water Council approval for use with potable water and these are listed in their document, Water Fittings.

Woven Asbestos

Asbestos can be spun into a yarn which can be woven and the incorporation of metal reinforcement will result in an increase in its tensile properties. The resulting weave is soft and compliant but is permeable. This is overcome by impregnation with heat and oil resistance compounds which results in a sealing material with a service temperature up to 230°C capable of high strength and heat resistance with a degree of compressibility that will overcome typical flange irregularities. The maximum service range can be extended by using a reinforcing agent, a low carbon steel wire up to 600°C for dry heat applications and stainless steel wire up to 800°C for high pressure and temperatures where a corrosive media is in contact.

Asbestos Millboard.

Asbestos millboard consists of asbestos fibre bonded by starch or sulphide compounds. This is a material of low mechanical properties, particularly fragile in handling and cutting and is therefore frequently used as a filler material inside a metal sheath. As it has no elastomeric content its dry heat resistance is excellent with service temperatures up to 500°C. Typical applications are exhaust gaskets.

ASBESTOS SUBSTITUTES

Health hazards associated with asbestos have led manufacturers of sealing products to seek alternative materials. These substitutes include materials such as glass fibre and mineral wool for jointings and gaskets. Other materials such as graphite fibres, PTFE, hemp and cloth are used in gland packings. The resulting products have similar operating parameters to those that they replace. For example glass fibre jointings may be used for water, steam, refrigerants and chemical applications up to 475°C and a pressure of 14MPa.

Millboard is available made from mineral wool plus inert fillers with a service temperature up to 1000°C.

PAPER

Papers, both plain and impregnated, are used for seals. Impregnated papers can be made resistant to oils, petrol and most organic solvents and depending on the type of paper and the impregnation agent they have a maximum service temperature of 120°C. Plain paper seals find uses as shims and dust seals. Their main disadvantage is dimensional instability with changes of humidity, this can pose a storage problem.

PLASTICS
Data Sheet PL15 PL32.

The principle sealing material is PTFE, it is virtually chemically inert and can be used for applications over a temperature range of -250 to +260°C. Its principle disadvantage is that it is liable to cold flow with a lack of recovery. The properties of PTFE seals can be improved with filling agents such as glass fibre. In situations where the corrosion resistance is important PTFE envelope seals may be used which consist of a PTFE covering over an insert material that will withstand the physical parameters of the system. PTFE is also available as unsintered cord which can be formed into seals and then compressed to a flat form. Another use is in the form of tape where it is used as a thread seal, see Section 4.7.1.4.

VULCANISED FIBRE

Vulcanised fibre consists of fibrous cellulose (paper) which is swollen to gelation by a solution of zinc chloride. The paper is layered and after pressing is washed to remove excess zinc chloride. The material is dried to shape under compression. This produces a dense solid fibrous material that can readily be machined and can be produced in rigid or flexible forms.

Vulcanised fibre absorbs moisture but because of its dense nature it is not possible to impregnate it with moisture resisting materials. Where this may be a problem they can be well dried and varnished such as with electrical insulants. Any moisture loss from the material will result in a dimensional change and the physical properties of the material may vary in the longitudinal or transverse directions.

The toughness and relative low cost of vulcanised fibre make it a useful constructional material. It is recommended that it is only used in liquids within a PH range of 6-8 and at temperatures below 100°C (see BS5292). It finds applications as washers, face seals and electrical insulants.

METAL

Metallic or part metallic gaskets have the advantage of high mechanical strength and are used where rigorous conditions may prevail. They are also widely used to extend the usefulness of other gasket materials beyond their normal limits by compensating the loss of strength in the weaker component.

Metal clad fibre.

Metal covered soft fibre material such as asbestos or glass fibre using copper, iron or aluminium provides an economical seal for service at temperatures in excess of the core material. The metal covering can either totally encapsulate the core or can be left open on the side remote from pressure application. This type of seal finds uses as flange seals for steam, hot water, hydrocarbons, weak acids and alkaline solutions and also for cylinder head and exhaust manifold gaskets on internal combustion engines and compressors.

Spiral wound

Spiral wound (edge wound) seals for high pressure use possess recovery properties not matched by some other forms of seals. Variations in sealing stresses such as those met during thermal cycling and vibration can be accommodated in the seal.

Spirally wound seals comprise a continuous strip of pre-formed metal spirally wound and inter-leaved with a filler material. Normal practice is to compress the seal to a predetermined thickness. The number of plies and the ratio of filler to metal plies gives known compression characteristics which can be chosen to suit particular flange design and loading. In service the spring action of the gasket accommodates stress changes due to temperature and pressure. The metal ply can be made from carbon steel, stainless steel, monel or nickel with a filler material of asbestos or PTFE.

A range of service parameters are available depending on the seal and the filler materials. The following are typical:-

Pressure range -   carbon steel $17.5 - 105$ N/mm^2
                    stainless steel $21 - 210$ N/mm^2

Temperature range - PTFE filled up to 220°C
                    asbestos filled up to 500°C

For flat or raised face flanges an inner and/or outer support ring of low carbon or stainless steel may be used. The outer ring has three functions.:

-    to control the compression on the spiral wound portion,
-    to centre the gasket,
-    to support the outside of the gasket and resist pressure induced by radial stresses.

Where inner and outer guide rings are fitted the recovery characteristics of the gasket are further enhanced at the expense of requiring a higher load to obtain the required compression.

Spirally wound seals find applications in high pressure steam systems, for example as flange and valve bonnet seals, feed water lines, boiler components, high temperature gas lines and others involving hydrocarbons, acids and alkalis.

667

Corrugated metal

Each corrugation of the seal shall be concentric and follow the edge of the joint. The concentric peaks tend to intensify the sealing stress and, if required, the volume between can be filled with a sealing media which would take up any irregularities on the flange face. For corrugated metal seals complying with BS5292 the following metals may be used for the indicated application. Further technical data on the metals may be found on the material data sheets indicated:-

Metal	Application	Data sheet
Copper	Gas	NF 11
Brass	Gas	-
Lead	Gas meter flanges for connection purposes	NF 34
80/20 copper/nickel	Water (hot & cold) and steam	-
304 stainless steel	Steam	FM24

For water and steam the following pressure and temperature limits are:-

- cold water up to a pressure of 20 bars,
- hot water up to a pressure of 3.5 bars and a temperature of 100°C,
- saturated steam up to a pressure of 2 bars.

4.7.1.2 GLAND PACKING

Gland packing is widely applied to pumps, compressors and valves. The original tallow loaded rope packing has been replaced by a wide range of seal materials, they come in square or round sectioned materials, generally incorporating a lubricant, which have resistance to corrosive conditions and high pressures and temperatures. Spirally winding with lead or aluminium foil or the use of graphite fibres and foil can extend the working parameters. The lubricants used include oils, greases, PTFE, waxes or solid lubricants such as graphite, molybdenum sulphide, mica or talc. Mechanical strength is obtained by the use of various fibres, such as hemp, cotton, flax, rayon, nylon, asbestos, graphite and metallic fibres. The fibres are twisted or braided together to provide the required rigidity and porosity for the lubricant.

Gland packing compounds come in either coiled materials or as prepressed or moulded rings in sets for standard shaft and housing sizes. A typical gland seal arrangement would be five turns of coiled material or five prepressed seals.

Although packed glands tend to develop leakage this can easily be reduced by tightening the gland nut without removing the component from the system. Replacement packings are low cost and recent developments are extending the pressure and temperature limits. Temperature limits vary with the base material and typical values are indicated in Table 4.7/2. Other factors influencing the choice of packing are shaft speed, packing lubricant and nature of fluid.

668

Grades of gland sealing materials have National Water Council approval for use in valves and pumps for contact with potable water. The local water authority should be contacted to ensure that the correct materials are used.

The choice of material will depend upon the working space, the compression system, temperature and pressure range; allowable friction, frequency of valve operation and accessibility.

Material	Lubricants	Max shaft velocity (m/s)	Max temp°C (unloaded)	pH range	Temp°C/Pressure (bar)
Cotton	grease/ graphite	10	100	6-8	80/0.6 20/1.6
Hemp	grease/ graphite		100	5-9	
Asbestos (white)	dry		500		
Asbestos (white)	Grease/oil /graphite	10	125	5-10	80/0.6 20/1.6
Asbestos (white)	PTFE	10	200	3-12	150/0.6 80/1.6 20/4.0
Asbestos (white) + wire	graphite		750	4-11	
PTFE	graphite	20	380	0-14	300/0.6 80/2.0 20/3.0
PTFE	PTFE dispersent	10	260	0-14	150/0.6 80/1.6 20/7.0
Graphite		35	+600	0-14	
Glass yarn	lubricated		600		

Table 4.7/2 Typical properties of gland packing materials.

669

4.7.1.3 SEAL RINGS

Seal rings which deform under the load applied by compressing the seal between flat faces such as flanges (elastomeric materials or metals) or caused by pressure applications (elastomeric materials).

RUBBERS AND ELASTOMERS

Elastomeric toroidal 'O' and 'U' rings are widely employed as flange seals where closure forces are low. A nominal load is required to deform the 'O' ring section within its locating groove. Alternatively either the internal or external pressure can deform the seal causing a reaction between the seal and the housing surfaces. 'U' rings operate in a similar manner except that the deflection of the moulded lip will usually require less effort than for an 'O' ring. Under pressure conditions sealing is achieved by the seal lips being pressed intimately against the adjacent surfaces and the U section retaining its integrity of shape.

Several elastomeric materials are used as ring seals, the choice depends on the fluid, temperature and pressure parameters of the system. Examples are butadiene-acrylonitrile (nitrile) chloroprene (neoprene), ethylene/propylene, fluro-carbon (viton) and silicone (see Section 4.6). They find applications as valve and pump shaft seals, push fit pipe seals, hot or cold and sewage pipe seals, pressure line seals and flange seals. When in contact with potable water or foodstuffs the lubricant used must be acceptable to the relevant authority.

METAL

These come in solid or hollow cross-sectional shapes and in a variety of metals such as lead, copper, brass, aluminium, soft iron, stainless steel, nickel or monel.

Sealing stress requirements are invariably high compared to other sealing systems. For this reason most designs seek to intensify the load over small contact areas such as oval or octagonal toroidal seals for piping systems operating at very elevated pressures. To function these seals require very high closure pressures. Metal rings find applications at temperatures up to 870°C and pressures of 7-70 N/mm^2.

Hollow or pressurised 'O' rings are available for vacuum or gas seals, particularly at elevated temperatures. A good finish to the mating surfaces is required for these to be effective.

Another form of metal seal is the olive associated with compression fittings. This consists of an annealed tubular component (olive) which slips over an associated pipe diameter. As the retaining nut is tightened the olive is deformed against sealing face and at the same time it is compressed on to the tube. This double action seals the tube to the compression fitting and prevents fluid leakage. Generally the olives are copper or copper alloys, (see Section 3.2.4).

PRESSURE SENSITIVE

Tapes are applied to external surfaces of ducts and pipework insulation as an economical method of sealing systems. Their principle purpose is to act as a moisture and dust barrier, to prevent heat leaks and in ducting systems to prevent air leaks. They are produced from a variety of materials and a selection of adhesives. Relative tape material properties are indicated in Table 4.7/3:-

Table 4.7/3 Tape materials.

Property	Teflon	Metalic	Glass cloth	Polyester	PVC	Polyethylene
	(Relative performance, 6 excellent - 1 poor)					
High temperature resistance	6	5	4	3	2	1
Backing thickness	2	6	5	1	4	3
Moisture barrier	5	6	1	3	2	4
Conformability	4	1	2	3	5	6
Low temperature flexibility	6	3	5	2	1	4
Acid resistance	6	1	5	2	3	4
Solvent resistance	6	5	3	2		4
Resistance to recovery	3	5	6	2	4	1

Typical pressure sensitive adhesives used for tapes are based on rubber, acrylic or silicone. Each adhesive has limitations and some of these are outlined below:-

Table 4.7/4 Tape adhesives.

Property	Material		
	Rubber	Acrylic	Silicone
	Relative performance		
	(3 Excellent, 2 Good, 1 Poor)		
Initial tack	3	2	1
High temperature resistance	1	2	3
Ageing	1	2	3
Ultimate adhesion to steel	2	3	1

The compatibility between the adhesive and backing material and the base materials is important since solvent attack may occur on plastics materials and paints and the plasticiser may migrate and attack the base materials. Some materials are subject to degradation by ultra-violet radiation. General information on the backing materials may be found in Section 4.4.

Thread sealing tape is generally manufactured from PTFE materials. This plastics material posseses exceptional thermal properties with a service range of -20 to +230°C, chemical inertness to most chemicals as well as good ageing and weathering properties. This method of thread sealing is dry and clean to apply and the excellent frictional properties of the tape gives lubricating qualities during the tightening of the joint. PTFE thread sealing tape can be used for sealing both metal and plastics joints on steam, water, oil and gas (including oxygen) systems. In general it is not recommended that PTFE tape be used above a pipe size of 40mm.

To obtain an adequate covering the tape should be applied to the male thread shoulder and wound direct on to the pipe thread, usually with a 50% overlap, in the same direction as the thread so that it tightens as the connection is screwed up. The plastic nature of the PTFE allows it to readily conform to the thread form.

4.7.1.5   HEAT - SHRINK SEALS

These seals are applied to the outside of ducts, to buried mains or to any pipe joint that needs protection from the environment. They can either be sleeves or in strip form and can be coated with a heat activated mastic or adhesive. By applying heat to external seals they shrink and protect the joint. They are made from irradiated plastics material (including polythylene), heated and then stretched to two or three times the original size. On cooling they retain these dimensions but when heated above their crystaline melting point they revert, or attempt to revert, to their original size and shape. As the heat shrink material shrinks onto the pipework the mastic or adhesive exudes out sealing the joint. Alternatively 'O' rings can be placed round the pipe and the heat shrink sleeve seals onto them. Care must be taken in selecting the correct size of shrink seal for the pipe. A shrinkage of about 50% on the sleeve diameter is required. If the allowable shrinkage is less than that recommended then undue stresses may develop which could cause the sleeve to split and the joint to fail. The heat for shrinking must be applied evenly around the sleeve.

4.7.2. COMPOUNDS

Compounds are available in two forms:-

- mastics,
- sealants.

Mastics are materials compounded to remain in a plastic state permanently. Although a surface skin is usually formed the inner part of the material remains relatively soft and plastic. Mastics show little recovery when subjected to deformation. Typical mastics are bitumen, butyl and oil based materials.

Sealants are applied in a plastic state and are converted, by an addition or by the action of moisture, into an elastomeric material. They are usually capable of accommodating much more movement than mastics and have improved durability. Typical of this type are materials based on polysulphides, silicones or polyurethane.

Mastics and sealants can be used in either a butt joint or lap joint mode. Lap joints are subjected to shear movement while butt joints are subjected to tensile forces. A lap joint protects the sealing material from the environment but may produce more problems in application than a butt joint. If the sealing material is to be removed during a maintenance programme then a butt joint may be preferable. Joint design and preparation are important factors.

The joint gap should take into account the tolerances on the component dimensions and the assembly accuracy achievable on site. It is essential that the maximum joint movement does not exceed that recommended by the manufacturer. All mechanical loadings should be taken through metal/metal contact and not through the sealing material.

The correct choice of depth : width ratio for each type of sealing material minimises local stresses which could promote premature failure. The ratio should range from 3:1 to 1:2 depending on the material. It is also important to achieve a minimum depth of sealing material to ensure adequate adhesion to the joint side. The supplier of the material should be consulted as to its suitability. To maintain the required depth : width ratio in butt joints back up strips should be used at the joint root to minimise adhesion to the back of the joint to obtain maximum accommodation of joint movement and to provide a base to force the sealant to make good contact with the joint faces.

BITUMINOUS

This is mainly used for sealing water proofing work and for sealing between concrete blocks. These materials are applied by hot pouring and where the joint is deep great care should be taken to avoid entrapment of air.

BUTYL

This is a one part non-hardening material with reasonable mechanical properties which is cured by solvent release. Butyl materials exhibit excellent low gas permeability, weatherability and resistance to water and the tear strength is one of the best for elastomers. The resistance to oils and solvents is poor and they should not be applied below 5°C due to retardation of the cure.

Butyl mastics are based on butyl elastomers or degraded butyl elastomers used alone or in combination with solvents, oils, fillers and extenders. They are produced in a wide range of compositions resulting in compounds varying from soft and sticky to hard. They can be made skin forming, non-drying or self vulcanising by solvent evaporation. Butyl mastic may be used for glazing or bedding in but longitudinal cracking may occur rapidly in joints which move. These materials are applied cold in contact with ferrous and non-ferrous metals, plastics, wood, brick, concrete and ceramic tiles and primers are not required.

The advantages of butyl sealants are low modulus, fairly good adhesion, low surface preparation and excellent water immersion resistance. The disadvantages are high shrinkage, low recovery and very long cure time.

OIL BASED PIPE JOINTING COMPOUNDS

Oil based sealing materials are designed for joints with little or no movement. Oil based materials are easy to apply, have no handling, storing, or mixing problems, require limited preparation and are relatively cheap. They contain a high solids content which results in little or no shrinkage.

Oil based compounds are used in the sealing of screwed pipe for gas and water applications. For lubrication additions such as molybdenum disulphide or graphite are sometimes included. The actual constituents of the compound must be compatible with the pipe material and also with the fluid flowing within the pipe and the compound must withstand the temperature and pressures of the system. A reinforcing agent, such as hemp, may be applied to the compound to improve its sealing properties.

When using organic based compounds on potable water systems the material must satisfy the requirements of the local water authority. Some types of material may be capable of supporting micro-biological growth.

4.7.2.2 SEALANTS

POLYSULPHIDE

Polysulphide is a non-rigid hardening sealant with great resistance to oils and solvents, oxidation, ozone and weathering. Compared to elastomers with similar characteristics the mechanical properties are low. These materials are available as one or two part systems.

The one part system is cured on exposure to atmospheric moisture and the rate of cure is dependent on the degree of penetration through the skin. They should only be used where early and excessive movement are not likely to occur. One part systems have low shrinkage and good adhesion. The cure time is much longer than the two part systems.

After mixing a two part system has a pot life of up to 4 hours, depending on the mix proportions and environmental conditions. High temperature and humidity accelerate the cure and vice versa. They have good flexibility, elasticity, elongation, durability and they possess good flow characteristics for filling irregularities. Two part systems can accommodate a larger movement of joints than one part systems. One and two part polysulphide systems will not cure at temperatures below 5°C. Polysulphide sealants extrude well from caulking guns and the surface of the seal may be tooled prior to curing. They adhere well to steel, aluminimum, glass and procelain without a primer but a primer may be required for concrete and wood. Polysulphide sealants with intumescent additions find applications as a gap filling fire barrier.

SILICONE

Silicone is a non-rigid hardening one part sealant which cures rapidly to an elastomer by moisture absorption from the atmosphere. It has a wide service temperature from -40°C to +220°C. Silicone sealants have excellent resistance to weathering, moisture, ultra-violet radiation and ozone, however they have low tear resistance. Because silicone is a high recovery sealant it remains under stress when the joint is deformed leading to rapid tearing if the sealant is cut or punctured. The sealant exhibits no shrinkage, excellent flexibility, excellent durability, and good heat and chemical resistance.

Silicone sealants retain their gunning charateristics over a wide temperature range but a skin is rapidly formed and any tooling of the surface should be completed quickly. During curing a small amount of acetic acid by-product is formed which may be corrosive to some materials, e.g. lead, brass, copper and concrete.

Depending on the relative humidity sections of 3mm become solid in about 24 hours but the curing time is longer where the sealant is partially or completely confined. Silicone sealants will bond to ferrous and non-ferrous metals, plastics, rubber, glass, ceramics, wood and asbestos cement. In some cases a primer may be required and it is imperative that the joint is clean. Even though the sealant is capable of being coloured it tends to pickup dirt.

Silicone sealants are expensive compared to other sealants but are justified where non-contamination of a fluid is important or where high temperatures are to be experienced.

POLYURETHANE

Polyurethane is a non-rigid hardening sealant which is available as a one or two part system. The one part system is available as a non-sag grade while the two part system is available in both self-leveling and non-sag grades. Polyurethane sealants are capable of handling wide joints and large movements without failure. They possess good resistance to oils and solvents but are affected by continuous high humidity or water exposure. They are generally regarded to be a very good weathering sealant with good resistance to ultra-violet radiation and ozone. Maximum adhesion to surfaces requires surface preparation and priming. Polyurethanes have negligible shrinkage, high compressive set resistance, abrasion resistance and tear resistance.

One part systems cure by reacting with moisture in the atmosphere. The cure rate is slow and the elastomeric properties are attained for a considerable period. The diversity of the polymer enables the formulation of sealants with widely varying properties, some of them give off carbon dioxide causing swelling.

Two part systems cure chemically enabling optimum properties to be achieved more rapidly than one part systems. A range of sealants can be formulated resulting in a wide range of properties. To achieve these properties polyurethanes must be mixed completely and uniformly with a more shearing action compared to that required for other sealants.

Although the cure is accelerated by heat and humidity and is retarded by low temperatures, polyurethane can tolerate colder installation conditions than polysuphide.

Polyurethanes adhere well to ferrous and non-ferrous metals, glass, plastics, ceramics, wood, brick and concrete.

676

ACRYLIC

Acrylic based sealants may be either solvent or water emulsion based. They are one part sealants applied by guns and have excellent adhesion without the use of primers. The addition of fillers produces non-sag grades. Acrylic sealants cure by solvent release and there is an associated shrinkage. The cure time is long and skinning is slow. Though these joints have good water resistance and will tolerate intermittent water exposure, such as rain or condensation, they should not be used for total immersion. Acrylic sealants are resistant to oils, have a service temperature range of -40°C to +130°C and have good chemical resistance. They have a strong odour which can contaminate foodstuffs and be offensive. Ideally the joints should be narrow or with a limited movement, the sealant in wide joints may wrinkle and become unsightly. The sealant is thermoplastic and may have to be heated before it can be extruded from guns, developments are in hand to produce low temperature sealants.

Acrylics are non-rigid hardening sealants and find applications as general purpose seals and caulking. As a non-hardening sealant they are used for pipe joints, liquid gaskets and general purpose seals and caulking.

ANAEROBIC SEALANTS

Anaerobic sealants are a recent addition to the sealant field. They are finding applications for thread sealing and joining tube to fittings in place of soldering. They are cured by the absence of oxygen at room temperature but they require close tolerance fittings with gaps limited to 0.5mm to obtain maximum physical properties. These sealants will cure rapidly when applied to copper, copper alloys, iron and steel, but a longer cure time will be required for aluminium, aluminium alloys, stainless steel, zinc or cadmium. In some cases the manufacturer may recommend the use of a priming agent. The service temperature ranges from -50°C to +150°C but at elevated temperatures the tensile properties of the anaerobic joint will be reduced, perhaps by as much as 50%. Between +50 and +150°C the strength is inversely related to the temperature but is dependent on the joint configuration.

Compared to other sealants anaerobics are expensive but only small quantities are applied to the jointing face. The sealant has a pot life of about 1 year in normal storage conditions and the surfaces to be sealed should be clean and grease free. They should not be used for joints which may have to be dismantled for service work or alterations to existing installations. Anaerobic sealants find applications for hot and cold water, gas and chemical plant. The sealant manufacturer should be consulted to obtain the correct formulation for the desired application.

PIPE JOINTING MATERIALS

BS1806	: 1962	Dimensions of toroidal sealing rings (0 seals and their housings).
BS1832	: 1972	Oil resistant compressed asbestos fibre jointing.
BS2494	: 1976	Materials for elastomeric joint rings for pipework and pipelines.
BS2815	: 1973	Compressed asbestos fibre jointing.
BS3063	: 1965	Dimensions of gaskets for pipe flanges.
BS4375	: 1968	Unsintered PTFE tape for thread sealing applications.
BS4518	: 1982	Metric dimensions of toroidial sealing rings (0 rings) and their housings.
BS4865	: -	Dimensions of gaskets for pipe flanges to BS4504.
Part 1	: 1972	Dimensions of non-metallic gaskets for pressure up to 64 bar.
Part 2	: 1973	Dimensions of metallic spiral wound gaskets for pressures 10-250 bar.
BS5292	: 1980	Jointing materials and compounds for installations using water, low pressure steam or 1st, 2nd and 3rd family gases.

SEALANTS

BS5215	: 1975	One part gun-grade polysulphide based sealants.
BS5889	: 1980	Specification for silicone based building sealants.

Index

Acetal, 469
  copolymer resin, 503
  glass fibre laminate, 559
  homopolymer resin, 501
Acrylic, 469, 505
Acrylonitrile butadiene styrene
  (ABS), 471, 507
  glass filling laminate, 561
Adhesive bonding, 417
Adhesives data sheets
  bitumen, 437
  cyanoacrylate, 439
  expoxy, 441
  expoxy, phenolic, 443
  expoxy, polyamide, 445
  expoxy, polysulphide, 447
  natural rubber, 449
  neoprene, 451
  nitrile rubber, 453
  phenolic, neoprene, 455
  phenolic, nitrile, 457
  polyester, acrylic, 459
  polyruathene, 461
  polyvinyl, acetate, 463
Advisory services, 7
Aluminium, 307, 588, 608
Aluminium data sheets
  grade 1050A/1200, 322
Aluminium alloys, 308
Aluminium alloy data sheets
  aluminium copper 4, 332
  aluminium copper 2011, 336
  aluminium magnesium 5251, 324
  aluminium manganese 3103, 326
  aluminium silicon 1, 334
  magnesium manganese 6082, 334
  LM2 casting, 328
  LM6 casating, 330
  LM25 casting, 338
  silicon magnesium 2014A, 332
Aluminium bronze, 312, 376, 378,
  380
Amino resins, 481
Anodising, 630
Asbestos fibre, 664
Asbestos substitutes, 665
Asphalt coatings, 599
Automatic controls, 225

Bacterial attack, 20
Bituminous surface coatings, 598
  coal tar pitches and bitumen, 599
  asphalt, 599
Boilers
  cast iron, 211
  welded steel, 215
  shell, 219
  water tube, 223
Bonding, 394
  adhesive 417
Brazing, 401
  alloys, 406
  fluxes, 408
  methods, 402
  parent metals, 403
Bronze, 311
  welding, 406

Calorifiers, 194
Cast iron, 241
  grey, 242
  nodular and malleable, 244
  high alloyed, 245
Cast iron data sheets
  austenitic flake alloy, 265
  austenitic nodular alloy, 267
  blackheart, 259
  grey, 255
  pearlite, 261
  spherical or nodular, 263
  whiteheart, 257
Cellular plastics, 485
Cellular rubbers, 640
Ceramic surface coatings, 602
  vitreous enamel, 602
  cement, 602
Cisterns, 179
Coatings
  bituminous, 598
  ceramic, 602
  inorganic, 593
  metallic, 583
  plaster and rubber, 600
  temporary, 603
Controls, 225
  control valves, 225
  controllers, 225

sensors, 225
Convectors
  natural, 202
  fan, 208
Copper, 309
Copper data sheets
  high conductivity C103, 340
  wrought copper C106, 342
  wrought copper C107, 344
Copper alloys, 310
  brass, 310
  bronze, 311
  copper alluminium, 312
  copper-nickel, 312
  low alloys, 312
Copper alloy data sheets
  aluminium bronze CA102, 376
  aluminium bronze CA103, 378
  aluminium bronze CA106, 380
  brass CZ106, 346
  brass CZ105, 348
  brass CZ110, 350
  brass CZ111, 352
  brass CZ112, 354
  brass CZ114, 356
  brass CZ121, 358
  brass CZ122, 360
  brass CZ126, 362
  brass PCB1, 364
  brass DCB1, 366
  brass DCB3, 368
  brass SCB1, 370
  copper beryllium CB101, 386
  cupro-nickel, CN102, 382
  cupro-nickel, CN107, 384
  gunmetal LG2, 372
  gunmetal LG4, 374
Corrosion, 40
Corrosion, forms of, 41
  bacterial, 42
  bi-metallic, 41
  crevice, 42
  dezincification, 41
  graphitisation, 42
  impingement, 42
  protection, 46
  stress, 41
  surface or pitting, 41

water composition, 44
water source, 43
Corrosion protection, 20

Drainage, *see* Sanitation
Data sheets
  ferrous metals, 254
  jointing and bonding, 426
  non-ferrous metals, 320
  plastics, 499
  rubbers and elastomers, 643
  surface coatings, 608

Elastomers, and data sheets, 632,
  636
  butadiene acrylonitrile, 636, 646
  butadiene styrene, 636, 648
  butyl, 637, 650
  chloroprene, 637, 652
  chlorosulfonated polyethylene,
  638, 654
  ethylene propylene, 638, 656
  silicone, 639, 658
Electrical current, stray, 20
Environments, 16
  arctic region, 18
  buried, 19
  desert, 18
  immersion, 19
  indoor, 17
  mountainous region, 19
  outdoor, 16
  temperate region, 17
  tropical region, 17
Epoxide resins, 481
EVA microcellular foam, 487
Expanded polystyrene, 486
Expansion vessels, 198

Factors, conversion, 12
Factors, and units, 11
Fibrous reinforcement, 488
Filled plastics, 490
Fire protection, 87
  foam systems, 92
  hose reel systems, 89
  hydrants, 90
  risers, dry, 90
    wet, 90
  sprinkler systems, 95
Flanges, pipe, 128
Fluxes, 399, 408
Foam plastics, *see* Cellular plastics
Fusion welding, 411
  methods, 412

Gaskets and jointings, 663
  asbestos fibre, 664
  asbestos substitute, 665
  cork, 663

metal, 666
paper, 665
plastics, 665
rubber bonded cork, 663
rubber and elastomers, 663
vulcanised fibre, 666
Gland packing, 668
Glass cloth, 495
Glass fibre mat, 495
Glass fibre tape, 495
Glass fibre tissue, 495
Glass reinforced plastics, 493
Glass rovings, 495

Hardness conversion factors, 14
Heat emitters, *see* Radiators,
  Radiant heaters, Convectors
Heat generators, *see* Boilers
Heat shrink seals, 671
Heating, *see* Space heating
Hose reels, 87
Hydrants, 90

Inorganic surface coatings, 593
  anodising, 593
  chromate, 593
  phosphating, 593
Insulation, thermal, 230

Jointing and bonding, 394
Jointing and bonding data sheets,
  426
  thermal methods
    copper phosphorous brazing
    alloy, 435
    silver based brazing alloy, 433
    soft solder 40/60, 427
    soft solder 60/40, 429
    soft solder 96/4, 431
  adhesives, *see* Adhesive data
  sheets
Jointings, *see* Gaskets and jointings

Lead, 313
Lead data sheets, 388

Mastics, 674
  bituminous, 674
  butyl, 674
  oil-based compounds, 674
Metallic surface coatings, 583
  aluminium, 588, 608
  cadmium, 588, 610
  chromium, 588, 612
  copper, 589, 614
  lead, 589, 616
  nickel, 586, 618
  silver, 590, 620
  tin, 590, 622
  zinc, 590, 624

Nylon, *see* Polyamide

Packaging, 603
Paints, 594
  air drying, 596
  cured by calalytic action, 597
  heat drying, 597
  water based, 598
Phenolic, 483
Pipe
  copper and copper alloy. 110
  plastics, cold water, 118
  plastics, hot water, 125
  stainless steel, 114
  steel, 105
Pipe fittings
  butt-welded fittings, 140
  capillary fittings, 135
  compression fittings, 137
  flanges, 128
  grooved fittings, 142
  screwed fittings, 132
Plastic and rubber coatings, 600
  chlorinated polyethylene, 601
  epoxy, 601
  polyamide (nylon), 601
  polyethylene, 600
  polyvinyl chloride, 601
  ptfe, 601
  rubber, 601
Plastics, 465
Plastics materials, 467
  cellular, 485
  filled, 490
  glass reinforced, 493
  laminated, 485
  thermoplastics, 469
  thermosetting, 481
Plastics data sheets, 499
  cellular plastics
    phenolic, 547
    polyurathane, flexible, 543
    polyurathane, rigid, 545
  glass reinforced
    polyester/glass fibre cloth, 577
    polyester/glass fibre mat, 575
    polyester/glass fibre roving, 579
  laminates
    abs/glass filling, 561
    acetal/glass fibre, 559
    epoxy/cotton, 555
    phenolic/asbestos, 553
    phenolic/cotton, 551
    phenolic/paper, 549
    nylon 66/glass filling, 557
    polycarbonate/glass filling, 567
    polypropylene/asbestos filling,
    569
    polypropylene/glass filling, 573
    polypropylene/talc filling, 571

ptfe/bronze filling, 565
ptfe/glass filling, 563
thermoplastics
  acetal copolymer resin, 503
  acetal homopolymer resin, 501
  acrylic, 505
  acrylonitrile butadiene styrene
    (abs), 507
  chlorinated pvc, 535
  polyamide, nylon 6, 509
  polyamide, nylon, 11, 513
  polyamide, nylon 12, 515
  polyamide, nylon 66, 511
  polybutylene, 519
  polycarbonate, 517
  polyethylene, high density, 521
  polyethylene, low density, 523
  polyethylene, cross-linked, 525
  polypropylene, 527
  polyvinyl chloride plasticised, 531
  polyvinyl chloride rigid, 533
  ptfe, 529
thermosets
  epoxide resins, 537
  phenolic, 539
  polyester, 541
Polyamide (nylon), 472, 484
Polybutylene, 475
Polycarbonate, 474
Polyester, 484
Polyethylene (Polythene), 475
Polyethylene, cross-linked, 477
Polyethylene foam, 486
Polytetrafluoroethylene (pfte), 478
Polyurathene foam, 486
Polyvinyl chloride (pvc), 479
Precautions checklist, 98
Pumps
  centrifugal, 167
  domestic, 173
  positive displacement, 176

Radiant heaters, 205
Radiators, 200
References, 3
  general, 3
  components, 4
  materials, 4
  services, 3
Resins, 481, 489
Risers, dry and wet, 90
Rovings, 495
Rubbers and elastomers, 632, 635
  cellular, 640
  natural rubber, 635
Rubber data sheets, 643
  natural rubber, 644

Sanitation
  internal drainage, 76

roof drainage, 82
waste drainage, 84
Sealants, 675
  acrylic, 677
  anaerobic, 677
  polysulphide, 675
  polyurathene, 676
  silicone, 675
Sealing materials, 660
  solid, 662
  compounds, 673
Sealing rings, 670
Soil composition, 19
Soldering, 394
  alloys, 399
  fluxes, 399
  methods, 396
  parent metals, 397
Soldering data sheets
  soft solder 40/60, 427
  soft solder 60/40, 429
  soft solder 96/4, 431
Space heating
  domestic heating, 49
  high temperature hot water
    heating, 57
  low temperature hot water
    heating, 52
  medium temperature hot water
    heating, 55
  steam heating and condensate, 59
Sprinkler systems, 95
Steel, carbon, 245
Steel, carbon, data sheets
  grade 151–360, 269
  grade 161–430, 271
  grade 161–480, 273
  grade 320, 275
  grade 360, 277
  grade 410, 279
  grade 460, 281
  grade 490 Nb, 283
Steel, low alloy, 247
Steel, low alloy data sheets
  grade 245/240, 285
  grade 503, 287
  grade 620/440, 289
  grade 620/460, 291
  grade 621, 293
  grade 622, 295
  grade 660, 297
  grade 762, 299
Steel, stainless, 248
Steel, stainless, data sheets
  austenitic type 302/304, 301
  austenitic type 316, 303
  austenitic type 321, 305
Steel pipe sizes, 15
Stray electrical currents, 20
Surface coatings, 583

bitumous, 598
ceramic, 602
inorganic, 593
metallic, 583
plastic and rubber, 600
temporary, 603
Surface coatings data sheets, 608
  inorganic
    anodising, 630
    chromate, 628
    phosphating, 626
  metallic
    aluminium, 608
    cadmium, 610
    chromium, 612
    copper, 614
    lead, 616
    nickel, 618
    silver, 620
    tin, 622
    zinc, 624
Surface protection, 583
  pickling methods, 585
  surface coatings, 584

Tanks, 183
  calorifiers, 194
  cisterns, 179
  cylinders, 187
  expansion vessels, 198
Tapes, 671
  pressure sensitive, 671
  thermal sealing, 671
Tapes, wrapping, 599
  petroleum jelly tapes, 599
  synthetic resin or plastic tapes,
    600
  coal tar and bitumen tapes, 600
Temporary coatings, 603
  oils and grease, 603
  packaging, 603
  strippable fibre, 603
  volatile corrosion inhibitor, 604
  wax, 603
Thermal insulation, 230

Units and factors, 11
Units, SI, 11
Units, SI multiples and
  sub-multiples, 13

Valves
  butterfly, 161
  check, 149
  float operated, 157
  gate, 143
  plug, 163
  screw-down (globe), 153

Water, in pipes and tanks, 20

Water services
  chilled, 73
  cooling, 71
  domestic cold, 62
  domestic hot, 66
Water source and composition, 20

Welding
  bronze, 408
  fusion, 411
  plastics, 416
  resistance, 409
Weldable metals and alloys, 410, 413

Wrought iron, 241

Zinc, 313
Zinc alloy data sheets
  BS1004A, 390
  BS1004B, 382